AACN MANAGEMENT SERIES

FINANCIAL MANAGEMENT IN CRITICAL CARE NURSING

AACN MANAGEMENT SERIES

FINANCIAL MANAGEMENT IN CRITICAL CARE NURSING

EDITED BY

Donna L. Bertram, RN, MBA, CNA

Vice President, Nursing
Penrose-St. Francis Healthcare
Site Administrator
Penrose Community Hospital
Colorado Springs, Colorado

Judith L. Wilson, RN, MPA, CNA

Assistant Chief, Nursing Service
Department of Veterans Affairs Medical Center
Denver, Colorado

WILLIAMS & WILKINS
BALTIMORE · HONG KONG · LONDON · MUNICH
PHILADELPHIA · SYDNEY · TOKYO

Editor: Susan M. Glover
Associate Editor: Marjorie Kidd Keating
Copy Editor: Jacquelyn Durbin
Designer: Norman W. Och
Illustration Planner: Ray Lowman
Production Coordinator: Anne Stewart Seitz

Copyright © 1991
Williams & Wilkins
428 East Preston Street
Baltimore, Maryland 21202, USA

All rights reserved. This book is protected by copyright. No part of this book may be reproduced in any form or by any means, including photocopying, or utilized by any information storage and retrieval system without written permission from the copyright owner.

Printed in the United States of America

Library of Congress Cataloging-in-Publication Data

Financial management in critical care nursing / edited by Donna L. Bertram, Judith L. Wilson.
   p. cm.—(AACN management series)
 Includes index.
 ISBN 0-683-00616-9
   1. Intensive care nursing—Finance. 2. Intensive care nursing—Economic aspects.
I. Bertram, Donna L. II. Wilson, Judith L. III. Series: Management series (Baltimore, Md.)
   [DNLM: 1. Critical Care—economics. 2. Economics, Nursing. 3. Financial Management—methods. WY 77 F491]
RT120.I5F46 1991
362.1'74'0681—dc20
DLC
for Library of Congress   91-7465
                                                                                    CIP

                                                        91 92 93 94 95
                                              1 2 3 4 5 6 7 8 9 10

To all those individuals who influenced our lives, professionally and personally, but especially our golf partners
Jerral E. Bertram
and
Donald R. Wilson

Foreword

The change in payment philosophy that occurred in 1983 heralded a new initiative in health care. Hospitals found themselves in unfamiliar territory financially, as an expensive cost based payment system was replaced by the diagnostic related groups (DRGs) of prospective payment for Medicare patients.

This change fostered an appreciation for the risks and rewards of the fixed payment system. Chief executive officers and trustees mandated intensive educational programs for a wide range of personnel. No longer was the hospital's Chief Financial Officer *solely* responsible for understanding and directing the health care institution's finances. Instead, a number of hospital employees were educated to share in increasing responsibility for cost containment and budgetary control.

As Medicare refined its financial reimbursement system, other payors adopted the prospective payment model or endorsed deep discounts to tighten remuneration. Increasing numbers of health care journals articles and continuing education programs addressed various aspects of financial management. Concepts such as *revenue centers, depreciation, accounts receivable*, and *rate setting* became the foci of lengthy Board of Trustees meetings as cost centers responsible for *variance from budget* were intensely scrutinized.

Increasingly available "high-tech" monitoring equipment and treatment options became commonplace, particularly for critically ill patients. Concomitant with greater use of expensive technology was a growing appreciation for the enormous impact of professional decisions on the financial viability of the institution. Initiatives aimed at physicians and nurses to control expenditures in the face of an escalating nursing shortage led to further scrutiny of resource allocation.

The establishment of a federal Commission on Nursing, in response to the 1987 shortage of hospital staff nurses, was one effort to evaluate and correct resource utilization. However, as the Inspector General noted in a report to the Commission, few chiefs of nursing service were actively involved in the overall budgeting and financial operations of their institution, stimulating the following recommendation[a]:

Health care delivery organizations, nursing associations, and government and private health insurers should collaborate to develop and implement methods for costing, budgeting, reporting and tracking nursing resource utilization, both to enhance the management of nursing services and to assess their economic contribution to their employing organization.

This book is another effort in that direction. It fills a much-needed void for nurse managers. Like other texts, it explains financial management principles. But it is unique in illustrating application of those principles with anecdotes and situations from clinical settings.

Contributing authors come from a range of backgrounds: rural, urban, inner city, private and public institutions, and small and large facilities. They write with a concise practical style which contributes to the reader's understanding and transference of knowledge to the clinical environment.

Part I covers the basic principles and terminology of finance, establishing a foundation for Parts II and III. The processes of planning and budgeting are explored in Part II, with vignettes illustrating the development of both capital and operating budgets. Part III describes the process of variance and variance analysis,

---

[a]Secretary's Commission on Nursing Final Report, Vol. I, December 1988, p. vi, Department of Health and Human Services.

while Part IV explores the macroeconomic issues that will impact hospital finances both now and in the future.

Although this book was written for the critical care manager, it has potential application to a much larger audience. Sound strategic planning based on financial principles is critical to organizational survival. Knowledgeable nurse managers have an opportunity to make a decided impact on the fiscal health of their institution. In our struggle with the concept of empowerment in the health care delivery system, the importance of a sound understanding of financing and financial knowledge becomes transparently clear. Nurses who use this book will be well on their way to accruing real power, as financial management is a skill that will be in ever greater demand in our future health care delivery systems.

Carolyne K. Davis, RN, PhD
National Health Care Advisor
Ernst & Young

Preface

Financial management encompasses one of the most important aspects of any critical care nurse manager's job, and every nurse, whether a direct caregiver or a chief nursing executive, manages resources of information, manpower, materials, money, and time. The success of the health care facility depends, to a large extent, on the competency of the nurse management team and their ability to manage resources effectively and efficiently. Many nursing programs lack courses on budgeting concepts, information processing, time management, and the accounting and financial principles necessary to prepare nurse managers for financial accountability. This text provides the basics of financial management and the specific information and strategies needed to perform financial responsibilities. This book enables first-line managers and others to understand, plan, implement, and evaluate the scope of activities in financial management. For managers of critical care units that utilize high levels of manpower, materials, time, information, and money, the study of financial management is crucial in an environment of limited and constricted resources and is necessary for success in meeting the organization's goals.

The financial management arena and the critical care environment are linked in an integrative model (see figure shown below). The critical care arena consists of the patient, the staff, and the nurse manager in a dynamic interaction. The financial management arena of the health care market relates to the patient as a resource consumer as well as a revenue supplier; the staff serve as the resource providers of care; and the critical care nurse manager coordinates the planning and controlling functions of financial management. These interactions are also dynamic. The American Association of Critical-Care Nurses (AACN) model for critical care nursing practice provides the balancing framework for the processing of the integrative model for financial management in critical care. The use of the nursing process with the AACN *Standards of Nursing Care of the Critically Ill*, the *Code of Ethics*, and the *Scope of Practice* provides the guiding principles to be used in the financial environment.

This book leads the nurse manager through the nursing process with the utilization and supply of resources as they affect patients, staff, and management. The nurse manager's role as a planner and controller in financial manage-

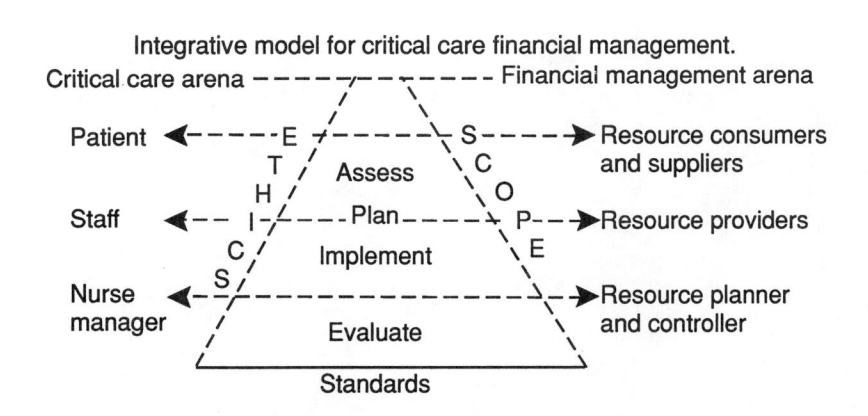

Integrative model for critical care financial management.

ment incorporates the AACN position statement, "Role Expectations for the Critical Care Manager," (see Fig. 1.1). The role is explained throughout the text with scenarios and anecdotes. A combination of theory and practical applications in critical care financial management provides the reader with information which leads to improved decision making about planning and controlling resources. As each facility may use different tools, formulas, and methods in the application of financial principles, this book presents a variety of different methods rather than supports only one. In this way the nurse manager can challenge old or traditional ways through exposure to new methods which may result in better decisions.

Part I introduces the critical care manager to the fundamentals of financial management. This introduction and assessment section includes: historical, hospital, and nursing perspectives on health care economics; a discussion of factors influencing health care; basic terminology; and accounting principles. The tools of financial management, types of budgets, the budget cycle, and financial statements are also included. Practical applications of these concepts facilitate the efficient operation of the critical care unit.

Part II presents the planning and implementation phases of financial management. This section includes the planning and budgeting processes for personnel, capital, and operating budgets. Staffing methodologies, presentation and approval of budgets, and management information systems are presented. This section provides the critical care nurse manager with the tools for a comprehensive understanding of budgets necessary to carry out the budgeting responsibilities of the position.

The evaluation component of financial management is discussed in Part III. Surveillance monitoring through variance reporting and controlling functions provides the critical care nurse manager with an evaluation process that can be applied practically in the service setting. Various records and reporting mechanisms are discussed to provide an overall picture as well as useful examples. The importance of reimbursement, program planning, and evaluation completes this section.

Part IV relates the health care system to changes that have implications for financial planning at the unit level. Economic perspectives, hospital organization, issues and trends, and future directions are discussed. This section gives the critical care nurse manager an appreciation of the entire scope of the financial arena in health care.

This book systematically presents the tools, process, and information needed by the nurse manager to handle financial management of the critical care unit efficiently and effectively. Each chapter is based on theoretical principles supplemented by practical applications, which results in a text that is a useful and valuable management tool. The content will enable the nurse manager to achieve personal, unit, and hospital goals as well as assist staff and others to appreciate the complexities and components of fiscal responsibility.

Donna L. Bertram, RN, MBA, CNA
Judith L. Wilson, RN, MPA, CNA

Contributors

Donna L. Bertram, RN, MBA, CNA
Vice President, Nursing
Penrose-St. Francis Healthcare
Site Administrator
Penrose Community Hospital
Colorado Springs, Colorado

Ann S. Bines, RN, MS, CCRN
Clinical Nurse Manager
Olson Post Anesthesia Recovery Room
Northwestern Memorial Hospital
Chicago, Illinois

Dorothy E. Black, RN, BSN
Head Nurse, Surgical Intensive Care
Department of Veterans Affairs Medical Center
Denver, Colorado

Suzette Cardin, RN, MS, CCRN
Nurse Manager
Coronary Care Unit/Coronary Observation Unit
UCLA Medical Center
Assistant Clinical Professor
UCLA School of Nursing
Los Angeles, California

Virginia J. Davis, RN, MSN
Director, Medical-Surgical Nursing
Harris Methodist-Fort Worth
Fort Worth, Texas

Jeanene DeLong, RN, BSN
Director, Patient Care Information Systems
Harris Methodist-Fort Worth
Fort Worth, Texas

Joanne M. Disch, RN, PhD
Clinical Director, Medical Nursing, Emergency
    Services and Dialysis
Hospital of the University of Pennsylvania
Associate Professor, School of Nursing
University of Pennsylvania
Philadelphia, Pennsylvania

Rhonda Easton, RN, BSN, MPA
Coordinator, Nursing Management Systems
Penrose-St. Francis Healthcare
Colorado Springs, Colorado

Roberta M. Fruth, RN, MS, CCRN
Practitioner-Teacher
Rush Medical Center
Chicago, Illinois

Karen Ginter, RN, MS
Director, Patient Care Services
Highland Park Hospital
Highland Park, Illinois

Dolores S. Gomez, RN, MN
Director, Critical Care/Medical-Surgical Nursing
Desert Hospital
Palm Springs, California

Peggy J. Maddox, RN, MSN, CNAA
Deputy Director for Nursing
Clinical Center
National Institutes of Health
Bethesda, Maryland

Christine A. Mayrose, RN, BSN, CCRN
Nurse Manager
Department of Veterans Affairs Medical Center
Grand Junction, Colorado

Katherine D. McCord, RN, MSN, CCRN
Administrative Director, Critical Care and
    Emergency Departments
Penrose-St. Francis Healthcare
Colorado Springs, Colorado

Patricia McGill, RN, MSN
Assistant Director, Congressional Relations
American Nurses Association
Washington, DC

Linda F. Samson, RN, PhD
Assistant Professor
Clayton State College
Marrow, Georgia

Sandra Small, RN, MSN
Director, Critical Care
Baptist Medical Center
Little Rock, Arkansas

Robert Squier, RN, BSN, CCRN
Supervisor, Ambulatory Care
Department of Veterans Affairs Medical Center
Denver, Colorado

Cathy Rodgers Ward, RN, MS, CCRN
Director of Nursing Systems
UCLA Medical Center
Associate Clinical Professor
UCLA School of Nursing
Los Angeles, California

Judith L. Wilson, RN, MPA, CNA
Assistant Chief, Nursing Service
Department of Veterans Affairs Medical Center
Denver, Colorado

Laura C. Young, RN, MSN
Vice President, Nursing
Harris Methodist-H.E.B.
Bedford, Texas

Contents

Foreword vii
Preface ix
Contributors xi

PART I: INTRODUCTION AND ASSESSMENT

1 Financial Management 2
 Judith L. Wilson, RN, MPA, CNA
 Donna L. Bertram, RN, MBA, CNA
2 Accounting Concepts 18
 Laura C. Young, RN, MSN
3 Basics: The Tools of Financial Management 32
 Sandra Small, RN, MSN
4 Financial Statements 43
 Donna L. Bertram, RN, MBA, CNA
 Katherine D. McCord, RN, MSN, CCRN

PART II: PLANNING AND IMPLEMENTATION

5 Budgeting Methods 56
 Judith L. Wilson, RN, MPA, CNA
6 Budgeting Process 81
 Peggy J. Maddox, RN, MSN, CNAA
7 Capital Budgets 98
 Dorothy E. Black, RN, BSN
 Judith L. Wilson, RN, MPA, CNA
8 Personnel Budgets 118
 Ann S. Bines, RN, MS, CCRN
 Karen Ginter, RN, MS
9 Staffing Methodologies 131
 Virginia J. Davis, RN, MSN
 Donna L. Bertram, RN, MBA, CNA
10 Operating Budgets 144
 Robert Squier, RN, BSN, CCRN
 Christine A. Mayrose, RN, BSN, CCRN
11 Management Information Systems 163
 Jeanene DeLong, RN, BSN
12 Budget Presentation and Approval Process 172
 Cathy Rodgers Ward, RN, MS, CCRN

PART III: EVALUATION AND CONTROLLING

13 Variance Reporting 178
 Rhonda Easton, RN, BSN, MPA
14 Controlling 198
 Donna L. Bertram, RN, MBA, CNA
 Katherine D. McCord, RN, MSN, CCRN

15	Reimbursement Analysis 211
	Patricia McGill, RN, MSN
16	Program Planning and Evaluation 221
	Roberta M. Fruth, RN, MS, CCRN

PART IV: ECONOMIC AND FUTURE PERSPECTIVES

17	Economic Perspective 234
	Linda F. Samson, RN, PhD
18	Hospital Organization 249
	Suzette Cardin, RN, MS, CCRN
19	Issues and Trends 264
	Dolores S. Gomez, RN, MN
20	Future Directions 275
	Joanne M. Disch, RN, PhD

Glossary 283
Index 289

Part I

INTRODUCTION AND ASSESSMENT

Chapter 1

Financial Management

JUDITH L. WILSON, DONNA L. BERTRAM

Every culture has myths and folklore. Both serve to provide a sense of nationalism and autonomy to the culture during a particular era or time in history. However, they often reflect a heritage based in fancy rather than fact and therefore must change to accommodate progress when empirical evidence requires change. The myths and folklore of health care are particularly vulnerable to the march of progress. Critical care nursing provides ample testimony of our ability to respond productively in a dynamic and challenging environment.

In the past 4 decades American medicine has been revolutionalized by scientific and technological advances of a magnitude unparalleled in earlier periods. The home remedies used by our grandparents have been replaced by sophisticated modalities of treatment administered by highly trained and educated providers in complex facilities. When old remedies are swept under the carpet, new myths spring up like mushrooms and are nurtured by a favorable environment. An examination of the contemporary problems facing the health care industry today reveals that these myths—like some mushrooms—can cause problems when swallowed indiscriminately.

One such myth is that the financial management of hospitals is "different" and not subject to the same rules that govern other businesses. Concerns over rising health care costs in the 1970s raised questions from the public and private sectors about the validity of this myth, and initiatives to control costs followed. By the 1980s the myth was being openly challenged by government regulation and legislation. Financial management, planning, and control, once trivial considerations in the operation of hospitals, have gained considerable visibility from pressures in the present environment.

Another myth is that Americans don't ration health care. In fact health care is rationed by the prohibitive prices of insurance for some uninsured families, by the cost of unreimbursed care for insured individuals, by the cost of care for those unable to pay, and by the barriers to service access that exist in some cases. Uncollectible accounts, including bad debt, charity, and managed care discounts have risen from 17.1% in 1985 to 27.6% in 1989. Reports that charity care write-offs have tripled for some hospitals make others wary of providing care without assurance that payment will be forthcoming (1).

One other important but complex issue is the folklore surrounding competitiveness in international markets. Some believe the cost of health care in our country raises prices of U.S. commodities and therefore jeopardizes our competitive position in the world market. And lastly, public funding of health care is perceived to have a negative impact on national savings (2), resulting in fewer resources available for other public needs such as education and environmental improvement programs. This causes us to look for more fact than folklore and introduces the issue of hard choices. How will we spend our dollars?

This chapter provides historical and hospital perspectives on the impact of economics and finance on health care, and specifically on critical care, cites the role of the critical care nurse manager, identifies factors influencing health care, and provides an overview of economic theory within the present cost contained health care environment.

OVERVIEW

Historical Perspective

The rather dismal state of financial planning within hospitals was recognized during the 1970s. Drebin (3) blames administrators, boards of directors, and regulators for supporting the erroneous attitude that hospitals are not subject to the same financial pressures as other businesses and that they should not be expected to employ the same financial systems or goals. According to Drebin this attitude helped to create an industry that consumes billions of dollars a year, but is unable to quantify its product or production costs or explain why costs outpaced the average rate of cost increases in the economy. He sees the basic problem as a lack of financial data upon which to make sound financial management decisions and cautions that without adequate financial information there is a risk of inappropriate allocation of resources (3). Why were hospital financial managers so unprepared for the major upheaval brought about by the changes in reimbursement methods seen in the 1980s?

Hospital Perspective

This question takes us back to the post-World War II (WWII) era. During the 1950s and early 1960s hospitals were busy keeping up with medical advances by providing bigger, better, and more facilities and services. The environment was one of growth without external constraints on spending, and money was cheap and plentiful. The government encouraged building through Hill-Burton funds and no one was counting. Financial management was simply not a top administrative priority. Up until the 1960s capital funds for hospital projects were primarily provided by philanthropy, grants, and internal reserves, and there was little incentive to evaluate capital spending. From 1968 to 1976 funding from government grants and philanthropy fell from 44% to less than 18%. This forced hospitals to turn to debt financing for capital projects and funding from this source increased almost 30% (4). These trends continue today, and this source of money is neither cheap nor plentiful.

Third-party reimbursement also played a key role in the hospital industry's lack of concern with financial management. Increased service usage meant increased revenues, and hospitals, assured of reimbursement by insurance carriers, felt financially secure in this arrangement. However, as insurance became an increasingly higher percentage of total revenue, the payors' interest in controlling costs increased. With the arrival of Medicare in the 1960s, it became more important for hospitals to determine charges on a cost basis. As hospital costs continued to rise, so did the government's interest in what constituted these "costs." Additionally, the hospital industry did not anticipate that the government would change the "costs" it would reimburse. These changes initiated the beginning of cost containment and control, and regulations have been in effect since the end of the 1960s.

Efficiency, responsiveness, accessibility, quality, and sophisticated technology were demands driving the health care system in the 1970s. One of the forces supporting innovation and change was the retrospective reimbursement system. Payment based on charges rather than costs stimulated entrepreneurial interest in providing solutions to the problems. Solutions provided were innovative, creative, and profit motivated. New organizational structures were introduced including Health Maintenance Organizations (HMOs), Preferred Provider Organizations (PPOs), nursing home chains, mergers that produced conglomerate giants, and parent holding companies with diversified business enterprises. For-profit hospital organizations entered an industry formerly dominated by altruistic goals and values. The financial forecasts for these new organizations, based on a seemingly unlimited supply of dollars, were tempting even to the lay investor uninitiated in the business of health care.

As the 1970s ended, prospects for these new organizations had many in health care optimistically buzzing about new challenges and opportunities. The outnumbered pessimists found their voices dimmed by the melodious hum of success and dollars in the bank. The myth of this success that promised to revolutionize health care delivery depended on purchasers to provide a continuous flow of dollars into the industry. The obscured voices of the 1970s became increasingly amplified as the decade ended and the message was clearly transmitted. The voices were saying cost constraint, cost constraint, cost constraint. But still, the 1980s began promising a revolution in health care with new organizations and opportunities, and with the problems of the 1970s on the mend. What happened?

The two largest purchasers of health care, government and large private employers, protested that their combined 80% contribution to financing health care was costing too much. Strategies to control costs through their combined purchasing (market) power have had a profound effect on the health care industry since the early 1980s. The government introduced prospective payment and set clear limits to reimbursement based on diagnosis related groups (DRGs). In addition to the governments focus on health care costs, insurance companies and businesses also jumped on the bandwagon in the late 1970s. Seeing the utilization of health care increasing with escalating costs, these groups developed initiatives to control their costs. The use of second opinion, changing benefit structures, and management of utilization led the way to new insurance products, managed care groups, automation of claims, and increased auditing. Both government and private employers embraced the concept of competition and hoped to control costs through the traditional American marketplace.

Herzlinger (5) reviews the scenarios of the 1970s and 1980s and the factors influencing health care and concludes "that the issues have not been resolved and that the failure was almost entirely that of management, not of strategy." Citing evidence to support that efficiency was not achieved, quality is questionable, and responsiveness and accessibility are continuing problems, this article goes on to explore why the "revolution" failed. One reason provided is that entrepreneurs devoted their energies toward marketing, creative accounting, and innovative financial arrangements rather than to the operation of the organization. The opportunity to cut costs and improve quality, according to Herzlinger, failed in four key areas: operational administration, human resource management, control systems, and development of a management philosophy.

Convincing examples of failure in each of the four areas are contrasted with examples of success. Extracting from these examples, she offers hope for the future if the focus is on increased productivity, reduced costs, rewards and recognition for employee contributions, and business based financial structures and control systems. As a last note, she predicts success for those who develop philosophies based on the mission and goals of the organization and then ensure that the services promised to meet customer needs are delivered (6).

Nursing Perspective

Involvement in the decision-making processes of the organization has been touted as an opportunity and a challenge for nursing. In fact health care is in a state of turmoil. No one knows exactly what programs or activities will work. Blame for the current state of affairs is easily placed on Medicare, managed care, and rising numbers of uninsured. Since the 1960s when Medicare was introduced, the percent of gross national product (GNP) spent on health care has doubled. This increase in spending is often cited as a problem, but the fact is no one knows if this is enough, too much, or not enough. To what are we comparing this increase in spending? This question leads to some interesting observations. First, we forget that institutional health care is a fairly recent phenomenon. Prior to 1940 (WWII era) nurses were employed by home health (public health) organizations, or they cared for patients at home when the women in the home could not provide this care. This changed during the 1940s when it became acceptable and necessary for women to work. Women who previously provided care in the home now needed alternatives to care for sick and ailing family members.

Those injured in the war also needed a place for rehabilitation and treatment. Hill-Burton funds first approved by Congress in 1946 provided the money for construction of facilities, and hospitals proliferated.

Prior to the 1960s, young women were encouraged to seek careers in teaching or nursing. The myth of a woman's role as wife and mother being "the" career for all women changed with women's liberation in the 1960s and 1970s. As women entered the business, scientific, legal, and engineering professions, we saw nursing education change from a hospital based training program to a college based education. The entry into practice issue introduced by the American Nurses Association (ANA) in 1965 created debate, diversity, and dilemmas. The ANA position paper, "Educational Preparation for Nurse Practitioners and Assistants to Nurses," identified the bachelor of science in nursing (BSN) degree as the professional educational base for entry into practice (7). The purpose of this paper was to standardize nursing education into two levels of practice, professional and technical, in order to meet rapid technological advances, patient demands, complex decision making, scope of responsibility, and career mobility (8). Complete consensus on and resolution of this issue have not yet occurred. In the late 1980s, accelerated degree programs for RNs to achieve a BSN were still limited in number. In 1990 the state of Colorado broke new ground. Through a voluntary effort the Colorado Articulation Project developed straightforward, consistent degree programs for all schools in the state for the RN to BSN and LPN to ADN.

Nursing management changed when hospital administrators began to look at nursing as the hospital's largest labor force with the largest personnel budget. With the shift from cost based reimbursement to prospective payment, hospital administrators looked to nursing for efficiency, productivity, and effectiveness. Prior to this time, many nurses with diplomas had been promoted to management positions as head nurses, supervisors, and directors of nursing. Power, influence, and responsibility varied depending on the facility. Many directors of nursing were responsible for the students in the school of nursing as well as nursing services in the hospital. In 1951 the W.K. Kellogg Foundation funded a study that promoted additional education for nurse administrators (9). Hospital administrators and nursing managers began to see the value of including nurses in the decision-making arena of the hospital. Nurses in the 1980s entered the executive arena of hospital management. The multiple and complex issues of higher acuity, changing work force, increased regulation, expensive technology, changing focus from inpatient to outpatient services, physician relationships, specialized personnel, and maintaining quality create a need for an educated nursing administrator. The nursing management team plans and sets priorities, designs and implements the nursing budget, focuses on personnel management, assesses and changes nursing practices, and seeks to meet patient outcomes within the parameters of cost and length of hospital stay. Many nursing managers of critical care units are responsible for millions of dollars in the revenue, operating, and capital budgets. They are expected to focus on cost containment, efficiency, and productivity. The pressures on the nursing manager will increase as reimbursement issues change, operating margins decrease, physician relationships change, and sick patients compete for scarce resources. The pressure to use less expensive labor in critical care poses unique challenges for the manager. The knowledge of managing fiscal resources will become more important in the years ahead.

REVIEW OF LITERATURE

Florence Nightingale challenged those who are "in charge" to do what was proper for themselves and to ensure that everyone else does what should be done (10). The role of the critical care manager involves a knowledge base, skills, and abilities in the clinical practice arena as well as in management in order to bring about a cost effective, efficient, and quality outcome unit. The manager may seek out information about nursing cost, impact of nursing on patient outcome, cost comparisons of various deliveries, and other cost strategies. The nursing research on these aspects of critical care currently is in the formative stages. More emphasis and effort on studies of nursing costs in critical care using comparable measures must be done.

COSTS, UTILIZATION, AND QUALITY

Costs

Wilson et al.(11) identified nursing as a major hospital cost component and reported a wide variation of nursing cost for the patient day and stay within one DRG. They reported on how various studies of nursing costs widely vary due to nursing practice differences and various methodologies of reporting costs. Their study looked at myocardial infarction with complications (DRG 121). The allocation of nursing labor cost was the focus of a study done by Barkyte and Glandon (12). They found that nursing costs could differ depending on the type of cost allocation method. The method they used accounted for patient acuity in identifying direct nursing care costs.

A large group of ICU patients were studied by Munoz et al. (13), who looked at hospital cost, resource utilization, and outcome by age. They found that the hospital cost per patient was highest for those aged 75–80 years of age with $20,942 spent per patient. This study revealed a longer length of stay, sicker patients with high outliers, and greater mortality in the age group over 65. An earlier study by Munoz et al. (14) looked at cardiology patients who died. They also concluded that there is a significant financial risk to hospitals under the DRG reimbursement model.

Identifying that high turnover rates affect costs, quality, and productivity, Mann (15) reported on the use of a human capital perspective in analyzing costs associated with ICU turnover. Using a human capital ICU retention model, Mann looked at the value of wages and productivity for the individual nurse and for the hospital's investment.

Health care economist Jeff Goldsmith linked the issues of quality, benefit, and cost in a recent *Harvard Business Review* article (16). Concerns over the issue of whether using a highly technological and costly procedure may affect patient outcome and quality of care must be weighed against using other alternatives that may generate a similar outcome without the cost. Citing data from 60 hospitals on patients with pulmonary edema and respiratory failure (DRG 87), Horn (17) found higher costs associated with the most severely ill patients. Making a case for appropriate payment levels, her concern is that hospitals will develop strategies to avoid treating the most severely ill and most costly patients. Horn recommends the computerized severity index (CSI) tool to quantify the burden of illness so that appropriate adjustments in reimbursement ensure both access to and quality of care.

Utilization

The question of a more efficient use of the ICU was proposed by Turley and Edwardson (18). They suggest that the benefits of critical care have not been thoroughly documented, that costs from critical care hospitalization can be reduced, and that because of criteria based admission procedures that are poorly administered or lacking, ICUs are not being utilized efficiently. In one study the admission criteria to ICU revealed that 15% of all ICU admissions were unnecessary (19).

Reviewing the literature, Spivak (20) concludes that 10–42% of ICU admissions could be admitted to lower cost intermediate care settings without compromising care. He proposes that significant cost savings could be realized by diverting 10% of the patients routinely admitted to ICUs. He cites teaching hospitals as having 13% low risk ICU admissions while community hospitals may have 40% or more of their ICU admissions in this category. Spivak concludes that efficiency could be realized through the use of strict admission and discharge criteria, diversion of low risk patients to intermediate units with the capacity for noninvasive monitoring, and alternative sites for care including the home.

Another strategy for decreasing ICU costs comes from a study of 706 patients done by Henning et al. (21) who found that 40% of MICU patients and 30% of SICU patients were admitted for monitoring only and never received active interventions. The cost containment recommendation by this group was to organize ICUs according to severity of illness rather than by medical and surgical diagnosis. The researchers propose that concentrating services in a centralized area will improve utilization and could result in cost savings. The major administrative drawback was seen as resistance by nursing and medical staff to combining medical and surgical patients in either an ICU or an intermediate care unit.

Reviewing the history of ICUs, Thibault (22) reminds us that the explosive growth and belief in intensive care occurred without data to support the efficacy of outcomes and without a systematic method to account for costs. He cites major studies conducted in the 1970s and 1980s as lacking evidence to support that outcomes are better or that resource utilization is justified.

Practice guidelines and feedback to physicians were linked to decreased ICU and hospital length of stay in a study of 1145 consecutive admissions with an initial diagnosis of chest pain, pulmonary edema, or syncope (23). The study collected data over three 6-month periods. The first 6 months established baseline data. During the second 6 months two feedback mechanisms were initiated: daily review of ICU patients, and weekly review of patients cared for by medical house staff. In the third 6-month period only daily reviews of ICU and monitored patients were done. Mean hospital and ICU lengths of stay fell significantly during the two feedback periods as compared to the baseline period data. An additional finding of this research is of interest. Patients reporting dissatisfaction that their hospital length of stay was "too long" prior to the feedback intervention were more likely to report their length of stay as "just right" during the intervention. The researchers suggest that validation of these findings could reduce ICU utilization by 10% nationwide (23).

A pulmonary noninvasive monitoring unit was used for 94 patients with a cost savings of $173,000 in a 1988 study (24). The researchers suggest this alternative to traditional intensive care settings to cut costs and maintain quality (24).

Quality

Studying the effects of prospective payment on the quality of care provided to medicare patients, Kahn et al. (25) evaluated 16,758 pre- and post-prospective payment system (PPS) patients with six diseases: congestive heart failure, acute MI, pneumonia, cerebrovascular accident, hip fracture, and depression. Researchers looked at outcomes of care, process of care, and discharge status. Data on the 14,012 patients with medical diagnoses were published in a series of reports where the findings are summarized (25). Draper et al. (26) present the design and sampling methods used to study 8404 pre-PPS and 8354 post-PPS Medicare patients and conclude that the sample is representative relative to hospital and patient variables.

Keeler et al. (27) studied sickness at admission and, using an average of 19 variables, concluded that sickness at admission increased following PPS. Thirty-day expected mortality due to sickness at admission was 1% higher in the post-PPS group. This study also found that high rather than normal blood pressures in ICU patients, especially cardiac patients, were more favorable and that reweighting variable parameters by specific diagnosis led to better predictions of outcomes.

Using explicit review techniques, Kahn et al. (28) found that better nursing care and better cognitive performance of physicians led to improvement in the process of care post-PPS as compared to pre-PPS. Improvements were associated with decrease in adjusted mortality rates post-PPS (28). Similarly, Rubenstein et al. (29), using an implicit review, report that despite more patients being discharged in unstable condition, the quality of care improved post-PPS. While 25% of patients were judged to have received poor care in 1981-1982, only 12% fell in the poor care category in 1985-1986. In the same sample, instability at discharge was found to increase post-PPS from 10% to 15%. Sixteen percent of patients discharged in unstable condition were dead at 90 days post-discharge, compared to 10% of patients discharged in stable condition (30). Comparing outcomes, Kahn et al. (31) found that hospital length of stay decreased 24% for all patient diagnosis combined, and in-hospital mortality went from 16.1% pre-PPS to 12.6% post-PPS. More patients were discharged to nursing homes post-PPS, and 1% had prolonged nursing home stays. The researchers concluded that PPS was not associated with worse outcomes in this study.

Summarizing the entire study, Rogers et al. (32) present three conclusions: (*a*) mortality following hospitalization has not been affected; (*b*) improvements in processes of care have continued post-PPS; and (*c*) a patient is more likely to be discharged while unstable. Recommendations are to continue to monitor the effects of prospective payment as pressures to contain costs increase.

While the above reports indicate that quality of care has been unaffected or improved post-PPS, careful interpretation is needed. The study data were collected during the 4 years preceding and following PPS, and we are now into its eighth year. Other factors such as the nursing shortage, effects of technology, changes in peer review, and the long-term impact of patients discharged in unstable condition should be considered. Perhaps the most valuable aspects of the study are the tools used in evaluation. The study is publicly available for continued research efforts.

AACN Studies

The American Association of Critical-Care Nurses (AACN) conducted a study in 1983 on research priorities in critical care nursing (33). These priorities blend clinical outcomes and practice concerns that need to include cost implications (see Table 1.1).

In 1990 the AACN published "Outcome Standards for Nursing Care of the Critically Ill" (34). This dynamic and bold work focuses on quality outcomes based on nursing diagnoses and nursing interventions used by nurses in the delivery of care to the critically ill. While these outcome standards define quality in terms of the patient, the editors believe that "quality care can be cost effective care." By identifying patient outcomes that are based on process standards, it is possible to control length of stay, complications, and costs.

In 1985 the AACN began a demonstration project to look at excellence, caring, high quality, nurse satisfaction, and cost containment in an ICU en-

Table 1.1. Research Priorities for Critical Care Nursing[a]

1. Sleep patterns of critically ill patients
2. Burnout
3. Orientation programs
4. Effects of stimuli on intracranial pressure
5. Weaning patients from ventilators
6. Patient classification systems
7. Incentives to retain nurses
8. Staff stress
9. Patient positioning and its effects on patients' cardiovascular and pulmonary status
10. Staffing patterns
11. Preventing infections in patients with invasive lines and/or undergoing invasive procedures
12. Suctioning patients on ventilators
13. Research utilization
14. Methods of assessing and relieving pain

[a]Reprinted from Lewandowski L, Kositsky A. Research priorities for critical care nursing: a study by the American Association of Critical-Care Nurses. Heart & Lung 1983;12:38.

vironment. The project was designed to look at cost effectiveness while meeting five values about critical care nursing. Central to the project was the belief that incorporating the values of an all RN staff, a high proportion of CCRNs, use of standards in the care of the critically ill, nurse-physician collaboration, and participative management would promote a cost effective and quality outcome unit. This study (35) revealed that when the values were present the outcomes were:

- Nursing turnover was less than 8%.
- Critical care nursing charges were only 11% of the total hospital charges.
- Mortality was 50% less than predicted.
- Morale was high.
- Unit functioning was viewed as very effective by physicians.

This important work challenges critical care managers to incorporate these values into their own work settings.

Concerns about the nursing shortage, working conditions, salary and benefits, educational opportunities, and professional image prompted a 1988 report by the AACN nursing economics task force (36). In the document, problem statements and strategies are presented to assist the critical care manager in maintaining a cost effective unit. One strategy that promotes cost savings is that of self-governance. Roberts (37) reported that with the estimated cost of replacing one staff nurse ranging from $10,000 to $80,000 the advantage of employee participation through a successful shared governance program which promotes satisfaction and commitment is difficult to argue against.

Role of the Critical Care Manager

The current environmental pressures and political structures within health care challenge the nurse manager of today. A clear understanding of the role of the critical care manager is necessary for staff, physicians, and the executive management team. Identified in "Role Expectations for the Critical Care Manager" are four primary management accountabilities: clinical practice, personnel, fiscal, and environmental (38). The integration of these four areas facilitates the coordination of the resources necessary to meet quality and cost goals of the institution. The clinical manager in critical care is the key that links all the players and resources.

The role of fiscal management is becoming more crucial in an arena of cost containment. The critical care manager needs to:

1. Identify and understand the fundamentals of financial management.
2. Assess, plan, implement, and evaluate the budget process.
3. Understand, monitor, and report variances with identifying strategies for control.
4. Communicate priorities, objectives, and outcomes to subordinates, peers, physicians, and others.
5. Coordinate the work of the entire unit by appropriate productivity measures and resource allocation.
6. Understand health care trends and issues as they relate to the hospital's financial and economic viability and future directions.

FINANCIAL MANAGEMENT AND NURSING

The future of health care is uncertain and uncertainty leads to change. Whether planned (proactive) or unplanned (reactive), change is inevitable and presents both challenges and opportunities. Many of these opportunities can be maximized by nursing if we are willing and able to accept the challenges. Challenges that involve financial planning and control functions will be among the top contenders for nurses seeking opportunities to influence health care in the future. To develop expertise in financial planning and control is crucial for success.

A review of the industrial literature shows that uncertainty within an organization increases when forces create dependency on external environments. With uncertainty goes risk. Gupta and Govindarajan (39) suggest that the ability of a manager to accept challenges and take risks in an environment of change and uncertainty will produce more effective performance results than managers that are faced with maintaining operations. Both willingness to take risks and tolerance for ambiguity were hypothesized to increase effectiveness of strategy implementation with new programs (39).

While it may be unrecognized by many first line nurse managers, the capacity to accept challenges and take risks can be one of the most rewarding and satisfying aspects of their jobs. Breaking a rule for a special request, confronting a "difficult" physician on policy, proposing a costly but necessary program to ensure staff competence, or implementing needed admission and discharge criteria in the face of physician opposition are all examples of risks—and hopefully rewards. Another strength not often recognized by nurses is their expertise in applying the nursing process. Used daily in the care of patients, this systematic problem-solving approach is scientifically based; produces excellent assessments, plans, and evaluations; and is potentially applicable to any clinical or administrative situation. The management process of planning, organizing, directing, and controlling is in fact almost identical to the nursing process.

Another aspect to consider is that uncertainty has led to the prevalence of contingency theory as the dominant organizational theory used in management today. Contingency theory is based on the supposition that responsiveness to situations, the environment, or internal and external circumstances is of prime importance in management. Situational management refers to the practical application of this theory. Sound judgment and self-confidence enable nurse managers to take calculated risks when outcomes are unknown.

Innovation and creativity are valued in today's society. Nurses have always been resourceful. We are experts at improvising. So, understanding our strengths and equipped with problem-solving and interpersonal skills, flexibility, and adaptability and protected by the armor of experience and self-confidence, let us proceed to apply these skills to the challenges and opportunities of the future. Financial management is one such challenge and opportunity.

The AACN identified "Role Expectations for the Critical Care Manager" (Fig. 1.1). In the section under fiscal management the nurse manager and the institution are expected to:

1. Establish a valid statistical base for budgetary decision making.
2. Facilitate the development of a realistic annual budget which may include revenue, personnel, supplies, and capital equipment.
3. Establish accurate nursing productivity measures.
4. Review budgetary variances regularly to assure appropriate use of resources.
5. Promote cost effective unit operations.
6. Anticipate the impact of institutional financial status on unit operations.

These role expectations were developed by the AACN to assist managers in four role components: clinical practice, personnel, environment, and financial management. Often nurse managers do not have formal preparation in financial management. On-the-job training, trial and error, and informal networks often are the nurse manager's only recourse in gaining skill in financial management. The nurse manager needs to understand practical principles and methods involved in accounting, finances, budgeting, economics, and health trends.

The AACN in the position statement resolved "that the manager of a critical care area is a baccalaureate prepared professional nurse who is clinically experienced in the areas of administrative responsibility. . . ." Nurses who return to school to achieve a BSN can take undergraduate courses in financial and managerial accounting, economics, and computer science. These courses introduce basic concepts and prepare the manager for better decision making. Graduate education in nursing administration, business, or a combination degree offers greater breadth and depth into financial concepts.

Each institution develops a budget process using accounting and financial management principles. The first-line manager who already possesses basic skills in these areas will be able to adapt without much difficulty. Understanding the more intricate aspects of cost accounting, cash flow, investments, debt financing, rate setting, revenue enhancement, accounts receivable, profit, and return on investment offer the manager a complete view of the total picture of financial management. Sound financial management is based on a full understanding of the financial operations of a hospital.

Sound financial management is essential to the survival of hospitals in today's economically constrained environment. In order to accomplish financial management, the critical care nurse manager must have an understanding of the financial operations of the hospital; be comfortable using financial terminology; be able to interpret, evaluate, and apply financial data; and appreciate the value of financial planning and control in the context of hospital mission, accomplishments, and achievement of goals. On a broader perspective, an understanding of the factors influencing health care is also necessary.

Role Expectations for the Critical Care Manager

IN *NURSING, A SOCIAL POLICY STATEMENT*, the American Nurses' Association defines nursing as "the diagnosis and treatment of human responses to actual or potential health problems." Critical care nursing is that specialty within nursing which deals specifically with human responses to life threatening problems (1).

Nurse managers "coordinate available resources to efficiently and effectively provide professional nursing care of a quality consistent with nursing care standards and at a cost compatible with the fiscal and other resources of the health care organization" (2). Management of a critical care environment presents a particular challenge because of the magnitude of resources utilized, the timeliness of nursing intervention that is required, the sophisticated technological and clinical interventions that are used, the depth of the data base necessary for decision making and the degree of collaboration needed among disciplines.

WHEREAS, the role of the critical care manager is defined as the coordination and integration of human and material resources necessary to care for a population of critically ill patients

WHEREAS, the trend in administration of patient care units is decentralization, with concurrent increased expectation and responsibilities of the nurse manager

WHEREAS, in response to environmental changes, nursing decisions must also reflect a business orientation

WHEREAS, the vital link between institutional goals and implementation at the unit level is the critical care manager,

THEREFORE, BE IT RESOLVED THAT the manager of a critical care area is a baccalaureate prepared professional nurse who is clinically experienced in the areas of administrative responsibility and competent in the application of management principles,

AND the critical care nurse manager formally participates in institutional planning and decision making that have an impact on the scope of critical care nursing practice and the critical care environment,

AND the critical care nurse manager has responsibility, authority, and accountability for implementation and maintenance of critical care nursing standards.

Implementation

The critical care manager is the leader and role model for professional nursing practice. The management of critical care also requires a knowledge base, skills, and competencies in clinical nursing and administration. It is the shared responsibility of the nurse manager and the institution to develop and maintain administrative accountabilities that include but are not limited to:

Clinical Practice Management
- Implementation of a valid and reliable patient classification system
- Implementation and maintenance of critical care nursing standards
- Direction and coordination of a selected delivery system of patient care
- Provision of support for critically ill patients and their families
- Incorporation of regulatory mandates into critical care practice
- Demonstration of sensitivity to ethical and legal ramifications of nursing practice in the critical care setting
- Delineation of needed knowledge, skills, and competencies of nursing staff and provision of staff development
- Incorporation of current research, new interventions, and technological advances into nursing practice
- Implementation of ongoing quality assurance activities

Personnel Management
- Interviewing applicants and hiring qualified critical care staff
- Staffing unit(s) to ensure 24-hour nursing coverage appropriate to patient care needs
- Facilitating staff input into decisions affecting nurse practice
- Identifying and planning for development needs of the staff
- Providing appropriate and timely information to staff as a basis for sound decision making
- Conducting timely and periodic performance appraisals based on pre-established standards, and following up appropriately
- Disciplining individual staff as delineated in institutional policy and procedure
- Demonstrating knowledge of labor law applicable to the institution

Fiscal Management
- Establishment of a valid statistical data base for budgetary decision making
- Facilitation of the development of realistic annual budget which may include revenue, personnel, supplies and capital equipment
- Establishment of accurate nursing productivity measures
- Regular review of budgetary variances to assure appropriate use of resources
- Promotion of cost effective unit operations
- Anticipation of the impact of institutional financial status on unit operations

Environmental Management
- Development, implementation, and evaluation of unit goals in concert with departmental and institutional goals
- Implementation and maintenance of structure standards for critical care nursing
- Establishment of effective communication channels to assure coordinated nursing care
- Promotion of a collaborative practice with other health care disciplines to assure an integrated approach to care of the patient
- Implementation of a risk management program to prevent, minimize, or correct risks to patients and staff based on institutional policy and procedure

With the unique combination of clinical, fiscal, and management expertise, the critical care nurse manager is in a key position to promote effective and cost efficient care of patients in the critical care environment.

REFERENCES

1. American Association of Critical-Care Nurses. Definition of critical care nursing. Newport Beach, CA: American Association of Critical-Care Nurses, 1984.
2. American Nurses' Association. Roles, responsibilities, and qualifications for nurse administrators. Kansas City, KS: American Nurses' Association, 1978.

Figure 1.1. AACN Position Statement: Role Expectations for the Critical Care Manager (adopted by AACN Board of Directors, June 1986).

FACTORS INFLUENCING HEALTH CARE

The health care system that exists today is influenced by consumers, social forces, public policy, technology, and providers. Providers include institutions, professionals, services, and delivery systems (Fig. 1.2).

Consumers

For our purpose, the consumer is primarily the direct recipient of health care, i.e., the patient, and in some cases the patient's family. Consumers of health care have changed over time in several ways; they are better educated, healthier, and older. Their expectations for health delivery systems have shifted from a focus on cure and treatment of disease to include the component of care in keeping healthy. Evidence of this shift is seen in the increased years of life expectancy as consumers adopt healthier lifestyles by meeting nutritional needs, psychological and physical fitness needs, and giving up unhealthy habits such as smoking. Still, when sick, and regardless of ability to pay, consumers often want the best that our system has to offer. This means a hi-tech, hi-touch, no-barriers-to-care expectation that has been the norm for 3 decades. What our system fails to realize is that sick patients simply need help. They are not consumers shopping around for the least costly service or comparing second opinion prices or looking for sales. While stipulations for reimbursement are being increasingly imposed by third-party payors, sick patients continue to access inpatient health care services primarily through physicians. Reinhardt (40) reminds us that over half of annual health care expenses are attributed to only 5% of the population and that 10% of the population accounts for over 70% of the health care dollars spent. While there is much concern about the 37 million Americans who have no health insurance, one has to wonder just how much of a burden they place on the system. Over three-fourths of the uninsured are full-time employees and their dependents. Typically they are low-income families unable or unwilling to allocate 20% of their income to private health insurance. As consumers, they receive only about half of the health care received by insured families with higher incomes. The issues are access and, as profit margins fall for hospitals, who will pay?

Consumer issues related to access, care, and the increased numbers of underinsured and uninsured will continue to be debated in the next decade as questions of who gets care and who pays are decided. For example, most health care dollars are spent in the consumer's last year of life, with the majority (two-thirds) spent in the last two weeks of life. Ethical concerns will continue to be voiced as the quality of life is argued against morbidity and mortality data.

A major consumer issue facing our society today is aging America. This issue will have implications for all aspects of our lives and specific impact on health care. By 2020, 17–20% of the population in America will be over 65 years of age. The largest growing segment of our population is the age group over 85 years of age. This is a change from today, with about 13% of the population over 65 and about half of this age group over 75. Compare this to 1970 when 10% of the population was over 65 and only 4% was over 75.

The elderly will have considerable clout in influencing everything from the food we eat, to the advertising that influences the products we buy, to the entertainment we seek, to the laws we live by. For example, the 1989 Repeal of the Catastrophic

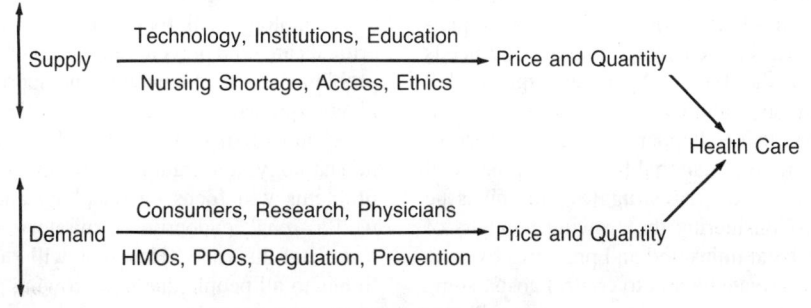

Figure 1.2. Factors influencing health care.

Health Care Bill passed in 1988 was largely due to political influence of the population over age 65.

As consumers of health care, the elderly will need both acute and chronic care. Eyes, joints, and essential organs wear out with age. We will see an increased need for such things as cataract surgery, lens implants, joint and organ replacements, and dialysis. Because of complex health problems, many of these patients will require critical care services.

Social Forces

Social forces influencing health care include the changing labor force, environmental issues, political influence, and the shift to a global economy/society. Environmental forces focus on safety, healthy lifestyles, and high-risk populations (exercise, diet, nonsmoking environments, war on drugs, etc.) Political clout will be exercised by baby boomers concerned about funding health care for the elderly and by the elderly also concerned with funding their own health care.

The changing labor force will have the most significant impact on nursing as we see a dwindling supply of 18- to 24-year-olds entering the labor market. Nursing has traditionally recruited from this age group, and we will be challenged to look at other entrants in the future. Minorities, the handicapped, mothers, and retirees may enter nursing, and each group presents unique challenges. The average nurse today is female, white, and 40 years old. Changes in traditional nursing systems will be required to assimilate new entrants into the profession.

Public Policy

In the public policy arena, cost constraints and regulatory issues will continue. Questions of quality vs. cost will be a challenge that nursing needs to address in the 1990s. Americans spend $1.8 billion a day on health care ($663 billion a year). The response to the Pepper Commission recommendations to go to national health insurance will be of interest as Congress struggles with this issue once again. Considering the growing numbers of underinsured and uninsured and pressures by government and private payors to control costs, some form of social health policy reform seems likely. This will present increased ethical concerns as the issues of access to care and rationing of care are openly challenged. Will everyone over the age of 65 be required to have a living will? Are social benefits derived from the treatment of AIDS worth the cost or should the money be spent on research? These and other tough questions will require hard choices.

Technology

In the area of technology, new equipment such as management information systems, integrated patient data systems, and clinical decision-making trees, as well as self-care products, will continue to be introduced. New preventive measures will come from genetic and other research endeavors. Occupational hazards such as AIDS, radiation, pollution, and hazardous wastes will continue to challenge us. The issue of who will fund capital equipment expenditures will challenge hospitals as credit ratings are scrutinized and payors are less willing to absorb these costs.

Technology is more advanced, more abundant, and more frequently used in the American health care system than in other countries. Hospitals, forced to evaluate investments in capital equipment, are likely to spend their shrinking dollars on technologies that will reduce costs, increase efficiency, focus on outpatient or home care alternatives to inpatient care, and maintain or enhance quality. Incentives for purchasing costly technology for inpatient care have come from physicians, who demand the newest and best; from consumers, who expect high-tech care; and from competition among hospitals for these two customers. Disincentives to these forces are now in effect as hospitals delay capital equipment replacement, hoping to extend the life of present technology, or postpone purchases expecting better prices when second-generation technology comes on the market (20).

Technology will focus on two major thrusts: critical care, and prevention/control of chronic care problems. Critical care will include organ transplantation, cardiovascular diagnostics and therapies, neurosurgery, high-risk obstetrics and neonatology, and trauma. Preventive/chronic care problems will focus on oncology and AIDS, as well as renal, endocrine, respiratory, and musculoskeletal disorders. Hospitals will stop being all things to all people due to narrowing margins and economies of scale.

Advances in technology have created some of

the ethical dilemmas in health care today. Sustaining life may be possible, but is not always desirable. This problem will increase as our population continues to age. For example, there are many issues to be resolved in cases of organ transplantation when supply, availability, and distribution questions are asked.

Providers

Hospitals will have three departments, ER, OR, and critical care, and will continue to discharge patients to expanded ambulatory care and hospital-based home care services. Diversification will continue as hospitals move into health promotion and specific markets such as women's health. Cost constraints along with morbidity and mortality data may promote large high volume regionalized medical complexes.

Physicians will experience changes in their practices, income, and payments. Some physicians, frustrated with hospital administration, will look for more opportunities to offer services independent of the hospital. The proposed payment scheme of resource based relative value scale (RBRVS) may create conflicts among physicians and hospitals. Astute hospitals will look for greater collaboration with physicians through joint ventures and patient care management delivery systems.

The health care system in the United States is struggling with many complex challenges, including:

- Costs that are rising at 10% annually;
- Costs that exceed price increases in the general economy;
- Excess capacity of inpatient beds, including critical care beds in some community hospitals;
- Rising consumption of total GNP;
- Excess supply of physicians;
- Shortage of nurses and allied health care workers;
- Increasing pressures to contain costs by the two largest purchasers of health care, government and private business;
- Shrinking (or stable but modest) profit margins;
- Increasing numbers of uninsured and underinsured;
- Poor credit ratings and shrinking sources of capital;
- Uncertainty and instability in the future.

Economics

Can the health care industry achieve the economic goal of efficiency? Can the health care services produced be distributed equitably among the population? These two questions move us from the world of financial management to the broader economic issues that influence health care. Without a basic understanding of the economic challenges specific to the health care industry, an appreciation for why nurse managers should study financial management would be incomplete.

"Economics is concerned with the efficient utilization or management of limited productive resources for the purpose of attaining the maximum satisfaction of human material wants" (41). This definition assumes that individuals, if free to do so, will choose to purchase the type and amount of goods and services that will provide them with the most satisfaction. It also assumes a rational customer with full information on both the benefits and prices of all available choices.

The three basic questions that economists seek to explain are what, how, and for whom? The function of an economic system is to determine what will be produced by a society (outputs), how it will be produced (methods and allocation of resources), and who will benefit from the output (distribution of income) (42). The ideal market economy, driven by profit and competition, responds to these conditions in the most efficient way. A free market system responds naturally by producing goods and services in just the right amounts and in the most efficient combinations. This balance of supply and demand is referred to as market equilibrium. Imperfect markets, those unable to operate efficiently or to maintain equilibrium, are subject to control through government regulation.

Economics examines efficiency and equity questions through optimization and equilibrium techniques. Optimization refers to the allocation of scarce resources in the most efficient (least cost) manner. Marginal analysis, including the study of marginal benefits and marginal costs, is the basis for optimization techniques. In theory, and assuming an efficient price, consumers will maximize their satisfaction by allocating their resources in such a way that the marginal benefit of the last unit (of a good or service) produced will equal the marginal cost of producing that unit. There are many variables that affect the selection decisions of consumers. For example, price, income, personal values, perceived benefits, and changes in alternative choices all influence consumer demand. Optimization techniques are used to predict how changes in price and income affect consumer behavior.

Equilibrium in markets is studied using supply and demand analysis. Using this tool economists can forecast changes in price, quantity, and total expenses associated with a change in health policy. They can also investigate why health care prices are rising faster than prices in other markets.

Gross National Product

One economic indicator of market activity is the gross national product (GNP). GNP is defined as "the total value of goods and services produced in a nation during a specific time period (as a year) and also comprising the total expenditures by consumers and governments plus gross private investments" (43). The *Economic Dictionary* illustrates GNP as the sum of consumer expenditures plus gross private domestic investment, plus government purchases of goods and services plus net exports (44).

GNP = Consumer Purchases
+ Gross Private Domestic Investment
+ Government Purchases + Net Exports

GNP is a measure of final goods and services produced. Goods or services that are intermediate, or only used in the production of the final product, are not included in the GNP. For example, under Medicare the government purchases care for a patient with the diagnosis of uncomplicated myocardial infarction (DRG 122) at a reimbursed rate of $3590. This is the final service purchased. Therefore, all of the "intermediate" services and goods including nursing care, diagnostic tests, supplies, drugs, dietary, and so forth are not part of the final GNP. Obviously, if the service costs more than the purchase price, the GNP will be underreported; if the service costs less than the purchase price, the GNP will be inflated.

Reports that health care consumes 11.1% of GNP simply mean that of final goods and services produced, 11.1% or about $600 billion per year are spent on health care. Of this percent, about 4% is spent on inpatient hospital care; and this has remained fairly constant over the past few years. The amount of GNP consumed by critical care services is not well documented but is estimated at 1% (22).

ECONOMICS OF THE HEALTH CARE SECTOR

The problems of rising costs and inequitable distribution of health care are brought to our attention daily as the media broadcasts that sick children are refused care because of inability to pay, and that a car made in Detroit costs an extra $700 because of the increasing cost of health insurance (40). Solutions to the problems are less abundant but can be sought through economic analysis.

There are three basic choices to be made in product/service markets. The first two address efficiency, and the third is concerned with equity. The choices can be posed as questions:

1. How much should be spent on health care and what should be the composition of services?
2. What is the best method for producing the services?
3. What method will be used to distribute health care to society (45)?

These questions raise complex and interrelated issues about what criteria will be used to measure one choice against another. If the criteria of least cost and consumer preference are used, then the free market economy will prevail. If other criteria based on values, assumptions, and special interests are used, the results will be different.

Some of the problems in applying economic techniques to the health care sector are the difficulties in defining what criteria is to be used. Standards such as number of hospital beds per thousand population and number of hospital days per DRG imply only one standard criterion can be applied. Consideration of optimizing alternatives is then limited. To illustrate this issue the example of substitution and compliments is useful. Substitution refers to exchanging one system or provider for another to achieve efficiency and equity goals. The substitution of a nurse for a physician, in some cases, is more efficient and effective than physician provided services. Who receives payment for the service differentiates substitution and complementary roles. If the nurse receives the payment it is substitution. If the physician receives the payment for services rendered by a nurse then the role is complementary.

Professional organizations protect the tasks performed by their members and limit infringement through state practice acts. The American Nurses' Association (ANA), with the support of other nursing organizations, participates in activities to protect the professional practice of registered nurses. The American Medical Association (AMA) protects the practice of physicians. These political arenas are powerful deterrents to change in pricing and delivery of health care.

Controlling expenditures in the health care market can be approached from the demand side, the supply side, or a combination of the two. Americans traditionally have encouraged entrepreneurship in their marketplaces and have shied away from government regulation. In the health care marketplace this has led to one of the best health care systems in the world. It is dynamic, technologically advanced, innovative, and expensive. Reinhardt (40), comparing health care systems in developed nations, presents our open-ended, entrepreneurial systems as "plagued by excess capacity . . . and rapidly growing costs." He points to other countries that effectively control costs on the supply side of the market through regional planing to limit resources such as beds, technology, and sometimes, physicians. He admits that controlling capacity creates monopolies which then require the addition of price control to limit the exploitive power that monopolies have in the market (40).

Early programs aimed at controlling the supply side of the health care market included the certificate-of-need (CON) laws, regional health planning, rate review, and budget review. Supply side controls are based on the premise that an increase in the supply of services will lead to an increase in demand and inflationary prices result. By controlling supply, demand decreases and costs can be controlled. These programs or their adaptations exist in many states today. Unfortunately they have been disappointing in achieving their intended objectives. More recent efforts to control supply include regulating the amount that providers can charge based on past practice, and restricting payment for certain procedures to specific providers; for example, designating which hospitals will be reimbursed for heart transplants. Some states have initiated rate-setting programs that establish reimbursement for all payors in the state. Another strategy influencing the supply of health care professionals is the federal government financing of education with low-cost loans or no-cost repayment programs. The success of these programs depends on how the outcome is measured.

Strategies undertaken to control demand include the increasing use of copayments and higher deductibles. The intent is to control demand by increasing consumer out-of-pocket expenses for health care. Demand is also decreased by the managed care concept. HMOs, for example, use less inpatient care per capita of insured than traditional systems. Queuing or increasing the time consumers must wait for elective procedures is another method of controlling demand.

Americans assume that health care is available, easily accessible, and equally administered to all in need. This assumption has been fostered by public policy initiatives enacted for the purpose of ensuring access to quality care regardless of ability to pay. The goal of public policy has been to avoid a two-tiered health care system whereby citizens dependent upon publicly funded health care have limited access to providers and treatments while citizens with private insurance or resources have unlimited access. This goal of equality in both access and quality is sound from a clinical standpoint; i.e., providers want to deliver services to those in need of health care and sick patients expect that they will receive health care services. But from a purely economic point of view, the goal becomes less clear and conflicts arise. This state of affairs has resulted in additional ethical conflicts in health care when questions arise regarding the allocation and distribution of scarce resources. For example, should people who smoke be eligible for mechanical ventilation? Should obese people with related cardiac conditions be eligible for coronary care? These are tough questions facing our nation.

Challenges for nurses include giving up old roles and functions, recognizing the impact of role change on present relationships, and developing strong first-line managers. Nurse managers will be expected to design systems and services that meet changing consumer and provider demands, provide cost efficient systems, provide quality based services with defined outcomes, problem solve with multidisciplinary health care teams, and reduce barriers to recognition and rewards for nurses through negotiation, influence, and marketing (46). The challenges are great, but so are the opportunities.

Knowledge of the financial and economic factors that influence health care provides an advantage in responding with vision and confidence.

CONCLUSION

Financial management is increasingly becoming an essential component of the critical care nurse manager's role. Expectations for cost efficiency while maintaining quality patient outcomes requires more sophisticated skills in planning, organizing, and controlling human and material resources. This chapter has reviewed the historical events leading to the present financial crisis in the health care industry and discussed the economic environment as it impacts health care. The focus has been on the effects of cost constraints in critical care with special emphasis on the changing role of the critical care nurse manager. Recent efforts by the AACN to address financial and economic issues have been presented throughout the chapter.

REFERENCES

1. Southwick K, Mayer D. Recession watch: hospitals, in a slowdown, the strong survive but weak facilities' woes may intensify, and DRGs are wild cards. Healthweek 27 Aug. 1990:15.
2. Reinhardt UE. Health care spending and American competitiveness. Health Affairs Winter 1989;8:5–21.
3. Drebin ME. Financial information systems: the key to hospitals' survival. Hospitals 1978;52(12):88–90.
4. Lightle MA. '70s see new approaches to capital financing for hospitals. Hospitals 1978;52(12):135–141.
5. Herzlinger RE. The failed revolution in health care—the role of management. Harvard Business Review March–April 1989:96.
6. Herzlinger, pp. 97–103.
7. McCloskey JC, Grace HK. Current issues in nursing. 2nd ed. Boston: Blackwell Scientific Publcations, 1985:472.
8. McCloskey, p. 213.
9. McCloskey, p. 279.
10. Nightingale F. Notes on nursing: what it is, and what it is not. Philadelphia: J.B. Lippincott Co., Facsimile 1859, p. 24.
11. Wilson L, Prescott PA, Aleksandrowicz L. Nursing: a major hospital cost component. Health Services Research Feb. 1988;22(6):773–796.
12. Barkyte DY, Glandon GL. Issues in nursing labor costs allocation. Journal of Nursing Administration Dec. 1988;18(12):16–19.
13. Munoz E, Josephson J, Tenenbaum N, Goldstein J, Shears AM. Diagnosis-related groups, costs, and outcome for patients in the intensive care unit. Heart & Lung Nov. 1989;18(6):627–633.
14. Munoz E, Chalfin D, Birnbaum E, Mulloy K, Cohen J, Wise L. Hospital costs, resource characteristics, and the dynamics of death for hospitalized patients in cardiology diagnosis related groups. Heart & Lung March 1989;18(2):164–171.
15. Mann, EE. A human capital approach to ICU nurse retention. Journal of Nursing Administration Oct. 1989;19(10):8–16.
16. Goldsmith JA. Radical prescription for hospitals. Harvard Business Review May-June 1989;3:67, 104, 111.
17. Horn SD. The financial impact of quality care. In: Parrills JE, ed. Critical decisions: key issues in the recovery of the critically ill. Burlington, Ontario, Canada: B.C. Decker, Inc. 1988:109–118.
18. Turley RM, Edwardson SR. Can ICUs be more efficiently used? JONA 1985;15:25–28.
19. Sebilia AJ. Critical care unit. Critical Care Nurse 1984;2:36–37.
20. Spivak D. The high cost of acute health care: a review of escalating costs and limitations of such exposure in intensive care units. Am Rev Respir Dis 1987;136:1007–1011.
21. Henning RJ, McClish D, Daly B, Nearman CR, Jackson D. Clinical characteristics and resource utilization of ICU patients: implications for organization of intensive care. Critical Care Medicine March 1987;15(3):264–269.
22. Thibault GE. Evaluating intensive care unit outcomes. In: Parrills JE, ed. Critical decisions: key issues in the recovery of the critically ill. Burlington, Ontario, Canada: B.C. Decker, Inc. 1988:57–76.
23. Eagle KA, Mulley AG, Skates SJ, Reder VA, Nicholson BW, Secton JO, Barnett GO, Thibault GE. Length of stay in the intensive care unit. JAMA 1990;264:992–997.
24. Krieger BP, Ershowsky P, Spivack D. One year's experience with a noninvasively monitored intermediate care unit for pulmonary patients. JAMA 5 Sept. 1990;264(9):1143–1146.
25. Kahn KL, Rubenstein LV, Draper D, et al. The effects of the DRG-based prospective payment system on quality of care for hospitalized medicare patients: an introduction to the series. JAMA 17 Oct. 1990;264(15):1953.
26. Draper D, Kahn KL, Reinisch EJ, et al. Studying the effects of the DRG-based prospective payment system on quality of care: design, sampling, and fieldwork. JAMA 17 Oct. 1990;264(15):1956–1961.
27. Keeler EB, Kahn KL, Draper D, et al. Changes in sickness at admission following the introduction of the prospective payment system. JAMA Oct. 17, 1990;264(15):1962–1968.
28. Kahn KL, Rogers WH, Rubenstein LV, et al. Measuring quality of care with explicit process criteria before and after implementation of the DRG-based prospective payment system. JAMA 17 Oct. 1990;264(15):1969–1973.
29. Rubenstein LV, Kahn KL, Reinisch EJ, et al. Changes in quality of care for five diseases measured by implicit review, 1981 to 1986. JAMA 17 Oct. 1990;264(15):1974.
30. Kosecoff J, Kahn KL, Rogers WH, et al. Prospective payment system and impairment at discharge. JAMA 17 Oct. 1990;264(15):1980.
31. Kahn KL, Keeler EB, Sherwood MJ, et al. Comparing outcomes of care before and after implementation of

the DRG-based prospective payment system. JAMA 17 Oct. 1990;264(15):1984.
32. Rogers WH, Draper D, Kahn KL, et al. Quality of care before and after implementation of the DRG-based prospective payment system: a system of effects. JAMA 17 Oct. 1990;264(15):1989.
33. Lewandowski L, Kositsky A. Research priorities for critical care nursing: a study by the American Associaton of Critical-Care Nurses. Heart & Lung 1983;12:35–44.
34. American Association of Critical-Care Nurses. Outcome standards for nursing care of the critically ill. Laguna Niguel, CA: AACN, 1990.
35. AACN. Demonstration project. Newport Beach, CA: AACN, July 1988.
36. AACN. Nursing economics task force final report. Newport Beach, CA: AACN, Aug. 1988.
37. Roberts WL. Self-governing. Personnel Management in Critical Care Nursing. Baltimore: Williams & Wilkins, 1989, pp. 37–46.
38. AACN. Role expectations for the critical care manager, Newport Beach, CA: AACN, June 1986.
39. Gupta AK, Govindarajan V. Business unit strategy, managerial characteristics, and business unit effectiveness at strategy implementation. Academy of Management Journal March 1984;27:30.
40. Reinhardt UE. Providing access to health care and controlling costs: approaches abroad, options for the U.S. Princeton University, 1990;1–17. Paper reproduced in proceedings book. ANNA Conference, Washington, D.C., April 1990.
41. McConnell CR. Economics: principles, problems, and policies. 8th ed. New York: McGraw-Hill, 1981:3.
42. Haveman RH. The economics of the public sector. 2nd ed. New York: John Wiley and Sons, Inc., 1976:27.
43. Gove PB, ed. Webster's Third New International Dictionary of the English Language. Springfield, MA: Merriam Company, 1971.
44. Moffat DW. Economics Dictionary. New York: American Elsevier Publishing Co., 1976.
45. Feldstein PJ. Health Care Economics. 3rd ed. Albany: Delmar Publishers, Inc., 1988:5.
46. Curtin LL. Designing new roles: nursing in the '90s and beyond. Nursing Management Feb. 1990;21:7–9.

Chapter 2

Accounting Concepts

LAURA C. YOUNG

Accounting concepts and principles comprise a body of knowledge that is often foreign to nurse managers. The rules that govern accounting are new and different to nurses. However, because of the growing importance of fiscal responsibility in health care, the nurse manager's success depends on mastering at least the basics of accounting. Basic accounting concepts when applied in financial operations will benefit the critical care nurse manager in daily decision making. Critical care nurse managers, like other nurse managers, utilize resources as part of their jobs. Because of the major role financial management plays in the success of the hospital, it is essential that nurse managers understand and apply financial and accounting concepts to manage resources efficiently and effectively.

Accounting is an activity which is an integral part of the management control process (1). The purpose of accounting is to provide quantitative information, much of which is financial, that can be used in making decisions. Using the information provided requires an understanding of how the data are gathered and compiled, the limitations of the data, and the extent to which the measurements are precise or estimated.

Accounting is a system for accumulating financial data about a business or organization. Through the process of accounting, the business can accurately track and record in a timely fashion those activities through which the business acquires, maintains, and/or disposes of cash. The interpretation of the data is another function of accounting. Interpretation of variations between reporting periods and unusual variances from budget, for example, is very important to the manager who must take the information and utilize it in decision making.

The process of accounting is quite similar to other management processes or problem-solving processes. There is a planning phase in which plans are made to generate a profit or a margin. Creating the plan involves assessment of many factors including: internal and external environment, historical financial trends, mission, objectives of business/organization, strengths, weaknesses, opportunities, and threats to business. Implementing the financial plan includes development of budgets and projections or forecasts. Evaluating the results of the financial plan, implementation, and reporting or communicating the performance are steps which then determine the need to revise the plan if needed.

There are two types of accounting that are differentiated by the audiences served. The first type is known as financial accounting, which primarily serves people outside the firm, such as governmental agencies (Internal Revenue Service, Health Care Finance Administration), investors, or creditors. Costs in financial accounting are classified by the function or object of the expense (administrative expenses, salaries, rent). Financial accounting reports are developed using basic accounting systems and include information that can be obtained from this normal accounting system. Financial accounting is used by outside groups in deciding such things as whether to provide a loan to the business or whether to invest in the business.

Managerial accounting differs from financial accounting in several ways. Those persons inside the business (managers) are served by managerial accounting, which provides information about future transactions, alternatives to previous transactions, forecasts, etc. Managerial accounting reports are more specific reports for specific users rather than the general type of reports one sees with financial accounting. Costs in managerial accounting are classified according to whose responsibility or under whose control they fall or by what happens to the costs with changes in level of activity.

An example of the difference between financial accounting and managerial accounting is helpful. Financial accounting would report, for example, the actual dollars spent for salaries, while managerial accounting would separate those salary dollars into dollars which are fixed without regard to a change in volume and a variable which would be expected to change with a change in volume. The reports received by managers are usually managerial accounting reports.

Whether the focus is on managerial or financial accounting, it is important to start with understanding the terms and concepts used in accounting. These concepts and principles have been long accepted by the accounting profession, having evolved over many years of experience. The generally accepted accounting principles are so well accepted that the American Institute of Certified Public Accountants and many other accounting organizations require their members to disclose in financial statements of audited companies any deviation from these generally accepted accounting principles (GAAP) (2). This chapter will provide a basic description of the most commonly used general accounting principles.

GENERAL ACCOUNTING PRINCIPLES

The financial statements of a health care organization audited by a certified public accountant (CPA) may read as follows:

> The preceding financial statement fairly presents the financial position of MY HOSPITAL as of September 30, 1990, and the results of its operations and changes in its financial position for the year ended, in conformity with consistently applied generally accepted accounting principles.

The purpose of that statement is to assure that those general principles of accounting have been used from year to year and that comparisons of financial position are, therefore, apple-to-apple comparisons.

Accounting Entity or Going-Concern Concept

For the purposes of accounting, each business is defined and treated as a separate entity from the person, group, or organization which may have created it. This separation is necessary to record the business transactions of the business as distinct from those of another business or those of an individual or group (3). For example, if MY HOSPITAL is such a hospital owned by me, this principle would be violated if my bills for clothing or expenses incurred on my vacation were paid by the hospital and, therefore, appeared on the expense ledger for the hospital. There would be a mixing of the business of the hospital and my personal business.

Health care institutions, which are owned by corporations or are part of a government agency, may create complications in defining the entity. Legal definitions of such facilities are sometimes different from the accounting definition. The clear separation is important if the financial information is to be useful and accurate.

One scenario in understanding this principle would be if a corporation that owned several hospitals paid the salaries of several key executives of MY HOSPITAL. In the scenario, the salaries are not charged back to MY HOSPITAL. As a result, the expenses do not appear on the accounts. The reason this may create a problem is that there is not an accurate picture of the hospital's real expenses, which are used in determining rates and in determining contracts with third-party payors.

Transaction

A transaction is a piece of business which is carried on. It may be the sale of an item or service, a purchase, a payment, or a change in something. In accounting, transactions are identified, recorded, and reported daily for managers. Business papers are used to record transactions. These business papers include invoices, sales receipts, the cancelled check or a copy of it, and bills. From the invoice, receipts, checks, etc., an entry is made in the ledger and journal. It may seem that accounting entails duplication, with assets and liabilities, revenues, and expenses recorded in many places. However, there is good reason to have multiple recording of transactions.

Whenever a transaction occurs such as a purchase of supplies, one invoice usually lists all supplies purchased. To trace the expense and payment of each item to the correct department and link the invoice to all the items recorded in various places, multiple recording is needed. The ledger (or general ledger) is a group of accounts which may be entered in a bound book, a loose-leaf notebook, or a computer program. The ledger provides a separate page for each account and may consist of thousands of accounts in a health care facility. The transactions from the invoice will also be recorded in the journal, which identifies each transaction or item by date with notes to link it to the ledger.

For example, if your hospital purchased three chairs and multiple office supplies from MY OFFICE SUPPLY, the transaction would be recorded from the invoice to the general ledger in separate entries for each department for "office supplies" and "office equipment," designating which department received each chair or supply. The journal entry would note the invoice number and the separate accounts to which the information is recorded, as well as the date of the transaction. From the general ledger, the information accumulated is recorded regularly (usually monthly) to financial statements for the department and for the business as a whole.

Transactions may be credit or cash transactions. Cash transactions are those in which cash payment is made at the time of the purchase of services or products. Credit transactions are those in which services or products are provided, but payment is delayed for a period of time. Most transactions in health care facilities are credit transactions.

Accounts Receivable

Accounts receivable are an asset for accounting purposes. Accounts receivable are assets that have been earned through the exchange of products or services, but have not yet been received. In health care organizations, because of significant delays in receipt of payments from third-party payors, such as insurance companies, Medicare, and HMOs, accounts receivable are generally the largest category of current assets. Current assets are those assets which are expected to be converted to cash within a short period, usually 1 year (4). The amount of accounts receivable which is posted or recorded in the accounting books may significantly affect the flow of cash. An example of this is reflected in a patient who is admitted for a coronary-artery bypass graft and develops complications requiring a 6 week hospital stay. After discharge, the patient's insurance company is billed (usually within 5 days after discharge). Payment from the insurance company is made 30–90 days or longer after billing. This means payment for services may occur more than 4 months after services are provided.

The companies and staff who provide equipment and services for the hospital won't wait this amount of time for payment. This creates cash flow problems. The relationship of accounts receivable to cash may be exemplified by the manner in which hospitals are paid. The hospital provides care, but does not receive payment for weeks after the patient is discharged. In fact, during the first two quarters of 1990, the average hospital accounts receivable was 75.5 days (5). There is a point at which accounts receivable must be converted to cash so that the organization can pay those bills that are due.

There are many factors that may impact the conversion of accounts receivable to cash. One factor is that patients are hospitalized from days to weeks, but bills are not usually generated until after discharge. Even at that point, bills are not completed and sent until charges are turned in or entered into the computer and until the medical record has been properly coded. Under the current reimbursement system, such coding requires classification by diagnosis related group (DRG) and the signature of the physician confirming the correct diagnosis. The longer the delay in generating a bill, the longer will be the delay in receipt of cash. Further delays in payment may occur if insurers hold payment until they audit or review the medical record against the bill to assure accuracy of the charges billed. There is a need for an efficient system which can assure that coding occurs concurrently with hospital stay, that the physician confirms the correct DRG diagnosis, and that the bill is generated as soon after discharge as possible.

Collection of accounts receivable is yet another important aspect of this part of financial management. Billing a third-party payor or a patient does not assure payment. Besides the usual delays associated with payment, further delays may occur when the bill is disputed or when an audit of the bill is requested. Audits are common today in the business services department of most health care providers. Audits are reviews of the bill against the medical record documentation. Lack of documentation of an item on the bill results in a denial of payment of that item. For example, a patient who has potential for skin breakdown may need a special type of bed for which there is a daily charge. However, even when the bed is ordered by the physician, if the documentation does not reflect use of the bed each day, the third-party payor may refuse to pay for rental of the bed for that day.

Obviously, nurses can positively, or negatively, impact reimbursement by documentation practices.

Controversy between health care providers and third-party payors also surrounds the area of preapproval (or precertification) of services. Many third-party payors refuse to pay for any service not preapproved (including some emergency services). Although the patient is still responsible for payment, this practice results in significant delays in collection of accounts.

Accounts Payable

Accounts payable is the term used for the debt owed by the hospital to a creditor for products or services provided. Accounts payable is usually the largest single type of short-term debt (6). It is listed as part of current liabilities on the liabilities side of the balance sheet. The reason this type of credit is important is the implication it has in terms of business. If supplies are purchased using short-term credit, the payment is usually not due for 30 days. The money that will be used to pay for the supplies remains in an account earning interest for the 30-day period. Since the creditors who owe money to the health care institution often practice similarly, holding their cash as long as possible to earn interest, it is equally important that health care institutions manage financial resources in such a way as to earn interest when possible. Because of this business practice, some suppliers of products and services will provide a discount to the buyer for rapid payment (such as within 10 days).

Realization Principle (Recognition Principle)

An accounting principle that is particularly useful in organizations that have large amounts of money owed to them is the principle of realization or recognition. This principle, also related to accrual accounting, does three things. First, it defines revenue as the inflow of assets which are exchanged for services or products. Second, the amount of that revenue is measured by the actual cash received, as well as the equivalent cash of other assets received. Finally, it requires that the revenue be recorded as revenue at the time it is earned. In the hospital setting, an example of how this principle is applied occurs daily. A patient who is admitted and treated in the intensive care unit for 5 days receives the service from admission to discharge. Although the patient or his insurance company are not as a general rule billed until after discharge, and although payment for services is not received by the hospital until some time later, the revenue of the hospitalization in ICU is recorded by accounting at the time the service is rendered. In fact, the revenue from the day of admission is usually recorded the following day and certainly before the patient is discharged. The revenue that is recorded is listed as an asset called accounts receivable, which means it is earned but not yet received. Once received, it becomes cash. Similarly, accounts payable is money owed, but not yet paid. Table 2.1 illustrates an example of the realization principle.

In this example, only cash and accounts receivable are identified as assets. The initial balance of $50,000 is changed in the example by three entries. Entry number one is revenue generated by a patient hospitalized in the ICU. The charges for the hospitalization are $5025. The amount added to the accounts receivable column is also added to the fund balance to keep the equation equal. In the second entry, another patient has outpatient surgery with a resultant charge of $3150. This, too, is accounts receivable. On the other side, the same amount is added to the fund balance. The third entry occurs when $7500 is received from a patient or his insurance company. The fund balance is used to maintain the balance on the liabilities side and is unchanged in this example.

ACCRUAL ACCOUNTING

One of the general principles of accounting related to costs and revenue, as discussed earlier in this chapter, is the principle of recognition or realization. According to this principle, revenue is

Table 2.1. Realization Principle

	Assets		=	Liabilities	+	Fund Balance
	Cash	Accounts Receivable	=	Accounts Payable	+	Fund Balance
	$50,000					$50,000
(1)		+5,025	=			+5,025
	50,000	5,025				55,025
(2)		+3,150	=			+3,150
	50,000	8,175				58,175
(3)	+7,500	−7,500	=			
	$57,500	675				$58,175

recognized in the accounting books at the time it is earned, whether or not the actual cash is received. It is on this principle that accrual accounting is based. Accrual accounting differs from the cash basis, where revenues are only reported as being earned in the period in which they are actually received as cash. Costs or expenses are deducted in the accounting period when cash is actually disbursed with a cash basis accounting system. On the other hand, accrual accounting reports revenue when earned and expenses are deducted when incurred even if not yet paid. One example of this type of accounting can be seen in Table 2.1 in which the revenue generated was recorded at the time the service was provided or delivered, although cash payment was received at a later date. Table 2.2 expands the realization principle to expenses which have been incurred.

In Table 2.2, the first transaction is recorded when an ICU patient receives services which incur charges of $5025. To maintain the balance between the assets and liabilities sides, the $5025 is added to the accounts receivable column for assets and to the fund balance column for the liabilities side of the equation. In transaction two, $18,000 worth of equipment has been purchased on credit and added to the department. The expense is added under equipment on the assets side and under accounts payable on the liabilities side. In the third transaction, $4025 in cash received from the insurance company is added under cash on the assets side and subtracted from accounts receivable. No change is made on the liabilities side because the total is unchanged. Notice that the totals on the assets and liabilities sides remain equal.

Further application of accrual accounting includes the recording of hours staff work for pay and vacation-time accrual. In most health care facilities, employees work a period of time before they are paid (usually 2 weeks). In fact, employees may wait an additional 2-5 days following the end of a pay period before they actually receive pay. Although the cash outflow for salaries does not occur until several days following the end of the pay period, and although employees work usually two weeks before they are paid, in accrual accounting salaries are recorded as "wages due to employees" as the worked days pass. How quickly this is recorded is determined by the sophistication of the time clock/computer system. Some systems record hours worked and wages due daily, and others at the conclusion of the pay period of each week. Similarly, vacation pay is usually recorded as vacation wages/pay due at the time the vacation hours are earned rather than when the hours are used by the employee.

Accrual accounting is useful for most health care organizations, because it presents a clearer picture of the financial position of the organization. This type of accounting provides reports which are comparable from one period to another, whereas the cash basis approach does not. It should be noted, however, that available cash cannot be overlooked. One financial difficulty faced by hospitals is inadequate cash flow to comfortably maintain operations. One can understand the difficulty by picturing all inflow and outflow tied up in accounts receivable and accounts payable. At some point, accounts receivable must become cash to pay accounts payable, or the business' success is endangered.

Table 2.2. Accrual Accounting

	Assets					=	Liabilities + Fund Balance	
	Cash	+	Accounts Receivable	+	Equipment	=	Accounts Payable	+ Fund Balance
Transaction (1)	$50,000					=		$50,000
			+5,025			=		+5,025
	50,000		5,025					55,025
Transaction (2)					+18,000		+18,000	
	50,000		5,025		18,000	=	18,000	55,025
Transaction (3)	+4,025		−4,025					
	$54,025		$1,000		$18,000	=	$18,000	$55,025
					Total $73,025	=	Total $73,025	

COST VALUATION AND MONEY MEASUREMENT

Cost Valuation Principle

The cost valuation principle is an accounting principle in which the actual cost of goods or services are recorded and appear on financial statements at that actual cost. The cost of the goods or services may not, in the mind of the purchaser, be the true value. For example, the purchase price of a defibrillator in ICU might be lower than the retail price because a new model is coming out. The hospital would, of course, like to list the asset at the higher price since it would improve the overall financial position of the hospital as a business. However, general accounting principles require listing each item at its cost. This avoids future concerns about who determines the value and how it is to be determined.

Money Measurement Principle/Duality Principle

Money measurement and duality are closely related accounting principles. The principle of money measurement refers to the fact that accounting is concerned with measuring financial assets and liabilities. In accounting, the method of measurement is money. Therefore, all resources (or assets) and liabilities are measured in terms of dollars.

The principle of duality requires that the financial statement called the balance sheet will always balance. Although the balance sheet is discussed at length in Chapter 4, it is important to recognize that the assets side of the balance sheet must be equal to the liabilities side. Since, hopefully, assets of a business will exceed liabilities, the excess is listed on the liabilities side as a "fund balance" for most health care organizations (7). A clearer way to picture the duality principle is to use the following equation:

$$Assets = Liabilities + Fund\ Balance$$

All transactions which occur daily are accounted for on both the assets side and the liabilities side of this equation. Table 2.3 illustrates this principle further.

MY HOSPITAL decides to purchase a new ultrasound machine and an office building. The equipment is purchased with cash, while the building is purchased with 10% cash and financed with 90% bonds. Each of the transactions is recorded in dollars as a change in assets and liabilities. The changes will always balance on both sides. Each time assets are increased or decreased, liabilities also are increased or decreased by the same dollar amount.

Stable-Dollar Concept/Stable-Monetary-Unit Concept

Although the dollar measurement used in accounting is not a stable unit of measure, the stable-dollar or stable-monetary-unit concept is an accepted practice in accounting. The value of the dollar or other monetary unit changes over a period of time because of such things as inflation. However, to convert dollars (monetary units) spent in previous years to current value would require some level of subjectivity. For example, inflation and the value of the dollar against foreign currency would need to be considered (especially in purchases of equipment from other countries). This is contrary to the objectivity principle of accounting. For that reason, general accounting practice treats the monetary measurement as if it were stable from year to year. It should be noted that this and many other general accounting principles provide a basis for comparison which is sound. However, these principles are not necessarily applied in determining current worth of a business, since the cost for replacement and the current value of an item may have changed dramatically over time.

MATCHING AND COST RECOVERY PRINCIPLES

The matching principle requires that expenses be matched with the revenues those expenses helped to generate. Because revenues may actually be generated over a period of several months, and expenses needed to produce the revenue may occur in a different reporting period, this principle's purpose is to match expenses to revenues in the same reporting period. This requires an adjustment process, which allocates to a specific reporting period the portion of a transaction which is applicable to the period.

An example of this principle may be seen with a patient who is hospitalized over several months. Although the patient is not actually billed until after discharge, as a general rule, the charges are

Table 2.3. Duality Principle

- Before transactions:

Assets		Liabilities	
Cash	500,000	Notes Payable	10,000,000
Buildings	10,000,000	Fund Balance	1,500,000
Equipment	1,000,000		
Total	11,500,000	Total	11,500,000

- Transaction 1

Assets		Liabilities	
Cash	400,000	Notes Payable	10,000,000
Buildings	10,000,000	Fund Balance	1,500,000
Equipment	1,100,000		
Total	11,500,000	Total	11,500,000

Assets: Increase in equipment, decrease in cash of $100,000.
Liabilities: No change.

- Transaction 2

Assets		Liabilities	
Cash	300,000	Notes Payable	10,000,000
Building	11,000,000	Bonds Payable	900,000
Equipment	1,100,000	Fund Balance	1,500,000
Total	12,400,000	Total	12,400,000

Assets: Increase $900,000 (Building increased $1,000,000; cash decreased $100,000)
Liabilities: Increase $900,000 (Bonds payable)

---

kept current as accounts receivable revenue and reported for each reporting period to maintain this principle and match the expenses of salaries and supplies incurred to produce the service.

One type of cost (or expense) to a business is bad debt. Although this is discussed later in this chapter, it is important to note that this expense, under the principle of matching, should be matched to the revenue associated with it. A bad debt is an account that is not paid by the customer. Bad debt losses are not known until some months after the revenue is recorded as accounts receivable. To match these bad debts to the revenue, there must be an estimation of what bad debt losses there will be for the period. This may be adjusted from period to period with any recoveries of bad debts (collections) being noted on the revenue side of the records.

Principle of Materiality

The write-off of bad debts usually occurs several months following the generation of the associated revenue. This means that there cannot be matching of revenue and expense in the same reporting period. Although estimation of these expenses is common, direct write-off may be used in some facilities or in some situations. This is permitted under the accounting principle of materiality, which says that adherence to an accounting principle is not required if that adherence does not have a material effect on the business' income or if adherence is extremely difficult or expensive. For example, if the amount of write-off for patients is small compared to overall revenue, it does not really matter when the write-off is recorded.

Objectivity Principle

The principle of objectivity is closely associated with other general accounting principles. This principle is based on the theory that accounting information cannot be useful unless it is based on objective data. Objectivity is the reason that cost is used to determine value for the purposes of accounting, since cost is established between buyer and seller, and is therefore considered to be objective and would prevent future disputes as to determination of value.

Continuing Concern Concept

The concept of continuing concern assumes that financial reports and records are completed for a business, which is continuing to function as a business, and which requires its assets in order to operate. It assumes that the assets of the business are not for sale and, therefore, would not have a change in objective value. This concept is tied to both the cost and objectivity principles, which place the value of assets at their cost without regard to any change in market value. Under this concept, the value of monitoring equipment would be on the records at original cost regardless of age or updated technology. This particular concept does not apply when financial statements are being prepared for a business which is for sale.

COST CENTER VS. REVENUE CENTER

Cost centers refer to those departments or groups of departments which incur costs but do not produce revenues. For example, engineering and housekeeping are cost centers. Revenue centers are those departments which generate revenue by providing direct services to patients. This does not imply that a department which does not produce revenue directly is unimportant. Departments that provide support services are necessary to the function of those departments which do provide direct services to patients. However, because of the implication that "cost" centers are less important than "revenue" centers, the term "responsibility" center has been created to refer to those departments which have some separate controlling management, receive resources, and produce services. What comprises a responsibility center may vary from one institution to another. In a small hospital, the facility as a whole may be the responsibility center. In large institutions, each unit or deparment may be a responsibility center. The major factor is that the department has responsibility for the financial operations. Resources that are provided to the responsibility center should result in production of services. For example, a critical care unit may be a responsibility center. The unit is provided with nurses, equipment, and supplies plus utilities, housekeeping, management services, and maintenance. In exchange, the unit provides patient care services in the form of hours of care provided and patient days counted and charged.

Revenue

Revenue is the inflow of assets in exchange for services or products which are sold. Revenue is not necessarily cash. In accounting, revenue is recorded at the time it is earned so that it might be considered accounts receivable. It is an increase to the assets side of the balance sheet resulting from earnings. In health care organizations, revenue is often the amount that is charged for services, and it does not consider what portion of charges, if any, will not be paid due to such factors as bad debt or charity.

Revenue is also one of the primary portions of the operating budget. The process for determining revenue projections for the coming year is discussed in Chapter 6. In health care organizations, the sources of actual revenue include patient room and nursing charges, medications, diagnostic services, medical supplies, procedures (such as surgery), treatments (such as physical therapy), and use of equipment (such as specialty beds or hypothermia units). The charges that are associated with each of these items become the actual revenue recorded for the patient. Other sources of revenue for health care organizations may include the cafeteria, office space rental, seminar fees, and the gift shop.

Charge

A charge is the amount of money that has been set for a product or service as its price. It is what the facility providing the service or product has determined as the value. The charge is the anticipated revenue from the service or product, without consideration of what will become cash. Charges are determined by many factors. These factors include the original costs for the product and the costs associated with providing the service. The mix of patients that receive a service or use a product also may influence the charge that is set. Competition is yet another factor in the determination of a charge. The section on rate setting will further explain how charges or "rates" are set.

Expenses

Expenses may be defined as the services or products that are consumed in operating the business. Expenses may be categorized as those necessary for operations (operating expenses) of the health care organization. These include salaries, supplies, depreciation, equipment repair, minor equipment, insurance, and contract fees. Expenses related to the purchase of major equipment are called capital expenses. These are expenses for equipment or a project, which have a lifetime of greater than a pre-set time, and cost over a predetermined amount. The predetermined time frame and cost may vary from facility to facility, but one year and $500 are commonly used figures.

Expenses may be categorized by their relationship to fluctuations in volume. For example, in a hospital setting the salary expenses on a nursing unit should vary with the census. If there are more patients to be cared for, there will be a need for more nurses and, therefore, salary expenses will rise. This is called a variable expense. Other variable expenses include forms, office supplies, medical supplies, and sterile supplies. Fixed expenses are those expenses which do not change in response to any volume change. Examples of fixed expenses include equipment depreciation, a manager's salary, or interest. Semivariable expenses are those expenses that include elements of variable and fixed expenses, such as utilities, monitor technicians' salaries, or food costs.

Expenses may also be categorized by how they are assigned. Direct expenses are costs that are assigned directly to the department which incurred them. These include salaries, supplies, and some equipment. Indirect expenses are those which are difficult to assign and are allocated to a specific department based on some calculation or proration. Examples of this type of expense would be the cost of utilities, security services, or interest expenses.

Costs

In financial accounting, the terms expense and cost have been differentiated based on when the liability was incurred. Expense is referred to as a cost assigned to the income statement for a specified period, while cost refers to the initial expenditure or the initial liability incurred (8). This is somewhat confusing since depreciation, for example, is identified on cost reports as a cost, although it is actually the amount of amortized prior cost. Because of the confusion, most resources use cost and expense interchangeably.

The classification of expenses may be discussed with reference to the type or categories of costs in health care. Another important point about such costs or expenses is the methodology used to determine the categorization. The method used to determine whether expenses (costs) are direct or indirect is traceability. A cost which is traceable to a given cost objective would be called a direct cost. Those which cannot be traced to a specific cost objective are indirect. This supports the previous definition of direct and indirect expenses.

Another way in which costs are classified (variable vs. fixed) is determined by the relation of the costs to output. A proportional rise in costs with a rise in output (or volume) is the cost referred to as variable, while those referred to as fixed are not related to the change in output. In health care, output generally refers to volume of patients, procedures, and visits, but outputs may also refer to complexity. For example, patient classification systems differentiate between levels of care required by patients, and acuity levels are tied to the hours of nursing care provided for those patients.

Costs may also be differentiated as controllable or noncontrollable. This differentiation is not a simple one. It implies that the department manager can influence the controllable group of costs. The difficulty is in determining which costs and to what extent they are controllable by the manager. For example, does the manager have control over fixed administrative costs (one type of indirect expense)? On the other hand, some indirect expenses (such as equipment maintenance) can be controlled by the manager. The differentiation related to control of costs, then, is often determined within the institution based on the organization's philosophy regarding the responsibilities of managers.

Discussion about cost would not be complete without including how costs are actually measured. In the business of health care, departments may be differentiated by whether they provide services directly or indirectly. Those departments which provide services directly to the patient (nursing units, clinical departments) are considered direct or revenue departments. Those which provide support services are considered indirect or non-revenue departments (administration, security, finance). Costs for the indirect departments must be assigned in some manner to the direct or revenue departments for decision-making reasons. It is extremely important, for example, to know the full operations cost in the intensive care unit (including costs for administration, housekeeping, etc.). Then the charge for ICU can be reasonably determined in order that contracts with third-party payors can be accurately negotiated. If only direct costs are used, the charge may not cover the full cost of operation or the payment negotiated may not result in a satisfactory margin.

The method of cost allocation used determines how indirect costs are distributed. There are three methods currently used: step-down, double-distribution, and simultaneous-equations (9). The proportion of allocated costs which are assigned to a revenue department must also be determined. Allocations may be determined based on percentages of services used (fiscal), square feet cleaned (housekeeping), hours served (pastoral care), etc. For example, if ICU occupies 10% of the square feet of the building, ICU might be allocated 10% of costs of cleaning the building. Step-down allocation is a commonly used method for allocating the costs of nonrevenue departments to revenue departments. Table 2.4 demonstrates how costs are allocated by the step-down and double-distribution methods. The simultaneous-equations method establishes a system of equations which are used to compute mathematically correct allocations. While more accurate, this method is also more time consuming and more difficult. Depending on the allocation method and the cost-apportionment method used, the cost allocation may be quite different. See Table 2.4 for the example of the type of difference which may occur. The process of allocating costs is called allocation accounting.

Decision making about charges and expenses is a key responsibility of nurse managers. A number of considerations about costs should be included in the decision-making process. As plans are being made for a department's budget, consideration should be given to costs which are avoidable. Avoidable costs are the costs that can be eliminated if a specific activity is discontinued. For example, if a hospital has a cardiac rehabilitation program which is a joint effort of serveral departments, and a decision is made to cut the program in half because of need for cost containment, the costs which can be eliminated are the avoidable costs. Caution must be used in identifying avoidable costs. In this example, the avoidable costs would only be those costs related to 50% of the volume. Fixed costs such as secretarial support or indirect allocated costs would still be incurred as would equipment needed in the program. The costs which are unavoidable and are not affected by the decision about cutting the program are referred to as sunk costs.

Consideration in decision making about expenses should also be given to incremental and opportunity costs. Costs which would result from anticipated action in decision making may be called incremental. For example, if a decision is made to expand the cardiac rehabilitation program, many of the fixed and allocated costs might be unchanged. However, there would be incremental costs associated with the expansion. Opportunity cost is the value lost when one option is chosen over another, thereby giving up the benefits of the option not selected. For example, with the cardiac rehabilitation program, if the physical space could be leased to a group of physicians instead of being used for the cardiac rehabilitation program, the benefits (rent) lost would be the opportunity costs. It is evident that many factors should be evaluated during decision making related to financial operations.

Depreciation

Depreciation is an expense that is recorded somewhat differently from most expenses. Because major pieces of equipment are used for long periods, the cost is deducted as an expense over the useful life of the equipment. This process is called depreciation. For example, the intensive care unit purchases an intra-aortic balloon pump for $35,000 and expects to use it for 7 years. Each year, one-seventh of the usefulness will expire and one-seventh of the cost ($5000) will be depreciated each year. This method is called straight-line depreciation. The depreciation is recorded on the financial statements as an expense, under a heading "accumulated depreciation" or "allowance for depreciation."

To figure simple or straight-line depreciation, one must divide the useful life of the equipment or building into the total expense or cost. To determine the monthly depreciation, one would need to use months of useful life instead of years. The example below is used to demonstrate how a monitor, with a useful life is 5 years (60 months) and which cost $6,000, has a monthly depreciation of $100.

$6000/60$ months $= \$100$/month depreciation

In determining depreciation, it is important to consider any salvage value of equipment and subtract that before dividing by the equipment's useful life.

28 INTRODUCTION AND ASSESSMENT

Table 2.4. Cost Allocation

	Nonrevenue Departments		Revenue Departments		Total Costs	Explanation
Step-down	A	B	C	D		
• Direct Cost	500	1000	10,000	20,000	31,500	• Total Direct costs for departments
• Allocate Dept. A 20%, 30%, 50% to Dept. B, C, D	−500	+100	+150	+250		• Allocation to Departments B, C, D from A—20% to B; 30% to C, 50% to D
	0	1100	10,150	20,250	31,500	
• Allocate Dept. B New amount to other dept. (C&D) 55%, 45%		−1100	+605	+495		• Allocation of new total from Department B to C & D—55% to C, 45% to D.
		0	$10,755	$20,745	$31,500	• New total equals old total
Double Distribution	A	B	C	D		
• Direct Cost	500	1000	10,000	20,000	31,500	• Total direct costs for departments
• Allocate Dept. A 50%, 20%, 30% to Dept. B, C, D	−500	+250	+100	+150		• Allocation to Departments B, C, D from A—50% to B, 20% to C, 30% to D.
	0	1250	10,100	20,150	31,500	
• Allocate Dept. B 20%, 50%, 30% to Dept. A, C, D	+200	−1000	+500	+300		• Allocation to Departments A, C, D from B (original amount) 20% to A, 50% to C, 30% to D
	200	250	10,600	20,450	31,500	
• Allocate Dept. A (new amount) 50%, 20%, 30% to Dept. B, C, D	−200	+100	+40	+60		• Allocation to Dept. B, C, D from A (new amount) 50% to B, 20% to C, 30% to D
	0	350	10,640	20,510	31,500	
• Allocate Dept. B (new amount) 60%, 40% to Dept. C & D		−350	+210	+140		• Allocation to Dept. C & D from B (new amount) 60% to C & 40% to D
		0	$10,850	$20,650	$31,500	

There are formulas used to perform accelerated depreciation calculations. These formulas result in better tax deductions for business and are sometimes used in health care institutions. The result of using this type of calculation is that equipment is depreciated more rapidly and the expense for the business is higher in the given year. In both methods used for depreciating equipment or other assets, it is required in general accounting principles that the cost of assets, their accumulated depreciation, and the method used for depreciation be disclosed (usually in a footnote). Table 2.5 illustrates how this is accomplished.

Note that the book value or remaining value after depreciated cost of the item is also noted. This is a very simple example of how depreciation is re-

Table 2.5. Depreciation[a]

Assets	Cost	Accumulated Depreciation	Book Value
Monitors	$100,000	$20,000	$ 80,000
IABP	35,000	5,000	30,000
Defibrillator	8,000	1,000	7,000
TOTAL	$143,000	$26,000	$117,000

[a]Note: The straightline method of depreciation was used for calculations.

corded and how the remaining value of assets are determined.

Bad Debt

Although financial management seems to require managing only revenues and expenses in such a way as to produce something left over for the company, there are additional factors which must be included in financial calculations. One such factor is called bad debt. Bad debt is the amount of charges which are uncollected from patients who have the ability to pay. Bad debt is deducted from revenue as an allowance. This differs from charity care, which is uncollected revenue from patients who are unable to pay.

Bad debt losses from revenue are a serious problem in health care, comprising larger percentages than seen in most other businesses (10). This is related to the perception by many consumers that health care is a right. Therefore, consumers may pay health care bills only after other bills are paid. This growing problem has resulted in many health care institutions implementing policies seen for some time in other types of businesses, such as requiring advance deposits for elective services, accepting credit cards for services provided, and openly utilizing collection agencies and legal proceedings to collect unpaid bills.

The amount of bad debt in a hospital is dependent on several factors such as the population served by a facility and the hospital's mission. A facility whose mission is to provide services to a population where employment is variable or unstable is likely to have a higher percentage of bad debt (and charity). Facilities which serve more affluent populations have less such problems. A tertiary care facility or referral center is also likely to have higher bad debt ratios because the wider range of services unavailable elsewhere results in transfer of complicated and costly cases to the facility. To control bad debt, many hospitals have adopted preadmission financial screening or means test policies. If a hospital provides such screening prior to admission and decides to admit elective cases on ability to pay, the percentage of bad debt is likely to be lower than when such financial considerations are ignored.

Health care organizations, to operate efficiently and effectively, must evaluate bad debts and determine causes and reasonable solutions. Requiring a deposit or arranging for credit are strategies which have been used successfully to reduce bad debt. Because emergency services result in treatment for some patients that do not pay, bad debts cannot usually be eliminated. However, managing bad debts is essential in successfully managing financial operations.

RATE SETTING

Rate setting is a process used by a health care facility to determine its rates or charges. There are three major steps which must occur. The first step is determination of financial requirements. A break-even analysis is one way to determine financial requirements. This analysis is a means by which the costs of providing a service or product are determined and the anticipated rate for the service is identified in a comparison. This permits the manager to evaluate whether sufficient volume can be generated to recover costs and make a sufficient profit to make the new service or product worthwhile. This type of analysis can also be used by managers to reevaluate rates periodically. Over a period of time, the costs for providing a service may change and there would be a need to increase the charge or rate of the service.

For example, in one hospital the rate for daily use of the intra-aortic balloon pump (IABP) was set 3 years ago based on the fact that the cardiovascular surgeons set the timing and calibrations, did the troubleshooting, and stayed with the patient on the pump. As the cardiovascular ICU developed and grew, the nursing staff assumed these functions, and changing technology required the purchase of a newer machine. Changes in practice should be considered in looking at the cost of the service to determine the point at which the department will break even. A simple calculation to further explain this concept might be helpful. If the ICU has 20 patient uses per year of the IABP, and the costs for the service for a year (salaries, equipment depreciation, and supplies) are $10,000, a charge of $500 per patient use would result in break even. If there are 40 patients uses per year, a charge of $250 would break even.

Once the financial requirements have been determined, other steps must be followed to set the rates for services or products. The allocation of financial requirements to revenue departments must occur as discussed previously and rate setting must be performed in such a manner as to produce good cash flow.

The health care organization's financial requirements include operating expenses, capital, and profit. Operating expenses are those financial requirements necessary to operate the facility from day to day. The amount of bad debt and charity care influence financial requirements since these amounts are lost revenue. Purchases of equipment, renovation/expansion projects, and "capital" expenses are generally covered by the organization's profit. Health care organizations usually refer to their profit as the "margin" from operations. This operating margin must be sufficient to meet short- and long-term needs. For health care facilities which are investor owned ("for-profit" facilities), a return to the investors is also drawn from the margin from operations. Both expenses and profits must be given consideration in setting rates.

Once the organization's financial requirements have been determined, the allocation of expenses from nonrevenue producing departments to revenue producing departments must be accomplished. Each revenue producing department must know what expenses they will be expected to cover. Data from previous years may be used to project expenses. Third-party payors have specific requirements which may influence the allocation process, but generally allocation is determined by services provided by nonrevenue departments to the revenue departments. After this allocation has occurred, a comparison of current rates or charges and expected revenue can be made. A department's revenue is based on the volume forecast or anticipated for the following year.

The final step in rate setting is to ensure the needed cash flow. This is accomplished by comparing expected revenues based on current charges (rates) to desired revenues. From this evaluation, it can be determined which departments will need to have adjusted rates. The methods used to determine the amount of adjustment may vary from department to department, and the proportion of expenses allocated to a specific department may influence the adjustment decision. For example, if current rates for ICU will generate inadequate revenues to produce a reasonable margin, rates in ICU might need to be increased.

One method for determining the amount of adjustment is called surcharge. This method bases the set charge or rate on the cost, plus an amount or a percentage. This method is heavily dependent on accuracy of costs. Another method used is called hourly rates, and is based on a time factor (after initial calculation of costs) for a set time period. The relative value method determines the relative value of a procedure or service compared to other procedures or services. The rate or charge is then set by that resulting value. For example, if a procedure requires twice as many resources to generate revenue, the charge might be twice as much. If the performance of a cardiac output requires twice as much time and supplies as noninvasive blood pressure (BP) monitoring, the charge for cardiac output may need to be twice that of the BP monitor. With each of these methods, the financial requirements for a department are compared to the costs of providing the services.

Ratio of cost-to-charge method involves determining the ratio of costs of providing the procedure to the charge needed to generate a satisfactory margin. For example, if the financial requirements for the ICU to generate a satisfactory margin are $330,000 and costs for operation are $300,000, then the ratio would be 3.30:3.00 or 1.10:1.00. This ratio could be used to calculate the rates needed for the future. An example of how this might work in ICU would be through applying the ratio to the current charge of $100. This results in a new rate of $110.

Regardless of the method used to set rates, it is important to consider also how rates compare with those of competing facilities. It is not uncommon to find facilities which set their rates based only on the competitor's rates. Since this does not consider the costs for providing the procedure or service, this method for setting rates is not recommended. Instead, the rate offered by the competitor should be one factor in determining the best rate or in considering whether the service should be offered at all.

Flow of Revenue

The flow of revenue and cash through the hospital business services is complex. However, it is important to understand the flow and the impact of that flow on the operation of the hospital. Once services are provided and billed, there is often a delay of 90 days or longer before payment is received. However, the hospital must purchase supplies and pay salaries of staff soon after the services are actually provided. Because of the delay involved, hospitals must monitor the cash flow continually, assuring that adequate cash is kept in accounts to meet current expenses.

In the purchase of supplies and equipment, several factors are considered. Occasionally, vendors will discount costs for supplies if payment is made within a specific time frame. On the other hand, holding the cash in an account which generates interest may earn additional cash for the hospital. The purchasing and finance department must determine which alternative is better, given the specific circumstances.

Another important consideration in the flow of revenue is purchase of capital equipment. Capital equipment purchases are made from the margin generated by a hospital. If the margin is inadequate or if the revenue flow is unsatisfactory, there may be a need to delay purchase of equipment. Maintaining a good revenue flow and cash flow, then, is important to maintaining updated technology, as well as meeting current expenses.

SUMMARY

The critical care nurse manager needs as much financial information as possible to make good management decisions. The American Association of Critical-Care Nurses' (AACN) position statement on the role of the critical care nurse manager identifies the specific responsibilities in efficiently and effectively utilizing resources, including personnel and finances, in the operation of critical care units (11). The critical care nurse manager must be knowledgeable about accounting concepts and principles and how these are applied in practice. Having an adequate understanding of the terminology utilized in financial circles is essential to successful communication with those individuals who are ultimately responsible for the financial success of the organization. Collaboration and involvement in financial decision making are very important for any nurse manager who wishes to succeed. Additionally, the organization's success depends upon the effectiveness of each manager in operating the department. Financial management has two major goals which must be remembered by every manager. Generating profit is a goal necessary to maintain services, develop new services, expand the plant, and purchase new technology. Maintaining the viability of the organization is also a critical goal for hospitals, as well as other businesses. Generating a profit is essential to this viability.

Health care organizations are complex businesses influenced by governmental regulation, third-party payor and reimbursement issues, and the trends in technology and health care practice. Competition is thriving among health care businesses which makes financial management a key role for managers. The Nursing Economics Task Force of AACN has identified the multiple economic issues facing critical care nursing, and has developed strategies for addressing those issues (12). AACN's demonstration project includes a focus on the cost effectiveness of operating critical care units which place emphasis on high quality and collaborative practice (13). This focus offers many opportunities and challenges to the critical care manager who is willing to recognize its importance and who is committed to understanding and succeeding in the area of financial management.

REFERENCES

1. Cleverley WO. Essentials of health care finance. 2nd ed. Rockville, MD: Aspen Publishers, Inc., 1986:253.
2. Pyle WM, Larson KD. Fundamental accounting principles. 9th ed. Homewood, IL: Richard D. Irwin, Inc., 1981:4, 12.
3. Pyle and Larson, p. 13.
4. Young L, Hayne A. Nursing administration—from concepts to practice. Philadelphia: W.B. Saunders Co., 1988:198.
5. Hospitals. September 5, 1990:22.
6. Brigham EF, Gapenski LC. Financial management: theory and practice. 5th ed. Chicago: The Dryden Press, 1988:654–655.
7. Cleverly, pp. 51–54.
8. Dominiak GF, Louderback III JG. Managerial accounting. 5th ed. Boston: PWS-Kent Publishing Co., 1988:19n.
9. Cleverly, pp. 202–203.
10. Young, p. 159.
11. AACN. Role expectations for the critical-care nurse manager. Newport Beach, CA: American Association of Critical-Care Nurses, 1986.
12. AACN. Nursing economics task force—final report. Newport Beach, CA: American Association of Critical-Care Nurses, 1988.
13. AACN. American Association of Critical-Care Nurses demonstration project. Newport Beach, CA: American Association of Critical-Care Nurses, 1988.

Chapter 3

Basics: The Tools of Financial Management

SANDRA SMALL

Budget is a word often feared by managers. The budget process is thought by many to be a time of intense negotiation and communication compressed into a few weeks of a fiscal year. In reality, however, the budgeting process is an ongoing, dynamic process which occurs all year long.

The budget can be one of comprehensive, institution-wide focus or can be limited in scope to a single department or unit. However the budget evolves, it is defined as a plan for the future expressed in quantitative terms (1). Budgeting then becomes a process of identifying probable revenues and consequential expenditures for the organization or sub-unit. It is the process by which decision makers allocate resources to support particular programs that ultimately serve the strategic plan of the organization as a whole for the coming year (2). As such, the budget must be tied to the organization's strategic plans, which include long-term objectives (over 3–5 years) and short-term objectives (those which must be accomplished within the next fiscal year).

In today's health care environment of fixed reimbursement and competition, planning for the future while maintaining an eye on the present with a view to maintaining flexibility and responsiveness is an essential process for hospital management. There are several advantages to budgeting:

1. Provides a framework of goals and objectives to serve as bench marks against which performance can be measured;
2. Coordinates activities of the entire organization;
3. Provides managers a way to formalize planning efforts;
4. Provides managers a vehicle to communicate plans in an orderly way;
5. Requires managers to give planning top priority to maintain fiscal responsibility (3).

There are several components to the budget process, which can be grouped into two divisions: quantitative and qualitative. The quantitative division deals with revenues, expenses, and capital budgets, while the qualitative division deals with goals, objectives, and accomplishments. This chapter will review the budget process, financial status and terms, and discuss the basics of revenue, expense, and capital budgets. The intent is to provide the essential building blocks for further discussion.

BUDGET PROCESS

The budget process can be approached utilizing the nursing process: assessment, planning, implementation, and evaluation. The nurse manager must actively participate in all four phases of the process.

Assessment is the data gathering phase. Examining historical trends for census, patient acuity, and procedures will assist the manager in planning for future needs. For example, if the acuity and census have risen steadily over the past 2 years and overtime has become a necessity on a routine (daily) basis, the manager may consider using this data as justification for additional full-time equivalent (FTE) employees to adequately meet patient needs and control budgetary expenses. Assessing equipment needs, new program requirements, or plans for future directions with key physicians is an absolute must. Discussing ideas with other departments is an integral part of data collection, because no one area exists in isolation. For example, the emergency department can plan a renovation project for a second x-ray room; however, if prior agreements with the radiology department are not made, issues of who will staff the new area and who will incur revenues and expenses may present problems. If the intensive care unit plans to open four more beds in the next fiscal year, how will this move impact respiratory care, pharmacy, radiology, housekeeping, the laboratory, and admissions? If a transplant program will be added in the next fiscal year, who will be impacted and how? If the census has gradually decreased over the past 2 years, are there thoughts to close beds or decrease program offerings? How effective has the manager been at maintaining operations within budget for the current fiscal year? Are some accounts over budget while others are significantly under budget? These, and many other questions must be considered when assessing financial data.

In the planning phase, the nurse manager must have access to the strategic plan and the hospital's goals and objectives for the next fiscal year. In order to meet the needs of the patients, the desires of the staff, and reconcile the wishes of physicians, the nurse manager must integrate these plans to coincide with the overall mission, goals, and direction of the organization. If a commitment has been made to decrease expenses, the manager may not want to request 10 new positions unless these positions are required to support a new program or procedure which will increase the revenue base or fulfill a requirement to meet other objectives. Mutual planning with other departments becomes mandatory. The nurse manager would not want to plan for opening more beds if respiratory care is planning to decrease service personnel. Today's hospital environment calls for integrated communication among managers at all levels.

Planning and development of the budget must produce a credible document and supplemental proposals for change. If 10 nurses are required to fulfill an objective, do not ask for 20 hoping to have 10 approved. Patient acuity systems, census, trends, physician input, and impact statements from other departments should provide the nurse manager sufficient data to justify appropriate requests. For example, if one account is overspent and a trend is likely to continue, can monies be shifted from another account during the budget process which will take care of anticipated needs and yet not add dollars to the bottom line? Planning is not confined to the 2 weeks from when budget packets are distributed until budgets are completed. The nurse manager must use the monthly monitor and variance statements to determine what changes will be required during the fiscal year, as well as in future years.

Implementation of the budget requires the nurse manager to be attentive to many areas. Patient care assignments should be coordinated to staffing and patient needs. Ongoing monitoring of scheduling, staffing, use of supplies, patient care activities, and changes in practice is the responsibility of the nurse manager in budget implementation. Systems must be examined and analyzed to determine how patient needs can be met in the most cost efficient way possible. Education of staff and physicians assists the manager in achieving budgetary objectives.

Each month the manager must evaluate how the budget was maintained as compared to what was planned. If the census was higher than expected and supplies were overspent, the expense may be justified if the supplies were directly related to patient needs. Each expense which is over budget should be thoroughly investigated. If the census was down and the expenses were up, there is clearly a problem that must be identified. In today's health care environment, fiscal responsibility requires the efforts and involvement of all providers.

REVENUES, EXPENSES, AND PROFIT

Revenues

The revenue of an organization is shown in the first section of the income statement. Revenues reflect charges made for care, not what the hospital receives. Gross revenues primarily come from three major sources: patient care, operations not directly related to patient care, and nonoperating sources. Examples of these major sources include inpatient and outpatient revenues attached to units of activity (patient days, number and types of procedures, number of visits) multiplied by a designated rate. Operations not directly related to care include office space rental, cafeteria charges, transcription fees, gift shop revenue, television rental fees, or fees from educational programs. Gifts or donations, grants, sales of equipment, interest income, or income from taxation (state- or county-supported institutions) are included in nonoperating revenues (4).

Adjustments are made to the gross revenues by subtracting allowances for bad debt, charity, and contractual allowances. Bad debt represents accounts which are deemed uncollectible, while charity represents patient care rendered to people who are known in advance to be unable to pay.

Contractual allowances are the difference between the charges for services and the payments

Table 3.1. Statements of Revenues and Expenses for Years Ended December 31, 1991 and 1990

	1991	1990
Patient Service Revenue	$46,839,242	$39,729,079
Deductions from Revenue		
Charity and other discounts	916,054	759,179
Allowance for contractual adjustments	8,403,773	7,026,982
Provision for bad debts	2,723,574	2,010,446
	12,043,401	9,796,607
Net Patient Service Revenue	34,795,841	29,932,472
Other Operating Revenue	146,806	99,598
Total Operating Revenue	34,942,647	30,032,070
Operating Expenses		
Salaries	15,322,308	13,632,079
Employee benefits	2,411,642	2,299,454
Supplies and other expenses	8,785,646	7,849,560
Professional fees	1,366,882	954,332
Depreciation	1,571,809	1,419,325
Cost of drugs sold	1,698,119	1,338,760
Utilities	676,340	649,240
Interest	190,662	241,901
Dietary, net of cafeteria sales	96,035	89,078
Insurance	396,342	427,201
Direct medical education costs allocated from affiliated entity (Note 5)	511,494	549,496
	33,027,279	29,450,426
Income from Operations	1,915,368	581,644
Nonoperating Revenue		
Interest income	621,950	488,601
Other	40,051	36,791
	662,001	525,392
Revenues Over Expenses	2,577,369	1,107,036

due from third-party payors such as Medicare, Medicaid, and private insurance. Negotiating payment for services through health maintenance organizations (HMOs), preferred provider organizations (PPOs), or other third-party reimbursements have recently increased the disparity between charges and expected payments. Room rates and procedure charges can be adjusted, but there is a point at which all the increases are in vain if the reimbursement is fixed due to a high percentage of Medicare patients or other contractual agreements for adjustments or discounts. What remains after these adjustments are made is defined as net revenues. See Table 3.1 for examples of revenues and expenses.

Revenues from patient care also are dependent on patients and doctors selecting a certain facility and the determined course of therapy. The critical care nurse manager has an opportunity to impact this selection process. Obviously, the ability to provide certain programs and services for the patient is essential. Many physicians will base a decision regarding patient placement upon the condition of the equipment and the skill level of the nurses in the critical care unit. Physicians want to know their patients are receiving quality care. For these reasons, physicians become the nurses' customers, and as customers, the physicians need the opportunity to provide input and receive feedback regarding the quality of service provided.

The patient and his family are customers too. Perceptions regarding the care the patient receives are determined in nonscientific terms. Patients want to know the nurses care about them as individuals and will help them understand and adjust to their surroundings. Families want a trusting relationship with the nursing staff. As customers, they base their opinions on interactions rather than skills.

The staff are customers too. The critical care nurse manager must select a staff to provide highly skilled care in a sophisticated technical atmosphere, and blend their skills with compassion, intellect, and caring. The manager who empowers the staff with the autonomy to practice professionally will be rewarded with staff satisfaction. The challenge for the nurse manager is to bring all three customer groups together in such a manner that all have a positive experience.

Marketing theory says that for each patient who is treated there are three other people who will be impacted. The patient and the other three will tell all their friends about their experiences in the critical care environment and their hospital stay. Suddenly, one positive or one negative experience has a significant impact on whether other customers will choose the hospital. Physicians, while measuring the quality of care from a different viewpoint, make similar judgments.

Good customer relations are essential for today's nurse manager. Good programs and equipment are certainly basic tools, but the positive relationships established with the customers keep people returning. The impact of quality service is not remote from revenues at all. In fact, quality service and a positive customer environment have a direct impact on the hospital's budget.

Expenses

Expenses in the operating budget include all the costs associated with maintaining the ongoing operations of the organization. Expenses are divided into two categories: direct expenses, which are considered controllable by the line manager, and indirect expenses, which are not generally within the manager's control.

Most direct expenses are budgeted by the manager and fall into two categories: salaries and supplies and other expenses. Some direct expenses, e.g., financing costs, depreciation, and employee benefits, may be budgeted for each unit in the hospital by the accounting department.

Methodologies of budgeting salaries vary by hospital. Some managers budget salaries by multiplying an average salary rate by the required number of FTEs allocated to the unit. This method is relatively simple but by averaging salaries the method fails to consider potential promotions, clinical advancements, or other alterations in the staffing pattern which could have a financial impact on the unit. Other managers develop salary budgets based on the current staff's actual salaries, adjusted for vacant positions. While it is more time consuming, developing a budget based on actual salary figures is far more accurate and can integrate projected salary increases and promotions into the budget. Either method is acceptable, although the use of computers and spreadsheet software makes budgeting by actual dollars relatively easy and far more accurate. Adjustments must be made to current salary figures, including replacement for nonproductive time (for vacations, holidays, illness), overtime, educational leave, promotion, merit raises, differentials, on-call pay, charge nurse pay, orientation expenses, and other sources of expenses related to wages. Chapter 8 will discuss the personnel budget in greater detail.

Supplies and other expenses are developed as line items, which means each line has its own charge code. Separation of expenses allows for easy tracking of usage and allows for accurate comparison of dollars expended against dollars budgeted. A sudden surge in spending in a certain line item can be immediately noticed and should have a logical explanation. For example, the line item for repair has $500 budgeted for the month of June, but reports show that $1500 was spent. Investigation reveals that a bronchoscope was sent for repairs unexpectedly, and this explains the $1000 variance for the repair account. Another example is when the telephone line item exceeds budget because a tele-family program was implemented. The critical care nurse manager must ascertain whether the overages are intermittent, impacting the budget only temporarily, or whether the overage will continue throughout the year. Evaluation of expenses and variances from budgeted amounts then becomes a planning tool for the future. At annual budget preparation time, the nurse manager can reallocate dollars to project expenses more accurately without necessarily increasing the total budgeted amount. However, evaluation may indicate increases in some areas are necessary.

Direct unit expenses are charged to the unit and include items from central supply, storeroom, telephone, pharmacy, maintenance and repair of equipment, travel and education, medical fees, dietary, patient care items, suture, and, of course, a line item for miscellaneous needs (see Table 3.2). These items are different from supplies which are charged to the patient, e.g., intravenous start kits and Swan-Ganz catheters.

Indirect expenses are expenses which are allocated by an established formula (e.g., square footage occupied) throughout the hospital. Indirect expenses are necessary to maintain operations of the hospital's physical plant. Examples of indirect expenses include administrative fees, electricity and plumbing costs, environmental services (housekeeping), and educational institutions, i.e., school of nursing costs and insurance fees. While some of these costs can be controlled at the unit level through volume or usage, most indirect expenses are not controlled at the unit or department level. And, while important to the total operation of the institution and necessary to understanding operating expenses, indirect expenses historically have not been a top priority as areas targeted for maintaining financial control.

Profit

Simply put, profit or net income is what remains when expenses are subtracted from revenues. His-

Table 3.2. Budget Projection Worksheet, Department CVICU

Account Number	Account Name	1991 Budget	1990 Projected	1990 Budget	Percent Change (projected)	Percent Change (budget)	Projected Cost per Unit	Budget Cost per Unit	Percent Change
525050	Professional Fees	$12,000	$12,000	$12,000	0.00%	0.00%	$4.49	$2.41	−46.33%
530112	Suture	$1,900	$1,453	$900	30.76%	111.11%	$0.54	$0.38	−29.63%
530114	Patient Care Items	$1,000	$2,000	$2,000	−50.00%	−50.00%	$0.75	$0.20	−73.33%
538010	Storeroom	$37,100	$35,000	$35,000	6.00%	6.00%	$13.09	$7.47	−42.93%
538510	Central Supply	$3,180	$3,000	$3,000	6.00%	6.00%	$1.12	$0.64	−42.86%
538610	Pharmacy	$250	$250	$250	0.00%	0.00%	$0.09	$0.05	−44.44%
538710	Drug Store	$60	$60	$60	0.00%	0.00%	$0.02	$0.01	−50.00%
544010	Print Shop	$1,500	$1,500	$1,500	0.00%	0.00%	$0.56	$0.30	−46.43%
546010	Marketing	$7,000	$0	$0	100.00%	100.00%	$0.00	$1.41	ERR
551010	Miscellaneous	$9,010	$8,000	$8,000	12.63%	12.63%	$2.99	$1.81	−39.46%
553510	Dietary	$2,350	$1,850	$1,850	27.03%	27.03%	$0.69	$0.47	−31.88%
572010	Maintenance Contr.	$12,980	$3,000	$3,000	332.67%	332.67%	$1.12	$2.61	133.04%
573010	Repairs-Equipment	$3,180	$3,463	$3,000	−8.17%	6.00%	$1.30	$0.64	−50.77%
582610	Telephone Expense	$300	$300	$300	0.00%	0.00%	$0.11	$0.06	−45.45%
587010	Education & Travel	$8,000	$8,000	$8,000	0.00%	0.00%	$2.99	$1.61	−46.15%
	Total Budget w/o Salaries	$99,810	$79,876	$78,860	24.96%	26.57%	$29.88	$20.09	−32.76%
	Salary Budget	$2,120,236	$1,984,533	$1,951,187	6.84%	8.66%	$742.44	$426.69	−42.53%
	Total Budget w/ Salaries	$2,220,046	$2,064,409	$2,030,047	7.54%	9.36%	$772.32	$446.78	−42.15%

torically, not-for-profit institutions have set their goals at a minimum profit with operating profit margins of 1–4%, while for-profit institutions establish margins at 10–15% (5). Competition in health care, shifts from expensive inpatient care to less expensive outpatient care, and an aging patient population that is increasingly dependent on care reimbursement have refocused hospitals from increasing rates to controlling expenses in order to ensure the necessary profit margin. Creative utilization of supplies, standardization of supplies, and creative use of personnel provide opportunities for the nurse manager to contribute significantly to the financial viability of the institution.

TYPES OF BUDGETS

Revenue Budget

The revenue budget represents the activity forecast for the hospital. Revenue reflects the charges anticipated from the projected patient days, number of procedures, or number of visits, developed during the budget process. Historical trends must be reviewed in order to make educated guesses on anticipated patient activity. In addition to reviewing trends, the budget must also include new programs or new procedures which will bring new revenues to the institution.

Operating Budget

Operating costs annualize the revenues, adjustments, and expenses, including salaries, which are required to maintain the ongoing day-to-day activities of the institution. The operations must include any medical fees or commissions, any purchased services, professional liability insurance or other kinds of insurance, all financing costs, and depreciation expenses (6).

Personnel Budget

Personnel costs are a portion of the operating budget. In the labor-intensive environment of a hospital, personnel consumes a majority of the dollars spent. Nursing, the division which provides most of the direct care, is the most labor-intensive area of the hospital and may represent close to 40% of the entire personnel budget or more.

The personnel budget must address regular salaries, replacement for vacation and sick time, overtime, on-call pay, educational needs, fringe benefits, anticipated increase in wages, and employee turnover resulting in recruitment and orientation expenses (7).

Capital Budget

The capital budget is usually divided into two parts, capital equipment and capital projects. Capital equipment usually has a minimum dollar determination, e.g., $500, and durability of 1 year or longer; it is also defined as necessary for operations or it provides services to more than one patient (see Table 3.3). Capital projects include construction to remodel a portion of the facility, acquisition of land, or new construction. Capital projects must address equipment and other needs.

Capital budgets are done separately from the revenue and expense budgets, but are presented concurrently to the board of directors for approval. Most of the money to finance the capital budget will be obtained through profit generated by operations, although other forms of financing might be obtained for buildings and major construction projects. Each request for a capital item must be received with supporting documentation as to whether the equipment is a replacement item or new. If the item is a replacement, documentation must establish why the old equipment no longer suffices. This may be due to increased repair costs or a designated need for state-of-the-art equipment based on program requirements and physician requests. New items must also be justified through change in program or patient care requirements.

Prioritization in capital budgets is a must. Based on the hospital's mission and goals for the next 3–5 years, capital equipment and projects must support those goals. The hospital must determine its most pressing needs and pursue those needs first. As capital resources diminish, the board of directors must decide whether the ambulatory care center is more important than the critical care expansion, if both cannot be done simultaneously. At the unit level, the critical care nurse manager must decide which items are essential and submit those items as top priority. Concern for patient safety, new patient services, new revenues, patient satisfaction, and staff safety can guide the nurse manager in decision making.

Once approved, capital budgets are not automatically implemented. Bids for equipment and

Table 3.3. 1991 Capital Equipment Budget

Date: October 25, 1990		DEPARTMENT: CCU		
Priority	Budget Description	New Item Replacement	Approx. Cost	Month Needed
1.	Life Pak 10	Replace	9500	April
2.	Intra-aortic Balloon Pump	Replace	36000	April
3.	Suction Regulators	Replace	2250	April
4.	Wheelchair (1)	Replace	1000	May
5.	Network Work Station	New	2600	May
6.	Cardiac Chairs (3)	New	1800	May
7.	Doppler (2)	Replace	1200	June
8.	Desk Chairs (6)	Replace	2000	June
9.	Scales	New	3000	June
10.	IV Poles (5)	Replace	1000	June
11.	ECG Cables (6)	Replace	900	July
12.	Geri Chair	New	2500	July
13.				
14.				
15.				
16.				
17.				
18.				
19.				
20.				
21.				
22.				
23.				
24.				
25.				

Sr. Vice President _____   63750

Vice President _____

Director _____

construction may be necessary to obtain the best possible price from competing vendors. The purchasing and biomedical departments should be actively involved in equipment selection to provide counsel regarding pricing, durability, repairability, functional efficiency, and safety.

Substitution for previously approved capital items can be made throughout the fiscal year. Each institution determines the authority levels for substitution. For example, the administrator may approve substitutions up to $10,000. Items exceeding that limit must be forwarded to the board of directors. Capital budgets represent monetary investment in the institution's goals and objectives, since they represent major purchases or alterations to the physical plant. Capital budgets are often projected for a 3–5 year period and must be developed, approved, and implemented with great care. Capital budgets are discussed in Chapter 7.

BUDGET CYCLE

Budgets are based on fiscal years (FY), meaning there is a starting date and an ending date between which the institution earns either a net profit or loss. Many teaching hospitals have fiscal years coinciding with the medical school year, such as July 1 through June 30. Other hospitals have fiscal years coinciding with the calendar year, such as January 1 through December 31. Public hospitals usually establish their fiscal year to coincide with the government (federal, state, or local) FY. What is important is that the dates of the operating fiscal year are constant so that periodic comparisons can be made.

The budget cycle is a series of events that occur throughout the fiscal year. This cycle has several distinctive phases (8). Phase one is the strategic planning phase. Strategic planning by top administration and the governing body sets the vision or direction for the institution, and is usually developed for a 3–5 year period, and updated annually.

From the long-term perspective of the strategic plan, the operational plan, or phase two, can be ascertained. During this phase the hospital can determine where the emphasis will be placed over the next fiscal year by developing goals and objectives for the organization.

Phase three is an administrative phase. The budget preparation materials are developed and disseminated by the financial department. Projections for units of activity (volume) should be determined and approved. Phase four concentrates on communication. The administration introduces the strategic plan and organizational goals for the next fiscal year. Department goals and objectives must complement those of the organization. This phase allows the managers to gather input from staff and key physicians about new technologies which could impact the future of the department or hospital. Communication from accounting regarding new budget materials or forms occurs during this phase.

Decision making and initial projections (implementation) of the plan commence in phase five. The budget preparation usually starts midway through the fiscal year. Using 6 months of actual data, managers must project year-end expenditures. These expenditures then become the baseline for the next fiscal year's spending. The conversion of plans into identified needs are negotiated with administration with tentative approvals established.

Phase six quantifies the plans. This is the computation and clerical phase where the previous plans are converted into the traditional budget. Budgets are completed at the department level, integrated by accounting into the comprehensive or master budget, and forwarded to the administration for a final review.

The administration recommends the budget to the governing body, e.g., board of directors, for approval in phase seven. Traditionally, this approval occurs at the final board meeting for the fiscal year. A typical budget calendar is found in Table 3.4.

The final phase of the budget cycle is implementation of the approved budget. Monitoring systems are established to compare the actual expenditures against the targeted amounts. Plans are implemented and revised as necessary, and the budget cycle repeats.

Presentation and negotiation of the budget are discussed in Chapter 12.

FISCAL DEPARTMENT ORGANIZATION

Many variations in the organization of fiscal departments exist, depending on the institution's size, its complexity, and the chief executive officer's preferences. However, the chief financial officer (CFO) is normally a key member of the administrative team, where budgeting is concerned.

The CFO has several duties. These range from ensuring the organization has enough cash available to meet financial obligations, and appropriately investing cash assets, to obtaining capital funding at the lowest possible cost (9). In addition to these duties, the CFO monitors all accounts, controls payroll and related tax issues, and monitors regulatory and governmental agencies to determine how they impact health care. The CFO oversees and reviews data regarding census, admissions, charges, and number of Medicare and Medicaid patients. This person also ensures that patient are billed, reimbursement is received or collection attempted, and that the hospital's bills are paid in a timely fashion to maintain an appropriate credit line. The CFO is intimately involved in establishing daily care rates, procedure charges, and in developing the strategies for financing new equipment (10). The majority of this information is prepared with the assistance of the medical records and admissions departments in a smaller institution, and the CFO delegates most of these functions in a larger institution. Nonetheless, the CFO is accountable for advising the governing body and management team regarding the organization's fiscal viability.

Development of the Annual Budget

The CFO or a designee may organize or develop the master document for the annual budget and present it to the administration for approval. The CFO may provide the appropriate data and instruction to the department level managers for preparation of the budget. The major benefit to the

Table 3.4. 1991 Planning Calendar (For the 1991–1993 Strategic Plan)

Timing	Activity
January	Annual Update of Corporate Strategic Plan
February 15	Corporate Planning Session—Communications of Corporate Strategic Plan to Hospital Administrators
March 30	Annual Update of Hospital Strategic Plans—Proposed Revisions Completed
April	Hospital Administrative Planning Sessions—Review of Hospital Strategic Plans, development of Administrative Objectives and preparation for Director's Planning Session
May	Hospital Department Director's Planning Session—Communication of Corporate Strategic Plan and Review of Hospital Strategic Plan and Administrative Objectives as a basis for development of Departmental Objectives
May 31	Hospital or Administrative Objectives Due to Senior Vice President
June 15	Departmental Objectives Due to Vice Presidents for Initial Review
July 2	Procedure Budget Estimates Due to Accounting
July 16	Corporate Review of Administrative and Departmental Objectives
July 25*	Budget Packages and Departmental Objectives Distributed to Department Directors
August 15*	Department Budget Requests and Departmental Objectives Due to Administrators for Review and Refinement
September 17*	Final Hospital Budgets to Accounting
September 28*	Budget Comparisons Complete
October 19*	Final Decision on Expense and Revenue Budgets
November 1	Final Review of Departmental Objectives for Alignment with Approved Budget
November 9	Final Administrative Approval of Strategic Plans and Budget
November 29	Present Budgets at Quarterly Board Meeting
Quarterly	Review Sessions—Held for the Purpose of Reviewing Progress Toward Hospital Objectives and Making Strategic Adjustments Mandated by Environment Changes and Market Responses to Implemented Actions

*Budget dates are tentative to be set by the Accounting Department

department manager preparing the budget is that plans for new programs, new equipment, and increases or decreases in beds can be incorporated into the process at its inception rather than later. In a small institution, the CFO will usually be intimately involved in decisions regarding programs and equipment. For a large institution, with many large departments or divisions, the CFO may not know the plans or needs of each area.

Besides providing data, the CFO must educate other managers regarding the budget process. Each year, the overall process must be reviewed with all managers who will be involved in budget development. The introduction of new forms, computer systems, limits for spending, and regulatory measures should be presented. While an institution's overall budget process may not change drastically each year, there is some refinement. Budget in-services can serve as a review for the experienced manager or as an initial learning device for the new manager.

Following the educational preparation, the CFO and the finance department should serve as consultants. It is important for these individuals to be available to the managers as the budget is being prepared.

Once the budget package is returned to the finance department, the CFO must accumulate revenues and expenses in order to project the estimated profit margin. The CFO must also review the budget to ensure its completeness and accuracy before presentation to administration. The CFO must understand the rationale for each budgetary projection and be ready to answer any query presented. Once the administration's concurrence has been secured, the budget is ready for presentation to the board of directors for approval.

The budget process, while sounding simple, represents a multitude of complex plans and negotiations. The administration, and ultimately the board of directors, must carefully plan the direction for the organization. If a multimillion dollar ambulatory center is to be built, then financing must be secured, construction contracts must be negotiated, and equipment must be purchased. Such a building may mean that another area of the hospital must wait another year to expand or will have equipment purchases rescheduled. If the hospital commits to maintaining state-of-the-art equipment and programs, these objectives must be financed through profits from operations or other sources such as debt or foundation grants and donations. The rising cost of personnel must be considered in light of increased competition for scarce professionals, and the need for attractive wage benefit packages should be considered in the budget process.

The CFO must be involved as financial strategies are set to ensure the hospital's fiscal viability. Tough decisions must be made when perceived needs are great but available dollars are declining. Without a clear vision of the goals for the institution, these decisions become impossible, so it is imperative that strategic planning begin and continue throughout the budget process.

Monitoring and Reviewing the Budget

Once approved, the budget must be implemented. The finance department must monitor the budget throughout the fiscal year. Monthly statements must be prepared and made available to the managers at all levels to inform them of progress in meeting budgeting goals.

Each monitor statement should identify the account and amounts budgeted vs. spent for each line item. The statement should include the current month and cumulative data year-to-date. The cumulative data are important to help determine whether a monthly overexpenditure is a one-time occurrence or a trend. The statement may also provide comparisons against the previous year.

The critical care nurse manager should review monthly budget statements carefully to establish whether the data are accurate, to identify trends in overspending, or to spot errors due to inaccurate data entry. For example, a $4000 expense in the dietary account may have been a repair bill which was entered incorrectly. Errors of this nature require corrections so accounts can accurately reflect the expenditures. Another example would be an increase in salary expense when the census was below budget. To justify the expense, managers must carefully examine the assignment of personnel, paid time off, acuity level of the patients, and whether unusual circumstances prevailed. These factors help ascertain if there is a pattern needing immediate correction. It is also important to review revenues to be sure they coincide with the level of activity. If revenues are low while procedures exceed budget, there may be discrepancies in data entry that need to be investigated. Chapter 13 presents information about variance reporting.

Business Planning

The financial department should take an active role in the development of business plans, especially those plans that involve the implementation of new programs. The CFO or a well qualified designee will likely be a member of the planning committee along with representatives of marketing, planning, computer services, and clinical departments. The finance department can offer major contributions in the internal analysis portion of the business plan by examining opportunities from the fiscal point of view. Having a financial adviser as part of the planning team from the beginning helps provide an understanding of the financial goals and objectives of the business plan. Determining the projected revenues and costs of new programs to establish a break-even volume utilizes the finance department's expertise.

FOCUSED ANECDOTE

Scenario

A large tertiary hospital had established a strategic plan in which increasing the number of admissions from the county in which it resides was considered an important goal. One of the major objectives was to market the emergency department (ED) to increase the number of visits, because approximately 30% of the ED visits converted to admissions. The director of the ED was notified to develop a business plan.

Action Steps

The ED director assembled a task force to help develop the business plan. The task force members included representatives from marketing, planning, nursing, the medical director and other key physicians, and an industrial engineer. The director of accounting served as a consultant. This task force assisted the director in thorough internal and external analyses utilizing a SWOT (Strengths, Weaknesses, Opportunities, and Threats) exercise. The census and financial statements from the previous 5 years were examined. From these analyses, goals were prepared. Three-year objectives and objectives for the next fiscal year with accompanying strategies and action plans were established. A portion of the goals and objectives is presented below as an example.

Goal 1. The emergency department shall maintain a leadership position in the provision of quality, patient-centered, emergency services.
Objective 1. Increase the number of visits by 10% in the next 3 years.
Strategies. Two-track approach ("Express Care" and Trauma); add occupational medicine program; target marketing.
Action Plan.
1. Recruit secretarial staff and RN to support program.
2. Contract with a physician to serve as medical director for the occupational medicine program.
3. Obtain a computer and appropriate software to support programs.
4. Market "Express Care," occupational medicine, and trauma.

Goal 2. The emergency department shall utilize a market-oriented approach in the development and delivery of emergency services.
Objective 2. Increasing the number of visits in the immediate county by 2.5% in the next 3 years.
Strategies. Target marketing; customer orientation.
Actions.
1. Target market in the western portion of the county.
2. Distribute brochures especially prepared to target market.
3. Establish a telephone survey the day after the ED visit to determine satisfaction.
4. Work with the marketing department to determine trends in dissatisfaction or suggestions to improve image.

Goal 3. The emergency department shall recruit, develop, and retain human resources consistent with the needs of the organization.
Objective 3. Increase staff to accommodate increase in both ambulatory and trauma business as evidenced by an increase in authorized positions.
Strategies. Administrative support; systems evaluation.
Actions.
1. Budget for 5 FTEs for RNs.
2. Hire qualified RNs to fill vacancies.

Given the above program goals and objectives at budget time, it was clear that projected visits had to be increased and that the director had to include salaries and positions for one secretary, five RNs, and one medical director. In addition to personnel, expenses had to be budgeted for marketing activities. For the capital budget, a personal computer and software became essential items.

During budget negotiations, the six new positions were questioned. The director easily demonstrated how removing the six positions would effect several objectives established in the business plan. The positions remained in the budget.

In the next fiscal year, the positions were added to the staff and qualified people were hired. The occupational medicine program was implemented. The computer was purchased and brought on-line. By year-end, approximately 4% more visits had been achieved; the budget plan had been exceeded for this initial year.

The budget is a plan expressed in quantitative terms. Budget decisions cannot be made in isolation, but must be made in relation to the goals of the organization and its strategic plan.

REFERENCES

1. Garrison R. Managerial accounting. Homewood, ILL: Business Publications, 1988:321.
2. Strasen L. Key business skills for nurse managers. Philadelphia: J.B. Lippincott Co., 1987:119–120.
3. Garrison, p. 324.
4. Young L, Hayne A. Nursing administration from concepts to practice. Philadelphia: W.B. Saunders Co., 1988:196.
5. Strasen, p. 38.
6. Strasen, p. 60.
7. Stevens B. The nurse as executive. Rockville, MD: An Aspen Publication, 1985:203.
8. Berman H, Weeks L. The financial management of hospitals. Ann Arbor, MI: Health Administration Press, 1982:509–541.
9. Young, p. 203.
10. Stevens, p. 291.

Chapter 4

Financial Statements

DONNA L. BERTRAM,
KATHERINE D. MCCORD

You need to order the special modular cardiac and respiratory monitors. You submit the necessary paperwork. Your director announces that the financial officer has just put a freeze on all capital purchases because of cash flow difficulties. What does this mean?

Financial statements describe fiscal behavior by generating a picture of the assets, liabilities, and net worth of an organization at a given point in time. Assessing the financial condition of an organization is done routinely to see whether the organization can remain viable if it pursues goals with the same level of activity. The basic information needed to make this determination is contained in financial statements.

While critical care nurse managers may not look at financial statements routinely, understanding the components and interrelationships of financial documents provides insight into the overall financial health of the institution. This is important because critical care units generate revenues and contribute to the operating and capital expenses of the hospital. With the ability to read and interpret financial statements, the manager gains a better understanding of the reasons for financial decisions and an appreciation for the importance of financial management. It also enhances the nurse manager's credibility in communicating financial management decisions to staff and physicians.

This chapter focuses on three important financial statements: the balance sheet, income statement, and statements in cash flow. The purpose of footnotes, auditing, and commonly used ratios is also discussed.

TYPES OF FINANCIAL STATEMENTS
Balance Sheet

The balance sheet is an important financial document that presents a snapshot of the assets, liabilities, and fund balance of the hospital. The balance sheet is produced at the end of an accounting period and represents the financial status at this point in time. Most hospitals generate this document at the end of each month and at the end of the fiscal year, but accounting periods can be any time period, such as a day, a month, a quarter, or a year.

The term "balance" provides the nurse manager with a clue that there is something significant about a document having two sides that equally balance. This equality requirement does not tell us much about the financial health of the hospital, but it represents a fundamental accounting principle whereby transactions of the hospital are shown on one side of the balance sheet as assets and on the other side as liabilities and fund balance. The two sections counterbalance:

$$\text{Assets} = \text{Liabilities} + \text{Fund Balance}$$

Usually, the assets are listed on the left and the liabilities are on the right (see Table 4.1). Occasionally a balance sheet is displayed in a top down format rather than in a left to right fashion.

Assets

In Table 4.1, the first sections show assets. An asset is any resource owned and controlled by the hospital, or any business or individual. Examples of assets are petty cash, savings accounts, supplies, equipment, vehicles, and buildings.

The balance sheet is organized to report current assets first, and fixed or long-term assets second. Thus, assets are listed in order of their liquidity, which refers to how quickly resources owned can be converted to cash. Liquid assets can be converted to cash quickly, usually within one year.

Current assets are the most liquid and include

43

Table 4.1. Balance Sheet

Nicest Hospital
Balance Sheet
June 30, 1990 (in 000s)

Assets		Liabilities and Fund Balance	
Current Assets		Current Liabilities	
Cash	$225	Accounts Payable	$597
Accts Receivable	460	Accrued Expenses	433
Inventories	195	Payroll Deduction	145
Total Current Assets	$880	Total Current Liabilities	$1,175
Fixed Assets		Long-Term Liabilities	
Land, Bldgs	900	Long-Term Debt	625
Equipment	1,500	Fund Balance	1,480
Total Fixed Assets	$2,400		
Total Assets	$3,280	Total Liabilities and Fund Balance	$3,280

cash, savings, accounts receivable (that which is owed to the hospital), and inventories.

Fixed assets are items that have a life longer than one year, are not easily bought and sold in the normal course of business, and have a specified dollar value. Fixed assets include buildings, property, capital equipment, and patents. These resources may be described as long-term assets, as they cannot be converted to cash quickly.

The current assets and the fixed assets are added together to arrive at total assets. This detailed listing of assets shows all the resources owned by the hospital.

Liabilities

Opposite the assets description are the liabilities and fund balance. A liability is an obligation that the hospital, agency, or an individual owes to someone for a good or a service. A liability is a claim against an asset and arises from an event that has already happened. Examples of liabilities are utility payments due, loan payments, wages payable, insurance premiums due, and interest due. A liability is the opposite of an asset.

Liabilities, like assets, are listed in the following order: current first, long-term second, and finally the fund balance. Current liabilities include all obligations which must be paid within 1 year and include wages, supplies, rent, utilities, or premiums. The balance sheet in Table 4.1 shows accrued expenses for rent and utilities, and a payroll deduction for the wages payable.

Long-term liabilites are due beyond 1 year. For example, a loan payment due each year for 10 years would be classified as a long-term liability. The first 12 months of a loan payment is a current liability. From the thirteenth month and beyond, the mortgage payment would be a long-term liability.

Fund Balance

The fund balance is the amount that remains after all the liabilities have been deducted from the assets. Owner's equity is the term used by a privately held company that shows the amount which has been invested in the company. The amount in the fund balance can also be called stockholders equity, retained earnings, or net worth. Fund balance is a term more commonly associated with the hospital. It decreases through loss or the withdrawal of cash or other assets.

All of the liabilities, current and fixed, and the fund balance are added together to give the total liabilities of the hospital. This total equals the total listed on the asset side of the balance sheet.

Income Statement

The income statement identifies the profitability of a hospital or a business. It summarizes revenues and expenses and tells what occurred in the organization over a period of time, usually a month or a year. This statement is also referred to as the profit or loss document, the statement of earnings, the results of operations, or the statement for revenues and expenses. The income statement provides a better measure than the balance sheet of how well an organization is performing financially. It shows the results of all the operations or activities of the hospital and the impact on the hospital's wealth.

Revenues

Revenues represent any monies that an organization receives or is entitled to receive. Revenues come from providing a service for a fee, selling a product, or receiving funds from grants or gifts. Examples of revenues for the hospital include patient room and board, procedures billed, rent paid to the hospital, supplies sold to patients, and sale of old equipment.

Revenues generally come from three sources in a hospital. Revenue is generated from patient services and from nonpatient services. The latter (from nonpatient services) is often called nonoperating revenue. Patient service revenues include all of the charges billed for services and products provided to a patient by the hospital. The revenue amount based on charges is called gross revenue. For example, daily intensive care charges, procedures, supplies, medications, and therapy charges comprise gross revenue generated by the patient. Patient services can be divided into inpatient and outpatient revenues. Nonpatient service revenues come from patient-related business proceeds such as the gift shop, cafeteria, and parking garage. Nonoperating revenues are those not related at all to patient care. These may include rent from an apartment building the hospital owns, catering services, management fees, grants, and gifts.

Adjustments

Adjustments to gross revenue are required in a hospital setting. Adjustments include any deductions due to contractual allowances, charity, bad debt, and discounts. Hospitals bill actual charges, but often must settle for less than the amount actually incurred. Contractual allowances come, for example, from Medicare, Medicaid, health maintenance organizations (HMOs) and preferred provider organizations (PPOs). For example, an open heart surgery patient covered by Medicare consumes $19,475 of goods and services, but Medicare only pays $12,650 under the diagnosis related group (DRG) for the hospital. The difference of $6825 is a contractual allowance. Often these allowances represent the largest deductions from accounts receivable.

Charity is the unreimbursed amount given to the underinsured or uninsured. If the patient pays part of the bill based on a sliding scale or some other arrangement, the amount paid is deducted from the amount owed and the remaining amount due is adjusted on the income statement as an allowance.

Bad debts occur when the patient is billed for all services but never pays. Like most businesses, hospitals may wait a reasonable time period for the patient to pay the bill. When the bill is not paid after repeated attempts to collect, the amount due is written off as a bad debt.

Discounts occur when certain groups or individuals receive a percentage of the amount billed as a deduction from the bill. The discounted amount is an allowance, as it is less than the amount due to the hospital. Sometimes this is called a courtesy allowance. Clergy, employees, and physicians may receive a discount when hospitalized or when using pharmacy or laboratory services.

Expenses

Expenses include any costs that the hospital incurs in order to produce the revenues. Examples of expenses include salaries, benefits, supplies, utilities, repairs, maintenance, travel, education, and interest due on loans. Expenses are amounts the hospital owes to someone else.

Expenses can be direct or indirect. A direct expense is one that is easily traceable to an actual service, good, or person. An example of a direct expense is the hourly wage paid to the critical care nurse. An indirect expense is one that is harder to trace and attach to a service, good, or person. An example of an indirect expense is the service of the chaplain in critical care. Part of the chaplain's time is allocated to the unit, unless the chaplain is considered in the unit's staffing complement.

Operating expense are often separated into categories by departments or functional areas. These include:

- Nursing Services
  —Medical-Surgical Units
  —Critical Care
  —Surgical Suite
  —Maternal/Child
  —Behavioral Medicine
  —Skilled Nursing Facility

- —Emergency
- —Rehabilitation
- Ancillary Services
  - —Laboratory
  - —Pharmacy
  - —Radiology
  - —Nutrition
  - —Therapies (Respiratory, Physical, Speech)
- General Service Areas
  - —Housekeeping
  - —Laundry
  - —Pastoral Care
  - —Medical Records
  - —Security
  - —Social Work
  - —Maintenance
- Financial Service Areas
  - —Accounting
  - —Admitting
  - —Business Service
  - —Collections
  - —Data Processing
  - —Insurance
  - —Materials Management
- Administrative Areas
  - —Development
  - —Medical Affairs
  - —Public Relations
  - —Planning
  - —Quality Management
  - —Risk Management
  - —Volunteer Services
  - —Officers and Board of Trustees

Net Income

After all the expenses are tabulated, profit can be calculated by subtracting the expenses from the revenues.

$$\text{Profit} = \text{Revenues} - \text{Expenses}$$

Net income or profit is the difference between the revenues (amount in) and the expenses (amount out). When revenues exceed expenses, there is a profit. A deficit or a loss occurs when expenses are greater than revenues. How well a hospital is able to earn an excess in revenue over expenses involves many management decisions.

Tracking the financial performance occurs over a period of time called the fiscal year (FY). The FY represents 12 months and can be a calendar year (January 1 to December 31) or another period (July 1 to June 30). The hospital chooses the most appropriate year for their business. Many hospitals compare the current year to the past year on the income statement (see Table 4.2).

Statement of Cash Flows

The term, statement of cash flows, is relatively new. Before 1988 hospitals and other businesses generated a document called change in financial position. This document was often confusing and unclear to the reader. The newer document, statement of cash flows, provides information about where resources came from and what happened to them during a specific accounting period.

Changes in the hospital's cash flows provide more information about how fund balances have changed over the fiscal year. Often the income

Table 4.2. Income Statement

Nicest Hospital
Income Statement
Year Ending
June 30, 1990 (in 000s)

Revenue	
Inpatient Revenue	$19,250
Outpatient Revenue	23,475
Gross Revenue	42,725
Deductions From Revenue	
Charity	1,310
Bad Debt	867
Discounts	910
Allowances	6,545
Total Deductions	9,632
Net Patient Revenue	33,093
Nonpatient Revenue	312
Total Revenue	33,405
Operating Expenses	
Nursing Services	9,250
Ancillary Services	5,126
General Services	2,350
Financial Services	1,535
Administrative Services	1,960
Insurance	415
Interest	95
Depreciation	1,169
Total Expenses	22,421
Excess (loss) of Revenue	
Over Expenses	10,984
Nonoperating Revenue	200
Net Income	$11,184

statement and the balance sheet lack the specific information needed by managers to make decisions. The governing body and investment agencies also like to know the cash flow activities for the facility. The flow of these funds can affect many decisions. Activities that generate or consume cash present a good picture of the hospital's financial health. These activities include operating, investing, and financing.

A statement of change in cash flows is often generated for the annual report, but many hospitals submit this document monthly with the other two financial statements. Information about liquidity changes, and how and why these changes are occurring due to operations, fund raising, gifts, major sales, grants, or the use of fixed assets, is contained in the report.

The changes in the statement of cash flows assist in the determination of how well operations, assets, controls, and cash flows are being managed. Looking at this statement allows the manager to determine if a capital freeze is necessary, if more debt can be funded internally, and if current debt could be repaid.

This statement identifies working capital and cash flows. Working capital indicates current assets, sometimes called funds. Accountants describe working capital as the excess of current assets over the current liabilities. The American Hospital Association and the Healthcare Financial Management Association (HFMA) define working capital as:

Working Capital

= Current Assets − Current Liabilities (1)

Income from operations, sale of long-term assets, such as buildings or property, and borrowing new money are all sources of working capital. Working capital is used to purchase long-term funds to build inventory or have cash for unanticipated needs. Looking at working capital over a time period gives management a very detailed tool which identifies trends in fund flows (2).

Depreciation does not involve the actual exchange of cash. As the plant, property, and equipment are acquired, a formula is established for the rate of depreciation. Depreciation is the concept of using up a resource over time. The amount that is depreciated is deducted as an expense, but no actual cash results. This amount can be added into the statement of cash flows (see Table 4.3).

FOOTNOTES TO FINANCIAL STATEMENTS

Often items in the financial statements need further explanation. Footnotes provide clarification or more detail to assist the reader in interpreting the information in the financial statements.

Footnotes to the financial statement may appear in the year-end report. These footnotes may describe the following activities:

- Discussion of third-party payors' activities;
- Summary of significant accounting methods;
- Description of depreciation methods;
- Description of long-term debt;
- Discussion of pension plan;
- Discussion of unusual amounts in revenues.

An example of a footnote follows:

Note 1: Basis of Presentation of Accounting Policy
Liability Insurance: The hospital's professional and general liability insurance is underwritten by the Best in the West Insurance Company. There is a $50,000 umbrella excess coverage policy. Professional liability is provided up to $5000 per occurrence. Premiums charged for the coverage were $4995 for FY 90.

AUDITING

Auditing occurs internally and externally. The internal audit serves to ensure that the hospital is adhering to certain policies and procedures, that financial transactions are accurate, and that internal controls are established and effectively used. External auditing provides an objective appraisal of the financial documents by someone not connected with the hospital.

Internal auditing includes many functions. For example, it may be used to ensure accurate distribution of payroll checks. To verify that only authorized personnel are receiving paychecks, the internal auditor may centralize check distribution and require employees to present identification before they receive checks. Other examples include the auditor investigating the use of overtime, studying how patient valuables are secured, reviewing expense reports for receipts, monitoring education expenses, and determining whether any

Table 4.3. Statement of Cash Flows

Statement of Cash Flows
Paradise Hospital
Year Ended December 31, 1990 (in 000s)

CASH FLOWS FROM OPERATING ACTIVITIES	
Net income (loss)	$6,686
Adjustments to reconcile net income (loss) to net cash provided by operating activities	
Depreciation	7,822
Equity in results of subsidiaries and affiliated operations	(210)
Net changes in current assets and liabilities	
Accounts Receivable	(1,742)
Inventories and Prepaid Expenses	(215)
Accounts Payable	308
Other current liabilites	1,476
Other changes	(1,006)
TOTAL ADJUSTMENTS	6,433
NET CASH PROVIDED BY OPERATING ACTIVITIES	13,119
CASH FLOWS FROM INVESTING ACTIVITIES	
Additions to property and equipment	(8,462)
Net decrease in assets whose use is limited	(1,747)
Other changes in investments and other assets	(110)
NET CASH USED IN INVESTING ACTIVITIES	(10,319)
CASH FLOWS FROM FINANCING ACTIVITIES	
Payments of long-term debt	(873)
Transfers	(20)
NET CASH USED IN FINANCING ACTIVITIES	(893)
INCREASE (DECREASE) IN CASH AND INVESTMENTS	1,907
CASH AND INVESTMENTS, BEGINNING OF YEAR	(1,718)
CASH AND INVESTMENTS, END OF YEAR	189

conflicts of interest are occurring. Internal auditing is done by an employee of the hospital and is considered an internal means of control.

External auditing involves the use of an outside and disinterested party, such as a certified public accountant (CPA) or a firm that does public accounting. The Securities and Exchange Commission (SEC) requires publicly held companies to issue an annual report to their stockholders that contains audited financial statements. The independent audit forms the basis for the professional accounting firm's opinion (3). The written report may state:

> We have audited the accompanying balance sheets of Paradise Hospital as of June 30, 1990, and 1989, and the related statements of income and changes in fund balances and cash flows. We conducted our audits in conformity with generally accepted accounting principles. In our opinion, the financial statements present fairly, in all material respects, the financial position of Paradise Hospital.

The financial statements are the responsibility of the hospital's management as they reflect the results of operations. The auditor's opinion usually appears on the annual report and states whether the financial statements actually represent what occurred. The auditor's opinion is not an absolute guarantee of the truth, but best reflects what was presented in the statements. The CPA or accounting firm provides a means of assuring reliability of the financial information, rather than certifying the absolute accuracy or correctness of amounts reported in the statements.

The audit is an examination following certain rules and standards called generally accepted accounting principles (GAAP) (4). The auditor randomly reviews accounting records, looks for errors, and identifies strengths and weaknesses of internal controls. The auditor will then render an opinion, which is like a stamp of approval. The auditor seeks to obtain assurances that the financial statements are free from any major misstatements.

The rules for accounting are established by the

Financial Accounting Standards Board (FASB). This group identifies universally acceptable rules and offers technical rulings on how a firm discloses its financial picture.

RATIO ANALYSIS OF FINANCIAL PERFORMANCE

Overview of Ratio Analysis

The objectives of analyzing financial statements serve to evaluate past performance, identify financial interrelationships, and predict future performance. Comparisons are done between accounting periods which look at how the organization performed in relation to their industry averages. After an analysis of the financial statements, better managerial decisions can usually be made.

Ratios are helpful tools used to assess overall financial operations, determine current financial position, and reveal any potential problems. Many ratios exist which facilitate management effectiveness.

A ratio is computed by dividing one number by another. It is a relation of one amount to another. Ratios can be expressed as a percentage (95%), a decimal (0.95), a fraction (¼), or an integer (4 to 1). Financial analysts rely on several ratios trended over time to evaluate performance in different areas. One ratio in isolation has little meaning (5).

The HFMA publishes a report called "The Hospital Industry Financial Report" (HIFR). The information in the report comes from the audited financial statements of those hospitals that subscribe to the Financial Analysis Service. Hospitals may submit their audited financial statements voluntarily to HFMA (6). Collective data from hospitals is compiled and reported based on trends and comparisons to peer groups. The U.S. is divided into five regions and there are six categories of hospitals based on bed size for each region. Many chief financial officers (CFOs) subscribe to this service and receive the report (7).

There are at least 30 ratios that can be used to analyze financial statements. This section will identify some of the more commonly used and important ratios for hospitals.

There are four categories of ratio analysis:

1. Liquidity ratios;
2. Leverage or capital structure ratios;
3. Activity ratios;
4. Profitability ratios.

Liquidity Ratios

Liquidity refers to how well an institution can meet its obligations. Liquidity ratios are used to determine how well a hospital could meet its current obligations by liquidating its assets. Cash poor indicates that there may not be enough cash to pay current claims. There may be something basically wrong if the hospital shows poor liquidity ratios.

Liquidity ratios include current ratio, days in patient accounts receivable ratio, and days cash on hand ratio. There are other liquidity ratios not discussed. Paradise Hospital's balance sheet and income statement will be used. (See Table 4.4 and Table 4.5.) The current ratio equation follows.

$$\text{Current Ratio} = \frac{\text{Current Assets}}{\text{Current Liabilities}}$$

The current ratio is one of the most commonly used ratios for liquidity. Current ratio values indicate the hospital is in a position to meet its current liabilities. However, a high ratio does not necessarily indicate that the hospital is managing all its financial resources well. Other ratios must also be evaluated.

Paradise Hospital in 1990 shows a current ratio of:

$$\text{Current Ratio} = \frac{\$7,780}{\$4,136} = 1.88$$

Paradise Hospital has 1.88 times more assets than current liabilities. The median for the U.S. hospitals in 1988 was 2.037 with a range of 1.491–2.715 (8). The range varies by bed size and geographic area. The current ratio trend in hospitals has been constant over 5 years.

Days in Patient Accounts Receivable

$$= \frac{\text{Net Accounts Receivable}}{\text{Net Patient Revenue}/365}$$

This ratio helps us look at the average time receivables are outstanding. Solvency, with cash coming in and going out, is a prime consideration when looking at a possible worsening of financial

Table 4.4. Balance Sheet

Paradise Hospital
Balance Sheet
December 31, 1990 (in 000s)

	12-31-90	12-31-89
Assets		
Current Assets		
Cash	189	141
Accounts Receivables	6,525	5,253
Less Adjustments	76	39
Net Accounts Receivable	6,449	5,214
Inventories	950	695
Prepaid Expenses	192	201
Total Current Assets	7,780	6,251
Property, Plant, Equipment		
Land	564	520
Construction in Progress	95	147
Buildings and Equipment	39,510	34,746
Less Depreciation	7,822	6,847
Total Property, Plant, Equip	32,347	27,828
Total Assets	40,127	34,746
Liabilities and Fund Balance		
Current Liabilities		
Accounts Payable	2,359	3,122
Notes Payable	950	975
Accrued Expenses	798	437
Due to Restricted Funds	29	42
Total Current Liabilities	4,136	4,576
Long-Term Debt	465	394
Mortgage	7,813	6,892
Total Liabilities	12,414	11,862
Fund Balance	27,713	22,884
Total Liabilities and Fund Balance	40,127	34,746

Table 4.5. Income Statement

Paradise Hospital
Income Statement
Year Ended December 31, 1990 (in 000s)

Patient Service Revenue	$54,129
Adjustments and Uncollectable	22,445
Net Patient Revenue	31,684
Other Operating Revenue	3,937
Total Operating Revenue	35,621
Operating Expenses	
Nursing Services	11,405
Ancillary Services	5,474
General Services	2,281
Financial Services	1,825
Administrative Services	3,193
Insurance	1,370
Interest	684
Depreciation	3,650
Total Operating Expenses	29,882
Net Operating Income	5,739
Nonoperating Revenue	947
Excess (loss) of Revenue Over Expenses	6,686

position. Often the hospital has little control over when the funds come in from the government, third-party payors, or self payors. Monitoring the number of days that go by before bills are paid is very important to the hospital. The longer that bills due to the hospital are unpaid, the less efficient the hospital becomes.

Paradise Hospital in 1990 shows:

Days in Accounts Receivable

$$= \frac{\$6,449}{\$31,684/365} = 74.3$$

The days in accounts receivable reveal the amount of time in days it takes for the hospital to collect on what was billed. For Paradise Hospital it takes 74.3 days on an average to experience cash from its accounts receivable. If days in accounts receivable are too high, the hospital may have problems with collection and billing systems. A high number leads to management actions in medical records, nursing, pharmacy, billing, and other areas. Charts held on the nursing unit too long may delay the billing process. The median in the U.S. in 1988 was 74.588 days with a range of 61.978–88.842. The trend is an increase in days in accounts receivable (9).

Days Cash on Hand

$$= \frac{\text{Cash} + \text{Marketable Securities}}{(\text{Total Operating Expense} - \text{Depreciation})/365}$$

This value indicates how long the hospital could continue paying its obligations if there were no more money coming in. Days cash on hand is a measure of liquidity determining how much cash is available to continue paying daily expenses. Too little cash on hand may signal difficulty, just as too much could imply the hospital has not taken advantage of putting the cash to work.

Paradise Hospital's days cash on-hand in 1990 was:

$$\frac{\$189}{(\$29,882 - \$3,650)/365} = 2.63$$

Paradise Hospital could pay for all daily bills for only 2.6 days before cash runs out. This is cause for concern. The U.S. median for hospitals in 1988 was 17.628 with a range of 6.859–35.692 (10). High values imply a greater ability to pay short-term obligations. However, hospital managers need to decide how much cash on hand is the necessary safety valve.

Leverage or Capital Structure Ratios

The ratios of leverage measure the amount of debt the organization has in relation to its fund balances. The greater the debt of the hospital, the greater the risk of being unable to meet all financial obligations. These ratios are useful in determining a longer-term assessment of the hospital, as leverage ratios show the extent of the resources involved in short- and long-term debt and reflect the hospital's ability to pay interest and principal. Leverage ratios are important to debt financiers and bond-rating agencies, as they reflect the ability of the hospital to handle more debt.

$$\text{Debt to Equity Ratio} = \frac{\text{Long-Term Debt}}{\text{Fund Balance}}$$

This ratio represents the amount of debt in relation to the fund balance. The higher the amount of debt or the lower the fund balance, the higher the ratio. The hospital may not be able to carry additional debt. The hospital that has less debt than the fund balance provides an assurance to debt financiers that the hospital is a good risk.

Paradise Hospital in 1990 shows the following debt to equity ratio:

$$\frac{\$8,278}{\$27,713} = 0.29$$

This means that 29% of the fund balance is matched by debt. The U.S. median in 1988 was 0.547 with a low of 0.140 and a high of 1.194 (11).

Times Interest Earned Ratio

$$= \frac{\text{Net Income} + \text{Interest}}{\text{Interest}}$$

A hospital's current interest expense becomes important when looking at the financial condition. This ratio looks at how current interest is being met from the net income. Failure to pay the interest on time could result in a demand to pay back the entire amount borrowed. The hospital must manage its revenues and debt so that the interest can be paid on time.

Paradise Hospital reported in 1990 the following times interest earned ratio:

$$\frac{\$6,684 + \$684}{\$684} = 10.77$$

Paradise Hospital is in a good position. The U.S. median in 1988 was 2.357 with a range of 1.099–5.242. The values have been declining over the past few years (12).

Activity Ratios

The financial manager must question the efficiency of the hospital's assets in contributing to the operating revenues. The ratios that provide this information are the activity ratios. They focus on the relationship between the level of revenues to the amount of assets. Sometimes these ratios are called asset management ratios or efficiency ratios. These ratios compare inputs to outputs.

Total Asset Turnover Ratio

$$= \frac{\text{Total Operating Revenue}}{\text{Total Assets}}$$

The number of dollars or revenue produced reflected in total operating revenue is compared to the total assets. This ratio determines the extent to which all of the assets are being used to produce revenue. A high ratio indicates that the hospital's investments in assets are being used effectively. The services that are contained or used in the assets are what generate the revenue.

Paradise Hospital's total asset turnover ratio in 1990 is:

52 INTRODUCTION AND ASSESSMENT

$$\frac{\$35,621}{\$40,127} = 0.89$$

The hospital is making fairly good use of its total assets. The median for hospitals in 1988 was 0.896 with a range of 0.731–1.145 (13).

Fixed Asset Turnover Ratio

$$= \frac{\text{Total Operating Revenue}}{\text{Total Fixed Assets}}$$

Fixed asset turnover ratio focuses on the efficiency of the fixed assets in producing revenue for the hospital. Most health care facilities invest in fixed assets. This ratio is important in determining whether these investments are being used efficiently. A high ratio shows that the fixed assets are being managed effectively in generating revenues. As the buildings and plant become older, less revenue may be needed to make up the asset's cost. This is because depreciation lowers the cost of the assets. A low ratio implies that the assets are not being used efficiently or that the facility and its assets are new with less depreciation.

Paradise Hospital shows in 1990 the fixed asset turnover ratio of:

$$\frac{\$35,621}{\$32,347} = 1.101$$

The hospital industry reported in 1988 that the median was 1.770 with a range of 1.399–2.299 (14). This ratio shows both inpatient and outpatient revenues.

Inventory Turnover Ratio

$$= \frac{\text{Total Operating Revenue}}{\text{Inventory}}$$

Inventory management is important for the critical care manager and the hospital. Inventory sitting on the shelf is not producing revenue. Cash was used to purchase the inventory. It is important for the critical care nurse manager to manage inventory and its turnover, so that increased cash can be invested. A high value indicates that inventories are turning over rapidly or that there are shortages which may be reducing the revenue. A low value indicates that items are not producing revenue because of overstocking or that items are no longer in use but still on the shelf.

Paradise Hospital's inventory turnover ratio is:

$$\frac{\$35,621}{\$950} = 37.5$$

The median in the hospital industry in 1988 was 58.178 with a range of 37.870–95.076 (15).

Profitability Ratios

Profitability ratios measure how efficiently the hospital organization is running. Even though a hospital may be not-for-profit, an excess of revenues over expenses is needed for continued operation. This is extremely important for the hospital to remain financially viable.

Operating Margin Ratio

$$= \frac{\text{Net Operating Income}}{\text{Total Operating Revenue}}$$

Operating margins are important to hospitals because the hospital does not want to experience financial difficulties or claim bankruptcy. This ratio is the amount of any dollar of revenue that the hospital gets to keep. The higher the ratio, the more financially effective the hospital is in generating net income.

Paradise Hospital reported in 1990 the following operating margin:

$$\frac{\$5,739}{\$35,621} = 0.16$$

In 1988, the overall trend in hospital profitability was downward. The median was 0.015 with a range of −9.922–0.044. As hospitals face increasing allowances and discounts due to contractuals, bad debt, and charity, operating margins continue to decrease (16).

$$\text{Deductible Ratio} = \frac{\text{Deductions from Revenue}}{\text{Gross Operating Revenue}}$$

Deductions from revenues can be significant if a hospital has a high percentage of Medicare and Medicaid patients, and many agreements with third-party payors. Bad debt and charity add to these deductions. Deductions can significantly impact the hospital's profits. The deductible ratio measures the relationship of the gross operating revenues that will not be realized in cash because of the deductions from revenue. A high ratio could mean profit may be minimized. The hospital manager needs to look at the hospital's rate structure, collection methods, contract management, and its charity care write-off policies.

Paradise Hospital reported its deductible ratio as follows:

$$\frac{\$22,445}{\$54,129} = 0.41$$

The industry median for hospitals in 1988 was 0.236 with a range of 0.158–0.318 (17).

$$\text{Return on Equity Ratio} = \frac{\text{Net Income}}{\text{Fund Balance}}$$

The return on equity ratio is a measure of profit for every dollar of the fund balance. The hospital managers want the investments to generate a financial return. This ratio ties profitability to the fund balance and includes the ability of the organization to raise nonoperating revenues. Factors that go into keeping revenues high include minimizing allowances and discounts, controlling expenses, and maintaining nonoperating revenues.

Paradise Hospital's return on equity ratio is:

$$\frac{\$6,686}{\$27,713} = 0.24$$

The ratio of 0.24 shows Paradise Hospital is generating an excellent financial return. The hospital industry reported in 1988 a median of 0.067, with a low of 0.009 and a high of 0.122 (18).

Using Ratio Analysis

Using only one set of ratios makes it difficult to determine the financial position and performance of a hospital. Ratios are one method in the analysis process. Ratios become more valuable when they can be compared to standards in the health care industry. The HFMA provides this information for hospitals. Ratios vary by geographic area, size of the hospital, the time of calculation, and the hospital's unique environment.

A set of ratios showing trends over 3–5 years are more useful than looking at ratios from one point in time. Examining past trends may help set the direction for the future.

CONCLUSION

This chapter provides a look at financial statements, footnotes, auditing, and ratio analysis. Understanding these various components and the implications of the decisions that need to be made is a critical area for the hospital manager. Viable organizations result from good financial and economic decisions. The critical care nurse manager is concerned with efficiently and effectively operating the unit, communicating with the clinical staff, and contributing to the overall success of the hospital. Increased understanding of these concepts helps the critical care nurse manager meet goals and expectations.

REFERENCES

1. Mark BA, Smith HL. Essentials of finance in nursing. Rockville, MD: Aspen Publishers, Inc., 1987:151.
2. Bolandis JL. Hospital finance. Rockville, MD: Aspen Systems Corporation, 1982:135–138.
3. Horngren CT. Introduction to financial accounting. Englewood Cliffs, NJ: Prentice-Hall, Inc., 1981:7–10.
4. Horngren CT. Introduction to management accounting. 6th ed. Englewood Cliffs, NJ: Prentice-Hall, Inc., 1984:532.
5. Cleverley WO. Essentials of health care finance. 2nd ed. Rockville, MD: Aspen Publishers, Inc., 1986:118–149.
6. Cleverley WO. Hospital industry financial report 1984–1988. Westchester, IL: Healthcare Financial Management Assn., 1989:3.
7. Cleverley, pp. 5–7.
8. Cleverley, p. 48.
9. Cleverley, p. 50.
10. Cleverley, p. 54.
11. Cleverley, p. 58.
12. Cleverley, p. 66.
13. Cleverley, p. 72.
14. Cleverley, p. 74.
15. Cleverley, p. 78.
16. Cleverley, p. 26.
17. Cleverley, p. 32.
18. Cleverley, p. 44.

Part II

PLANNING AND IMPLEMENTATION

Chapter 5

Budgeting Methods

JUDITH L. WILSON

Hospitals today must be operated as businesses. Achieving the goal of delivering high-quality care at the lowest reasonable cost requires sound financial management skills. Financial planning and budgeting have become more sophisticated in the past 20 years due to increased regulation of the health care industry and efforts to contain costs. Operating as businesses demands the application of business strategies. Simply stated, this means providing services and products that generate profits.

Budgeting is basic to sound financial management. The need to develop budgets implies scarcity and budgeting is the process used to arrive at a purposeful distribution of scarce or limited resources. Historically, budgeting has been used as a method to control expenditures. Today budgeting is a financial tool for planning, managing, and controlling resources. Critical care nurse managers are often responsible for capital, operating, and personnel budgets that encompass large expenditures for human and material resources. These budgets are comprehensively and expertly covered in other sections of this book.

The purpose of this chapter is to present the various tools and techniques used in budgeting along with the formats or styles of budgets that the nurse manager may encounter. The first section provides an overview of budgeting, the second section describes historical stages of budget development, the third section discusses the basic types or formats used in budget making, and the last section addresses specific budgeting and business strategies including cutbacks, product line management, and business plans. After the introductory section, the chapter is arranged chronologically to demonstrate how budgeting techniques emerge in response to changing needs for the controlling, planning, and managing functions of budgeting.

OVERVIEW

Budgets

A budget is a financial plan. Household budgets are based on anticipated income and decisions on how income will be spent or saved. Portions of income may be allocated to housing, food, education, transportation, insurance, entertainment, savings, and so forth. Each category of expense can be thought of as an account. If spending increases in the housing account, for example, because a home is purchased, then income must increase to cover the additional amounts required; spending (or savings) in other accounts must be adjusted downward; the household must incur debt; or assets must be exchanged. It is possible for all four—or any combination—of these situations to occur. A hospital budget similarly expresses its financial plan by forecasting anticipated revenue and then systematically allocating the dollars it expects to spend on labor, supplies, capital equipment, and other items or projects. A hospital budget contains information on how funds or revenues are to be obtained, how much they are projected to be, how much will be spent to support the generation of revenue, and what the difference is expected to be (profit or loss).

Hospital budgets are usually organized around departments or service units. The unit manager, or some other individual, is assigned responsibility for planning and controlling the unit budget. The measures of performance established in every budget are standards to be achieved. This requires the managing functions of coordinating, monitoring, and evaluating actual performance against established standards. Restating the definition, a budget is a planning, managing, and controlling tool used to accomplish the goals and objectives of the organization in a cost efficient and effective manner.

A budget document expresses the hospital's plan in dollar amounts for a specified period of time. The critical care budget should reflect the goals and objectives of the hospital and the intensive care unit.

Budgets usually encompass a period of 1 year and coincide with the hospital fiscal year. This allows the hospital to establish consistency in formulating annual operating budgets and establishing routine time frames for monitoring and reporting budget performance. Reports may be done for any accounting period, but generally cover one month or one quarter with cumulative data reported at year end. Budgets can be generated for longer than one year. Five-year facility plans include budgets for projects planned beyond the current fiscal year, major construction or expansion programs, and capital equipment needs. Short-term budgets of 1–6 months are also submitted during the fiscal year for unexpected events. Examples would be temporarily contracting for laundry service during delays in the installation of new equipment, or a special program for management development using outside consultants and trainers. Strategic planning may also include projected budgets based on changes in demand for health care services or changes in hospital mission. It has been suggested that budgets should cover longer than one year to reflect strategic planning.

Some institutions have adopted the concept of a "rolling" or continuous budget to address the problem of ending a budget year without a new budget in place. In effect, these budgets roll over every quarter by retiring the completed quarter and adding a new quarter projection. This allows management to always have a budget for 1 full year. Continuous budgets are especially useful for projecting cash budgets when planning depends on the availability of cash at a future date (1).

Budgeting

Budgeting has long been debated by experts including V. O. Key, who argued that there should be a rational method of allocating "X dollars to activity A rather than to activity B," and Wildavsky, who argues that the notion is utopian and a practical impossibility (2, 3). For our purposes, budgeting is a knowledge based process that is systematic and ongoing and that incorporates information on past and present financial performance into decisions about the future.

Budgeting takes place within the political environment of the hospital and nurse managers must appreciate that having power and influence at top levels of the organization is essential to maintaining control over nursing service. Attention to structure, economy, process, and outcome are important in the political arena. Structure refers to who has the power to make budgetary decisions and whether the organization (and nursing service) is centralized or decentralized. Economy considers the resources of the organization and how these are distributed. While nursing cannot have everything it asks for, neither should it settle for less than its fair share. Process has to do with how change is made in the hospital. Who is involved and what support is necessary? Process is closely linked to strategy and wise managers find out which strategies work and which are unsuccessful. Outcome is the consequence of budgetary decisions and may include giving up a desired program for an essential one (4). Structure, economy, process, and outcome are interrelated and the relationships are complex within the political environment. There are many players, many motives, and many intricacies to consider when positioning for influence within the organization. Sensitivity to people, timing, and financial pressures present major challenges for nurse managers as they negotiate for limited resources to ensure quality clinical programs.

Centralized vs. Decentralized Budgets

Budgets can be either centralized or decentralized. A centralized budget means that planning and control are done at top levels of the organization and input into decisions is beyond the influence of first-line managers. Decentralization places responsibility and accountability at the lowest level of the organizational hierarchy that has the knowledge and the skill to make responsible decisions. Decentralization is a term often used to describe structure, function, responsibility, and authority. Unfortunately it is often misused and confusing. The problem evolves from the tendency to change structure and function without a change in management philosophy. Decentralization, when viewed as a philosophy, is much easier to understand. The question to be answered is, who has the authority for decision making? If authority is at the responsibility level, you have decentralization. If it is not, you have a change in structure with centralized authority.

The current trend in management is to decentralize. Thus, the critical care nurse manager is increasingly responsible for the unit level budget. The accompanying expectation is that increased responsibility will lead to increased accountability for improved financial management. If head nurses and staff nurses are to be truly involved and responsible for establishing and adhering to a budget plan, they must have the authority to enact the controls that are necessary to achieve the budget objectives. When not given the authority to control, the budget responsibility is delegated rather than decentralized.

There are many ways that decentralization can be applied. The inclusion of staff nurses in the budgeting process has great potential for ensuring commitment to the budget and participation in programs aimed at controlling costs. In practice, responsibility and authority are often shared and require skill in negotiating changes that impact the bottom line.

Why centralize? Control at the top is necessary during periods of major reorganization or mission changes. Corporate mergers are one example. Also, the philosophy of management influences this decision. Why decentralize? The operational levels of an organization often have the best information to make decisions. When flexibility and timeliness are important, decentralized structures work best. A centralized structure may be too cumbersome to respond rapidly to changes at the operational level. Competence of first-line managers is critical in a decentralized system.

Flexible Budgets

One technique for negotiating changes to the budget is through the flexible budget. Flexible budgeting allows adjustments to be made based on changes in revenues, expenses, or volume. Static or fixed budgets are developed for one level of expected activity. With the rapid changes in health care and third-party reimbursement, the static budget is too rigid. Flexible budgets correct for this fault. An understanding of fixed, variable, and semi-variable costs is necessary in making adjustments or explaining variances reported in the budget:

- Fixed costs—do not change with volume;
- Variable costs—vary with volume;
- Semi-variable costs—vary with volume, but not directly (5).

For example, suppose that the number of patients requiring an intra-aortic balloon pump (IABP) increases from 5–10 cases per month.

Number of cases with IABP	5	10
Fixed costs (HN salary)	$5000	$5000
Variable costs (IABP and catheter)	$1500	$3000
Semi-variable costs (maintenance)	$ 100	$ 120
Total	$6600	$8120

The fixed costs for administrative salaries are unchanged with the increase in volume. Variable costs for equipment and supplies increase as volume increases. Semi-variable costs increase, but not in direct proportion to volume. In the above example, the variance is an excess of $1520 over what the static budget projected. Without a mechanism to adjust for variances in volume, expense, and revenue changes, the nursing budget may be grossly overextended by year end. The flexible budget provides the means to ensure realistic financial outcomes based on actual rather than projected performance.

Flexible budgeting is more sophisticated than fixed budgeting. It allows the nurse manager more autonomy in responding to budget variances and also provides a better understanding of the impact of changes in volume, acuity, expense, and revenue. Variance analysis can produce better quantification of the causes of the variance if flexible budgets are used (6).

STAGES OF BUDGET DEVELOPMENT

There are three major stages of budgetary development. Each stage can be identified with one of the three primary functions of budgeting; control, management, and planning. Characteristics of budgets in each developmental stage are influenced by a dominating function that can be viewed as an orientation toward budgeting. Table 5.1 summarizes characteristics of the three budget stages.

Table 5.1. Comparison of Budgeting Stages

Stage	Control	Management	Planning
Information base	Expenditures Economy measures	Costs of services Productivity measurements	Future mission Broad goals Program analysis
Communication of budget priorities	Bottom to top	Bottom to top	Top to bottom
Implementation focus	Operational level First-line managers	Planning level Middle managers	Strategic planning Top management
Budget control	Centralized	Decentralized	Decentralized
Budgeting responsibility	Shared all levels	Shared all levels	Centralized

Control Stage

The control orientation is based on controlling objects of expenditure. Classification of expenditures required to operate programs are listed and then examined for funding justification. While originally intended as a planning tool focusing on functional work units, in practice, control over items of expenditure predominated (7). The priority on controlling expenditures places less emphasis on management and planning aspects of budgeting. Control budgets are characterized by centralized decisions on actual spending. However, planning occurs throughout the organization, and line managers participate in communicating operational needs upward through management channels. Budget makers of the 1920s and early 1930s ignored "visionary" proposals for management-focused budgets and concentrated on developing forms that neatly contained item by line expenditures. Gradually this preoccupation with accounting procedures and control gave way to the need for coordinating functions, and sometime in the 1930s administrators replaced accountants as budgeting officials. With this change came performance budgets.

Management Stage

Performance budgeting is management oriented. Its goal is to measure work efficiency by relating outputs, or what is to be accomplished, to workloads, expenses, and revenue. Performance budgeting is a product of both cost accounting and scientific management. In the early literature, performance budgeting is considered a management tool and the budget document is referred to as a work program (8). Performance budgeting focuses on work activities or programs to be managed and upward communication of budgetary needs. The control of expenditures is decentralized to the work unit, and planning is dispersed throughout the levels of the organization. Performance budgeting gained recognition and support until the 1950s when it was challenged on the grounds that the work to be accomplished was seen as an end and not the means to achieving program outcomes. The entry of program budgeting followed.

Planning Stage

Program budgeting considers what is to be achieved and measures the effectiveness of outcomes. Its end product orientation is determined by the mission and goals of the organization. Planning is the essential ingredient of program budgets. The planning function, which occurs at higher levels of management and is strategic in nature, tends to overshadow the management and control aspects of budgeting without precluding them. Approved plans are communicated downward to managers who assume responsibility for controlling budgetary allocations. The value of planning budgets lies in the ability to make decisions about resource allocations based on what end product is desired. The goal is to support policy and mission by providing data on: (a) the costs and benefits of programs, (b) alternative programs, and (c) outcome measurements (7).

Planning budgets have been influenced by increased use of economic analysis, informational and decisional technology (cost-benefit and cost-effectiveness analyses), and the convergence of planning and budgetary processes. As analysis entered the budget model, budget makers with backgrounds in economics and system analysis also entered the budget scene.

BUDGET FORMATS

Different budget orientations have produced specific formats or techniques for budgeting. Table 5.2 compares the three basic budget types: line-item budgets (LIB); performance budgets, including management by objectives (MBO) and zero-base budgets (ZBB); and planning program budgets (PPB). It also includes product-line budgets (PLB) discussed later in this chapter.

Line-Item Budgets

Line-item budgeting is, simply, the technique of listing each expense item on a separate line. The budget document may be detailed, listing every expense item, or it may group expenditures into categories such as salaries, equipment, travel, and other service charges. Capital expense items may be in the line-item budget or may be a separate budget request. Individual items or categories are approved or disapproved by the official or body with approval authority and, if approved, the money allocated must be spent for the item (category) specified. Line-item budgets are referred to as traditional because they have been used since budgets originated. In the public domain, the first executive budgets were produced in 1921 (9). At that time, public budgets were used for control to keep expenditures down and to prevent waste and corruption from misuse of public funds.

Line-item budgets have been influenced more by accounting principles than economic or budgetary theories. They address resources needed to maintain programs and activities rather than broader questions of mission, policy, or alternative uses of resources. Despite budget reform and the entry of performance and planning budgeting techniques, line-item budgets continue to be used in both public and private sectors.

The original form of "one line for one item" has been modified to include activity areas and lump-sum categories that allow more flexibility in the use of funds. However, control is still central to line-item budgeting. The focus is on inputs and what is to be purchased with the resources. The expectation is that economy will be realized by tight controls on spending. The technique is characterized by assembly from the bottom up, with the lowest organizational unit submitting expense estimates to the next higher supervisory level for review, and that person submitting the budget up to the next administrative level, and so on. Line-item budgets are closely aligned to the incremental theory of budgeting. Incremental budgets start with last year's base and add (or subtract) an amount calculated by some predetermined criteria or projected change in services to arrive at a new budget request. Requested increases are generally justified at each

Table 5.2. Budgeting Types and Purposes

Type	Focus	Purpose	Question	Measurement
Line-Item Budgets (LIB)	Expenses Resources needed	Control over expenses	What is to be bought?	Economy
Performance Budgets (ZBB) (MBO)	Output	Management of expenses and revenues related to work loads	What is to be accomplished?	Efficiency
Planning Program Budgets (PPB)	Outcome	Planning and programming	What is to be achieved?	Effectiveness
Product-Line Budgets (PLM)	Profit Product markets	Revenue generation	What is to be sold?	Profitability

step of the budgeting process by supporting data in the form of footnotes or attached memoranda.

The advantages and disadvantages of line-item budgeting are:

- Advantages
  —Simplicity in calculations and presentation;
  —Simplifies decision making (facts and figures are easier to agree or disagree on than policy or program issues);
  —Reduces conflict, because issues are monetary;
  —Promotes collaboration and compromise in decisions by committee;
  —Accepted as traditional;
  —Consistent with political system (fragmentation, specialization, special interests);
  —Does not force partisan political stands.
- Disadvantages
  —Alternative programs or levels of service are not considered (cost/benefit is ignored);
  —Strategic planning is undervalued as operational control is emphasized;
  —System and economic analysis has little impact;
  —Present oriented;
  —Not comprehensive (may be in conflict with organizational priorities);
  —Inhibits change and innovation;
  —Means oriented rather than ends oriented.

Advantages and disadvantages are, or course, a matter of opinion and considerable dispute exists on the merits of line-item budgeting as compared to other budgeting options. Examples of line-item budget formats are found throughout this text; see Chapter 10 on operating budgets.

Planning, Programming, and Budgeting System (PPBS or PPB)

Planning, programming, and budgeting treats the processes of planning, management, and control as compatible and complementary, but not coequal, elements of a budget system. In theory, planning is centralized and primary in PPB, and operational management and control responsibilities are delegated to line managers (7). PPB was developed by the Rand Corporation and adopted by the Department of Defense in 1961. The goal was to improve the quality of budgetary decision making. In 1965, President Johnson instituted PPB in all federal departments with the expectation that budgets reflecting program goals would lead to decisions made on quantitative comparisons of costs and benefits rather than on neutral line-item budget requests. Experience in the private sector is based on the same goal, but has been less publicized.

PPB has four main characteristics: (a) specification of objectives, (b) specification of alternative methods for achieving objectives, (c) extensive use of analysis in determining costs and benefits, and (d) use of analysis throughout the process and into the future (9). Implementation of PPB requires each department to submit a program memorandum stating goals and objectives, and a program and financial plan outlining the future consequences of current year decisions. Special studies providing the analytical basis for budgetary and goal decisions are attached. The whole process sounds like a reasonable, achievable improvement to line-item budgeting. Unfortunately, the experience of the government proved anything but the case, except possibly in the Department of Defense. What went wrong?

New budgeting techniques may be easier to conceptualize than to operationalize. Implementation is a key factor and often lacks the thorough planning that change requires. Education and training, practice, realistic time frames and expectations are all necessary. If lacking, the system will flounder and managers will revert to tried and true budgeting processes. The primary problem with PPB is that it lacks procedures for, and relevance to, daily operational realities. Defining boundaries and responsibilities for programs that overlap into other services is also a major PPB problem.

PPB is useful at the strategic planning level and may be used in hospitals to establish mission, broad program goals, and initiatives for the future. As goals are translated into operational objectives and then converted to budgeted dollars, the system is probably used more than many realize. It has simply been adapted to a more usable form. Whether any long-range planning is practical, in view of the rapid internal and external changes in health industries, remains a question for the 1990s.

The advantages and disadvantages of PPB are:

- Advantages
  —Promotes understanding of problems, program concepts, and alternatives;
  —Increases informational data on program inputs and outputs;

— Uses analysis to facilitate decision making;
— Program accomplishments can be measured;
— Relates policy decisions to overall budget planning;
— Allows comparison of related programs;
— Futuristic.
- Disadvantages
— Focuses on what will be done, ignores how to do it;
— Budgets are stated as long-range plans rather than intermediate or short-term objectives;
— Fails to provide an operational tool to guide implementation by first-line managers;
— Lacks a mechanism to evaluate efficiency;
— Focuses on new or expanding programs rather than evaluation of ongoing activities;
— Requires well-trained administrators and qualified analysts;
— Expensive in terms of time, energy, and expertise required;
— Poor history of success.

Management by Objectives

Management by objectives (MBO), while not exclusively focused on financial management or budgeting, is used for the planning, controlling, and evaluating functions of management. A system of management by objectives and self-control was used by Dupont after World War I (WWI) and General Motors used the term "Management by Objectives and Self-Control" during the 1920s. In the public sector, the concepts of MBO were recommended by Gulick and associates after studying federal government organization in the 1930s (10). In the 1950s, Peter Drucker developed the system known today as management by objectives. The system enjoyed wide popularity in the private sector as a method to improve worker motivation and productivity (11). MBO remains a management technique that is alive and well in many industries today. The Office of Management and Budget implemented management by objectives under the Nixon Administration in the early 1970s. However, like many of the budget reforms in the public sector, MBO was short lived and judged unsuccessful by most critics (12).

Management by objectives is described by Drucker as a philosophy of management as well as a method of managing (13). Philosophically, it is closely aligned to decentralization and participative management with a focus on self control and effectiveness of results. Management by objectives assumes that employees will be responsible contributing members of the organization when given the opportunity to participate. As a managerial method, MBO is a system that promotes the integration of goals and objectives throughout the various organizational levels while providing the opportunity for individuals to establish objectives at each level. The process is carried out by planning objectives, implementing activities toward objective achievement, and evaluating results.

The interactive or planning phase involves the superior and subordinate in negotiating objectives that are clear, measurable, time specific, and relevant to the overall goals of the organization. Objectives are prioritized according to importance, and the best alternative for achieving the objective is determined. Interactive planning involves managers and staff in establishing the actual objectives they will be held accountable for achieving.

The second phase of MBO, implementation, consists of doing the work necessary to accomplish the objectives. Managers should be delegated sufficient authority and given adequate time and resources to achieve objectives. Support from top management gives credibility to MBO and communicates that it is important to the organization. There should be standardized procedure manuals and forms for periodic reporting. Training needs should be addressed to ensure that the process is understood and can be completed effectively. Time is often a problem when implementing new MBO systems. Results may be expected too soon or in greater amounts than can be realized. This is particularly true in large, complex organizations such as hospitals when new programs are initiated. Critical care managers need to appreciate that evidence of success will require time and patience.

The final phase of MBO is evaluation. This phase entails more than reviewing and measuring results at the time specified in phase one. Monitoring of objectives is ongoing and an important component of MBO. The manager reviews objectives monthly and reports formally on progress every quarter or semi-annually. Negotiation is an integral part of MBO when objectives are established and at each review. Assessment of progress may mean restating the performance measure or adjusting the time frame for completion.

Structurally MBO can use either a top-down or a bottom-up approach but, as originally intended, it is more effective if decentralized. Overall mission and broad goals established by top administration are communicated to middle and first-line managers who then plan the activities, programs, and resources necessary to goal accomplishment. The bottom-up approach requires extensive communication at each management level and is time consuming. However, the advantages of active participation, effective communication, and acceptance of responsibility for decisions offset the efficiency sacrificed by this approach. Additionally, goals and objectives established at levels of the organization closest to the product are likely to be more realistic and achievable. A decentralized structure encourages motivation, creative thinking, and commitment to objectives.

There are four areas that objectives routinely address: services, management, relationships with others, and personal and professional growth. Service objectives include such things as level of services, new services, cost of services, different methods of delivery, and elimination of programs or services. Management objectives have to do with planning, programming, measurement and evaluation criteria, productivity, staffing, cooperative programs with other services, and organizational change. Objectives for relationships with others might consider the need to maintain, establish, strengthen, change, or terminate affiliations and roles. Specific relationships to examine are superiors, subordinates, other departments, work teams, outside agencies and organizations, and customers. Personal and professional objectives are related to growth and development that directly or indirectly affect job performance and potential for the future.

Writing objectives can be a considerable challenge to the uninitiated manager. There are many resources available to help with this task. It is important that objectives be stated as specifically as possible. Vague objectives make it too convenient to ignore them; thus, little progress will take place and results will be disappointing. For example, an objective to reduce critical care cost per patient day is too vague. A better objective would be stated: reduce average critical care costs per patient day by 10% in the next 12 months. To avoid vagueness, consider the following format:

- To (action verb) (single key result) by (target date) at (cost).
- To (reduce) (average critical care costs per patient day by 10%) by (May, 1992) at (present quality level).

Another format is:

- (Do what) to (whom or what) to/for (what purpose) using (what resources) by (when).
- (Reduce) (overtime) to (within budget) using (self scheduling) by (September, 1991).

Objectives should be understandable, measurable, achievable, and feasible. Understandable means the objective can be translated by superiors and subordinates and there is mutual agreement at both levels on how it will support the overall division or hospital goals. It should, of course, also be understood by the writer. Interpreting organizational objectives into terms that can be understood by staff is also a responsibility of nurse managers.

Measurable refers to the concrete, definable, and quantifiable results expected. Without clear standards by which to measure outcomes, it will be difficult to determine if the goal was met. This is often a difficult task, particularly in health care. Keep in mind the measurements of quantity, quality, time, and cost when writing objectives. Other criteria are:

- Purpose (outcome)—What is to be accomplished?
- Target date (time)—When will it be accomplished?
- Measure (standard)—What quantity, quality, cost?
- Actor (individual)—Who is accountable?
- Action—How will it be done?
- Judge—Who will decide?

Achievable is the same as saying an objective can be accomplished. Is it reasonable within the present organization and within the time available? Is the objective consistent with organizational goals? Is the standard for measurement set too high? These questions must be asked to determine achievability.

Feasible refers to what may be done. To determine feasibility requires looking at the impact of the objective on the operation of other departments and services in the hospital, and at regulatory constraints. Feasibility also requires that adequate resources, skills, and time are available to complete the objective.

Management by objectives can enhance the management functions of planning, controlling, monitoring, and evaluating. It increases participation and thus commitment at all levels of the organization. MBO is results oriented and can lead to service improvement and change within the organization. Because it involves everyone in planning, resistance to change is decreased. MBO offers the opportunity to control the work environment and to determine work methods. Finally, MBO is collaborative in nature and leads to team building and improved communication.

Disadvantages of MBO include lack of administrative support and involvement, excessive paperwork, failure to follow through with implementation plans, lack of training, expectations that are too high or too low, and unrealistic expectations for immediate results (11).

Zero-Base Budgeting

Zero-base budgeting (ZBB) has a longer history than is generally recognized. In 1924, E. Hilton Young, a budget authority from England, suggested the concept (14) which was advocated by Verne B. Lewis in 1952 (15). In 1962, the U.S. Department of Agriculture used a "ground up" budgeting approach similar to ZBB, but the method was declared unsuccessful. ZBB was popularized by Peter Phyrr, who initiated it at Texas Instruments for the 1970 budget year (14). The technique came to the attention of the newly elected governor of Georgia, Jimmy Carter, who implemented ZBB in the state of Georgia and subsequently in the federal government after he was elected President. During the 1970s, ZBB was implemented in several other states and in hundreds of private businesses. ZBB is plagued by a dismal history and early demise in the public sector, but has enjoyed more success in the private sector. ZBB continues to have intellectual appeal, as it promises to achieve greater efficiency through review, analysis, and improved decision making.

ZBB is a method of budgeting that starts at ground zero without considering what has occurred in the past. It requires a fundamental evaluation and complete justification of all programs and activities annually. Because of this requirement, ZBB has been criticized as "naive and impractical, if not downright mischievous" (16). Justifying why any money at all should be spent does seem a tedious and unnecessary chore to impose on nurse managers every year, but adaptations are possible. In practical applications of ZBB, many adaptations have been made and the annual review of all programs is often not enforced. The purpose of ZBB is to insert rationality into the budget process by requiring unit level managers to examine purposes, methods, and resources related to programs. This places responsibility for program continuation on the service manager. Mission statements, broad goals, and general direction are issued by the governing body, but actual construction of the budget is done at the operational level. ZBB is similar to MBO in respect to placing responsibility and authority for budget implementation and control at the first-line supervisory level.

ZBB is characterized by emphasis on the total budget request. Existing programs are thoroughly evaluated along with new programs and changes in current program levels. ZBB expands the question, On what basis shall X dollars be allocated to activity A rather than to activity B?, by substituting the question: At what point is an increase in program A more important than an increase in program B, or programs C, D, and E? Unlike line-item budgeting, which builds on the past year's base and assumes continuation of existing programs, ZBB questions the need for all programs. Programs may be expanded, reduced, eliminated, or "traded off" to make room for expansion in other areas (17). ZBB is most useful to program managers because the basic elements of the process are developed at the service or unit level.

The basic elements of ZBB are: (a) identification of decision units, (b) development of "decision packages," and (c) ranking of decision packages. The decision unit is a grouping of discrete activities, functions, or operations. The unit can be a traditional budget unit such as a critical care unit or it can be a special program or project such as a cardiac rehabilitation program. McGrail states that decision units can be "structured around service areas, products, markets, customer groups, regional areas, capital projects, or anything else that can logically be tied to the organization's mission or long-range objectives" (18). Units must be large enough to permit meaningful review, but small enough to allow decisions to be made. For example:

- Nursing Service ⟩ Too Large
- Critical Care Unit ⟩ Just Right
- Salary ⟩ Too Small

Identification of the decision unit is the most crucial part of the process, since everything is built on the decision unit.

A decision package is developed for each decision unit. The purpose of the decision package is to inform the decision maker about what the chosen program or activity will accomplish, what it will cost, and what alternatives have been considered. The decision package includes:

- Purpose (goals and objectives);
- Consequences of not performing the activity;
- Measures of performance;
- Alternative courses of action considered;
- Costs and benefits.

According to Phyrr, the identification and evaluation of alternatives to each decision package is key to successful zero-base budgeting. He suggests considering two types of alternatives: (a) different ways of accomplishing the work or the same function, and (b) different levels of input to accomplish the function (19).

Funding is usually identified at three levels: (a) a minimum level below which it is unrealistic to operate a program or activity, (b) the current level of operation, and (c) an increase in operations. The manager writes a brief explanation of what services can be provided by whom at the various levels of funding. The objectives, responsibilities, and methods to accomplish the objectives are spelled out in the decision packages.

The ranking process can be a considerable management challenge. Unit managers rank their decision packages, identifying priorities from among the packages and levels of funding. Rankings should reflect decisions that produce the greatest benefit to the organization. The packages are then sent up the chain of command, the next higher level of management repeats the process, and so on until the budget is finalized. Critics of ZBB point out that expecting top executives to rank and choose from among thousands of decision packages is an impossible task. Several adaptations in the ranking process have been made. For example, committees at each management level choose top priorities and eliminate some packages. Cuts at certain funding points (such as 50%) can be stipulated at each level. This makes the job of top management more manageable (20).

ZBB has been broadly criticized for its failure to produce expected budget cuts in the public sector. It has been branded as oversold and impossible to do (21). Public budgets are different from private industry budgets. First, they primarily try to control expenditures (inputs) rather than outputs. The scope and purpose of public budgets are also different. It should be remembered that most efforts toward budgetary reform in the public sector reflect current administration initiatives that may be too short lived to demonstrate the results expected. Performance in the private sector has generally been rated as positive in corporations using ZBB. ZBB has been criticized for being unwieldly. The paperwork is voluminous in some systems. For example in 1977 the state of Georgia had 17 different forms for their ZBB budgeting process. Requiring justification for every program and activity every year is also unreasonable. A 16-bed critical care unit with a 95% occupancy is likely to be continued without extensive justification every year. Still ZBB is useful for analyzing present operations and stimulates thinking about better ways to operate programs. Table 5.3 is an outline of typical instructions for a ZBB budget proposal. An example of how ZBB can be used is provided in the section on cutback management.

The advantages and disadvantages of ZBB are:

- Advantages
  —Relates cost/benefit analysis to specific programs;
  —Improves information flow and decision making;
  —Encourages participation in the budgeting process at all management levels;
  —Opportunity costs are more clearly identified;
  —Enhances the planning function of budgeting;
  —Links allocation decisions to expected results;
  —Promotes comprehensive analysis of alternatives (innovation and change is possible);
  —Flexibility and responsiveness to changes in activity levels are enhanced (costs and revenues);
  —Potential for eliminating nonproductive programs.
- Disadvantages
  —Managers have difficulty divorcing their judgment from the past;
  —Data required is hard to compile;
  —Overlapping activities are hard to separate into discrete decision units;
  —Paperwork is excessive and time consuming (increases budgeting costs);

Table 5.3. ZBB Form Completion Instructions

1. Department:	Name of organizational department
2. Division:	Name of department or division
3. Unit:	Specific service unit, cost or revenue center, or product-line section
4. Fiscal year (FY):	Year proposal will be implemented
5. Decision package:	The descriptive title of the subject of the package and its number in relationship to alternatives, e.g., 1 of 3, 2 of 3, 3 of 3
6. Ranking:	The initial ranking by the unit or service manager beginning with the number 1 as the highest priority
7. Purpose:	Describe the activity or service in relationship to the problem it is intended to resolve or the objective it is supposed to achieve.
8. Actions:	Describe the actions and methods to accomplish the purpose (what will be done and how).
9. Benefits:	Describe tangible (quantitative) benefits first, then intangible (nonmonetary) benefits. Include only general amounts or broad statements. Specifics are addressed later. Relate benefits to purpose (step 7).
10. Consequences:	Identify the impact of not approving the package on other services, functions or activities not mentioned in step 9.
11. Quantifiable data:	Describe the measures used to support the objectives and purpose of the activity or program. Include work load measures, cost-benefit, problem trends, and cost or revenue data.
12. Required resources:	Enter current year (CY) amounts budgeted. Enter amounts requested for next year (NY). Enter % of current year to next year = NY/CY.
13. Alternatives and cost:	Alternative levels of activity or service are explained in this section. Decision packages are developed for each alternative, i.e., 1 of 3, 2 of 3, 3 of 3, with each package compared to the others. If different levels of activity have been excluded, an explanation of why a lower level was not possible is necessary.
14. Alternatives:	Different ways of performing an activity or providing a service are considered here. Describe why the previous system was not chosen and why the present system is preferred. Include cost analysis.
15. Costs:	Enter net costs in this section. Compare with step 11. Costs should be approximately equal.
16. Attachments:	Special analysis or justification reports can be attached to each package if necessary for clarification of the decision package. In general these attachments should be brief and to the point.

—Accounting and control systems must be adjusted;
—Ranking is difficult, since many decision packages overlap;
—Undermines production budgeting, as it is controlled by the input/output relationship;
—Managers resent "new" methods if "old" methods are perceived as adequate.

ZBB is a budgeting technique with characteristics of performance budgets, i.e., it relates inputs and outputs to workloads and accomplishments. The criterion measurement is efficiency. In theory, each program or activity of an organization is systematically detailed, evaluated, and prioritized. Decisions to continue, discontinue, or modify programs are then made. And this is done every year! The minimal result should be a very efficient corporation. Employees should benefit from more autonomy, participation, and commitment to objectives. Ultimately, the patient should receive quality care delivered in the most cost-efficient way. Implementation of new budgeting techniques requires the education and support noted in the discussion of management by objectives. Without adequate preparation, the difference in what is and what ought to be may result in something less than desirable. ZBB has appeal in its potential for identifying cost-efficient work methods and structures. It therefore may be a useful tool for nurse managers in reviewing delivery systems and designing new systems for the future.

BUSINESS STRATEGIES

Cutback Management and Downsizing

The phenomenal growth in critical care technology and services over the past three decades has been matched by the increased demand for critical care nurses. These trends are expected to continue throughout the 1990s. In 1988, despite 194,000 employed critical care nurses, a 13.8% vacancy rate existed nationally. The study reporting these numbers also predicted that the need for critical care nurses would double in the next few years (22). Predictions that the number of critical care beds will increase by 30% in the 1990s support the conclusion that discrepancies in the supply of, and demand for, critical care nurses will worsen. So why are we talking about cutback management and downsizing services? There are three reasons. First, cutback management is a strategy foreign to many nurse managers; second, it is a difficult one to implement; third, cutbacks will be necessary in some hospitals.

In the pre-1983 era of retrospective cost reimbursement, critical care units were considered money-makers. In the current era of prospective reimbursement, the reverse may be the case. For example, under diagnosis related groups (DRGs) the payment for coronary artery bypass graft has been steadily adjusted downward. Another problem is that many ICU patients are "outliers," i.e., their length of stay exceeds the DRG breakeven point. Thus, many critical care units may be identified as money losers. Hospitals must produce revenues in excess of expenses to maintain financial viability. From a business perspective, cutting programs that cost more than they are reimbursed for is prudent financial management.

There are, however, many aspects to making the decision to cut services. Internal and external forces alter not only what services are delivered in specific hospitals, but where specialized programs such as cardiac surgery and organ transplantation are provided. Issues (and decisions) will be driven by complex and interdependent political, social, economic, technical, and clinical considerations. For example, data on "the more you do the better you are" are basically a clinical and technological consideration, but the push to regionalize transplant centers will be driven by economic, social, and political forces as well. The decision to close an underutilized critical care unit in a community or rural hospital may be economically sound, but may prove impractical in view of social and clinical pressures to keep the unit open.

Another issue is the projected number of hospital closures and/or conversions to other than acute care facilities. It is estimated that about 15% of the nation's hospitals will close by 1995; and with a 50% occupancy rate nationwide, half of the acute care beds will either close or be dedicated to other services (23, 24).

A final issue is that corporate mergers and acquisitions are increasingly common strategies used by hospitals in response to financial pressures. Mergers have affected over 20% of hospitals in the northeast and nearly 30% of hospitals in the southwest and many in other sections of the country have merged or are considering the possibility (25). Mergers involve the combination of two or more hospitals while acquisitions refer to one hospital buying another. Both are financially motivated with incentives being more economical operations and improvements in net profits. Results of mergers frequently include restructuring and downsizing.

Restructuring is done to increase productivity and achieve economies of scale. Examples include terminating unprofitable services, adding new services, and combining departments such as purchasing to take advantage of quantity price discounts. Downsizing is done by cutbacks and may include elimination of management positions and positions associated with terminated services. It is estimated that the hospital industry will downsize by 18% with a loss of almost 500,000 full-time equivalents (FTEs) during the 1990s (26). Combined, these issues may change not only what we do as critical care nurses, but where we practice.

One thing is certain, change is inevitable, ongoing, and dynamic. Predictions aside (who would have predicted the recent social and political upheaval in Europe?), the topic of cutback management in critical care may become a reality at least in some situations and in some hospitals.

Foremost in the decision to include cutback management in this chapter is the problem itself. What manager wants to tell a staff nurse that he or she is no longer needed? How do we reconcile goals and commitments made to provide the best critical care services with the reality that critical care is excluded in long-range hospital planning? These tough questions are addressed in the discussion of cutback management or downsizing.

Cutback management is a strategy for systematically downsizing operations in response to organizational change. Managing change is difficult in the best of circumstances. In this case it is complicated by an environment of increased competition for scarce resources and excess bed capacity. Most management theory assumes growth or at least maintenance of the organization. Therefore, cutting services is a strange challenge for managers and one that creates considerable stress throughout the organization. Economic conditions force managers to develop different approaches to budgeting resources in the face of decreased services. Knowing the typical problems associated with organizational decline is a first step in planning. Problems encountered in declining organizations include:

1. Refusal of managers to confront the realities and necessities;
2. Inability to cut back one element without affecting the entire organization;
3. Increased need for control at all levels of the organization;
4. Increased need for analytical tools to minimize the risks of decision mistakes;
5. Difficulty in rewarding managers involved in contracting services and terminating employees;
6. Ensuring adequate communication throughout the organization and to the public;
7. Anticipating consequences of decisions;
8. Overcoming resistance to change.

Levine identifies three decisions that managers must make when approaching the cutback process: (a) whether to adopt a strategy to resist decline or adjust to it, (b) what tactics to adopt given a decision on the strategy, and (c) deciding how and where cuts will be made if deemed necessary. Strategies to resist decline include:

- Diversify into other businesses or services;
- Threaten to cut vital or popular programs;
- Cut a visible service to rally client support;
- Identify a richer revenue base;
- Seek philanthropic support;
- Investigate new investment sources;
- Improve productivity;
- Use less-costly delivery systems.

Strategies to adjust to decline include:

- Cut low prestige programs;
- Share services with other organizations;
- Cut unprofitable programs;
- Reorganize;
- Refinance or negotiate terms of debt;
- Change leadership;
- Install rational choice techniques like zero-base budgeting;
- Mortgage the future by deferring maintenance and capital equipment purchases or projects;
- Ask employees to take early retirement, pay cuts, leave without pay (LWOP);
- Defer raises, freeze hiring;
- Improve forecasting capability to avoid future problems;
- Sell surplus property or equipment;
- Exploit everything possible (27).

Levine suggests three general approaches when cutbacks are inevitable. When cuts entail 3% or less, stretching can be used. This approach uses attrition to reduce supervisory and support staff while maintaining direct care givers to sustain present levels of service. Using labor saving technology, deferring maintenance, and postponing capital investment are also used in stretching. Rationing is used for cuts of 3–5%. Some services are cut, hours are decreased, new fees are initiated where possible, positions vacated are abolished, and overtime is eliminated. Cuts of 5–10% require layoffs, facility closings, program reductions, and terminations. Budget reductions of greater than 10%, according to Levine, are not cutback management but rather new program or service initiatives that require major restructuring around new missions and goals (27).

In deciding whether layoffs are a necessary response to organizational decline, Perry suggests six questions for managers to ask. Three of the questions will be discussed here. First, are personnel cuts necessary? This depends on the expected duration and the severity of the situation. Unless the financial situation is severe and permanent, other options such as lowering prices to increase market share or restructuring debt are suggested. The second question to ask is, are there alternatives to layoffs? Managers who react to financial losses without considering anything but terminations fail to appreciate the many options available. In addition to suggestions already noted, Perry lists job sharing (splitting full-time positions), work sharing (reduction in hours and pay), decreasing paid time off, demotion, and early retirement or resignation with provisions to rehire former employees as part-time consultants. The third question seeks an answer to the dilemma, is there a best alternative? Perry recommends strategies that decrease quantity, i.e., numbers of hours worked, as less hazardous and more acceptable to employees than decreasing what they are paid for their work through wage concessions (28).

Before implementing cutbacks, several issues need to be addressed by management. Table 5.4 lists these issues and factors associated with them. Using the outline to guide the planning, implementation, and evaluation phases of downsizing will prevent many of the problems that are sure to arise without thoughtful planning.

Experience with Downsizing

Faced with an extensive downsizing operation, Rozboril's challenge was to reconcile three seemingly conflicting objectives: (*a*) maintaining the quality of patient care, (*b*) ensuring fair and equitable treatment of employees, and (*c*) operating cost effective services. Rather than starting with present staffing levels to decide on cuts, she suggests beginning at zero base and restructuring the nursing organization based on projected volumes, types of patients, and identified nurse:patient ratios. Systematic analysis of all positions led to a variety of strategies to achieve the targeted 190 nursing FTE reductions. Combining responsibilities, increasing the span of control, conversion of full-time to part-time, cutting nonessential functions, and giving nonnursing duties back to other departments accounted for a 31% decrease in administrative positions and a 59% reduction in support and educator positions. A 22% decrease in direct care givers was achieved by defining essential positions for each unit and building from zero base. The hospital used a five-step plan including attrition, early retirement, streamlining management positions, increasing variable staff by conversions to part-time, and terminations. Careful planning, timing, extensive communication, and monitoring of quality indicators were built into the downsizing operation (29).

Coping with cutbacks and layoffs was the focus of an article by Feldman and Daly-Gawenda, who reported results of interviews with nine directors or vice presidents of nursing who had been through the experience of "retrenchment" (cutbacks). The language used to describe cutback management was one of the issues mentioned. Nursing executives clearly distinguished between staff and management categories affected, and were careful to protect the hospitals' image and employment reputation. They found that policies and planning were important first steps in formulating management strategies. Coping strategies involved mechanisms to avert bad publicity in the community, squelch rumors among staff, decrease stress from harassment, foster open communication with affected employees, and reassure staff remaining on the job and the use of support systems for the nurse executives.

The media was generally handled through a designated person or public relations department. Internal rumors were controlled by newsletters, open meetings, rounds on all shifts and days of the week, and through the informal grapevine. Harassment was generally a minor problem for these nine executives; however, harassment was defined and perceived differently among the group. Communication and reassurance was seen as equally important for the employees left in their jobs as it was for those leaving. Visibility and availability were viewed as important for up to 1 year following retrenchment. Support systems included esprit de corpe of the management team, friends, colleagues, professional networks, and in some cases families. Counseling was also used for support. The effects of cutbacks affected the entire organization, as security was threatened and a sense of loss pervaded (30).

A staff reduction policy requires decisions on who will be terminated, and in what order, the method of job reassignment for remaining staff, and conditions and order for recall. While performance criteria may be favored, it has potential for charges of discrimination, unfairness, and costly legal suits. Seniority is therefore the usual criterion used. An exception to this method can be included in the policy to cover situations in which seniority alone would compromise patient care or the institution (31). For example, a sufficient number of staff with critical care skills may be jeopardized if seniority is the only criterion used.

Implementing a downsizing operation should:

- Use an organized systematic approach;
- Have a plan and written policies and procedures;
- Involve as many people as possible in the decision making;
- Encourage a team approach;

Table 5.4. Staff Reduction Plan

Objectives	Key Question	Actions/Strategies	Decision Responsibility	Expected Outcome
Phase				
I. ASSESSMENT				

Identify the Problem
Degree
Extent
Duration
Future
  Short-term
  Long-term
	Financially viable?	Data Collection
		Length of stay
		Utilization (census)
		Financial reports
		Productivity measures
		Classification system
		  earned vs. actual FTE
			Administrative Team
			(includes first-line and middle managers)
				Realistic financial outlook
				Reliable data to support decisions

Determine Type and Scope of Services	Is change needed?	Market Analysis
		No change
		Reorganization
		  Delete
		  Expand
		  Merge
		Contract services
		New ventures
			Governing Body Board of Directors	Verify or redefine mission and goals

II. PLANNING				

Determine Cost of Downsizing	What costs are involved?	Calculate
		Unemployment claims
		Termination pay
		  Severance
		  Accrued leave
		Benefits
		  Early retirement
		  Insurance
		Liquidation of investment plans
		Retraining
		Occupational counseling
		Referral service
			Personnel
			Fiscal
				Accurate picture of costs
				Accurate employee data
				  Seniority
				  Retirement eligibility
				    Now
				    Next 5 years
				    Vested
				    Not vested

Determine Required FTE by: Numbers Category Assignment Specialty	Which employees are essential to meet patient care needs? Will this conflict with seniority criteria?	Assess personnel required for services to be provided	Immediate Supervisors/ First-Line Managers	Ensure core component of caregivers needed for safe patient care

Communicate Potential Problem to Employees	What are the costs/benefits of early involvement?	Costs Insecurity Benefits Participation Trust	Immediate Supervisor	Understanding and commitment to plan
Determine Alternatives to Layoffs	What is the magnitude of the problem? What are alternatives?	Assess feasibility of: Decreasing personnel Attrition Early retirement Voluntary resignation Full-time to part-time Job sharing Reorganization Reassignment Decreasing costs Salary freeze Reduction in pay Reduce benefits Unpaid time off Eliminate overtime, differentials, special pay plans (Baylor)	Administrative Team Input from Employees	Decrease costs without layoffs Efficiency
Define Layoff Policy Objectives	What are priorities?	Define procedures for: Fair and equitable treatment Minimize disruption to services Communication mechanisms Rationale Procedures	Administrative Team Input from All Managers Selected Staff	Clear understanding of priorities
Define Legal Issues	What are legal liability areas?	Consider: Discrimination Bargaining contracts Special circumstances Medical leave Workers' compensation State statutes on wages, obligations Appeals procedures Review procedures	Personnel with Legal Advice	Protection from illegal practices

continued

Table 5.4. *Continued*

Objectives	Key Question	Actions/Strategies	Decision Responsibility	Expected Outcome
Develop Written Policy	What is to be included?	Define: Seniority Notification procedures Rights Termination pay and benefits Recall procedures Exceptions Responsibilities Legal implications Assistive services	Administrative Team Input from: Legal counsel Union	Decision on an administratively and legally sound policy that is fair and equitable
III. IMPLEMENTATION				
Communicate Plan to All Involved in a Timely Effective Manner	What? To whom? When? How? By whom?	Formal announcement to all managers Distribute plan, timetable, policies to all employees, trustees, physicians, volunteers, referring and affiliating agencies	Administrative Team Some responsibilities delegated to individuals, e.g., press releases, notification of personnel	Understanding of plan and rationale by all parties
Protect Image	How can negative publicity be avoided?	Prepare media releases Schedule press conferences		Positive community relations
Publicize Employee Alternatives	What are options?	Formal and informal meetings, individual letters, memos for general distribution and posting, personal phone calls, appointments	Administrative Team Employees	Voluntary cutbacks through resignation, conversions to part-time, early retirement
Complete Layoff Plan	What assistance is available?	Individual interviews inform employees of available assistance: Placement counseling Jobs available in community Referral and reference procedures Resume writing Unemployment application Educational opportunities Social services	Immediate Supervisor or Designated Individual/Service	Completion within identified timeframe Minimal disruption in continuing operations

Offer Reassignments	What are employee preferences?	Individual interviews with affected employees Revise schedules/schedule moves Curtail admissions to units targeted for closure	Immediate Supervisor First-Line Managers	Requests for reassignment Compatible skill/need matches
Maintain Open Communication	What is impact?	Publish new organization chart Visibility and approachability Rounds and meetings on all shifts Inform physicians and all departments	Administrative Team	Rumor Control Minimize nonproductive responses
Effective Transition	What are problems?	Develop relationships with new staff Review job description Identify and provide for training and orientation needs Encourage ventilation Recognize symptoms of grief	First-Line Managers	Minimize dysfunctional behavior and adverse impact on quality services
IV. EVALUATION				
Provide Cost-efficient Quality Service to Customers	Has downsizing achieved desired results?	Assess: Changes in data collected in phase I Skill/staff mix in relationship to patient needs Morale Customer satisfaction Impact of press coverage Impact on referrals and affiliations Cost of plan Benefits attained Adverse effects Report to governing body	Administrative Team and Legal Counsel	Viable financial position Effective delivery of services

- Collect the data needed to support decisions;
- Calculate the cost of the operation;
- Be communicated openly and honestly, both internally and externally;
- Allow reassignments to be selected by displaced employees;
- Treat people with dignity and respect;
- Be fair and equitable.

Cutback management is a technique of downsizing operations to reduce costs. It occurs in all industries when dollar outputs (expenses) exceed dollar inputs (revenues, profits). The process requires organizational change, and change theory should be integrated into management planning, implementation, and evaluation strategies. The change affects all parts of the organization and these effects are often long term. Considering the feelings, emotions, and future of those leaving the organization should be balanced by strategies to assist those remaining in the organization. Feelings of loss are normal and should be treated as a grieving process. Noer uses a poignant metaphor to illustrate why survivors of a downsizing operation feel fearful, anxious, depressed, and guilty. His story is about a loving family of six, caring parents and four obedient children, who sit down together for breakfast. The parents announce that due to budget problems two of the children must "go." The next morning only four sit down to breakfast and the "surviving" children, grateful but not very hungry, eat in silence, fearful of wasting costly resources (32). Disruption in this family, like disruption in a work group, may produce dysfunctional behavior.

Attention to productivity, quality, and morale is important. The process does not end with the layoffs. Insecurity may be manifested in physical, social, and psychological responses. Continued monitoring and astute awareness of symptoms indicating maladaptation are as much a management responsibility as making the cutback decisions. Both ensure the continued health of the organization.

Product-Line Management

Product-line management (PLM), also referred to as product management and service-line management, is a profit-driven business technique that relies on planning, managing, and marketing strategies to promote specific products or product lines to consumers. Product-line management became a prevalent business strategy used by manufacturing firms in the 1960s. Its popularity grew in response to consumer demands for quality products that were reasonably priced. With the advent of prospective payment in 1983, PLM has received increased attention in the health care industry.

Historically, hospitals have been organized along functional or departmental lines rather than product lines. Under cost-based reimbursement, there was little need for hospitals to justify the costs of their product or to produce competitively priced products. Changes in reimbursement, negotiated service agreements, and cost constraints have caused hospitals to reconsider this posture and some have altered their business practices to include product-line management. A 1986 survey of hospital executives reported that 48% planned to implement product-line management in the near future. While a follow-up survey in 1988 found that only 19% actually had adopted this business strategy, the majority of those implementing product-lines reported improved financial position because of it (33).

Characterized by ties to the planning function of management, PLM aims to establish a relationship between service mix and health care markets, and to increase market share by offering competitively priced or unique products. A product can be defined as the final good or service offered in the marketplace. One problem with identifying hospital products is that many intermediate goods and services contribute to the final product. For example, a patient with a diagnosis of acute myocardial infarction (AMI) receives nursing care and dietetic, laboratory, radiology, and pharmacy services as components (intermediate services) of the product "patient care." Each of the components could be a product line if its service constituted the end product. A patient education program, for example, could be a nursing end product.

Two other problems are raised in the AMI example. First is the interdisciplinary nature of the services needed. Many PLM plans include a matrix organizational structure. Matrix organizations violate both traditional management principles and bureaucratic organizational structure. Span of control (how many people one supervisor can effectively manage) and unity of command (one boss) are challenges to traditional management, and the hierarchical chain of command is a challenge to bureaucratic structure. While these challenges may be legitimate—and even past due—they create change and invite the surly companion of change, resistance, to enter the scene. It should be noted that matrix organizational structures are neither prerequisites nor requirements of product-line initiatives. Other organizational structures can and have been used. The second problem in the AMI example is the designation of patient care as a product line. Patient care is much too broad to be meaningful for the planning, managing, and marketing strategies essential to PLM. Smaller and more specific product arrangements are needed to focus these planning, management, and marketing functions. Products such as DRGs, programs, procedures, or clinical services typically comprise hospital products.

Product lines are organized around the concept of strategic business units (SBUs), which are discrete or mini-businesses within the overall organization (34). Strategic business units as used in industry refer to the operational units or divisions defined by the organization's structure and control systems. Ideally, SBUs are decentralized units organized around specific product lines and markets under the direction of a manager responsible for performance of the unit. In reality, SBU managers may be responsible for more than one product line, depending on activity levels and how like services are clustered organizationally (35). Hospitals contain multiple businesses that provide specific services to meet consumer/patient demands. A patient that needs obstetric and pediatric care is not likely to need geriatric care—at least not at the same time. Therefore, one SBU may be established for obstetrics and pediatrics and another designated for geriatrics. The type and number of SBUs will depend on the hospital's mission, competitive position, service activity level, market share, and business plan strategies for the future.

At the present time, DRGs are the most logical method of arranging product lines because reimbursement is dependent on the DRG category and it makes sense to track cost according to the revenue generation source. The issue here is that having close to 500 products becomes problematic. Grouping like DRGs into efficient sized groups under one manager resolves this issue (36).

DRGs and competition for market share have promoted efficiency in hospital operations and paved the way for the adoption of managerial accounting systems. They have also promoted a concern about what services a hospital will offer. DRGs define the products that a hospital "sells" and thus challenge institutions to manage by product. Competition similarly challenges institutions to manage according to the services or products that it offers. Unfortunately, management accounting has focused on the concern with efficiency rather than on the concern about selecting the services and products that will be sold. The fixation on efficiency may be dysfunctional in some product markets.

Managerial accounting evolved in industry at the turn of the century along with mass production and scientific management. Its primary focus is on efficiency as it deals with routine processes in mature or declining organizations. The product cycle in mature industries is a design-sell-produce model. This allows production standards and costs to be determined prior to selling the products. The concern in these markets places production and accounting for efficiency first and product marketing and service selection second.

In contrast, industries that focus on service selection deal with nonroutine processes in start-up, high-tech, or rapidly changing growth organizations. The product cycle in this case is sell-produce. Marketing strategies become primary in selling a product or service that may not be thoroughly designed or is too new for standardized production and cost data to be relevant (37). Traditional accounting practices that focus only on efficiency fail to appreciate the opportunities offered by nonroutine managerial decisions related to developing products or services.

Hospitals need accounting information that serves both purposes (efficiency and product selection), if they are to remain viable and profitable. DRGs provide a standard base product that can be costed out by the traditional accounting system. However, management decisions to offer product lines that generate new activity and increase revenue, while eliminating unprofitable services that do not warrant asset commitments, are ill served by traditional accounting orientations.

To illustrate this, consider the two ways in which profits can be increased. A strategic profit model considers two pathways to improve the rate of return on assets (profits) (37). The first pathway takes the traditional approach of raising net income relative to net operating revenue. The focus is on efficiency measures to increase profits by increasing net operating revenue, decreasing operating expenses, or increasing nonoperating revenue. Budgets start with projections of expenditures in the traditional approach. Profits are increased primarily by keeping expenditures down.

The second pathway focuses on asset turnover by selecting profitable services for asset investment and disinvestment in assets and services that are unprofitable. Asset management requires forecasts of utilization (volume and case mix) and payor mix. Budgeting starts by projecting revenues based on the forecasts. This approach blends strategic planning with financial planning and promotes a philosophy of change and growth. Profits are realized by managing assets and increasing revenues.

Case mix reimbursement is aimed at efficiency in providing services to keep costs down. The goal is to identify standard costs of treating specific patient case types and then reimbursing according to the standard. This effectively places constraints on physician control over the use of resources and reassigns control to the payor and the hospital. Patients become the product lines through their diagnosis related group. This model resembles the stable mature organization that relies on accounting, budgeting, and variance reporting to maintain financial viability. Competition for new, emerging, or growth markets requires a different financial strategy. Accounting systems that are responsive to changing environments and uncertain markets require different accounting information to project financial outlooks. Product-line management is consistent with both routine and nonroutine management decisions and offers potential for capitalizing on market opportunities to organizations that recognize the importance of being able to respond quickly and flexibly in today's marketplace.

Implementing a product-line system can be a considerable challenge. It entails major change throughout the organization as roles, relationships, power bases, and services are restructured. The change to PLM should begin with a clear mission statement and a well-developed business plan (38). Time, communication, patience, and education will be required to ensure success.

Proponents of product-line management view it as an opportunity to budget rationally and to instill sound business practices into hospital operations. The potential for increasing profits and remaining financially viable are positive attributes along with the possibility of improving productivity. Fundamental changes needed in budgeting and accounting systems are seen as major challenges. Supporters caution that PLM may be inappropriate for some hospitals, such as small community facilities with a limited number of services, and admit that adaptation in outpatient settings is problematic (39).

Skeptics cite conflicts in traditional hospital roles and regulatory mandates as the major deterrents to PLM (40). Four popular concerns are discussed here. The first is that hospitals are driven by mission and regulation rather than by profit motives. The argument is that hospitals, because of internal and external forces, cannot eliminate services based on financial considerations. The second issue is that the hospital mission includes programs that are provided because of a commitment to community service. For example, there is frequently a commitment to research and education programs and to extended care services that depends on financial support from profit making services to offset losses. The benefits of these programs and services would be lost in a strict product-line business approach. The third concern is responsiveness to changing reimbursement trends and is tied to the first issue of regulation. The argument is that hospitals respond slowly to the need for new products and services because of traditional structure, function, and imposed regulations. In contrast, less structured and regulated industries can respond quickly to changes in market demand by providing new products or services. The conclusion is that PLM will not work in hospitals. The last concern is an ethical one having to do with access to care. If hospitals provide only profitable services, the care now delivered to those unable to pay the full price would be stopped, and services needed but deemed too expensive would be eliminated (41).

The advantages and disadvantages of PLM are:

- Advantages
  —Fosters competitive pricing (efficiency);
  —Increases profit margins (revenues);
  —Organized and systematic;
  —Improves management decision making;
  —Flexibility in adjusting to economic environment;

—Responsive to changing health care needs;
—Increases accountability to the consumer;
—Potential for reducing duplicative services;
—Promotes optimal use of resources.
- Disadvantages
—Lack of adequate accounting and information systems;
—Competitive markets may increase problems of rationing and access;
—Skeptical attitudes and resistance by many;
—Ethical issues (may eliminate needed but unprofitable services);
—Complex organizational structure challenges traditional lines of authority;
—Threatens traditional roles and functions;
—Disrupts power bases in the organization;
—Promotes fragmentation.

Table 5.5 summarizes the comparison of four budgeting techniques discussed in this chapter.

Business Plans

A business plan is a formal document that presents in detail the business being proposed and what the expected performance measurements and outcomes will be over a specified time frame. The plan serves several purposes. It commits ideas to a written format that serves as a guide to plan, operationalize, manage, and evaluate the business venture being proposed. It allows others (potential investors or supporters) to critically analyze the plan. The plan is a blueprint that can be reviewed, updated, and revised as required by new information or changes in the business. Finally, it is a tool to facilitate goal accomplishment and decision making.

Business plans vary in format, length, depth, and purpose. Detailed plans are probably unnecessary for every new activity or product but should be considered for major programs, projects, or service changes (42). A business plan should be written by the person responsible for its implementation. The value lies in ownership of the plan. The unique ideas and strategies expressed in the document require entrepreneurial efforts and firm commitments if success is to be achieved.

Components of a business plan may be very detailed and all-inclusive or abbreviated depending on purpose and need. A general master plan is presented in Table 5.6. A sample business plan is presented in Chapter 3. The presentation of budgets in Chapter 12, and program planning and evaluation in Chapter 16 offer additional considerations on presenting the plan to specific audiences and eliciting support. The U.S. Small Business Adminstration has detailed examples of business plans and is an excellent resource for information.

CONCLUSION

Budgeting is a necessary skill for critical care nurse managers. A knowledge of the different

Table 5.5. Comparison of Budgeting Techniques

Time Orientation	Budget Organization	Funding Request	Method of Justification
LIB—past to present	By expense category	Previous year base + or −	Incremental adjustments
PPB—future (ignores past)	By program	Projected program costs	Cost/effectiveness analysis Comparison with other programs Inputs to outcomes
ZBB—present (eliminates past)	By ranked decision packages	Zero-base + alternative levels of goal achievement at various funding levels	Cost/benefit analysis Comparison of alternatives Inputs to outputs
PLM—present to future	By product or service	Projected revenues Profit forecasts	Profit maximization Market analysis Outputs to inputs

Table 5.6. Master Outline for a Business Plan

I. Cover Sheet
   A. Name of venture/purpose
   B. Author
   C. Date submitted

II. Index (include subtitles)

III. Executive Summary: Pull key ideas from the finished plan. Be brief. Include:
   A. Brief overview of proposal essence
   B. Financial summary
   C. Brief goals
   D. Purpose: explain business, objectives, methods

IV. History
   A. Describe product/service and current market
   B. Organizational structure (regulated/nonregulated)
   C. Trends: economic, social, technologic, regulatory
   D. Milestones: financial and clinical
   E. Setbacks and losses: yours/others and why they won't happen again

V. Management
   A. Note key responsibilities
   B. Organizational chart: identify essential positions
   C. Key individuals: highlight key actor accomplishments
   D. Compensation: salary, bonus, stock options
   E. Board of Directors
   F. Support positions: legal, patents, advertising, consultants

VI. Product/Service Description
   A. General description: why is it needed and who will use it
   B. Describe the value of the service

VII. Market Research: This section should be detailed and believable. Present data to support the proposal. Use charts and graphs.
   A. Customer demographics: who needs the service
   B. Industry profile: who else provides the service
   C. Projections: 3–5 years
   D. Regulation impact
   E. Primary or secondary market: other providers

VIII. Competition Analysis: Describe real and potential competitors by name, price, performance, market share and profitability
   A. Show market share by dollars and volume
   B. SWOT assessment: competitors and self. (Strengths, Weaknesses, Opportunities, Threats)
   C. Identify proposal impact on competitors

IX. Marketing Plan
   A. What (goals)
   B. How (to be achieved)
   C. What (will be done)
   D. Who (will do it)
   E. Internal and external resources
   F. Service warranties
   G. Customer guarantee/problem handling
   H. Advertising
      1. Methods
      2. Promotions
      3. Expenses
   I. Projections
      1. First year by month
      2. Quarterly after first year

Table 5.6 *Continued*

- X. Operations Plan
  - A. Present facilities and future requirements
  - B. Capital equipment list with budgeted amounts
  - C. Labor force (FTEs) needed and availability
  - D. Address:
    1. Labor unions
    2. Wage rates
    3. Availability of service to users
    4. Access to service: transportation/eligibility
  - E. Long-range plan: 1–5 years
    1. Space
    2. Labor
    3. Capital equipment
    4. Inventory financing

- XI. Legal
  - A. Consider past litigation and judgments
  - B. Legal structure/type of organization

- XII. Design and Development
  - A. Describe past, present and future research and development
    1. Cost
    2. Time
  - B. Schedule: show timeframe from idea to full operation
  - C. Risks and problems: describe plans for minimizing impact of price cutting
    1. Industry trends
    2. New competition
    3. Excess costs
    4. Delay costs
    5. Lack of labor pool

- XIII. Unique Factors and Opportunities: This section is devoted to the last chance to plead the case.
  - A. Highlight goals
  - B. State % of profit generation
  - C. Return on equity
  - D. Position in industry
  - E. Why this is unique
  - F. Opportunities: joint ventures/mergers

- XIV. Glossary of Terms: Define all technical terms, industry buzz words

- XV. Financial Data
  - A. Historical: current year plus 5 previous years (if available)
  - B. Profit and loss projections
  - C. Cash flow projections
  - D. Balance sheet
  - E. Supplemental financing
    1. Tax effects
    2. Credit position
    3. Impact on long-term debt
    4. Financing arrangements

- XVI. Proposed Use of Proceeds
  - A. Profits and use
  - B. Use tables and graphs

- XVII. Appendix of Support Data
  - A. Resumes
  - B. Product brochures
  - C. Customer lists
  - D. Testimonials
  - E. Sample agreements
  - F. Analysis data

techniques and purposes of budgets is valuable in developing unit level documents for planning, controlling, and evaluating financial performance. One technique may be appropriate for the annual budget while another may be more suitable for developing a proposal for new programs and services. Business strategies included in the chapter may assist with specific problems such as cutback management or with role development in assuming management of a product-line. This chapter has also presented comparisons of the stages of budgetary development and various budgetary techniques along with advantages and disadvantages of each.

REFERENCES

1. Esmond, TH Jr. Budgeting procedures for hospitals. American Hospital Association, 1982:15.
2. Key VO. The lack of a budgetary theory. Reprinted in Public Budgeting and Finance Summer 1981:86 (originally published in The American Political Science Review, 1940;34:1137–1144).
3. Wildavsky A. The politics of the budgetary process. 3rd ed. Boston: Little, Brown and Co. 1979:128–130.
4. Swansburg RC, Swansburg PW, Swansburg RJ. The nurse manager's guide to financial management. Rockville, MD: Aspen Publishers, Inc., 1988:76–78.
5. Mark BA, Smith HL. Essentials of finance in nursing. Rockville, MD: Aspen Publishers, Inc., 1987:139–140.
6. Francisco PD. Flexible budgeting and variance analysis. Nursing Management 1989;20:40.
7. Schick A. The road to PPB: the stages of budget reform. Reprinted in Classics of public administration. Oak Park, IL: Moore Publishing Co., Inc., 1978:253–256. (originally published in Public Administration Review 1966;26:243–258).
8. Schick, p. 258.
9. Leloup LT. Budgetary Politics. 2nd ed. Brunswick, OH: Kings Court Communications, Inc., 1980:5,268.
10. Drucker PF. What results should you expect? A users guide to MBO (originally published in Public Administration Review, vol. 36. Jan/Feb 1976:12–19). Reprinted in Shafritz JM, Hyde AC. Classics of public administration. Oak Park, IL: Moore Publishing Company, Inc., 1978:427.
11. Albanese R. Management. Cincinnati, OH: Southwestern Publishing Co., 1988:258–260.
12. Wildavsky, pp. 185–186.
13. Drucker, p. 428.
14. Suver JD, Brown RL. Where does zero-base budgeting work? Harvard Business Review Nov–Dec 1977:76–77.
15. Lewis VB. Toward a theory of budgeting. Public Administration Review 1952;12:42–54.
16. Taylor GM. Introduction to zero-base budgeting. The Bureaucrat 1977;6:33.
17. Taylor, p. 36.
18. McGrail GR. Budgets: an underused resource. JONA 1988;18:29–30.
19. Phyrr PA. Zero-base budgeting. New York: John Wiley & Sons, 1973:6.
20. Suvac, p. 78.
21. Schick A. Zero-base budgeting and sunset. The Bureaucrat 1977;6:12–13.
22. American Association of Critical Care Nurses. Summary analysis of critical care nurse requirements. Newport Beach, CA: AACN 1988:1–8.
23. The future of healthcare: changes and choices. Arthur Anderson and the American College of Healthcare Executives 1987:6–7.
24. U.S. Hospitals. The future of health care. Touche Ross June 1988:4–10.
25. Fink CA. The impact of mergers on employees. Health Care Supervision 1988;7:59–60.
26. Cherskov MM. What's driving upcoming mergers. Hospitals January 5, 1987:36–40.
27. Levine CH. Organizational decline and cutback management. Public Administration Review July/Aug 1978:316–325.
28. Perry LT. Cutbacks, layoffs, and other obscenities: making human resource decisions. Business Horizons July/Aug 1985;28:68–75.
29. Rozboril AJ. Systematic downsizing: an experience. JONA Sept 1987;17(9):19–22.
30. Feldman J, Daly-Gawenda D. Retrenchment: how nurse executives cope. JONA June 1985;15:31—37.
31. Roberts JD. Nursing staff reductions: plans, process, and aftermath. Nursing Management March 1989;20(3):70.
32. Noer DM. Layoff survivor sickness: a new challenge for supervisors. Supervisory Management March 1990:3.
33. The future of healthcare: changes and choices. Arthur Anderson and the American College of Healthcare Executives 1987:14–15.
34. White RE, Hamermash RG. Toward a model of business unit performance: an integrative approach. Academy of Management Review 1981:6:213–214.
35. Gupta AK, Govindarajan V. Business unit strategy, managerial characteristics, and business unit effectiveness at strategy implementation. Academy of Management Journal 1984;27:31.
36. Bird GA. Product-line management and nursing. Nursing Management 1988;19:47.
37. Covaleski MA. The shifting nature of management accounting practices in the health sector. In: Wolper LF, Penna JJ, eds. Health care administration. Rockville, MD: Aspen Publishers, Inc. 1987:137–146.
38. Hesterly SC, Robinson M. Nursing in a service line organization. JONA November 1988;18:32.
39. Solovy A. Hospitals must budget by DRGs, payors. Hospitals June 5, 1989:34–39.
40. Solovy A. Limited use for product management in hospitals. Hospitals January 20, 1989:72.
41. Yano-Fong D. Advantages and disadvantages of product-line management. Nursing Management 19 May 1988:30.
42. Vestal KW. Writing a business plan. Nursing Economics May/June 1988;6:121.

Chapter 6

Budgeting Process

PEGGY J. MADDOX

The process of budgeting has become more important in recent years because of rising health care costs and the emphasis on cost containment. Budgetary projections guide decision making by managers at every level in the health care system. Budget documents should be organized, comprehensive, and related to the organization's strategic plan. Nurse managers must be aware of the relationship of unit operational plans to the strategic plan, and of the importance of their unique areas of program responsibility as they influence the performance of the entire health care organization. The budget is a formalized plan that sets direction for the unit within the strategic plan of the facility. The purpose of this chapter is to present a comprehensive approach to budget planning and development that will yield effective results for nurse managers.

ORGANIZATIONAL PLANNING

To ensure optimal performance and attain organizational goals, managers utilize strategic planning and strategic management applications. As an operational plan, the budget is one of the most widely employed methods for managerial planning and control. While the budget does not in and of itself determine or control operations, it is a powerful management tool used to assure organizational goal achievement when coupled with management action. The budget defines the standard by which operational performance can be evaluated. As a plan, it is the statement of management's knowledge, experience and goals, expressed in quantitative and financial terms.

To approach budgeting from a sufficiently comprehensive frame of reference, nurse managers must first understand the relationship of unit, program, and department plans to the long-term performance plans and strategies of the health care organization.

Budget and Strategic Planning

According to Drucker, "Strategic planning is a continuous, systematic process of making risk-taking decisions today, with the greatest possible knowledge of their effects on the future; organizing efforts necessary to carry out these decisions; and evaluating results of these decisions against expected outcomes through reliable feedback mechanisms" (1). Strategic management goes beyond strategic planning to include thinking and action. Strategic management involves managers making informed decisions which enable their organizations to reach established goals. In the ever-changing and increasingly competitive health care environment of the 1990s, informed managers make decisions resulting in the least risk with the greatest reward. The goal of strategic management is to enable managers to take actions that strengthen the competitive position of the organization and optimize goal attainment and performance (2).

Budgets are useful for two managerial functions, planning and control. Budgetary planning involves establishing goals and objectives in quantitative terms and identifying the resources and performance levels that will be required. Budgetary control involves the ongoing process of comparing actual performance results against those planned, and making corrections or modifications during the budget cycle.

The responsibility for strategic planning rests at the highest level of an organization's management hierarchy with the governing board and chief executive officer. They determine the organization's mission and goals, and develop the strategies that will be undertaken to achieve these goals. The process of strategic planning focuses attention on the future, in order to position resources and take actions that support adaptation and change. Planning enables the organization to take advantage of new opportunities.

Strategic plans are developed to guide long-term (3–5 year) organizational performance. Operational plans are typically developed by first-line and mid-level managers to guide short-term (1 year) program performance. Although decision responsibility for the strategic plan rests with executive management, the planning process itself usually involves managers throughout the organization. The strategic planning process involves assessment of current environments (internal and external), anticipates future conditions, and establishes future goals (including competitive position). Planning and control for the organization in its entirety is accomplished by integrating all unit, program, and department operational plans (budgets). Budgets developed by nurse managers serve as one of many operational plans that support the organization's long-term strategy and goals.

Integrated Budget Programming

A number of important organizational considerations should be incorporated into preparation of the budget. The nurse manager should be familiar with the organization's strategy and its current priorities and operational assumptions. Comprehensive programming creates the foundation upon which a successful budget is based. Finkler cites a number of essential organizational programming prerequisites:

1. The statement of environmental position;
2. The statement of organizational goals and objectives;
3. Identification of organization-wide assumptions;
4. The specification of program priorities;
5. The specification of measurable operating objectives (3).

Nurse managers should understand the importance of these elements and seek information from these prerequisites for incorporation into program budgets. Incorporation of these elements into individual budget requests will tie the individual unit or program budget to overall organizational goals and priorities. Such as approach is more likely to yield favorable decision support for budget requests.

Nurse managers should be aware of the significance of their individual program responsibilities and performance results as they impact the organization. The nurse manager can start the integration process for the unit by asking the following:

1. What type of patients, and how many of each type, are in the unit?
2. What strengths, weaknesses, opportunities, and threats exist with this patient mix?
3. What is our capacity and how do we actually compare?
4. What hospital goals will impact the unit and what will be the results?
5. What are the hospital assumptions for inflation, contracts, discounts, wage and merit changes, technology improvements, etc.?
6. What programs does the unit offer, how are they prioritized, and how do those priorities fit into the overall plan?
7. What results in quantifiable terms do we want to achieve in volume, mix, productivity, revenue, etc.?

While much rests on the shoulders of managers to understand and incorporate into operations, organizational structures, processes, and functions have been developed to ensure coordination and integration of decentralized initiatives.

ORGANIZATIONAL PREREQUISITES

The development of budgets demands commitment, participation, and accountability from individuals throughout the organization. Prerequisites associated with effective financial planning and control ensure that information needs and decision processes are supported and that there is organizational consistency and coordination. Although not exhaustive, the following organizational prerequisites are widely recognized:

- Delineation of organizational structure that assigns individual responsibility and designates cost or departmental centers;
- Organization of the accounting systems chart of accounts to parallel managerial responsibility;
- Maintenance of a system of data collection for statistical and financial data (historical and concurrent);
- Development of a budget calendar which identifies tasks, responsibilities, and timetables;
- Designation of a budget decision authority and process.

These structures and functions assist in managing the people and processes associated with budgeting by supporting wide organizational participation and ensuring consistency and accountability among managers and systems.

In order to meet certain functional requirements, data must be collected and made available; the organization must specify assumptions, limitations and goals; systems and processes must serve the needs of managers (not vice versa); and managers must work together to achieve organizational goals and priorities. While most health care organizations spell out functions, processes, structures, and timetables in a budget manual, there is more to managing the budget process than a manual can provide. Organizations must create the environment and the expectations which (when coupled with effective planning and control) support effective budget processes and outcomes.

Because each health care organization will approach financial management and budgeting differently, nurse managers should become familiar with the methods of their own institution. This will enable them to participate effectively in the budget planning and decision processes.

BASIS OF BUDGET DEVELOPMENT

To facilitate budget development and subsequent decision making, a basis for budgetary projections is required. Forecasted data is utilized to meet this need. Analysis of historical data, experience, and knowledge provides the basis for projecting future operations. Nurse managers should begin development of the budget with the collection of pertinent historical and current data. Such data includes resource utilization and trends for revenue and expenses.

The type of budget process employed determines the nature of data required. Historical budgets utilize prior year expenses as the basis for new year budget proposals. Forecast or statistical budgets are similar in that they use historical and other data (e.g., program changes anticipated) to establish expense levels. Both the projected and forecasted levels of activity serve as the basis for budget levels requested. Flexible and trended budgets likewise utilize historical data such as expenditure patterns and activity levels to determine how the budget changes within a given time period. Only the zero-base budget does not utilize historical data to determine budget requests.

Forecasting is the practice of predicting the future. It is utilized extensively in strategic management to anticipate change and develop action plans in uncertain environments. It is used at the operational level to provide information upon which budgets and decisions will be made and as a managerial tool for planning, quantifying plans, and controlling costs (4). Comprehensive planning requires the use of forecasted data to support budget requests. Indeed, historical and forecasted data serve as the best foundation of a well-prepared budget. Nurse managers need to become familiar with the various types of budgets and understand the unique data requirements of each. Additionally, nurse managers should know that organizations expect managers to explain and defend their budgetary projections and requests. Forecasting techniques are discussed in greater depth later in the chapter.

BUDGET FORMULATION PROCESS AND CALENDAR

Most health care organizations plan and control budget activities through an annual budget calendar. The budget calendar serves a variety of planning purposes: it is an activity guide; it identifies and describes budget task requirements and responsibilities; it defines the annual budget cycle; and it sets target dates for completion. Budget calendars may be formatted in any number of ways. Typically they will be found in a time line or Gant chart format which specifies budget tasks and deadlines. The nursing department follows the budget calendar and facilitates budget activities using internal department planning and review. The top nurse executive usually evaluates nursing department budget requirements and provides a nursing department calendar to facilitate and control budget requests for all units and programs.

While each organization's budget calendar is unique, selected activities are typically identified with timetables for completion. Swansburg identifies three stages which capture activities associated with budgeting:

1. Formulation stage;
2. Review and enactment stage;
3. Execution stage (5).

The formulation stage will usually begin 6 or more months prior to the new budget year. During this stage, managers obtain and analyze pertinent data and make forecasts about program activity levels, operational expenses, and revenues. The review and enactment stage includes such activities as preparation, revision, and presentation of budgets to the nursing department and the budget officer. In the execution stage, expense and revenue budgets are implemented and then evaluated and revised as appropriate. Table 6.1 illustrates an organization's budget calendar.

Budget Assumptions

The master budget for the health care organizaton comprises numerous operational plans (unit, program, department) which must be closely coordinated and managed. In order to ensure uniform budget submissions, standardized assumptions are specified by health care organizations and all budget managers are required to utilize them in budget projections. They ensure organizational uniformity for budgetary performance. Assumptions about utilization levels, variable rates, costs, and personnel management expectations are typically standardized. Assumptions are utilized in developing budgetary forecasts. Examples of organizational budget assumptions are:

- Inpatient days will decrease/increase by __%;
- Overtime utilization levels will not exceed __%;
- Outpatient services will be based on __ visits/yr;
- Inflation rate adjustments will be __%;
- Merit increases may not exceed __;
- Operational expenses will be reduced by $__;
- Reduce FTE by __%.

Organizational assumptions are incorporated into the budget along with additional information concerning changes in utilization or professional practices for each unit or program. Historical data should be obtained about activity level (volume) and utilization by unit or program. Because each organization will collect and report data differently, nurse managers should identify what data is recorded and what reports are issued. Likely organizational sources for data are the admissions, medical records, payroll, accounting, nursing, and data processing departments.

It is important that nurse managers know that a wide range of reports and reporting systems exist in most health care organizations. Reports are typically of two general types, program reports and financial reports. Program reports are designed to meet the manager's informational needs about program activity and quality, e.g., numbers and types of patients and services delivered. Financial reports are designed to meet informational needs about costs, expenses and revenues, and budget variances. Data in both managerial and financial reports may initially be found uncorrected until a final report is presented. It is important to ensure that congruent and accurate data are used in making budget projections. Cross-checking data for congruence among sources will ensure organizational consistency and accuracy.

Essential information about the organization that should be considered in developing forecasts is:

1. The organization's mission, goals and priorities;

Table 6.1. Budget Calendar, Budget Year Beginning Oct. 1, 1991

Target Data	Tasks	Responsibility
June 1991	Develop department goals and objectives	Department managers
June 1991	Determine expense budget components and line items	Department managers, Budget Director
June 1991	Develop capital expense plan	Department managers
July 1991	Prioritize and develop institution's capital expense plan	Capital equipment committee, budget committee
July 1991	Determine department work standards and volume forecasts	Budget Director, Nurse Executive
July 1991	Determine revenue projections	Budget Director, department managers
July 1991	Prepare preliminary revenue and expense budgets	department managers
September 1991	Seek final budget approval and implementation plan	Budget Director, Nurse Executive, department managers, governing body

2. Budgetary assumptions (including variable standard rates, costs and performance standards);
3. Capital expenditure needs;
4. Volume and utilization forecasts;
5. Cash flow objectives;
6. Revenue and expense reports.

A wide variety of data are utilized to quantify budget needs and requests. Types of data and possible organizational sources are shown in the table below.

Data	Sources of data[a]

Unit Activity Data
  Average daily census
  Monthly average patient census
  Percent occupancy
  Yearly census
  Monthly patient days
  Yearly patient days
  Average length of stay
	A,B,D,E,F

Personnel Utilization Data
  Average hourly rate (by job category)
  Paid productive hours (by job category)
  Regular hours
  Overtime hours
  Differential hours (by category)
  Premium and special pay hours (by category)
  Paid nonproductive hours (by job category)
  Vacation, sick, holiday, other
	C,D,E,F

Productivity data	D,E,F

Supply Utilization Data
  Supply and expense variance data
  Monthly supply utilization data (including costs)
	D,E,F

Unit Work Load Data
  Patient classification data (including hour required variances)
  Nursing hours per patient day
  Revenue per patient day
  Allowances and discounts
	D,E,F

[a]Key: A = Admissions; B = Medical records; C = Payroll; D = Nursing; E = Accounting; F = Data Processing.

Utilization of Historical and Forecasted Data

Forecasted data is utilized to meet the information needs of managers in preparing and executing budgets. Indeed, most health care organizations base budgetary projections on historical and forecasted data (6). When historical information is not available, projections may be based on industry norms or standards such as those reported by the American Hospital Association (in *Monitrend*), state hospital associations, and the Healthcare Financial Management Association's Financial Analysis Service, to name a few.

Two data bases of historical information are utilized to project the next year's budget, prior year data and current year data. Because the current year is in progress, data will not be complete. Incomplete data are "annualized" or estimated using current activity and utilization levels. An example of annualized data for patient days is illustrated in Table 6.2. Using the data in Table 6.2, 6 months of data are known, and the remaining 6 months must be estimated from the utilization level for the year-to-date in order to arrive at an annualized total with projections for 12 months.

Another method of estimating patient days is to compare current budgeted patient days with current actual patient days, in order to project next year's utilization volume from trends. Table 6.3 illustrates this method. If no significant change in internal and external operating factors is projected, historical data and trends serve as the most reliable and accurate basis for forecasting activity levels and budget requirements (7).

Forecasting is used in budgeting to predict in quantitative terms what a unit, program, or institution expects to produce in a given period of time. Nurse managers are frequently expected to forecast future trends in patient census, supply utilization, and personnel utilization. Work load and activity level schedules organize and format data so that trends may be observed. Sections A, B, and C of the Appendix illustrate schedules (forms) that are useful for this purpose.

Quantitative forecasting results in projections of future activity levels based on historical trends. Georgoff and Murdick describe four types of methods into which most forecasting techniques are categorized:

- Counting: Market testing and survey methods;
- Time-Series: Moving average, exponential smoothing, adaptive filtering and others;

86 PLANNING AND IMPLEMENTATION

Table 6.2. Annualized Patient Days Fiscal 1991 Year-to-Date

FY	Months	Days	Patient Days	Average Patient Days/day	6-month Estimated Total	Total
FY 1990	12	365	4380	12	XXXXXXX	4380
FY 1991	6	181	1840	10	1840	3650

Table 6.3. Projected Patient Days for Fiscal Year Ending December, 1991

	Projected Patient Days			
Month	Current FY Budgeted	Current FY Actual	Variance	Projected Patient Days
Jan	300	330	+30	320
Feb	308	308	0	308
Mar	310	341	+31	330
Apr	360	330	-30	340
May	341	372	+31	360
Jun	360	330	-30	350
Jul	372	341	-31	350
Aug	341	341	0	341
Sept	310	310	0	310
Oct	310	310	0	310
Nov	330	310	-20	320
Dec	279	279	0	279
TOTAL	3921	3902		3918

- Judgment: Historical analogy, delphi technique, naive extrapolation, scenario method, and others;
- Causal: Correlation, regression, econometric models, leading indicators, and others (8).

Nurse managers should be aware of the most commonly employed forecasting methods. Among them, moving averages, least squares, and regression analysis are particularly useful to nurse managers. The process of forecasting is managed in four steps:

1. Collect data;
2. Graph data;
3. Analyze data;
4. Prepare predictions.

Nurse managers examine data trends using activity schedules that compare prior year and current year (to-date) data.

When more quantitative methods of forecasting are desired, a number of mathematical techniques are useful.

Moving Average Method

The moving average method is useful in projecting future patient days. As a time-series method of projecting future activity, this method is sensitive to monthly trends and is more accurate than data derived from annualization. A commonly utilized application is to project patient days for a given unit or program. Below is an example of the application of moving averages, the weighted moving average equation.

$$\text{Forecast (f)} = \frac{3M^1 + 2M^2 + 1M^3}{6}$$

where M^1 equals current month data, M^2 equals 2 months ago data, and M^3 equals 3 months ago data. Table 6.4 illustrates a weighted moving average.

Least Squares Method

Another time-series method of forecasting is the least squares or simple regression method. It is useful in identifying trend lines and developing volume forecasts. Nurse managers will find it useful in identifying annual patient day trends. Simple regression assumes that a straight line superimposed on graphic or time-series data of volume or activity level will project the subsequent year's activity. The formula and explanation of the least

Table 6.4. Example of Weighted Moving Average Application to Calculate Average Patient Days/Month

Month	Patient Days	Calculation
Jan	279	
Feb	308	
Mar	300	
Apr	279	(3×300) + (2×308) + 279/6 = 299
May	270	(3×279) + (2×300) + 308/6 = +291
Jun	240	(3×270) + (2×279) + 300/6 = 278

squares (simple regression) method is provided below and in Table 6.5.

$$\hat{y} = a + bx \text{ (simple regression equation)}$$

$$\hat{y} = a + b_1x_1 + b_2x_2 \text{ (multiple regression equation)}$$

Figure 6.1 depicts the projection of patient days in graphic display. The first reaction of many nurse managers who are new to working out forecasted numbers is one of intimidation. Keep in mind that these formulas are neither memorized nor typically computed manually. Formulas are used when the need to employ them is identified and computers are utilized to make computations. The illustration is important to provide the underlying principles behind a useful forecasting technique.

Multiple regression techniques are used to examine the impact of more than one variable (i.e., patient work load and volume) on a particular outcome.

Table 6.5. Least Squares Method of Projecting Patient Days Simple Regression

	Projected Patient Days		
Years (X)	Patient Days (Y)	(X) (Y)	X squared
1986 (yr0)	3650	0	0
1987 (yr1)	3285	3285	1
1988 (yr2)	4015	8030	4
1989 (yr3)	3650	10950	9
1990 (yr4)	4015	16060	16
$\Sigma x = 10$			
	ΣY	ΣXY	ΣX^2
Totals 10	Total = 18615	Total = 38325	Total = 30

(x = # of years) (Y = # of pt. days) Average $\bar{X} = 2$ Average $\bar{Y} = 3723$

By solving for Y using the least squares method of forecasting, the nurse manager can project or forecast patient days for 1991.

$$\hat{Y} = a + bx$$

$$b = \frac{\text{sum}XY - n\overline{XY}}{\text{sum}X^2 - n(X^2)} \qquad a = \bar{Y} - b\bar{X}$$

$$\frac{38325 - (5)(2)(3723)}{30 - (5)(4)} \qquad 3723 - (109.5)(2) =$$

$$\frac{38325 - 37230}{10} \qquad 3723 - 219 =$$

$$b = \frac{1095}{10} = 109.5 \qquad a = 3504$$
1991 projected patient days

Expense Budget

The expense budget comprises two components, the wage-and-salary budget, and the non-salary-and-wage budget. Although separate and distinct components of the non-salary-and-wage budget, capital and expense items are treated similarly in that they are projected based on a common set of assumptions about the amount and quality of care to be provided. Expense items are differentiated as to whether they are fixed (nonvariable) or variable as a function of program activity level changes.

The salary and wage budget portion of the expense budget includes three general categories of personnel expenses:

1. Variable salaries and wages;
2. Fixed salaries and wages;
3. Employee fringe benefits.

The largest item in a health care organization's expense structure is employee salaries. Salary projections are typically based on either average hourly cost per employee at a given utilization level or actual employee salaries paid. Salary expenses may be divided into three categories: productive time, nonproductive time, and fringe benefit factors.

The categories of nonproductive time will vary in organizations, but commonly include vacation, sick, holiday, personal, and education time. Fringe benefit costs associated with the personnel budget include annual salary increases (e.g., merit increases), health insurance, life insurance, and FICA (social security contribution). Productive salaries are typically divided into direct patient care and indirect patient care categories. Direct patient care salaries are attributable to care givers who actually deliver (at the bedside) patient care services. Direct patient care hours are sometimes referred to as variable care costs because they vary as a function of changing patient volume and acuity. Indirect patient care salaries are associated with nonvarying or fixed personnel costs, such as those for management (head nurses, off-shift supervisors), clinical consultants (educators, clinical specialists) and clerical and technical support (unit secretaries, supply managers). Wage and salary expense projections are based on projected hours of work multiplied by the average hourly rate of each employee category. Fringe benefits are most often computed as a percentage of total salary costs (e.g., FICA = 7.2% of employee salaries). Section D of the Appendix illustrates a sample format for wage and salary expense requests.

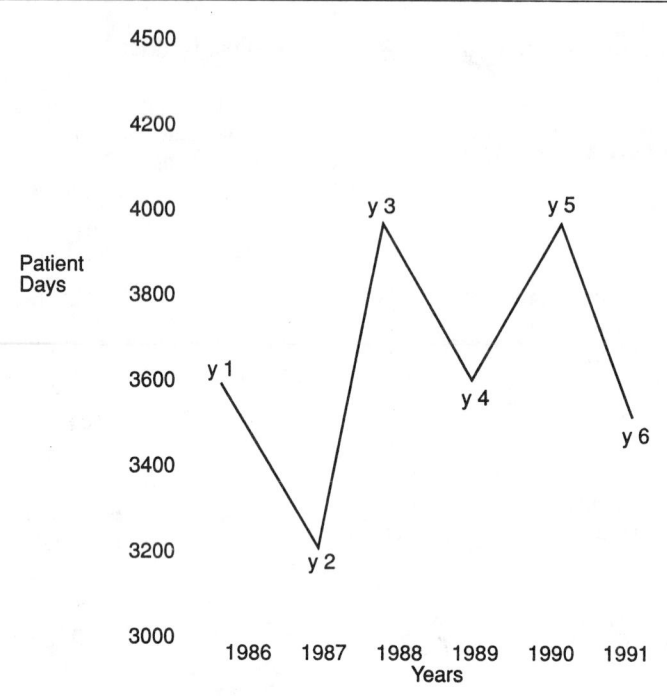

Figure 6.1. Least squares projection of patient days graphed.

Other Expense Items

The non-salary-and-wage portion of the expense budget includes expense items not related to personnel salary and wage costs. This includes the daily supplies consumed and the minor equipment used on a patient care unit. The number and type of items in this portion of the expense budget are defined by each organization. There are numerous categories of items that usually will be specified in the budget manual under expense codes. The following fixed and variable items are typically included in this portion of the budget:

1. Fixed expenses
    Dues and subscriptions;
    Education and training;
    Travel;
    Rentals;
    Insurance;
    Repairs.

2. Variable expenses
    Office supplies;
    Medical-surgical supplies;
    Pharmaceuticals.

In preparing the supply budget, statistical methods of expenditure projections within the year are utilized (9). After projections of service volume for the next year are identified, calculations for annual expenses are made for each line item. The factors that nurse managers consider in analyzing and planning for the other expenses are volume, clinical indicators (patient mix and acuity), price, and program and technology changes projected. Section B of the Appendix illustrates a sample expense analysis schedule.

The supply component of the budget is typically the second-largest component of the expense budget after personnel expenses. Health care organizations usually base the supply budget on historical utilization levels adjusted for inflation. Using this method, calculations are made by taking prior year actual expense data and dividing it by service units to obtain cost per unit of service. This is multiplied by the projected volume of activity expected and a preestablished inflation factor. In the following example, if a unit's year-to-date medical supply costs were $22,000 from January through July (7 months), and the preestablished inflation adjustment is 5%, the projected cost for medical supplies for the new budget year will be $39,600. Projected supply expenses calculations follow.

$22,000 (Annualized Medical Supply Costs YTD) ÷ 7 × 12 (Annualizing Factor) = Projected Annual Supply Costs of $37,714.

Annualized Supply Costs × Inflation Factor = Projected Medical Supply Costs
$37,714 × 1.05 = $39,600.

Sections C and D of the Appendix illustrate non-salary-and-wage expense analysis schedules.

Capital Budget

The capital budget comprises expenditures for items that will have a long-term (greater than 1 year) impact on the types of services to be provided by the organization, and for acquisition costs that exceed established limits (e.g., $500 per item). Components of the capital budget usually include the following items:

1. Land (not a nursing responsibility);
2. Land improvements (not a nursing responsibility);
3. Buildings (not a nursing responsibility);
4. Fixed equipment;
5. Major movable equipment;
6. Minor equipment.

Program or unit capital budgets may include only movable and minor equipment. Fixed equipment is usually associated with the physical plant of the facility and has a depreciable life of greater than 10 years. Major movable equipment is not fixed but movable and meets the preestablished limits of useful life and cost. Some organizations may include physiologic monitoring equipment in this category.

Each organization establishes criteria for capital equipment and the organization's budgeting responsibilities. Examples of criteria used to differentiate major movable from minor equipment would be 3 years useful life and $500 for minor equipment and 5 years useful life and $1000 for major movable equipment. Examples of major movable equipment include IV pumps, therapeutic beds, and portable monitoring equipment. Minor equipment is typically depreciated over 3 years or less and is requisitioned and managed by programs. Examples of minor equipment include many surgical instruments, bedpans, and heat lamps.

Reasons for making capital expenditures vary. They may include replacement, new service, accreditation requirements, or quality and efficiency improvements. The rationale for capital purchases is essential information for the decision making process and includes the urgency of need. The nurse manager prioritizes the equipment accordingly. Organizational decisions about capital equipment acquisition are critical in our health care financing environment. These purchases impact organizational cash flow and costs may not be "passed on" to some payors. This change has been created by the new prospective payment system. The advent of the Medicare prospective payment system has created considerable debate in the hospital industry as to how capital-related costs will be reimbursed (10).

Commonly employed mathematical methods for determining whether or not to make a particular capital acquisition are those which evaluate profitability. While an in-depth discussion is beyond the scope of this chapter, the discounted cash flow calculation methods most commonly utilized are: pay-back period, net-present-value (NPV), and internal rate of return (IRR).

Discounted cash flow analysis (NPV and IRR) calculations assist organizations in determining profitability in the following manner: NPV is utilized to determine whether a project earns more or less than a desired rate of return, and IRR determines interest rate for finding the future value of money in today's dollars. Such information is useful in conjunction with information about clinical need and impact in determining whether to make, defer, or deny a particular capital expense, based on profitability.

Development of capital budget proposals is time-consuming and requires a considerable level of justification detail. Hoffman describes a 7-step approach to the development of capital budgets (11). She suggests that nurse managers employ the following steps in preparing capital budget requests:

1. Gather data;
2. List alternatives;
3. Prioritize requests;
4. Analyze cost:benefit;
5. Recommend an action;
6. Implement plan;
7. Evaluate plan.

Each organization will specify the timetable, format (forms), and data requirements for capital equipment justifications and requests. It is not uncommon for capital equipment requests to be projected 3 years or more into future budget planning, in order to evaluate and finance acquisitions. Section E of the Appendix illustrates an example of a capital equipment request and justification form.

Computerized Assistance in Managing Budgets

Although budgets can be compiled and analyzed manually, computers are widely used and preferred over manual methods in budget preparation and management. Computers offer advantages to budgetary planning and control by introducing increased accuracy, ease of managing complex data calculations and analyses, and increased time efficiency in formatting and manipulating data. Nurse managers should familiarize themselves with the computer resources and support available in their institutions. Today's sophisticated health care organizations employ both mainframe computers and microcomputers to facilitate budgeting processes. Microprocessor computers are particularly useful to nurse managers for use in scheduling staff, in planning and monitoring budgets, in unit record keeping/data tracking, and for word processing.

For budgetary support purposes, the electronic spreadsheet is useful for numerical calculations and for request formatting using microcomputers. A number of commercially available software applications for electronic spreadsheets are available. These applications support sophisticated numerical calculations which allow various statistics, graphing, and planning functions.

A spreadsheet comprises a series of rows and columns which create cells into which data may be inserted. The size of cells can be adjusted to accommodate small or large numbers and text. Additionally, formulas which perform mathematical functions may be programmed into cells to automatically perform a wide variety of calculations and adjust totals to reflect changes. The graph capabilities of the most widely available spreadsheets support line, bar, and pie-type graphs. It is well worth investing time and attention to learn and utilize a computerized spreadsheet application (12).

Electronic file and database management applications are also useful to nurse managers in tracking and storing large amounts of data. Database programs create fields and layouts for data of all types. Once a database is established it is readily manipulated to add, delete, and update information, and to generate reports and display information. Electronic databases are superior for ease and timeliness of data tracking, filing, and retrieval.

Computer applications are essential to support accurate, time-efficient, and easy budget planning and control functions. They offer considerable advantages over manual methods for accuracy and sophistication of statistical support calculations and for database management.

SUMMARY

Organized, standardized budget planning and control processes and functions enable health care organizations to implement wide managerial participation and accountability in budgeting. The unit or program budget should be prepared as an operational plan for the organization's goals. Nurse managers need to understand the structures, processes, and responsibilities as they relate to the strategic plan and management of the competitive position. Additionally, nurse managers should learn a wide variety of sophisticated applications and methods for tracking, quantifying, analyzing, and forecasting for the planning and execution of budgets. Whenever possible, computer assisted applications are employed to ensure accuracy and ease of data handling.

REFERENCES

1. Drucker P. Management: tasks, responsibilities, policies. New York: Harper and Row, 1974:125.
2. Fox DH, Fox RT. Strategic planning for nursing. Journal of Nursing Administration, 1983;13(5):11–17.
3. Finkler S. Budgeting concepts for nurse managers. Philadelphia, PA: W.B. Saunders Co., 1984:19.
4. Finkler S., pp. 108–109.
5. Swansburg RC. Management and leadership for nurse managers. Boston, MA: Jones and Bartlett Publishers, 1990:134–188.
6. Covert RP. Expense budgeting. In: Cleverly WO, ed. Handbook of health care accounting and finance. Rockville, MD: Aspen Publishers, Inc., 1982:261–278.
7. Herkimer AG Jr. Understanding hospital financial management. 2nd ed. Rockville, MD: Aspen Publishers, Inc., 1986:122–123.
8. Georgoff D, Murdick R. Manager's guide to forecasting. Harvard Business Review 1986; 64(1):110–120.
9. Hoffman FM. Projecting supply expenses. Journal of Nursing Administration 1985;15(7):21–23.
10. Buerhaus PI. Incorporating hospitals' capital-related costs within Medicare prospective payments. Nursing Economics 1986;4(5):227–235.
11. Hoffman FM. Developing capital expenditure proposals. Journal of Nursing Administration 1985;15(9):32–33.
12. Finkler SA. Microcomputers in nursing administration: a software overview. Journal of Nursing Administration 1985;15(4):18–23.

Appendix Chapter 6

APPENDIX 6.A. EXPENSE ANALYSIS SCHEDULE

Revenue/Cost Center: _____ Fiscal Year: _____ Manager: _____

| Item Description | Prior Year ||||| Current Year ||||| Projected Year |||||
	QTR1	QTR2	QTR3	QTR4	TOTAL	QTR1	QTR2	QTR3	QTR4	TOTAL	QTR1	QTR2	QTR3	QTR4	TOTAL
Bandages/Dressings															
Wound Care Kits															
Ostomy Appliances															
Sutures															
IV Catheters/Needles															
Bed Pans/Urinals															
Specimen Containers															
Infusion Cassettes															
IV Tubing															
Disposables															
Drainage Devices															
Pharmaceuticals															
Non-Pharmacy															
TOTAL															

APPENDIX 6.B. EXPENSE ANALYSIS SCHEDULE

Revenue/Cost Center: _____ Fiscal Year: _____ Manager: _____

Description	Prior Year	Current Year	Projected Year	Justification
Books & Periodicals				
Office Supplies				
Travel				
Education & Training				
Printing				
Equipment Repair				
Equipment Lease				
Minor Office Equipment				
TOTAL				

APPENDIX 6.C. PERSONNEL EXPENSE BUDGET

Revenue/Cost Center: _____ Fiscal Year: _____ Manager: _____

POSITION	HOURS/DOLLARS	Prior Year	FTE	Current Year	FTE	Projected Year	FTE	Justification
HN	Total Hours							
	Total Dollars							
UC	Total Hours							
	Total Dollars							
RN	Total Hours							
	Total Dollars							
LPN	Total Hours							
	Total Dollars							
NA	Total Hours							
	Total Dollars							
ANNUAL GRAND TOTAL HOURS								
ANNUAL GRAND TOTAL DOLLARS								

Note: To convert hours to FTE, divide by 2080.

APPENDIX 6.D. WORK LOAD ANALYSIS SCHEDULE

Revenue/Cost Center: _____ Fiscal Year: _____ Manager: _____

	CATEGORY	Jan	Feb	Mar	Apr	May	Jun	Jul	Aug	Sep	Oct	Nov	Dec	Total	Comments
PRIOR YEAR	Patient Days														
	Nursing Hrs Req'd														
CURRENT YEAR	Patient Days														
	Nursing Hrs Req'd														
PROJECTED YEAR	Patient Days														
	Nursing Hrs Req'd														

APPENDIX 6.E. BUDGET YEAR CAPITAL EQUIPMENT REQUEST FORM

The "Capital Equipment Request Form" must be completed for each item of equipment which costs in excess of $1000 and has an estimated useful life in excess of 3 years.

A) The following sections are to be completed by the Department Head:

1) Requesting Department: _____ Dept. No. _____
   Prepared by _____ Date of Request _____ Date Equip. Needed _____

2) What is requested? (Enter below a short descriptive title for the equipment being requested.)
   _____
   _____

3) Equipment (Complete the following concise statements.)

   a) Description of Primary Equipment: Model No.   Quantity
      _____   _____   _____
      _____   _____   _____
      _____   _____   _____

   b) Description of Accessories/Options: Model No.   Quantity
      _____   _____   _____
      _____   _____   _____
      _____   _____   _____

4) Will this equipment require additional staffing?   Yes _____ No _____
   If answered yes, complete the following information:

                                                        Annual
      Job Title: Manhours   Salary
      _____   _____   _____
      _____   _____   _____

5) Will any existing equipment be traded in or scrapped?   Yes _____ No _____
   If answered yes, complete the following equipment information:

      Description: _____ Trade in _____ Scrapped _____
      Model/Parts/Serial No. _____ _____ _____
      Manufacturer _____
      Estimated Purchase Date _____ Dept. Charged _____
      (Proceed with price quotations) _____ Date _____
                                              Administrator

B) Description of the Equipment:

Briefly describe the actual service to be provided by this equipment, including services that are presently provided that will continue with the purchase of this equipment, along with new and/or additional services that will result with the acquisition of this equipment.

C) Justification of Need—Department Head/Manager:

On an attached 8½ × 11 sheet, prepare a detailed justification of the acquisition of this equipment using one or more of the following types of justification:

1. Revenue Producing:

    This type of justification is used for any equipment that produces a services which is chargeable to a specific patient regardless of whether it is an existing or new test, exam, treatment, procedure, or service.

2. Cost Reduction Equipment:

    Any nonrevenue producing equipment that increases productivity, reduces staffing or operating cost or replaces worn out equipment should use this type of justification.
    Examples: Eliminate or reduce maintenance cost, supplies, or the purchase of outside services, etc.

3. Medical/Psychological:

    Equipment of this nature can be justified if said service is not presently available and the medical/psychological wellbeing of the patient may be impaired. The department head and chief of the clinical service should collaborate and co-sign this justification. The purchase of this equipment is necessary even though the purchase may or may not generate revenue or said revenues are not adequate to cover the operation of the equipment.

4. Repair vs. Purchase:

    Compare the cost of repair or overhauling of equipment to that of purchase. Equipment can be justified if the repair/overhauling expense is prohibitively expensive.

D) The Director of Purchasing is responsible for obtaining all price quotations and the information below on all equipment being disposed of. As soon as said information is obtained it will be forwarded to the department head for inclusion in the original "Equipment Request" form.

E) This section is for the use of Capital Equipment Review Committee only.

        Return for further justification
        Approved
        Not approved

Signature of Review Committee Chairman   Date

Chapter 7

Capital Budgets

DOROTHY E. BLACK, JUDITH L. WILSON

Capital budgeting has taken on new importance as hospitals face reduced inpatient revenues, increased operating costs, competition, changing clinical practice, and reluctance on the part of third-party payors to reimburse for capital expenditures. The paradox is that the need for computerized systems to assist in making informed and financially sound decisions has never been greater, yet hospitals may be unable to afford them. It is readily acknowledged that the prospective payment system has had a profound impact on the financial management of daily hospital operations. While less apparent in the short term, this system may have even graver consequences for future capital budgets.

Capital budgets include durable fixed and movable assets with a price above a specified amount (usually $500) and an estimated life of greater than 1 year. The physical plant, land, and major equipment fall into the category of capital assets. Until the advent of prospective payment, capital acquisitions were reimbursed by third-party payors based on costs. Although there were limits, retrospective reimbursement generally provided incentives to invest in the newest and most technologically advanced equipment. Since the mid-1980s this situation has been replaced with one of uncertainty. Reimbursement is likely to be less than the full cost of capital expenditures and may be absent altogether. Medicare, for example, reimburses capital expenditures at 15–25% less than cost and imposes time consuming legislative procedures on the approval of payment for new technology (1, 2). The point is that capital budgeting will become a greater challenge in the future and the potential impact on critical care makes this a particularly cogent concern for the critical care nurse manager.

This chapter focuses on the capital equipment budget from the perspective of the critical care nurse manager, presents methods to evaluate capital equipment purchases, considers leasing as an alternative to purchase, and briefly discusses depreciation and other funding sources.

CAPITAL BUDGETING

Ventilators, intra-aortic balloon pumps, defibrillators, intravenous infusion pumps, and continuous electrocardiogram and hemodynamic monitoring systems are examples of capital expenditure items needed to provide care to critically ill patients. The ability to develop a capital budget is an essential skill for critical care nurse managers as it directly impacts patient care and staff satisfaction. One responsibility of management is to provide workers with the tools and equipment necessary to do a quality job. In the high tech world of critical care this responsibility takes on greater magnitude than in most general nursing units. The nurse manager plays a significant role in planning for equipment that meets the needs of patients and staff. Knowledge in financial management is necessary to communicate effectively with other departments involved in the capital budgeting process, to improve the management of critical care programs, and to achieve the goal of cost efficient quality care.

The health care organization is the first consideration in the development of a capital budget. Managers must appreciate that the difference between for-profit and not-for-profit agencies affects services, caseload, and available funding. The primary difference between not-for-profit and for-profit hospitals is that not-for-profit hospitals are exempt from federal income tax, state property tax, and corporate income tax. Although not-for-profit agencies have an advantage because of their tax exempt status, investor-owned hospitals have the advantage of being able to diversify into businesses related or unrelated to health care. Not-for-profit hospitals, especially public hospitals, often provide mandated services such as charity care. Investor-owned agencies have more options in selecting what services they will provide and to whom. They may choose to discontinue an unprofitable service. Not-for-profit hospitals with mission objectives and competition may not have this choice. Sources of funding for capital equipment and capital projects are also affected by a hospital's for-profit or not-for-profit status. Chapter 18 presents a comprehensive discussion of hospital structure and ownership.

In addition to understanding the type of organization, it is necessary and even more important for the unit level manager to know the hospital's strategic and financial plans. Where is the agency going in the next several years? As the patient diagnosis determines the plan and the critical path outlines the day-to-day interventions based on expected outcomes in managed care, the strategic plan sets directions for the future and the financial plan offers the time line for disbursement of funds in the health care organization. Financial plans must take into consideration "market activity, organizational goals, prior performance, trends in third-party reimbursement, regulation, competitors' activities, and provider attributes" (3).

In order to do capital budgeting a knowledge of the terminology is required. Planning articulates specific outcomes to be achieved and the strategy to be used. Strategic planning involves the long-term goals and directions of the organization. Medium-range planning is specific to the unit or program level and often includes targeting capital budget funds for use in the next 1–5 years. Short-range plans are incorporated into the annual budget to distribute resources during the current fiscal period. Budgeting is the process that defines how the plan will be implemented at the tactical or operational level of the organization. Capital budgeting is the process of planning and decision making for capital assets. This includes determining future assets, financial feasibility, evaluation of asset operations, and integrating capital expenditures with long-range financial plans. Capital budgeting includes planning for disbursement of funds needed for land acquisition, plant development or expansion, and capital equipment expenditures. The strategic plan is influenced by market activity such as the types of patient services that are in demand, market share, the availability of personnel, the resources necessary to deliver the product, and physician specialties. For instance, consider the technological requirements needed for a laser surgery program, and the factors that go into the decision to expand, develop, or discontinue this service. Another example of strategic planning would be the development or expansion of a cardiac surgery program. Market analysis should support decisions made at the strategic planning level. It should be recognized that changes in existing programs and the development of new programs must also consider the impact on current hospital capacity. If a critical care unit has maintained an occupancy rate of 90–100% over the last 3 years, expansion will require an increase in the number of critical care beds, budgeted positions, and capital equipment. This may be unrealistic in a unit having difficulty staffing the present work load. Information provided by the critical care manager can impact planning for the overall agency. "The department budget is the fundamental information base from which the overall budget is calculated" (4). Once the goals of the organization are clear, the department manager's responsibility for goal achievement is established.

For the manager of a critical care unit, a clear knowledge of the planning process for capital expenditure items is imperative. More now than in the past nurse managers are expected to be involved in budgeting. In view of this trend, nurse managers must become familiar with the procedures necessary to complete the capital budgeting process.

Hospitals vary in their approach to reviewing and approving capital equipment requests. Generally, the approval process involves the following:

- Goals are established for the hospital.
- Calls for capital equipment requests go out to managers (usually at the beginning of the fiscal year for next year's budget).
- Managers submit requests including justification and an indication of priority need to the budget or capital equipment committee.
- Preliminary data on all requests is gathered and a priority is assigned. (Priorities can be based on critical needs such as regulatory or safety recommendations, essential needs, and needed but nonessential items.)
- Cost/benefit studies may be conducted.
- Comparisons of requests are completed.

- Prioritized lists are submitted to the chief executive officer/board of directors/chief financial officer and first cuts are made.
- Targeted projects and requests are returned to managers for in-depth documentation of justification.
- Proposals are returned to the budget committee.
- Rankings are completed using financial analysis (subjective information is also considered).
- Final recommendations go to the chief executive officer/board of directors.
- Final funding is approved (subject to availability of financial resources).

Whatever procedure is used, nursing must be involved. The importance of having a nursing representative on the budgeting committee cannot be overemphasized. Decisions by committee can be influenced by persuasive argument. The risk of arbitrary decisions is too great without nursing input. This is especially relevant in the environment of competition for scarce resources that exists in hospitals today.

Based on financial performance from previous fiscal years, the critical care unit's ability to function within set budgetary constraints or guidelines can be evaluated. This information, along with budget projections for the next fiscal year, determines the new budget. The overall organizational budget is developed and the guidelines are shared with each department or unit so they can be implemented. If the unit or program is unable to maintain costs within these guidelines, justification for exceeding the set guidelines is needed. The decision to deny requests, seek further funding, or shift funding from one program to another is made at the chief executive level. Normally, a list of capital equipment needs is solicited from the unit or program manager on an annual basis. These lists are reviewed and prioritized by mechanisms specific to each hospital. An equipment committee, a budget committee, or some other arrangement may be used. Recommendations are made at the chief executive level where it is determined whether the capital equipment expenditures will fit the strategic and financial plans of the agency. Table 7.1 presents a partial listing of capital equipment for a surgical intensive care unit (SICU). The table depicts purchase cost and date along with replacement date. This type of report is helpful in planning capital equipment budgets.

In situations where the unit is to expand, or a new unit is needed, careful evaluation of the projected floor plan is vital. Specifically, the plans for electrical outlets, plumbing, and room design and their effect on patient privacy should be considered. The list for capital equipment items with justification for each item can be extensive and may include, for example, beds with or without weight scales, refrigerators for patient medications and staff, furniture, e.g., patient reclining and nonreclining chairs with or without tables, and furniture for staff. Patient and staff safety is a major consideration and includes infection control, e.g., an adequate number of sinks must be available for hand washing. As the manager of a critical care area plans for capital budget items, it is essential that the proposal submitted to the executive committee mirror the overall goals and mission of the agency while addressing specific unit needs. A capital equipment request is illustrated in Table 7.2.

At the unit level, the first step of the capital equipment budgeting process is to establish the goals and objectives of the unit. A profile of the unit includes: patient case types, acuity levels, average daily census or overall occupancy rate, and the average length of stay. Nursing considerations are staffing and skill levels of staff. Future trends such as physician specialities and emerging technologies, and the clinical vs. research focus of the unit should be considered. The projected time frame of an item's useful life is important in planning for capital equipment items. For example, is this a 1-, 5-, or 10-year plan? A 1-year plan will be prioritized with other immediate needs while a 5- or 10-year plan will be treated differently. Another area of significance is the community. Community considerations include: market, or patient population; community health needs; and growth or anticipated growth that will be influenced by incoming industry. When the first step in the budgeting process is complete, the goals and objectives at the unit level will be clear.

The second step is to develop a list of new and replacement equipment items along with a justification for each item. Justification will ensure that equipment needs and anticipated benefits are based on defined goals and objectives. Justifications should address standards of care, standards of practice, and professional organization recommendations. Along with justification, the priority of each item must be listed. Priorities are linked to goals and

CAPITAL BUDGETS   101

Table 7.1. Capital Equipment Report

Capital Equipment Report
Department Intensive Care
SICU

Page 1

Description	UI	Serial Number	Unit Cost	Acq Date	Repl Date	Quantity on Hand for Period Ending 09/28/90 Date

Monitor blood pressure. An electronic module item is complete with an alarm circuit. Designed to be used with a physiological system or as a self-contained single item.

Monitor bld pressure   EA   0MA89   2,200.10   04/85   04/98   1
                                1 6515-8576
                                2 Blood pressure sensors
                                3 Model 1000
                                4 With extra cuff

/   /   /   /   /   /   /   /   /   /   /   /   /   /

Page 2

Patient data management system. A physiological monitoring system. Data and commands from terminal and recalls the data catagories for vital signs, lab results, staff notes, fluid balance, medications, acid-base.

Patient data system   EA   25,605.06   10/85   10/95
                              1 6516-8086
                              2 4-bed telemetry patient central station
                              3 With single channel recorder

Monitor cardiac and respiration. An electronic item designed to provide a continuous audible and/or visual indication of heart rate and rhythm, and respiration rate.

Moni cardiac resp   EA   G6G00485   2,131.50   01/87   01/95   1
                              1 PM 6516-8218

/   /   /   /   /   /   /   /   /   /   /   /   /   /

Page 3

Blood pressure control apparatus, intra-aortic. A mobile apparatus used in the temporary control of coronary blood flow by inserting a balloon catheter into the thoracic aorta.

Blood press cont app   EA   1484   24,988.50   04/85   4/93   1
                                 1 PM 6515-7670
                                 2 Balloon pump

Blood press cont app   EA   1427   33,985.00   01/87   01/95   1
                                 1 PM 6515-8252

   No. of records   2   58,973.50   Total 2

Pacemaker, cardiac. An electronic item designed to stimulate, by electrical impulses, contraction of the heart muscle at a certain rate through the closed chest wall or directly to the heart.

Pacemaker cardiac   EA   EH0000606R   2,055.00   10/79   10/92   1
                                1 6515-8614
                                2 MOL 5330
                                3 SICU

Pacemaker cardiac   EA   EH002087R   2,295.00   01/82   01/92   1
                                1 6515-6801

Physiological monitoring system, intensive care. A complete centralized system consisting of components necessary to provide the measurements, alarm, and recording functions to monitor patients in intensive.

Phys mon sys int care   EA   254,046.85   12/85   12/93   1
                                  1 6515-8615
                                  2 Consists of 12 monitors and 6 cameras
                                  3 SICU

Table 7.2. Capital Equipment Request

Hospital Form 123

1. Department: <u>Nursing</u>
2. Location: <u>SICU</u>
3. Cost Center: <u>1114</u>
4. Date of request: <u>5/91</u>
5. Item requested: <u>Defibrillator</u>
6. Number requested: <u>1</u>
7. Model #/Vendor: <u>WX 73A   ZAP Corp.</u>
8. Address/Phone: <u>one place, USA 555-5555</u>
9. Cost: Each: <u>$7000</u>   Total: <u>$7000</u>
10. New _____   Replacement __X__
11. Priority: Urgent _____ Explain _____
    Essential __X__ Nonessential _____
12. Date needed: <u>FY91</u>
13. Cost savings/revenue generating: yes _____ no __X__ Est. amount _____
14. Space/FTE requirements: __N/A_____
15. Equipment use: Clinical: __X__ Nonclinical _____
16. Justification: <u>Current equipment outdated and due for replacement. Cost of repairs increasing. This is essential equipment to ensure the safety of patients at risk for cardiac arrest.</u>
17. Department Approvals:
    Nurse Manager: _____ Date: _____
    Department Head: _____ Date: _____
18. Organization Approvals:
    Financial Officer: _____ Date: _____
    Budget Committee: _____ Date: _____
    Chief Executive Officer: _____ Date: _____
19. Comments: _____

---

objectives. Some hospitals rank order equipment as follows: patient safety and care, new revenue, new technology, reduction in staff, and physician requests. Additional information may be required to help decision makers maximize the available funds.

Step three is evaluating the present equipment systems for possible upgrading. An example would be adding new modules to cardiac monitoring. If upgrading the present system is not feasible consider integrating the current system with new equipment acquisitions.

At this point the criteria for equipment purchase have been established. The fourth step of the process then begins. This involves the solicitation of information from vendors. Vendors should be allotted a reasonable time frame to respond. Once the information is returned, the number of vendors should be narrowed to a range of two or three who are then requested to make presentations to the selection committee members. Considerations in the vendor selection process include using the established justifications. Justifications promote concentrating on the benefits to be obtained from equipment purchase and include: desired capabilities, need to upgrade capabilities, training time, and ease of use. Attention to special features should be avoided unless they are absolutely necessary. Special features often result in unnecessary expense. Other major considerations in vendor selection include cost, serviceability, availability, and post-purchase support. Some hospitals request vendors to work with the buyer of materials management rather than directly with the clinical manager. This may help avoid the "high pressure" sale or a quick buy due to a promised vendor discount. It will also conserve the nurse manager's time. Table 7.3 outlines questions to consider in assessing vendors and products.

The fifth and final step is the actual selection of the capital equipment items and implementation. Implementation can be difficult without prior planning. It is during this phase that the results of effective planning and the benefits based on justified objectives will be realized. The final phase also includes the evaluation process which should be initiated immediately and can be measured in cost effectiveness, efficiency, quality, and satisfaction levels.

Case Scenario

Perhaps the best method to assimilate the process of purchasing a capital equipment item is by example. It has been established that the surgical intensive care unit (SICU) must increase from a 10-bed unit to a 14-bed unit. The purchase of a continuous electrocardiogram (ECG) and hemodynamic monitoring system is necessary. As the manager of the SICU it is essential to establish a group of committee members who will aid in the selection process. Consider clinical and administrative services that will be impacted by the acquisition and utilization of the equipment. A representative from purchasing service is needed as the purchase agreement is the responsibility of this service. In some institutions the vendor contacts must be made through the purchasing department. Biomedical engineering should be represented to oversee installation, integration of the new system with the current system, and maintenance. Physician involvement would include the chief of surgery, especially for input regarding the development of any new programs that will have a significant impact on the type of monitoring system necessary to meet patient care requirements. The SICU medical director is also included, and in this case, a physician representative from anesthesiology service is needed. Monitoring equipment used in the operating room (OR) and in the SICU should be compatible. Nursing members will include the head nurse, a staff nurse, and the cardiac clinical specialist or nurse educator who will provide ongoing training for nursing staff members. Optional personnel for the committee could include the architect, interior decorator, and hospital planner if numerous changes are occurring throughout the agency.

Committee members review the profile of the unit. In this example, it is noted that the SICU consistently maintains an occupancy rate of 90%, the acuity level of the patient population is increasing, and trending reflects a longer average length of stay. However, a percentage of the patients, specifically the open heart surgery patients, could transfer to the general unit sooner if telemetry was available. Of significance is the fact that these open heart surgery patients, who are not true SICU patients (according to set criteria), continue to remain in an ICU bed, which promotes poor utilization of beds and nursing staff. This is a management and physician issue that must be addressed. Future considerations are expansion of the open heart surgery program by 30% over the next 5 years. Available nursing staff for the critical care areas is on the decline, and the outlook at present offers no improvement. The present equipment is 6 years old and due for replacement in 1993. Delays in replacing parts have been documented and the warranty has expired. The alternative of purchasing 4 new units now and 10 new units in 1993 was evaluated using objective and subjective criteria. Based on this information, the goals and objectives are set. The goal is to purchase a continuous electrocardiogram and hemodynamic monitoring system for a 14-bed SICU that will meet the patient care requirements. Additionally, telemetry capabilities for four "dual purpose" beds is requested. A list of desired capabilities with justification for each is developed. The system must have the ability to provide a wide range of information because of the high acuity levels of the patient population. Features that would best meet the needs of the patients are: capabilities for drug calculations, ST elevation detection, pacer spikes not counted as heart beats, trending, arrhythmia alarms, and event recall. The system must be user friendly with minimal time required to access information. The electrocardiogram monitoring system should be compatible with the OR system to provide a smooth transition from the OR to the SICU, and to promote familiarity of equipment between anesthesia and nursing staffs. The telemetry component will promote better utilization of beds and staff. Compatibility of equipment is an important issue. Transducers, intra-aortic balloon pumps, and module transferability must be con-

Table 7.3. Assessment Areas for Vendor and Product Selection

I. Vendor Specifications
  A. Design Philosophy

    Consistency and trend in design philosophy during the company's manufacturing history?

  B. Product Scope

    Major products comprising the product scope?

  C. Technological Expertise

    Firm's expertise in technology development relative to medical instrumentation?

  D. Cost of Ownership

    Determining the life cycle cost of equipment in the following areas:
    1. Five-year service contract price for 5-day 8-hour coverage; parts, labor, travel included?
    2. Mean time between failures?
       (Source of substantiating data?)
    3. Average cost of repair?
    4. Average turn around time on a service call due to equipment breakdown?

  E. System Development Support

    Support capability:
    1. Preinstallation
       —On-site equipment definition and feasibility/capability review (a telemetry antenna survey for example)?
       —System definition including detailed equipment layout and wiring diagrams?
       —Assistance with site preparation?
       —Development of installation and staff training schedules?
    2. Installation—ability to provide field system verification and calibration?
    3. Documentation—ability to provide complete and accurate operating manuals, service manuals?

  F. Maintenance and Service
    1. Service in the local area?
    2. Average response time?
    3. Round-the-clock service coverage?
    4. Technical support for biomedical engineers by phone?
    5. Technical training support available?
    6. Maintenance programs available?
    7. Spare parts program? (location and type of parts stocked, ordering and response times, and length of time parts are maintained for product models.)

  G. Training
    1. Company provided training?
    2. Training cost?
    3. Qualifications of training staff? Availability of training on an ongoing basis, and the flexibility of meeting specific hospital needs?
    4. Availability of audiovisual programs?
    5. Training duration and coverage?

  H. Compatibility
    1. Does the equipment utilize instruments from other vendors? If yes,

Manufacturer?	Model Number?	Description?
_____	_____	_____
_____	_____	_____
_____	_____	_____

    2. For equipment not manufactured by the company, who will do the servicing?

    3. Operating conditions (temperature and humidity)?
    4. Product flexibility (color schemes, wall mounting, locating in modular walls, and meeting different hospital environment situations?

Table 7.3. *Continued*

  I. Clinical Data
     Is there unbiased clinical data available to support product claims?
  J. Code and Agency Approvals
     Does equipment carry UL approval? Does it conform with codes and all local, state, and federal safety rules and regulations?

II. Instrument Specifications
   A. Bedside Station
      1. Do the bedside monitors minimize the risk of counting pacer spikes as heart beats?
      2. Can the heart rate at the bedside be derived from pulse or pressure wave-forms?
      3. Do the bedside monitors provide an adequate HR current for neonatal patients (if appropriate)?
      4. Do pressure monitors provide single pushbutton automatic transducer balance and amplifier calibration?
      5. Do pressure monitors provide beat-to-beat measurement and systolic peak detection triggered by the ECG "R" wage?
      6. Do respiration monitors provide automatic rate counting threshold adjustment? And a means to prevent counting of cardiac activity?
      7. Does the cardiac output computer provide microprocessor based, component level self-diagnostics?
      8. Does the cardiac output computer provide digital display of cardiac output, body temperature, or injectate temperature?
      9. What is the range and accuracy of the cardiac output computer?
   B. Central Station
      1. Are the central station products compatible with all bedsides provided by the manufacturer?
      2. How many bedsides can be shared by one central station strip chart recorder?
      3. Will this recorder provide strips which include pre-alarm traces, even if all beds go into alarm at the same time?
      4. Does the central station have a software heart rate and alarm mechanism that is independent of the bedside?
      5. Does the central information center provide trend plots?
      6. Does the central information center eliminate respiration artifact?
   C. Arrhythmia Monitoring
      1. What arrhythmia algorithm is used?
      2. How many keys, pushbuttons, or switches are needed to operate the arrhythmia system? Describe their function.
      3. What are arrhythmia alarm categories?
      4. Can arrhythmia reports be automatically scheduled?
      5. Can arrhythmia alarm events be selectively stored for recall and edit purposes?
      6. Are arrhythmia trends automatically updated with edited beat classifications?
      7. Can arrhythmia trends be correlated to the patient's medication administration? If so, how many drugs can be individually selected for each patient?
      8. How many beds can be accommodated by the arrhythmia computer?
      9. What hospitals are using the arrhythmia system?
   D. Patient Data Management
      1. How is the patient information transferred from the emergency room, to the operating room, to the SICU?
      2. How are patient data management systems linked together?
      3. How many beds can each system accept data from simultaneously?
      4. How many parameters can each system accept simultaneously?
      5. How many patients' files can each system manage?
      6. How many bedside video terminals can each system support simultaneously?
      7. How much does each video terminal cost?
      8. What is the manufacturer and model number for the page printer?
      9. How many seconds does the graphics printer take to produce one page?

sidered. This system must comply with current standards of practice, and provisions for upgrade capabilities must be clearly defined.

After completing the list of desired capabilities along with the benefits that will be derived, the present system is evaluated for the possibility of upgrading rather than purchasing a new system. Perhaps the same benefits can be achieved at minimal cost. If upgrading is possible, feasibility studies are required to determine cost effectiveness. In this example, upgrading was determined to be inefficient.

It is now time to select a vendor. "This process should include assessment of the manufacturer's financial stability and commitment to the product and product line, as well as of its reputation for providing initial support and ongoing service" (5). When requesting information from vendors, questions should be specific. Often, the best resources for evaluating equipment performance are other health care workers presently using the system. The vendors should be narrowed to a maximum of two or three, and each requested to make a presentation to the committee. It is important that all committee members be present for each presentation. Adequate time should be scheduled for the presentation and an initial evaluation should immediately follow each presentation. Trial usage in the clinical area with manufacturer support is highly beneficial and allows for staff input on the type of system that is to be acquired. Evaluations should be documented during trials. Table 7.4 provides an example form for this purpose.

Training manuals and operating guides should be reviewed to evaluate ease of use, clarity, organization, and comprehensiveness. In addition to the cost of the system, supplies such as ECG paper, ECG leads, cables for invasive monitoring, and adapters for balloon pumps must be evaluated. Cost information also includes delivery and installation, service contracts, warranties, failure rates, down time (time needed for repairs), and training for both clinical and biomedical staff. In evaluating post sales support, the location of the manufacturer and distributorships must also be explored as this can directly impact response time for service and supplies. It can also impact availability of personnel for ongoing training and consultation. Sole source justification may be required if the cost of the selected equipment item does not stay within the guidelines set at the executive level or if the chosen vendor is not under contract with the hospital. For instance some federal and multicorporation agencies are under contract or have agreements with specific suppliers. However, if the selected equipment is unavailable from these companies, sole source justification can be used to obtain the needed item. The equipment that best meets the identified need at the least cost should be chosen and implementation at the unit level can be initiated. Section A of the Appendix provides an example of sole source justification.

The considerations for implementation are numerous and can be overwhelming if a plan is not developed. A committee of key people includes: unit manager, clinical specialist and/or nurse educator, staff nurse, representative from biomedical engineering, vendor sales representative, and manufacturer-supplied clinical implementation specialist. Each committee member should be assigned specific responsibilities and target dates for completion. Of major concern is the installation of the monitoring system and the impact that it will have on patients and staff. The number of beds that can remain open during installation should be determined. The date for closure of beds must be set, and the service chief needs to be informed so admissions can be controlled. Before installation can begin, the physical, environmental, electrical, and logistical properties of the unit must be thoroughly explored. These include the location of the central station and ease of access and visibility, location of amperage and quantity of electrical outlets, adequate air conditioning, noise from printers and alarms, and dust control. Certain specifications must be met for equipment to function properly. Committee members who have been carefully selected will ensure that all areas are researched prior to the installation date.

It is essential that staff be kept informed of plans. It is beneficial to keep a temporary set-up of the chosen monitoring system at one bedside so that staff have the opportunity to become familiar with the system's capabilities. A format for training should be adjusted so that patient care concerns do not interfere with training. Consider training away from the agency to allow staff to concentrate on new information. The method for orientation of new staff members should be determined. In addition to operating and training manuals, unit resource nurses and video tapes can be useful. Once the system is in place a method for ongoing evaluation is essential. Errors are often operational; however, system deficits may be present

Table 7.4. Equipment Evaluation Form

LOCATION _____ NURSE ( )
PHYSICIAN ( )
TECHNICAL ( )

Please evaluate this equipment: omit those questions that do not apply. Provide additional comments, if desired, on last page.

1. General
    a. Clarity of graphical display
        1. Fixed trace with erase bar
        2. Moving trace

    b. Clarity of alphanumeric display

    c. Number of traces
        1. At bedside
        2. At central station

    d. Central station monitoring
        1. Number of patients accessible
        2. Types of information available

    e. Bedside data entry/display

    f. Color (monitors)

    g. Remote bed monitoring

    h. Patient data transfer, bed to bed

    i. Remote graph start

    j. Size
        1. Bedside
        2. Central station

2. Arrhythmia Monitoring
    a. Waveform recall (duration, number of events)
        1. Speed of recall
        2. Ease of recall
        3. Editing capabilities (relabeling)
        4. ECG (actual) waveform recall
        5. Blood pressure waveform recall

    b. Histogram display
        1. Event/drug markers

    c. Relabeling provisions

Table 7.4. *Continued*

    d. Lead fail indication
       1. General
       2. Specific

    e. Multilead analysis/simultaneous analysis
       1. Hardwired beds
       2. Telemetry beds

    f. Alarm structure selectable

    g. Pacemaker rejection/accommodation

    h. Telemetry monitoring

3. Physiological Monitoring
    a. Pressure monitoring
       1. Ranges
       2. How many monitored/displayed
       3. Invasive, noninvasive or both
       4. Provision for plotting/graph

    b. External calibration with hg manometer

    c. Damping correction for tubing sets

    d. Automatic measurement of end diastolic PAW pressure

    e. Total number of waveforms (parameters)/bedside
       1. Monitored
       2. Simultaneously displayed

    f. Trend plot displays
       1. Episodic/continuous
       2. Event/drug markers

    g. Thermal Dilution C.O.
       1. Waveform (washout curve) display
       2. Storage/recall of washout curves
       3. Rejection of bad waveforms
       4. Averaging of readings
       5. Inline or probe (or both) injectate temp.
       6. Notification of arrhythmias during procedure

    h. Respiration monitoring

    i. Cardiac calculations
       1. Integrated with C.O. calculation
       2. Storage/recall of how many sets

Table 7.4. *Continued*

- j. Pulmonary calculations
- k. Renal calculations
- l. Temperature monitoring
  1. Number of temp. avail/module
  2. Changes in temp. indicated
  3. Celsius/Fahrenheit selectable
- m. Left ventricular function curves
- n. Fluid volume or weight (blood, urine)

4. Computer Interfacing
   a. Technically feasible
   b. Vendor collaboration
   c. Cost

5. Maintenance
   a. Schools
   b. Ease of service
   c. Accessibility of boards
   d. Spares

6. Nursing In-service

7. Overall Preference

8. Comments

and immediate detection and follow-up are required.

Capital budgeting is not unlike effective utilization of the nursing process. A plan is devised based on accurate assessment of current and anticipated needs. Equipment justifications are based on expected outcomes, and ongoing evaluation is used to determine effectiveness. The skills necessary for capital budgeting are used by the manager of a critical care area in daily clinical practice. It is important that we expand our knowledge base to include the principles involved in budgeting because as unit managers we have assumed a greater responsibility for the overall delivery of patient care and our input is vital.

FINANCIAL ASPECTS OF CAPITAL BUDGETING

Managing capital budgets in the 1990s will become an increasingly complex task as organizations respond to the challenges of higher costs, lower inpatient revenues, competition for market share, and pressures from physicians and consumers for state-of-the-art technology. How hospitals respond to the conflicting demands of cost constraint and high tech service will require creative solutions. Higher costs and lower inpatient revenues are inconsistent with the philosophy of providing all services to all patients.

Nurse managers need to be familiar with the terminology and techniques of financial analysis to the extent necessary for interpreting results and communicating with financial personnel. Knowledge is also important in understanding why some capital projects are funded and others are disapproved or delayed. The actual calculations and preparation of the analysis reports are usually done by the fiscal, purchasing, or data processing departments.

Financial Analysis Techniques

Objectivity aids decision making by quantifying the costs and benefits in various requests. Comparison of the costs and benefits can facilitate the selection process. It is unlikely that all requests will be funded in any given year and the quality of the justification data in a proposal may provide the cutting edge that determines what gets funded.

While hospitals have used strategic planning to project capital needs, the combination of competition and leaner budgets has introduced new challenges. Market-based strategic plans are necessary to ensure financial viability in the future. This includes assessing the hospital's and competitors' positions so that realistic priorities can be established.

Quantitative techniques such as net present value analysis allow a comparison among alternatives. Goal programming provides the means to measure specific proposals against diverse goals. Development of 3–5 year business plans can provide information valuable to capital budgeting decisions (5). Business plans are discussed in Chapters 3 and 5. This section presents the more commonly used quantitative techniques of return on investment, net present value, internal rate of return, payback method, and return on assets.

Return on Investment

One important concept in any long-term financial transaction is the time value of money. A dollar today will have a different value 1 year from now. The following discussion illustrates this idea. Return on investment (ROI) is a measure of profitability calculated on the expected revenues that can be generated from the cost of the investment. It is important to consider ROI when undertaking the purchase of capital equipment, and it should be used as a test when evaluating new equipment proposals. The relationship of annual income to profits, return on assets, and return on investment is shown below:

$$\text{Profit} = \frac{\text{Net Income}}{\text{Total Income}}$$

$$\text{Return on Assets} = \frac{\text{Gross Income}}{\text{Assets}}$$

$$\text{Return on Investment} = \frac{\text{Net Income}}{\text{Gross Income}}$$

$$\times \frac{\text{Gross Income}}{\text{Assets}}$$

$$= \frac{\text{Net Income}}{\text{Assets}}$$

Basically an investment will result in a profit as long as the rate of return exceeds the interest rate. For example, the purchase of an intra-aortic balloon pump (IABP) at $35,000 is expected to generate income of $12,000 per year for the 5 years of its useful life ($500 per use calculated at two uses per month multiplied by 5 years). Assume that the hospital wanted a full ROI in the first year. At two uses per month the cost would increase to $1,458 per use just to break even ($35,000/24 uses = $1,458). Further assume that investing the $35,000 instead of purchasing the IABP would yield 9% interest, or $3,150. To make the purchase decision requires a ROI greater than 9%, say 10%. So the IABP is purchased if the cost can return $1,604.16 per use ($35,000 + 10% or $3,500 = $38,500/24 = $1,604.16 per use). Did the hospital make money?

This becomes slightly more complicated and includes consideration of interest rates and the present value of money. Continuing the example in a 1-year time frame, the first consideration is interest rates, as shown in the following equation.

Cost × Rate of Interest × Time (in years)

= Interest

$35,000 × .09 × 1 = $3,150

The $3150 represents simple interest. At the end of the year the hospital would have $38,150 ($35,000 + $3,150). If purchasing the IABP and charging $1,604.16 per use for the 24 uses, the hospital would have $38,500, or a profit of $350 ($38,500 − $38,150 = $350). This represents a 1% ROI, not a $350 ROI, because the value of money is time related. To discount (or adjust) for the present value of money requires the reverse of the interest rate computation. For example, if $35,000 today is equal to $35,000 + $3,150 ($35,000 × .09) = $38,150 in 1 year, then thinking in reverse from future to present, $38,150 a year from now is only worth $35,000 today.

The above example is oversimplified for the sake of illustration and the sanity of those who are not mathematically inclined. It assumes the hospital paid cash and fails to take into consideration the usage patterns, time of reimbursement, and other factors. In reality the interest rate earned (or paid on a loan to finance the IABP purchase) would be compounded. Assuming compounded rates annually, the interest earned (or paid) in the first year would earn (or be charged) interest during the second and subsequent years. For example:

Year	Investment	Rate	=	Interest
1	$35,000	9%	=	$3,150
2	38,150	9%	=	3,434
3	41,584	9%	=	3,743
4	45,327	9%	=	4,079
5	49,406	9%	=	4,447
				$18,853

Assuming the IABP is purchased with a 5-year loan at a compound interest rate of 9% annually, the actual cost of the equipment is the sum of the purchase price plus the interest paid or $35,000 + $18,853 = $53,853. Put in the perspective of present value, $53,853 5 years from now is equal to $35,000 today. The sum that would need to be borrowed = $53,853.

Discounting dollars to present value in evaluating purchase decisions is a valuable tool. It is highly sensitive to the discount rate that is used and the time value of money. Evaluating various interest rates for various time frames can be translated to cost-benefit ratios. Comparisons of alternative equipment purchases is another advantage of present value analysis in determining ROI (6). There are formulas for calculating present value at a given interest rate over time, and for calculating income streams for future years. Tables are available to make computations easier as are financial calculators and software computer applications.

Net Present Value and Internal Rate of Return

Both net present value and internal rate of return are considered preferable analytic techniques because they are based on the value of money concept and use interest rate in computations. Net present value relates investment decisions to the cost of capital discounted over time. Internal rate of return assumes cash inflows or revenues that then can be reinvested to earn interest. This method may overinflate the return on investment if the revenue can only be invested at lower rates rather than at the same or greater rates of interest.

Payback Method

Payback method refers to the number of years required to recover the initial investment. Consider the IABP example. The cost of $35,000 is paid in cash and the expected life of the equipment is 5 years. Expected revenue is $500 per use and the usage is projected at two cases per month. Payback is calculated by multiplying the expected revenue per year and adding each year to the next. For example:

Year	($500 × 12 months × 2 per month)	Cumulative
1	$12,000	$12,000
2	12,000	24,000
3	12,000	36,000
4	12,000	48,000
5	12,000	60,000

The payback for the IABP purchase occurs in year three when the purchase price of the equipment is recovered. This method has obvious flaws. It fails to account for the time value of the money, it assumes the technology will be useful over an extended time, that the usage is constant over time, and that the equipment will be efficient. Payback methods may be of general use in evaluating purchases and estimating the time required to return the original investment (7).

Return on Assets

Return on assets (ROA) is defined as the net income divided by total assets. It is a measure of performance used by management to analyze various business strategies (8). In health care the investment in capital assets is an expensive proposition. Having large amounts of money tied up in assets that fail to produce revenues or revenues in proportion to the investment is impractical. ROA can be improved through efficient use of resources or by increasing the activity related to the asset; for example, the hospital may increase the number of procedures done.

One word of warning in using financial analysis, there are many assumptions to be considered and many factors that can influence final decisions. Using more than one method of analysis provides information for comparing financial outcomes. The important point is that analysis is a tool and should assist in decision making rather than be the absolute determinant.

Depreciation

Depreciation is a financial concept encompassing the decreasing value of capital assets, equipment, and buildings as they wear out or become obsolete over time (land can also be depreciated but this is unusual and therefore excluded from this discussion). The deterioration of the physical plant and capital equipment is treated as an allowable expense for income tax purposes, and is treated as a deduction from assets for accounting purposes. Depreciation is often misunderstood by managers because it is a paper rather than a cash transaction. The expense is accounted for on financial statements without the actual exchange of money. One way to think of depreciation is as a business expense that reflects the cost of doing business.

There are several accepted techniques for calculating depreciation, and organizations may use more than one method depending on the asset involved and the objective to be achieved. Variables in selecting one technique over another include: (*a*) life of the asset, (*b*) tax advantages and disadvantages, (*c*) changing technology, and (*d*) preference of the financial officer or governing body. There is disagreement on the best choice for calculating depreciation even among experts (9).

Three methods of calculating depreciation are practiced: straight-line, sum-of-the-years in digits (also referred to as sum-of-the-years-digits), and double declining balance. Straight-line depreciation assumes that the deterioration of the asset occurs at a constant rate each year. A ventilator that cost $10,000 with a useful life of 10 years and no salvage value would be depreciated at $1,000 per year ($10,000 divided by 10 years).

Straight-line depreciation is often used to depreciate the hospital structure because it is generally accepted that buildings depreciate at a fairly constant rate and that the same dollar figure may be used from one year to the next. Equipment depreciation is another matter. Rapid changes in technology may render equipment obsolete before it reaches the estimated useful life. This discrepancy in technological vs. useful life presents problems in planning for new equipment and in depreciating old equipment. For example, a ventilator with a technological life of 5 years but a useful life of 10 years may be considered for accelerated depreciation. This means depreciation will be calculated at higher rates in the initial years after purchase. Because depreciation is an allowable income tax deduction, accelerated methods result in less tax being paid in the higher depreciation or initial years and thus a tax advantage is gained. Lower taxes make more funds available for investment. This tax advantage assumes that the tax rate will remain the same or decrease. If tax rates increase, the advantage of accelerated depreciation may be questionable.

Both sum-of-the-years-digits and double declining balance are accelerated depreciation techniques. Salvage value of the equipment is subtracted in calculation of straight-line and sum-of-the-years-digits methods. The entire historical cost is used to calculate depreciation in the double declining method but an amount similar to salvage value is left at the end (10). Sum-of-the-years-digits is calculated in the first year using the following formula.

$$\$35{,}000 \times \frac{5 \text{ (years of life remaining)}}{\substack{15 \text{ (sum of total years} \\ 5+4+3+2+1=15)}}$$

$$= \$11{,}666.66$$

Sum-of-the-years-digits is calculated in the second year as follows, and so on.

$$\$35{,}000 \times \frac{4}{15} = \$9{,}333.33$$

Double declining depreciation is calculated by dividing the actual cost by half the number of estimated years of life in the first year, and in subsequent years the remaining balance is divided by half the number of estimated years of life. The equation below is used in the first year.

$$\$35{,}000 \div 2.5 \text{ (half estimated life)} = \$14{,}000$$

In the second year the following equation is used, and so on.

$$\$21{,}000 \div 2.5 = \$8{,}400$$

Debate over allowable depreciation centers on three main issues: (a) historical vs. replacement cost, (b) the estimated life, and (c) what part of depreciation should be included in reimbursement schedules. The first issue seems simple. The actual purchase price of the asset is the logical figure to use because it will reflect the allocation of costs over the period in which they are used. Replacement costs should be a separate issue. However, some hospitals prefer to use price adjusted levels to fund depreciation accounts. This ensures the cash reserves needed to invest in replacement equipment at higher prices (1). The second issue is estimated life. The American Hospital Association and most hospitals have a standard chart for estimating the useful life of capital assets. Depreciation is sometimes negotiated with third-party payors. The third issue is the most troubling to hospitals. If Medicare and other third-party payors are unwilling to adjust reimbursement (or will only pay part of the costs) to include an allowance for capital assets, hospitals must bear this cost.

Depreciation is the responsibility of the accounting department but a general understanding of the mechanism is helpful to nurse managers. The erosion of the hospital's capital base is important in the high-tech environment of critical care. Without the money to replace outdated technology, hospitals and critical care units will be faced with more "down time" as equipment wears out, repairs become more frequent, and obtaining parts causes lengthy delays in service.

Recording Capital Assets

The institution's balance sheet reflects the acquisition as an increase in equipment assets and, depending on the financing method, either a decrease in cash assets or an increase in liabilities. The bottom line is the same in either case. The example below illustrates changes in the balance sheet when a ventilator is purchased on short-term debt.

Assets	
Equipment	$1,000,000
+ ventilator	10,000
Total	$1,010,000
Previous Assets	$5,000,000
+	10,000
Current Assets	$5,010,000

Liabilities and Fund Balances	
Accounts Payable	$1,000,000
+ ventilator	10,000
Total	$1,010,000
Previous Liabilities	$5,000,000
+	10,000
Current Liabilities	$5,010,000

Purchase vs. Lease Decisions

Essentially all equipment can be leased. The decision to lease rather than purchase equipment requires an understanding of the types of leases, the advantages, and what reimbursement conditions apply. Leasing gives the institution (the lessee) the right to use equipment that is owned by another (the lessor).

There are two main types of leases to consider:

(*a*) operating and (*b*) capital lease option. The operating lease is generally used for short-term needs or low volume usage. The purpose is to obtain the service needed without incurring high capital costs. The payment agreement may be based on a minimum use period or a per use fee. The hospital can deduct the cost of the lease and interest as a business expense but the equipment belongs to the lessor. The capital lease option is basically a conditional sale and the hospital has the option of renewing the lease or of purchasing the equipment at a specified time. This type of agreement treats the equipment as property owned by the hospital and therefore depreciation as well as the interest portion of payments can be deducted for income tax purposes. A third type of lease, known as a true lease, allows the lessor to benefit from the tax advantages of ownership and the hospital to benefit by deducting rental payments as tax deductions. True leases include leveraged leases that provide lower rates for high tech equipment while decreasing the risk associated with obsolescence (11). Leasing options may become more diverse as hospitals seek new ways to manage capital.

There are several advantages to leasing. First, the cost of the lease may be reimbursed by third-party payors. This serves to minimize the cost differences between lease and purchase. A lease may provide better service since the lessor has a vested interest in maintaining equipment for optimal performance. Leasing makes cash available for other uses by the hospital and limits the investment in fixed assets. The risks of technological obsolescence are borne by the lessor rather than the hospital. Lastly, leasing is attractive when the cost of money (interest rate) is high (12).

The type of lease determines how it is accounted for in the hospital's financial reports. As with any expenditure, leases should be carefully evaluated before commitments are made. In some cases they may be more expensive than purchase.

In a recent survey of hospitals, leasing was cited as an emerging trend in the acquisition of high priced technology. Helicopters, air ambulances, and magnetic resonance imagers were the most frequently leased items, with ultrasound, lithotriptors, and mobile imaging also often obtained through rental or shared agreements (1). The sources providing lease options include product manufacturers, equipment dealers who sell or lease the products of several manufacturing firms, and independent leasing companies who make it a business to lease equipment.

CAPITAL FINANCING

A comprehensive discussion of debt financing is beyond the scope of this chapter. However, the nurse manager needs to understand how the current environment impacts the dollars available for capital expenditures. The basic scenario is the one depicted throughout this book. Since the advent of prospective payment system (PPS) in 1983, hospital profit margins have fallen and capital costs have continued to rise. Decreasing profit margins combined with decreased length of patient stay, decresed census, and increased cost of capital expenditures equate to an increase in costs per discharge. The problem can be demonstrated by supposing that 1000 patients per month are discharged and fixed expenses for debt financing are $1000/month. The redistributed cost is one dollar per patient. Now suppose that patient discharges fall to 500 per month while fixed payment on debt remains the same ($1000/month). The cost per discharge is now two dollars per patient. Assuming that patient discharges mean a lower average daily census, then revenues will decrease as patient census drops. The ratio of debt service to income therefore rises.

>Debt = $1000/month
>Income/1000 patients = $1,000
>Ratio = 1:1
>Debt = $1000/month
>Income/500 patients = $500
>Ratio = 2:1

This ratio increase means that more of the hospital's cash must be spent to service debt when there are less cash dollars available. The example is oversimplified to make a point. Taken further, what happens when more cash is needed to pay for fixed expenditures and less cash is taken in?

Suppose you have a combined family income of $10,000 per month and a fixed mortgage payment of $2,000 per month. Imagine that one income earner is terminated and income drops to $5000 per month. The mortgage payment (fixed) remains $2000/month.

Cash In = $10,000/month
Cash Out = $2,000/month
Ratio = 5:1
Cash In = $5,000/month
Cash Out = $2,000/month
Ratio = 2.5:1

What happens? First there is a loss of negotiating (credit) power. Then there are several options:

- Cut spending (decrease services and products);
- Refinance (at possibly higher rates);
- Defer maintenance (long-term risk);
- Sell the house (hospital);
- Increase income.

Some of these options are unrealistic for both households and hospitals.

Long-Term Debt

The capital budget may require the incurrence of long-term debt. Long-term refers to debt repaid over a period greater than 1 year. The decision to finance the acquisition of fixed assets with debt should take into consideration the facility's leverage ratio, or the proportion of debt to equity. This ratio will be used by lenders to determine the amount of risk associated with the loan.

Sources of Capital

Internal funds from operating margins are generally used to purchase lesser capital equipment items that do not qualify for tax-exempt financing. Gifts to the hospital are another method of acquiring equipment that is below a certain cost. Cash reserves from funded depreciation accounts is an internal source of funding for capital needs.

Depreciation is typically placed in an escrow or savings account to ensure the availability of funds when capital purchases are approved. The amount of money in these accounts often determines the level of funding possible for a hospital during a given year. In other words, there is a finite amount of dollars set aside for capital equipment. Of course, if hospitals use depreciation funds to cover operating expenses, this amount will fall short of capital equipment requests. Nurse managers need to be aware of how capital funding occurs so they can accept the rationale when requests are disapproved.

Internal funds from profits, gifts, and funded depreciation (sometimes at price adjusted levels) continue to be the primary sources of capital (1).

Financing Methods

Bonds are one mechanism used by hospitals to finance capital expenditures. Bonds are legal contracts between the issuer and the purchaser where the issuer pays an agreed upon interest rate. Bonds are usually issued to finance major construction or renovation projects and, therefore, additional or replacement capital equipment purchases in existing facilities are usually financed by other methods. Exceptions might be a hospital purchasing a magnetic resonance imager (MRI) that in itself is expensive but also may require renovation or construction to accommodate the equipment. Similarly, a hospital building a new critical care wing might issue a bond to cover the total costs of construction and equipment.

Bond rating, the risk associated with a hospital's ability to pay principal plus interest on issued bonds, is an emerging concern as hospital operating margins fall and their financial viability is questioned.

Bank loans are a source of capital but the cost of commercial loans is more expensive than tax-exempt financing and therefore used less often.

Equity financing has attracted interest in health care recently. Raising capital through partnerships or sale of stock provides the benefits of low cost capital, no interest debt burden, leverage by improving net worth and debt to equity ratios, acquisition through stock options, and personal incentives such as stock options and partnerships (13). The major disadvantage to equity financing is the dilution of ownership.

As health care continues to be challenged to cut costs, new and innovative financing mechanisms are likely to emerge. At the present time financing through taxable and tax-exempt bonds, public stock offerings, joint ventures, limited partnerships, and sales of streams of business to other institutions are all options for raising capital.

CONCLUSION

Capital budgeting will continue to receive attention as hospitals struggle with uncertainty and the risks of investing large sums in unprofitable projects. Critical care nurse managers must be prepared to justify their capital equipment needs. This chapter discusses the preparation of a capital budget, methods used to evaluate needs and products, and present financial aspects that affect capital purchasing decisions. Familiarity with the process and the terminology will enable nurse managers to negotiate for resources from a position of strength.

REFERENCES

1. Anderson HJ. Survey identifies trends in equipment acquisitions. Hospitals Sept 20, 1990:30–36.
2. Health Technology, Mar/Apr 1988;2(2):54–60.
3. Mark BA, Smith HL. Essentials of finance in nursing. Rockville, MD: Aspen Publishers, Inc., 1987:91.
4. Mark, p. 134.
5. Health Technology, Sept/Oct 1988;2(5):174–175.
6. Musgrave RA, Musgrave PB. Public finance in theory and practice. 3rd ed. New York: McGraw-Hill Book Company, 1980:184–185.
7. Mark, pp. 218–19.
8. Covaleski MA. The shifting nature of accounting practices in the health sector. In: Wolper LF, Pena JJ, eds. Health care administration. Rockville: Aspen Publishers, Inc., 1987:144.
9. Mark, p. 42.
10. Berman HJ, Weeks LE. The financial management of hospitals. 4th ed. Ann Arbor, MI: Health Administration Press, 1979:66–69.
11. Cerne F. Equipment leasing: a question of economics. Hospitals Nov 5 1987:86–87.
12. Mark, pp. 226–227.
13. Shields GB, Schnebel DJ. Financing of health care facilities. In: Wolper LF, Pena JJ, eds. Health care administration. Rockville, MD: Aspen Publishers, Inc., 1987:214, 224–225.

Appendix Chapter 7

APPENDIX 7.A. SOLE SOURCE JUSTIFICATION ZAP ELECTRONICS SERIES A MONITORING SYSTEM

The Ultra Medical Center has received approval to purchase a new monitoring system for the surgical intensive care unit (SICU). Based on a review of potential suppliers, we conclude that ZAP Electronics Series A uniquely fulfills our requirements.

Software developments in monitoring are in a constant state of change. The Series A is totally software based, the core of which is a unique microprocessor in each bedside unit. Applying this powerful processor to tasks at the bedside has some important and unique abilities.

Some of these unique functions include: the ability to see multi-leads from the same patient on the display simultaneously. Also, the system looks at and processes four leads simultaneously for purposes of arrhythmia analysis. This particular feature will greatly enhance diagnostic information. Additionally, multi-lead arrhythmia analysis comes standard in each bedside and is not dependent on a central processing computer. This obviates the problem of "down-time" on a central computer affecting all other units linked to it.

Traditionally, arrhythmia analysis linked to SICU monitoring has been structured rigidly in terms of arrhythmia calls. The Series A offers the unique advantage of "QRS shape review" allowing much greater nurse and physician input into the instrument's arrhythmia decision-making process.

The system also uniquely calculates and displays pulmonary artery wedge measurements. This resolves the problem of inconsistent measurements and difficulty in transcribing them accurately.

Also, ZAP provides a writer that will document four simultaneous waveforms. This device replaces three separate devices now in use i.e., a printer plotter, a multichannel recorder, and a video hard copy unit. Additionally, ZAP offers a unique 5-year warranty on the function modules solving the problem of service for many years.

The screen presentation is designed in such a way that data is presented in a clear and precise manner.

The technique of stroke writing resolves the problem of nurse eye fatigue while watching the screen for protracted time periods and produces data resolution much finer than anything available.

In conclusion, it was found that from the standpoint of system design, extended module warranty, and unique features, ZAP's Series A exclusively fulfills our requirements for monitoring.

Attachments
    Cost Estimate
    Financial Analysis
    User Evaluation Summaries

Chapter 8

Personnel Budgets

ANN S. BINES, KAREN GINTER

Nurse managers devote more time and energy to planning and controlling the personnel budget than to any other aspect of the operating budget. The personnel budget accounts for the largest expense in nursing budgets. Because nursing is more labor intensive in critical care, the personnel budget becomes a significant challenge to the critical care nurse manager. The challenge is to schedule the hours of care needed for quality patient outcomes according to the available skills, hours, mix, and preferences of staff. A thorough understanding of the components to be considered and the variables that affect the personnel budget will enable the nurse manager to proceed with confidence.

The personnel budget for a critical care unit is constructed from a knowledge of the personnel resources needed to accomplish the work of the unit and the corresponding costs.

Understanding the work of the unit is imperative in determining resources needed. The unit manager determines work load by identifying the nursing care needs of the patient population and projecting average patient acuity. Through this process, the unit manager develops strategies and objectives which are specific and pertinent to the upcoming budget. These strategies and objectives support and are congruent with the organization's overall mission, goals, and plan. The critical care manager recognizes that the plans may change as new programs and priorities emerge and that resource needs may vary from one fiscal year to the next.

Fiscal year objectives may refer to the quantity of work, such as patient days or census, as well as to those more programmatic in nature such as personnel, skill, mix, or staff orientation. The quality of work in patient outcomes and productivity must be identified with the process. Objectives have an impact on the number of full-time equivalent positions (FTEs) and their associated cost. The specific unit objectives and the assumptions about how the unit works will impact the personnel budget. Understanding and articulating all elements considered when developing the budget is key to defending and justifying a budget document.

The personnel budget is built based on assumptions which reflect quantity of activity, programs, structure, and functions. The resulting budget is a plan indicating FTE and dollar requirements needed to achieve objectives, and is a statement of financial outcomes or targets to be met. Actual unit performance can be measured against these targets. As the budget is implemented, variables and realities will be reported. Understanding the reports of variances from budgeted targets can only be accomplished if the original assumptions and methods for building the budget were logical and well documented.

This chapter identifies the components of the personnel budget and presents a variety of methods used by different hospitals in calculating staffing. Different approaches are used by hospital managers dependent upon the level of sophistication of the patient acuity system, availability and use of computer software programs, and degree of accuracy required. Each unit manager needs to be familiar and comfortable with the staffing methods used for budget planning.

FACTORS DETERMINING FULL-TIME EQUIVALENT POSITIONS

The critical care nurse manager considers many factors in determining FTEs for the upcoming fiscal year. Budgeted patient volume, direct care hours per patient day, indirect care hours per patient day, fixed FTEs, and FTE type are the components to be determined. These components of a personnel budget need to be viewed in relation to acuity, standards of practice, organizational culture, and costs.

Some hospitals determine FTEs through management engineering methods. These systems are designed to meet the following behavioral objectives of the management process: planning, organizing, leading, delegating, and controlling (1). Others use industrial engineering techniques to analyze work, work flow, time, and type of worker. This approach involves work sampling done by direct observation or chart review. Time and motion studies may be done to look at frequency, distance, length of time for task completion, and type of provider. The various times and frequencies are statistically computed for a projected census and result in the calculated number of FTEs needed.

Nurse managers may utilize a more descriptive, objective determination of staffing needs by calculating volumes and acuity, incorporating standards of care and practice for specific patient populations, and determining nurse:patient ratios based on identified needs. Each hospital may utilize standard formulas to convert these factors into FTEs. A variety of these formulas are presented.

Patient Volume

Patient volume is probably the single greatest factor in determining the number of budgeted FTEs, as it represents a quantifiable measurement of a patient care unit's work load.

Patient volume can be expressed as an annual or monthly number of patient days or as an average daily census (ADC). It is a statement of how many patients are to be cared for throughout a given time frame. A patient day is the equivalent of one patient in a bed at census time, which is often at midnight. An average daily census, multiplied by the number of days in a fiscal year, will indicate the annual patient days for the unit. For example, your critical care unit has a capacity of 19 beds. Your average daily census is 15. The annual patient days are 5475 (15 × 365). This may be reported as an occupancy rate of 79% (15/19). Volume projections are generally reported monthly.

Within the institution, the census or patient volume may fail to accurately reflect the activity and work load. Numbers of admissions, transfers, and types of patients may change rapidly from day to day. Some hospitals calculate patient census on the number of admissions multiplied by the average length of stay (Table 8.1). This type of census calculation reflects patient type, numbers, and average length of stay. The nurse manager may wish to compare the numbers of elective or scheduled admissions to emergency admissions. This figure may add information when considering staffing and scheduling patterns. Seasonal fluctuations of patient census also need to be identified; for example, if your unit is in a sun-belt state, you may see more admissions in the winter months.

To date, little work has occurred in calculating staffing based on patient outcomes and nursing diagnosis. Some hospitals with sophisticated data bases and computerization of data elements may have the information on nursing care that will help a manager determine staffing.

Bed Capacity vs. Occupancy

Occupancy is a percentage of total bed capacity. It is normally calculated by dividing average daily census by the capacity. Understanding the impact of bed capacity vs. occupancy leads to other assumptions in the budget-building process.

If a unit covers staffing needs with its own staff (part- and full-time staff permanently assigned to the unit), the impact of bed capacity vs. occupancy is great. When increasing staffing to meet high occupancy, success can be achieved if the difference between bed capacity and occupancy is minimal. If a unit routinely uses supplemental staffing options (float staff, on-call staff, "in-house PRN," outside agency staff, etc.), budgeting for a greater difference between bed capacity and occupancy can be tolerated. There are more resources available to be used at the peak times with this option.

In a unit that covers staffing needs without supplemental staffing options, the unit manager uses creativity and flexibility to meet patient needs. The manager discusses with the director how much latitude or "flex" is given in overtime, extra shifts, and part-time work over the allocated FTE. Productivity figures, patient outcome, physician preferences, and staff morale must be considered when occupancy nears bed capacity. If trends in increased occupancy remain constant for 2–3 months, discussions about FTE increases should be considered. The increased patient days will be reflected in the monthly reports. The unit manager must weigh the risks of overstaffing and the potential for future layoffs against being understaffed and facing subsequent morale issues. Staffing up to unit capacity can avoid discussions

Table 8.1. Census Calculation

DRG Class	Admissions		Length of Stay		Patient Days
DRG 122	350	×	3.1	=	1,085
DRG 110	145	×	2.9	=	420
DRG 121	110	×	10.2	=	1,122
DRG 88	210	×	8.7	=	1,827
DRG 95	76	×	13.4	=	1,021
	891			Total:	5,475
	Admissions				Patient Days

on bed closures, control the cost of expensive supplemental staff, and can assure the availability of specialized nursing staff as it is needed. However, productivity may be affected and will need to be monitored.

Direct Care Hours per Patient Day

Direct care hours refer to the "hands on" worked hours in providing nursing care to a patient over 24 hours. This calculation involves the patient classification system. Patient classification tools assist the manager by providing a methodology for determining the hours of care needed for a certain acuity and volume of patients. The amount of resources needed is based on patient care requirements for a given shift or day, and on the number of patients present for that period. Optimally, the patient classification tool should recommend the direct care hours per patient day that are needed. This information is then used to plan the direct care hours projected for a budget. The direct care hours required for a given volume of patient days converts into the core variable FTEs needed by that unit. The term variable implies that the core number of FTEs can vary as volume changes or as the amount of care per patient day varies. More intense care of patients will be reflected in higher direct care hours needed.

Determining FTEs for direct care hours can be done in a variety of ways. Three methods are discussed. Twenty-four hours of care are available each day; however, because of personal rest and time away from the patient doing nonpatient activities, less than 24 hours are provided. Nurse:patient ratios represent one method for determining hours of care (Table 8.2).

Based on hours of care needed, the direct care

Table 8.2. Nurse to Patient Ratios

Hours of Care	Nurse to Patient
24	1:1
16	1:1.5
12	1:2
8	1:3
6	1:4
4	1:6
2	1:12

hours in FTEs can be calculated. For example, you decide to deliver 16 hours of direct care for the 5475 patient days in your unit. The calculation would be:

$$\frac{16 \text{ hours} \times 5475 \text{ patient days}}{2080 \text{ (number of hours of FTE)}} = 42.1 \text{ FTEs}$$

You would need 42.1 FTEs to provide 16 hours of direct care every day for the 5475 patient days.

A second method involves average daily census, acuity, and work load (2). Your average daily census is 15 patients. These patients are divided in the acuity system as follows:

Type	Hours per Day	Acuity Constant	Census
II	8	1.0	2
III	12	1.5	8
IV	16	2.0	5

You next calculate the work load index (WLI) as follows:

Type	Hours per Day	Acuity Constant	Census	Weighted Census
II	8	1.0	2	2.0
III	12	1.5	8	12.0
IV	16	2.0	5	10.0
			15	24.0

$$\frac{\text{Weighted Census}}{\text{Census}} = \frac{24.0}{15}$$

$$= 1.6 \text{ Average WLI for Unit}$$

The weighted census is 24.0 with a WLI of 1.6. This translates into 12.8 (1.6 × 8 = 12.8) hours of care per patient. Converting this to FTEs, you would use the calculation:

$$\frac{12.8 \text{ hours of care} \times 15 \text{ census} \times 365}{2080 \text{ hours of FTE}}$$

$$= 33.7 \text{ FTEs}$$

A third method uses the number of patient days by type of diagnosis related group (DRG) and the classification category for the hours required to determine staffing hours (3).

DRG	Patient Days	Acuity Hours	Staff Hours Required
122	1,085	12	13,020
110	420	16	6,720
121	1,122	12	13,464
88	1,827	20	36,540
95	1,021	20	20,420
	5,475		90,164

$$\frac{\text{Staff Hours Required}}{\text{FTE}} \quad \frac{90,164}{2,080} = 43.3 \text{ FTEs}$$

These last two methods require knowledge about the patient classification system and trends about patient population type.

Indirect Care Hours per Patient Day

Another category of FTEs is determined by unit function and structure. Indirect care FTEs are related to indirect patient care functions. These functions refer to the activities that are not hands-on care, such as secretarial or monitoring functions, and management positions. For example, if a charge nurse is excluded from patient care assignments, due to other responsibilities such as responding to all hospital cardiac arrests, trauma calls, or administrative tasks, this position must be accounted for within the FTE budget over and above those FTEs allocated for direct patient care assignment. Other examples of indirect patient care positions may be equipment technicians and research protocol nurses.

Decisions must be made regarding the work load and need for these FTEs each shift. For example, you determine that a secretary is needed every shift. As there are 21 shifts a week (assuming three shifts of 8 hours each for 7 days), you will need 4.2 FTEs. (One FTE works 5 days a week or 0.2 each shift; therefore, 21 shifts × 0.2 = 4.2 FTEs). Perhaps you decide that the research protocol nurse is needed three shifts a week. This translates into 0.6 FTE (0.2 a shift × 3 shifts).

Indirect care hours are productive paid hours, providing the activities support patient care. Each facility decides what job classification is assigned as indirect care.

Replacement Time Positions

The personnel budget must include the costs of replacing staff while they are in a nonduty pay status (nonproductive paid time). An FTE represents 2080 total paid hours in a calendar or fiscal year (40 hours a week × 52 weeks). A percentage of this time is devoted to nonwork time, such as vacation, holiday, ill, education, or official business time. When these employees are not working, they may need to be replaced; therefore, the budget must account for the replacement.

Some hospitals use a straight percentage factor such as 10% to calculate the FTEs for direct and indirect care, assuming replacement is needed. For example:

43.3 FTEs Direct Care
× 10% = 4.30
4.2 FTEs Secretary
× 10% = 0.42
0.6 FTE Research Nurse
× 10% = 0.06
1.0 FTE Equipment Tech
× 10% = 0.10
49.1   4.88 FTEs needed for replacement

The budget requires 49.1 FTEs, plus 4.9 FTEs for replacement, for a total of 54 FTEs.

Other hospitals calculate the amount of nonproductive hours for each employee. In this circumstance, the nurse manager would identify the following:

1. Average vacation days taken;
2. Average holidays taken;
3. Average sick days taken;
4. Continuing education days;
5. Any official business days.

These would be added up in hours, multiplied by the number of FTEs, and divided by 2080 to convert to replacement FTEs. In the example below, you have 49.1 FTEs, and you discover the average employee used:

17 vacation days	× 8 hours =	136
8 holidays	× 8 hours =	64
5 sick days	× 8 hours =	40
2 continuing education days	× 8 hours =	16
0.5 official business day	× 8 hours =	4
	Total:	260 hours

$$\frac{260 \text{ hours} \times 49.1 \text{ FTE}}{2080} = 6.1 \text{ FTEs needed for replacements}$$

If a critical care course is offered for beginning or advanced clinical nurses, the time in the class must be allocated as nonpatient care time and be covered for replacement purposes. If replacement time is not allocated, overtime and use of supplemental staffing may increase.

The basic standard should be consistent across all units, with adjustments based on assumptions or objectives of specific units. For example, a unit which requires and pays staff to obtain special training may need a higher percentage of replacement time to cover the paid time off. If extensive training or orientation occurs during the staff member's first year of employment, the replacement time may also vary according to unit turnover. The length of time a new employee is not "counted" in staffing patterns can vary from unit to unit. This, as well as the specific unit's turnover, needs to be considered when budgeting for nonproductive time related to orientation and training.

The total of all replacement time FTEs should be based on the average amounts of nonproductive paid time expected for a fiscal year.

Management and Other Unit-Based Positions (Fixed Full-Time Equivalent Positions)

Fixed or overhead positions are budgeted for unit managers, clinical specialists, and nursing education and training positions, if applicable. FTEs in these categories represent positions which are responsible for overall management or specialized nursing functions that are generally unaffected by changes in patient volume or acuity. Thus, replacement time for these positions is usually unnecessary. The exception explained below is for management positions. This practice varies by institution.

These positions are considered fixed or overhead positions. In some cases, a position is split. One example is a relief charge nurse position that is 60% fixed and 40% variable. The budget will reflect a 0.6 FTE for management and 0.4 FTE for direct patient care. This means the relief manager assumes a routine patient assignment 40% of the time and performs a managerial or nondirect role function 60% of the time. Other fixed clinical positions might vary by volume in certain situations. For example, if a patient care service such as a pacemaker clinic or cardiac rehabilitation program is provided by a clinical specialist, the number of FTEs required might change as the demand for service changes. With increased demand, it might be appropriate to budget 1.5 FTE based on volume demand and to hire full- and part-time staff with the assumption they will cover each other for nonproductive paid time as needed, and not budget for the extra replacement time per FTE.

The number of management and other fixed positions are ultimately determined by unit structure and function. Fixed positions are largely determined by the size and complexity of the cost center (unit) and by the organizational definition of role responsibilities. For example, the greater the scope of the manager's role and the more decentralized the management environment, the greater is the need to allocate a 100% fixed FTE to the position.

FACTORS WHICH NEED NOT AFFECT FULL-TIME EQUIVALENT POSITIONS

Scheduling Patterns

The use of varied shift-scheduling patterns need not affect the FTEs required for direct patient care. Once the variable direct care FTEs are determined, how shifts are designated is more a matter of matching the patterns of work load with the scheduling of the work force. Eight-, 10-, and 12-hour shifts are commonly used in critical care for the benefit of patients, employees, and unit function. Shifts may overlap where predictable peak levels of activity dictate a need. For example, a surgical unit with a high volume of postoperative admissions occurring after noon and into the evening hours might use an 11:30 a.m. to midnight, 12-hour shift in order to assure adequate coverage for the high volume of patient care required during those hours. Overlapping shifts can be very functional when matched with work load. The unit manager must justify the need and variance. Units with consistent levels of work load over a 24-hour period need to avoid overlapping shifts to achieve cost-efficient services and effective use of personnel resources.

Part-Time vs. Full-Time Staff

A unit with an appropriate mix of part- and full-time staff can accomplish an even distribution of scheduling. This ratio may also be able to provide staff with every other weekend off, or more, depending on numbers. Assuming that one of a unit's objectives is an every-other-weekend-off staffing pattern and this unit has no part-time staff, the result may be overstaffing during the week and average or understaffing on the weekend. Part-time staff who work every other weekend may work less weekday shifts, which can correct the uneven weekday scheduling, while keeping total FTEs within the budgeted positions. Meeting staff needs for weekends off can be solved by many creative options. Weekend 12-hour shifts, the use of part-time staff, and weekend bonuses are options that can be used to accomplish appropriate staffing. Patient care needs must be met by adequate staffing every day within the budget parameters. The unit manager and staff can work on effective options that fit the patient, unit, staff, and budget needs.

Incentive Weekend Plans

Generally speaking, incentive weekend plans do not affect the FTEs needed. These are scheduling plans that offer a salary incentive to staff who choose to work only weekends (12-hour shifts, or three or four weekends per month) at inflated rates of pay. The dollars required are accounted for in the salary budget; however, this type of option does not decrease or increase the required direct care FTEs.

Minimum Staffing

Critical care units, which have a low average census and do not have the budgeted patient days to justify a predetermined level of staffing, must at least budget for minimum staffing. This is the type of unit which may have frequent census fluctuations requiring flexible staffing. In this case, the use of unit-based PRN staff, an on-call system, and overtime (within reason) may be necessary if the unit is self-covering.

Some nurses are willing to be crosstrained and oriented to other areas. If census is down in their unit, they may accept a reassignment to another unit. In this case, the nurse's worked hours are charged to the reassigned unit. This ensures that the salary budget of the unit with a low census is accurate.

Discussion needs to occur regarding priorities. For example, today your census is 10 and you have three RNs who are not needed. One decides to take a benefit day, one is willing to take a day off without pay, and the third is willing to work in the emergency room (ER). A few hours later you receive four patients: a post-code patient from the medical unit, a cardiac catheterization patient with ventricular dysrhythmias, an acute MI from the ER, and a postoperative open heart. Do you request the nurse from the ER to come back? What if they are busy and short staffed? Do you call the nurse back who took a benefit day? Do you utilize overtime? These questions must be considered before implementing a minimal staffing plan.

Student Employees

When nursing students are hired, they should be accounted for within direct or indirect care FTEs. Students may be employed in positions they are qualified to fill as nursing assistants, student technicians, or unit secretaries. In other cases, students may be hired temporarily to fill vacant staff nurse positions, which would be budgeted direct care FTEs. This can be done on a seasonal basis, depending on the pattern of staff nurse vacancies and the availability of students. In any case, students can fill any budgeted position; and, as long as they function within an appropriate job description, the unit can tolerate holding a position vacant while the student is employed. Students may be hired into unbudgeted temporary positions during seasonal periods of high census without compromising the unit productivity.

If students are consistently employed throughout the fiscal year over and above the required direct and indirect FTEs and, if the unit is fully staffed, the FTEs should be reflected within the budget and so designated. This may be done as a means of recruitment. These FTEs may be needed for only part of the year and can be budgeted based on the expected hours to be paid. For example, one FTE can be filled by several students all working full time for a short period of time.

FACTORS DETERMINING THE SALARY BUDGET

After all the determinations are made for finding the staffing numbers, the salary budget can be determined. Several factors determine the salary budget, including the base wage rate, specialty or certification pay, raises and salary adjustments, differentials and bonuses, overtime, on-call and call back pay, and supplemental and agency staffing. Each of these factors incur dollars to be expensed and added to the personnel budget.

Base Wage Rate

The base wage rate for a position is the hourly rate of pay paid to an employee before adding all other wage enhancements, e.g., differentials, bonuses, and overtime. The average base wage rate is the actual, average hourly rate paid to all employees in a single job classification. For example, the average base wage rate for staff nurses might be $15 per hour or for nurse aides may be $8 an hour. An average base wage rate will vary by job classification. The average base wage rate per job classification determined at the end of 1 fiscal year is the basis for setting the base salary dollars for the next fiscal year budget. This amount may need to be multiplied by a factor, if across-the-board adjustments are made for competitive market or retention purposes. The gross, weighted, average wage rate for the cost center can be determined by dividing the total budgeted salary dollars by the total budgeted paid hours (Table 8.3). Using the average base wage rate in the budget process is not as accurate as using the actuals.

Specialty Pay or Certification Pay

When the base wage rate is adjusted for staff working in a specialty unit or for staff with credentials (certifications) beyond the minimum requirements, the FTEs affected can be assigned the higher base wage rate; or if specialty or certification pay is handled as a differential, the dollars per hour for all hours paid in this category can be calculated and added to the base salary dollars. For example, certification pay would be calculated as follows:

$$\text{Total Certified} \times \text{Differential} \times \text{Hours} = \text{Budget Dollars}$$
$$35 \times \$2 \times 2{,}080 = \$145{,}600$$

The total certified amount needs to include those nurses currently certified, assumptions about any newly certified nurses, and any who do not maintain certification.

Paid time-off to obtain certifications is factored into the replacement time FTEs. Other expenses related to paying fees to maintain certification are usually handled within a nonsalary expense account (i.e., continuing education account).

Merit or Step Increase Raises

Merit or step increase raises should be factored into the salary budget. Merit factors may range from 0 to 8%. Some hospitals budget for the average. If all merit dates are at the same time, then the factor increase can be multiplied by all affected for the number of months in the fiscal year. For example, all merits for RNs occur in January, but the fiscal year starts in July. In this system, the merit factor of the average, 4%, would be applied for all RNs for 6 months.

Many hospitals implement merit on the employee's hire date. In this system, some hospitals expect the unit manager to be very accurate and

Table 8.3. Base Wage

Job Class	Numbers in Class	×	2080	×	1990 Base Wage	=	Total Yearly	×	Percent Increase 1991	=	1991 New Total
RNs	43.3	×	2080	×	$15.00	=	$1,350,960	×	1.05%*	=	$1,418,508
Secretary	4.2	×	2080	×	$8.00	=	$69,888	×	1.03%	=	$71,985
Research RN	0.6	×	2080	×	$18.00	=	$22,464	×	1.05%	=	$23,587
Equipment Tech	1.0	×	2080	×	$10.00	=	$20,800	×	1.00%	=	$20,800
Unit Manager	1.0	×	2080	×	$22.00	=	$45,760	×	1.05%	=	$48,048
Clinical Specialist	1.0	×	2080	×	$20.00	=	$41,600	×	1.05%	=	$43,680
Totals:	51.1										$1,626,608

Total Budgeted Hours = 106,288

Average Base Wage = $\dfrac{\$1{,}626{,}608}{106{,}288}$ = $15.30

* 5% increase due to market.

calculate the merit for each employee individually. This can be done with a spreadsheet on a computer. In other hospitals, it is assumed that the merit review dates are relatively evenly staggered throughout the year, so the average merit factor of 4% is halved to 2%, but calculated for all staff the entire year. This method of giving the 2% to all staff accounts for those hired at the end of the fiscal year, who would wait for 8 or 9 months before their merit was due. For example, Barbara was hired in April, 1990 with a merit due in April, 1991. The fiscal year starts in July, 1990, so from July to April, Barbara is not eligible for the merit. From April to June, Barbara would receive her merit amount, but the budget impact is only for 3 months rather than the entire year.

Differentials and Bonuses

Charge nurse, shift, weekend, and holiday differential dollars should be added to the salary budget by identifying all hours to be paid at the various differential rates, totaling this amount, and adding it to the salary budget. A spreadsheet through a software program can be very helpful.

Bonuses can be budgeted based on knowing how much is to be paid out, frequency, and the type of activity. For example, if the institution implements a $1,000 bonus for recruiting a nurse into the night shift and it is projected that 10 new hires would be recruited, $10,000 would be added to the salary budget for bonuses.

Overtime

Overtime occurs due to absenteeism, increased volume, increased acuity, mandatory meetings and minimal staffing. In the perfect world, if a unit budgeted FTEs to cover all needed paid hours for all unit functions, overtime would be nonexistent. Due to daily changes and unscheduled activities, some amount of overtime exists. Overtime is additional productive time paid at a higher rate of pay. Overtime is budgeted based on a projection that identifies the unit's historical amount of overtime and any additional amounts that may be needed for the new fiscal year (4).

Overtime is identified by the hospital and must meet state and federal guidelines. In some hospitals, overtime is paid after 40 hours of work, in others after 8 or 12 hours of work. The pay for overtime is often called premium pay and is usually the rate of pay for the hours worked at time and a half or at double time. Most hospitals do not like to go over 3–5% of the salary dollars for overtime.

The unit manager determines the percent of hours for each job class to be paid at the overtime rates. This amount is added to the personnel budget. For example, it is determined that 1% of the total budgeted hours will be overtime. A quick determinant is to use the average base wage rate to calculate dollars. In Table 8.1, total budgeted hours are 106,288 with a base rate of $15.30. At 1% overtime, 1063 hours will be paid at time and a half.

$$\$15.30 \times 1.5\% \times 1{,}063 = \$24{,}396$$

This amount covers the overtime pay. Some hospitals separate the premium pay of $7.65 (which is the additional amount added to the base rate) and put this amount in overtime pay and the base rate of $15.30 as regular hours.

On-Call and Call Back

Using a paid on-call system is one method of assuring availability of staff when using "flex-time" because of high census. On-call means the staff are available by phone or beeper to be called back into work if needed. "On call" may be for a shift, for 24 hours, or for a week. The staff member on call receives on-call pay for the hours of being on call. This rate of on-call pay per hour is totaled and added to the salary budget.

Some hospitals will pay an additional amount for travel time, if called back to the hospital. The rate of pay when called back is usually at the employee's regular rate of pay, unless it results in overtime.

For example, Stephanie is on call from Friday at 3 PM to Monday at 7 AM for the cardiac catheterization laboratory. On-call pay is $2 an hour. Stephanie receives 64 hours of on-call pay at $2, or $128. She will receive 1 hour travel time and her rate of pay, if called back.

Supplemental Staffing

Supplemental staffing from outside agencies or through per diem in-house pools usually costs more per paid hour than average base wage rates. The premium for these paid hours must be determined and added to the salary budget. The hours may already be accounted for in the FTE budget. However, this may not include orientation or continuing education hours. The total impact on the salary budget must be calculated.

Nurse manager Ruth has negotiated with her director, Mike, to cover two FTE vacancies with supplemental staff. Ruth decides to use the hospital's in-house pool. She identifies that the per diem nurse earns $20/hr. As she plans on covering two vacant positions, she will budget $83,200 for this staffing (2 × 2,080 × $20/hr).

Employee Benefits

The cost of employee benefits, such as social security tax, worker's compensation, life insurance, and pension, affects the budget. In some hospitals, this is calculated centrally by the finance department and allocated to each area. In other hospitals, it is the unit manager's responsibility to calculate employee benefits. The finance department will provide the current percentages for calculations.

DEVELOPING THE BUDGET FOR A CRITICAL CARE UNIT

The unit that will be used to develop the following budget is a 19-bed critical care unit for predominantly cardiovascular patients. The unit provides direct care by RNs and has ancillary staff.

Steps in Developing a Budget

I. Budgeted Patient Volume (Patient Days)

15 patient ADC × 365 = 5475 Patient Days
Occupancy is 79% (15/19)

II. Direct RN Care Hours per Patient Day (Method 3)

DRG	Patient Days	Patient Classification System Acuity Hours	Staff Hours Required
122	1,085	12	13,020
110	420	16	6,720
121	1,122	12	13,464
88	1,827	20	36,540
95	1,021	20	20,420
	5,475		90,164

$$\frac{\text{Required Hours}}{\text{Numbers of FTE @ 2,080}} = \frac{90,164}{2,080} = 43.3 \text{ FTEs}$$

PERSONNEL BUDGETS   **127**

III. Indirect Care Hours per Patient Day

Secretary:	4.2 FTEs
Research RN:	0.6 FTEs
Equipment Tech:	1.0 FTE
	5.8 FTEs

IV. Total Direct and Indirect FTEs

Direct:	43.3
Indirect:	5.8
	49.1

V. Replacement Time for Direct and Indirect (Nonproductive Time)

17 Vacation days	× 8 hours =	136
8 Holidays	× 8 hours =	64
5 Sick days	× 8 hours =	40
2 Continuing education days	× 8 hours =	16
0.5 Official business days	× 8 hours =	4
		260 hours

$$\frac{260 \text{ hours} \times 49.1 \text{ FTE}}{2080} = 6.1 \text{ FTEs needed to replace}$$

During Critical Care Course:

10 days twice a year for 20 staff

$$\frac{10(d) \times 8(h) \times 2(yr) \times 20(staff)}{2080 \text{ hrs}} = \frac{3200}{2080} = 1.5 \text{ FTEs needed}$$

Total replacement = 7.6

VI. Fixed FTEs
1 Unit Manager:
1 Clinical Specialist: $= 2.0$ FTEs

VII. Total All FTEs

Direct Care	43.3
Indirect Care	5.8
Replacement	7.6
Fixed	2.0

58.7 × 2,080 = 122,096 Total Hours

VIII. Calculate Salaries (two methods shown)
  A. Average Base Rate Method

  58.7 Total FTEs × $15.30 base wage × 2,080 = $1,868,069

  (This includes all direct, indirect, fixed, and replacement FTEs.)

  B. Job Classification Method
    1. RNs
      a. 43.3 FTEs
      b. Replacement $\dfrac{43.3 \times 260 \text{ hrs}}{2080} = 5.4$

128 PLANNING AND IMPLEMENTATION

    c. Total of 48.7 × $15/hr × 2,080 = $1,519,440
    d. Replacement during course

$$1.5 \times \$15/hr \times 2{,}080 = \$ 46{,}800$$

2. Secretary
    a. 4.2 FTEs
    b. Replacement $\quad \dfrac{4.2 \times 260 \text{ hrs}}{2080} = 0.5$
    c. Total of 4.7 × $8/hr × 2,080 = $ 78,208
3. Research RN
    a. 0.6 FTE
    b. Replacement $\quad \dfrac{0.6 \times 260 \text{ hrs}}{2080} = .07$
    c. Total of 0.67 × $18/hr × 2,080 = $ 25,085
4. Equipment Tech
    a. 1.0 FTE
    b. Replacement $\quad \dfrac{1.0 \times 260 \text{ hrs}}{2080} = .13$
    c. Total of 1.13 × $10/hr × 2,080 = $ 23,504
5. Clinical Specialist
    Total of 1.0 × $20/hr × 2,080 = $ 41,600
6. Unit Manager
    Total of 1.0 × $22/hr × 2,080 = $ 45,760

                  Total Salaries = $1,780,397

IX. Calculate Specialty Pay
    A. All RNs who achieve CCRN are paid $2/hr plus receive the cost of the exam or recertification fee reimbursed.
    B. Calculate Costs
    Currently 20 RNs are certified and 10 more have signed up for the February exam. All are AACN members. Assuming all 10 pass, the costs are:

        30 × $2 × 2,080   = $124,800
        10 @ $125 (cost of exam) = $ 1,250
        20 to recertify at $100   = $ 2,000
                        Total: $128,050

X. Calculate Merit
    A. Assume a 4% merit is given to all employees at start of fiscal year. Cost:

$$55.7 \text{ FTEs} \times (\$15.30 \times .04) \times 2{,}080 = \$70{,}904$$

($15.30, the average base wage, × 4% gives the new amount of merit.) Assume two vacancies and separate merit for head nurse.
    B. Individual method can be done on a spreadsheet with actual amount.

XI. Calculate Differentials and Bonuses
    A. Differentials
        1. Charge Pay $1/hr (covers hours when unit manager not available and other shifts)

$$16 \text{ shifts/wk} \times 8 \text{ hrs} \times 52 \text{ weeks} \times \$1 = \$ 6{,}656$$

2. Evening Pay $2/hr (assume one-third of RN staff work evenings = 16.2 FTEs)

$$16.2 \text{ FTEs} \times \$2/hr \times 2{,}080 \text{ hrs/yr} = \$ 67{,}392$$
$$1.4 \text{ Secretaries} \times \$2/hr \times 2{,}080 = \$ 5{,}824$$

3. Night Pay $3/hr (assume one-fourth of RN staff work nights = 12.2 FTEs)

$$12.2 \text{ FTEs} \times \$3/hr \times 2{,}080 \text{ hrs/yr} = \$ 76{,}128$$
$$1.4 \text{ Secretaries} \times \$3/hr \times 2{,}080 = \$ 8{,}736$$

4. Four staff rotate evenings and nights

$$4.0 \text{ Staff} \times \$2.50/hr \times 2{,}080 \text{ hrs/yr} = \$ 20{,}800$$

5. Weekends $1.50/hr (assume every other weekend) starting Friday at 3 PM to Monday at 7 AM)

$$47.5 \text{ FTE} \times \$1.50/hr \times 64 \text{ hrs} \times 26 = \$118{,}560$$

6. Holidays at $12/hr (assume eight holidays)

$$30 \text{ FTEs} \times \$12/hr \times 24 \text{ hrs} \times 8 = \$ 23{,}040$$

B. Recruitment Bonus = $ 10,000

XII. Calculate Overtime
Assume 3% of total budgeted hours with base wage of $15.30

$$122{,}096 \text{ hours } @ \; 3\% = 3{,}663 \text{ overtime hours}$$
$$3{,}663 \times \$15.30/hr \times 1.5 = \$ 84{,}066$$

XIII. On-Call and Call Back
Assume 64 hours every weekend on-call for 2 FTEs at $2 an hour.

$$64 \times 52 \times \$2 \times 2 \text{ FTEs} = \$ 13{,}312$$

Assume 12 call backs for average time of 4 hours plus 1 hour travel at $15/hr for two staff.

$$12 \times 5 \text{ hours} \times \$15 \times 2 = \$ 1{,}800$$

XIV. Supplemental Staffing
Use of two per diem nurses at $20 an hour

$$2 \times 2{,}080 \times \$20 = \$ 83{,}200$$

XV. Summary
The resulting budget for the critical care unit is summarized in Table 8.4.

APPROVAL PROCESS

The personnel budget for a critical care unit is usually quite expensive and of major interest to an organization. It is desirable to build a budget with all factors and assumptions clearly understood and documented. The budget should not overstate needs, yet should be realistic and agree with objectives. If budget targets for productivity and expense are to be met, the budget must be achievable. If any aspect of the budget must be reduced, it is best to know where those compromises can be made as it may affect the managing of the unit. The manager's ability to articulate the budget accurately and objectively can be a key factor in obtaining budget approval.

CONCLUSION

Various methods can be used to determine the personnel budget. Once the numbers and levels of

Table 8.4. Personnel Budget Fiscal Year 1991

	Cost Center: Critical Care Unit 1810	
010	Salaries—Regular	$2,077,663
020	Salaries—Overtime	84,066
030	Salaries—Differentials	337,136
040	FICA	179,918
050	Health Insurance	49,765
060	Life Insurance	6,220
070	Other	2,488
	Total Employment Cost:	$2,737,256

FTE Cost per Patient Day:

$$\frac{\$2,737,256}{5,475} = \$499.95/\text{day}$$

Gross Weighted Average of Salaries and Benefits:

$$\frac{\$2,737,256}{122,096} = \$22.42/\text{hour}$$

staff are determined, the various costs can be calculated. The unit manager must be aware of hourly wage, overtime, differentials, merit review, replacement costs, and use of supplemental staffing.

REFERENCES

1. Gillies DA. Nursing management: a systems approach. Philadelphia: W.B. Saunders Company, 1982:178.
2. Finkler SA. Budgeting concepts for nurse managers. Orlando, FL: Grune & Stratton, Inc., 1984:70–73.
3. Kirk R. Nurse staffing and budgeting. Rockville, MD: Aspen Publishers, Inc., 1986:13–19.
4. Finkler, p. 75.

Chapter 9

Staffing Methodologies

VIRGINIA J. DAVIS, DONNA L. BERTRAM

Mary Wilson, RN, has recently accepted the position of nurse manager of a 12-bed critical care unit (CCU). Mary knows from her interviews that the unit has an 83% annual occupancy rate. The patient population focuses on postoperative coronary artery bypass grafts, myocardial infarctions, dysrhythmias, and post-angioplasties. Mary was told that this unit is budgeted for 39.1 full time equivalents and currently has six vacancies. The staff had told Mary that their current staffing situation is of prime importance. Several of the unit's informal leaders are concerned with meeting patient care needs, overtime, and recruitment issues.

As the new nurse manager, Mary is interested in staffing the unit within the hospital's guidelines for productivity and budget allowances. She also desires to meet patient care needs and quality outcomes. Mary generated a list of questions to get her started on understanding the CCU's picture. The questions are:

1. What are the standards of care for patients in the unit?
2. What are the staffing standards and how were they developed?
3. What type of patient classification system is being utilized and how accurately does it reflect patient needs and staffing?
4. What are the unit's productivity standards and its work load index?
5. Why are there six vacancies; how long have they been vacant; and what is being done to recruit?
6. What staffing options are available and what is the skill mix of staff? and
7. What strategies have the staff developed for meeting unit needs?

Mary knows that staffing accounts for the largest expense in the operating budget, so understanding the steps and complexities of staffing will lead to decisions for control. She realizes that management works with people to accomplish work outcomes, so her goal is to balance the appropriate number and type of employees to meet and improve patient care within the budget. Mary decides to investigate the standards of patient care, staffing standards, patient classification, productivity, turnover, work load, staffing options, and staff participation. This chapter provides information that will help answer Mary's questions.

STANDARDS OF CARE AND STANDARDS OF PRACTICE

Mary is familiar with the work done by the American Association of Critical-Care Nurses (AACN) on standards. She found a copy of *Standards for Nursing Care of the Critically Ill* and reviewed the definitions for structure, process, and outcome. A structure standard identifies the following: the environment where care is given, the organizational relationships with other departments, equipment, physical facilities, and staffing. A process standard specifies methods, actions, and functions for nursing care delivery. The results to be achieved are the outcome standards (1). The new book she purchased also contains excellent information about patient care outcomes resulting from nursing care delivered. Mary agrees with the definition, "a standard is a statement of quality that serves as a model to facilitate and evaluate the delivery of optimal nursing care" (2).

Standards of care and standards of practice often are confusing to staff. A standard of care is what the patient can expect while hospitalized. A standard of practice is what the nurse implements to achieve patient outcomes. Often a standard of care is called a patient-care standard and the standard of practice may be identified as a practice guideline. The following simplified example clarifies these two standards.

Standard of Care	Standard of Practice
1. The patient can expect to be safe from injury while hospitalized.	1. The nurse will administer medications according to policy.
2. The patient can expect to be free from infection.	2. The nurse will appropriately follow the handwashing policy.
3. The acute myocardial infarction patient can expect to be pain free upon discharge.	3. The nurse will manage pain control with the patient and provide instructions upon discharge.

Mary remembers that standards have been promoted by the American Nurse Association, the Joint Commission on Accreditation of Healthcare Organizations (JCAHO), the AACN, and other nursing organizations. She knows that the focus today is on outcome standards, but she reviews the CCU standards to ensure that structure and process standards are covered. Some examples she finds are:

- Structure
  1. All electronic systems, electrical equipment, and patient-supplied electrical equipment used in the CCU are inspected and documented as safe:
     a. Before initial use;
     b. After repair;
     c. Quarterly;
     d. By a biomedical engineer; and
     e. Removed from patient care if unsafe.
  2. Emergency equipment and supplies are readily accessible, centrally located, and inspected every shift to ensure completeness and proper functioning.
- Process
  1. The critical care nurse will collect assessment data on admission, every shift, during a change in condition, and on transfer from the unit.
  2. The critical care nurse will document findings through the use of the exception model of charting using data, action, response, and evaluation formats.
- Outcome
  1. The patient will be free from constipation on discharge.
  2. The patient's pain will be controlled while in the CCU.

Mary is encouraged that this unit has developed standards. She will want to work with the staff in using AACN's outcome standards, which promote quality care. She is excited about the integration of these outcome standards into practice and decides to ask for volunteers to serve on a task force to review and implement them in the unit.

Standards are formalized statements that establish a level of performance against which the quality of structure, process, or outcomes can be judged (3). Standards serve as a measuring tool to compare performance. A written standard alone is not the ultimate authority, but must be considered along with the nurse's judgment, the patient's circumstances, and acceptable practice.

Staffing

Hospital policy, regulatory considerations, method of care delivery, patient needs, standards of practice, projected patient days, anticipated acuity, and physical layout are all considerations when establishing a staffing plan for a nursing unit. Other factors to be considered are the expected cost per patient day, availability and educational levels of personnel, and contingency conditions. Staffing, Mary knows, includes integrating all these activities into providing an adequate number of the right type of employee on every shift every day. She needs to review the hospital's staffing philosophy, master staffing plan, staffing policies, staffing objectives, what shifts are customarily used, and how the work is distributed on each shift throughout the week.

The hospital's staffing philosophy identifies matching the knowledge, skills, and abilities of each employee to the needs of the patient or area assigned. The hospital where Mary is employed identifies the need for registered nurses (RNs) in critical care supplemented by ancillary personnel for nonnursing tasks. Additionally, management supports certification in the nursing specialty. The hospital's administrator had learned about AACN's demonstration project from the director of special care services. The administrator was impressed that a higher number of certified critical-care registered nurses (CCRNs), in critical care, had a positive effect on mortality, morbidity, quality, and retention (4). Convinced that certification is a better measure of knowledge and skills than the number of education programs a nurse attends, she decided to promote achieving CCRN status by offering a salary differential for certified nurses.

Included in the hospital's staffing philosophy was the issue of decentralization. Each unit manager has 24-hour responsibility and accountability for unit staffing. An internal professional resource team provides a pool of nurses available to help meet unit needs.

The master staffing plan identified that 4-, 8-, 10-, and 12-hour shifts are available. It explained routine start times, vacation and holiday requirements, and core staffing for average daily census. The unit staffing plan was consistent with the hospital's master staffing plan. The critical care director would review Mary's plan for the next fiscal year and when it was approved, forward it to the vice president for nursing.

Mary next read the unit's staffing policies and plan. The unit policy identified minimum numbers of staff, qualifications, annual skills review, continuing education requirements, and the renewal process for special privileges. The policy also described the collaborative efforts of the unit manager with the medical director and their designees in meeting the goals and objectives of the unit. In this policy, Mary read about the admission criteria, the divert process, and how pediatric patients would be cared for while in the unit. Mary made a note to check how the competencies were maintained for CCU nurses who delivered pediatric care. The unit policy addressed reassignment, rotation, on-call, call back, and call-off situations. Mary learned about priorities in using full- and part-time nurses, internal resource teams, and agency nurses. She also read about medical associates who had clinical privileges. These medical associates are employees of a physician and have a limited scope of practice.

In reviewing the unit's staffing objectives, Mary found the following:

1. A professional, registered nurse staff would supervise patient care.
2. Secretaries crosstrained as nurse technicians would be assigned to every shift to do non-nursing and secretarial duties.
3. A 1:1 ratio would be used for all Type V patients and a 1:2 ratio would be used for Type IV patients.
4. A clinical nurse specialist (CNS) was budgeted for the unit.
5. Flexibility was encouraged through the use of 4-, 8-, 10-, and 12-hour shifts.

Mary determined that an adequate weekly staffing pattern was established. She was aware that predicted patient census and acuity determined CCU's budgeted positions. Mary understood that her position and the CNS position are excluded from direct care giver hours category. The secretaries enter computer data including charges, physician and nurse orders, and stock requests; answer the phone, intercom, and call lights; greet visitors to the unit; and perform nurse technician duties. Their positions are included in the fixed indirect hours category.

Given the critical nature of the CCU patients, the distribution of work activity was fairly evenly spread among 7 AM–3 PM, 3 PM–11 PM, and 11 PM–7 AM shifts. Mary noticed, however, an increased work load on the 7 AM–3 PM shift, which was associated with an increase in patient and physician activity. The resulting work load distribution was 40% on 7 AM–3 PM, 30% on 3 PM–11 PM, and 30% on 11 PM–7 AM The work load tended to be greater Tuesday through Friday due to the surgery and cardiac catheterization schedules.

Mary noted that the method of care delivery was primary nursing. Mary is concerned with the nursing shortage, retention, and increasing acuity of the patients. She plans on learning more about case management and innovative ways to deliver critical care. She knows that home care nurses are taking care of critically ill patients. She makes a note to meet the home care nurses and learn how they might work together in the future.

Before Mary calculates the staffing plan, she needs to know about the patient classification system, productivity, work load, and turnover.

PATIENT CLASSIFICATION SYSTEMS

Patient classification systems (PCSs) provide a means for differentiating among patients based on their requirements for nursing care. Florence Nightingale in the 1860s identified the value of differentiating between medical and surgical patients because of their unique and separate needs.

Interest in PCS increased in the 1980s due to a nursing standard in the JCAHO survey process and the need to better identify staffing needs related to patient acuity. Greater emphasis on cost effectiveness caused hospital managers to focus on better staffing methodologies. With increasing technology, shorter length of patient stay, higher acuity, and the nursing shortage, the need for efficient and effective nursing care requires that patient classification systems or acuity systems be accurate, reliable, and valid.

In the 1960s the first type of PCS was developed at The Johns Hopkins University and was used to predict nurse staffing levels from shift to shift (5). Many PCSs have been abandoned, changed, or improved in order to provide more useful information. Mary knows that many nurses use the acuity system inappropriately, believing that getting credit for nursing care results in more staff. DeGroot identified that the PCS determines, validates, and monitors individual patient care requirements over time in order to determine staffing, patient assignments, budget planning, case mix analysis, cost of nursing services per patient, variable billing, and maintaining quality (6).

There are two general types of patient classification systems in use. The first is the prototype system, which generally describes the characteristics of patients typical to each category, and then matches patients to fit those general characteristics. The second system is called factor and is based on a number of indicators or descriptors of direct care requirements which are separately rated, timed, and then combined to designate a score which places the patient in a category (Table 9.1). The prototype system is subjective and has the potential for variability caused by those rating the patient. For example, two nurses rating the same patient at the same time may classify the patient differently. The factor type system identifies more objective data in describing the direct care indicators. It does not include all of the specifics for each patient, but groups like functions as major indicators of patient needs. A factor type system can be done in two ways: the forecasting mode is based on anticipating patient needs; the second method is to choose the indicators that have actually been done for the patient. Either methodology for factor type PCSs tends to be more accurate and objective than the prototype system (7).

A PCS is a management information tool. It does not provide the answers to Mary's questions by itself. Mary discovers the unit uses a factor type system that is considered useful and reliable. The PCS had several attributes which contributed to Mary's sense of confidence with the system. This system:

Table 9.1. Prototype and Factor Classification Systems

I. Prototype
  Category I: Patient self-care or requires partial assistance. Patient has short-term acute, episodic problem.
  Category II: Patient has chronic disease with an acute illness. Requires assistance.
  Category III: Patient has severe chronic or severe acute illness. Requires constant assistance.

II. Factor
  Points: 2 Complete bed rest
           3 Complicated dressing change
           3 IV with prn meds
           6 Total feed
          10 Two invasive lines
           8 Patient teaching of new skills

  Category I: 0–10 points
  Category II: 11–20 points
  Category III: 21 + points

1. Predicts nursing care requirements for individual patients;
2. Validates the amount of care given and reflects attributes of individual patients;
3. Requires less than 1–2 minutes per patient and is easy to use;
4. Evaluates trends of care delivery by shift and care-giver level through an audit trail;
5. Is applied throughout the hospital so that group care requirements are similar;
6. Is analyzed yearly for accuracy, applicability, and reliability;
7. Relates nursing care requirements to staffing, shift by shift, and week to week for each unit;
8. Receives support by the staff, as they perceive it differentiates between patients and indicates the appropriate number of hours of care; and
9. Maintains a high degree of inter-rater reliability.

Mary supports the use of inter-rater reliability. Inter-rater reliability indicates the degree to which different nurses agree when classifying the same patient independently of each other. Mary discussed the content validity of this PCS with the director of nursing systems. Content validity means the tool measures what it is supposed to measure; refers to the amount that the tool samples; and indicates that items are progressively weighted in relationship to one another. For example, simple and complex functions are weighted differently. Mary also knew it was reliable in that it provided consistent results.

Mary knows the process involved in identifying indicators and developing standards to be used in PCS. The development of these standards are based on current staffing practices, community and professional standards, administrative needs and desires, nurses' opinions, and management or industrial engineering judgments. This process establishes standards that indicate the average nursing time and category of employee required by patients in each acuity level. Often a panel of clinical nurses will identify, with the manager, all of the critical indicators involved in providing nursing care. Each of these data elements needs to be identified by level of care giver performing the task, what knowledge is needed, and the time needed by the average person to perform the indicator. The goal is to identify the fewest indicators that accurately predict patient care needs. More is not better. Then, weights are assigned to the indicators. For example, a patient with an intra-aortic balloon pump may reqire an RN for a longer period resulting in a higher weight than a patient with an oxygen mask. The indicators must be identified for all three shifts and decisions about the distribution of the work made. Samplings, time and motion studies, and review by a panel of nurse experts help with this process.

Two methods used in developing or updating classification systems are time studies (recording the time it takes to complete an activity) and work sampling observation (recording the activity observed at specified time intervals). Both methods document the level of care giver engaged in the activity and include "personal time" activities such as breaks. Observers are trained for this assignment, which is actually a type of observation research. Sometimes the two methods are combined and the data integrated into the classification system.

Several years ago, both of the book editors were involved in "second generation" data collection to update a "first generation" staffing methodology using medical and surgical patient classification systems. The classification system defined four discrete levels or acuity categories for patients and the nursing hours of care needed for each acuity level. Preparation for the "observer" (as the name badges read) role included a week of intensive training. Background, rationale, procedures for observing and recording data, and how the data would be analyzed and used were included in the training. Each of us was assigned to a four-member RN team. Teams were then assigned to each of the hospitals selected as a study site. Data was collected for three 24-hour periods, including one 24-hour period on a weekend. The 24 hours were divided into 12-hour shifts with two nurses working each shift. Observations were made and recorded by each nurse every 10 minutes. The actual timing of observations and the location of the observation were selected at random. Additionally, questionnaires on staffing, unit activity, census, and work loads were completed by charge nurses each shift. Data were compiled and analyzed, and new classification hours per patient day for the four category levels in medicine and surgery were published. The work sampling study provided the validation for the tool. The experience was enlightening and turned a former skeptic of classification systems into a firm believer in them. When well designed and used correctly, they are a powerful management tool.

Some systems build in a constant factor to include both patient and staff activity. The patient constant includes bathing, bed changing, and meals. The staff constant includes personal rest and wait times. The points and times are added separately to determine the categories for each type of patient classified. For example, in Mary's unit there are five categories of patient care requirements (Table 9.2). Most of the patients in this unit will be in category IV and V, requiring 12 hours and 20 hours of care per day, respectively.

Coupled with the PCS data, standards had been set for the CCU. These standards relate to the percentage of work done on each shift, what level

Table 9.2. Patient Classification

Patient Classification System Type	Hours Per Day
I	3
II	5
III	8
IV	12
V	20

of personnel are needed, and what level is needed for unit operations. These standards help identify the number and level of staff, assuming the mix of level IV and V patients remains at what was projected (Table 9.3). From this, 168 hours of care a day are required. Then the distribution of the activity is calculated for the amount needed on each shift. The fixed, indirect care providers are added with the shifts they work each week. In this example, a factor of 10% is calculated for nonproductive time. The shifts per week (0.2 a shift) are multiplied by the productive (100%) and nonproductive (10%) to determine paid full-time equivalent positions (FTEs) to meet the projected type of patients. From this a schedule can be established (Table 9.4).

Mary has clarified patient care standards and PCS development with her staff. She feels comfortable that the classification standards are weighted and valued so that the sicker critical patient who requires more direct nursing care accumulates more hours. She decides to look at productivity next.

PRODUCTIVITY

Productivity is a measure of efficiency and quantifies the relationship of outputs to inputs as a result of certain processes. Productivity takes labor, materials, and equipment and converts them into services and goods. It is defined as a ratio of outputs to inputs (8). It can also be viewed as the ratio of revenues received to cost of production; standard hours to hours worked; or patient outcome to nursing care (see Fig. 9.1). Integrating these aspects shows how productivity with inputs and outputs affects the care process.

Productivity measures in the manufacturing industry in the first part of the century related to standard hours for production of the renowned "widget" and the material costs of its production.

Table 9.3. Staffing Calculations

Average Daily Census = 10
Average Acuity = Type IV = 4
Type V = 6

Work Distribution by Shift
7–3   40%
3–11 30%
11–7 30%

Shift Configuration   8 hours
Hours of care/day   4 pts × 12 hrs (Type IV) = 48 hrs/day
6 pts × 20 hrs (Type V) = 120 hrs/day
168 hrs/day

168 hrs/day
8 hrs/shift = 21 shifts/day

21 × 40% = 8.4   7–3 shifts
21 × 30% = 6.2   3–11 shifts
21 × 30% = 6.2   11–7 shifts
             21 shifts

21 shifts/day × 7 days/week = 147 shifts/week

Head Nurse =   5 shifts/week
Clinical Nurse Specialist =   5 shifts/week
Secretaries =   21 shifts/week
Care Givers =   147 shifts/week
                              178 shifts/week

Nurse Manager =   5 shifts/week = 1 FTE × 110% =   1.1
Clinical Nurse Specialist = 5 shifts/week = 1 FTE × 110% =   1.1
Secretaries =   21 shifts/week = 4.2 FTEs × 110% = 4.6
Care Givers =   147 shifts/week = 29.4 FTEs × 110% = 32.3
                            178 shifts/week = 35.6 FTEs × 110% = 39.1 FTEs paid

STAFFING METHODOLOGIES

Table 9.4. Staffing Schedule

	S	M	T	W	TH	F	S	Total Shifts
Head Nurse		1	1	1	1	1		5
Clinical Nurse Specialist		1	1	1	1	1		5
7–3								
Secretary	1	1	1	1	1	1	1	7
RNs	8	8	8	9	9	9	8	59
3–11								
Secretary	1	1	1	1	1	1	1	7
RNs	6	6	6	7	7	6	6	44
11–7								
Secretary	1	1	1	1	1	1	1	7
RNs	6	6	6	7	7	6	6	44
								178

$\dfrac{178 \text{ shifts/week}}{5 \text{ shifts/week}} = 35.6$ full-time positions

$35.6 \times 110\%$ (includes nonproductive time) $= 39.1$ FTEs

39.1 FTEs $\times 80\% = 31.3$ FTEs as full-time positions

39.16 FTEs $\times 20\% = 7.8$ FTEs as part-time positions

$$\text{Productivity} = \dfrac{\text{Output}}{\text{Input}}$$

$$\text{Productivity} = \dfrac{\text{Revenue Received}}{\text{Cost of Production}}$$

$$\text{Productivity} = \dfrac{\text{Standard Hours}}{\text{Hours Worked}}$$

$$\text{Productivity} = \dfrac{\text{Patient Outcome}}{\text{Nursing Care}}$$

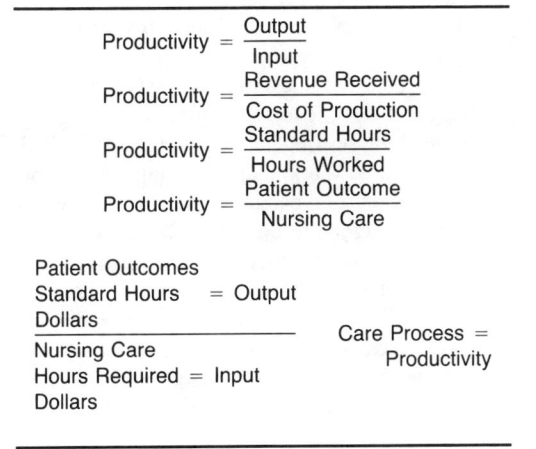

$$\dfrac{\begin{array}{l}\text{Patient Outcomes}\\ \text{Standard Hours}\\ \text{Dollars}\end{array} = \text{Output}}{\begin{array}{l}\text{Nursing Care}\\ \text{Hours Required} = \text{Input}\\ \text{Dollars}\end{array}} = \begin{array}{l}\text{Care Process} =\\ \text{Productivity}\end{array}$$

Figure 9.1. Productivity.

A plant manager could easily determine the productivity of the plant by comparing actual hours and actual material costs (inputs) for widget production to the established standard for production and the amount actually produced (outputs). Productivity could be affected by an increase or decrease in labor costs, material costs, labor hours, or demand.

Mary knows that staff often have problems with the concept of productivity. She believes that there is a lack of understanding and a fear about focusing more on the business side than on the patient side. She wants to make sure she understands productivity, how to manage it, and its effect on quality and cost.

When examining a unit's productivity, the words efficiency and effectiveness must be considered. Mary remembers the old adage, "Efficiency is doing things right, and effectiveness is doing the right thing." Mary will need to determine if the established care and practice standards make a difference in relationship to patient outcome. Determining if the output produced is valuable to the patient is another component of productivity. Mary knows the importance of the question "what is a better way?" because it leads to a more productive environment. She also is aware that costs are important, as the direct and indirect care provided are inputs to be compared to the outputs of the revenue received. Dollars and hours per patient day are important measures of productivity.

In measuring nursing productivity, Mary wants to know the comparison of direct worked hours to earned hours from the acuity (PCS), and the total paid dollars to man hours worked. She knows that this data is available and can be understood. The CCU's productivity will present a picture of the unit's performance (Table 9.5). In Mary's analysis, she sees that the earned hours by the acuity system as compared to staffed hours provided a 99.6% productivity for the patient care side. She also had 128 hours of paid time off and 74.3 hours of secretarial, management, and clinical specialist time. When the patient hours of direct care are added to the other paid hours, she had 823 hours compared to a budget of 612 hours resulting in actual paid productivity of 74.4%.

Mary understands that productivity on the output side results in patient outcome, standard hours, and budgeted amounts; while on the input side are the nursing care provided, actual employee hours, and actual dollars. The meeting of these two forces involves a care pathway. For example, some of the patients in the CCU have unstable angina, which is DRG 140 with an average LOS of 4.1 days and a DRG payment of $2103. Mary knows that balancing inputs and outputs in the nursing care of this patient affects productivity. Mary and her staff have identified nursing actions for the care pathway of this patient (Table 9.6).

Outputs in this situation related to effectiveness are the clinical outcomes of pain control, dysrhythmia treatment, and patient and family understanding of the disease. The nursing actions taken are the inputs of effectiveness. The input part of this efficiency productivity ratio can be the patient's actual length of stay in the CCU. The productivity ratio that examines value would include the output of revenue received and the input of costs for providing the care for this patient. Mary is assured that the care pathway format for identifying standards of care and practice is valuable and will provide adequate information for measuring the unit's productivity in terms of efficiency, effectiveness, and value. She believes this will improve quality.

Mary is responsible for managing productivity. She can do this by monitoring and controlling amounts of paid time off, flexing staff to volume and acuity, monitoring and controlling all non-regular pay such as overtime and premiums, and trending what was budgeted and earned from the acuity system. Mary discovered an article which identified high employee morale as the primary condition in being able to attain and maintain productivity (9). She makes a note to review this article again. Mary decides that to improve productivity, she can utilize participative management, quality improvement programs, flexible staffing schedules, and promote the clinical advancement program. She believes that these methods will lead to higher employee morale. She remembers that the staff had concerns about work load and turnover. She now focuses on these aspects.

WORK LOAD

Work load is determined by the patient census and acuity. The PCS provides a mechanism for reliably quantifying the nursing care hours needed. The PCS used in Mary's CCU has five acuity classifications. Each level has a number of assigned hours which comes from the work standards identified in the factor type system. Historical census and PCS data provide information for projecting staffing and work load. This information is useful in establishing staffing patterns and justifying budgeted positions. Work load, or the amount of work to be done, must be balanced with the numbers of personnel assigned to do the work (Table 9.7).

Work load index (WLI) is a term used in conjunction with many classification systems. The WLI is derived from the constants given to each acuity type. The premise is that one acuity type is the norm and this normative acuity type is given the constant of 1.0. All of the other acuity types are driven from

Table 9.5. Unit Productivity

		Productive Hours			
Volume	Reg Care Hours	Other Hours	Earned Acuity Hours	Total Staffed Hours	Patient Productivity
34	554	66	618	620	99.6%
		Other Paid Hours			
Fixed	PTO		Total Budgeted	Total Actual	Budget Productivity
74.3	139		612	833	73.4%

Table 9.6. Patient Plan

Unstable Angina
DRG 140
Average Length of Stay 4.1
DRG Payment $2103

Clinical Outcomes:
  Pain controlled with activities of daily living throughout CCU stage.
  Dysrhythmias detected and treated prior to progression to lethal stage while in CCU.
  Patient and family understand disease process prior to discharge from CCU.

Common Complications:
  Hemodynamic instability
  Lethal dysrhythmias
  Progression to acute myocardial infarction

CCU Stay	Day 1	Day 2	Day 3
Nursing Actions	IV maintenance Cardiac monitoring Vital signs at 1 hr × 4, then at 4 hr. I & O Bathroom privileges Teaching module to patient Admission assessment Pain control	Implement module Shift assessment	To med surg area Telemetry QID VS DC I & O Ambulate Begin discharge instructions
Nursing personnel	RN	RN	RN
Hours of care	12	12	5

Table 9.7. CCU Work Load

Census × Acuity = Work Load

PCS Type	Hours per day	Number of Patients	Nurse: Patient	Total Earned Hours
I	3			
II	5			
III	8			
IV	12	4	1:2	48
V	20	6	1:1.2	120
				168 Hrs earned

168 hrs ÷ 8 hrs = 21 shifts

Work Load Determination

Number of Patients/Type × Number of Hours/Type = Hours Earned

$$\frac{\text{Number of Patients/Type} \times \text{Factor Type}}{\text{Total Number of Patients}} = \text{Work Load Index}$$

Total Census × Workload Index = Weighted Census

the norm. Average WLI can be used to project patient days for the unit and can easily transfer into needed hours and staffing. By using the WLI, one can see that the med surg unit with 20 patients will need about the same numbers of nursing care hours as the CCU with 10 patients. WLI of 1.0 translates into 8 hours of care per day per patient, and WLI of 2.1 translates into about 16.5 hours of care per day per patient. Census multiplied by the unit's WLI gives a weighted census. The number of hours earned, the work load index, and the weighted census are all mechanisms which help the CCU compare its productivity to established standards. See Table 9.8 to determine work load.

Nurses often refer to "heavy" patients. Usually the nurse is expressing that the WLI is greater than anticipated. This is why using the WLI and weighting the census can be helpful for staffing. Nursing work load may increase due to various external factors such as seasonal fluctuations, weather conditions, community issues, political pressures, and economic conditions. Predicting external factors can be based on historical trends, but are not absolute.

TURNOVER

Turnover in a nursing unit is another source of valuable information that can affect morale, budget, recruitment, and retention efforts. Turnover is defined as the percentage of employed nurses who leave their jobs during a time period (10). Turnover can significantly impact cost and quality in managing patient care needs.

Table 9.8. Work Load Index

PCS Type	Hrs per Day	Constant	Average Daily Census	Weighted Census
I	3	.4		
II	5	.6		
III	8	1.0		
IV	12	1.5	4	6.0
V	20	2.5	6	15.0

$$\frac{6 + 15}{10} = 2.1 \text{ Average WLI for CCU}$$

Med-Surg Unit Average Work Load Index = 1
CCU Average Work Load Index = 2.1

Med-Surg Predicted Census = 20
20 × 1 = 20 Weighted Census

CCU Predicted Census = 10
10 × 2.1 = 21 Weighted Census

The computation of turnover is:

$$\frac{\text{Number of Terminations}}{\text{Average Number of Employees}} \times 100\% = \% \text{ Turnover}$$

This provides for both part- and full-time employees. Turnover rates for nursing units need to be determined by category of personnel, e.g., RNs, LPNs, secretaries, as well as for the unit as a whole. The information can be enhanced by looking at the tenure of those terminated and the reasons. Reasons for turnover may be avoidable or unavoidable. Avoidable turnover includes any reason in which the job failed to meet the expectations and needs of the employee. This type of turnover is more controllable than unavoidable turnover. Unavoidable turnover occurs due to relocation, marriage, family, childbearing, or illness.

Turnover is costly in any industry, but these costs may be greater with professional positions. Turnover is of critical importance when the demand for nurses exceeds the available supply. The costs of turnover include:

1. Recruitment costs including advertising, printing, travel, giveaways, postage, telephone, and salary of the recruiter.
2. Hiring costs of interview and relocation expenses, processing by unit manager and personnel (direct labor costs), and physical examination.
3. Orientation costs of materials, room, labor costs of instructors, refreshments, audiovisuals, copying, transportation to other facilities, and computer costs.
4. Training costs of unit orientation, labor costs of preceptor or buddy, materials, decreased productivity, and increased supplies.
5. Terminating costs: labor involved, exit interviews, return of hospital property, and follow-up letters or phone calls. Delays from the termination to a new hire must also be costed.

The ability of the manager and staff to identify correctable turnover trends may prove invaluable to retention initiatives. The turnover information, if tracked fully, may identify problems that can be addressed. For example, if the part-time RN turnover rate is lower than the full-time RN turnover rate, questions regarding scheduling and flexibility arise. If RN turnover rates are greater at 9 months of tenure and again at 24 months of tenure, further exploration is in order. The turnover at 9 months may be due to an inadequate orientation, lack of inclusion in the work group, or failed expectations. The turnover at 24 months may demonstrate a lack of opportunity for growth and challenge.

Trends in turnover and its costs provide an opportunity for clarification and identification of actual or potential problems. The unit manager needs to ask the following questions:

1. What is an acceptable percentage of turnover?
2. What short- and long-term trends are noted?
3. What are the reasons for the turnover?
4. How does the turnover rate compare to national, state, and local reports?
5. How much is it costing the unit?
6. What strategies have staff identified in decreasing turnover?
7. What are hiring practices and interview skills?
8. Does the job description represent the performance criteria required?
9. What guidance and support are available to new staff?

Actions on the part of the entire unit can be reviewed. Goals discussed and agreed upon may affect the unit's turnover rate. Some turnover is acceptable and inevitable. Monitoring and maintaining an acceptable level requires the unit manager to carefully analyze and improve the hiring, orientation, and continued learning process.

STAFFING OPTIONS AND STRATEGIES

Mary, in discussions with staff, realizes that the unit is experiencing some problems with the six vacant positions. This accounts for 30 shifts a week that must be covered by overtime, part-time, or other means. Mary has some ideas and strategies for meeting the current needs which include self-staffing, use of supplemental staffing, and adjusting hours to match work loads.

Self-staffing is a strategy that has several advantages for both staff and managers. Self-staffing is possible when the staff of the unit agree to accept the authority, responsibility, and accountability for the development of schedules which will assure appropriate staffing for the unit. This strategy requires a commitment on the part of the manager to serve as a teacher, trainer, mentor, and coach to the staff in assuring completion of the task. As important as the manager's commitment is the staff's commitment to establish schedules that meet patient, unit, and hospital needs as well as provide equitable scheduling for all staff. The self-scheduling process enables staff to participate on a professional level in controlling their own work schedules. It often results in staff understanding the complexities of the staffing process. The manager retains ultimate responsibility for meeting patient care needs. Many units which convert to self-staffing commit to a responsibility for controlling the staffing budget, which means minimal use of overtime, outside agency, and supplemental staffing. The self-staffing unit, in exchange for their commitment, may receive the positive benefits of continuing education days or not being reassigned to other units. Greater autonomy and self control leads to a professional work setting.

Another alternative to filling vacant positions on a short-term basis is the use of supplemental staffing. This refers to staff provided from a source outside the unit, but within the hospital. Mary plans on networking with the managers of the emergency department and cardiac catheterization laboratory to see if nurses from those areas would like to be crosstrained to the CCU. She also will discuss the hospital's per diem pool with her director. Considerations directly related to patient care are skill level, competency, and familiarity with unit operations, policies, and procedures. She knows she must factor orientation time, competency, verification, supervision, and per diem availability. Continuity of patient care and assimilation into unit culture are important.

Advantages of supplemental staffing are realized when use is short term and for a specific purpose. For example, supplemental staffing can be cost effective and productive with unexpected but temporary increases in patient census and work load. Disadvantages include extra supervisory requirements, training needs, lower productivity potential, higher cost, and decreased morale of existing staff. If supplemental staffing is not used, Mary will utilize overtime and look to outside sources.

Mary seeks to be flexible and adjust the work load to staff and time needed. At the next staff meeting, she plans on discussing an analysis of the peak times and recommending some new scheduled hours. This matching of hours to the work load may be of interest to some staff who would consider a change in their work schedule.

STAFFING METHODOLOGY

Mary now has a thorough understanding of her unit and its needs for staffing. She now collects the statistics and materials needed to calculate staffing.

1. Standards Using PCS:

Classification	Patient Days	Hours Per Day	Staff Hours Required
I	0		
II	0		
III	0		
IV	1,460 × 12.0	=	17,520
V	2,190 × 20.0	=	43,800
Total	3,650		61,320

$$\frac{\text{Required Hours}}{\text{Patient Days}} = \text{Average Nursing Care Hours per Patient Day}$$

$$\frac{61,320}{3,650} = 16.8 \text{ Hours per Day}$$

2. Flexible FTE (Direct):

   16.8 Hrs per Day × 3,650 Patient Days
   = 61,320 Required Hrs

$$\frac{61,320 \text{ Required Hrs}}{2,080 \text{ Hours of FTE}} = \frac{29.5 \text{ Total Direct}}{\text{Productive FTEs}}$$

3. Fixed FTE (Indirect):

   Secretary:
   21 shifts × 0.2 FTE/shift = 4.2
   Clinical Specialist:
   5 shifts × 0.2 FTE/shift = 1.0
   Nurse Manager:
   5 shifts × 0.2 FTE/shift = 1.0

   Total FTE Productive (Fixed): 6.2

4. Nonproductive FTEs (two methods are shown):
   a. Factor Method

   29.5 Direct FTE + 6.2 Fixed FTE = 35.7
   Total FTE × 110% (100% productive + 10% nonproductive) = 39.3 FTE

   b. Average Nonproductive Hours

   15 vacation days × 8 hours = 120 hours
   9 sick days × 8 hours = 72 hours
   9 holidays × 8 hours = 72 hours
   3 education days × 8 hours = 24 hours
   288 hours

   35.7 FTEs × 288 Hrs = 10,282

   $$\frac{10,282}{2,080 \text{ Hrs/Year}} = \frac{4.9 \text{ FTE needed}}{\text{to cover}}$$

5. Total FTE Adjusted
   a. Factor Method: 39.3
   b. Average Nonproductive Hours:

   35.7 + 4.9 = 40.6 FTEs

One can see that the method used to cover the nonproductive hours can vary depending on what method is used. For example, if Mary did not plan on replacing the 6.2 fixed FTEs, the FTEs requiring replacement would be using a factor of:

29.5 × 110% = 32.5 FTEs

Using average hours:

29.5 × 288 = 8496 / 2080 = 4.1
4.1 + 29.5 = 33.6 FTEs

Mary would then add back the fixed (nonreplaced) FTEs so her total would be:

32.5 + 6.2 = 38.7
or
33.6 + 6.2 = 39.8

Mary discusses with her director the method that is used in the hospital.

CONCLUSION

Standards, productivity, patient classification, turnover, work load, and staffing in the critical care unit affects patient care. Through examining the interrelatedness of these concepts in managing the unit and asking the right questions, Mary Wilson and the CCU staff can use the information to develop a unit that is efficient, effective, productive, professional, and provides services that are valued.

REFERENCES

1. American Association of Critical-Care Nurses. Standards for nursing care of the critically ill. Reston, VA: Reston Publishing Company, Inc., 1981.
2. American Association of Critical-Care Nurses. Outcome standards for nursing care of the critically ill. Newport Beach, CA: AACN, 1990:1.
3. Gillies DA. Nursing management a systems approach. Philadelphia: W.B. Saunders, 1983:97–180.
4. American Association of Critical-Care Nurses. Demonstration project. Newport Beach, CA: AACN, 1988.
5. Giovannetti P, Moore-Johnson J. A new generation patient classification system. JONA No. 5 May 1990:33–40.
6. DeGroot HA. Patient classification system evaluation. Part 1: essential system elements. JONA No. 6 1989:30–35.
7. Gillies DA, pp. 221–223.
8. American Hospital Association. Strategies: productivity measurement and management. Chicago, IL: A.H.A. 1986.
9. Fifield F. What is a productivity excellent hospital? Nursing Management, No. 4 April 1988:32–40.
10. Gillies DA, p. 247.

Chapter 10

Operating Budgets

ROBERT SQUIER, CHRISTINE A. MAYROSE

The hospital administrator, Jane Ceo, informs the vice president of nursing, Marge Don, that each intensive care unit (ICU) will plan, control, and evaluate its own operating budget in the next fiscal year (FY). Marge decides to begin the project in the medical intensive care unit (MICU) by assigning the head nurse responsibility for the unit's operating budget for the remainder of the current fiscal year. Marge discusses the responsibility of the project with the director of critical care, Dee Rector. Dee, who is excited about this opportunity, informs the MICU nurse manager, Chris Medunit, about the project. Chris, bewildered and overwhelmed, asks Dee, "How do I begin? Where do I start?"

The planning and control of the operating budget is an essential financial function in every health care organization. The budgeting practicalities of providing adequate supplies, ordering minor equipment, arranging for repairs and maintenance, and allowing staff opportunities to attend training and education programs confront every critical care nurse manager.

An understanding of how costs are allocated to maintain the routine operations of the unit over the fiscal year is a prerequisite to assuming the fiscal responsibilities. This chapter presents and analyzes a practical case scenario of how Chris, as a critical care nurse manager, plans and controls the costs produced by general and patient-care supplies, drug and dietary items, utilities, minor equipment, advertising, education, and fixed overhead. While the personnel budget is technically part of the operating budget, a separate chapter has been devoted to this topic (see Chapter 8). Personnel expenses are, therefore, only superficially addressed in the last section of this chapter.

The fiscal management responsibilities contained in the American Association of Critical-Care Nurses (AACN) position statement, "Role Expectations for the Critical Care Manager" [1], serve as themes to explore and use in constructing an operating budget for a critical care unit. The nursing process is used for presentation and analysis of the operating budget in this chapter.

NURSING PROCESS

Although the delegation of this new responsibility appears, at first, overwhelming, components of the nursing process (assessing, planning, implementing, and evaluating) provide Chris with a familiar framework for addressing the challenge. The effective critical care nurse manager already uses the nursing process in planning and controlling clinical and administrative programs. This familiarity facilitates the application of the problem-solving process in planning and controlling an operating budget.

Because of the key role that nurse managers play in supervising daily unit activities and operations, the first-line manager offers the organization the best opportunity to predict trends in patient census and acuity, as well as to control and plan for supply and equipment needs. Knowing that health care confronts an uncertain economic future and that administration will continue to exert pressure on nurse managers to improve the efficiency and effectiveness of care, Chris anticipates competition for scarce financial resources [2]. This translates into reducing or maintaining costs at the unit level through sound financial management.

A critical care manager's role in controlling costs and realizing how an institution's potential revenues will impact unit operations is consistent with two of AACN's listed fiscal management responsibilities. These are promoting cost effective unit operations and anticipating the impact of institutional financial status on unit operations [1].

Assessment and Planning

Initially, Chris needs to decide about the level of sophistication or complexity required by the operating budget. A critical care manager must ascertain how much detail will be necessary and how operating costs are allocated to respective departments (3). In making these assessments, a critical care manager considers the size of the hospital, the available resources, the institution's managerial cost accounting system, and the expectations of management (4). The capability of measuring costs and attributing them to a medical or nursing diagnosis, a procedure provided, or a specific patient underlies whatever approach a critical care manager decides to select.

Cost Distribution Report

Chris learns from her director that their hospital reports quarterly and annual costs in a cost distribution report (CDR). The CDR identifies service costs generated by patient care activity during each quarter of the fiscal year, accumulated costs for year-to-date, and annual costs at fiscal-year end. The CDR classifies expenses into numeric department accounts and then charges these numeric accounts to the specific unit that used them. The CDR views the unit generating the expenses as a cost center. A cost center is the point where control and accountability over the incurrence of costs are found (5). A nursing unit is usually referred to as a cost center, but some hospitals refer to their units as revenue centers. Other cost centers may exist within a unit. For example, a cardiac catheterization laboratory may be a cost center within an MICU. All hospitals use similar methods to charge expenses to specific cost centers and accounts. Each cost (revenue) center has a designated account number for the purpose of assigning and tracing costs. Methods are described in Chapter 2.

In this example, the 1990 CDR reflects expenses charged to MICU's account (1117.00) from the following accounts: diagnostic radiology (222), laboratory (223), pharmacy (224), library (226), nuclear medicine (229), nursing service (241), dietetic (243), and supply (281). A portion of MICU's CDR report is illustrated in Table 10.1.

Figure 10.1 represents the MICU CDR. As shown by the graph, MICU's greatest costs came from nursing salaries, and the laboratory, pharmacy, and supply accounts.

Chris can, at a minimum, rely on the financial data found in the 1989 and 1990 hospital CDRs to plan MICU's 1991 operating budget.

Chris observes that supply items represent the fourth most expensive category of expenses in the CDR. Laboratory and pharmacy accounts are the second and third largest expenses for MICU. These costs are outside the direct control of the nurse manager.

Patient Diagnostic Categories

Dee reminds Chris that budgets aim to measure costs by attributing them to a final product or service. Hospitals face a difficult challenge, since their product is patient care and identifying all costs is complex (6). Dee explains that a hospital may define its product to be patient days and acuity levels, or types of patient cases such as diagnosis related groups (DRGs) or nursing diagnosis (ND) (7, 8).

Chris views MICU nurses caring for patients with recurring classes of illness and proposes to use a combination of the patient's nursing diagnosis and DRG as the MICU product. Chris will try to relate as many operating costs as possible to a patient's nursing diagnosis or DRG.

Forecasting Method

Chris realizes that there are alternative methods available to plan the budget. She recognizes that many operating expenses are difficult to identify and measure. Each institution internally defines costs through their own unique system and selects a method that is consistent with their objectives (9).

Chris selects a simple and pragmatic method to plan MICU's budget. First, she collects data from the 1989 operating budget and the calculated projection for the remainder of FY 1990. The 1991 operating budget will be constructed by multiplying the annual historical costs by a chosen factor. The factor could be a relative value based on case mix, patient acuity, patient length of stay, or a cost-plus or incremental approach. Chris selects the 1991 forecasted health care inflation rate as the factor to use in planning the 1991 MICU operating budget.

This method does have limitations. It avoids questions about worker productivity, a unit's efficiency, and the accuracy of allocated expenses

Table 10.1. Cost Distribution Report

1990 CDR REPORT
Cost Account Center #1117.00
Medical Intensive Care Unit

Cost Account	Number Description	FTE Costs	All Other Costs	Total Costs
222	Diagnostic radiology	23,524	17,641	41,165
223	Laboratory	108,589	99,930	208,519
224	Pharmacy	45,310	134,081	179,391
229	Nuclear medicine	2,100	1,513	3,613
241	Nursing service	864,864	4,364	869,228
243	Dietetic	43,448	11,544	54,992
281	Supply	42,773	89,474	132,247
	Total direct cost:			$1,489,155

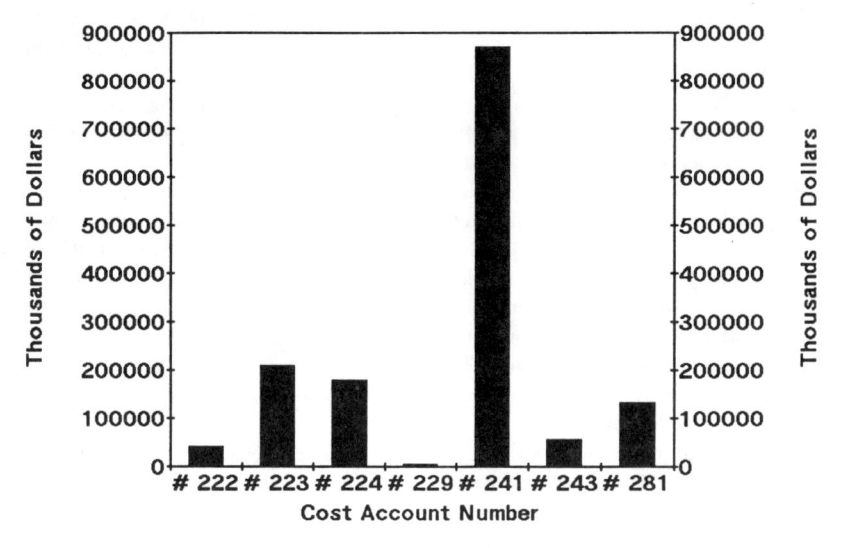

Figure 10.1. MICU cost distribution report FY 1990.

(10). Additionally, the prediction of the inflation rate may prove false or it may vary by cost category. Critical care nurse managers forecast the changes in patient volume and complexity, since these changes will impact use of supplies and minor equipment, staff education needs, staffing, and other expenses. In this case, Chris anticipates the MICU case mix and patient complexity for 1991 will remain unchanged.

The 1990 costs for supplies, minor equipment, dietary, drugs, education and training, advertising, lab, and other expense categories are multiplied by the anticipated inflation rate. This is an approach that requires accurate information and is tedious, but does not require much analysis.

Chris finds that the precise historical data needed are difficult to obtain. While most of the information is available, the data base is scattered, since it has been maintained by other departments and department managers. Information must be retrieved to develop an accurate historical summary of operating costs for the intensive care unit. Of course, Chris knows she can always extract cost data from the hospital CDR. While these data may be accurate for the hospital overall, the allocation methods may be discriminating.

Because there is a clear and direct relationship between the volume of supplies used and patient case mix, predicting changes in patient populations becomes critical. The number of patients with acute MI admitted to an MICU, for example, affects the utilization of ECG pads, laboratory tests, laboratory tubes, angiocatheters, IV lines, and medications. Likewise, an increase in open heart surgery cases in a surgical intensive care unit (SICU) increases the number of pulmonary artery catheters used. The number and types of supplies or drugs used by a unit depend on the volume, complexity, and acuity of ICU patients. This aspect of planning an operating budget becomes an educated guess, based on collected historical trends and data, information known on proposed changes in programs, and practical experience from managing daily operations.

Chris reviews the medical intensive care unit's historical data, work load, and staffing with Dee. During the last year, the medical intensive care unit operated 10 beds and averaged a 90% occupancy rate. The unit admitted 800 patients. Twenty-four full-time RNs staffed the unit, excluding fixed full-time equivalent (FTE) staff.

The patient case mix comprised 30% uncomplicated MIs (DRG 122), 20% GI bleeds without complications (DRG 175), 15% acute pneumonias without complications (DRG 90), and 35% other diagnoses. In each of the three identified diagnostic categories, patients had an average length of stay (ALOS) of 4 days. Data for the other 35% of the diagnoses proved difficult to retrieve.

Dee and Chris agree that a system to capture MICU's specific operating costs is necessary. Chris anticipates better data collection will require computerization of the patient data, MICU operating costs, and MICU supply and drug usage.

TYPES OF OPERATING COSTS

Chris continues her consultations with her director by reviewing various aspects of an operating budget, and Dee continues her role as mentor to Chris by discussing types of operating costs.

Fixed and Variable Costs

There are two basic kinds of costs, fixed and variable (11). By definition, fixed costs are those that do not change despite fluctuations in activity or work load. They include rent or mortgage, taxes, interest on loans, administrative salaries, and depreciation of equipment and buildings. In distinction, variable costs fluctuate with changes in activity or work load levels. Variable costs include linens, meals, patient and administrative supplies (IV fluids/tubing, dressing supplies, hygiene supplies, pencils, pens, paper, etc.).

Semivariable Costs

Dee continues by telling Chris that semivariable costs have characteristics of fixed and variable costs (12). Examples of semivariable costs include the payroll and utilities. The fixed component would be the rate, while the variability would be the amount of actual usage. Staff nursing salaries are fixed for specific periods of time. The total amount paid for nursing salaries might vary, however, depending on the census of the unit. As an illustration, if the patient census of a 10-bed MICU fell to five, staff nurses might be required to take leave without pay. Salaries of the staff nurses then vary with the patient census.

Direct and Indirect Costs

Costs can be classified as direct or indirect (13). Direct costs are those that can be traced to a specific function, cost center, or product. In a nursing budget, direct costs are routinely related to direct patient care. For example, salaries and supplies are direct costs.

Indirect costs do not relate directly to patient care and are transferred to the unit or department cost account center by the accounting methods used by the hospital. Examples include housekeeping, utilities, and administrative salaries. For more detail, refer to Chapter 2.

Medical Intensive Care Unit Cost Accounts

Chris continues to apply the nursing process to building an operating budget by assessing the specific operating costs in the MICU.

Chris finds that the cost of supplies is a large expense in a critical care unit's budget. She learns from Dee that buying and distributing patient supplies is a major focal point of the hospital's cost containment efforts.

The supply budget funds the supplies and noncapital equipment a unit requires to operate (14). Supply costs originate from paper and office supplies, central supply items, minor equipment, and pharmacy items.

A critical care nurse manager projects the needs of a supply budget from historical costs, taking into account anticipated changes in case mix and patient complexity. The astute nurse manager recognizes that new technology, inflation, and changes in clinical practice can impact both planning and controlling an operating budget.

General Supplies

The hospital in the case example has a distribution center for ordering and dispensing administrative supplies. These supplies include such items as pencils and pens, paper, typewriter ribbons, management forms, paper clips, and chart forms.

The distribution manager informs Chris that the projected annual 1991 expenses to the unit's cost center account are $5000. From a review of the 1990 CDR, Chris finds that MICU was charged $4500 for administrative supplies. The difference between the 1990 and 1991 budget for administrative supplies represents an 11% factor for inflationary forces. She agrees with the estimate for MICU's 1991 administrative supply costs.

Drug Costs

Budgeting for drug costs represents a considerable challenge to Chris. Physician practice, new products, research, updated therapies, patient acuity, case mix, consumer demands, new diseases, infection control, and quality improvement influence the amount and type of drugs used in the unit. New and more expensive drugs may unexpectedly increase the costs and utilization of drugs.

Chris plans to assess drug costs by determining the historical costs and multiplying them by the expected rate of health care inflation. To be consistent with her general approach, Chris intends to track the retrospective data on drug costs and relate these costs to a patient's nursing diagnosis or DRG.

Every hospital pharmacy department has some method of monitoring drug costs. The pharmacy may distribute drug costs to the MICU as a cost center, to the patient as a consumer, or may combine methods. Chris visits the director of pharmacy and learns that pharmacy charges MICU's cost account for all the drugs used by patients in a fiscal year. Composite information is recorded in the hospital's CDR, but the pharmacy is unable to inform Chris what drugs a particular patient or patient diagnostic category used during a stay in MICU.

Chris intends to propose a system that will provide the specific pharmacy costs for every MICU patient and each diagnosis. This would introduce a system, currently existing in some hospitals, that bills patients directly for pharmacy costs. However, under prospective payment systems, pharmacy costs are generally included as part of a patient's hospitalization charges.

Forecasting Supply and Drug Costs

Chris traces the costs of supplies and drugs for the three most common diagnostic classes and places the data into a computer information base.

The collected data shows the average drug and supply costs for three diagnostic classes:

1. Uncomplicated MI: $59.96;
2. Uncomplicated GI Bleed: $152.10;
3. Acute Pneumonia: $354.36.

These costs reflect the 4-day ALOS. Hard-copy printouts of the patient diagnostic category data appear in Tables 10.2, 10.3, and 10.4.

Chris assumes these individual diagnostic cases represent average costs. The costs of the uncomplicated MI are multiplied by 240, or the number of the uncomplicated MI cases for the last year. The costs of the GI bleed are multiplied by 160, which represents the number of GI cases last year. Finally, the costs of acute pneumonia are multiplied by 120, or the number of acute pneumonia cases from last year. The total costs for these three diagnostic categories are summed. The sum is multiplied by 11%, or the expected 1991 health care inflation rate (15). This results in a total estimate of $90,186 (dollars rounded). (Calculated expense $81,249 × 11% = $8,937 + $81,249 = $90,186.)

Detailed data on the 35% of other patient cases from last year are unavailable. Chris knows a large proportion of these cases were complicated and that their ALOS exceeded 4 days. Some of these complicated patient cases required expensive interventions, including additional respiratory equipment and respiratory therapy, intra-aortic balloon pumps, multiple transfusions, numerous antibiotics, monitoring lines and equipment, several cardiac drugs, physical therapy, one-to-one nursing care, and other costly therapies.

However, without detailed information, an educated guess guides this year's budget proposal. Chris estimates that the costs of the complicated patient cases are twice the costs of the uncomplicated case mix. The complicated cases fell within the 35% of patients in the unknown patient mix.

Table 10.2. Supply and Drug Costs DRG 122

Patient #: 523-59-0878
Patient Name: Rector, Robert
Nursing Diagnosis: Cardiopulmonary, #Y28.0
DRG: Uncomplicated MI, #122

Summary of Supply Items

Item	Item Name	Item Cost	Items Used	Total Cost
501	PKG ECG electrodes	.21	4	.84
560	Nasal cannula	1.42	1	1.42
915	Oxygen bubbler	1.77	1	1.77
1296	IV tubing	4.85	1	4.85
2323	Nitro tubing	5.25	1	5.25
1910	Package 4 × 4 gauze	.50	4	2.00
720	Tape	2.58	1	2.58
2415	18 G. needles	.18	6	1.08
1150	Urinal	2.58	1	2.58
1160	Bedpan	3.45	1	3.45
1800	Emesis basin	.70	1	.70
1809	Wash basin	3.28	1	3.28
1225	Angiocath	1.40	1	1.40
1345	Lab collection tubes	.55	5	2.75
821	Box unsterile gloves	8.86	1	8.86
	Total costs of supplies:			$42.81

Summary of Drugs Used

Drug	# Used	Unit Cost	Total Cost
IV heparin	4	3.09	12.36
IV nitro	1	.68	.68
ASA tabs	4	.09	.36
500 cc NS	5	.75	3.75
Total drug costs:			$17.15
Total drug and supply costs:			$59.96

Chris derives her estimate from an analysis of the CDR for MICU's 1990 annual drug and supply costs. The CDR shows that the supply and drug costs, excluding FTE costs, are approximately double what is estimated for the three major case types. Chris assumes this difference resulted from the complicated cases.

Thus, Chris multiplies the total drug and supply costs calculated for 65% of the case mix by a factor of 2 and adds the 11% inflation factor. This results in a forecast of additional supply and drug costs of $180,373 for 1991. Table 10.5 summarizes the calculations.

Laboratory Costs

Chris visits the manager of the inpatient laboratory. She finds that the laboratory has no system to attribute laboratory costs to patients or patient diagnostic categories. The laboratory maintains data of the tests ordered by MICU and charges the cost to the unit. The 1990 laboratory costs, excluding FTE costs, recorded in the CDR were $99,930. Chris adds the 11% inflation factor, reaching a figure of $110,922 for the 1991 budget.

This is one area that will benefit from improved data collection. The proposed information system will relate specific laboratory tests ordered and their costs to patients and their diagnoses.

Dietary Costs

Purchasing and preparing food and serving meals often represent uncontrollable costs for a critical care unit. Salaries of dieticians, dietary aids, and kitchen staff, as well as the costs of kitchen space and equipment contribute to MICU expenses. Usually, these are indirect costs of patient care and

Table 10.3. Supply and Drug Costs DRG 175

Patient #: 523-58-0879
Patient Name: Rector, Joe
Nursing Diagnosis: Gastrointestinal, #Y28.2
DRG: UGI Bleed, #175

Summary of Supply Items Used

Item	Item Name	Item Cost	Items Used	Total Cost
501	Pkg ECG Electrodes	.21	4	.84
560	Nasal cannula	1.42	1	1.42
915	Oxygen bubbler	1.77	1	1.77
2121	Central line tray	31.00	1	31.00
1296	IV tubing	4.85	1	4.85
843	Protective gown	2.25	8	18.00
1910	Package 4 × 4 gauze	.50	4	2.00
720	Tape	2.58	2	5.16
2415	18 G. needles	.18	6	1.08
1150	Urinal	2.58	1	2.58
1160	Bedpan	3.45	1	3.45
1800	Emesis basin	.70	1	.70
1809	Wash basin	3.28	1	3.28
1225	Angiocath	1.40	1	1.40
1345	Lab collection tubes	.55	5	2.75
1355	Blood set	7.79	1	7.79
821	Box unsterile gloves	8.86	1	8.86
482	Connecting tubing	6.45	1	6.45
927	NG tube	5.75	1	5.75
305	Suction cannister	18.38	1	18.38
	Total supply costs:			$127.51

Summary of Drugs Used

Drug	# Used	Unit Cost	Total Cost
NS & 20 KCl	8	1.30	10.40
Cimetadine	8	.95	7.60
MVI & folate	8	.30	2.40
Thiamine	8	.28	2.24
Vit. K	1	1.95	1.95
Total drug costs:			$24.59
Total drug and supply costs:			$152.10

are allocated to cost centers based on the number of meals delivered or served. In some hospitals, meals may be a separate billing item and, thus, a direct cost to patients.

Knowing the cost of serving breakfast, lunch, dinner, and snacks for each patient and for each patient illness category is the ideal objective. Information on dietary costs should come from fiscal reports, but it may be obtained from the dietary department or purchasing department. Chris must have accurate cost data to prepare budget requests.

Chris depends on cost information acquired from the dietary service to project variable dietary costs for 1991. Using the formula (cost of meals per day) × (number of patients) × (length of stay) = total dietary costs, one finds that the total dietary costs for MICU for 1991 are, rounded to the next dollar, $53,168. (These costs exclude costs for tray waste and coffee or snacks provided for staff or visitors. Chris learns that these costs are charged to the dietary department's own cost center account. Of course, another institution might deal with these costs differently and so might this department when the issue is recognized.)

Table 10.4. Supply and Drug Costs DRG 90

Patient #: 523-58-0880
Patient Name: Rector, Roy
Nursing Diagnosis: Impairment in Airway
DRG: Acute Pneumonia, #90

Summary of Supply Items Used

Item	Item Name	Item Cost	Items Used	Total Cost
501	Pkg ECG electrodes	.21	4	.84
560	Nasal cannula	1.42	1	1.42
915	Oxygen bubbler	1.77	1	1.77
548	Nebulizer & tubing	4.50	1	4.50
1296	IV tubing	4.85	3	14.55
1221	Heparin lock	.30	1	.30
1910	Package 4 × 4 gauze	.50	6	3.00
720	Tape	2.58	2	5.16
2415	18 G. needles	.18	6	1.08
1150	Urinal	2.58	1	2.58
1160	Bedpan	3.45	1	3.45
1800	Emesis basin	.70	1	.70
1809	Wash basin	3.28	1	3.28
1225	Angiocath	1.40	1	1.40
1345	Lab collection tubes	.55	5	2.75
1597	Incentive spirometer	16.00	1	16.00
821	Box unsterile gloves	8.86	1	8.86
482	Connecting tubing	6.45	1	6.45
305	Suction cannister	18.38	1	18.38
1730	ABG kit	5.45	1	5.45
	Total supply costs:			$101.92

Summary of Drugs Used

Drug	# Used	Unit Cost	Total Cost
1000 cc NS	3	.93	2.79
Alupent bottle	1	2.05	2.05
500 cc aminophyline	2	3.35	6.70
Tylenol tabs	10	.09	.90
Antibiotics	24	10.00	240.00
Total drug costs:			$252.44
Total drug and supply costs:			$354.36

Table 10.6 illustrates the calculations to reach this total.

Minor Equipment Costs

Minor equipment encompasses the category of products that fall outside of capital equipment. The differentiation of minor equipment from capital equipment is defined by the hospital cost accounting system. Minor equipment usually possesses a short span of use, often less than 1 year, and is less than a specified dollar amount, e.g., less than $500. In contrast, capital equipment requires larger investments and has a longer average use than does minor equipment. Sometimes, minor equipment is termed durable minor equipment.

Assessing and planning for minor equipment needs depend on the types and numbers of patient care categories a critical care unit serves. The minor equipment ordered by a surgical intensive care unit might differ from that of a medical unit.

Confusion over what is minor equipment may arise when, for example, one digital thermometer costing $250 is placed in the minor equipment category. However, a unit order for 10 digital thermometers with a cost of $2500 is considered a

Table 10.5. Forecasted Supply and Drug Costs Fiscal Year 1991

Projected Supply and Drug Costs for MICU in 1991 Cost Account Center 1117.00**

1. Uncomplicated acute MI
   a. 800 (total patient census for 1990) × .30 (percentage of Uncomplicated MI cases in 1990) = 240 MI patients.
   b. 240 × $59.96 (average cost for MI UOS in 1990) = $14,390.00 in rounded dollars.

2. GI bleed without complications
   a. 800 × .20 (percentage of GI Bleed without complication in 1990) = 160 GI patients.
   b. 160 (# of GI Bleed Patients) × $152.10 (average cost for GI UOS in 1990) = $24,336.00 in rounded dollars.

3. Acute pneumonia without complications
   a. 800 × .15 (percentage of Acute Pneumonia in 1990) = 120 pneumonia patients.
   b. 120 × $354.36 (average cost for acute pneumonia in 1990) = $42,523.00 in rounded dollars.

4. All other costs
   a. Sum totals from #1, #2, and #3 above: $14,390 + $24,336 + $42,523 = $81,249.
   b. $81,249 × 2 (estimated factor for the remaining 35% of patient categories) = $162,498.

5. Inflation factor
   a. $243,747 (costs from #4 a+b above) × .11 (expected inflation rate for health are in 1990) = $26,812.00 (dollar rounded).

6. Total 1991 estimated operating supply and drug costs: $270,559.00 (243,747 + 26,812 in #5 above)

**These calculations exclude FTE costs or labor costs.

Table 10.6. Forecasted Dietary Costs Fiscal Year 1991

MICU Dietary Costs

a. MI patients: # of patients = 30% × 800 = 240
   $17.71 × 240 × 4 days = $17,000 (dollar rounded).
b. UGI bleed: # of patients = 20% × 800 = 160
   $17.71 × 160 × 2 days* = $5,667 (dollar rounded).
c. Acute pneumonia patients
   # of patients = 15% × 800 = 120
   $17.71 × 120 × 4 = $8501 (dollar rounded).
d. All others 22,000
e. Total dietary costs: $53,168.00 (a+b+c+d)

*Although UGI patients length of stay was 4 days, these patients received meals for 2 days.

---

capital expense. Hospitals differ in how accounting departments treat this issue.

Chris reviews the minor equipment requirements and requests for 1991. Table 10.7 illustrates the calculations and the items included in this expense category.

Repair and Maintenance Costs

Another aspect to direct and indirect costs is those costs that are attributed to MICU from another department. For example, engineering and biomedical engineering departments produce an indirect cost for a nursing unit and other hospital units, but incur direct costs of their own. The labor of engineers or biomedical employees and the costs of the equipment parts used are direct costs to the engineering or biomedical departments, but are indirectly related to patient care.

Hospitals vary on how they account for the engineering department's costs of labor, materials, parts, and administrative salaries. Chris learns that the hospital engineering and biomedical departments allocate the costs of parts, labor, and materials to the unit cost center receiving the service, while their respective administrative salaries are charged to their department cost center salary accounts.

Adding new electrical outlets and electrical lines, checking and repairing digital thermometers or ECG machines, painting rooms, changing door locks, replacing worn carpet, repairing IV pumps, clearing wall suction lines, monitoring equipment on a routine schedule, and fixing a broken faucet represent services that engineering, biomedical departments, or some other service might provide to MICU. The costs of checking the electrical system in MICU or of maintaining the boiler plant arise from engineering service. Costs for parts and labor to repair MICU's plugged wall suction lines are another instance of engineering department costs. The costs for labor and replacement parts used to repair a pulse oximeter arise from the biomedical department. In these examples, MICU is charged for engineering and biomedical costs as a specific cost center account.

Allocations of indirect costs to the specific unit department vary according to each hospital's particular managerial accounting system (16). Indirect

Table 10.7. Minor Equipment Budget Fiscal Year 1991

Anticipated Minor Equipment Needs for Fiscal Year 1991 Medical Intensive Care Unit
Cost Account Number 1117.00

Item	Quantity	Unit Cost	Total Cost
Bedside cabinets	2	150.00	300.00
Bedside chairs	2	150.00	300.00
Chartholder carts	1	150.00	150.00
Commode chairs	2	250.00	500.00
Fax machine	1	525.00	525.00
Hampers, linen	2	45.00	90.00
X-ray illuminator	1	300.00	300.00
IV wheelchair holder	1	30.00	30.00
IV poles, mobile	4	150.00	600.00
Ophthalmoscope	1	300.00	300.00
Overbed tables	3	150.00	450.00
Patient walkers	1	200.00	200.00
Pencil sharpener	1	25.00	25.00
Scanners	11	160.00	1,760.00
Sphygmometer, portable	1	170.00	170.00
Sphygmometer, wall	2	100.00	200.00
Spotlight, rechargeable	1	20.00	20.00
Transducer holders	2	100.00	200.00
		Total Cost:	$6120.00

costs may be allocated on a percentage based on square feet, numbers of equipment items checked, number of work orders generated, labor time, and so forth.

Engineering and biomedical managers meet with Chris and review their MICU work order schedules, parts used for equipment and repairs in MICU, and the hours of labor required to maintain MICU's equipment and physical environment on a regular schedule. This figure is $15,000.

The engineering managers point out that their costs are allocated to respective cost center accounts in an equitable manner. As a high-tech area, MICU can expect higher indirect costs than can a low-tech unit. The replacement parts used and the labor required to repair and maintain the intensive care equipment, for example, make MICU's indirect costs higher than those of a general medical or surgical ward.

Utility Costs

There are several methods that can be used to determine utility costs for individual units. First, the total amount of energy (electricity, natural gas, generator costs) and water used by the hospital should be determined. Engineering can then allocate costs based on actual consumption, or by retrospective annual usage studies, or on the square feet of the unit. Each of these methods is acceptable and represents the variable portion of semivariable costs. The fixed portion is the rate per kilowatt of energy. Together, the fixed rate and one of the equations for usage will determine the total utility costs.

Chris consults the engineering service and learns that MICU occupies an area of 4550 square feet. The engineering service informs Chris that each square foot is allocated $1.41 for annual utility operating costs. This means that 4550 square feet multiplied by $1.41 equals, in rounded dollars, $6416. Chris finds MICU avoids charges for the cost of water and the expense of maintaining the emergency generator, since these costs are distributed to another hospital cost center account.

Recruitment Advertising Costs

Advertising is an area that is usually overlooked by nurse managers preparing operating budgets. However, with the documented shortages facing the nursing profession, it is one item that nurse managers cannot afford to ignore.

In many institutions, advertising responsibilities fall to the human resources department. This arrangement may allow nonnursing departments to have a large amount of control over frequency of advertisements and the amount expended. In this situation, nurse managers need to maintain a close working relationship with the advertising director. Decisions on content, design, media type, and frequency can prove to be invaluable to timely and effective recruitment programs.

Several types of media can be effectively used to advertise for professional staff. Television, newspapers, professional journals, and radio advertising can be productive but costly. Television and radio advertising tend to be too expensive for most hospitals. The cost for one 2 inch by 3 inch advertisement in a newspaper or journal may run anywhere from $200–$400, or more, depending on the geographic area and the media used. Half-page or full-page sizes, color, or special graphics add to the cost.

Less costly methods of recruitment may place considerable time and energy requirements on the nurse manager or nurse recruiter. For example, exhibits at national or local conventions can recruit experienced, qualified staff. Exhibits at universities or open houses at the facility can attract new graduates. Often, staff nurses are interested in recruiting and represent the organization at special functions. The costs associated with staff or manager travel, hotels, and per diem expenses should be included in the budget request.

Of all methods of advertising, the most effective and least costly may be word-of-mouth publicity. Because every staff nurse is a potential recruiter, each should be thoroughly familiar with the specific attributes and incentives provided by their hospital. Flyers advertising benefits with specific information on such things as tuition and educational funding programs, scholarships, and upward mobility opportunities can be distributed to staff periodically. Opportunities to communicate positive aspects of employment occur in places as unlikely as the supermarket line and church socials to more likely places such as professional meetings. The hospital should recognize staff recruitment efforts with "finders" bonuses, authorized absence (paid time) to attend professional meetings, and other personal and monetary incentives to encourage positive publicity. Budgets should include funds for these promotional activities.

Both short- and long-term effectiveness of recruiting practices were the focus of a study done by Labig in 1987–1988 (17). The lack of research on recruiting methods specific to health care workers and inconsistent results from recruitment effectiveness reported by other industries led to a comparison of six long- and short-term recruiting strategies.

The study was conducted in 32 Oklahoma hospitals and included 294 experienced and 191 inexperienced applicants. A 1-year follow-up to determine turnover and performance measures was conducted. Labig found that outcomes of recruitment vary depending on whether short- or long-term criteria are evaluated. Efforts that produce better short-term results, such as newspaper advertisements, did not produce long-term results, such as higher performance and retention. Recruiting students during clinical rotations resulted in greater retention, but not in better performance, and required more time from contact to hire date. Advertising costs varied widely in this study—from $25 to almost $3000 per applicant. While this study cannot be generalized, Labig suggests tailoring recruitment efforts to specific needs of the hospital in terms of qualifications and short- or long-term objectives.

Chris plans to place two advertisements in a local newspaper and one ad in a professional journal. The newspaper charges $300 for the type of advertisement planned. The journal charges $400 for the planned advertisement. This results in $1000 for 1991 advertising expenses, or

$$(\$300 \times 2) + (\$400 \times 1) = \$1000$$

This minimum level of planned advertising supplements the usual method of replacing staff by training in-house nurses. Depending on the response to advertising, hiring experienced nurses may be less expensive than training inexperienced nurses. While offering a critical care course is viewed as a retention strategy, the drain on the medical-surgical areas may be acute at times. Additionally, the staff conducting the course benefits from an occasional break.

Education and Training Costs

Education and training is another area of the operating budget that Chris cannot afford to overlook. The amount of time and money spent on continuing education and training may affect staff performance and nursing practice standards. In some institutions, this is budgeted at the department division level rather than by unit. For example, the nursing education department may assume responsibility for budgeting training cost. This is not recommended for two reasons, responsibility and control (18).

Staff nurses and unit managers jointly share responsibility for maintaining critical care skills, and both should be included in the planning of educational programs and their expenses. Because managers are responsible for providing equitable opportunities for education and must justify the associated costs, they should have control over the funds allocated to cover the expenses.

In planning the budget for staff development, several areas should be assessed:

1. Individual staff nurse needs;
2. Unit needs;
3. Available resources (tuition money, education days, etc.);
4. Anticipated needs (new programs, standards, procedures, and practice).

Joint responsibility for continuing education requires time, effort, and communication. Staff nurses need to keep nurse managers informed of individual goals and the educational programs needed to meet these goals. The nurse manager should identify needs and provide guidance and direction to assist the staff nurse in selecting educational experiences that promote professional development.

The Joint Commission on Accreditation of Health Care Organizations (JCAHO) states that "All personnel are prepared for their responsibility in the special care unit through appropriate orientation, in-service training, and continuing education" (19). This standard supports Chris in her efforts to establish a reasonable education budget. Every unit should be staffed by qualified, well trained nursing personnel. Specific training needs will be dictated by the type of unit, specialization levels, performance standards, and skill levels of the staff. For example, a critical care unit (CCU) manager with a "new" staff and a large volume of cardiac angioplasty patients may identify the need for staff to be proficient with intra-aortic balloon pumps. The increased possibility of utilization combined with the lack of experienced staff would constitute a valid education request.

Once training needs are identified, the nurse manager reviews mandated requirements and assesses what resources are available. In some facilities, each employee is entitled to a set amount of paid education time as a benefit. Labor contracts may establish a set percentage of base pay or set number of days the employee may use for educational purposes. The provisions vary widely and managers need to be cognizant of facility policies, labor agreements, and state regulations regarding continuing education for relicensure prior to outlining a staff development budget. Each state regulatory (licensing) authority will be able to outline the educational requirements for relicensure. Provisions for education agreed upon through the collective bargaining process will be in the negotiated agreement contract if one is in effect at the hospital. Hospital policies related to leave should also be reviewed. In the case of public institutions, statutory regulations may apply to the type of leave, restrictions, and approving authority. While these should be incorporated in hospital or personnel policies, familiarity with actual statutes is recommended.

The resources available may be difficult to determine. Most hospitals provide tuition reimbursement of some sort. Control over these funds may be by committee or be a centralized point or may be decentralized to department and/or unit level based on an allocation formula.

However the education budget is set up, the one point that Chris keeps in mind when granting education leave or approving the allocation of funds is equity. Whatever funds are available should be distributed fairly. It is a good idea to keep a log noting each staff nurse's attendance at continuing education courses. The record could reflect the course title, the date of attendance, the cost of the course, travel expenses (if paid by the facility), the number of paid days, and a list of the course objectives. In facilities where staff are given a certain amount of funds per year, this record will be helpful in deciding who can attend a program. It also gives Chris the opportunity to consider sending one staff member to a more costly program in the event that all staff members have not used their funds. Again, this is where Chris must be careful to give each staff nurse a fair chance to utilize education days and dollars.

Once needs and resources are assessed, planning how to meet the needs with the resources available begins. Alternatives that benefit the entire staff should be weighed against sending one or two individuals to expensive workshops. Teleconferences, video tapes, and slide tapes are some examples. Initially, teleconferences may be more costly; however, if purchased, they may be able to reach more staff and be used over and over again. In the end, they may pay for themselves. In some facilities, video tapes or slide tapes can be made on-site. This option should be explored for orientation classes, critical care courses, or on-site educational seminars, because they can be utilized more frequently for a fraction of the cost of presenting the topic initially. In some instances, these options will not exist and one individual will have to attend the workshop. It is always a good idea to have the participant present the information gained to the entire staff at a specified and agreed upon date following the conference.

Another option that managers should consider is shared agreements. These can work in two ways:

1. Between an employee and employer;
2. Between facilities or institutions.

Agreements between employees and employers are made when the employer offers the employee an opportunity to gain new knowledge and experience. For example, if an employee wishes to train in the critical care area, the employer would provide the structured classes and hands-on clinical experience. The employee, however, would be asked to commit to working in the ICU for a set period of time. Pay-back time in return for tuition reimbursement while obtaining a degree is another example of shared agreements.

In shared agreements between facilities, there are any number of arrangements that can be negotiated. Managers must be creative in order to assure an equitable exchange of resources without overextending personnel or the budget. Facilities can share instructors for nursing education; or, they can alternate sites for certain classes, thus sharing the responsibility. Universities can agree to "giving" a facility a specified number of class openings or credit hours in return for employees of the hospital serving as faculty for students or presenting at a seminar. Networking within the health care community can prove to be very beneficial in exploring and exercising these options.

Implementing and evaluating an educational budget will be an ongoing process. It will be the manager's decision as to what method works best for the unit. Nurse managers will be responsible for evaluating what methods of educational delivery fulfill the educational needs of the staff/unit for the least amount of money.

Nursing Turnover Costs

Citing the lack of research on the cost of turnover and inconsistency in the literature reporting costs, Jones proposes the nursing turnover cost calculation methodology (NTCCM). This tool measures direct and indirect costs of nursing turnover and has potential for standardizing the way hospitals measure the costs of nursing turnover (20).

Jones applied NTCCM in her 1988 investigation of turnover costs in four acute care hospitals in the Southeast. Hospitals ranged in size from 239 to 611 beds, with an average of 355 beds. The nursing personnel budget ranged from $6 million to $11 million, with an average of $8.3 million. Averaging all hospitals in the study, Jones reports a 26.8% turnover costing hospitals an average of $902,590 in 1988 or about 11% of the average salary budget. The study calculated direct and indirect costs. Direct costs were attributed to advertising and recruitment, unfilled positions, and the hiring process. Indirect costs included termination, orientation and training, and decreased productivity. The average cost of turnover per RN was $10,198 with a range of $6,888–$15,152. This study reports costs that exceed some estimates of turnover costs and are less than others. It does point out that a systematic and standardized process for determining turnover cost is lacking and further research is needed.

In this study, costs associated with unfilled positions accounted for 35% of total cost per RN turnover. Orientation and training was the next costly category, followed by advertising and recruiting, decreased productivity, hiring, and termination. Considerable variation existed in the ranges of costs reported. Costs of unfilled positions ranged from $1358 to $7794 per RN. This raises questions about how hospitals track and report turnover costs. Jones cites limitations of the study as difficulty in obtaining accurate data, sample size and generalizability, and nonspecificity to specialized areas (21).

Costs vary in other reports; however, the secretary's Commission on Nursing cites the average cost of replacing a nurse at $20,000 (22).

Literature specific to critical care is scarce. Costs of recruiting critical care nurses are reported as

$7,324–$9,042 in one California hospital, but detailed information on how the costs were calculated is incomplete (23).

Based on previous experience, Chris anticipates six RN vacancies for MICU in the next fiscal year. From past experience, Chris expects to fill all vacancies from in-house applicants. This practice serves retention and recruitment goals. However, these in-house transferees lack ICU experience and training.

Nursing education provides a 12-week critical care course every 4 months for nurses new to critical care. The nursing education department provides the information that the cost for the program is $2000/nurse based on six participants per course (SICU and CCU also use this training course to fill positions). These costs include salaries for the nursing educators, administrative expenses, indirect costs for space and utilities, and costs for equipment and supplies.

Multiplying nursing education costs by the number of MICU trainees ($2000 × 6) equals $12,000. In addition, each nurse receives a salary during the 3-month ICU course, and is assigned with another experienced ICU nurse who serves as a preceptor and mentor during clinical training. With a projected 1991 average salary and benefit cost for each nurse of $40,000, the 3-month orientation for six nurses costs $60,000. This figure is reached by dividing each nurse's $40,000 average salary by 4, or the cost of a nurse's 3-month salary and benefits. This results in $10,000. Multiplying this figure by 6, or the total number of 1991 vacancies, equals $60,000.

Further, each ICU nurse has three paid educational leave days available to use each year. This means an average cost of $462 for educational leave days ($40,000 divided by 2,080 (total work hours for a full-time nurse in a year) equals $19.23 (hourly average salary and benefit rate); and $19.23 × 8 (regular hours of duty) × 24 (number of staff) × 3 (number of educational leave days) equals $11,077 (rounded to nearest dollar).

Summing the cost from nursing education, educational leave days, and orientation, ($12,000 + $60,000 + $11,077) equals a figure rounded to the next dollar of $83,077.

Library Costs

Costs for specific textbooks and journals ordered for MICU by the hospital library are charged to the unit. In addition, services of the librarians, subscription costs for nursing journals, and photocopy costs of pertinent articles for nursing staff also are charged to MICU as a cost center. From the hospital cost distribution report, Chris finds that the library charged the unit $3600 for 1990. Chris estimates that in 1991 the library costs will be $4000.

IMPLEMENTATION

Chris aims to have better information to plan MICU's 1992 operating budget. She perceives that she has expended more effort in collecting and preparing the data for 1991's estimated budget than will be necessary in preparing 1992's budget. Chris decides to consult with the automated data processing (ADP) department to determine how to use the hospital information system to track the various classes of costs she has identified.

Meeting with the ADP coordinator, Chris explains her needs and inquires about the possibility of a high-tech work station that she recently read about. The article describes how clinical support representatives manage unit and patient information through an automated system of computers, fax machines, and copiers. The work station concept has appeal in its ability to manage both quality and cost information efficiently (24). The coordinator agrees that the work station sounds ideal for the system Chris has in mind, but points out that the need for people, time, and money makes the idea impractical in the near future. The coordinator suggests they work with the present system for now while watching other hospitals for reports of work station performance. Chris and the coordinator decide to implement a bar-code labeling system and to install a fax machine and an additional computer terminal to facilitate information transmission and processing. The ADP coordinator will be responsible for programming and equipment needs. Chris leaves the meeting confident that the computerized information system will organize data, prepare reports, forecast supply and drug requirements, forecast costs, analyze data, and track the supplies, the drugs, and the minor equipment used by a critical care unit.

For example, the computer program will examine each product separately and maintain records of available supplies. Further, the program's data base will record the minimum number of each item required on the unit and determine what items to replace from central supply. Historically, nurses have hoarded essential supplies such as pressure tubing to ensure that necessary items are always available. But the practice of keeping excess supplies on units is inefficient. This system would eliminate costly stockpiling, while providing information to allay nurses' fears about running out of essential products. It would also provide a measure to protect supply losses from theft. Table 10.8 illustrates how the information system will record the inventory supply data for MICU for a specific day.

A terminal that networks with the hospital computer system becomes imperative. How much information is entered by nurses at the unit level, compared to input by supply technicians or ward secretaries, becomes an important practical consideration. At a time when nurses voice concern about the number of nonnursing duties they perform, Chris anticipates some resistance to entering the data from staff.

In this case example, Chris plans to have all stocked supplies and drugs come with detachable bar-code labels. When an MICU nurse administers a drug or uses a supply item, the nurse scans the label with a hand scanner. The label includes information about the particular item used and its cost. Chris thinks most unit nurses will support this approach to inventory control and tracking costs.

A ward secretary or unit nurse will attach a bar-coded label to the top of each patient's charge record. The label identifies the patient by social security number and includes the codes for the patient's nursing diagnosis or diagnosis related group. The patient's charge record is scanned daily.

Consequently, the information data base system can track the cost generated and attribute the cost to each specific patient and the diagnostic classification. The computer also maintains a cumulative ledger of costs of each diagnostic category, as well as the accumulated costs for patient supplies. Chris will use the information system data base to forecast the drug and supply costs for the 1992 operating budget.

Table 10.8. Daily Supply Usage Report

Delivery Point Summary Report for MICU
Central Supply
July 13, 1989
Page 1

Cost Unit Account Number 1117.00
Medical Intensive Care Unit

Item	Item Name	Quantity	Level	Cost	Issues
109	Catheter-foley 16 Fr. 5 cc	8	6	3.04	2
222	K-Thermia blanket	1	0	18.01	1
510	Nasal cannula	25	21	8.74	4
518	Bag-leg urine	6	4	4.12	2
482	Connecting tube 72 inch	20	15	18.00	5
572	Salem sump tube	6	5	3.42	1
819	Glove/sm/exam/10's	2	1	16.38	1
1000	CVP dressing tray	10	8	11.00	2
1006	Sputum trap	6	5	5.70	1
1015	Urine spec. contain	8	7	18.00	1
1730	Blood gas kit	10	9	54.40	1
1941	Sponge 4 × 4 unfilled	2	1	2.96	1
2124	Chest tube 36 Fr.	1	0	4.98	1
2306	Introducer kit.	4	3	72.04	1
2309	Swan-Ganz cath.	4	3	96.10	1
2310	Catheterization tray	12	10	21.97	2
4590	Swan-Ganz cath bridge	40	38	50.00	2
4595	Dual injection site	5	3	4.75	2
8006	Pegboard intubation	3	2	181.68	1
Total item costs:				$595.29	

General and bulk supplies are more difficult to attribute to any specific patient diagnostic category. For example, pens, pencils, paper, paper clips, printer ribbons, staples, Band-Aids, syringes, and needles represent a few of the innumerable items difficult to charge to a specific patient category. As these supplies are delivered, they become charged to the unit's cost center account. Costs for these supplies could be charged to a patient if a bar label is attached to them. Some hospitals have automated equipment that labels syringes and syringe needles for bar-code reading. This permits the costs of these items to be related to a patient account, unit account, or diagnosis.

Preparing a critical care budget requires extensive data collection and tracking. Information systems can provide a solution for this need.

EVALUATION

Chris aims to relate costs to a patient's medical or nursing diagnosis. This permits an evaluation of each individual case and building an information base involving similar cases. Determining the norm of costs expended for a particular diagnosis will assist in future budget projections.

The hospital's fiscal or managerial accounting department produces a statement of expenses. The statement includes the amount budgeted, the amount actually spent, variances, and a year-to-date cumulative. The report includes lists of specific categories of expenses and amounts budgeted. From the comparison of what was spent and what was budgeted, Chris learns if the budget balances, is less than projected, or exceeds the plan. When the budget varies, Chris expects to write a variance analysis with justifications.

However, the information system could provide Chris with ongoing data about how well the unit's costs correspond with the targeted budget. If there was a variance in the budget, Chris could realize it before the accounting system presented a formal report about the budget overrun, since the cost data would be available to her through the information system. This allows for a regular review of budgetary variances to assure appropriate use of resources.

With continuing good information, Chris can take actions to investigate budget variations. This assumes, of course, that the causes for going over or under budget have been identified. Chapter 13 goes into detail on the topic of variance reporting.

Suppose, in one case scenario, that during the second quarter, an unanticipated surge in MI admissions results in the unexpected administration of expensive drug treatment modalities and increased use of supplies. One drastic action to control the budget includes capping the number of MI patients admitted to the ICU. Clearly, this decision requires the approval of the hospital's chief executive officer and medical director. In the final analysis, Chris recognizes that the increased expenses associated with increased census will result in additional revenue. Controlling expenses to ensure that revenue is sufficient is a challenge for all health care providers in the current environment.

SUMMARY

Chris expects the operating budget's data base to improve. Her projection for next year's operating budget is based on fragmented data. Much of the data was provided to her from other departments and retrieved from multiple sources. With the implementation of the medical informatics system, Chris is confident about forecasting, planning, and controlling next year's budget. These goals are consistent with AACN's critical care manager role expectations of establishing a valid statistical data base for making budgetary decisions and facilitating the development of realistic annual budgets.

Summarizing the scattered data collected and collated from 1989 and 1990, Chris forwards the following operating budget for 1991 through the director and vice president to the chief executive officer. Chris includes the staff salaries in her operating budget.

In this example, nurse staffing guidelines for critical care are based on a patient classification system. The classification system recognizes differences in the demand for nursing care and, based on specific criteria, separates patients into categories ranging from the least (category I) to the most demanding (category III). Analysis of work sampling identified the three discrete groups of patients in the critical care classification categories.

The demand for nursing care is expressed in hours per patient day (HPPD), and categories are specific to critical care. The classification system reflects the difference in required nursing care time among patients within the critical care unit. The hours per patient day by category are listed in Table 10.9.

Staffing requirements can be calculated based on the categories. To obtain the FTE required to staff a unit, multiply the average daily census (ADC) in each category by the required hours per patient day times the 7 days in a week. This number is then divided by the average hours worked (AHW) by one full-time employee. In this case, the average number of hours worked per week is 35.2. This accounts for an average of 4.8 hours per week per employee that are taken as paid time off. This average estimate may vary by hospital. An example of the calculation is shown in Table 10.10.

In the budget the FTE was rounded to 24 and multiplied by the average annual salary of staff RNs working in MICU (24 × $40,000 = $960,000). The figure of $40,000 includes base salary plus overtime, holiday pay, and shift and weekend differentials. The FTE refers to staff nurses needed for direct patient care and excludes FTE for the head nurse and unit secretaries, which are accounted for under administrative salaries.

Another simple method for calculating FTE is shown in Table 10.11.

This method uses a factor of 1.6 to estimate the number of FTEs needed to staff a unit based on average work load by patient category. The factor 1.6 represents one FTE plus replacement for paid time off, i.e., 7 days per week multiplied by 8 hours per day equals 56 hours divided by 35.2 equals 1.6. Some hospitals use a factor of 1.4 or 1.8 depending on the estimated paid time off each full-time employee will use. This method is also useful for hospitals that do not have patient classification systems. If the estimated staff needed per 8-hour shift is five, then five multiplied by three shifts per day equals 15. Fifteen times 1.6 equals 24 FTE. This factor does not work for 12-hour shifts, because the employee is really working one and one-half shifts. A factor of 2.4 must be used in this case (1.6 + 0.8 = 2.4). For example, 10 instead of 15 staff would be needed for the same 24-hour coverage if 12-hour shifts are used. Ten multiplied by 2.4 equals 24 full-time staff.

One other calculation can be used to estimate staffing in the absence of a classification system. The desired number of patient care hours is multiplied by ADC times 7 days and then divided by AHW (35.2). A unit that staffs with a nurse-to-patient ratio of 2:1 is shown in the following example:

Desired Hours × ADC × 7 ÷ 35.2 = FTE
12 × 9 × 7 ÷ 35.2 = 21.5 FTE

This method has the obvious drawback of being insensitive to quantified patient care needs. Meth-

Table 10.9. Required Hours per Patient Day (HPPD) by Category

Bed Section	Category HPPD		
	I	II	III
Critical Care	11	16	24

Table 10.10. Required FTE

Category	ADC	×	HPPD	×	Days	÷	AHW	=	FTE
I	6	×	11	×	7	÷	35.2	=	13.0
II	2	×	16	×	7	÷	35.2	=	6.4
III	1	×	24	×	7	÷	35.2	=	4.8
Total									24.2 FTE

ADC × Required HPPD × 7 days ÷ AHW = FTE

Table 10.11. FTE Calculation

Category	ADC	×	HPPD	÷	Hrs/Shift	=	FTE/24 Hrs
I	6	×	11	÷	8	=	8.25
II	2	×	16	÷	8	=	4.00
III	1	×	24	÷	8	=	3.00
Total							15.25 × 1.6 = 24.4 FTE

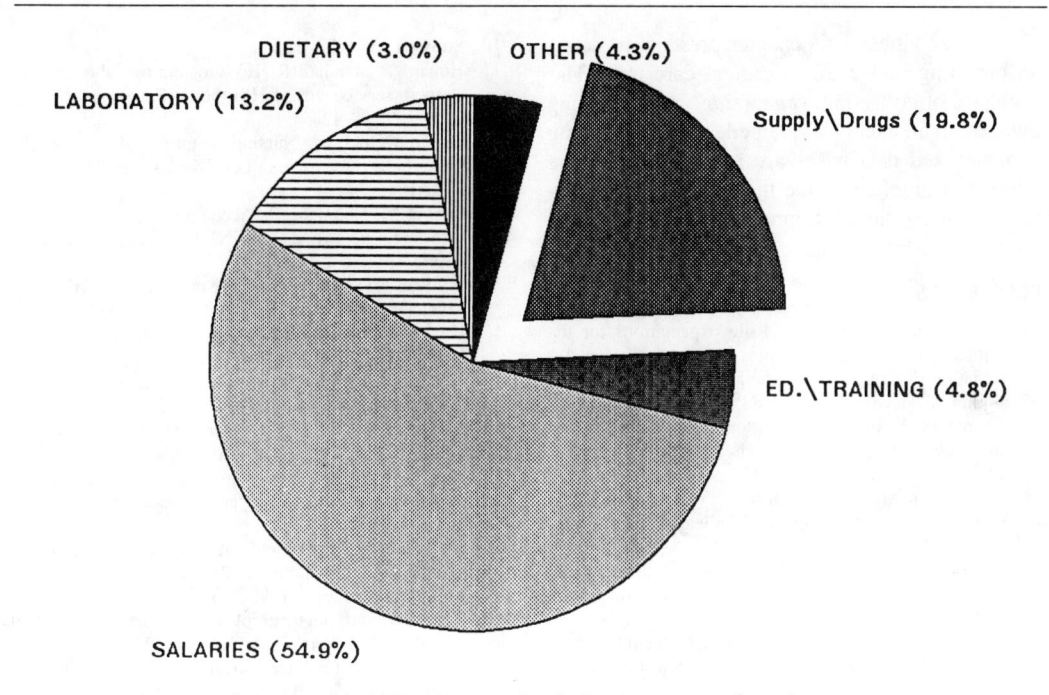

Figure 10.2. MICU 1991 operating budget (percentage of costs).

ods based on valid and reliable patient classification systems are recommended. Chapter 8 on personnel budgets explores this issue in detail and provides additional examples of projecting FTE requirements.

Table 10.12 illustrates the operating budget proposal.

Knowing how graphical representations assist in presenting data, Chris compares the percentage of account costs to the total budget by creating a pie chart. She sums the costs for administrative supplies, minor equipment, repair and maintenance, utilities, advertising, laundry, library, and x-ray together in the "other" category. The greatest percentage of account costs are for salaries, patient supplies/drugs, laboratory, dietary, and education and training.

The finance committee and the board of trustees review and approve the 1991 operating budget for MICU (Fig. 10.2) Chris expects that this budget will promote cost effective unit operations. An ongoing effort to educate physicians and staff about the budget will promote success of the 1991 budget proposal.

CONCLUSION

Operating budgets are essential to efficient and effective utilization of resources in conducting daily

Table 10.12. MICU Operating Budget Fiscal Year 1991

Proposed 1991 Operating Budget for MICU
Cost Account Center 1117.00

Cost Category	Amount
A. Patient supplies and drugs	$346,316.00**
B. Administrative supplies	$5,000.00
C. Dietary	$53,168.00
D. Minor equipment	$6,120.00
E. Repair and maintenance	$15,000.00
F. Utilities	$6,416.00
G. Advertising	$1,000.00
H. Education and training	$83,077.00
I. Nursing salaries and benefits	$960,000.00
J. Laundry	$1,400.00
K. Laboratory	$231,456.00
L. Library	$4,000.00
M. X-ray	$36,000.00
Estimated 1991 MICU Operating Budget:	$1,748,953.00

**This figure includes the FTE costs (labor). It assumes that labor costs increase supply and pharmacy costs by a factor of 28%, which is the aggregate estimate based on the MICU 1990 CDR report for supply and pharmacy FTE costs. Thus,

$270,559 × .28 = $75,757 (dollar rounded)
$270,559 + $75,757.00 = $346,316

The labor costs would be allocated to each patient and diagnosis according to the patient's length of stay. These costs would be added to the patient's charges by methods established by the hospital information system.

hospital activities. This chapter presents in detail an operating budget for a critical care unit. The problems of collecting, organizing, and analyzing data are realistically explained. Solutions using computerized data bases are recommended. The tables and graphs provide the illustrations necessary to display and interpret data used in typical operating budgets.

REFERENCES

1. AACN position statement: Role expectations for the critical care manager. Newport Beach: American Association of Critical-Care Nurses, 1986.
2. Sorkin A. Health care and the changing economic environment. Lexington: Lexington Books, 1986:5–6.
3. Strassen L. Key business skills for nurse managers. Philadelphia: J.P. Lippincott Co., 1987:105–106.
4. Amatayakul M. Finance concepts for the health care manager. Chicago: American Medical Record Association, 1985:168.
5. Granof M, Neumann B. Accounting for managers and investors. Englewood Cliffs, NJ: Prentice Hall, [in press,] 1990.
6. Porter-O'Grady T. Nursing finance: budgeting strategies for a new age. Rockville: Aspen Publishers, 1987:99—100.
7. Amatayakul M. Finance concepts for the health care manager.Chicago: American Medical Record Association, 1985:68.
8. Fitzpatrik J. Nursing diagnosis: translating nursing diagnosis into ICD code. AJN April 1989:493–495.
9. Hogan A, Marshall R. How to improve allocation of support service costs. Healthcare Financial Management 1990:44–46.
10. Strassen, pp. 122–123.
11. Hogan A, Marshall R. How to improve allocation of support service costs. Healthcare Financial Management 1990;44:42.
12. Porter-O'Grady T. Nursing finance: budgeting strategies for a new age. Rockville: Aspen Publishers, 1987:104.
13. Granof M, Neumann B. Accounting for managers and investors. Englewood Cliffs, NJ: Prentice Hall, [in press,] 1990.
14. Sullivan J, Decker P. Effective management in nursing. Menlo Park: Addison-Wesley Co., 1988:451–452.
15. Health Care in the 1990s: forecasts by top analysts. Hospitals 1989:34–46.
16. Henke E. Accounting for nonprofit organization. 4th ed. Boston: Kent Publishing, 1986:225–227.
17. Labig CE. Effectiveness of recruiting resources for staff nurses. JONA 20(7/8) July/Aug 1990:12–16.
18. Blaney D, Hobson CJ. Cost effective nursing practice: guidelines for nurse managers. Philadelphia: J.B. Lippincott, 1988:219–221.
19. Joint Commission Accreditation Manual for Hospitals. Chicago: Joint Commission on Accreditation of Health Care Organizations, 1990:246.
20. Jones CB. Staff nurse turnover costs: part I, a conceptual model. JONA April 1990; 20(4):18–22.
21. Jones CB. Staff nurse turnover costs: part II, measurements and results. JONA May 1990;20(5):27–32.
22. Secretary's Commission on Nursing, Final Report, vol 1. Washington, DC: Department of Health and Human Services, Dec. 1988:28.
23. Mann EE, Jefferson KJ. Retaining staff: using turnover indices and surveys. JONA 18(7/8) July/Aug 1988:20.
24. Hardy JC, Douglas M. High tech workstations on nursing units. Nursing Management July 1990;21(7):62–63.

Chapter 11

Management Information Systems

JEANENE DELONG

FINANCIAL INFORMATION MANAGEMENT FOR NURSE MANAGERS

The increasing complexity of care required by current patient populations, and pressure to be fiscally competent and accountable requires that the nurse manager have quick access to useful, reliable information. It is imperative that nurse managers be involved in the selection, purchase, and placement of computer hardware, in the evaluation of their information needs, and in the review and recommendations about the choice of software applications (1). In order for nurse managers to intelligently assist in the hardware and software purchase they must become familiar with computer terms, abilities, and usage. The manager could start with a class on personal computers to learn about the keyboard, monitor, hard disk drives, floppy diskettes, memory, and processing. The next step is mastering computer terms, such as MIS (management information systems), NIS (nursing information system), and HIS (hospital information system).

The MIS usually consists of the financial aspects of the health care facility: pricing for rooms, procedures, and supplies, salary dollars budgeted, and other items that assist the manager when assessing, monitoring, and managing the budget. The MIS is dependent upon the HIS and NIS for accurate information so trends, revenues, and expenses can be shared with the manager. The HIS consists of an admission, dismissal and transfer system, laboratory, radiology, materials management, pharmacy, and charge capture systems. The HIS supports the day-to-day clinical operations of the health care facility and supplies information to the MIS. The nursing information system is fairly new to the health care setting. This system supports nursing at the bedside. The NIS, through input by nurses, captures clinical data from the patient. This system also supplies information to the HIS and MIS.

Nursing, the key element in patient care, is at the hub of the information wheel. Nurses utilize the information process daily and contribute to the information required by nurse managers. The information process for the nurse clinician may be described as follows:

1. Gathering information; the process of accumulating data necessary for the work day, such as report at change of shift.
2. Generating information; the process of creating additional data necessary to continue nursing activities, such as an assessment.
3. Recording the information; recording is the process of documenting patient information and nursing activities.
4. Retrieval of information is the process of searching for information previously stored, such as laboratory results, or a previous admissions record.
5. Exchange of information, also known as communication, is one of the most important steps in the information process (2) (see Fig. 11.1).

As clinical information is entered into the computer it is coded, priced, and/or formatted so the manager can review reports on the monthly patient days or visits, the procedures required by the patients, the costs of patient care per day, and diagnosis related group (DRG) information. This information is used by the nurse manager to formulate the financial plan and goals for the nursing unit.

Computers are simply tools that make it easier for the manager to receive quick and reliable information for the decision-making process. They are excellent at storing large quantities of data,

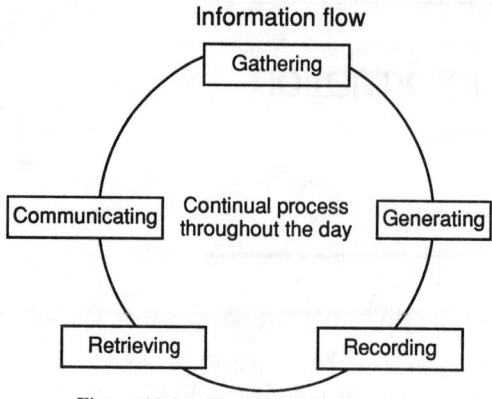

Figure 11.1. The information process.

sorting data, "flagging" items outside of normal parameters, and projecting what may be needed in the future based on historical or assimilated data. Data elements are the bits and pieces of information that are entered into the computer, such as a patient's age or diagnosis, or an employee's salary. Once a logical grouping of data is achieved it can be used to make a decision. For example, the nurse manager may ask "What if we increase the number of telemetry beds?" With the use of information stored by the computer about telemetry beds, the manager can determine the occupancy of the current telemetry beds, the waiting time for patients requiring telemetry beds, and the revenue generated by telemetry usage. The manager can then review this data, along with the expense of purchasing additional telemetry units, possible restructuring of personnel, education of personnel, etc., and make an informed decision about an increase in telemetry beds.

Having enough of the right data at the right time to assist the manager in making intelligent decisions is important. Let's review the following scenario of not having enough of the right data. A nurse manager is approached by the nursing and medical staff about purchasing an additional intra-aortic balloon pump (IABP). To begin the justification process, the nurse manager needs to gather information about current usage, maintenance problems, service calls, functionality and depreciation of the IABP, cost of a new IABP, cost of the maintenance contract, cost of supplies for the IABP such as paper, batteries, cables, etc., and the time frame for depreciation. Once the appropriate information is gathered, the manager can then compile the expected expenses; compare the expenses with projected revenue; and forecast the return on investment. If the nurse manager is unable to retrieve an accurate and/or complete history of IABP usage, the ability to adequately justify the additional purchase cannot be made.

A management information system may provide data to the manager to assist in the decision-making process (3). Types of data the nurse manager requires may include the following types of information:

- Revenue dollars generated for a particular unit on a monthly basis;
- Number of admissions by a particular diagnosis;
- Number of patient days by month by nursing unit;
- Pattern of equipment usage;
- Expense of staff education;
- Salary dollars;
- Lost charges.

This information is used by the nurse manager to formulate the financial plan and goals for the nursing unit, to investigate financial problems and their etiology, and determine how the problem effects the financial plan. If we return to our scenario of the IABP, the nurse manager will need to investigate the effects of the capital purchase on the budget, and balance that with possible opportunity cost, lost revenue if the service is not provided as marketed.

HARDWARE

Before purchasing computer hardware, the nurse manager needs to examine where they are now, where they want to go, and how to get there. As previously discussed, education is important, because knowledge is power. In this case, it is the power to make the right decision. Other issues to be addressed include:

- Budget, how much can be spent on hardware?
- Type of hardware currently used, will the hardware to be purchased be compatible with current hardware?
- Current operating system, will the hardware to be purchased be able to communicate with the current hardware?
- What service contracts and/or support does the manufacturer offer?
- Would current users recommend this hardware?

- Type and volume of data the manager requires;
- Physical access to the computer.

Computer hardware is the keyboard, monitor (screen), processing unit, and printer. The processing unit size determines the amount of memory and the processing power of the computer.

Access to hardware is important for the manager and determines the ease of information retrieval from the computer. For example if 15 managers have to share one terminal or a personal computer that is in a locked room in the basement, then access is very poor. However, if the manager shares a terminal or personal computer with two or three other managers in their office area, then access is better. Another consideration to be made is the ability to manipulate data. Usually in the budgeting process the nurse manager is asked frequently to review the budget and cut costs, reduce full-time employee complement, and/or reduce salary dollars by 3%. Data manipulation, also known as correcting, adding, removing, or modifying data, is used to achieve the desired outcome of reducing the budget.

There are three common types of computer hardware: mainframes, minis, and micros. Mainframes are large computers, minis are mid-size computers, and micros are known as personal computers.

Mainframes, also known as "hosts," have a large storage capacity and powerful multiple-processing abilities. Most health care institutions either own or share a mainframe. Large and/or complex software applications such as "admissions, dismissals and transfers" (ADT), order entry and results reporting, such as laboratory, pharmacy, radiology, respiratory therapy, and materials management are usually present on the mainframe. The mainframe utilizes these orders, in combination with a large on-line price book to generate patient billing and revenue for the health care facility. Mainframes, depending on size, can support 250-plus users at a time, this is probably another reason they are so popular with large institutions. Mainframes, because of their large storage capacity, can hold or provide a wealth of historical information. They are excellent for storing what was actually recorded. However, they can be restrictive when attempting to manipulate data for "what if" brainstorming. Historical information is helpful in forecasting future financial needs of the nursing unit. The powerful processing ability of the mainframe supports such applications as payroll, in which the computation of hours worked is multiplied by the hourly wage to produce a unit budget. Number crunching, such as reviewing how a 10% reduction in patient days across the hospital would affect revenue, is another way the mainframe can be used. Information from the mainframe may also assist the manager in the justification of capital expenditures and new ventures. The mainframe may also interact with a bedside system. The information generated can be used to research and improve billing of nursing services. Nursing tasks or nursing diagnoses can be sent from the bedside system to the mainframe. The mainframe may correlate the task or diagnosis with the price book and translate this information into a bill for nursing care delivered.

There may be drawbacks in any mainframe system. One may be report definitions that may restrict the manager to one format of information retrieval. An example would be revenue earned from the IABP is in report "G456," while usage is in report "H238," so multiple reports may have to be used. Unfortunately this requires the manager to manually enter, with each new addition, the pertinent data into their own personal computer for data manipulation, or the manager may choose to use paper and pen to do the calculations.

Also it may be difficult for the mainframe and the personal computers to communicate with each other, because their operating systems require complex translations, and this can be frustrating to the manager. However, future trends indicate that the need to standardize communication is a must and a solution is being addressed.

Options for minimizing drawbacks could involve the following steps. When dealing with multiple reports, work with the management information department to define useful reports and then present in detail these new report definitions. Remember, put the specifications together first, then discuss with the management information department what outcomes are desired from the data gathered.

The following illustrates a report definition scenario. The nurse manager is asked to put together a "price package" for care of patients with myocardial infarction (MI) with cardiac catheterization. There are many elements which may make up the total price package. These elements may be laboratory costs, radiology costs, supply costs, nursing costs, etc. When the manager discusses with MIS personnel the reports required to package these costs, the desired outcome will be total costs for acute MI with cardiac catheterization. The detail required includes all costs as billed to a specific number of patients; this gives an average cost and a place to start the "price packaging" determinations.

Future communications will enable the manager to "export" data from the mainframe, and then study, manipulate, and redefine the data based on patient care needs. This information can then be "imported" back to the mainframe so other users can review the changes. Future mainframes will become a centralized support system and will support decentralized processing.

The second type of computer hardware is the "mini." Minis have more computing power and storage capacity than the personal computer, but not as much as the mainframe. Minis are usually set up on a network, which allows communication between all computers on the network. Depending on the size of the mini, it can support 5–35 users at a time. In the health care setting you may see minis set up in departments; for example, radiology can utilize a mini to track their supplies and usage of their equipment, and support sophisticated imaging and voice-to-text technology (4). The mini will allow multiple person access so many radiologists can dictate at one time. Another item to be addressed when installing a mini system is space for the computer. The space for the computer needs to be cool, protected, and have its own fire protection. The issue of cabling to terminals attached to the mini needs to be addressed, along with printer placement. Before making a decision to purchase a printer, the volume of printing, number of persons using the printer, quality of printing, and speed of the printer need to be determined. Problems may occur if the minis network cannot talk to the mainframe for billing and scheduling purposes. This problem can be addressed by working closely with your vendor and your management information department on a communication solution.

Micros, also known as personal computers, can support one user at a time. Personal computers are excellent for manipulation of data; however, if the personal computer and the mainframe cannot communicate and share data, the manager must manually load data on the personal computer. The manager must ensure accuracy of projections by using the most current data. Once again, work closely with your management information department on finding a possible solution. Personal computers may have a hard drive internal storage and one or more disk drives. The disk drive allows the user to save data to or restore data from floppy or hard disks. One advantage of the storage to the hard drive is faster retrieval of information. However, if many managers are using a personal computer, floppy disks are a good way to allow the managers to keep their work with them and save hard disk memory for day-to-day operations. Remember when using floppy disks to protect them from damage by placing them in their covers when not in use and designating a dry, dust-free storage area. Hard disk drives should be protected from heat, cold, dust, and jarring.

ESSENTIAL VS. NONESSENTIAL INFORMATION

The information systems used by health care facilities collect copious amounts of data, and it is up to the decision makers to discover what information is essential. One way to harness the massive amount of information collected by the computer is to work with your staff and other managers in establishing what information is essential for decision making. Once these items have been identified, the next step is to determine which items complement each other to give the manager a clearer picture. When this identification is complete, it can be shared with the management information department to create the report definition which is loaded into the system. Nonessential information discovered in this process should be questioned. Why is the nonessential information being collected; should continued collection be stopped; and, could the space occupied by this data be better utilized?

After the nurse managers have the information collected and organized, and have a format in mind for reporting the information, it may be helpful to sit down with the analysts from the management information department. When discussing the report desired with the analyst it is good to remember that the computer deals best with simple logic, such as yes/no questions (Fig. 11.2). The MIS analyst may also need to know where the information is captured or who generated the information. Revisions are sometimes necessary, but the time spent now will save many hours in the future.

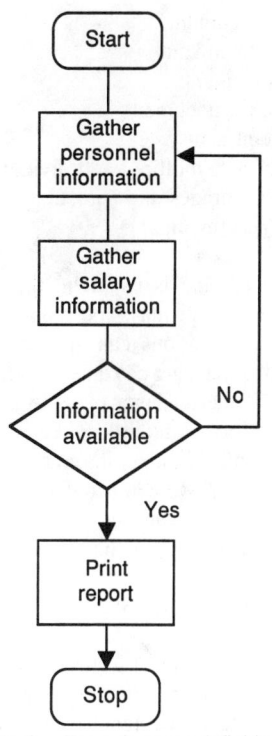

Figure 11.2. Example report definition flow.

SOFTWARE

There are many software packages on the market for the personal computer: spreadsheet applications, word processing applications, data base management applications, and many others. Each of these software applications can assist the manager in information evaluation. A summary of their functions will be discussed.

Software is the instruction given to the computer. When learning about new software remember to take your time to practice and explore. For some it may be helpful to take a class at the local college or university on the use of spreadsheet software packages, word processing packages, and data base management packages. Others may want to learn on their own, utilizing the guide sent with the software, or viewing an instructional videotape. Some health care facilities may offer classes to employees to instruct them about specific software packages in use in the health care facility.

It is helpful for the manager to know the hospital's long-term goals, plans for use, and allocated funds for computer enhancement before approaching a consultant. It is also important to be familiar with the software applications the health care facility uses, mainframe applications, applications used on minis, and software applications for use on the personal computer. Take time to learn how the mainframe applications create, review, and use data. This familiarity will give you insight into what your facility values and how they operate. Consultants may be used for guidance in the purchase process; they can supply expertise and solutions that are not political or traditionally mandated by the health care facility.

Armed with knowledge about software programs (with some effort) the manager can write personalized, small, helpful programs known as macros. These macros can be written to use on the personal computer. Macros can be written to do calculations. For example, when asked to reduce salary dollars by 3%, the use of an appropriate macro may require less than five keystrokes, saving hours of manual calculations. Macros can also be designed to calculate, i.e., what percentage of expenses is salary dollars, or the mean number of patient days per month, or the annual sum of lost charges.

Spreadsheets

There are many spreadsheet software packages on the market. These packages are useful for organizing data and utilizing graphs to present data. Spreadsheets can assist the manager in reviewing and projecting salary dollars, expenses, and capital expenditure items.

Spreadsheet applications have other uses, such as:

- Create a worksheet;
- Revise a worksheet;
- Print a worksheet;
- Build a pie chart from worksheet data;
- Build a line graph from worksheet data;
- Build a bar graph from worksheet data;
- Create macros (small set of instructions);
- Use mathematical functions;
- Use logical functions;
- Use financial functions;
- Use statistical functions.

One of the useful functions of a spreadsheet is financial calculation capability. This function can assist in calculating depreciation. For example, the unit has just purchased an intra-aortic balloon pump

(IABP) for $50,000. The useful life of the IABP is 7 years and the salvage or resale value will be $15,000. By supplying this information to your spreadsheet, the computer can compute the yearly depreciation expense.

Another useful function of the spreadsheet program is the graph capability. Graphs give visual representation of raw data and may help the manager analyze trends quickly and efficiently (Fig. 11.3).

Trends, such as acuity or census, can be displayed in a graph so the manager can quickly and clearly review areas of interest (5). A graph may also be built to review length of stay by diagnosis, either medical or nursing. If you plan to use graphs for justification purposes it would be wise to invest in a quality plotter. A plotter is a piece of hardware designed to draw graphs. Small desk-top plotters contain six to eight color pens. Plotters can create overhead transparencies or graphics on regular or glossy paper, and with color, the graph message can really stand out.

Word Processing

The functions of most word processing software applications include the following:

- Create a document;
- Revise a document;
- Print a document;
- Spellcheck a document;
- Merge documents;
- Add, subtract, multiply and divide;
- Calculate averages and percentages;
- Create line drawings.

Word processing is useful to the manager for writing memos, agendas, and reports. Most word processing applications can also store document formats so the manager can quickly process a memo or agenda. If the manager plans to use word processing for formal reports and/or formal correspondence, an investment in or access to a quality printer is a must. Remember, the content of your document may be great, but without a clear, clean, and readable presentation the message may be lost.

Data Base Management

Data base management software applications give an organized way of managing information. Data input formats can be designed to suit the manager's needs for loading data. The computer can then sort, find, or highlight information based on search criteria entered by the manager. The following are

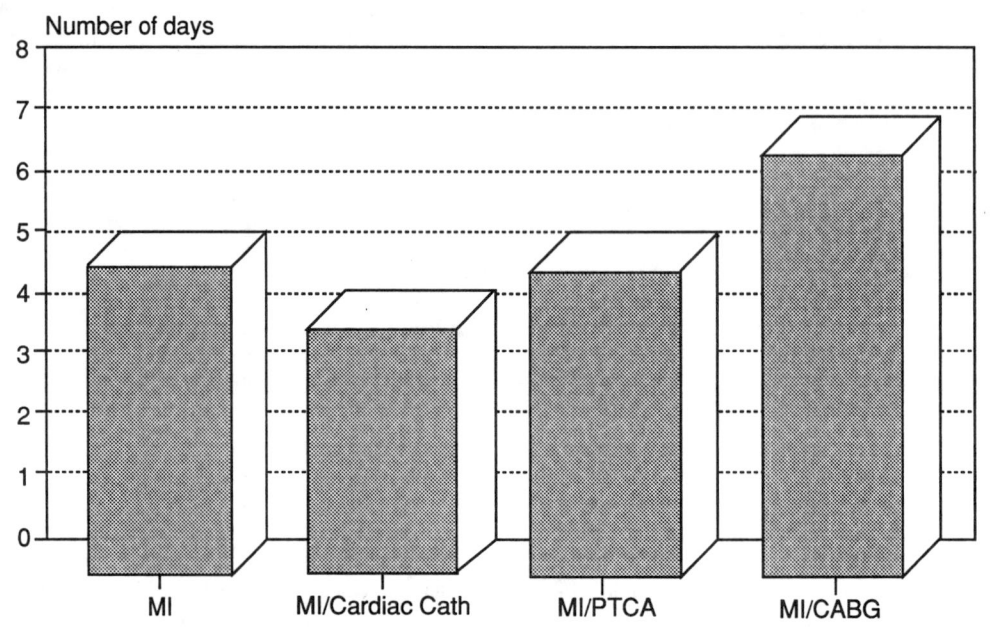

Figure 11.3. Length of stay by cardiovascular medical diagnoses.

the functions of most data base management software applications.

- Create a form design;
- Add data;
- Search update data;
- Print data;
- Redesign a form;
- Create reports;
- Create and use macros.

Data base management can be useful for many things, such as personnel management. The manager can design a format to capture their personnel's education level, certifications, continuing education hours/units, salary, expiration dates for basic and/or advanced life support, and other items (6). Once this information is loaded into the data base, the manager can use the search options to locate all employees with Certified Critical-care Registered Nurse (CCRN) certification or all employees who hold advanced cardiac life support certification.

Research can also be enhanced through the use of a data base management system. The computer is a tireless, efficient clerical assistant and can quickly search, categorize, and organize data. For example, an increase in urinary tract infections (UTI) is reported; there are many elements that can be captured and analyzed to discover why this has occurred. First, the researcher would need to design the data capture format, which may include patient name, diagnosis, presence of urinary catheter, type of pericare or catheter care rendered, etc. After this information is loaded, the researcher can then search for commonalities among the patients and perhaps determine the cause. The discovery of commonalities can be accomplished by entering search criteria into the computer, and requesting that all data be reviewed for this particular piece of information (7).

Electronic mail is another use of the computer. Use of electronic mail can reduce time spent in memo preparation and time wasted in telephone tag. Most electronic mail systems also allow for multiple person distribution, enabling the manager to quickly update all pertinent personnel at one time. Again, computer availability is important for timely electronic mail correspondence.

USES AND MISUSES OF INFORMATION SYSTEMS

The ability of the computer to rapidly retrieve, summarize, and compare large volumes of information has made it a useful tool for the manager. However, the computer is only as good as the software written for it and the data received is only as good as the data entered.

Misuses of the computer may cause the manager frustration from delays and unnecessary data review. Common misuses could include loading data that will not be utilized but consumes memory on your computer. Another misuse is reports that are not used by anyone. Data resident on the computer and printed on reports should be reviewed critically and decisions made on whether to continue to capture the data, change the format of the report, or discontinue the report. Storing unnecessary data, especially on a personal computer, can slow the response of your computer.

Examine data carefully and decide which pieces are necessary for you to make decisions. Work

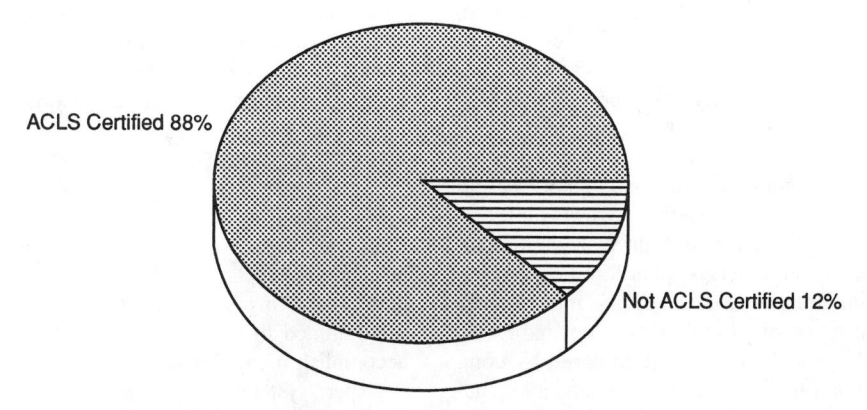

Figure 11.4. Percentages of certified RN staff in the intensive care unit.

with the data to design useful and meaningful reports. Clean up data that is irrelevant and/or old.

AUTOMATION VS. NONAUTOMATION

Automation, or to operate automatically, is beginning to enter the nursing realm. For the nurse manager the data captured on the financial and bedside clinical systems can supply a wealth of information. Bedside systems use automation to distribute data like urine output to a graph, a clinical flow record, or an intake/output record instead of the nurse entering the same value into three different records. In another example, if the bedside system supports nursing diagnoses, the manager can track costs by nursing diagnoses and use this data to bill the patient for nursing care delivered. Managed care models can also use bedside systems to track costs and nursing care delivered. Bedside systems can also collect valuable information for quality management monitoring and research (8). For example, the manager can use data from the bedside system to discover why length of stay is increasing. By tracking medication errors, outliers in managed care programs, and unmet outcomes of nursing diagnoses, the manager can study possible causes for increasing length of stay and work with staff on solutions.

Processes that aren't automated may require hours of manual entry and review to discover trends and/or causes. Without automation, the retrieval of the information may be difficult because it may come from many different sources. Also, the format of written information may vary from department to department and consistency of data collection may differ. Data manipulation using paper, pencil, and calculator may be more time intensive. Automation may be the answer; however, before automating a process, the benefits and possible hazards need to be investigated. If the process requires complex decision making, an expert system may be required. The cost of automation needs to be weighed against the current cost of the process.

Bedside computer systems that support the clinician at the bedside have mixed reviews for return on investments. Some studies have shown that after computerization nurses spent less time in clerical, communicative, and supply maintenance activities; however, this time was not redirected to bedside patient care. The time saved by computerization was spent in continuing education, administrative planning, and management tasks (9).

Other studies have shown a time savings of 15 minutes-1 hr per shift per nurse. If a health care facility experiences overtime, dollars may be saved through automation. Other results have determined that even though on-line charting has not been shown to take less time than manual charting, it does result in a more complete and legible chart with more frequent notations of date and time (10).

To receive the greatest return on investment from a bedside system, a communication via the mainframe to the HIS and MIS must be established. Without pharmacy, laboratory, radiology, materials management, and other department communications the patient care picture is incomplete.

Another issue to be addressed is nursing and medical staff acceptance. Acceptance can be encouraged if the hardware and software is reliable, available, fast, and user friendly (i.e., the use is consistent, F3 key always means Exit, etc.). The bedside system should also be self evident to the clinician and not require a lot of repeated reference in manuals or days of training. The system should also contain the correct vocabulary. Overviews and demonstrations are very important, and will give the staff an opportunity to become familiar with the system.

Once a bedside system is selected, education is the number one agenda item. Education on software packages can be accomplished in many ways, through lecture and demonstration, through self-paced studies in a learning laboratory, through a preceptor program, or all of the above. Whatever form is selected, it's important to allow the staff time to "play" and become familiar with the system and how it works.

Back-up procedures should be established in case of automated system failure. Back-up procedures could include saving data on diskettes, printing data on paper, designing forms to capture information if the system is down, and a process for entering information during down time.

EXPERT SYSTEMS

Computers are designed for repetitive tasks and following precise instructions. Humans are better at ideas, concepts, exploring, initiating changes, and discovering solutions. However, computers programmed to use human problem solving can accomplish many things.

Expert systems are designed to mimic human intelligence to solve problems. Expert systems utilize algorithms and rules of logic to emulate human decision making. Building expert systems requires research and observations of expert practitioners and how they reason on the job (11). Once the reasoning process is captured, it is then replicated into commands for the computer.

The manager can use an expert system for resource management in the following way. You have been asked to reduce the salary dollars for your nursing units. By loading personnel data into the system you can ask the system many questions. Such as, if salary dollars are reduced by 10%, how many full-time employee positions will need to be eliminated? Or if LVNs are used as monitor technicians instead of RNs, how many salary dollars can be saved? The system can quickly do the calculations and offer possible solutions based on the "human expertise used" in the programming.

Many may have also heard of artificial intelligence or AI. This system, also based on human logic and intelligence, can actually make a decision and follow through (12). An AI system may be in the critical care unit right now. There are infusion pumps on the market today that titrate drugs like nitroprusside, based on blood pressure parameters entered into the infusion pump by the nurse. Surgical departments may use AI in the form of robotics for the placement of femurs into the hip.

AI systems can be used in the financial realm in many ways. When preparing a budget to open a new critical care unit, the number of beds, cost of equipment, supplies, salary dollars, and other expenses can be entered into the system. With the appropriate data, the system can offer answers to questions about the number of patient days required to balance the budget or the number of patient days required to make a profit.

SUMMARY

The benefits realized from the use of computers will directly correlate to the availability of the computer, the availability of the required data, and the decision-making ability of the manager (13). The computer is a tool to assist the manager in assessing information, planning a solution, and evaluating the outcome (14). Managers who learn how to use the computer tool effectively will reap the rewards in time saved and better decision preparation.

REFERENCES

1. Ball MJ, Hannah KJ, GerdinJelger U, Peterson H, eds. Nursing informatics where care and technology meet. New York: Springer, Verlag Inc., 1988:206–211.
2. Bertram D, Bozeman E, Crooks C, DeLong J, Jundi A. Harris Hospital Methodist Nursing Practice Task Force: analysis of nursing activities and automation. July 1986:1.
3. Ball MJ, Hannah J. Using computers in nursing. Reston, VA: Reston Publishing Company, Inc., 1984:123–124.
4. Ball, p. 27.
5. Laborde JM, Dando A, Hemmasi M. Computer graphics: a tool for decision making in nursing. Computers in nursing Jan/Feb 1989:17.
6. Peterson J, Hannah KJ. Nursing management information systems. In: Ball MJ, Hannah KJ, GerdinJelger U, Peterson H, eds. Nursing informatics: where care and technology meet. New York: Springer, Verlag Inc., 1988:193.
7. Baker A. Computer applications in qualitative research. Computers in nursing Sept/Oct 1988:211.
8. Mowry MM, Korpman RA. Managing health care costs, quality, and technology product line strategies for nursing. Rockville, MD: Aspen Publishers, Inc., 1986:139.
9. Staggers N. Using computers in nursing: documented benefits and needed studies. Computers in nursing July/Aug 1988:164.
10. Hendrickson G, Kovner CT. Effects of computers on nursing resource use: do computers save nurses time? Computers in nursing Jan/Feb 1990:16.
11. Chase SK. Knowledge representation in expert systems. Nursing diagnosis applications. Computers in nursing March/Apr 1988:60.
12. Penrose R. The emperor's new mind: concerning computers, minds, and the laws of physics. New York: Oxford University Press, 1989:11.
13. Peterson, p. 203.
14. Charns MP, Schaefer MJ. Health care organizations: a model for management. New Jersey: Prentice-Hall, Inc., 1983:275.

Chapter 12

Budget Presentation and Approval Process

CATHY RODGERS WARD

Preparation of the budget package is only the first step in obtaining the necessary funds to manage and operate a nursing unit, division, or department. After planning and devising the best estimation of the amount of financial resources needed for the coming fiscal year, the critical care nurse manager must then seek institutional approval of this proposed plan or financial forecast. The process of budget presentation and approval is equally important as that of budget preparation. An excellent budget which is presented poorly is likely to be rejected. The critical care nurse manager must be prepared to present, defend, and negotiate for the financial package that is submitted. This chapter will outline the procedure for budget finalization including the approval process and strategies for budget acceptance.

FINALIZING THE BUDGET PACKAGE

The actual budget package to be submitted must look professional and organized. Before submitting the budget proposal, the nurse manager and (where available) the unit business manager perform a final review (Table 12.1). All components of the budget plan must be complete and without any sections left blank. Hospital finance departments usually have specified formats and forms for each nurse manager to complete. These formats should be followed exactly to prevent any confusion in interpretation of the data submitted. Formulas for deriving specific data (i.e., how to calculate benefits) are usually specified by the finance department and must be known and executed by the nurse manager. The order of the budget components submitted should be prioritized unless otherwise outlined by the finance department.

To avoid unnecessary embarrassing moments in the budget presentation process the final budget package should appear neat, legible, organized, and worthy of any corporate budget review. The nurse manager may seek assistance from the unit or departmental business manager to make sure there are no errors in the package and that the graphic display of data is optimum. This may include the use of computers and submitting the finalized proposed budget plan via computer disks with accompanying hard copies.

THE APPROVAL PROCESS

The hierarchy of the budget approval process may be simple or complex depending upon the organization. In some hospitals the unit nurse manager prepares the budget, consults with the director, and submits the plan directly to the hospital budget committee for approval. In other systems the unit nurse manager prepares the budget plan, proposes the plan to the divisional director who in turn seeks approval from the department director or chief nursing officer (CNO). The CNO then presents the entire department's budget to the hospital chief executive officer (CEO), the chief financial officer (CFO), and/or the hospital's budget committee (Table 12.2). The hospital's board of trustees has final approval of the institution's entire budget.

Responsibility for the budget preparation and proposal process seems to depend upon the size and type of the hospital. One study conducted by the Office of the Inspector General found that in nearly three-quarters of the hospitals surveyed, the

Table 12.1. Final Budget Presentation Checklist

_____	Budget package is complete
_____	Submitted format is correct as specified
_____	Absence of mathematical errors
_____	Absence of typographical errors
_____	Appears neat and organized

Table 12.2. Budget Approval Process

1. Critical care nurse manager and ICU staff	Discuss unit needs for coming fiscal year
2. Critical care nurse manager and unit business manager	Develop budget and perform final budget package review
3. Critical care nurse manager	Formulates and rehearses justifications and convincing arguments for proposed budget
4. Critical care nurse manager	Proposes budget plan to director of critical care
5. Critical care nurse manager and director of critical care	Propose budget plan to chief nursing officer
6. Chief nursing officer	Proposes budget to CEO/CFO or budget committee

Table 12.3. Nursing Budget Preparation (in percentages; n = 93)[a]

Stratum	Units Prepare CNO Reviews	CNO Prepares	Neither Prepares
500+ beds	93.5	6.5	0.0
Urban	83.9	9.7	6.0
Rural	58.1	29.0	12.9
Weighted Averages	72.4	18.6	9.1

[a]Reprinted with permission from Kusserow RP. Nurse participation in hospital decision making: Potential impact on the nursing shortage. *Nursing Economics* 1988;6:312–316.

unit managers prepare the budget for the chief nurse officer to approve, with this being particularly dominant in hospitals of over 500 beds in size. Approximately 18% of the CNOs surveyed prepare the budget themselves, and 9% reported having the budgets prepared and approved by others outside of nursing, mostly in rural hospitals (Table 12.3). Eighty percent of the 93 hospitals surveyed reported total control of the nursing budget by the CNO, once the budget was approved. In large hospitals (over 500 beds) all CNOs controlled the approved nursing budget (1).

Given this information it follows that for the majority of hospitals a crucial element in the budget approval process becomes the CNO's ability to convince the CEO of the nursing department's fiscal needs. Compatibility between the CEO and CNO is vital to the nursing department and has recently appeared as a topic of interest in the nursing administration literature. A recent study of decision-making styles of these two groups found that the majority (88%) of CEOs and CNOs are actually very similar in their decision-making styles and both groups prefer the thinking process to the feeling process to make judgments (2). The majority of CEOs and CNOs who worked together shared a common cognitive style and approach and the majority (87%) felt they worked well together. Both groups draw conclusions by ordering choices in terms of cause and effect, logical connections, and impersonal analysis. These characteristics of decision-making styles should be considered by the critical care nurse manager in presenting the intensive care unit (ICU) budget to the CNO for approval.

To seek approval of the budget the critical care nurse manager must be able to articulate the congruence of the goals of the institution and those of the ICU. These goals must be reflected in the proposed budget. The greater the value of the requested resources to the organization, the higher the probability of budget approval (3). For example, consider the critical care nurse manager who requests an increase in FTEs (full-time equivalent positions) for additional staffing to implement a new transplant program, despite the institution's announcement that there will be no increase in FTEs this fiscal year. This nurse manager must assess the value of the new transplant program to the institution as a whole, and then defend this proposal in terms that include a cost-benefit analysis of the revenue generation this program will bring to the organization.

Whether presenting to the divisional director or to the hospital budget committee, the nurse manager must be intimately familiar with the budget requests. The nurse manager must be very well versed in the number of FTEs, work load indicators, salary dollars, operating expenses, capital equipment dollars, total dollars, and total dollars per work load requested. How these figures relate to the previous year's budget (and the percentage of increase and decrease) should also be known as well as actual year-to-date costs.

The critical care nurse manager must be able to articulate clearly and succinctly the needs of the critical care unit. This includes the ability to speak to the number of nursing and support personnel, type of skill mix, amount of supplies, and essential equipment to safely operate the ICU. Frequently nurse managers are asked to cut the budget by a known percentage from the previous year. Identifying areas to cut should be done by the nurse manager in conjunction with the ICU staff very early in the budget process and may include discussion of a minimal level for safe patient care. Before the approval process begins, the nurse manager must know the "bottom line" figure at which the ICU can still provide safe patient care. To provide quality patient care the budget proposed will most likely be higher than this minimal safety figure, but it is important for the nurse manager to know the lowest level of financial resources that must be supported. Before any budget hearings the nurse manager should rehearse the justifications for the budget proposed and also arguments to defend this "bottom fiscal line."

Conversely, it is also the critical care nurse manager's responsibility to scrutinize the proposed budget carefully for excessive demands which are not easily justified. "Padding" the budget in anticipation of automatic cuts is risky and detracts from the manager's credibility in providing sound justifications.

STRATEGIES FOR BUDGET APPROVAL

As health care institutions continue to face increasing costs and decreasing reimbursements, critical care nurse managers will share in reductions through the ICU budget. Maximizing one's knowledge to obtain the proposed budgeted funds for the ICU will become increasingly important. Learning the art of strategy and the principles of negotiation can assist the nurse manager in obtaining the fiscal resources to operate an effective ICU.

The Art of Strategy

The concept of business strategy has only recently emerged in the health care management literature as a result of accelerated levels of uncertainty in health care environments (4). Strategy is not a new concept, however, in approaching a goal and in fact was addressed by ancient Chinese philosophers such as in Sun Tzu's classic "The Art of War" where the described objective is the achievement of triumph through tactical positioning without resorting to battle (5). These principles of strategy (Table 12.4) have been applied in many different situations since 300 BC and have relevancy for the nurse manager seeking budgetary approval. Before entering into this process the nurse manager must actively strategize to achieve the goal of obtaining the proposed budget.

The following case example will illustrate the use of these principles in the budget approval process:

> SJ is the nurse manager of the surgical intensive care unit (SICU). In the middle of the fiscal year she is told by the director of critical care nursing that she must decrease the next fiscal year's budget by 5%. The work load in the ICU is not expected to decrease. At the next SICU staff meeting SJ discussed the issue with the staff, and they identified areas for reduction which included adding more technician positions in lieu of professional nurse positions and also reducing supply costs. The staff also voiced concerns that to reduce staffing and supplies any more could jeopardize safe patient care. The calculated costs of the proposed reductions translated into a 3% budget cut instead of 5% as requested. SJ develops the proposed budget at 3% less than the current year.

In this example SJ must now strategize for gaining acceptance of this budget which she feels is a very sound proposal. Using the principles of strategy she must first *analyze the conflict* which in this case is the discrepancy between her boss's request for reduction vs. what the nurses believe can be safely reduced in the SICU budget. In analyzing this conflict the nurse manager will want to know more about where the 5% directive originated. Is

Table 12.4. Principles of Strategy[a]

1. Analyze the conflict.
2. Estimate the costs.
3. Develop an error-free strategy.
4. Position yourself for triumph.
5. Position your opponent for defeat.
6. Use camouflage.
7. Maneuver for advantage.
8. Move spontaneously according to the situation.
9. Cultivate allegiances.
10. Know the situation.
11. Mobilize with unity.
12. Execute a decisive thrust.
13. Use information to your advantage.

[a]Adapted from Wing RL. The art of strategy: A new translation of Sun Tzu's classic The art of war. New York: Dolphin/Doubleday, 1988.

the 5% reduction an expectation for all departments in the hospital or is it 5% for all nursing units or did the director assign cutback percentages to units based on perceptions of where reductions can be made? This type of information assists the nurse manager in making her case for 3% reduction.

In entering into this conflict situation the nurse manager must *estimate the costs* of any possible outcomes. If the objective is achieved and the 3% decrease is accepted, the nurse manager may encounter resentment from other nurse managers who were asked to cut their budgets by higher amounts. She may be viewed as rigid and uncooperative by her boss and by the institution. If she is unsuccessful in her objective and is forced to make the 5% reduction she may lose credibility with the staff as their advocate as well as the patient's advocate for safe care. Personal costs may also be great in this situation if the nurse manager has become emotionally invested in her position.

Developing an *error-free strategy* or plan of attack will be critical in achieving the objective. This includes the nurse manager knowing when to present her case to her boss. Presenting the 3% decrease to the director immediately after a speech from the CEO on cost containment or following a low census period in the ICU will not promote the objective. Timing of the presentation is one significant factor in the strategy.

Positioning yourself for triumph and your opponent for defeat are principles of strategy for the nurse manager to consider. Strategic positioning for the nurse manager includes acting with integrity at all times and executing methodical planning as opposed to emotional approaches. Positioning for triumph in this case means the SICU nurse manager will have to promote her plan with facts including staff or patient surveys, patient acuity data, quality assurance information, and perhaps data from other similar ICUs. If the 5% reduction is mandated hospital-wide, the nurse manager's task is to convince the director to support the 3% plan or to work with the director in finding other areas to reduce dollars and not jeopardize safe patient care.

The *use of camouflage* is of course a frequent strategy used to mask one's position usually through the use of illusion and avoidance of reality. This could include not allowing the position to be known (in this case the nurse manager not divulging her opinions about the safety level of patient care and this budget proposal) and remaining obscure about the plan. Although this approach may assist the nurse manager in remaining emotionally unattached to the proposal, it is not recommended in most situations as the illusion may backfire. In this case the director may read camouflage of the nurse manager's position as apathy and not seriously consider this proposal.

Maneuvering for advantage and moving spontaneously according to the situation are other principles of strategy according to Sun Tzu. For the nurse manager seeking budget approval these principles mean being able to maneuver into an advantageous position by knowing the plans and positions of others and acting swiftly to stay one step ahead of them. Sun Tzu warned "The overly reckless can be destroyed. The overly cautious can be captured." This quotation reflects the balance the nurse manager must have in approaching the situation in this case example. If the nurse manager recklessly and directly defies her boss by insisting on the 3% decrease, she will incite an emotional conflict and will surely not win approval. On the other hand if the nurse manager is slow to act, unprepared, and does not strategically maneuver into a win-win position, her plan will not be heard.

Cultivating allegiance and *mobilizing with unity* are also essential ingredients in achieving one's goals. The nurse manager who is seeking budget approval must establish positive relationships with all parties involved in the process prior to entering into the negotiating phase. Soliciting the support of the ICU medical director in planning the budget, for example, may lend credence to the critical care nurse manager's case for the proposed budget. Letters of justification for capital equipment which are jointly written by the nurse manager and the physician unit director may be viewed positively by the hospital budget committee especially if there are physicians who serve on the committee. Getting to know the hospital finance director may also behoove the nurse manager who may want to seek financial advice regarding creative budgeting.

Knowing the situation also means knowing when to back off or retreat. In this case example it may be that all department heads have been asked to reduce their budgets by 5% throughout the hospital and there is absolutely no money to be allocated otherwise. In this situation the nurse manager must present her case clearly and logically, thoroughly examine other places to make reductions, and finally be prepared to potentially accept rejection of her budgetary plan if all strategies have not achieved the goal. It is helpful to always be prepared for rejection of the initial budget plan proposed and to have a fall back position before entering into the negotiation phase of the budget process.

If this happens the nurse manager could *execute the decisive thrust* which would probably include direct confrontation. In this case the SICU nurse manager would have to be willing to fight this battle up the organizational hierarchy. This is not advisable unless the nurse manager is absolutely certain of her inability to find other solutions and of her ability to influence others in the budget approval process. The nurse manager must "pick her battles" wisely and decide if a 2% reduction is truly worth the fight.

A better solution for this SICU nurse manager would most likely be to note the principle of *using information to your advantage*. For instance this SICU nurse manager could go back to the SICU staff with information regarding the hospital's need to cut an additional 2% and propose an incentive plan for the staff whereby any savings over the additional 2% could be returned to the nurses of that unit or to the unit as a whole to be spent at their discretion. This would provide an incentive for a win-win solution for both the hospital and the staff. Another possible solution would be to invent mechanisms to increase revenue generation for the hospital which would be equivalent in dollars to cutting an additional 2% from the budget. This might include implementing variable billing in certain patient populations based on acuity of the patient. Another form of revenue generation could be providing unit-based preceptoring and education services to other hospitals who have a need to learn specialty skills in critical care.

The nurse manager may need to propose such "intrapreneurial" concepts during the budget approval negotiations. These ideas express an entrepreneurial orientation but are developed within the organization (6). For those organizations that are open to intrapreneurialism, the nurse manager is a likely candidate to promote innovative behaviors with new business ventures within the organization. The budget approval process may provide an opportunity for the nurse manager to display these innovative behaviors.

The critical care nurse manager may also find the principles of negotiation helpful in acquiring a sound budget (7). Fisher and Brown of the Harvard negotiation project urge focusing on the relationships of those with whom one is negotiating and not simply on the content of the negotiation (8). The theory which describes this phenomenon is referred to as the theory of unconditionally constructive relationship management and assumes that outcomes of all negotiations depend upon the relationships of the parties involved. Under these assumptions a good "working" relationship is deemed to be one that is able to deal well with differences. The critical care nurse manager will encounter many relationships along the budget approval path and must remember to look for solutions that are unconditionally constructive for all parties.

CONCLUSION

Budget approval processes will continue to present challenges for the critical care nurse manager. Submitting a budget which is organized, orderly, and precise will facilitate acceptance of the proposed plan. Being ready to defend the proposal with sound and logical rationales will also aid the nurse manager in securing the desired financial package. The nurse manager who is prepared for this process through the use of principled strategy has an advantage to receive approval for the fiscal resources necessary to effectively manage the intensive care unit.

REFERENCES

1. Kusserow RP. Nurse participation in hospital decision making: potential impact on the nursing shortage. Nursing Economics 1988;6:312–316.
2. Freund CM. CNO and CEO decision-making patterns and compatability: Part 2, using the MBTI. Journal of Nursing Administration 1989;19:15–20.
3. Porter-O'Grady T. Nursing finance: budgeting strategies for a new age. Rockville, MD: Aspen Publishers, 1987.
4. Luke RD, Begun JW. The management of strategy. In: Shortell SM, Kaluzny AD, eds. Health care management: a text in organization theory and behavior. New York: John Wiley & Sons, 1988:463—491.
5. Wing RL. The art of strategy: a new translation of Sun Tzu's classic The art of war. New York: Dolphin/Doubleday, 1988.
6. Pinchot G III. Intrapreneuring: why you don't have to leave the organization to become an entrepreneur. New York: Harper & Row, 1985.
7. Ward CR. Negotiating. In: Cardin S, Ward CR, eds. Personnel management in critical care nursing. Baltimore: Williams & Wilkins, 1989:138–144.
8. Fisher R, Brown S. Getting together: building relationships as we negotiate. New York: Penguin Books, 1988.

Part III

EVALUATION AND CONTROLLING

Chapter 13

Variance Reporting

RHONDA EASTON

Susan Stewart is a new manager in a 15-bed intensive care unit (ICU). She has been involved in the budget preparation process by assessing the unit's needed resources and planning for new programs and services. Now the new fiscal year has begun, the new budget has been implemented, and the next step to be carried out is the ongoing, yearlong evaluation process.

In this institution, unit managers are held accountable for financial performance and must explain variances in the budget. Susan hopes that the various budget reports will serve as useful management tools throughout the year. She read an article by McGrail which cautioned about budgeting games between line management and top administration, whereby managers "stretch" or "pad" the budget, and administrators, not knowing where the overexpenditures are, make random cuts and disapprovals to counteract the built-in slack (1). Although a novice in this area, Susan feels that she has a realistic budget with which to work, and she hopes that "games" aren't the norm for the facility. The finance team has shown its respect for her expertise as a health care provider, and she has gained an understanding of their financial perspective of operations. She is eager to test her competence in promoting cost effective unit operations.

Susan's director, Leslie Miller, has served in a mentoring role during the budget planning and implementation processes and is now prepared to continue that guidance during the evaluation phase. Positive patient outcomes are a shared goal of this manager-director team, and they view the budget as a means to that end. Philosophically, they agree on another of McGrail's statements (2):

> ". . . to say a (budget) variance is positive because it is less than the budgeted expenditure is where the organization fails to utilize the budget to its fullest. Organizations following this standard practice assume the reduced input level or cost resulted in an adequate output level or result. If this is the case, then the division has performed well. However, if the end product does not match the planned activity level or if the program or project was not completed thoroughly, the action is just as harmful as if the budget was overspent."

In the critical care arena, the "product" or end result is the achievement of desired patient outcomes. Susan and Leslie have planned, cooperatively with other hospital departments, a budget that will serve their patient populations more comprehensively than before. For patients with ineffective breathing patterns and altered gas exchange, they have planned resource acquisition and utilization with the respiratory department. Only the previous year, patient oxygen therapy had been delayed at times because of turf issues about control of oxygen tanks and flow meters, a scenario they did not want repeated. With the cardiology and surgical services, they have planned for the delivery of thorough, yet efficient, services for patients with altered cardiac output. Diagnostic testing, surgery, stabilization, and rehabilitation are the range of services. Each department knows its specific accountabilities for providing uninterrupted services.

Susan is anxious to learn and to carry out her new responsibilities. She makes a note on her "to do" list to discuss with Leslie the tools available in their institution for evaluating budget performance.

DATA BASES

There are many data bases designed for storing, tracking, and trending statistical data. Leslie explained that, when formatted well and when shown in relation to a number of variables which impact the production of patient care services, the comparative data can give managers many answers related to budget variances.

Generally, data bases are automated. They are most helpful when different hospital computer programs communicate with one another. It is possible to keep data manually, but it becomes a more cumbersome and time consuming process. "Our data bases are usually designed to report biweekly, monthly, and fiscal year-to-date statistics," reported Leslie. "The biweekly reports correspond to payroll periods, and they give managers a timely report which allows prompt course correction when something is out of line. The monthly and fiscal year-to-date reports correlate with finance department data and give a more detailed picture of certain revenue and expense variances."

EXPENSE PER PATIENT DAY

Leslie had explained to Susan during the budget planning process that most hospitals set a standard or target against which to measure performance. These standards are frequently calculated per patient day or use some other volume indicator. The advantage to this approach is the adjustment that can be made with a flexible budget system.

The flexible budget concept is one that adjusts expenditure increases when volume or patient acuity changes. Hopefully, the increased expense will be matched by increased revenue when the increase is volume-related. Acuity-related changes may not be matched by revenue increases, but maintenance of quality outcomes justifies the expenditure.

Conversely, if volume or acuity requirements decrease, so do the allowable expenditures. This encourages cost efficient spending and appropriate adjustments downward in staffing and supply expenditures. Volume and acuity predictions are rarely, if ever, accurate as the year is played out. There is no crystal ball which can foretell the deviations in patient mix, market share, and other variables. So, organizations modify the standard budget to reflect these activity variances through a flexible budget.

Even in a flexible budget, some line items will be "flexed" and some will be fixed (unchanged from the original budget, regardless of other variances throughout the year). Leslie explained that certain maintenance costs for the new cardiac monitors will not change during the year; therefore, the maintenance is a fixed cost. Also, the unit has a part-time medical director whose salary is set for the next 12 months, regardless of activity in the unit; so that expense is also a fixed cost. Some of the things that will "flex" up or down to reflect changes in volume and acuity are staffing, supplies, equipment rentals, and other direct care expenses.

Leslie demonstrated this concept by reviewing a budget variance report from the previous year. In Table 13.1, line items titled "salaries," "medical-surgical (med-surg) supplies," "solutions," and "drugs" have budgeted amounts based on an average monthly census of 342 patient days. When the volume dropped in April to only 276 patient days, a volume-adjusted expense figure is given. However, for line items titled "textbooks" and "contract costs," the "volume-adjusted" amount is the same as the original budget; those items are not adjusted for volume because they are "fixed" expenditures.

The first variance column demonstrates the difference between budgeted expenditures and allowable expenditures "flexed" for the actual number of patient days. In this case, $23,098 in salaries should have been saved because of the lower than budgeted volume. But, the account overran the "flex" budget by $1541. Leslie explained that the variance was caused by staff members using additional vacation hours when they were called off. Any amount followed by a "F" is a favorable variance, or below the allowable budget expenditure. Any amount with a "U" is an unfavorable variance, or exceeds allowable budget expenditures.

Leslie brought Susan's attention to the third column again. Note that for "medical-surgical supplies" the actual expense did not adjust downward as the flex budget required for the lower volume. "This is where management evaluation and decision making comes in," said Leslie, "And many times it takes a bit of detective work to figure out if our performance is poor or if something else is affecting the results. Last year, we budgeted a 7% increase in the costs of med-surg supplies, but actual increases were closer to 10.5%. When we realized the unexpected cost increases for supplies, we took steps to be even more cost effective than usual; and by fiscal year-end our budget performance had improved."

It is important to note that when volume decreases, the total actual expense per patient day may increase slightly because fixed expenses must

EVALUATION AND CONTROLLING

Table 13.1. Budget Variance Report for April

	Budget Expense	Flex Volume-Adjusted Expense	Actual Expense	Variance Flex-Budget	Variance Actual-Flex
220 Salary	119,690	96,592	98,133	23,098(F)	1541(U)
360 Supplies	742	599	787	143(F)	198(U)
380 Drugs	240	194	183	46(F)	11(F)
540 Solutions	68	55	53	13(F)	3(F)
810 Textbooks	36	36	0	0	36(F)
963 Contracts	187	187	187	0	0
Patient Days	342	276	276		
Expense/Pt Day	354	354	360		6

F = favorable variance; U = unfavorable variance.

be divided among fewer patients. But if volume increases, we gain efficiencies and may see a slight decrease in expense per patient day because fixed expenses are spread among more patients.

Not all hospitals use the flex budget format, but it is easy to calculate allowable expenses for volume changes. The calculation is done by dividing actual volume by budgeted volume, then multiplying the result times the budgeted expense:

$$\frac{276 \text{ actual patient days}}{342 \text{ budgeted patient days}} \times \$742$$

$$= \$598.81 \, (\$599 \text{ rounded})$$

"You mentioned that acuity also plays a part in flexible budgeting," Susan reminded Leslie. "Yes," Leslie responded, "some hospitals have adjusted supply expenses based on patient classifications." Francisco describes a system which, using an average supply cost per patient category, calculates allowable variances (3). Table 13.2 shows how volumes in each patient classification can be multiplied by the average supply cost for that classification. (Table 13.2 has been simplified to show this concept as an example.) The result can be compared to budget and evaluated as a favorable or unfavorable variance. Again, "F" indicates a favorable finding. You can see that, due to the number of patients in the higher classifications, the flexible budget called for increased supply expenditures, creating a $99 overrun of the original budget. But actual expenses were only $68, so this unit actually saved the hospital $31 of justifiable expenditures.

Table 13.2. Flexed Supply Budget Based on Average Costs per Classification

Patient Classification	Patient Days Per Classification	Average Supply Cost	Total Costs
I	2.50	$ 12	$ 30
II	3.25	68	221
III	4.70	273	1283
IV	9.65	167	1612
			3146

Total Costs Budget	Total Costs Flexed	Total Costs Actual	Variance Flex-Budget	Variance Actual-Flex
$3047	$3146	$3078	$99	$68(F)

PATIENT DAYS

Leslie explained that the patient day has become a typical volume measure for evaluating nursing expense and productivity performance. From the hospital's finance department come many reports, including such common performance indicators as "full-time equivalents per occupied bed." Although that indicator is a useful yardstick for hospital administrators to consider, it is not especially useful to nurse managers who are trying to determine which factors are adding to, and which are detracting from, their net productivity (4). Patient days are usually measured by financial systems at a specified time each day, e.g., patients who occupy a bed at midnight, because it matches the hospital charge structure for daily room charges.

Since the advent of prospective payment systems (PPS), a more significant volume issue has arisen. It is often advantageous for hospitals to treat patients on an outpatient basis, so many inpatient units care for patients who are not counted in the hospital's inpatient volumes. To reflect the additional work load for patients who may be present for only a partial day (for "short stay" visits or "observation" stays), the nursing unit may choose an "adjusted" volume indicator, such as adjusted patient days. This allows a conversion factor for these partial outpatient days.

In critical care, nurses often feel that patient days inadequately reflect the amount or type of work done, such as temporary admissions for cardioversion, responses to cardiorespiratory arrests on other units, consultations regarding a patient's condition on another unit, remote monitoring of patients with continuous electrocardiograms, etc. These units may also benefit from the conversion of certain patient care activities to adjusted patient days. Even more helpful is the development of acuity systems, an additional tool for measuring the needed nursing resources and for justifying budget variances; their impact is discussed later in this chapter.

Patient days, generally, are not constant. Nursing units may have dramatic fluctuations in the number of patients for whom care is required. These fluctuations may be seasonal or they may be day-to-day changes. For example, a pediatric respiratory unit may be able to anticipate increased patient volumes from December through March. Some surgical units know to expect increased admissions on Tuesdays and Wednesdays, because those are the days with the heaviest operating room schedules. The advantage of knowing these varying census trends is that it provides the opportunity to develop staffing plans to match the varying volume of work.

HIRING VARIANCES

Susan knew by now that personnel costs consume the majority of budgeted expenses. Health care is labor intensive and, contrary to other industries which have decreased manpower requirements by way of technological advances, health care has needed increasingly more manpower in its highly technological environment (5).

One of the first things a manager must evaluate and continue to monitor is the question, "How many people do I hire?" "First, let's get all of the terminology straight," cautioned Leslie, "Definitions are confusing from institution to institution and often cause us to compare apples and oranges unless we're careful."

Examples of how different nursing organizations may look at labor inputs include:

1. Productive time—all time spent working, including management and clerks.
   Nonproductive time—all time paid for vacations, illness (6).
2. Direct full-time equivalents—those hours devoted to hands-on care.
   Nonproductive full-time equivalents—benefit hours, paid but not worked.
   Fixed full-time equivalents—those hours devoted to indirect care; hours remain constant regardless of volume (may be managers, clerks, clinical specialist) (7).
3. Worked hours—only hours available for variable production, i.e., patient care.
   Fixed indirect labor—hours which are not variable for volume or acuity; may include training, in-service, managers.
   Paid hours—includes worked (patient care) and fixed hours, plus all nonworked benefit hours.

These are all different ways of looking at budget components. Number 1 is standard financial terminology for grouping different types of hours paid to employees. The categories in number 2 are all mutually exclusive, and when added together, make up the entire salary budget. The first two items in number 3, worked hours and fixed hours, are a portion of the third item, paid hours.

Employee time may be expressed in hours or full-time equivalent positions (FTEs). An understanding of FTEs is essential to budget evaluation. One FTE is based on an employee working 2080 hours per year, which is 40 hours per week multiplied by 52 weeks. Determining other equivalents is basically a calculation of ratios—the number of hours worked by a full-time employee. A full-time nurse works 40 hours a week. A part-time nurse who works 24 hours a week can have the full-time equivalent calculated by dividing 24 by 40; the result is 0.6 FTE.

Because many institutions calculate FTEs on a 2-week pay period basis, the 2-week calculation would be the number of hours worked by the part-time employee divided by 80. A 2-week equivalency chart would look like this:

    80 hours/2 weeks = 1.0 full-time employee
    72 hours/2 weeks = 0.9
    70 hours/2 weeks = 0.875
    64 hours/2 weeks = 0.8
    60 hours/2 weeks = 0.75
    56 hours/2 weeks = 0.7
    48 hours/2 weeks = 0.6
    40 hours/2 weeks = 0.5
    36 hours/2 weeks = 0.45
    32 hours/2 weeks = 0.4
    24 hours/2 weeks = 0.3

What is difficult for some new managers to grasp conceptually is the need for relief staffing. Monday through Friday staffing plus weekend relief staffing adds up to total FTEs needed to staff a unit. Hospitals are a 7-days-a-week business, no one can work without days off. A full-time nurse who works 10 days, or 80 hours in a 2-week pay period, is relieved by a nurse who works 4 days, or 32 hours a pay period. Thus, it takes 1.4 FTEs to cover one 8-hour position for a 7-day week; the 0.4 FTE provides relief to cover days off for the full-time nurse (1.0 FTE).

Consider a 10-bed ICU at maximum occupancy. With a 2:1 patient:nurse staffing ratio, the unit requires five nurses per shift, or 15 nurses for 24 hours. Multiplying 15 times 1.4 FTE equals 21 FTEs, the total number needed for 7 days/week coverage. While it seems more confusing when we look at creative staffing plans, like 12-hour and 4-hour shifts, every calculation comes back to the basic conversions listed above. It should be noted that these calculations do not include an FTE adjustment for benefits.

MASTER STAFFING PLANS AND POSITION CONTROL

All worked and paid hours convert to paid FTEs. One report that comes from most finance departments is a report of total paid hours converted to paid FTEs. The problem in evaluating the report is that it doesn't necessarily reflect the number of hired FTEs accurately, and it may be interpreted that nursing has exceeded allowable hired FTEs. If the nursing department has a position control system, data can be easily retrieved to demonstrate that overhiring is not the cause of the paid FTE variance.

Once needed FTEs for patient care are determined, a master staffing plan and position control system can be developed. It will help accomplish several things in the ongoing evaluaton of fiscal performance.

1. It prevents hiring in excess of budgeted levels, thus helping prevent "FTE creep." This is a situation where gradual increases in paid FTEs occur when not justified by volume or acuity needs.
2. It gives up-to-date vacancy levels, which substantiates the need for supplemental staffing. Because supplemental staffing may be more expensive and is often less productive than regular staff, the data helps evaluate dollar and productivity variances. It may also help support incentive programs for regular staff.
3. When integrated with an employee information data base, it can give up-to-date information about the individual employees filling each position, and special reports can be generated which help explore both financial and quality issues, e.g., how many staff members consistently work overtime hours, how many of the staff have greater than 10 years experience, etc.

Steps for Building a Position Control System

Step 1

First, see that the direct care, fixed position, and indirect care FTEs needed to staff the unit are budgeted in the "productive" (worked) hours category. For the 10-bed ICU just discussed, there were 21 direct care FTEs budgeted, plus 4.2 management and charge nurse FTEs (1.0 head nurse, 2.0 charge nurses, and 1.2 charge nurse relief), and 2.8 clerical position FTEs. Both the management and clerical positions are considered fixed indirect positions. The total FTEs needed to staff all positions in the unit equals 28. This method is generally used to determine total FTEs in the master staffing-position control system.

The calculation includes consideration of required staffing for 7 days a week, all year long. But, employees hired to fill a position in the staffing plan do not work all year without vacation time or without occasional illnesses. Should a unit hire extra FTEs for replacement of the staff's paid benefit time?

Many organizations use internal pools, speciality pools, on-call, or per diem status employees for replacement hours rather than including them in the master staffing plan. Some indirect care positions are not replaced during the employee's paid time off. Also, benefit hours are not used at consistent levels each pay period, and it is difficult to productively schedule FTE employees for a constant number of hours when they are hired solely for replacement of regular staff who are on vacation or sick leave. Some organizations multiply the average number of benefit hours used by each FTE in the nursing department by the total number of FTEs. The total may be used to determine the size of its internal pool.

For example, in the 10-bed ICU, the total paid FTEs would probably be close to 31 or 32 FTEs when nonworked benefit hours are added to the productive worked hours. That figure is based on a study which places total paid FTEs at 12–14% higher than productive worked FTEs (8). But the manager of the 10-bed unit may choose not to hire to the total paid level, for the reasons stated above.

Leslie explained to Susan that their budget had been built progressively, with known patient acuity levels as the basis for determining budgeted, direct- and indirect-care FTEs; then fixed hours were added; and finally, benefit hours were added. Their organization's preferred hiring level consists of those FTEs needed for patient care, plus those FTEs needed for fixed positions such as management. A pool of on-call speciality nurses supplements staffing during vacations.

Step 2

The second step is to determine how we place those FTEs into the staffing pattern. If we look at Table 13.3, we see such a tool (9).

The first Table 13.3A shows how the FTEs for a seven-bed critical care unit (CCU) were planned for each shift, and what positions are actually filled. For consistent volumes, and if the nursing market allowed, it would be ideal to have perfectly matched full- and part-time staff to always cover the 7-day work week schedule and to be able to rotate weekends off equitably. But, that is seldom possible. Census and work load fluctuate, staff members take vacations, and staff attend training courses. So, a manager must plan the staffing pattern based on average volume, trends in peak work load, and known replacement requirements.

Table 13.3B demonstrates the unfilled positions on each shift—0.6 registered nurse (RN) on the 7 am–3 pm shift, 0.7 RN and 0.2 unit clerk (UC) on the 3–11 pm shift, and 0.4 RN on the 11 pm–7 am shift. Table 13.3C adds the total unit vacancies and shows the total of 1.9 unfilled FTEs.

Step 3

The third step of setting up an effective position control system is to have a method for never hiring above the allowed level. All requisitions for hiring new staff must match a vacancy in the position control system. New FTEs may be added, when a continuing need exists over time due to increased volume and acuity requirements. At that point, most institutions have procedures for formal approval of increases above the level originally approved in the fiscal year budget. Other institutions will not make formal changes once the fiscal year is underway, but do allow managers, with executive level approval, to hire additional FTEs with justification of the variances made at year-end.

Once the system is set up and filled positions are listed, this data can be fed into any automated, cyclical staffing system. This can save the manager hours of manual schedule preparation time every few weeks. If coordinated with staff self-scheduling opportunities, the system can help improve morale. In general, nurses like a significant degree of autonomy in scheduling, and cyclical scheduling helps them plan their personal time far in advance. These systems can help correct the following common staffing variances:

- Scheduling too many people;
- Scheduling too few people;
- Scheduling the wrong skill mix;
- Scheduling inequitable rotations.

Budget variances can occur as a result of hiring too many people for the projected volume, or as a result of hiring too few, or from hiring a nonbudgeted mix of staff. Hiring too many FTEs can obviously lead to overstaffing, which creates a salary dollar overexpenditure.

The obvious variance created by hiring too few FTEs is a lower-than-budgeted dollar expenditure. This happens when understaffing occurs, and that creates the potential for unsafe or compromised

Table 13.3. Robert Wood Johnson University Hospital, CICU Position Control, Bed Capacity of 7[a]

	7–3		3–11		11–7	
CICU	Budget	Actual	Budget	Actual	Budget	Actual
HN	1.0	1.0 Hampton				
AHN	1.0	1.0 Captivo	1.0	1.0 Craft		
RN	1.0	1.0 Williams	1.0	1.0 Candela	1.0	1.0 Nolan
	1.0	1.0 Babish	1.0	1.0 Duncan	1.0	1.0 Reisman
	1.0	1.0 Benson	1.0	1.0 Sanchez	1.0	1.0 Ryan
	1.0	1.0 Pearson	1.0	0.8 Brown	1.0	0.8 O'Brien
	1.0	0.6 Miller	0.4	0.4 Matthews	0.2	
	0.6	0.4 Thomas	0.4	0.2 Olean		
	0.4	0.4 Reynolds	0.3			
	0.2	0.2 Clowe				
NA	1.0	1.0 Porter				
UC	1.0	1.0 Wright	1.0	0.8 Condon	0.5	0.5 Burton

CCU	7Bud	Act	Vacancy	3Bud	Act	Vacancy	11Bud	Act	Vacancy
HN	1.0	1.0	0.0	0.0	0.0	0.0	0.0	0.0	0.0
AHN	1.0	1.0	0.0	1.0	1.0	0.0	0.0	0.0	0.0
RN	6.2	5.6	0.6	5.1	4.4	0.7	4.2	3.8	0.4
LPN	0.0	0.0	0.0	0.0	0.0	0.0	0.0	0.0	0.0
NA	1.0	1.0	0.0	0.0	0.0	0.0	0.5	0.5	0.0
UC	1.0	1.0	0.0	1.0	0.8	0.2	0.0	0.0	0.0
	10.2	9.6	0.6	7.1	6.2	0.9	4.7	4.3	0.4

CCU	Total	Actual	Vacancy
HN	1.0	1.0	0.0
AHN	2.0	2.0	0.0
RN	15.5	13.8	1.7
LPN	0.0	0.0	0.0
NA	1.5	1.5	0.0
UC	2.0	1.8	0.2
Unit Total	22.0	20.1	1.9

[a]Permission requested and granted for use of material: McCabe, J.P. and Hartnack, J.L.P. FTE reports and fiscal management. Nursing Management, 1989:11;47.

patient care. More frequently, however, an overexpenditure occurs caused by using costly and less-productive supplemental staff in place of the regular, but unfilled, positions. Overtime pay may also cause overexpenditures and be reported as a variance.

Hiring a staff mix that was not budgeted can lead to dollar variances. A potentially positive variance can occur when a manager has budgeted for an all-professional staff, then uses some of the budgeted FTEs for clerical assistance. Astute managers took a new look at this issue when the Hay Group reported that 52% of med-surg nurses' time is absorbed by nonnursing tasks such as housekeeping duties, answering phones, and ordering supplies (10). Susan decided to evaluate her critical care unit to determine if there might be a similar finding and whether more clerical assistance would be beneficial to the professional staff.

Other circumstances may create FTE variances from budget even when the budget is flexed for patient volume and acuity requirements. Other departments, in their efforts toward cost containment, may ask or expect nursing to assume certain activities that the ancillary department performed in the past. Unless activities are integrated into the acuity or productivity system measurements, nursing may be picking up additional work which isn't reflected appropriately in system reports. A variance reporting system will miss an issue like this, so it is essential that a manager know the clinical areas well and recognize subtle or not-so-subtle shifts in work load. The manager must evaluate if nurses are performing professional duties that require licensure, and determine which duties are nonnursing tasks. When work load changes are negotiated as permanent shifts from one department to another, the acuity and productivity systems should reflect these changes.

From one budget year to the next, projected volumes may change significantly. Expanded or new services can mean that more FTEs are needed. Increased competition or shifting demographics can mean that fewer patients will be using services and fewer FTEs are needed. In the first case, the manager may have difficulties if the planned staff aren't available to hire. If the volume is expected to decrease, and too many FTEs are currently hired, plans to decrease staffing levels through attrition (as employees leave through usual turnover), transfers within the system, or immediate reductions will need to be made. In these instances, the personnel department must be consulted for guidance in fair and equitable practices. Are reductions and transfers going to be based on length of service, past performance, specialty skills, pay grade or title, or a combination of these and other criteria?

STAFFING VARIANCES

In many hospitals, staffing variances become apparent from reported data base information. The manager must be able to interpret the data in order to answer questions. What is causing the variance? Which hours are controllable? Which variances are justifiable? Which strategies are the most successful "course correction" techniques to bring the budget back into line?

Nursing should have a system for validating the reports generated by the finance department. Nursing may need a system to generate its own reports for tracking staffed hours and variances. The two tools of quality care and productivity must be evaluated and balanced. Neither productivity nor quality monitoring are new, but constant improvements are being made to give managers better information for decision making related to appropriate staffing levels. Productivity reports have gone from a basic variance report, as reported in percentages or variances in hours of care per patient day, to sophisticated reports full of data which can provide the manager with information about the source of variances and the budgetary impact of the variance. An example of a basic report might include:

Budget Hours per Patient Day	Actual Hours per Patient Day	Hours per Patient Variance	Productivity
14.0	14.73	0.73	95%

Without additional data, a manager might think that 95% is very good—why, in school that was an A! With additional data, the dollar impact of the unit's performance at that level is revealed. For a 2-week pay period, a variance of 0.73 hours per patient day multiplied by 210 patient days (a 15-bed unit at maximum capacity for 14 days) equals 153.3 paid hours over budget. At an average wage of $13.40 per hour, that equals $2,054.22 for one pay period. Continued performance at that level (a 0.73 hour overrun with maximum occupancy) would equal $53,409.72 (26 pay periods for the fiscal year multiplied by the $2,054.22 variance) in salary budget overruns for the fiscal year.

In Table 13.4, we see an example of the productivity report used by Susan Stewart's department. It gives timely management information when it is distributed to the managers within a week of the pay period. Then, prompt evaluations of performance can be made. The report clearly shows which payroll categories are considered productive hours, and which are considered nonproductive. Leslie spent many sessions with Susan reviewing this report, analyzing variances and their budget impact, and discussing ways to reconcile variances.

Inpatients and Outpatients

Both inpatients and outpatients are reported; both consume nursing resources, and at times, the outpatient activity is even more intense than inpatient care because time consuming professional activities such as patient assessment, health teaching and counseling, and admission and discharge protocols are delivered in a shortened time frame. Leslie explained that each type of outpatient activity had a conversion ratio to inpatient days based on length of stay, patient acuity, and other factors.

Table 13.4. Productivity Report

Payroll Period 23. April 15 to April 28, 1990

Unit	In Patient Days	Out Patient Days	Total Volume	Regular Care Hours	Holiday Hours	Overtime Hours	Purchased Hours	Earned Acuity Hours	Total Staffed Care Hours	PATIENT PRODUCTIVITY	Care Hours per Patient Day	Fixed Hours	Paid Time Off	Orientation Hours	Total Budgeted Paid Hours	Total Actual Paid Hours	BUDGET PRODUCTIVITY	Paid Hours per Patient Day
1606	414.00	8.00	422.00	1739.90	0.00	27.15	596.00	2540.66	2363.05	107.52%	5.60	156.00	46.14	16.00	2894.92	2581.19	112.15%	6.12
1607	379.00	6.50	385.50	1997.00	0.00	133.05	536.00	2673.41	2666.05	100.28%	6.92	236.00	505.62	8.00	2814.15	3415.67	82.39%	8.86
1608	367.00	8.00	375.00	1811.30	0.00	141.60	392.00	2314.07	2344.90	98.69%	6.25	156.00	236.41	0.00	2763.75	2737.31	100.97%	7.30
1611	376.00	31.50	407.50	2524.75	0.00	167.50	208.50	3172.09	2900.75	109.35%	7.12	430.00	197.94	0.00	3626.75	3528.69	102.78%	8.66

Productive Hours | Nonproductive

Total Volume

This figure is the sum of inpatient and outpatient activity. In a flexible budget system this is a very important number, because it drives the calculations for all dollar adjustments related to increased or decreased volumes. In many hospital systems, these figures are generated from reliable automated systems. If managers are required to report these figures from manual systems, they must be as accurate as possible. Carelessness in reporting can make a significant impact in allowable budget expenditures.

Regular Hours

Regular care hours are those hours paid at regular base rates of pay.

Holiday Hours

Holiday hours are paid at time-and-a-half or at double-time rates in most institutions. Holiday pay may create a variance from budgeted salaries if not included in salary calculations during the budget planning process. Managers must know personnel policies, understand how many holidays per year are included in holiday pay categories, and include the differential in budget planning.

Overtime Hours

Overtime hours are the hours paid at an overtime rate, usually time-and-a-half or double-time. The dollar impact of paying a premium above the regular hourly rate of pay is considered a variance. Depending on state labor laws, overtime may be paid for all hours over 40 in a week, over 8 in a day, or over 80 in 2 weeks. When alternative staffing plans are developed and implemented, it is wise to work with the personnel department to understand regulations that apply to pay rates. For example, if four 12-hour shifts are worked for a total of 48 hours in a week, is the last 8 hours at overtime pay, or can an agreement be signed with the employee that prescheduled hours are paid a regular rate? How does the hospital define its work week? Are unscheduled hours or hours worked above the hired FTE paid at an overtime rate? Hospitals now have many incentive plans which reward extra work days by extra pay. Overtime is approved in some institutions, because it is a morale booster and still less expensive than contracting for nurses from external agencies. If used for peak work loads, it is also less expensive than hiring additional FTEs.

Although overtime is an expense that hospitals have traditionally tried to eliminate or minimize, there is more of a trend currently to allow overtime. In some hospitals, overtime hours are routinely used as one strategy to help cover vacant positions; this may be earned by regular staff working more than normal hours, or it may be earned by nurses who are willing to be on-call, and when called in, earn call-back pay at overtime rates.

The problems inherent in the issue of overtime are money, quality, and productivity. Overtime hours obviously increase the actual salary dollars paid and can cause a unit to exceed budget. Some nurses who desire the extra pay will volunteer excessively and will work beyond their own stamina levels, so that quality outcomes are threatened. And, of course, there are nurses who need help with organizing their work and only earn overtime pay due to inefficiencies in time management. In these situations, the manager must assess what is happening in the clinical area, take steps to intervene, and then evaluate if the corrective action achieved the desired results.

Some hospitals have categories of employment which allow flexibility in staffing without the expense of overtime pay. A survey by the American Hospital Association in 1988 revealed that hospitals used per diem nurses, those contracted by the hospital to only work when needed, most frequently as a supplemental staffing mechanism (11). The per diem status employee is often paid at a percentage above base rate, such as a 10% differential; these rates usually are less than overtime rates.

Susan had heard of hospitals with "professional practice units" where nurses are salaried, where there is no reassignment out of the unit, and where the number of work hours depends on patient census and acuity (12). She thought that the idea would appeal to her professional staff. She wanted to explore whether she could replicate the experience of other hospitals which had been able to save money by eliminating overtime, on-call pay, and expensive agency fees. She had read of a hospital that was able to save $100,000 by this strategy, and was still able to pay its own nurses higher salaries and allow them autonomy through self-scheduling (13).

Purchased Hours

Purchased hours is the term Susan's hospital uses for the use of temporary agency nurses. This term indicates that the nurses are not paid through the employee payroll system, but through a subaccount in the operating budget for any contracted services from agencies outside the hospital. The same American Hospital Association report that Susan had reviewed regarding per diem staff, also revealed that temporary agency staff were used by hospitals most frequently to fill budgeted but vacant positions (14). However, the dollar impact of paying a premium to outside agencies for wages above internal rates creates a budget variance; those higher wage rates are not usually budgeted expenses.

"There are several problems associated with the use of temporary agency nurses," Leslie explained to Susan. "Even though some of the nurses assigned to us are very good clinicians, we still can't give them the same assignment our own nurses receive. The need for orientation to the physical layout, location of patient care supplies, unit philosophy, specific use of equipment, and what to do in emergencies detracts from the agency nurse's productivity and requires our own staff's time. If agency nurses deliver care that falls below established unit standards, quality may suffer. Financially the agencies hurt us; they charge fees which are two to three times the hourly wages of our own staff. Our nurses can't help but compare the salaries and flexibility of the agency nurses. It can create morale problems if agency nurse salaries are exaggerated, or if our salary plus benefit package cannot remain competitive in the local market. Our personnel department performs market studies at least yearly in order to make adjustments in salary levels. When only similar hospitals are surveyed, the data may actually be counterproductive and serve to keep salaries suppressed and compressed. But if agencies were included in these surveys, the information might help us by showing a higher average salary in our market area. This is another example of the need for good data and for not making hasty decisions before we understand which data are included in survey reports."

RELATIONSHIPS: SOURCE OF WORKED HOURS

Leslie explained to Susan that it is important to look at relationships of items reported on the productivity report. If there are usual volumes and acuity, then overtime and purchased hours should not exceed the unfilled FTEs reported in the position control system. (For the 2-week report shown in Table 13.4, she explained that all hours had to be divided by 80 to convert them to full-time equivalents.) If volume and/or acuity are increased, then supplemental staff may be needed for those reasons as well as for coverage of unfilled positions. "However, we got into a situation last year where purchased hours were excessive and we could not justify the need by high volumes, high acuity, or by our vacancy levels. This tool helped us evaluate those issues and to take steps toward development of better approaches to staffing."

There are times, of course, when hospitals may be faced with all three circumstances—increased volumes, high acuity, and high vacancy rates of staff. It is very difficult during those periods not to use costly alternative staffing mechanisms on a short-term basis. Other alternatives are to close beds or to compromise care by understaffing, neither of which is acceptable to the hospital with a commitment to quality care and meeting the health care needs of its community.

"Our job," stated Leslie, "is to take the time to evaluate and plan for longer-range proactive strategies in staffing, so that we don't keep reacting to crisis staffing situations." She was encouraged by Susan's enthusiasm to explore salaried options, per diem options, and creative incentive programs.

Acuity Hours Earned Divided by Care Hours Staffed Equals Patient Productivity

Patient care needs are expressed in many classification systems in terms of hours of care required. The advantage of this measurement is that it can be directly compared to actual staffed hours and a certain productivity picture can be obtained. This picture gives us a performance indicator of appropriate staffing levels for the given patients' needs. The productivity figure is calculated by dividing the "acuity hours earned" by "care hours staffed," and is multiplied by 100 so it can be expressed as a percent:

$$\frac{2540.66 \text{ acuity hours earned}}{2363.05 \text{ care hours staffed}}$$

$$= 1.0752 \times 100 = 107.52\%$$

In evaluating this percentage of productivity, we first and foremost must have a believable acuity system. Is it a valid system that measures what it is supposed to measure? Does it have high reliability results among individual users? If the answer is "yes" to these questions, the patient-care productivity percentage should be a good reflection of management's ability to staff correctly.

Some new managers might ask, "Aren't there other things which affect these results?" Again, relationships of reported data must be explored. What if the volume was low, and staffing levels had to exceed acuity requirements to meet basic safety requirements? Many nursing departments will move these additionally required hours into the fixed hour category to exclude them from the productivity calculation. Others may keep the hours in the actual care hours but accept the low volume as justification of a lower productivity.

Leslie asks, "Remember last year when the respiratory department asked our nursing staff to assume tasks normally assigned to their department, like setting up oxygen therapy devices and performing some of the diagnostic tests such as ear oximetry?" Susan recalls that respiratory therapists were barely able to keep up with the pediatric respiratory crisis during the winter months, so ICU nurses tried to help with the delivery of adult treatments. Leslie and Susan agree that the acuity system doesn't measure these additional activities. Leslie explains, "This situation we could justify, and we were able to prevent harsh feelings between departments because administration supported our team efforts."

Other areas to consider in evaluating low-productivity results are the skills of the person making staffing decisions, and the skills of the staff assigned to patient care. When a charge nurse is making decisions on how many resources are needed for patient care, is acuity system data interpreted correctly? If calculations are required for changes in volume due to admissions and transfers, is the charge nurse proficient in this function? Is there a tendency to ignore the formal systems and go by "gut feel" exclusively? Managers must evaluate the skills of management assistants and provide appropriate training in order to make well designed systems work as they should.

If staff consists of new trainees who are relatively inexperienced or unskilled, or of internal pool or agency nurses who are unfamiliar with the unit, it may be necessary to staff with more people than required by acuity system projections.

Care Hours Per Patient Day

Usually the required hours of care per patient day, based on historical trends, plus any known or anticipated change in patient mix, is built into the budget planning process. The budget gives us a standard or target against which actual results can be measured. This data can be trended over the course of the fiscal year whether acuity requirements are increasing, decreasing, or remaining fairly static. The cumulative data from the current fiscal year can then be used to project the next budget.

Fixed Hours

Fixed hours have generally been used to describe those hours which would continue to be staffed even if the census dropped to a very minimum level. Would the manager continue to work in a management capacity, in which case the hours would be fixed or static, regardless of variable volumes? Or would the manager move into staffing as a direct patient care giver, in order to increase the unit's efficiency and to stay in touch with the needs of patients and staff? In the latter situation, the hours should go into the actual staffed hours instead of fixed hours.

Would a secretary always be staffed regardless of volume because someone is needed to manage the unit's communication center? Or would the charge nurse assume some of the telephone, computer, and paperwork tasks? These questions can only be answered after evaluating individual unit size, unit structure, delivery systems, and philosophies.

When the decisions are made regarding assignments during low-volume periods, it then becomes important to have a flexible system of moving hours from one category to the other in the payroll, acuity, and productivity systems. For example, a manager may move into direct patient care, but is still reported in fixed hours. The patient care productivity may then look exceptionally high (in excess of defined targets, e.g., over 105%) and might raise questions about safe staffing levels and appropriate care. If these hours cannot be moved to match actual clinical staffing arrangements, false assumptions might be made, and "corrective action" might be requested when it is not needed.

Fixed, indirect labor hours include paid staff development time, such as preceptor time, mentoring programs, and training courses. These activities help develop and maintain staff competence and are hours committed for quality enhancement. They are, therefore, frequently budgeted in the fixed hours category. Variances in budget may occur when staff members attend more or fewer programs than were planned.

NONPRODUCTIVE HOURS

Benefit hours—those hours earned for vacations, sick time, bereavement leave, etc.—are considered nonproductive time. Orientation hours may be considered as productive or nonproductive, depending on payroll categories. Nonproductive hours are paid time to employees, so the hours impact salary budgets and budgeted productivity levels. The hours are also calculated into paid FTEs. When paid FTEs increase in hospitals, the organization will explore two primary areas, benefit accruals and hired levels of employees. Nursing is frequently one of the first areas to be explored, because it is the single largest FTE department in most hospitals. This is one reason why position control systems are beneficial, as they demonstrate that FTEs remain within budgeted levels and that system budget overexpenditures are not a result of overhiring practices. This can be invaluable information in an organization where staff cut-backs are mandated based on assumptions rather than complete analyses.

All paid hours convert to paid FTEs. This is a different and higher figure than hired FTEs, because the use of benefit hours require replacement of normal staff at the same time that normal staff is being paid for vacation or sick time.

See Table 13.5 as an illustration at this point. Usual staffing is five registered nurses (RNs) on the day shift, for a total of 5.0 FTEs Monday through Friday. Five RNs on weekends equals four shifts each for a 2-week pay period for an additional 2.0 FTEs. The total day shift staffing now is 7.0 FTEs. When a full-time RN goes on vacation and is replaced by another RN (perhaps an internal pool nurse, a per diem nurse, or a part-time nurse increasing hours), both are paid. One nurse is paid for the hours worked and the other nurse is on paid time off. The total paid FTEs during this period is 8.0 FTEs, instead of the usual 7.0 FTEs.

Paid Time Off

Many hospitals incorporate vacation pay and holiday pay into one category of nonproductive

Table 13.5. Variance Between Hired and Paid FTEs

Paid FTEs for normal staffing on 7 am–3 pm shift, for 2-week period:
5 RNs Monday–Friday (1.0 FTE each) = 5.0 FTE
5 RNs Saturday–Sunday (0.4 FTE each) = 2.0 FTE
Total = 7.0 FTE

Paid FTEs for normal staffing, plus vacation relief, for 2-week period:
5 RNs Monday–Friday (1.0 FTE each for 4.0 regular staff and 1.0 for replacement staff) = 5.0 FTE
1 RN on vacation, but receiving full pay = 1.0 FTE
5 RNs Saturday–Sunday (0.4 FTE each) = 2.0 FTE
Total = 8.0 FTE

paid hours. It would be ideal for budget management if these hours could be allocated for use evenly throughout the year; but, of course, requests for time off are uneven. Total budget productivity for all worked and paid hours may look exceptionally high during a pay period when few benefit hours have been used (see unit 1606 in Table 13.4). Conversely, total budget productivity for all worked and paid hours may look exceptionally low if too many staff members are granted vacation at one time (see unit 1607 in Table 13.4). Additionally, this latter situation may have a negative impact on patient care productivity because too many internal pool and agency nurses replace the usual staff. The unit manager is wise to set guidelines and limits for paid time off, so that productivity and quality do not suffer.

Sick time is a difficult budget item to anticipate, unless staff can give you advance notice of planned surgeries, maternity leaves, etc. Many managers budget on average use statistics for their particular unit, from total hospital figures, or even from state or national averages for sick time utilization. As with paid time off, these hours are generally not used evenly throughout the year, and will cause fluctuations in the total budget productivity figure. This category of paid time may also have an indirect affect on patient care productivity, depending on personnel policies of the institution. A prolonged leave of absence by one or more employees, when the position must be held for the employee's return, may cause increased float and agency use during the prolonged absence. The situation may, in turn, create salary variances, productivity variances, and decrease continuity and quality of care. The manager must understand personnel policies, which positions must be held open for absent employees, and at what point in the leave process the employee can be permanently replaced.

ORIENTATION AND OTHER HOURS

Orientation and education and training hours are also difficult to anticipate and will affect productivity salary figures negatively when this paid time exceeds budgeted allowances. The need for these hours is closely tied to turnover rates, expanded programs, and changing practice. See Chapter 9 for a detailed discussion of these costs.

Additional paid hours, such as bereavement leave for deaths in the nurses' family and jury duty, are usually of minimal impact unless a staff member is retained as a juror for a lengthy trial. Then, the impact may be similar to that of a leave of absence. Military duty obligations may produce situations, especially in times of national crisis or war, where the organizations must release regular staff to serve in their military units. It is important to understand hospital policy for these situations so appropriate evaluation of budget performance can be made.

Total Budget Hours ÷ Total Hours Paid

= Budget Productivity

Total budgeted paid hours are calculated by multiplying the target or standard paid hours per day by the total volume. This yields the total paid hours allocated by budget, adjusted for volume increases or decreases.

Total actual paid hours equals all hours paid through the payroll system for all categories of worked and paid hours, plus the purchased hours from agencies for supplemental staffing.

Total budget productivity is calculated by dividing the total budget hours (flexed) by the total actual hours, then multiplying by 100:

$$\frac{2894.92 \text{ total budgeted hours}}{2581.19 \text{ total paid hours}} = 1.1215 \times 100 = 112.15\%$$

At Susan's hospital, the chief nursing executive holds managers accountable for explaining variances not only in patient care productivity, which reflects appropriate staffing for patient care requirements, but also for total budget productivity. The latter is total budget performance for all worked and paid hours. At the beginning of the fiscal year, a standard is developed for paid nursing hours per patient day. This paid standard includes every payroll category described above.

Paid Hours per Patient Day

This indicator of performance, like acuity hours per patient day, gives managers a standard against which to measure budget performance. But this is a standard of total budget performance—patient care hours, fixed hours, and benefit hours, or, all productive and nonproductive hours. If the paid hours per patient day standard, or target, is exceeded by actual paid hours, the manager can work through the individual categories of the report to determine the source of overexpenditures. This paid hour per day indicator can be trended throughout the fiscal year, and can be used in next year's budget planning. The limitation of this indicator, if Table 13.4 and Table 13.5 are closely compared, is that productivity may be very high, yet the budget dollars may still be exceeded. To look only at the paid hour per day indicator may be misleading in regard to budget expenditures, because it assumes that hours are paid at the budgeted rate. Overtime, agency hours, and changes in skill mix may negatively impact an otherwise good budget performance.

New managers may ask, "Why is everything reported per patient day? Why don't we just get total budgeted hours to work with?" Again, we must return to the concept of the flexible budget, where resources are increased if patient days exceed projections, and allowable resources are decreased if volume falls.

DOLLAR VARIANCES

Leslie showed Susan the complementary report to the nursing productivity report. The variance report (Table 13.6) shows the dollar impact of a variety of budget components. "When we need to make corrections in budget performance, we first need to know which things are controllable and the level of control possible. We want to put our

Table 13.6. Variance Report

Unit	Overtime $ Variance	Purchased Hours $ Variance	Acuity $ Variance	Fixed Hours $ Variance	Paid Time Off $ Variance	Orientation $ Variance	Skill Mix $ Variance	Total $ Variance
1606	$178.42	$6,500.61	$719.05	$998.56	($5,199.57)	$56.89	$1,403.96	$4,658.21
1607	$791.40	$6,514.42	$2,549.00	$1,855.81	$776.23	($112.57)	($178.02)	$12,196.28
1608	$791.46	$5,045.53	($1,286.67)	$849.59	($2,037.49)	($197.58)	$1,950.83	$5,115.65
1611	$1,023.26	$2,467.12	($505.80)	$4,276.05	($3,646.76)	($244.36)	$657.17	$4,026.63

efforts into making changes that will make the most positive impact."

In Table 13.6, we see the dollar impact of the budget variances. This data assists managers in determining major problem areas and also in prioritizing plans for corrective action. The variance calculations already include adjustments for volume and acuity differences from budget (those factors which are considered uncontrollable and justifiable). So, the dollars shown here reflect controllable factors which the nurse manager must reconcile:

Overtime variance = (½ × average wage) × number of overtime hours (when overtime is paid at time-and-a-half)

Purchased hours variance = (average agency wage − average unit wage) × number of purchased hours

Acuity variance = {(actual staffed hours/patient day − earned acuity hours/patient day) × volume} × average wage

Fixed hours variance = (actual hours for non-volume-related activities − budget hours for non-volume-related activities) × average wage

Paid time off variance = {(actual paid benefit hours − budgeted paid benefit hours) × (actual volume/budgeted volume)} × average wage

Orientation variance = {(actual orientation hours − budgeted orientation hours) × (actual volume/budgeted volume)} × average wage

Skill mix variance = (actual RN% − budgeted RN%) × total paid hours × average RN wage

+

{(actual LPN% − budgeted LPN%) × total paid hours} × average LPN wage

+

{(actual NA% − budgeted NA%) × total paid hours} × average NA wage

+

{(actual secretary % − budgeted secretary %) × total paid hours} × average secretary wage

Total variance can be calculated by adding the above variance categories.

The above items represent variances which are controllable by managers. For a 2-week pay period, a variance may represent a normal fluctuation in hours, e.g., vacation time increases during a holiday season and may not be a cause for serious concern. However, if the fiscal year-to-date report shows consistent overexpenditures as the budget year is well under way, a plan of action should be developed and implemented to correct the variances. Managers have found self-scheduling systems, salaried staff systems, per diem supplemental staff, and other programs to be successful budgeting strategies while simultaneously promoting improved professional practice models and increasing staff morale.

TURNOVER

"When we looked at orientation hours on the productivity report, we mentioned that turnover of staff has significant budget impact," Leslie reminded Susan, "so let's take a closer look at that whole issue." They started with a literature review, and found that there is a positive side to turnover. Miller describes the benefits of turnover: opportunities for presenting new ideas, forced analysis of the work organization with improvements in efficiency and effectiveness, opportunities to recruit new skills, and involvement of the manager in employee career development (15).

But turnover can be excessive and may result in increased salary costs due to expensive replacement staffing, increased paid but nonproductive hours during training of new employees, lost productivity, low morale, and possible bed closures and lost revenue. Kerfoot believes that managers' excuses for turnover, such as poor nurse-physician relations, difficult patient populations, and inadequate physical environments, are not acceptable because those problems are within the control of the manager. She places the cost of replacing a single nurse "easily" at $50,000 dollars, including recruitment and advertising efforts and expensive overtime or agency expenses (16). The average time for a nurse to achieve 90–100% productivity is reported by Jones to be 6.7 weeks, and by Miller to be 24 weeks (17, 18).

Susan was especially interested in a study by Mann which specifically addressed ICU turnover and retention. First year on-the-job training and negative productivity, plus the preceptor's time equaled $17,194. It was 18 months before a nurse's net productivity value equaled the initial investment to train the nurse (19). Considering that it takes up to 90 days to recruit new nurses for critical care areas (20), Susan was beginning to feel that this problem could have serious consequences on the quality of care. She wanted to monitor this item closely and take steps to minimize any negative impact. Leslie explained how to calculate a turnover rate:

$$\text{Turnover rate} = \frac{\text{number of employee terminations}}{\text{average number of employees}} \times 100$$

She went on to explain the turnover report generated in the hospital's personnel department (see Table 13.7). It tracks turnover rates and the reasons for turnover. "Finding out why people are leaving our organization is very important, because it allows us to make improvements that will help retain employees longer," Leslie explained, "Our nurse recruiter does an exit interview with every employee, using a personalized, nonthreatening approach so the employee will feel comfortable to give truthful responses about why they are leaving."

Strategies to retain employees include approaches such as incentive pay programs, which may have significant budgetary impact. These programs are increasingly popular for evening, night, and weekend hours worked. As hospitals respond to staffing shortages throughout the year, some of these programs are developed to address urgent shortage situations. If the incentive salary differentials were not budgeted for the fiscal year, a salary variance will occur and managers must track those expenditures to justify the variance.

If turnover rates continue to climb, vacancies will increase, supplemental staffing may include untrained and unreliable performers, and the result will most likely be budget overexpenditures, low productivity, and less-positive patient outcomes. How much is justifiable because of uncontrollable conditions, and how much is unjustified because of poor management skills? One recent study indicates that 88% of nurses in the initial conflict stage of leave-taking could have been influenced by their managers to stay, if only better listening skills, words of encouragement, or problem solving had been attempted in response to their concerns (21). Exit interview results may provide valuable information for management.

BENEFITS

Nurse managers must be knowledgeable about benefits offered to employees, must know which benefits are paid directly from the manager's budget, and must know their level of control regarding benefit expenditures. In 1988 American Hospital Association's report of the hospital nursing personnel survey revealed that: over 50% of all hospitals offer tuition assistance, nurse mentorship programs, and crosstraining; recruitment and retention bonuses were the most common new policy

Table 13.7. Turnover Report

Unit: ICU						Year: 1990
	Jan	Feb	May	Apr	May	FYTD
#separations	0	2	1	4	2	9
Ave # employees	52	52	52	52	52	
% turnover	0%	3.8%	1.9%	7.7%	3.8%	3.5% ave
						17.2% cum

Reasons for separation FYTD:

Inflexible schedule	2	Spouse relocation	3
Job stress	1	Change in career	
Inadequate staffing		No promotion opportunity	1
Inadequate wage		Return to school	1
Inadequate benefits		Performance problems	
Inadequate training	1	Problems with supervisor	
		Problems with coworkers	

from 1987 to 1988; virtually all hospitals pay shift differentials; and more than 80% provide medical insurance, vacation time, continuing education, and parking for full- and part-time nurses (22).

Shift differentials are usually fairly constant, unless a significant change is made in the staffing plan during the course of the fiscal year. As base pay salary dollars are flexed for volume changes and acuity changes, so should shift differentials be flexed.

Vacation time is less constantly paid, so budget impact will fluctuate. Judicious allocation of vacation time during the year (not too many regular staff gone at any one time) is best so that productivity and budget don't suffer from too many expensive supplemental staff who are unfamiliar with the unit. Budget may be affected if employees are called off due to low census and choose to fill out their normal paycheck by using vacation time; then total paid hours may exceed budgeted levels for the actual patient volume. All earned vacation time is usually paid to terminating employees, so turnover will create excessive reported vacation expenditures for the pay period in which they occur.

An interesting variation in control of vacation hours is found in the finance department, which charges the nursing budgets as vacation time is earned, not as it is used. This allows more constant charges to the cost center, and is easier to plan and control. However, the actual dollars have not been spent, so the institution's budget reports may be misleading unless a special adjustment is made to reflect the difference between accounting transfers and actual expenditures. This method of accrual accounting is explained in Chapter 2.

Recruitment bonuses may come from a special personnel budget for hospital-wide recruitment efforts, or they may be charged to the nursing budgets where used. The same is true for retention incentives. It is likely that the latter are charged to nursing cost centers, because the bonuses or differentials are frequently calculated on base pay.

SUPPLY EXPENSE VARIANCES

Now that we've covered the issues related to staffing, wages, and benefit cost, we need to look at another portion of the expense budget, the expenditures for supplies. "It's been my experience that when supply expenses exceed budget, it is usually caused by unexpected increases in the cost of purchasing supplies, or from "hoarding" inventory on the unit, or from inexperienced or untrained nurses using too many supplies because tasks are carried out inefficiently or incorrectly the first time," Leslie cautioned.

"Remember when I spoke of last year's overexpenditure for supplies, even after flex budget increases for our higher volumes? Well, we had finally trained all of our nurses to use effective body-substance-isolation techniques when in contact with all patients, not just those patients that the nurses knew had actual or potential infectious processes. The nurses were using all of the appropriate protective barriers, and then we received word from central supply that there was a shortage on gloves. We couldn't compromise safety and infection control practices, so we went to another vendor and paid much more for the gloves that were in short supply. The change in practice combined with the increased costs from a noncontracted vendor resulted in a significant negative budget impact."

There are times when essential supplies such as transducers or pressure tubing are not delivered in a timely manner. This leads to a lack of trust in the supply department and nurses react by overordering and hoarding supplies to ensure that they have plenty on hand. Hospitals at times do not even know how much inventory they have, because it is "hidden" in decentralized cabinets and shelves. This inefficient practice adversely impacts on the individual unit's budget, because supplies are ordered in excess of patient volume, resulting in expenses which exceed revenue. This increased store of supplies on the unit may also lead to inefficient use, if it gives the perception that there is a "never-ending" supply; nurses may not consider or even realize the costs of dressings, intravenous supplies, and other items. It is always a good idea to make them aware of costs. A manager's job must include setting up appropriate ordering systems so that only supplies needed in urgent and emergent situations are maintained in unit cabinets, and other supplies come on the daily supply exchange carts in sufficient levels.

Quality experts have studied the issue of repeating tasks because they are not done right the first time; and they can demonstrate the increased costs and decreased quality that result from any failure to meet standards on the first attempt (23). When orientation and ongoing skills development programs are inadequate, or when too many internal pool and supplemental agency nurses are

196 EVALUATION AND CONTROLLING

used, there is a risk of inefficient use of supplies. Treatments may have to be repeated in order to get the desired result, simply because the nurse is unfamiliar with the supplies or equipment or with the unit's standard of practice for using them.

Most managers understand their obligation for assuring a competent staff, but they relate the issue only to quality outcomes for the patients. They need to also understand the budgetary impact of delivering care. Adopting a standard of "getting it right the first time" reflects a prudent cost containment strategy.

REVENUE VARIANCES

Revenue is probably one of the least controllable budget items for nursing cost centers, and it is most often the area of least understanding and experience for nurse managers. Critical care areas have little control over admissions; thus, control of revenue is difficult.

It is possible, through historical trends, to estimate the sources of revenue and to project that those trends will also occur in the subsequent year(s). It is helpful when hospitals report the payor mix, as shown in Table 13.8.

Managers may be able to influence revenue by developing and marketing new services that are projected to be reimbursed by specific payors. This may also necessitate recruitment of specialty physicians, such as cardiac surgeons or burn specialists.

Responsibility reports may or may not report deductions from revenue—such things as bad debt write-offs, charity, and contractual agreement deductions. If not reported, managers may evaluate their bottom lines as very favorable. But, when the actual adjustments are made, the reverse may be true. Medicare reimbursement may involve a 60% or more write-off, the difference between the hospital charges and the diagnosis related group (DRG) payment. Managers should understand their reports and if the figures are pre- or post-deduction status.

There is an area of revenue control, however, if charges are entered manually for patient care treatments and procedures. A manager should have a system of checking charges on a daily basis; waiting for the end-of-month report is too late to make corrections to the patient bill. Table 13.9 is an example of a daily charge-tracking system which may be reviewed by a designated clerical person, on a daily basis, to ensure correct charge entries. Managers must hold staff accountable for using charge systems correctly. Omissions may occur due to "forgetfulness," to a haphazardly developed or incomplete charge system, to unclear expectations of job responsibilities, or even to nurses' manipulation of the system based on their interpretation of whether the patient "can afford it." Reconciling budget variances may require the development of a new or different system; it is best to involve clerical staff, rather than professional staff, in this function whenever possible. Correction of lost revenue may require clarity of job role expectations, rewriting job performance standards, and/or employee counseling.

It is helpful to evaluate how much of the DRG prospective payment is being consumed by nursing care costs. Especially in critical care areas, where nursing care is only a portion of the total hospital stay, it is helpful to know how efficiently patients are being cared for and how quickly they are being transferred to step-down units. Table 13.10 shows a data base created by an automated patient-classification system; the system interfaces with the financial system when the patient is discharged so that the total nursing hours used can be matched with the discharge DRG.

This particular patient had a 9.7 day length of

Table 13.8. Payor Mix Variance

Dept: CICU　　　　　　　　Period ending: 11/30/90

Payor	Budget	Flex	Variance
Medicare	379,900	275,113	104,787
Medicaid	36,709	32,892	3,817
HMOs	141,355	221,287	(79,932)
PPOs	60,875	117,858	(56,983)
BC	61,696	51,012	10,684
Private	89,606	147,583	(57,977)

Table 13.9. Daily Patient Charge Report

Date: 9/12/90

Unit	Patient	Charge Item	Quantity
CICU	Smith, V.	Cardioversion	1
	Jones, B.	Telemetry	1
	Hill, J.	Telemetry	1
	Paul, L.	Telemetry	1
	Ng, M.	Swan-Ganz insertion	1
	Lafka, T.	Pacemaker	1

Table 13.10. Nursing Costs per DRG

DRG	Mean LOS	Act LOS	Var LOS	Total Nursing Hours	Cost/Nursing Hour	Nursing Cost/DRG	Reimb Rate
121 M.I. w/ comp.	10.3	9.7	(0.6)	93.05	$15.84	$1474	$6024

Nursing Diagnosis/DRG
Altered cardiac output
Altered gas exchange
Altered self-concept

stay and required 93.05 hours of nursing care during his hospital stay. At an average cost of $15.84 per hour, the total nursing care costs consumed $1,473.91 of the $6,024 DRG reimbursement rate. The major nursing diagnoses for the patient in this DRG are also reported, so nursing costs can be evaluated based on a nursing model of care. Susan saw this as an opportunity to trend data and expand the budget planning efforts next year to include more nursing diagnosis related planning.

"There's a lot of information available to me," said Susan, "I wonder if I'll ever learn how to use it all to make good management decisions for my unit." Leslie assured Susan that guidance would continue to be offered until Susan felt knowledgeable about the reports and competent to interpret the data. Together they reviewed the biweekly and monthly reports until Susan demonstrated competence in promoting cost effective unit operations.

REFERENCES

1. McGrail GR. Budgets: an underused resource. Journal of Nursing Administration, 1988;11:25–31.
2. McGrail, p. 27.
3. Francisco PD. Flexible budgeting and variance analysis. Nursing Management, 1989;11:40–43.
4. Betka RD, Lacusta MP. Productivity monitoring systems: their use in management planning, forecasting, and labor budgeting. Health Care Strategic Management, 1984;1:8–12.
5. Callahan D. Setting limits: medical goals in an aging society. New York: Simon and Schuster, Inc., 1987:143.
6. Hoffman F. Nursing productivity assessment and costing out nursing services. Philadelphia: J.B. Lippencott, 1988:91–92.
7. Kirk R, Dunaye TM. Managing hospital nursing services for productivity. Nursing Management 1986;3:29–32.
8. Lawrenz, Madden, and Assoc. Hours per patient day survey update. Perspectives on Staffing and Scheduling 1989;5:1.
9. McCabe JP, Hartnack JLP. FTE reports and fiscal management. Nursing Management 1989;11:46–48.
10. Mallison MB, ed. Misuse of RNs spurs shortage, says new study: only 26% of time is spent in professional care. American Journal of Nursing 1989;9:1223.
11. 1988 Report of the Hospital Nursing Personnel Surveys. Chicago: American Hospital Assoc., 1989:9.
12. Secretary's Commission on Nursing: Support studies and background information, vol II. Washington, DC: Department of Health and Human Services, 1988:V–5.
13. Secretary's Commission on Nursing, p. V–16.
14. AHA. 1988 Report of the hospital nursing personnel surveys. Chicago: American Hospital Assoc., 1989:9.
15. Miller JJ, Strategies: calculating the cost of staff nurse turnover. In: Nurse executive management strategies. Chicago: American Hospital Assoc., 1988;11:3.
16. Kerfoot K. Nursing management considerations: retention, what's it all about? Nursing Economics, 1988;1:42–43.
17. Jones CB. Staff nurse turnover costs: measurements and results. Journal of Nursing Administration, 1990;5:27–31.
18. Miller JJ, p. 6.
19. Mann EE. A human capital approach to ICU nurse retention. Journal of Nursing Administration 1989;10:8–16.
20. Moss J, Curran C. The nursing shortage becomes a growing human resource priority. Trustee 1987;5:13–16.
21. Landstrom GL, Biordi DL, Gillies DA. The emotional and behavioral process of staff nurse turnover. Journal of Nursing Administration 1989;9:23–28.
22. AHA. 1988 Report of the hospital nursing personnel surveys. Chicago: American Hospital Assoc., 1989:2.
23. Crosby PB. Quality is Free. New York: McGraw-Hill, 1979:11.

Chapter 14

Controlling

DONNA L. BERTRAM, KATHERINE D. MCCORD

With the focus on health care costs, nurse managers play a pivotal role in controlling the various resources under their direction. We are very labor intensive, especially in the critical care environment where the nurse:patient ratio is higher than elsewhere in the hospital. Additionally, critical care units (CCUs) reflect a high utilization of expensive supplies and equipment. A 1990 survey of hospital executives revealed that intensive care units (ICUs) and CCUs ranked as the third most unprofitable health care service provided by the hospital (1). Controlling these costly resources requires nurse managers to be integrally involved in organizational goals.

Cost control, cost containment, capitated costs, cost-benefit ratio, and cost effectiveness are familiar words in health care. Nursing is expected to contribute to cost control. One of the role expectations of the critical care manager is the "promotion of cost effective unit operations" (2). This chapter will identify the components necessary for the critical care manager to be more effective in controlling.

CONTROLLING COMPONENTS

Controlling is a management function of checking, directing, restraining, comparing, and regulating resources. Controlling costs consist of at least five components:

1. Participation;
2. Standards;
3. Expectations;
4. Comparison;
5. Decision making.

These components require the clinical manager to control the behavior of the employees to meet objectives and communicate and mediate with others in order to obtain the resources needed (3). Various reports and tools facilitate tracking the information needed for effectiveness. With the rapidly changing environment, the information needs to be timely and reports flexible enough to capture the experiences necessary to make decisions.

Participation

Participation starts with the budgeting function with the involvement of those who have direct control over the area. The clinical manager, staff, and physicians of the unit participate in budget planning, budget control, and decision making. These interrelated activities result in greater effectiveness and efficiencies of unit operations. The process is reflected in Figure 14.1.

Planning involves identifying organizational and unit goals and seeking input from all of the team members. The result of the planning process is budget development. The best time to control costs is at the start. The budget may serve as a standard by which performance can be measured.

Controlling is the process which helps assure that actual performance conforms with the standards. The result of controlling is greater effectiveness of resource utilization.

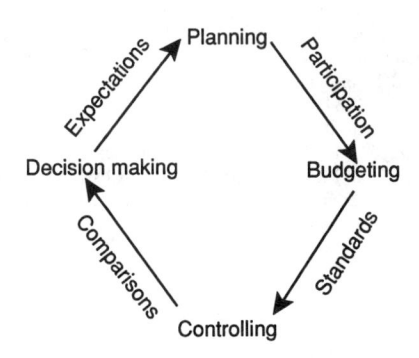

Figure 14.1. Controlling process.

Input on variances and outputs on productivity lead to the decision making process. Decision making uses the information generated by the control process to determine the next plan and the process repeats.

The first-line manager holds the key to controlling and seeking participation in the financial management process. It is imperative that clinical staff and others become involved, as they are the ones ultimately responsible for costs and resource use at the patient level.

The first approach in achieving clinical staff involvement is education. The clinical staff nurse needs to be educated regarding aspects of financial management and personnel control. This includes knowledge of the operating and capital budget, the costs and the charge of all the items and supplies used, and the expectations for cost control. Education is an ongoing process which needs repetition periodically in order to familiarize nurses with the importance of their involvement in cost control.

The second approach describes and emphasizes the staff nurse's role in controlling the actual performance of the unit in regard to personnel utilized, materials used, and services performed. Each nurse is a manager of a wide variety of resources. Not only can the clinical nurse make an impact on the financial performance of the unit, but including them can have long-lasting effects. A study by Kusserow indicates that nearly 80% of chief executive officers and 85% of nursing executives believe that including the staff nurse in the decision-making process can have a positive effect on nurse retention (4). Establishing a unit cost committee composed of staff nurses can provide education, greater control, and peer support (5). Clinical nurses are where the action occurs in patient care and their effect on cost control can be dramatic. Staff generate excellent ideas. One nurse noticed that after a transfer, the television and electric lights were left on in a vacated room. Her observation and working with housekeeping and others helped decrease the electricity merely by turning off unused equipment.

A positive function of control results in worker satisfaction (6). A satisfied worker is more apt to be productive and efficient. A nurse who understands financial ramifications, and exercises the needed responsibility and accountability to integrate this knowledge in practice, is a valuable asset to the manager and the organization. The nurse manager can provide guidance, reinforcement, and acknowledgement to subordinates to promote cost control behavior.

The demarcation between the roles of the physician and nurse is rapidly blurring. There is an increasing acceptance of the team concept where both physician and nurse are key members of the health care team. Collaboration lends itself to including the physician in the controlling process. Like the clinical nurse, the physician needs to be educated regarding the financial aspects of the unit. Physicians can be a major influence in suggesting items for the capital budget and supplies for the operating budget. Through education, they can be informed of the cost of the services and supplies provided. One approach used by the nurse manager reminds the physician of costs by suggesting a more economical approach. Examples include: (*a*) the nurse can suggest that a patient can be appropriately transferred from the critical care area to a less acute unit. The nurse is at the bedside 24-hours a day and is in a position to evaluate patient acuity and nursing care needed; (*b*) the nurse can give the physician a choice of a particular supply, explain the cost factor and seek input. The nurse can explain the use of the products committee and the need to standardize.

This active collaborative effort between physicians and nurses results in greater control at a unit level and helps the hospital meet financial goals.

Participation also involves the unit manager seeking information from others in finance, ancillary departments, and administration. Taking an active role, a unit manager may want to send memos to others recognizing their assistance in the control process. Participation includes attending budget meetings, educational opportunities, and seeking resources.

Standards

The operating and capital budgets serve as the measuring guidelines. The approved budget provides the basis for comparison and/or judgment of performance. It is important for the unit manager to be knowledgeable and proactive in meeting established standards. Using financial reports, the unit manager analyzes operational and financial performance frequently. The manager must know the amount of latitude allowed, understand work improvement methods, and appreciate the impact of cost on quality.

Reports help us keep track of the progress of the implementation of the budget and provide a means of control. Martin identified the importance of reports in being oriented toward the needs of the operational managers. Who receives reports should determine what information is reported, their frequency, and the format (7). Reports need to be timely so that action, if required, can be taken. The unit manager also needs to identify what reports the director and others expect from them.

One report tracks capital equipment. Some hospitals produce a current fixed asset list of major movable equipment. This report shows the acquisition date, cost, depreciation amount, serial number, hospital identification number, and location (Table 14.1). If an item is transferred to another department or replaced with a new piece of equipment, the unit manager works with finance to change the inventory for the unit so depreciation and asset evaluation can be correct.

The unit manager controls the ordering of capital equipment items. Often the capital equipment list appears in descending order by cost and identifies the month to be ordered. The unit manager needs to develop a system of tracking items ordered and/or substituted (Table 14.2).

Other reports may include charts or graphs comparing volumes to standard, acuity to standard, productivity to standard, expense reports of supply expense per patient day, or salary expense per patient day. Visualization often helps understanding (Fig. 14.2).

Each manager must explore with the immediate supervisor how much latitude or variance is allowed before reporting and action must take place. A rule of thumb may be to report variances within plus or minus 5% of the standard. The manager identifies how frequently to report and the approved format. The manager may be expected to report and justify FTE use and overtime on a routine basis (Table 14.3). Additionally, the manager needs to identify controllable costs and find out how other expenses beyond direct control are handled. For example, if central supply adjusts inventory and charges back some supplies to the unit without a paper trail verifying the reason, the unit manager cannot be responsible for this variance in the budget.

Work improvement methods can affect the productivity standard. (Productivity is discussed in Chapter 9.) Work improvement controls costs through analyzing the work and the people doing the work, seeks new ideas, examines outcomes, and assigns priorities. The concept behind work improvement is not to work harder, but to be smarter and decrease effort. In analyzing work and people, the following questions are helpful:

1. What activities take the most time?
2. What kind of skills and knowledge are needed?
3. Who is currently doing the work?
4. How do employees use those skills?
5. What tasks are spread too thin?
6. Where is the work done?
7. Who else could do the work?
8. Can the work be eliminated or changed?
9. What barriers are there to changing?
10. What factors would lead to success?

If there is no reason for doing something, seek to eliminate the task. When the place seems inappropriate, change where the work is being done. Sometimes a different person can do the work faster and be a cheaper substitute. Some work requires more people. Seek a complement such as an LPN. This work and people analysis leads to better control and efficiencies. Challenging traditional tasks is another control strategy.

All units determine quality outcomes expected for patients. Quality according to Crosby is "conforming to requirements" or doing the task in the right way the very first time (8). Control of quality involves staff participation in looking at patient outcomes, patient and physician satisfaction, and

Table 14.1. Equipment Inventory for CCU, December, 1990

Hospital Number	Item	Date Purchased	Cost	Serial Number	Depreciation	Location	Comments
M2403	Defibrillator	10/88	$8500	HP43796	$3682	2 Main	BioMed done
M181	Stretcher	8/86	$5000	59485	$4249	2 Main	
M9467	Computer	6/90	$12,000	IBM33904	$1200	2 North	Service Contract
M8435	IV Pump	12/89	$3000	I77433	$600	2 Main	

Table 14.2. Capital Items, Fiscal Year 1990–1991

Item	Vendor	Cost	Month	Date Ordered
Cardiac Monitors	Skyway	$48,832	October, 1990	7/90
Transport Monitor	STF	$12,965	August, 1990	8/90
BP Modules	Hi Tech	$ 8,700	March, 1991	
Bed with Scales	EasyGo	$ 8,500	May, 1991	
Cardiac Bed	HR	$ 8,500	March, 1991	
Neuro Monitors	HN	$ 5,000	Sept, 1990	10/90
Facsimile	QP	$ 2,450	Nov, 1990	1/91
Suction Regulators	STF	$ 1,500	June, 1991	

the environment. The clinical manager can question and quantify how well the staff are doing and seek input on how to improve. For example, the quality indicator is to prevent infection from peripheral intravenous lines. The manager notices that recently more patients are showing signs of phlebitis and are on antibiotic therapy. The manager checks charts, observes staff, and monitors sites. At the staff meeting, the manager reports the problem and observations. The staff decide to research the issue and validate the need to change the IV site more frequently. This aspect of improving quality may result in decreased antibiotic use for the patient, nurse intervention time, and pharmacy time.

Expectations

Individual managers must be held accountable for budget control in order to meet organizational goals. As the cost of health care continues to escalate, managers are increasingly responsible for monitoring and controlling expenses. There has always been an expectation to provide and maintain quality service. Today, an equal expectation exists to provide and maintain financial viability. Staff, physicians, and managers are challenged to control financial performance (9).

Three key components of controlling costs in personnel, material, and services were described by Mailbot, Binger, and Slezak (10). Each of these areas are key issues the critical care manager can be expected to control. Strategies are presented in each area.

Personnel Control

The budget planning process identifies the specific number of positions at each salary level that are planned and allocated. The manager develops a position control system to prevent accidentally overhiring. A monthly personnel budget report identifies positions filled, productive and nonproductive time, overtime, differentials, benefits, and dollars spent. The clinical manager may calculate the cost of direct care per patient admission. The manager monitors and reports the variances. Action steps for correction must be included.

Changing the clinical staff mix may lower the average salary cost per FTE. Utilizing licensed practical or vocational nurses and nurse aides may free RNs from performing some nursing tasks and nonnursing duties. The manager needs to determine the scope and distribution of the work and analyze the need for additional non-RN workers. AACN has a position paper on the use of technical support personnel in critical care (11).

Developing an internship and preceptor program for new graduates, as well as the experienced nurse with no critical care background, helps maximize their effectiveness and longevity in the unit. AACN has identified various strategies for integrating new graduates into critical care (12).

Monitoring overtime and evaluating alternatives can control the personnel budget. Some hospitals have elected to change from an 8–80 work time to a 40-hour work time. In the 8–80 work time, any work over 8 hours in a day and 80 hours in a pay period is overtime. Some hospitals employ staff at the outset on 12-hour shifts with the understanding by the employee that overtime will not be paid. If the unit is on 12-hour shifts, the overtime dollars can add up quickly. The 40-hour work time pays overtime for work greater than 40 hours in a work week. The manager can control overtime by analyzing the work environment and personnel performance. Challenging traditional start times of the shift may decrease overtime.

202 EVALUATION AND CONTROLLING

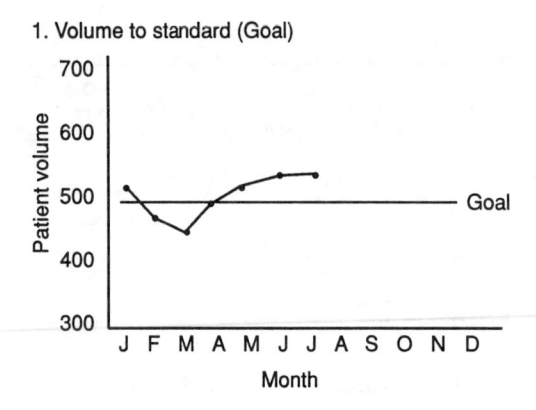

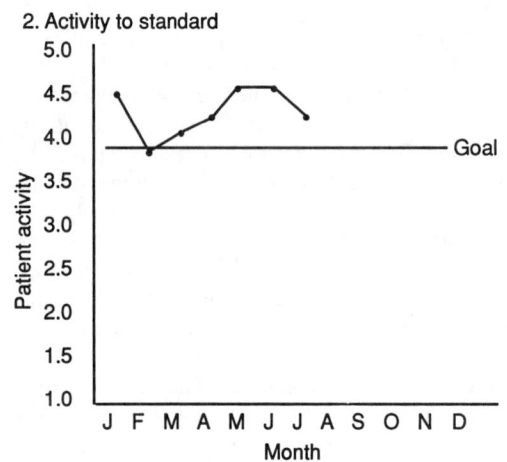

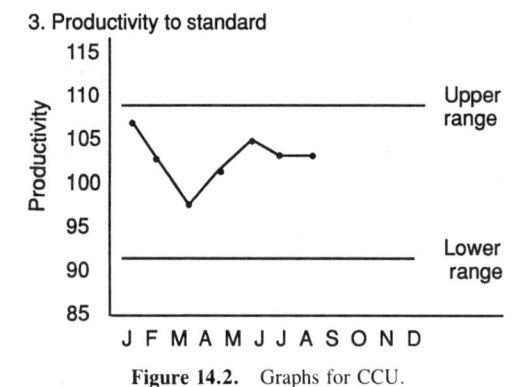

Figure 14.2. Graphs for CCU.

Develop variable 4-, 6-, 8-, 10-, and 12-hour shifts to better utilize clinical staff during peak times. For example, if a nurse is assigned to take care of the new open heart surgery patient on the day shift and the usual surgery lasts over 3 hours, the nurse may not need to arrive at the 7 A.M. time, but report later. Four-hour shifts can bridge the gap between 8 and 12 hours and decrease overtime.

Develop an on-call system to care for unscheduled acute admissions. The clinical manager can budget for these dollars in the planning phase. On the counter side, maintaining a go-home-early rotation list of staff can be used when census decreases. Options to be used may include absent without pay, use of benefit time, or trading a day off for another day.

Assign special projects to a nurse when an unavoidable overlap occurs. This nurse could research a quality problem, talk with families, or work on an orientation packet. This nurse could check on newly transferred patients or call discharged patients.

Monitor vacation, holiday, sick time, and any paid benefit time off. This requires the clinical manager to arrange scheduling and staffing to avoid overtime and costly agency replacement. For example, the manager desires to send six nurses from the unit to the AACN National Teaching Institute. In the planning process, budget money was allocated for six attendees and replacements in the unit. The manager knows the dollars are covered and now must work with remaining staff to ensure that additional dollars are not spent on overtime or agency utilization.

Establish an internal critical care pool to help with times of high census and low staffing. The clinical nurses in the pool need to keep their competencies current so minimum hours may need to be established. Seeking medical surgical nurses who may want to take care of the patients awaiting transfer can augment staffing. An exchange program with other areas such as emergency may provide additional resources.

Educate the staff and charge nurses on the process of controlling costs when the manager is unavailable. Post memos about changes in stock and emergency supplies. Assign one or two staff to do spot checks of costly items. For example, one unit discovered it was throwing pizza boxes in the hazardous waste containers. These containers cost the hospital $12.50 to purchase and the staff were using them improperly.

Monitor performance appraisals of staff and do not award raises for less than outstanding performance. A mixed message occurs when the manager identifies marginal performance, but yet awards a raise. Delay the raise until performance improves. Staff need to be terminated for failing to meet standards and expectations. Recognize and reward staff who perform above the standard and

Table 14.3. FTE and Overtime Report

Unit _____
Manager _____
Date _____

Full-Time Equivalents (FTEs)

	Current FTEs	Budgeted FTEs	Variance ± 5%	Variance Justification	Plan to Control FTEs
Current Period FTEs Dates _____					
Year-To-Date FTEs					

Additional Comments:
_____
_____

Overtime

	Current Period Overtime Hours	Current Period Overtime Cost	YTD Overtime Hours	YTD Overtime Cost	Variance ± 5%	Variance Justification	Plan To Control OT
Overtime							

Additional Comments:
_____
_____

contribute to unit success. Consider the use of incentive sharing, bonuses, or salaried status.

Absenteeism and turnover affect the nursing budget, especially when employees must be replaced through overtime, float pool, agency pool, or other alternatives. One sick day results in paying benefit and replacement time. Turnover results in higher cost due to replacement time, recruiter time, marketing dollars, orientation time, and lost productivity during the learning period. Counseling for absenteeism that is high puts the employee on notice that this behavior is unacceptable. Disciplinary action may be necessary or attention by the manager to the issue may correct the problem. Some hospitals have found that self-scheduling and peer pressure reduces absenteeism. Turnover can be controlled by proper hiring practices, skilled interviewing, clear expectations, positive reinforcement, promotion of professionalism, education, involvement, and salaried status. The AACN demonstration project revealed that a high percentage of CCRNs on the unit was one factor that promoted retention (13).

Consider hiring a clinical nurse specialist. Ahrens and Padwojski identify that an advanced clinical nurse can improve quality care, reduce length of stay, and save dollars through appropriate product acquisitions. They cited a $70,000 a year savings (14)!

Identify any workers compensation issues and aim for prevention. Controlling lost work due to on-the-job injuries starts with looking at what has happened on the unit and what can be improved. Examples are needle sticks, back injuries, slips, falls, and exposure to communicable diseases. Remind staff and physicians frequently about needle disposal and the cost to the hospital for follow-up. Our hospital identified a cost of $139 to process one needle stick. Back injuries can be minimized through education of body mechanics and having proper equipment available. Falls and slips can be minimized by working with housekeeping to identify wet floors and cleaning up spills immediately. Reminding nurses and others of the importance of hand washing can be a savings by preventing nosocomial infections. A safety education program increases staff awareness of safety issues and may save expenses related to lost work time.

Materials and Inventory Control

Identify the average level of supplies that are needed to meet average daily census and patient needs. In financial management the economic ordering quantity (EOQ) is the optimum quantity to be ordered each time an order is placed (15). The manager may need to work with materials management to ensure the adequacy of supplies and cost savings can occur when ordering in bulk. Maintain a small safety stock to guard against delays that impact patient care or increase costs due to overnight shipping or rental. This amount needs to be identified with the manager of materials and/or central supply. Using a red-line method or flag method of the time when supplies need to be reordered is helpful. Placing a red mark on the third to the last item or inserting a note "reorder" helps the designated staff keep inventory costs in control.

Evaluate supply inventory at least quarterly to prevent stockpiling and unused shelf items. Working with the staff and physicians on using present inventory before changing over to a new product can be cost effective. Working with central supply on the exchange cart system can also be a cost savings by limiting numbers of items available.

Coordinate with hospital purchasing the negotiation of the best price for quality supplies and products. Investigate with other areas such as the cardiac catheterization laboratory, surgery, anesthesia, and emergency areas for the use of the same product so greater savings can occur. Develop a products evaluation committee that works on standardization.

Consolidate products and trays whenever possible by working with clinical staff and physicians. Instead of separate thoracotomy trays for each surgeon, seek input and explain the reason for consolidation. Develop physician preference cards so the right supplies can be gathered quickly.

Establish protocols with vendors for free trial periods for a new product being considered. Provide the users with score sheets that identify quality, user friendliness, applicability, and durability. Notify materials management on any product concerns. Do not use unsafe equipment, but seek replacements. If there is a problem with a product, save the wrapper it came in as well as the product. The vendor may trade in problem products as well as outdated supplies.

Identify the educational needs of the clinical staff and physicians on new products, procedures, and supplies. Negotiate with the vendor for round-the-clock in-services and quarterly updates. Often new equipment and products are used improperly due to poor in-service. This can be costly and time consuming.

Limit special purchases of products for certain physicians. The medical staff may not be aware that there are established protocols for standardizing supplies. Meeting with physicians, providing explanations, and showing what is available controls costs.

Utilize accounting and finance resources to determine the benefit of rental versus purchase. This may depend on volume, availability of the product, the amount budgeted for rental, and whether the product can be substituted or exchanged.

Develop a unit culture that fosters cost savings. Often employees and physicians do not know the costs of various items. One unit was discovered to be throwing away a reusable item. A reward system for a cost saving tip or suggestion provides incentives for the employees. Some hospitals split the savings with the employees or give a bonus for the best suggestion.

Monitor with the pharmacy drug inventory of stock and emergency medications. Minimizing this inventory so that out-of-date drugs do not occur can save costs. Negotiate with the pharmacy to assume responsibility for checking the expiration date of drugs, providing delivery, and recording refrigerator temperatures. This saves nursing time.

Collaborate with ancillary departments in order to maintain all appropriate supplies within the designated areas. The matching concept requires that the unit receiving the revenue is also allocated the expense. An example would be if any equipment used for laboratory tests such as culture tubes and hemoccult slides needs to be expensed to the laboratory if they receive the revenue.

Charge all necessary patient items and credit the patient for those items unused. Many items can be reused after repackaging and resterilization.

Perform periodic bedside and environmental assessments. The bedside assessment includes checking all stock items needed such as IV supplies, airways, syringes, needles, swabs, ECG pads, etc. The environmental assessment occurs in each room so that items can be identified early to avoid costly repairs (Table 14.4).

Monitor items for pilferage. It is amazing what items can be removed from the hospital premises without anyone noticing. Microwave ovens, computers, printers, typewriters, refrigerators, chairs, lamps, and other items can walk out the door. Some hospitals bolt down such equipment. Others have security checks. All managers and employees need to question any suspect behavior.

Controlling Services

Investigate the benefit of using in-house services of biomedical or maintenance departments instead of incurring costly service contracts. Service contracts need to be evaluated with the warranty parameters and the cost included in the budget.

Examine nurse:patient ratios on all three shifts each day. Periodically assess, explain, and redefine the criteria of 1:1, 1:2, 1:3, and the need for 2:1. Investigate the impact of 1:3 ratio on stable patients awaiting transfer. Consider the acuity system in staffing needs. Some acuity systems tie the level of care giver to the task being done. Develop contingency plans before they occur. For example, a hospital in your community has closed and it was announced 3 months ago. They had been doing cardiology cases that will now come to your hospital. Planning for staff coverage and bed space can be anticipated in this situation.

Investigate the cost-benefit of performing some procedures in the patient room vs. a surgical suite. This takes coordination and input from the clinical staff and physicians. For example, tracheostomies, intra-aortic balloon pump insertion, and pulmonary artery catheter insertion, may possibly be done in the unit room, saving transport and/or time. It may be in the best interest of the patient not to be moved. Can infection be controlled? Are staff knowledgeable and skilled? How long will it take to train staff? Will this be additional revenue or an over expense? Answering these questions helps control costs and provide quality service.

Evaluate nursing practice and nursing research. Look at every procedure performed in the unit. Question the appropriateness, need, and national norms. Question how to do things better or differently. Seek input from the users of the system. Ask an administrator to spend some time in the unit to see if there are areas to be controlled.

Many critical care units are frequently at or near full capacity. Emergency rooms find that they hold patients for extended periods of time until a bed is available in the critical care unit. Some units are so short of qualified nursing staff that unlimited admissions would potentially compromise patient care. When these situations occur, many hospitals go on divert status, that is, critically ill patients are diverted to another hospital due to insufficient beds or not enough staff to care for additional admissions. Divert is a short-term solution that has long-term effects.

The advantage of divert is that it limits admissions to the critical care unit from the emergency medical system. Patients needing care may still enter the hospital via private auto and then be transported to another hospital if condition warrants.

The disadvantage of divert is twofold. First, there is a negative public relations effect on the community and physicians. Physicians and the community may choose to go to another institution if they are frequently turned away. Secondly, there is a significant financial impact to the physician and the hospital when divert occurs. Not only is there revenue lost on potential admissions, spin off revenue to the ancillary departments is lost. An indirect loss is possible when the physician chooses to take any elective cases to another hospital because of the negative experience with divert. Both the hospital and physicians may experience frustration when divert occurs.

The manager of the critical care unit must seek to avoid divert status. Several steps can be taken. Stringent, adhered to criteria for admission to and discharge from the unit need to be developed, distributed, and reviewed annually. AACN has admission and dismissal criteria established in a booklet (16). Physician directors or a liaison works closely

Table 14.4. Environmental Assessment

Date: _____
Department: _____
Unit: _____

Patient Rooms

Room #	Chairs	Elect Equip	Bed	TVs	Over-Bed Table	Bed-Side Table	Mini Blinds	Shelve Closet	Trash Cont.	Vents	Lt. Fixt	Walls	Wind.	Ceiling Tiles	Drape	Floor	Door	Nurs Unit	Tub, Sink, Commode

C-Cleaning   R-Repair   RP-Replacement   *SC-Safety Check with nursing management to monitor all admissions and discharges and takes steps to intervene when there is inappropriate use of the unit. Physician committees need to be frequently apprised of the criteria in order to prevent inappropriate use of the unit. Discharge planning should be a part of assessment. A close relationship is needed between the staff, the physician, and case manager or discharge planner. Designate an alternative location for chronic long-term patients who may be ventilator dependent, rather than use the acute care bed. The charge nurses should triage less critically ill patients who could be transferred to another unit if a bed is needed. This should be done each shift. Educate the staff to keep them informed of the patient and unit needs and their role in assessing the need for divert and using opportunities to avoid it. Consider alternatives of using the post anesthesia recovery area for patients or the need to cancel elective surgeries.

Some hospitals experience a low census and cannot keep critical care beds full. This may occur at certain times of the year, during vacations or meetings or due to competition. When this situation occurs, beds may need to be closed and staff redirected or downsized. During bed closings, the rooms may be repainted, cleaned, or decorated. The manager must determine the cost and benefit of keeping an ICU open when low census continues. In evaluation, the manager needs to consider many options:

1. Compare the revenue and the expenses. Evaluate the managed care reimbursement. What is the break-even point?
2. Evaluate the maintenance of clinical staff skills and competencies. Working with a pulmonary artery catheter once or twice a year makes it difficult to maintain skills. Consider rotation to other areas such as PACU or the emergency area.
3. Identify other needs that may not be met. For example, the CCU has a low census because the hospital does not have a cardiac program. Could the space be used for another service such as pediatrics, obstetrics, ventilator dependent patients, or skilled nursing home care?
4. In downsizing the staff, consider flexibility, hours, competencies, longevity, and wishes of the staff. Cutting back hours and layoffs can be very difficult. Can the staff work elsewhere in the system?

Comparisons

Part of managing unit cost involves comparisons. A comparison notes the similarities and differences from what was planned. This analysis and interpretation guides the manager in gaining insights to keeping costs in control. Many automated budget systems provide a comparative column. Most frequently, the actual costs are compared to last month or this year to last year. Some systems compare the actual amounts to what was budgeted and then offer a flexible budget column. The flexible column adjusts for volume and price differences. Merely comparing one column to another is inadequate and not helpful in cost control. Comparisons must be valid and identify the reasons for the variances. Factors that can be controlled must be identified and action must occur. The clinical manager cannot afford to rationalize poor results, pass the buck, or ignore issues.

The clinical manager may be expected to explain any variance of $\pm 5\%$. An example of a report of variance is shown in Table 14.5.

The unit manager seeing the comparisons needs to think about the problems that created the variance. Looking at all the alternatives and suggestions supports creative problem solving and results in cost control. Roehm and Labarthe identify the importance of looking at different methods and alternatives that may reduce costs. They present the following ideas: choose a new method, assign a dollar value to the new alternative, determine if there results a cost savings or a benefit, list the important trade-offs, and consider the feasibility of the alternative (17).

In controlling costs as a result of comparative analysis, clear objectives for action need to be communicated to those closest to the resource consumption. It takes a team effort.

Decision Making

It was stated earlier that the control process generates information so the decision-making process can be completed. Fleming states that decision making is concerned with the best, most rational choice among alternatives (18). In the decision-making process, management accounting constructs of cost accounting, differential accounting, and responsibility accounting are important for managers to understand.

Financial accounting tools and concepts are dis-

Table 14.5. Variance Report, CCU—January 1991

	Actual	Budget	Variance	Explain	Action
Revenue	$455,000	$396,000	14.8%	Patient days +74	None
Salaries	$116,100	$108,000	7.5%	Overtime × 12	Flex Staff
Supplies	$53,950	$51,700	4.3%		None
Other	$22,450	$34,000	33.0%	New monitors not purchased Depreciation not realized	

cussed in Chapter 2. Management accounting uses information as a means to an end. The end being planning, implementing, and controlling. Management accounting consists of three constructs. These are full cost accounting, differential accounting, and responsibility accounting (19). These three constructs are used in the controlling process.

Cost accounting is a major subfield of accounting. Full cost accounting measures the resources used in performing an activity. This includes all direct and indirect costs. Cost accounting collects information for reporting any costs that are incurred, and this data helps in making decisions regarding product or service strategy (20). Within the cost accounting process there are various cost systems which identify the costs of production, the costs of a particular job, and the estimate of the cost per unit of each service or product, which is sometimes referred to as the standard cost. The reason for this process is to determine a figure that fairly accurately reflects the cost of each unit that is produced. Some hospitals purchase a cost accounting system to help analyze the costs of production. Others have developed an internal system. Within nursing, cost accounting relates to patient care values often called relative value units or patient care units. All of the costs of production, the costs of the job, and the standard costs are calculated to determine a value. This can be very helpful information when nursing is asked to cost out its service so that a price quote can be given to a third-party payor.

Differential accounting looks at how expenses, revenues, and the utilization of assets would be different under one course of action as compared to another. For example, in the unit it is not uncommon to have three ventilator-dependent patients. As the unit has a capacity for 15 patients, these three patients may be keeping the acute care beds occupied. You may consider creating a separate unit for ventilator-dependent patients. You would use differential accounting to help in the decision-making process. You would calculate all the revenues, operating expenses, capital, construction, and other costs of the new unit based on projected occupancy rate. You would evaluate the current unit, the impact of three less ventilator-dependent patients, and the addition of three acute care patients and their turnover rate. What you are doing is going through a decision-making process using differential accounting.

Responsibility accounting traces expenses and revenues to the responsibility center directed by a manager. The budgetary process is an aspect of responsibility accounting and is explained in Chapter 3.

The nurse manager uses these constructs in decision making. Many authors use the label "problem solving" interchangeably with decision making. Both concepts are similar and involve the same approach; however, not all decisions are made based on a perceived problem. For example, decisions about whether to purchase or lease a piece of equipment does not involve a problem, but rather examines the best alternative approach. Using the process facilitates control by the manager.

Anthony and Reece describe the construct of differential accounting as the decision-making process, which can be called the alternative-choice process. They describe five steps:

1. Define the problem.
2. Select alternative solutions.
3. Express each alternative in quantifiable terms.
4. Evaluate the nonquantifiable factors.
5. Reach a decision (19).

These five steps are closely linked with what has been known as the "scientific approach" to problem solving. These are: defining the problem, gathering information, analyzing the information, developing possible solutions, and making decisions. The advantage to the differential accounting approach over the scientific approach is that the former uses a quantitative step which requires management to put into monetary terms the potential effect of the decision choices.

In the alternative choice process, the first step is viewed as the most difficult and most important. This is defining the problem. This requires the manager to identify symptoms and become proactive in continually assessing the potential for a problem or need. A key factor is involving staff in order to help define concerns and problems that need intervention. Staff involvement is crucial in the decision-making process; and through this learning method each staff member gains experience in identifying and solving problems.

One of the first indications of a problem might be a staff or physician's concern regarding equipment, supplies, or the staffing process. Another indicator is when management recognizes a discrepancy between the actual results and the planned results in attaining unit goals. In financial terms, this would be in the form of a variance on the budget reports. As soon as the problem is recognized, then the second step of selecting possible or alternative decisions begins. All choices need to be examined, even if some of them seem remote and questionable.

The third step involves expressing each alternative in quantifiable terms. One needs to look at the advantages and disadvantages of each decision as expressed in either negative or positive monetary terms. What would be the worst possible dollar loss? The best dollar gain? The most likely amounts? This is the approach that objectifies the data.

The fourth step looks at nonquantifiable factors. This is the subjective data. For example, changing a piece of equipment may be financially sound, but if the staff perceive it as inconvenient to use, this subjective data might carry more weight in the long run than the cost savings in the short run.

The final step is reaching a decision and acting on it. If there is not enough information the process may need to be repeated, or new information may have developed that changes the course of the ultimate decision.

Utilizing these five steps of the differential accounting approach of alternative decision making provides the manager with a better control process. An example will illustrate this process.

The issue is a decision to cut or eliminate all utilization of outside agency personnel.

Step 1. Define the problem.
  a. High cost of agency personnel—$150,000/month;
  b. Variance indicates actual cost is 10 times above projections;
  c. Medication incidents up to 25% by outside agency;
  d. Increased patient and physician complaints about agency nurses;
  e. Decreased morale of existing staff due to salary differential.

Step 2. Selecting alternative solutions.
  a. Continue to use at present rate;
  b. Stop all agency use;
  c. Limit agency to high usage areas with plan to phase out;
  d. Implement changes in wage and salary for existing staff.

Step 3. Quantifying alternative solutions.
  a. Continue to use at present rate;
     Advantage: Number of FTEs provided will meet patient needs;
     Disadvantage: Cost in dollars.
  b. Stop agency;
     Advantage: Use of internal staffing costs less;
     Disadvantage: Estimated divert cost due to:
       —Insufficient staff;
       —Cost of closing beds;
       —Cost of cancelling surgeries;
       —Cost of increased recruitment efforts.
  c. Limit agency to high-use areas;
     Advantage: Quantify cost of more beds in use;
     Disadvantage: Cost remains high.
  d. Implement changes in staff salary;
     Advantage: Quantify retention;
     Disadvantage: Quantify costs.

Step 4. Evaluate nonquantifiable factors.
  a. Continue to use at present rate;

Advantage: Less staffing concerns; less unrest regarding meeting patient needs;
Disadvantage: Questionable quality issues; physician and patient dissatisfaction; medication errors.
b. Stop all agency use;
Advantage: Improved control of patient care, own staff;
Disadvantage: Staff unrest; low morale due to short staffing; increased turnover; increased nurse:patient ratios; patient and physician complaints.
c. Limit agency to high-use areas;
Advantage: Less staff unrest;
Disadvantage: Staff resentment.
d. Implement new salary for existing staff;
Advantage: Improve morale; less turnover;
Disadvantage: Nothing may change.

Step 5. Reach a decision and act on it. During this phase, each alternative is examined in monetary and nonmonetary terms. This is an example of where the quantifiable factors weigh as much as the nonquantifiable factors. There is a cost with any of the choices. The manager decides which is the best choice after weighing what is in the best interest of the patient, the staff, and the organization.

The above process can be utilized for any decision ranging from purchasing or leasing equipment to developing a new graduate internship program.

After a decision is made at the management level, the next step is seeking administrative approval and support. A well prepared manager separates fact from fiction, supports all data, and presents proposals in a clear and concise manner using audio-visual support where appropriate.

CONCLUSION

The controlling process focuses on an evaluation of actual operational performance resulting from the planning process. The elements of control include an analysis of the performance of operating, revenue, and capital budgets. The components in the controlling process include participation, standards, expectations, comparisons, and decision making. Controlling requires commitment and action. The use of differential accounting can provide a mechanism for the manager in choosing among alternatives.

REFERENCES

1. Deloitte and Touche. U.S. hospitals and the future of health care. Boston: Deloitte & Touche, June, 1990.
2. American Association of Critical-Care Nurses. Role expectation of the critical care manager. 1986.
3. Covaleski MA & Dirsmith MW. Building tents for nursing services through budgeting negotiation skills. Nursing Administration Quarterly 1984;2:1–11.
4. Kusserow RP. Nurse participation in hospital decision making: potential impact on the nursing shortage. Nursing Economics 1988;6:312–316.
5. Holle L, Armocida PF. A practical approach to cost containment. Nursing Management 1988;10:82–86.
6. Marriner-Tomey A. Case studies in management practice, theory and research. St. Louis: C.V. Mosby, 1990.
7. Martin K. Controlling the budgetary plan. Nursing Management 1989;10:64.
8. Crosby PB. Running things: the art of making things happen. New York: New American Library, 1986:196.
9. Mark BA, Smith HL. Essentials of finance in nursing. Rockville, MD: Aspen Publishers, Inc., 1987:1–17.
10. Mailbot C, Binger J, Slezah L. Managing operating room budget variances. Journal of Nursing Administration 1990;5:19–26.
11. American Association of Critical-Care Nurses. Use of technical personnel in critical care settings. Newport Beach, CA: AACN, 1983.
12. American Association of Critical-Care Nurses. Itegration of new graduates into critical care. Newport Beach, CA: AACN, 1988.
13. American Association of Critical-Care Nurses: Demonstration project information. Newport Beach, CA: AACN, 1988:1–19.
14. Ahrens T, Padwojski A. Economic impact of advanced clinicians. Nursing Management 1988;6:64A–64F.
15. Brigham EF. Financial management theory and practice. Chicago: The Dryden Press, 1985:779–783.
16. American Association of Critical-Care Nurses. Guidelines for admission/discharge criteria in critical care. Newport Beach, CA: AACN, 1987.
17. Roehm HA, Labarthe S. Six steps to managing unit costs. Nursing Management 1987;2:58–62.
18. Fleming M. Managerial accounting and control techniques for non-accountants. New York: Van Nostrand Reinhold Co, 1984.
19. Anthony R, Reece J. Accounting text and cases. Homewood, IL: Irwin Inc., 1989.

Chapter 15

Reimbursement Analysis

PATRICIA MCGILL

With the increased emphasis on cost containment in health care, how providers are paid for the services they deliver has become an ongoing and hotly debated issue. Prior to 1983, hospitals and physicians were reimbursed by third-party payors for the actual cost of the services provided. When the prospective payment system (PPS) was implemented in 1983, payment for service for Medicare patients took a radical, and still controversial, step toward cost containment. This system pays a predetermined fee according to a diagnosis related group (DRG) that was intended to be payment in full for the service. Health care providers have seen a move toward increased cost containment by private payors as a result of the changes in the Medicare system. Private payors have relied on strategies that restrict or limit the type of insurance plan available, contracting with selected providers, or restricting services to certain hospitals or settings. Co-payments and deductibles in insurance coverage force consumers to be selective in utilizing health care services and to make discriminate choices. Unfortunately, this has led to a decrease in utilization of services for a less acute illness and an exacerbation of chronic health needs that are more costly to treat. There are concerns that this limitation by insurers is a form of rationing of health care services based on ability to pay and may lead to a two class system of health care based on the consumers' ability to pay. Ninety-five percent of insured patients no longer are covered by "traditional" health insurance. Health maintenance organizations (HMOs), preferred provider organizations (PPOs), and managed care have all been established to offer alternatives to the high cost of health care. As more payors have sought to contain costs and model their payment after prospective payment systems, the health care industry has been forced to look at how care is delivered in all settings. Nurses in critical care have felt the impact of prospective payment in their practice. Nursing administrators have been faced with the need to provide care to a high acuity patient while at the same time decreasing cost to match the amount of reimbursement provided for the service under the DRG system. Nursing managers and staff have had to adjust their practice to be more cost efficient while still providing quality care. This chapter will discuss how nurse managers can analyze the impact of reimbursement methods on their practice and adjust to the changes primarily on reimbursement under the DRG system, but with the recognition that these methods may be applied to any third-party payment mechanism.

DIAGNOSIS RELATED GROUPS

Diagnosis related groups were implemented in 1983 by the federal government in an effort to control increased Medicare spending. Patient diagnostic characteristics were developed according to a patient's principal diagnosis or surgical procedure and were related to the resources (nursing hours, laboratory and diagnostic tests, medication, etc.) consumed, with the assumption that resources varied with length of stay and type of hospital, urban or rural. The system predetermined the amount paid under Medicare for 467 diagnosis related groups with the rate for a patient's hospital stay fixed and set in advance. If costs are less than the rate, the hospital makes money on the rate reimbursed; however, if costs are more, then the hospital absorbs the loss. The incentive is to decrease cost by being more efficient and using less resources to provide patient care.

Congress approved prospective payment for Medicare patients because it perceived hospitals were inefficient and could provide services more cheaply, but there was no incentive to do so as long as they were being paid their actual costs for service. Health care spending has continued to increase through the years. Annual health care expenditures have risen from $249 billion in 1980 to $540 billion in 1988 with the greatest share of health dollars going to hospitals (1). In fiscal year 1990, hospitals received an estimated $47.3 billion in prospective payment system payments (2). Because Medicare is the largest single payor for health care, it has a major influence on the health care system. Total Medicare expenditures increased 11.4% in 1989 to $99.9 billion, the largest annual increase since 1983 (1). The Medicare program is the fastest growing government program with a growth rate larger than that of the defense budget.

Changes in Health Care under Prospective Payment

Health care is consuming increasing portions of the gross national product (GNP), and economists predict that it will reach 13% in 1995. Health care spending in the U.S. is now at 11% of the GNP, 39% of this for hospital care with intensive care unit (ICU) costs estimated to total almost 1% of the GNP (3). Intensive care units have steadily increased in the past 2 decades. In 1987 there were approximately 85,000 ICU beds in the U.S. according to American Hospital Association (AHA) statistics. This increase has generally been linked to the increased acuity of hospitalized patients. Increasing use of intensive care has been cited as a major factor in escalating hospital costs, with one study showing the ICU costs are 3.8 times greater than conventional hospital treatments (4). Intensive care unit costs have nearly doubled those of other hospital departments since 1983. The major factors are increased intensity of services and introduction of technological advances according to analysis of American Hospital Association data by the Prospective Payment Assessment Commission (ProPac) (5).

Reimbursement methods prior to the prospective payment system have contributed to the growth of intensive care services. Reimbursement for actual costs gave incentives to perform and provide as many procedures and services as possible. The availability of new technology as well as the increasing concern over malpractice issues has led to overuse of expensive diagnostic procedures. According to a 1984 office of technology assessment report, medical technology costs accounted for nearly one-third of the 107% increase in Medicare spending.

The pattern of health care in hospitals has changed since the introduction of the prospective payment system. During the early 1980s Congress made major cuts in the Medicare program. As health care expenses continued to increase, national health policy shifted from one of guaranteed access to health care to one of cost containment. This shift in policy encouraged for-profit enterprise and competition among health care providers to force the elimination of excess and duplication of goods and services. The "full service" hospital of yesterday is now defining its product-lines and eliminating those services that are not financially sound. Competition has in fact occurred, but hospitals are competing for the "private" and more profitable health care dollars, instead of those who are self-pay. Those patients who are uninsured, or have Medicare or Medicaid, are being seen in greater numbers in teaching and public hospitals. These sicker and more financially at risk patients are placing a disproportionate burden on hospitals. Admissions for Medicare patients declined from 1983 through 1986 due to a shift to outpatient surgical procedures. Inpatient occupancy rates have decreased from 74.9% in 1980 to 64.9% in 1989 and the number of beds has decreased by 40,381 in those years (6). The average length of stay (ALOS) dropped from 9.7 days in 1983 to 8.6 days in 1984 for elderly patients and has continued to decrease steadily (7). It is generally believed that DRGs fail to predict actual hospital costs because the patient's severity of illness is not considered. A 1986 study showed that 94% of the ICU sample were cost outliers and the ALOS for the general hospital population was 8 days compared to 22 days for patients in ICU (8).

Financial Impact of DRGs on Hospitals

The impact on practice caused by poor financial status of a hospital is often felt first in high technology areas that depend on large capital and operating budgets. An awareness of the financial status of the hospital is an expectation for nurses who practice in critical care. The financial status of a hospital is measured in a number of ways. One primary indicator of a hospital's overall financial status is the total margin. The total margin compares hospital revenues and expenses for all inpatient and outpatient care as well as nonpatient care activities. Interpreting Medicare cost report data on total margins is often difficult because of individual hospital accounting practices. According to American Hospital Association data, the total margin of 7.6% in the first year of prospective payment fell to 3.8% in the fifth year, a decrease of 50% (9). However, the decline in the prospective payment system margin over the same period was 82%. The PPS operating margin compares PPS payments to Medicare-allowable inpatient operating costs and provides a measure of how well hospitals are reimbursed for the costs that prospective payment is intended to cover (10). Medicare payments to hospitals have been unevenly distributed because of different characteristics of individual hospitals. Teaching hospitals have historically received larger than average payments under PPS due to higher costs per case and more discharges. Additionally, payments to hospitals have not been evenly distributed among hospital groups. Refinements to the system over the years have resulted in changes in the payment rate to rural vs. urban area hospitals, those that indirectly support teaching programs, hospitals that treat disproportionate shares of low-income patients, and those that incur financial loss due to cases with exceptionally long stays or high costs (outliers). Examples of payment policy changes include reductions in the indirect teaching adjustment; the addition of a disproportionate share adjustment; and separate update factors for rural hospitals, hospitals in large urban areas, and sole community hospitals.

The financial stability of a hospital is an issue that is very important for nurses who work in critical care. Much of the technology and equipment essential to critical care units is dependent on a hospital's ability to replace and update that technology to remain competitive. To replace and update very expensive technology, a hospital must have the capital available on a yearly basis. Additionally, there is growing evidence that shows financial instability in hospitals. The use of staff in selected areas has contributed to increased work load and shortages in the health professions. Hospital employment levels declined as admissions and ALOS decreased until 1986 when employment levels began to rise. Staffing levels increased from 3.7 FTEs per average daily census (ADC) in 1984 to 4.28 FTEs per ADC in 1988 (11). Hospitals have seen an increase in the number of nurses employed to care for high acuity patients, but a decrease in the number of ancillary support staff, which has led to a shifting of the work load to nurses.

Measuring Nursing Costs under Prospective Payment

The 1988 Secretary's Commission on Nursing final report recommended the need for an understanding of the cost of providing care to patients and the ability of nurses to utilize this information to manage care and make policy decisions (12). The ability to integrate cost considerations into care for patients will be an expectation of every nurse who delivers care in today's health care system.

Nursing care in many hospitals is incorporated in the daily room and board or per diem charge to patients. This method of billing for nursing care has led to a perception that nursing care does not generate revenue. Greater difficulty in demonstrating the cost effectiveness of nursing care occurs when nursing is included in the room rate. According to American Hospital Association data, 90% of patient care (the hospital's product) is delivered by nurses, and yet current research data demonstrate that total nursing costs average less than 30% of a hospital's operating budget (13). Any department which produces 90% of the product while consuming less than 30% of the budget is a profit center, not a cost center. Because nursing labor constitutes the single largest component of any hospital budget, it is often a logical target for increased scrutiny and budget cutting. The need to precisely determine nursing cost and demonstrate the ability to generate a profit is becoming essential to prevent cost cutting measures that will affect the quality of the product delivered. The nursing manager must demonstrate what costs are occurring within the unit and then be able to develop strategies that will bring the costs back into line with budget or to decrease costs in areas that will have less impact on patient outcomes. The manager determines how the cost matches the revenue generated for a specific type of patient (Table 15.1).

Patient Classification System (PCS) to Determine Nursing Cost

To develop a mechanism to determine the cost of nursing care requires a system to classify pa-

Table 15.1. Cost per Unit of Service

Unit	Budget	Actual	Variance	Percent
Adult patient days	541	524	−17	−3.1
Patient revenue/unit	$916.40	$923.26	−6.96	−0.8
Salaries per unit	$340.73	$354.65	−13.93	−4.1
Consumables per unit	$ 28.76	$ 24.40	4.06	14.3
Other supplies per unit	$ 3.84	$ 3.00	0.84	21.7
Total expense per unit	$373.03	$382.06	−9.03	−2.4
Gross margin per unit	$543.27	$541.19	2.07	0.4

tients and define and predict the resources needed to care for specific types of patients. Secondly, a mechanism for adjusting staffing requirements either up or down to meet fluctuating patient needs must be developed. The nursing manager must have the ability to integrate patient data obtained from the nursing system with existing financial information within the hospital's billing or accounting system.

Identification of the cost of nursing care became more of a possibility in the early 1960s when patient classification systems were developed that would project the average number of nursing hours for the delivery of patient care. As these systems evolved it was recognized that patients varied in their care requirements, and the systems were refined to measure the acuity of patients and how that affected nursing work load. With implementation of prospective payment, classification systems were further refined to link patient classification with the cost of nursing care. The use of patient classification systems became a mechanism to measure nursing resources and convert a patient's nursing care needs into a work load index to which a dollar figure could be attached. However, the varied requirements for care of individual patients have pointed out the difficulty in trying to measure severity of illness and the corresponding utilization of resources. Attempts to come up with a more equitable mechanism for measuring nursing resources have increased. Perhaps the best known measurement is the relative intensity measures (RIMS) developed in New Jersey. This system defined nursing resources in terms of minutes of nursing care received and assigned relative values to the time in determining cost. The relative values reflect intensity of illness for each patient and is correlated to nursing care delivered. The RIMS method has been criticized for its methodology, but it did represent the first attempt to separate nursing cost from room and board charges. Multiple studies have continued to search for the classification tool that would address severity of illness for the critical care patient population. Whatever the system used to measure case mix and severity of illness, it is important to remember that nursing judgment is very difficult to define and even harder to measure in terms of resource utilization.

With implementation of the prospective payment system, the cost of nursing care became an additional incentive for developing patient classification systems that accurately predict staffing requirements. Studies conducted at Strong Memorial Hospital in Rochester, New York in 1984, showed variability in nursing care of patients within the same DRG. The extent of variability in nursing care of patients within the same DRG was also demonstrated in a 1985 American Nurses Association (ANA) study that showed variance in nursing utilization patterns and cost related to the DRGs studied (14). The study was designed to be reproducible in order to facilitate replication studies. Although the study was small, it did provide data showing nursing cost and utilization of resources within defined DRGs that would contribute to development of a national data base for nursing care.

Efforts to develop costing models for nursing care have been limited by the difficulty in replicating studies that have been cited in the literature and the unavailability of costing data bases. The studies in the current literature are developed for the individual hospital setting. Data was collected and implemented to the institution's specific system, often making replication difficult. These studies have contributed to the recognition of the need for development of a broad data base for accurately costing nursing care that can compare data across institutions. In 1986, the Medicus Systems Corporation of Evanston, Illinois began a 6-month data collection program called "The National DRG Nurse Costing Study" to create a national data base to link nursing cost with the DRG system. Data was collected from Medicus client hospitals in different regions of the country. The hospitals were a variety of private, not-for-profit, teaching, and multi-health care system facilities. Over 24,000 patient records were studied for 40 of the most frequently treated DRGs to determine the cost per case of delivering nursing care. The study reported that cardiovascular DRGs require the highest percent of registered nurse (RN) cost and that nursing costs represented only 17.8% of Medicare reimbursement (15). A 1987 invitational conference on "Costing of Hospital Nursing Services" sponsored by the U.S. Department of Health and Human Services' (DHHS) Division of Nursing, recommended establishing guidelines to identify nursing resources utilized by individual patients so that institutions could develop systems according to a uniform standard (16).

Despite the initial opposition by nurses to patient classification systems, their use represents one of the first times that nursing has been able to document objectively the kind of nursing care required for specific types of patients and the amount of resources necessary to provide that care. This development of objective information has continued to yield data that can be used to demonstrate cost of care.

There are many patient classification systems available today that determine the number of nursing care hours necessary to care for a patient during a 24-hour period. A very simple method of determining nursing care costs can be made by determining the nursing care hours needed for each patient under a specific DRG and calculating the cost based on nursing personnel wages, benefits, and indirect costs. It is important to determine both direct and indirect nursing costs of patient care.

STRATEGIES TO ADDRESS THE COST OF CRITICAL CARE

Cost vs. Reimbursement for Care

One strategy that has been used to break down nursing costs has been to look at specific DRGs under an identified service line and determine what costs are attached to the specific DRG. This mechanism has been utilized with hospitals that have financial information systems where actual patient data can be studied from a retrospective review. For example, clinical nurse managers at Charleston Area Medical Center in Charleston, West Virginia pulled data for the previous 3 years to identify which DRGs were most common in their individual units. Using the hospital financial information network, each DRG was then analyzed for total cost, direct cost, total charges, and net revenue (Table 15.2). Managers were then able to identify those types of patients where a profit was not generated and change the delivery of care to bring the expenses more in line with the reimbursement. For example, in many coronary care units (CCUs), the protocol calls for routine laboratory and diagnostic testing at specified intervals. If the patient has a negative set of isoenzymes, then the protocol should be revised with subsequent tests being cancelled. Often the protocol continues, with unnecessary procedures being performed because of the habit of ordering diagnostic tests by a protocol. These additional tests are adding costs to the care of the patient.

Development of the service line model requires that the "service" be identifiable with a specific DRG. For example, a cardiac service might be divided into an invasive product line and a noninvasive product line. Medical cardiac and surgical cardiac DRGs are separated into two different services.

Identification of the service line would include determining the volume of patients within each DRG, the length of stay (LOS), and the resources needed to care for that patient. Development of a service line requires the input of all providers of care within the system. The ability to get the patient into the system and placed in the most appropriate care setting is just as important as the physician ordering the correct number and sequence of diagnostic tests. A patient with an acute myocardial infarction who is admitted to the emergency department of a hospital where there is no available critical care bed will use more resources

Table 15.2. Cost Analysis by DRG (Average Dollars/Case), Noninvasive Cardiac Services

DRG	Description	Total Cost	Direct Cost	Total Charge	Net Revenue
121	Complicated MI	7520	4741	11765	7387
122	Uncomplicated MI	5249	3352	7750	5139
123	Acute MI—died	5314	3611	9216	5660
127	Heart failure shock	4161	2554	7152	4754
140	Angina	2414	1482	3821	2790
143	Chest Pain	1913	1198	3248	2283

and have a longer LOS. An effective service line management would identify a system to triage and appropriately place patients who are admitted to the system.

Nursing Case Management

Professional nursing case management is a strategy being developed that addresses allocation of resources, effectiveness of care, and cost containment. It has been utilized in a variety of settings from community models to acute care in hospitals. Hospital-based nursing case management was first implemented at the New England Medical Center as an extension of primary nursing. Etheridge described outcomes of reduced LOS, reduced nursing turnover, and increased admissions. For the payor there was a cost savings gained from earlier transfer from high intensity care units to those requiring less intensity and fewer resources (17). Nursing case management utilizes the development of critical paths for treatment protocols and has been shown to reduce length of stay and utilize resources more efficiently, because care is coordinated and collaboratively provided. A critical path defines the timing of key events within an average patient's hospitalization and indicates what outcomes can be expected on each day. For example, a patient with a surgical procedure might have a critical path that determines extubation at 3 hours post operatively, invasive lines removed at 48 hours, and chest tubes removed at 3 days. Any deviation from this normal path would be addressed collaboratively by the health care providers in order to get the patient back on the established path. By quickly addressing deviations from the norm, patients' needs are addressed before they result in complications that affect LOS or the need for additional resources. The critical path provides a guideline for nurses to determine how much nursing resource to allocate to achieve the determined outcome. This approach enables managers to study the course of an individual's care throughout hospitalization. By analyzing the services provided and the resources utilized, managers can determine if the course of the patient's hospitalization could have been affected by using a different set or number of resources. The patient's hospitalization is looked at in its entirety, and a determination is made whether the cost is reasonable and if the outcome was what was expected for the treatment given.

Nursing case management has been utilized at several hospitals with striking results in costs and outcome. Carondelet St. Mary's Hospital in Tucson published data in 1989 that had been accumulated over 3 years that showed case management influenced financial data (18). The most dramatic results were demonstrated for patients within respiratory DRGs. Respiratory patients constituted 10% of all patients at Carondelet and the largest subgroup were those with chronic obstructive pulmonary disease. Two years before the study, DRG 88 constituted the greatest financial loss to the hospital of all Medicare patients. At the time of the report, DRG 88 was the highest revenue generator of all DRG categories. Instituting nursing case management resulted in decreasing the patient length of stay by 8.1 days, and a savings of $1,552 per case.

The ability to demonstrate cost saving by a nursing management strategy is a powerful incentive for hospitals to allocate adequate nursing positions and resources to ensure that cost effective care can be provided. Nursing managers who can show the ability to produce high quality patient outcomes, while still maintaining costs, will certainly be in a better position to negotiate for scarce resources at budget time.

In light of the continued emphasis on cost containment in health care, nurses will be required to develop an awareness of the financial outcome of their interventions as well as the clinical outcomes.

Alternative Care Givers

Just as hospitals are beginning to analyze which physicians provide the most cost effective care, in the future they will also begin to analyze which employees provide the most cost effective nursing care. We must begin to evaluate our patient care delivery systems and interventions for effectiveness in order to meet the changes that will be required in hospitals. This means that nurses in critical care must objectively look at the kinds of things they do and who does the task in the intensive care setting. The move toward all-RN staffs, that began with the increased acuity of hospitalized patients, may have contributed to the shortage of nurses. Critical care units have traditionally had a higher ratio of RN staff and have resisted the use of ancillary personnel due to the high degree of skill required to manage ICU patients. As a result, ICUs may be inefficiently using the staff in their unit, and the nurse may do every task in the ICU, whether it requires RN skill or not. Many critical care nurses resist giving up the routine tasks of patient care because of the opportunity to assess patients while bathing, weighing, and changing linen. Nurses in critical care units spend a great deal of time "nursing" the environment; they call lab reports, enforce visiting hours, order supplies, maintain equipment, in addition to the patient care they provide. Nurses must begin to evaluate what is needed in the care of critically ill patients and delegate those functions that do not require nursing time. Use of ancillary staff and support departments must be a priority in restructuring. When support personnel are cut from a budget, it is not cost effective to substitute a nurse and the time lost from care delivery to replace a dietary worker, pharmacy aide, or other technician. Nursing departments are affected when support personnel are cut from hospital budgets, and they must stop taking on additional functions. Nurse managers must begin to negotiate with support departments to do the tasks that take nurses away from the bedside. They must be able to demonstrate that it is more costly to use RN time and how that affects quality of care when these functions are shifted and assumed by nursing departments. Critical care nurses must develop the ability to delegate and use nurse extenders to ease the critical nursing shortage. The American Association of Critical-Care Nurses (AACN) and the Society of Critical Care Medicine (SCCM) formed a working group (in 1982) known as the Interorganization Liaison Group (ILG) that developed a consensus statement that became known as the collaborative practice model. The ILG continued to meet to develop strategies for addressing the shortage of critical care nurses. They concluded that use of nurse extenders was one solution to the shortage and developed a framework for using nurse extenders in the intensive care unit. The position statement on "Use of Nursing Support Personnel in Critical Care Units" was approved by both organizations and is available to assist with the development of ancillary positions in critical care units. The definition of nurse extender in a special care unit is "an individual who is not a registered nurse, but works under the direct supervision of a registered critical care nurse to implement specific delegated aspects of nursing care" (19).

As the acuity of hospitalized patients continues to rise, the amount of time required to care for patients will increase. This increased need for care givers may not be met with the current shortage of nurses unless alternate providers are used. To meet the demand for critical care staff, managers must continue to search for all available options. The recent American Medical Association (AMA) proposal for a registered care technician (RCT) points out that someone will suggest a solution if nursing does not do it. It will be increasingly important to look at how effectively staff are utilized in care delivery systems to obtain the best outcome in the most cost effective manner.

Appropriate Use of Critical Care Beds

As health care moves toward an all-payor DRG system, appropriate utilization of critical care resources will become increasingly important. A 1989 study reported the finding that patients in an ICU would have generated over $30 million in losses to the hospital under an all-payor prospective payment scheme. The losses resulted from a variety of factors, including severity of illness and hospital resource utilization. Additionally, they concluded that the current DRG hospital payment system appears to be inequitable for the patient who receives ICU treatment (20). The ability to demonstrate a cost-benefit ratio in treating the critically ill will emerge as a significant challenge to managers and clinicians. The increasing use of critical care will continue despite the cost of that care. The high use of critical care beds which increase hospital costs have been noted to result from a number of factors, including use of ICU beds by noncritically ill patients when other beds are available. ICU care is often requested for at-risk patients, because of the high concentration of nursing services in these units. Additionally, once a patient is admitted to the ICU, many physicians believe a commitment is made to continue aggressive treatment and are reluctant to move the patient out of the unit. When ICU beds are utilized ineffectively, the cost of care becomes higher than necessary. These costs are increasing the pressure to restrict and analyze admissions, discharges, and transfers to intensive care units. It is acknowledged that the best way to improve utilization is to reduce the admission rate by identifying those patients who will not benefit from intensive care. Generally these patients are not critically ill, or are terminally ill and their outcome and survival is not likely to be affected by intensive care. Evaluation of admission and discharge criteria for a critical care unit will ensure that beds are utilized most effectively. Development of these guidelines must be an interdisciplinary exercise, so that all providers who use the service will be in agreement about the purpose and desired outcomes. In order to realize cost effectiveness, all users agree that utilization of intensive care must be monitored for effectiveness, appropriateness of length of stay, and need for the technology and staffing provided in the ICU. Jointly developed policies regarding reduction of interventions, such as blood analysis, x-ray, routine monitoring, and more definitive policies for transferring "no code" patients, will result in savings of intensive care costs. Limiting the amount of ICU resources inevitably leads to concerns about rationing of health care and raises moral and ethical questions. In today's economic environment, values deemed important for cost effectiveness must be balanced with the values necessary for delivering care that does not generate ethical problems for nurses. The critical care manager must be able to document the cost of caring for a patient in intensive care and demonstrate appropriateness of staffing decisions as well as the utilization of beds. The ability to control costs, decrease LOS, and efficient utilization will increase the chance of getting a more realistic budget in subsequent negotiations. The manager of a critical care unit cannot manage cost and quality of care alone. Every nurse in a critical care unit must understand how their individual practice affects the patient outcome and the cost to the patient and the unit. Clinical practice must be evaluated in terms of its contribution to high quality outcomes that are cost effective. Staff must be able to evaluate common practices in their unit that are passed down from nurse to nurse without any foundation in clinical efficacy. Many procedures that are in fact habits can result in substantial savings to the patient when objectively looked at for effectiveness. For example, a unit policy that required daily changes of clean, dry incisional dressings with the bath, was revised to changing only when soiled and saved each patient approximately $30/day in dressing charges. The staff were able to document that daily inspection without changing an unsoiled dressing showed no increase in wound infection. This standard unit policy, passed to each nurse upon orientation to the unit, was contributing to increased cost for supplies that did not affect the patient outcome.

MANAGING REIMBURSEMENT IN THE FUTURE

Economics will continue to drive the health care system into the next decade. Management of the critical care environment of the future will involve the ability to utilize resources in a system that is receiving less reimbursement for a more critically ill patient. Economics and reimbursement will continue to impact the practice of nursing by requiring nurses to change how they deliver care within the constraints of the financial system of health care.

The future may see nurses managing caseloads of technology-dependent patients that will be cared for in the home after being stabilized in the critical care unit. This method of caring for patients is more cost effective and is being driven by the economics of reimbursement and the high cost of providing technology. Critical care units will increasingly be staffed with nurses who may not be direct employees of the hospital, but are under contract to provide "per diem" service. The need to have flexibility in staffing will drive this strategy. Decentralized decision making and involvement of the critical care staff will be essential to changing clinical practice and controlling the cost of providing high tech care. The nurse manager will depend even more on the skill of the critical care staff to manage clinical as well as fiscal outcomes of patient care. The critical care manager must be able to effectively utilize resources in an environment that will continue to compete for the shrinking profitable health care market. The ability to increase reimbursement levels may not be within the power of the nurse manager, but effective utilization of resources within the critical care unit is a strategy that can keep the unit competitive for scarce budget resources within an institution. The critical care manager must not only be able to analyze the impact of reimbursement on the budget of the critical care unit, but also be able to recognize how that reimbursement affects the financial situation of the hospital. The manager of a cardiac unit that generates 30% of the profit for the hospital must be sensitive to the budget requirements and capital investment that is needed to continue that profit margin and must be able to successfully defend the necessary budget outlay to other unit managers. Likewise, the manager of a critical care unit that is consistently losing money, cannot expect an increased budget without some strategic plan to demonstrate the cost-benefit ratio of the unit. The American Association of Critical-Care Nurses' position paper, "Role Expectations for the Critical Care Manager" cites accountability for fiscal management that includes anticipation of the impact of institutional financial status on critical care units, as well as the ability to appropriately utilize resources. In addition to fiscal management accountability, the manager must be able to maintain standards that meet institutional goals, promote collaborative practice, establish patient classification systems, and facilitate staff input into unit decision making. All of these accountabilities are applicable to the strategies we have discussed for addressing the cost of critical care service.

CONCLUSION

The prospective payment system has changed the way we deliver health care in the U.S. by shifting away from inpatient care toward other methods of delivering care. That impact on critical care has resulted in increasing numbers of patients who are more severely ill. Coupled with decreasing levels of reimbursement and shorter lengths of stay, the challenge to provide care within a specified cost and time frame has fallen greatly on critical care nurses. The expectation of delivering high quality care, with cost restrictions, has created a new dilemma for nurses. Care givers have traditionally acted in the best interest of the patient without consideration of the financial picture. Economic factors may now constrain the care giver and may limit the patient's trust in the care giver to act in his or her best interest when deciding what course of action to offer. Scarce resources may in fact cause conflict if quality of care is sacrificed in the interest of financial cost savings. In today's economic environment, values important for cost effectiveness must be balanced with values necessary for the delivery of adequate critical care nursing service.

Nurse managers must be involved in restructuring systems to make them more conducive to collaborative management of patient care. The National Commission on Nursing recognized decentralized administration of nursing services, participatory management, and shared governance models as highly valued elements in the delivery of nursing care. Models that push decision making to the care giver level and empower nurses with problem resolution ability are one of the best ways to demonstrate the costs and benefits of nursing within a hospital.

Nurses must be involved in the development of federal policies that impact the cost of health care, because any change in policy will affect nursing practice within hospitals. The health care agenda of the future will be vastly different from what we have seen in the past, and nurses have a great opportunity to participate in setting this agenda. Critical care nurses are in great demand for meeting the future health needs of our nation and must be prepared to work collaboratively with physicians and other health providers. The stage is set for nurses who can develop new roles and practices that can provide cost effective, high quality health care in an environment where the reimbursement dollar is shrinking and scarce resources are now a reality.

REFERENCES

1. Prospective Payment Assessment Commission. Medicare prospective payment and the American health care system report to the congress. Washington, DC, June 1990:9–10.
2. Unpublished Congressional Budget Office estimate.
3. Division of National Cost Estimates. National health expenditures, 1986–2000. Health Care Financing Review 1987;8(supp):1–23.
4. Wagner DP, Wineland TD, Knaus WA. The hidden cost of treating severely ill patients:charges and resource consumption in an intensive care unit. Health Care Finance Review 1983;5:81–88.
5. Prospective Payment Assessment Commission, p.50.
6. Prospective Payment Assessment Commission, p. 41.
7. Beebe K, Callahan W, Mariano A. Medicare short-stay hospital length of stay, fiscal years 1981–85, Health Care Financing Review 1985;7:119–25; and HCFA, Impact Report 1985; Pub. 03251, 3.6–3.10.
8. Galanes S, Harris G, Dulski R, Chamberlin W. The intensive care unit population within the prospective payment scheme. Heart & Lung 1986:15:5,515–520.
9. Prospective Payment Assessment Commission, pp. 52–53.
10. Prospective Payment Assessment Commission, pp. 30–31.
11. Nemes J. Hospital profit margins continue to stall. Modern Healthcare Nov. 3, 1989;52–53.
12. U.S. Department of Health and Human Services. Secretary's commission on nursing final report, vol 1. Washington, DC: U.S. Department of Health and Human Services, December 1988.
13. Curtin L. Who says "lean" must be "mean?" Nursing Management 1983;17:1,7–8.

14. American Nurses Association. DRGs and nursing care. Kansas City: ANA, 1986.
15. McCormick B. What's the cost of nursing care. Hospitals 1986;11:5,48–52.
16. U.S. Department of Health, Education, and Welfare. Costing hospital nursing services, report of the conference. Publication No. HRP-0907082. Springfield, VA: U.S. Department of Health, Education, and Welfare, August 1987.
17. Etheridge MLS, ed. Collaborative care: nursing case management. Chicago IL: American Hospital Publishing, 1989.
18. Etheridge P, Lamb G. Professional nursing case management improves quality, access and costs. Nursing Management 1989;20:3,30–35.
19. American Association of Critical-Care Nurses. Use of nursing support personnel in critical care units. Newport Beach, CA:AACN, 1989.
20. Munoz E, Josephson J, Tenenbaum N, Goldstein J, Shears A, Wise L. Diagnosis related groups, cost, and outcome for patients in the intensive care unit. Heart & Lung 1989;18(6):627–633.

Chapter 16

Program Planning and Evaluation

ROBERTA M. FRUTH

In the current economic environment of health care, program planning and evaluation can play a significant role in the allocation of resources. Administrators and funding groups often rely on program analysis to plan, budget, and manage programs. In addition, evaluations serve to demonstrate performance and establish accountability of the program managers. As decision makers learn to routinely use the information provided in program evaluations, managers will be expected to provide appropriate and timely analysis. The analysis offers a basis for the design of new program proposals and status review of current programs. Program evaluation is part of the planning and controlling process fundamental to the managerial role.

What is program evaluation? A program is a set of interrelated activities carried out to accomplish a specific set of goals. Several programs are easily recognized as common to many critical care units (CCUs): quality improvement programs, recruitment and retention programs, CCRN certification programs, and advanced cardiac life support (ACLS) programs. To successfully operate these programs, numerous activities, individuals, and resources need to be provided and coordinated. Program goals or desired outcomes for a given program may vary among organizations or even among CCUs within an organization.

For example, at Hospital Y many CCU managers are interested in ACLS programs for their staff nurses. Managers interested in ACLS programs usually use established programs offered outside the organization or establish their own program internally. In considering which is the better option the CCU manager must compare the two options.

Elements to be considered in the comparison include: target audience, qualifications to enter ACLS class, length of class, location of class, frequency of classes offered, schedule of class, tuition for registration, book fees, needed resources to offer class, maintenance of ACLS provider status, and staff coverage during ACLS class.

Nurses recognize the need for and value of evaluation. Our first exposure to evaluation is usually framed in the nursing process. Managers rely on evaluation techniques in planning and controlling activities. Evaluation involves a systematic assessment of the purpose, design, implementation, or utility of a program for the purpose of influencing decision makers. Program evaluations meet several organizational needs (Table 16.1). However, the ultimate goal in program evaluation is to provide useful information concerning the program's merits and operations to those individuals who determine the future of the program. Program evaluation contributes to decision making by examining the use of resources and achievement of goals. Two fundamental questions underlie program evaluation: Does the program work? and Is it worth it?

TYPES OF EVALUATIONS

Generally managers use one of two widely recognized types of program evaluation, formative or summative evaluation (1). Formative evaluation

Table 16.1. Purposes of Program Evaluation

1. Justify program development and implementation.
2. Determine the need for program modification.
3. Determine how to apply the program to other settings.
4. Determine the effectiveness of resource use.
5. Meet routine expectations of the organization.
6. Meet outside agency requirements.
7. Evaluate program manager's performance.

focuses on program elements during the developmental and implementation stages of a program. This type of evaluation aims at improving the program's implementation, delivery, and ongoing use of resources. Sometimes it is referred to as process evaluation or ongoing program monitoring. For example, in an ongoing structured in-service program the clinical manager reviews lecturer evaluations and attendance records, and compares this data according to the individual lecturers and times the in-services were scheduled. Through this formative evaluation the clinical manager may decide to offer more in-services in the early afternoon since attendance is greater at that time. This evaluation was done to examine delivery of the in-services and use of resources.

Summative evaluation, also called outcome or impact evaluation, focuses on the achievement of stated goals and objectives. The findings from a summative evaluation are often used to assess the overall program and determine the program's effectiveness. For example, in a new program developed to recruit staff nurses, a summative evaluation after 6 months would examine staff nurse inquiries in response to radio, newspapers, and journal advertisements and the number of staff nurses hired since the new campaign began, as well as the number of staff nurses hired compared to last year at the same time. The characteristics of the newly hired staff nurses, such as age, marital status, and educational status, could also be compared to institutional staff nurse characteristics to assess if any different sector of the labor market was reached. This evaluation focuses on the results of the program, that is, the number of new recruits. Although the intent of these two evaluations differs, elements in the evaluation process are similar.

Evaluation Process

As a systematic assessment of a program the evaluation process has identifiable steps (Table 16.2).

Define the Program

It is essential to clearly define the program that is being evaluated. Programs are created to address perceived needs or to resolve problems. The program definition should include the purpose, goals, objectives, intended audience, structure, and organization of the program. The purpose can be

Table 16.2. Steps in Program Evaluation

1. Define the program.
2. Define the purpose of the evaluation.
3. State the evaluation questions.
4. Design the evaluation project.
5. Identify data sources.
6. Collect data.
7. Analyze data.
8. Report the findings.

briefly stated in general terms. In a formative evaluation the purpose of an ACLS certification program could state:

> The purpose of the ACLS certification program is to improve emergency effectiveness by assisting the staff nurses of the medical intensive care unit to achieve ACLS provider status.

Goals are broadly stated and include terminal outcomes, but should be specific enough to be measurable. By defining the goals in measurable terms the manager establishes evaluation criteria (2). In the ACLS example, the manager could state what percentage of staff nurses will achieve ACLS certification and within what time frame:

> By the end of the first year of the ACLS program 80% of full-time nurses in the CCU will attain ACLS provider status.

These criteria establish outcome measures that can be readily evaluated. The objectives are narrow and specific and state what will change as a result of the program. Objective statements might include the frequency of ACLS training sessions offered, the number of ACLS instructors within the unit, the frequency of basic cardiac life support (BCLS) sessions, and the projected effect on staff nurse performance during cardiopulmonary resuscitation. These statements provide specific measures for evaluation purposes.

In defining the program the manager should identify the target audience. This information will be needed to accurately calculate the cost of the program, to direct marketing initiatives, to determine if the target audience is reached, and to judge if the program can be expanded to other settings or other groups. In defining the ACLS program, the manager must consider what staff members are targeted participants. Will all full-time registered staff nurses attain ACLS provider status? Will part-time staff nurses be included? Will staff nurses working special programs such as weekend plans or CCU float pools be included? These decisions affect how frequently the program will be needed and contribute to the cost of program implementation.

Decisions such as these influence the formative evaluation during the planning and implementation process. The critical care unit manager's input and knowledge are critical during these initial stages. The clinical and nursing perspectives offered by the nurse manager support realistic program development.

In describing the organization of the program the manager defines resources needed for program implementation. The description of program organization addresses how frequently elements of the program will be performed, what facilities will be needed, and what additional resources will be required. The manager must also define the program structure; that is, who is involved with program management and delivery and what reporting relationships will be established.

Program definition establishes the criteria for program implementation, management, and evaluation. It captures the essence of why, who, what, when, where, and how. This information directs data collection, resource evaluation, and data analysis. Thus program definition becomes an essential managerial task for the CCU manager.

Define the Purpose of the Evaluation

Decision makers use evaluations for planning and controlling functions. As they proceed through the decision-making process these individuals must compare alternative programs, consider resource utilization, and review various options. Factors such as program cost, required capital expenditures, degree of value, or length of time to return on the investment may influence decision makers choices on program initiatives.

The nurse manager must understand the reasons for program evaluation. For example, if the evaluation is requested to identify needed changes, an implicit message conveys ongoing administrative support. However, a manager may question the intent of continued administrative support if asked to justify resource commitment and examine program efficiency. Both requests address the need for an evaluation but the stated purposes of the evaluations send messages that lead to different approaches. These are subtle differences but astute managers learn to read the organizational messages as they move into the evaluation process.

Evaluations also serve unstated purposes. Evaluations can provide a whitewash to enhance a weak or politically favored program. They can also serve to undermine an expensive or unfavored program. Occasionally, evaluations are mechanisms used to postpone needed action or to support political posturing by key decision makers (3). The manager should consider what is the purpose of the evaluation and who will use the evaluation results.

Various individuals or groups may have access to the results of a program evaluation. The manager needs to consider the intended recipient of the evaluation results. In addition the manager should identify who actually makes decisions that impact the program. Program evaluations can be submitted to supervisors, management committees, finance committees, quality improvement committees, auditors, funding groups, outside agencies, staff, or clients. The targeted recipient will be interested in specific elements of a program. A finance committee will focus on the cost of needed resources and consider the benefits gained by the organization. A quality improvement committee may be more interested in the outcome measures of the program without consideration of program cost. Managers should organize program evaluations based upon the purpose of the evaluation. However it is important to remember that organizational documents, reports, and evaluations are often shared among numerous individuals and groups. Although managers target evaluation results for specific recipients they must be aware that the evaluation report may be shared with a broader audience. Program evaluations may serve multiple purposes and reach several audiences.

State the Evaluation Questions

Considering the purposes of evaluation and the potential audiences, the manager needs to identify the questions to be addressed in the evaluation. Questions focus and direct the evaluation process and should relate to the program definition. The questions should be framed in such a way that answers will provide meaningful, relevant information that contributes to decision making. In a formative evaluation the questions are phrased in future or present tense in order to project how the program should be structured and what resources will be needed. How will the ACLS program be accessible to all staff nurses? In a summative evaluation the questions examine how the program met its goals and objectives and are therefore stated in the past tense. Did the target number of staff nurses attain ACLS provider status?

In addition the questions should address two areas: program efficiency and program effectiveness. Efficiency considers the cost of operating a program, that is, resource consumption, in relation to the benefits delivered by the program to the organization. Effectiveness refers to how well a program reaches its goals. Effectiveness alone is rarely sufficient to justify a program; the outcomes obtained must be viewed in relation to efficiency, i.e., cost. Every staff nurse in the CCU may attain ACLS provider status through the established ACLS program. However, administrative decision makers with limited clinical expertise may not recognize any specific benefits realized by the organization and decide the cost of the program does not justify its existence. The CCU manager must be able to evaluate program efficiency as well as program effectiveness. In formative evaluations alternative options should be included in the program proposal. What is the cost of using established external ACLS programs? What will be the cost of operating an ACLS program within the organization? How long will it take for the targeted number of staff nurses to attain ACLS certification through an interval program vs. external programs?

Design the Evaluation Project

Designing the evaluation requires deciding what to measure or observe and how to collect the needed data. Stecher and Davis point out that no single evaluation approach fits the needs of all evaluations (4). The manager must select the approach that provides meaningful information to the evaluation's target recipients. The clinical manager can anticipate that the finance committee, the quality improvement committee, and the staff nurse advisory committee have different priorities and seek different types of evaluation information. In fact, the critical characteristic of any program evaluation is that the best possible information that is available is collected and that this information is relevant and credible to the target recipients (5).

In selecting the evaluation design several factors should be considered. The purpose of the evaluation, and the target audience will direct the extent and detail of the evaluation. The design may vary from a scientific experimental approach to one that examines only outcome measures. Scientific research designs and techniques can be useful, however, such rigorous methods are often unnecessary and budget and time constraints limit the practicality of such methods. Program evaluations are considered administrative functions or are elements of quality improvement strategies. As part of the scope of management, not research, program evaluations are often structured as quasi-experimental designs.

The evaluation design should identify what information is needed, what time frame the evaluation will cover, and what information sources will be used. In considering the design, five general aspects of a program that provide comprehensive evidence of program effects include: context characteristics, participant characteristics, program implementation or process characteristics, program outcomes, and program costs (6). Context characteristics include factors such as class size, location of classes, or sociopolitical considerations. Sociopolitical considerations would include if ACLS certification of staff is required by an external accrediting agency, if it is a community standard, or required by an internal policy. These would be significant factors in justification for the program. Participant characteristics include variables such as age, gender, education, prior or existing certification, employee status, professional goals, or clinical ladder placement. Program characteristics are defined by the activities, materials, staffing, and structure of the program. Anticipated program outcomes should be stated in the goals and objectives. The nurse manager should also expect and identify any unanticipated outcomes as well. An unanticipated outcome of an ACLS program for staff nurses may include less drug wastage during cardiac arrest situations. This could be a significant cost savings for the organization and helps justify continuing the program. Another unanticipated outcome could result if a high failure rate was experienced by the participating nurses. Staff nurse reluctance or resistance in participating in the program could present a significant challenge to the program managers. Program costs are calculated from the resources required to operate the program. The nurse manager should consider such resources as staff time, support personnel time, material, equipment, space, and associated fees, as well as hidden costs such as additional staff coverage needed to release staff to attend a class. The nurse manager should consider these five general program characteristics in the design of the evaluation, however few evaluations actually include all of these characteristics.

Another consideration in the design is the validity and reliability of the data used in the evaluation process. Briefly, data are considered valid when it measures what it is supposed to measure. Reliability refers to the consistency and stability of the measure, that is the item measures the same element every time it is evaluated (7). Issues related to validity and reliability arise when data are obtained from existing sources or have been collected for other purposes and are now being applied to the current evaluation process. This may be the only available data and may be useful but the nurse manager must recognize and state the limitations of some data. For example, information obtained from charts may not be complete, a page may be missing or illegible, so the data retrieved does not totally reflect the events of the cardiopulmonary resuscitation episode. Thus these data are not totally valid. A common clinical reality involves the revision of cardiac arrest flow sheets. If these flow sheets are revised during the time frame under review, information may be charted differently, categories or definitions of categories may be altered so the reliability of the data over the course of the evaluation period may be questioned. The data can be used but the evaluator must recognize and state the limitations of the data. The nurse manager needs to consider evaluation design with a reasonable and pragmatic point of view.

Identify Data Sources

Various management activities may contribute to program evaluation as they provide existing data to the assessment process. Managers may be able to integrate available information into program evaluation. Readily available data might include budget information, quality improvement data, mortality statistics, infectious disease statistics, staff absentee rates, or nurse recruitment and retention statistics. In the ACLS example an organization may have a cardiac arrest committee that reviews the operations and outcomes of all cardiac arrests. Their records may provide data that reflects changes in patient outcomes since the institution of the ACLS program. The use of existing sources of data can conserve both time and work in the evaluation process.

Other sources of information include other health care personnel, patients, significant others, program participants, program staff, patient charts, other hospital department or committee records, or external organization information or data. For example, national or regional statistics concerning a particular therapy may be available as a comparison to illustrate an improvement of patient outcome since the implementation of a given program. This information may be very beneficial in justifying the continuation of a program.

A wide variety of data collection and analysis techniques are acceptable for evaluation purposes. The nurse manager must consider the value of the data, its financial cost, and the time required by a given technique to determine its usefulness to the evaluation. Techniques include both quantitative and qualitative methods. Questionnaires, surveys, tests, interviews, observations, and subjective ratings by specific individuals are all considered acceptable data sources.

Collect Data

After the types and sources of data have been identified the nurse manager proceeds to the data collection phase of the evaluation. Developing a time schedule and a system to organize information as it is obtained are two approaches that will assist in organizing this phase. Some data can be generated from questionnaires, surveys, interviews, or observations. Often timing is critical and the data collectors must be ready to proceed on schedule. One roadblock in this phase is the expectation that data retrieval from existing sources will be easily accessible and readily available in a useful form. However, personal and political issues often complicate this process. The individual who controls the information may be on vacation, in the middle of a major project, or in some other way unavailable. Occasionally individuals or departments are reluctant to share information especially if they sense the information might be used to justify competing resources. Information is not always in the form that was anticipated and additional information might be needed to generate the required data. These various stumbling blocks require political suave and problem solving skills that are commonly needed by nurse managers.

Often an overall data collection guide can serve

as a useful tool to direct and clarify the process (8) (Table 16.3). This guide offers categories of data and questions that are common to many evaluations. It can be easily modified to meet specific needs.

Data Analysis

Data analysis involves performing procedures that will transform data into usable information for the purpose of program evaluation. Raw data rarely demonstrates a problem or a solution as well as transformed data. For example, the number of nurses who achieved ACLS certification through this program is 15. Based on the same data a stronger statement is 60% of the staff nurses achieved ACLS certification through this program. Often percentages, ratios, and simple comparisons present more meaningful information than simply reporting raw scores. Depending upon the type of data and techniques used in data collection, standard deviations, means, and variances may be appropriate and are relatively simple and useful techniques for program evaluation. More sophisticated statistical testing can include t-Tests, ANOVA's, correlation coefficients, and regression analysis. In order to correctly use these more sophisticated analysis procedures nurse managers may need to seek the assistance of a statistical or research consultant or an experienced nurse researcher. Critical care nurses have learned to use quantitative measures to provide sophisticated patient care, now critical care nurse managers are learning to use more sophisticated measures to support decisions and programs in complex environments.

Various data analysis techniques are available to evaluate cost effectiveness. Cost-benefit (C-B) analysis provides important financial information to nurse managers and decision makers. Cost-benefit refers to the relationship between project costs and project outcomes expressed in monetary terms (9). The C-B analysis can be developed through several well defined steps (Tables 16.4). Elements of the project are considered costs when a person or a program is unfavorably affected by the use of that element. Every program uses resources that could potentially have alternative uses. Any resource that is committed to a given program deprives the alternative program of that resource. Thus any resource use can be considered a cost (10). Both direct and indirect costs should be considered in C-B analysis. In the ACLS example, a direct cost would be the salary for the staff nurse attending the program; an indirect cost would be the classroom space allocated to the program.

Anticipated costs and benefits that are considered during program planning are referred to as ex ante C-B. Costs are estimated based on anticipated resource needs, and benefits are assumed to be achieved. The ex ante C-B analysis is part of a formative evaluation. For example, the unit manager may anticipate registering five staff nurses for each ACLS certification session and expect a 100% pass rate. Ex post C-B analysis is done at the completion of the program as part of the summative evaluation. Here the C-B calculations reflect actual resource investment and achieved benefits. The unit manager may have actually registered six nurses for each ACLS certification session with a 100% pass rate. During the ex post C-B analysis any unanticipated outcomes may also be recognized and included in the calculations (9).

Program outcomes are considered benefits when a person is better off or an outcome has improved because the program effected a change. As with costs, managers can identify both direct and indirect benefits associated with a program. Quantifying benefits in monetary terms is often more challenging than quantifying costs. Managers usually identify tangible and intangible benefits associated with a program. A monetary value can easily be assigned to a tangible benefit. In contrast when it is difficult to assign monetary value to a benefit it is referred to as intangible (11). Many of the programs in health care involve intangible benefits. The classic example of an intangible benefit in health care programs is a decrease in mortality. How do you value a human life in a C-B analysis? In fact, one standard method is to consider the individual's average salary and potential life income. However, many will argue that an average salary does not adequately reflect the true benefit of decreasing morality. Two techniques used in dealing with intangible benefits are shadow prices and nonquantification (11). Shadow prices refer to any reasonable ascription of value assigned to a good not openly traded in the market. The price assigned is what consumers would pay if they needed this good. Shadow prices are difficult to assign since the value of the item in the health care context can be emotionally laden. In the ACLS case example, a patient who never needs resuscitation may feel that a nurse certified in ACLS is worth an additional one hundred dollars. However a patient

Table 16.3. Data Collection Guide

Program Goals
- What are the stated goals of the program?
- How do you determine goals are achieved?
- What are stated objectives of the program?
- How do you determine objectives are achieved?
- Who identified the goals and objectives?
- Are there additional goals related to this program at other organizational levels? If so, what are those goals?
- Is the program required?
- What agency requires the program?
- What are unanticipated outcomes?

Target Audience
- Who should be a participant?
- Who are the participants?
- How are they recruited?
- Who benefits from the program?
- How do they benefit?

Program Organization
- Who directs the program?
- Who controls the program?
- Who staffs the program?
- How is the program structured?
- How is the program funded?
- What resources are required?
- Where is the program delivered?
- What programs compete for resources with this program?
- Who supports the program?
- Who opposes the program?
- How does this program fit into the organization?

Program History
- How long has the program existed?
- What are the significant changes since its inception?
- What are any recent significant changes?
- Who initiated the program?
- Where did the initial support come from?
- Have previous evaluations been done?
- What did previous evaluations show?
- Is this a highly visible program?

Program Process
- What activities are included in the program?
- Are there cycles that influence the program?
- Do activities vary within the program time table?
- What are the direct costs of the program?
- What are the indirect costs of the program?
- What are the tangible benefits of the program?
- What are the intangible benefits of the program?

Program Evaluation
- Who is the targeted audience for the evaluation?
- Who will receive copies of the evaluation?
- What are the current program issues?
- What decisions will this evaluation influence?
- When is the evaluation due?
- What support is available for the evaluation process?
- What information should the evaluation contain?
- Who should be interviewed during the evaluation?
- What is the main focus of this evaluation?
- What needed information is currently available?
- What needed information must be attained?
- How will existing information be attained?
- How will needed information be attained?
- What is the budget for the evaluation?

Table 16.4. Methodology for a Cost-Benefit Analysis

1. Identify decision makers and their values.
2. Identify program alternatives and assumptions.
3. Identify program costs.
4. Identify program benefits.
5. Value costs and benefits monetarily.
6. Discuss intangible benefits.
7. Calculate the cost-benefit relation.
8. Interpret the calculation in terms of the program.

who has been successfully resuscitated may feel that the same nurse is worth several thousand dollars. Thus it becomes difficult to assign a reasonable monetary value to this certification.

Nonquantification occurs when the attempt to assign any value to an intangible benefit is so difficult that no value is assigned. For example, what value can be assigned to the successful resuscitation of a healthy young child who happens to have an anaphylactic allergic reaction to medication prior to an appendectomy? Since it is so difficult to assign a reasonable value it may seem acceptable to consider nonquantification. However in their own way the individuals involved in the decision process will assign some level of worth. Each individual can overestimate or underestimate the value of the good or service thus significantly altering the C-B analysis.

Another issue in C-B analysis is that decision makers may differ on definitions of cost or benefit. The value of factors identified in the C-B equation are influenced by the organizational mission, the current organizational environment, and the decision makers. Increased organizational visibility and recognition may be seen as a benefit by one unit but not by another unit. Increased nursing morale may be a significant consideration for the nursing administrative team but not viewed as important by the financial committee. The inconsistencies in benefit definitions, especially the intangible benefits, complicates C-B comparisons between programs.

In determining C-B comparisons, program alternatives and assumptions need to be recognized. In the ACLS example, program alternatives may include an internal program, an external program, a program targeted only for the CCU staff, an institution-wide program, or no program. Program assumptions might include that all staff nurses will be paid for their class time, all registration fees will be reimbursed, and all book fees will be the responsibility of the nurse participant. Obviously these assumptions influence the cost calculations of the program. Cost calculations are also influenced by the method of calculating equipment costs. Rarely is the full cost of any equipment item calculated into one program budget. Depreciation or amortization costs are calculated over the life of the item. The ACLS program would calculate some costs for the use of the demonstration equipment for resuscitation. However, the full purchase and maintenance costs of this equipment would not be accounted only to this program.

Direct and indirect costs and benefits as well as tangible and intangible benefits must be identified and assigned values (Table 16.5). Maintenance costs are important factors in some program evaluations. For example every 2 years an individual must renew ACLS certification. A long-term plan should consider the costs of such a renewal.

After the monetary values have been assigned and the nonmonetary values considered, the overall C-B relation is calculated and interpreted (Table 16.6). The direct comparison of costs to benefits is demonstrated in Table 16.7. This direct comparison is calculated by subtracting the monetary cost from the monetary benefit to produce the net benefit. A more useful calculation to compare the efficiency of one program to another is the cost to benefit ratio. To determine this ratio, the monetary benefits are divided by the monetary costs. The program with the higher ratio demonstrates a better investment for the required resources. In the ACLS example, the internal program demonstrates the best cost to benefit ratio. This example does not quantify the intangible benefits, however the internal program benefits are stronger than the external program benefits. Decision makers may select programs with high costs over less expensive programs when the net benefit or the cost-benefit ratio indicates an advantage to the organization. In addition intangible benefits may be a significant strength of a given program and influence the cost-benefit relation beyond the monetary values.

The C-B analysis examines the economic efficiency of a program in monetary terms. In situations where monetary value is difficult or impossible to assign, cost effectiveness analysis may be used (9). Cost effectiveness examines the efficacy of a program in achieving stated goals and outcomes in relation to program costs. A cost effectiveness relation considers the net outcomes, that is, only

Table 16.5. ACLS Program Calculations

Program Costs for a 2-day Program
Assumptions: A total of 20 nurses will participate in the program. Five nurses will participate each quarter. Staff nurses will be paid as a workshop day to attend. Staff nurses registration fees will be paid by the organization. Staff nurses will pay for their required texts and handouts. Each session must enroll a minimum of 10 registrants. Nursing will support one ACLS instructor per session.

Costs Common to Internal and External Programs
   Direct
      Staff nurse time—16 hours @ $15.30/hour
   Indirect
      Staff nurse coverage—16 hours/participant
   Tangible Benefits
      Decreased drug wastage during CPR
   Intangible Benefits
      More effective CPR in CCU and hospital wide by CPR team
      More efficient CPR in CCU and hospital wide by CPR team
      Improved nursing morale

External Program Costs for a 2-day Program
   Direct
      Registration fees—$250/student

Internal Program Costs for a 2-day Recognition Program
   Direct
      Instructor time—16 hours @ $17.50/hour, 1 instructor/5 students
      Registration fee—$50/student
   Indirect
      Classroom—16 hours @ $20/hour
      Demonstration equipment—$70/session
      Instructor preparation time—4 hours @ $17.50/hour
   Tangible Benefits
      Tuition from nonstaff registrants—$100
   Intangible Benefits
      Control of class schedule
      Recognition as ACLS provider

Table 16.6. Cost Comparison of Internal vs. External ACLS Program

1. Common Costs
   Staff nurse class time
     —16 hours × $15.30 = $244.80 × 20 nurses = $4896.00
   Staff nurse coverage
     —16 hours × $15.30 = $244.80 × 20 nurses = $4896.00
   Decreased drug wastage during CPR
     —Savings of $5750 per year
2. External Program
   Registration fees
     —$250/student × 20 nurses = $5000
3. Internal Program
   Instructor time
     —16 hours × $17.50 = $280.00 × 4 = $1120
   Registration fees
     —$50/student × 20 nurses = $1000
   Classroom
     —16 hours × $20 hour = $320 × 4 = $1280
   Demonstration equipment
     —$70/session × 4 = $280
   Instructor preparation time
     —4 hours × $17.50 = $70 × 4 = $280
   Tuition from nonstaff registrants
     —5 registrants × $100 = $500 × 4 = $2000

Table 16.7. Cost-Benefit Comparison for ACLS Programs

Common costs: $4896.00 + $4896.00 = $9792.00
Common benefits: $5750.00
External program costs: $5000
Internal program costs: $1120 + $1000 + $1280 + $280 + $280 = $3960
Internal program benefits: $2000

	ACLS Programs	
	External	Internal
Costs	$14,792	$13,752
Benefits	5,750	7,750
Net benefits	−9,042	−6,002
B–C ratio	.389	.564

the outcomes attributed to the program. A retention program targeting staff nurses who have been employed 3 years or more may be instituted. Within 1 year, a significant decrease in attrition of this targeted group is recognized. In calculating the cost effectiveness of this program only nurses who have been employed 3 years or more and the changes in their attrition can be considered. Gross outcomes include all outcome changes and some may not be related to the program being evaluated. When using cost effectiveness analysis, monetary value is not assigned to outcomes but rather, the relationship between costs and outcomes is usually stated as cost per unit of outcome (9). If the retention program costs totaled $45,000 and attrition declined in the target population by 17% accounting for retention of eight nurses, the cost effectiveness ratio would be $5625 per nurse retained.

Another form of analysis is the cost feasibility analysis (11). Decision makers use cost feasibility analysis to determine if a program is affordable.

This technique is often used during the initial planning phase of a program. The costs of a planned program are calculated before implementation and compared with the available resources. If costs and resources do not balance, the program may be modified or eliminated, or additional resources may be sought for other areas or programs. For example, a bonus program offering dramatic incentives to staff nurses agreeing to work permanent off-shifts requires a cost feasibility analysis. Several different incentive packages might be considered during the process to determine which option would be affordable to the organization.

Data analysis involves calculations and quantification yet the nurse manager must often consider nonquantifiable factors and present the data to decision makers in a relevant context. A specific program could influence staff nurse retention. In a very competitive nursing market retaining staff nurses might be more feasible and more productive than trying to recruit nurses. A CCRN review program offered free to staff nurses might be a successful strategy for retention. The nurse manager may have to convince decision makers of the nonquantifiable aspects of such a program.

Report the Findings

Program evaluations can be presented in many different ways. The final report may be oral or written. As a written report it may be submitted as a business plan, an executive summary, an abstract, or detailed evaluation report. Guidelines may request specific data to be included or excluded, synthesis to be emphasized, or program recommendations to be suggested. It is critical for the nurse manager to recognize and follow stated guidelines. However, in developing the final report the nurse manager should consider several essential rules (Table 16.8). All reports exist within the context of the political environment in the organization. The nurse manager should consider the nature of the organizational environment when drafting the report. The information in the evaluation should be pertinent to the target audience and stated in meaningful terms. This often involves translating findings into usable information for decision makers. Data, figures, and graphs should accurately represent the projected or actual costs, benefits, or outcomes. Graphs and charts can simplify complicated information and allow the presenter to draw attention to specific data. Often the visual representation of information captures attention and focuses the reader toward a particular issue or point of fact. The nurse manager should consider that misrepresented data can undermine the program and lead to loss of program support.

Formative and summative evaluations tend to be presented in slightly different manners. A formative evaluation is used for planning and can be presented as part of a business plan. A business plan is formally presented to generate organizational support and resource commitment for a program. As a formal marketing document it is well organized and has a polished appearance. Although considerable time and effort are invested in preparing a business plan, often the target audience consists of many "5-minute readers." A one page abstract or executive summary is often critical to the success of the business plan. The reader can be enticed or rebuffed by that one page abstract or executive summary. The business plan includes all the elements identified earlier as part of the program definition. Projected resource needs and program outcomes should be specified. A market and competitive analysis should be included to justify the market share, market need, and potential for success. Business plans offer financial and program forecasts for 1, 2, and 5 years. Through the business plan the manager is seeking long-range support and commitment and must offer information and data to generate such a return.

On the other hand, the summative report reflects the program's accomplishments and impacts. It is usually written and often offers considerable detail. Because summative evaluation findings may be used for several purposes, several different reports may need to be generated. To be of greatest value the report should address the characteristics of the target audience. Audiences will vary on their focus, understanding, and needs. For example, graphs and tables illustrating various aspects of costs and benefits may be very appealing to the finance committee. However the quality improvement committee may focus on outcome measures and data collection techniques used to evaluate the

Table 16.8. Essential Rules for Writing Reports

1. Write clearly.
2. Avoid abbreviations and jargon.
3. Highlight the programs critical characteristics.
4. Keep the report relevant.
5. Always remember the audience.

program outcomes. Each committee may find the data presented to the other committee relatively useless. The nurse manager presents a more influential report when the pertinent data are readily available in a usable form. Graphs, tables, and diagrams are useful tools in presenting complicated data. Commonly decision makers focus on the general program description, conclusions, and recommendations. For this reason, the nurse manager should prepare these sections carefully. A well written evaluation report can generate and solidify program support.

SUMMARY

Today nurse managers are routinely expected to participate in or direct program evaluations. Nurse managers participate and coordinate formative and summative evaluations. Through their involvement they assist in defining the programs needed to operate their clinical units. The nurse manager's clinical expertise can help in developing realistic program goals and objectives. During these processes they identify direct and indirect costs and benefits related to the program being considered. In addition, nurse managers direct and critique the data collection and analysis required during the evaluation process. Often they present and defend the findings to various organizational committees and funding groups. Approaching this responsibility in an organized fashion, the nurse manager can present meaningful data and persuasive arguments to establish and maintain needed programs.

REFERENCES

1. Scriven M. The methodology of evaluation. In: Tyler RW, et al., eds. Perspectives of curriculum evaluation. Chicago: Rand McNally, 1967:39–83.
2. Patton MQ. Utilization-focused evaluation. 2nd ed. Newbury Park: Sage Publications, 1986:83–121.
3. Rutman L. Planning useful evaluations. Newbury Park: Sage Publications, 1980:33.
4. Stecher BM, Davis WA. How to focus an evaluation. Newbury Park: Sage Publications, 1987:22.
5. Fitz-Gibbon, CT, Morris LL. How to design a program evaluation. Newbury Park: Sage Publications, 1987:13.
6. Herman JL, Morris LL, Fitz-Gibbon CT. Evaluator's handbook. Newbury Park: Sage Publications, 1987:22.
7. Rutman L. Planning useful evaluations. Beverly Hills: Sage Publications, 1980:123–162.
8. Stecher and Davis, pp. 58–61.
9. Rossi PH, Freeman HE. Evaluation: A systematic approach. 3rd ed. Beverly Hills: Sage Publications, 1985:321–356.
10. Levin HM. Cost-effectiveness a primer. Newbury Park: Sage Publications, 1983.
11. Thompson MS. Benefit-cost analysis for program evaluation. Beverly Hills: Sage Publications, 1980.

Part IV

ECONOMIC AND FUTURE PERSPECTIVES

Chapter 17

Economic Perspective

LINDA F. SAMSON

OVERVIEW

The rising cost of health care services is one of the most significant environmental trends affecting critical care nursing today. As cost of care increases, individuals reduce the amount of income spent on preventative health care, thus increasing the likelihood of acute, life threatening illness. Reduced insurance coverage and an increase in the numbers of uninsured and underinsured also contribute to the significance of this trend. Health care spending reached $511 billion or 11.4% of the U.S. gross national product (GNP) in fiscal year 1987 (1). In 1989, 20 million Americans spent an average of 7.2 days in the hospital, and paid $260 billion for inpatient services alone (2). Analysts project that total health care spending will accelerate at 10% per year through 1995 and will reach 13% of GNP by the year 1991. The physician portion of the health care bill is expected to rise at a rate of about 15% per year (3). Increases in health expenditures have occurred despite prospective reimbursement and other cost containment initiatives.

Government expenditures on Medicare and Medicaid have increased at the same overall rate that health care expenditures have grown. The rapid escalation of costs in these programs has jeopardized services to some and reduced availability of services for others (4). In 1989, 24 states spent between 8% and 12% of their budgets on Medicaid, and 11 states spent over 12% of their budgets on health care services for the poor (5). Nationwide, Medicaid expenditures were $50 billion in 1989, a 10% increase over the previous year.

The environment of fiscal constraint has met competing demands for quality and reduced cost. Consumers of health care services demand improved quality while industries paying health care insurance premiums or subsidizing the costs of health care seek reduced cost for services. The new challenges for the health care industry are surviving in a cost constrained milieu while providing quality health care at reasonable costs. In order to accomplish these goals, hospitals must reposition themselves for better and more efficient resource utilization. Nurse managers and nurse executives must not only achieve economic efficiency at the unit or department level, they must also learn to speak the economic language of the industry.

This chapter will provide insight into the economic factors influencing health care delivery and strategies used by hospitals to enhance financial position and organizational stability. Key terms will be defined. A case scenario will be used to apply concepts and information presented in the chapter.

Supply and Demand in Health Care Markets

Economics is the study of efficient allocation of scarce resources among competing demands. It addresses four aspects of the economic system: what will be produced, how it will be produced, what quantity will be produced, and who will get what is produced (6). These factors are basic to an understanding of the competitive market. In a competitive or free market economy, demand for services drives the supply of services developed or offered. Demand indicates the level of interest in or need for a particular type of service, while supply refers to the quantity of services actually available.

In the current economic environment, supply of health care professionals, particularly nurses, is a major driving force in the determination of how much health care can be produced. This section will explore the factors that influence supply and demand in health care markets.

Factors Affecting Demand

A variety of factors affect an individual's demand for health care services. An understanding of the factors that most significantly affect demand will help nurse managers and nurse executives plan the most appropriate combinations of services. These factors are summarized in Table 17.1.

The individual's need for health care is essentially demand for treatment or prevention of illness. Demand is typically initiated by the individual. However, demand for service has also been created by the marketing of health promotion and disease prevention to a health conscious consumer. Offering cholesterol screening and risk assessment in the work place are examples of created demand. Once demand has been established, the health care system then combines various inputs to provide services. Factors influencing the individual's demand decision include incidence of illness or need for care, cultural and demographic factors, and economic factors (7). Demand for health care insurance coverage is related predominantly to the economic factors influencing demand.

The demographic factors most closely linked to demand are age, marital status, family size, and education. There is known to be an increased demand for health care services with increasing age. In 1985, those over 65 accounted for 11.9% of the population, up from only 9.2% in 1960. Due to longer recovery times and lack of needed convalescent and home care services, length of stay for individuals over the age of 65 is 1.5 times higher than the length of stay for the group aged 45–64. The rate of surgical procedures performed on the elderly is also 70% higher per 1000 population than for the age group 45–64 (8). Joint replacements, organ transplantation and intensive cancer therapy are just a few of the high technology treatments that are more commonly demanded in the elderly population.

The demand for certain types of services, such as obstetrics, occurs over a narrow age range. Beyond that time frame, the demand diminishes significantly. Single persons generally use more hospital care, regardless of age, than do married persons. This may be related to lack of available care givers at home to provide care. The per capita income is often lowest in large families, thus limiting resources to expend for health care services. Education is closely linked with the types of health care services demanded. Consumers with higher levels of education tend to seek preventive services and early treatment for illnesses. For example, mammography and pap smears are more commonly performed at recommended intervals in women with a college education than in those women without a high school education. These behaviors can reduce illness morbidity and reduce the economic burden (7).

The economic factors associated with demand for health care are income, price of services, value of the consumer's time, type of insurance, and amounts of copayments and deductibles. While income level plays a role in determining demand for health care in some groups, a more critical determinant is insurance coverage of the health care service. It has been argued that the increased availability of insurance, which reduces out-of-pocket expenditures for consumers, has significantly increased the demand for health care services in this country (9). Furthermore, workers have come to expect low cost or no cost health care coverage as part of employment benefits.

In a market economy, price influences demand in much the same way that income influences demand. Generally, price and demand are inversely proportional; for example, the higher the cost, the lower the demand. However, health care is unique in that some or all of the price is often paid by third-party payors. Thus demand may be high, even when total cost is high, because consumers are isolated from the full purchase price. This relationship is depicted in Figure 17.1.

Value of the consumer's time often influences both the quantity of health care services demanded and the way those services are delivered. Busy executives may participate in preventative services if the services are brought to them. Understanding this concept and the desirability of preventing costly illness, many corporations are providing preventative services and health promotion initiatives in the work place. At the other end of the continuum, critical care services provide the consumer with intense in-

Table 17.1. Factors affecting demand

Marketing of services
Health promotion
Incidence of illness
Cultural factors
Demographic factors
Economic factors
Availability of health insurance

236 ECONOMIC AND FUTURE PERSPECTIVES

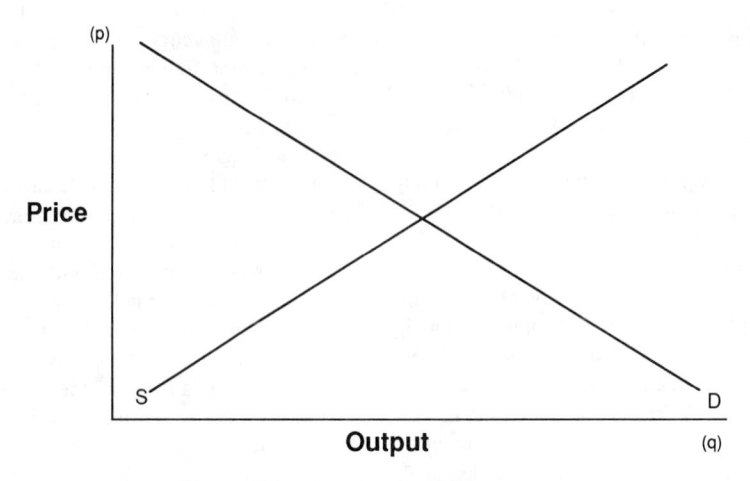

Figure 17.1. Relationship of price to output.
p, price; S, supply; D, demand; q, quantity.

teraction and contact. This type of interaction is often demanded even when the patient's medical condition no longer warrants that level of service.

Controlling Demand for Health Care

One of the most common methods of controlling demand for health care services is to increase the copayments and deductibles paid by individuals. When bearing a larger portion of the cost of care, individuals demand less services, are more likely to postpone treatment, and request more conservative approaches to care (10). A study conducted by the Rand Corporation with patients randomly assigned to full-pay and copay health care plans, found as much as a 50% reduction in costs with minimal negative impact on health status when substantial copayments were used (11).

Employers have also attempted to control demand for services by increased use of health maintenance organizations (HMOs) and preferred provider organizations (PPOs). The concept behind these methods of health care delivery is that a "gatekeeper" or primary care provider can regulate the volume of services consumed by an individual. Where HMOs and PPOs are available, employers often create financial incentives to employees who enroll, and disincentives for employees choosing plans that provide freedom of choice of physicians and fee-for-service reimbursement (8).

A final way in which employers and insurers have controlled demand for services is the use of preservice review of medical necessity. Under this system, individuals are required to notify the insurers' utilization review department prior to hospitalization or surgery. Without certification, the insurer or employer are relieved of financial obligation for the services rendered.

Hospitals may also require partial payment at the time of registration in order to reduce bad debt burden created by tightened insurance regulations. Payment of past bad debt and new partial payments may be facilitated by trends toward credit card acceptance and hospital loan programs.

State governments have reduced services under Medicaid and other initiatives by restricting eligibility. This has placed increased financial burden on the poor and the medically indigent (8). States have also adopted a variety of control methods to reduce lengthy hospital stay and resource consumption. For example, New Jersey adopted the Johnny Appleseed program to reduce inpatient obstetrics (OB) and neonatal intensive care unit (ICU) costs through the use of home visits. Case management is another method of control used by states and health care facilities.

Federal initiatives to reduce the demand for health care services are discussed in Chapters 15 and 19. Some of these initiatives include diagnosis related groups (DRGs), utilization review programs, and medical effectiveness initiatives. In addition, Medicare deductibles and copayments have been continuously increased just as they have been increased by private insurers. A newly adopted regulation requires care givers to complete all Medicare paperwork, rather than having the individual submit reimbursement forms to the government (12). Some argue that this regulation will adversely affect the supply of providers rather than contain demand for services.

Hospitals have also begun to create demand for services. Product-line management, market analysis, and targeted marketing represent techniques used to create demand. In critical care, effects of transplantation programs, specialized cardiovascular services, and trauma program marketing may increase or create demand for services.

Factors Affecting Supply

Underlying the supply of any good or service is the production function. The production function describes the relationship between the output of a good or service and the resources necessary to produce it. If the output is hours of care per patient in the critical care unit (CCU), the inputs would be the number and education levels of the nurses and support personnel in the unit. The production function would then demonstrate that the quantity of nursing care produced is related to the types and numbers of personnel and the characteristics of the critical care unit such as bed capacity, general acuity of patients in the unit, and length of stay of the usual patient in the unit. Production functions depend upon the concept of output maximization, or production of the greatest possible output, and may serve to increase demand. For example, the American Heart Association has increased demand for cholesterol screening through their educational programs to alert consumers to acceptable levels of cholesterol for coronary artery disease risk reduction.

Increased attention has been focused on the supply of nurses and especially critical care nurses over the past several years. A survey conducted for the American Association of Critical-Care Nurses (AACN) suggests that there will be a demand for at least 336,000 RN FTEs by the year 1995. The available supply of critical care nurses in 1988 was 194,000. This equates to a 75% increase in supply just to meet projected critical care staffing needs (13). Inadequate compensation, lack of professional autonomy, and unsatisfactory working conditions have all been cited as factors limiting the supply of nurses (14–18).

The effects of increased demand on supply must also be considered. Supply is affected by the number of hospital beds, their geographic distribution, and the occupancy rate. Occupied beds often increase demand for services. Furthermore, supply is affected by the availability of technological support for the services offered. An ICU bed is not a part of the supply of beds if there are no monitoring capabilities for the bed and its potential occupant.

Fiscal constraints, capitated reimbursement, the nursing shortage and underutilization are recent factors affecting the supply of hospital beds. Table 17.2 summarizes the factors affecting supply. Uncompensated care and bad debt, combined with institutional inefficiency have resulted in bed closings and consolidations of services in many geographic areas. Institutions with low volume have chosen to close beds or close the entire hospital. Finally, the nursing shortage has seriously limited the bed supply (19). Beds that cannot be staffed cannot be operated.

The nursing shortage is more appropriately viewed, not as a decrease in absolute numbers of practicing nurses, but rather as an increased demand by hospitals and other health care agencies for the services of nurses. Thus, the shortage can be viewed in terms of supply and demand concepts. Demand for professional nursing services has increased significantly while supply has increased more slowly. When demand outpaces supply, there is usually increased cost associated with acquiring the item or service in demand. However, in nursing, salaries have not truly reflected demand side economics. This may be due to ceilings on wages and the employee whose fringe benefits and tenure with the organization outweigh increased salary compensation offered by competitors.

The surplus of physicians is a more recent concern on the supply side of health care costs. It has been estimated that each physician results in medical care expenditures of at least $500,000 per year, since physicians, not patients, order services and they are the source of 70% of all health care ex-

Table 17.2. Factors affecting supply

Types of personnel
Numbers of personnel
Bed capacity of ICU
Patient acuity
Length of stay
Compensation
Professional autonomy
Technologic support services
Fiscal constraints
Capitated reimbursement

penditures (10). Surplus numbers of physicians, therefore, have the potential to greatly increase the proportion of income expended on health care services. Despite this, the only mechanisms available to control excess supply and production of physicians are to decrease medical school admission rates and reduce the fiscal incentives provided for medical education under capitated reimbursement. Attempts to regulate physician charges for services, while as yet limited, will influence demand for services rather than supply. When reimbursement for specialized services such as neurosurgery is limited, physicians will recommend more procedures, thus increasing demand, in order to maintain constant or increased income levels. Volumes may need to be regulated to prevent unnecessary utilization.

Implications of Supply and Demand Controls for the Critical Care Nurse Manager

Intense competition for consumer health care dollars has driven hospitals to carefully analyze new and existing programs and services. Realistically, attention must be directed toward profit maximization as well as cost containment. In order to accomplish this, critical care nurse managers will be increasingly called upon to establish a volume of care delivery which can achieve the profit maximization goal. Factors such as optimal unit size and occupancy rate to achieve profitability will be as important as physician desire to admit a patient in most hospitals. For example, hospital administrators have long known that newborn intensive care units are both costly to operate and poorly reimbursed. Research done on cost per case for newborns demonstrated that infants under 1500 grams at birth were likely to survive, but also to have hospital bills that significantly exceed reimbursement (20). The cost information from the study now allows nurse managers and nurse executives to identify the best mix of patients in a neonatal ICU. While nurses do not currently control admission decisions, in the future they may play a key role in limiting numbers of admissions, referral of infants to other facilities, or enhance the volume of more profitable services depending upon the mission and philosophy of the organization.

Case Scenario

Hospital Y is a 354-bed community hospital located in a metropolitan area. The hospital has always offered a full range of services including general ICU-CCU, ER, OB, pediatrics, and general medical surgical services. Specialized services, such as cardiac surgery, transplantation, burn, and trauma, have been referred to a university medical center about 10 minutes from Hospital Y. Recently several of the members of the medical staff have approached administration about the need to expand cardiothoracic services to include CABG procedures. Hospital administration must evaluate this request in light of other activities in the hospital's long-range plan, the available fiscal and human resources, an assessment of need for the proposed services, and determination of the impact of such actions on the hospital's overall financial position.

The issues raised in the above case scenario will be discussed throughout the following sections. Steps in the decision making process will then be reviewed, and an action plan formulated.

There are several issues related to supply and demand that will be necessary to consider in the proposal evaluation. The following questions must be answered.

Demand Issues

1. What percent of current volume of ICU admissions present with cardiovascular problems?
2. Has this percentage changed over the last 3 years?
3. Does the hospital have a cardiac catheterization laboratory?

Supply Issues

4. Is there a health planning and regulating mechanism that controls development of specialized, high cost services in the area?
5. If so, is there a demonstrated demand that has overextended supply?

Supply and Demand Issues

6. Are there large numbers of staff nurse vacancies in the existing ICU?
7. Does the proposal call for conversion of existing beds or addition of new beds for cardiothoracic surgery patients?
8. Can support services handle the added volume cost effectively or will there need to be changes in other departments to accommodate the service changes?
9. How will the need for additional FTEs be de-

termined as well as associated training costs, equipment needs, and impact on other support services?

Market Analysis

Feasibility or market analysis provides a framework for determining whether a proposed new service could survive in a given market. The usual goals for a new or expanded service are to increase market penetration or market share, improve the institution's financial position, and meet long-range goals as set out in the strategic plan. The primary components of the analysis are market assessment, provider assessment, and financial assessment (21).

The market assessment phase of the analysis determines whether there is a demand for the service in the target market area and if supply is adequate to meet demand. Factors that should be considered in this assessment include: usual geographic distribution of hospital admissions; demographic characteristics of the community such as age, sex, income level, education, and attitudes toward the hospital; and the nature of the competition. In addition, any regulatory constraints should be explored. Expanding an existing program should increase the hospital's market share, or proportion of the demand satisfied by the institution. A new program should enhance market penetration, or provide increased community awareness of the institution and its programs, thereby increasing the potential patient base.

The provider assessment helps to determine whether the needed physicians and support services are available to carry out the plan. In the case scenario, are there adequate numbers of cardiothoracic surgeons on Hospital Y's staff? Would they perform their surgical procedures at Hospital Y if the program was implemented, or do they prefer another facility? Does the anesthesia department want to see a CABG program developed? Will the anesthesia department provide the necessary back-up for the program? Is there an appropriately equipped and staffed cardiac catheterization laboratory?

The final phase of the assessment is the financial assessment. Costs to be considered are both direct and indirect planning and operational costs. Short- and long-term costs must also be analyzed and compared against revenue projections for the service. In the example, will renovations be required? What demands for additional staff must be met? What is the financial effect on other services within the hospital? For example, will radiology, laboratory, operating room, respiratory therapy, and pharmacy have additional costs related to the proposed program? If so, will costs be offset by revenue generated? Are there educational and training start-up costs? How long will it take to get the program operational if it is approved?

A market analysis can provide information for sound decision making in the current environment. Nurse managers and executives have a key role to play in such an analysis. They can provide the information about the demand for services and any marketplace competition. Nurse managers often can provide insight into the impact of the proposed service on staffing requirements for nursing and support services.

Financial Repositioning

In order to survive in the health care environment of the 1990s, hospitals and health care organizations are learning that new approaches and creative solutions to financial management are required. Having an affluent, well-insured patient population and DRGs with a high profit margin can help institutional solvency but they can't guarantee long-term viability. If the volume of services delivered is low, the cardiac catheterization laboratory underutilized, or reimbursement for services delayed, the institution's viability may be affected. Optimal control of fiscal resources, cash flow control, and debt management are important for achievement of institutional goals. Development of the institution's financial plan determines how the organization can best position itself to enhance profitability.

Investment

Since hospitals are often required to wait 90–120 days or longer for reimbursement from third-party payors and reimbursement levels do not support capital expansion and replacement of equipment, it has become increasingly important for institutions to find additional revenue sources. Investment offers one strategy for increasing revenue over the short- and long-term.

Short-term money market investment accounts allow working capital to earn interest until expenditures occur. Funds can be invested in these accounts for as few as 7 days, with interest at slightly lower rates than longer-term investments. Treasury bills (T bills) are an intermediate-term investment. Investment periods are at least 3 months and may be as long as 30 years. Interest rates on T bills are set at weekly auctions. Yield, or rate of return, on T bills often determines the yield on other short-term and intermediate-term investments. Stocks are considered a long-term investment, since prices fluctuate widely over the short term. While yields on stocks can be higher than other investments, the risk is also greater.

Capital investments are another strategy used by hospitals to improve financial position. Investments may be in the form of health related facilities or nonhealth related facilities. Capital investments will be discussed more completely in the section on diversification.

Prepaid Health Plans

Since the passage of the HMO Act of 1973, prepaid health care organizations have grown in number and type. As of January, 1988, 30.3 million people were enrolled in 653 HMOs of four basic types. The independent practice association (IPA) model accounted for about 58% of all HMO contracts. Group practice HMOs like Kaiser-Permanente accounted for about 14.5% of contracts. Staff models, using salaried medical staff and expanded role nurses, accounted for about 12%. The remaining 15% are organized in a network model, where the health plan administrator contracts with private or group practices to provide services (22). The PPO is a health financing arrangement in which a group of health care providers offers services on a predetermined financial basis to purchasers under terms that favor its selection (23). The PPO is similar to the network model HMO.

In order to protect or expand market share, hospitals increasingly seek to develop new relationships, or contract with existing HMOs and PPOs. Development of a new prepaid health program is often a response to requests from medical staff members, who see an erosion of their own practices due to prepaid health plans. Contracting with existing HMOs and PPOs can improve hospital cash flow, respond to local demand, and allow the hospital to attract a different case mix (21). Cash flow improvement occurs in two ways. First, in some arrangements, the hospital is paid a fee in advance of service. Second, even without a prepaid fee, time from billing to payment is substantially less than with traditional third-party payors. HMO and PPO contracts can also change the institution's case mix if desired (24). For example, contracting with an HMO that serves predominantly younger, employed families can expand OB services, which are usually high volume, lower cost services. However, not all low-cost services are financially profitable for institutions. Some can contribute to financial loss for the institution.

There are, however, problems associated with prepaid health plan contracts. First, in order to secure the contract, a discounted rate for services must be offered. If the discount is too great, the institution will erode its operating margin and may even lose money for each admitted enrollee. Second, unless the HMO or PPO is owned by the hospital, contracts are periodically reviewed and may be changed or terminated. Thus, if the hospital budget has been developed based on the volume of projected PPO or HMO services, significant budgetary problems can occur if the contract changes. Finally, there may be problems for the hospital if a particular specialty is not represented in the HMO or PPO and a patient is admitted with a specialized problem. For example, if a patient with multiple trauma is admitted and the HMO has no neurosurgeon, the hospital ethically and legally must find a way to provide the necessary services, even if they are unreimbursed.

Marketing

Health care institutions have come to recognize the value of marketing for both survival and growth. The marketing concept, which places primary emphasis on the consumer, arose as part of the evolutionary growth stage of business. Kotler has defined marketing as the analysis, planning, and control of carefully formulated programs designed to bring about voluntary exchanges of values with target markets for the purpose of achieving organizational objectives (25). Marketing relies on designing products to meet market needs and desires. Those products and services then are appropriately priced. Communication is critical to inform, motivate, and service the target markets.

Hospital marketing incorporates the needs and demands of five separate consumer "publics." These are patients, physicians, employees, unions, and governmental and regulatory agencies. Since each public needs and demands different services, the hospital must evaluate how well each consumer group is served and determine if better service is necessary (10).

Reallocation of Unused Beds

Excess inpatient bed capacity has forced hospitals to consider alternative uses for vacant beds, or face closure. During the 1980s, over 300 community hospitals closed, resulting in a 12% decrease in the numbers of rural hospitals, the number of emergency rooms dropped by over 100, and the number of state certified trauma centers fell by 323 (26). The trend toward closure or reallocation of beds is especially significant since the cost of vacant beds is more than just a loss of earnings for the hospital (27). Empty beds cause decline in use of support services, such as laboratory and radiology, reduce marketability of other programs within the hospital, diminish access to care, reduce jobs, and may influence community pride.

The evidence suggests that a large number of vacant beds are being assigned to other uses. During the period 1983–1987, nonacute care hospital beds increased by one-third from 104,911 to 143,955 (22). The major increases have been in alcohol and chemical dependency beds and rehabilitation beds. Growth in these areas may be related to both the increased need for these services and exclusion from restrictive federal and state reimbursement policies. Modest increases have occurred in psychiatric and long-term care beds. Long-term care and transitional care bed growth may have been limited by lack of health care benefits to cover those services.

As inpatient bed downsizing continues, there has been a growing trend toward increased outpatient service development (28). Outpatient charges now approach one-fourth of hospital revenues nationwide (29). While this trend is appropriate at the present time, there is concern that outpatient overbedding may develop in the future, producing excess bed supply costs and unnecessary treatment for consumers.

Diversification

Diversification is a strategy that attempts to spread the organization's financial risk by taking advantage of new market opportunities. It was adopted in the 1980s in response to declining inpatient revenue and loss of ancillary department revenue to private physician's offices. Diversification represents a business approach to health care financial management (30).

Diversification of services requires restructuring of the health care delivery system. Traditionally, the hospital corporate model (Fig. 17.2) has reflected a mission of humanitarian service rather than focusing on business aspects such as profit or positive fund balance and market driven service development. Appropriately, efforts to spread financial risk must consider both mission and financial viability.

Generally three types of corporate models have been developed to spread financial risk and increase revenue production opportunities. The first (Fig. 17.3) involves the traditional hospital corporation with a foundation which may be proprietary or not-for-profit. In this model, unrelated business income is channelled through a foundation. The foundation's income can then be used to support specific activities of the hospital corporation. The second model involves the development of two or more related corporations. The additional corporations may include a foundation, along with a corporation through which additional businesses, such as medical office buildings, parking garages, pharmacies, and long-term care facilities, operate. A third, and closely related model, involves a parent holding company (Fig. 17.4). In this model, the hospital and any other businesses function under the holding company. The holding company functions as a foundation and makes decisions about the allocation of revenue. Many of the proprietary hospital systems are arranged in this way.

Diversification can also be viewed in terms of vertical or horizontal integration. Vertical integration (Fig. 17.5) looks at providing all of the services a consumer of health care might need. Diversification of the hospital inpatient product thus logically moves to wellness and health promotion services, ambulatory illness-based care such as PPO and HMO development, and ambulatory support services, such as pharmacies, laboratories, physical therapy, outpatient surgical services, nonacute care inpatient beds, long-term care facilities, and home health agencies. Services are usually available on one campus with satellite sites. Vertical integration models also look to providing non-health related services, such as real estate transactions. The horizontal model of diversification (Fig. 17.6) looks at the totality of service needed to provide inpatient care and avoid the middle man.

242 ECONOMIC AND FUTURE PERSPECTIVES

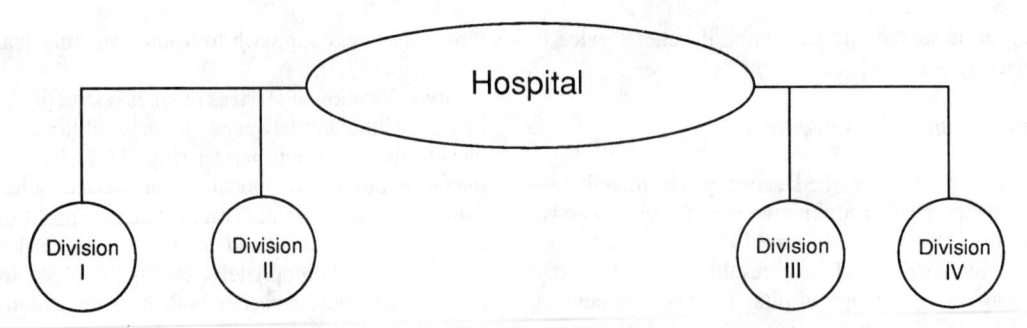

Figure 17.2. Traditional hospital corporate model.

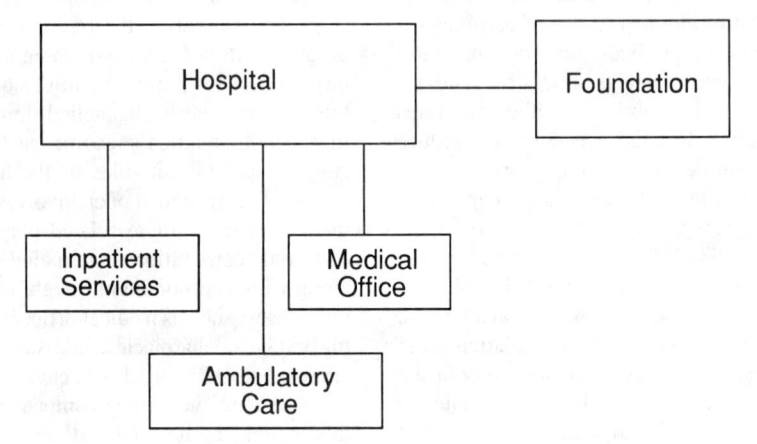

Figure 17.3. Traditional model with foundation.

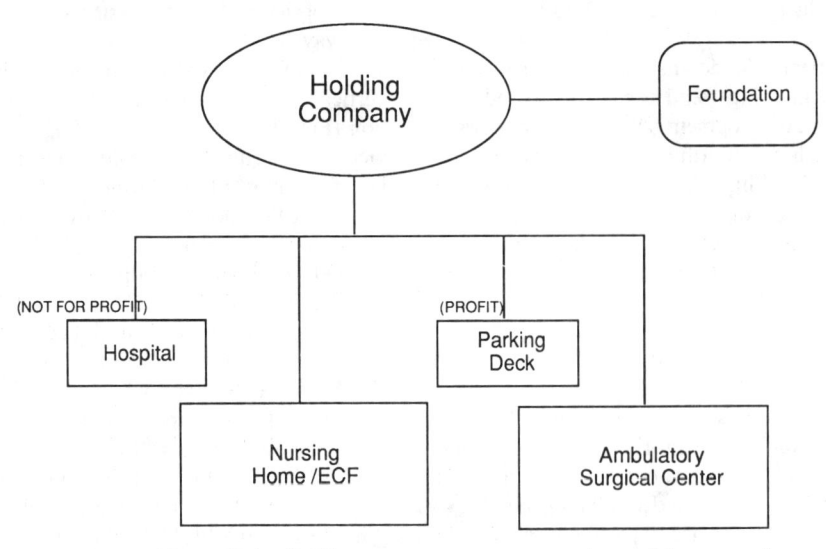

Figure 17.4. Holding company—parent corporation model.

Figure 17.5. Vertical integration.

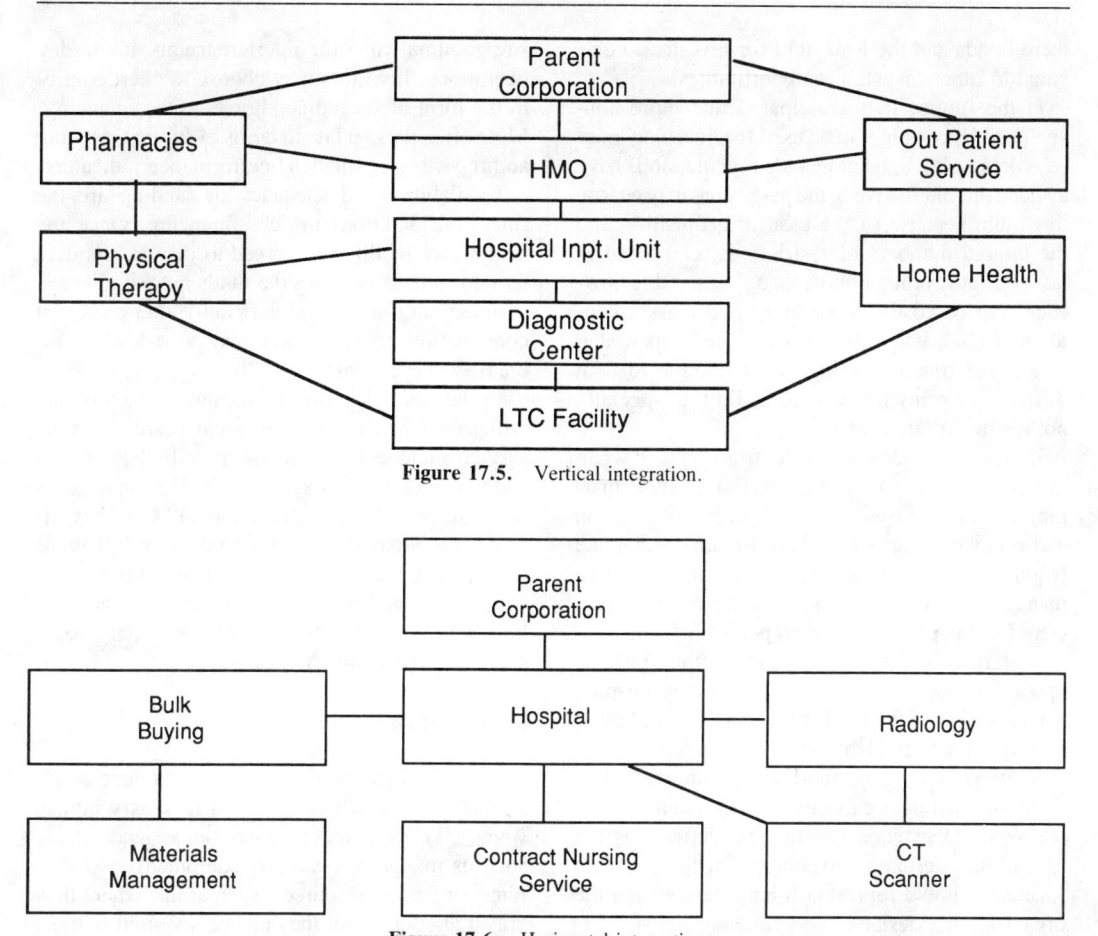

Figure 17.6. Horizontal integration.

The hospital may develop its own laundry services, materials management program, radiology services, and so on. Attempts by hospitals to acquire high-technology CT scanners and magnetic resonance imaging units are examples of horizontal integration.

Decisions about diversification are institutional and depend upon a variety of factors, such as available revenue for investment, basic hospital structure (proprietary or not-for-profit), characteristics of the community, and gaps in existing services. Decisions to diversify and the methods of diversification should be approached using the market analysis techniques previously described.

In the case scenario presented earlier, expansion of services in cardiothoracic surgery would be considered a horizontal integration of diversified services. Hospital Y is attempting to increase its share of the market by offering additional services. The question of whether these services are necessary or appropriate remains to be answered.

Debt Management

In the past hospitals have depended upon philanthropy, government grants, and long-term tax-exempt bonds for capital financing of physical construction, plant renovation, and major equipment. Philanthropy has now declined to the point that only about 3.9% of all financing for hospital construction is obtained from donations and gifts (31). Government grants represent less than 12% of all funds for hospital construction, with most of this reserved for underserved areas (32). Long-term tax-exempt bonds have funded more than 55% of hospital construction costs. However, there are concerns about the continued tax-exempt status of these bonds and the low yield for investors, compared to other investment opportunities.

In the future, it is anticipated that more conventional borrowing will be used for financing long-term debt. Although health care organizations have avoided this alternative in the past, more may choose this route because of the ease of acquisition and the limited numbers of restrictions, compared to tax-exempt revenue bonds. Long-term debt, however, can be costly depending upon market conditions. High bad debt rates and uncompensated care make funding of high cost, long-term debt difficult for many health care facilities, especially not-for-profit facilities.

Restricted funds, set aside from an excess in operating revenue over expenses (operating margin), can also be used to finance capital expansion and renovation projects. This funding technique requires sound financial planning and effective management to ensure an operating margin sufficient for this purpose. Fifteen percent of construction started in 1981 was funded from internal operations and, as of 1984, the average hospital had only 37% of the funds for replacement of plant and equipment available in investments.

Regardless of debt funding technique, a formally defined debt capacity ceiling should be established. Debt capacity may be defined as the ratio of long-term debt to equity. The limit on debt financing should represent a balance between the organization's desire to prevent financial risk exposure and the investment needs generated by the strategic plan (32).

Factors Affecting Debt Financing

The most important cost of debt financing is interest rate. Other factors that influence the cost of debt financing are issuance costs necessary to initiate the financing, including attorney and accountant fees, costs of the investment banking firm arranging the securities sale in public offerings, and reserve requirements in the form of debt service reserves and depreciation reserves. Reserves represent the funds that the institution must have available in cash or investments to protect the lender's interests.

Several factors other than cost affect institutional debt financing decisions. Degree of autonomy of decision making by the health care agency is a critical element. While investors desire low-risk investments, most institutional borrowers desire minimal investor interference in day-to-day operations. Investors may choose to exert control in the form of special conditions to the financing. Most often these relate to terms of future financing and reporting of financial performance indicators.

Availability and adequacy of funding are the final considerations in debt financing. Once the health care facility has agreed to increase its debt burden, it usually wants the funds quickly. Delays in obtaining funds can significantly alter projected construction costs. Delays may also lead to increased interest costs.

In the case scenario of Hospital Y, factors that will need to be considered to begin a cardiothoracic service include those things identified in the financial phase of a market analysis. How much debt does Hospital Y currently maintain? Can they afford capital expenditures for renovations? If funds are needed for the program, should tax-exempt bonds be issued or should conventional financing be undertaken? Are there grants or philanthropic sources of financing available?

Resource Utilization

Resources are the things used to produce goods and services which can be used to satisfy human wants (33). Resources may have an assigned value, such as manpower, money, equipment, and supplies, or be free resources, such as air, where they are so abundant that they can be acquired without regard for cost. All resources, however, can be used for a variety of competing purposes. Public immunization programs are an example of public goods while the same immunizations, administered by private physicians are private goods, or use of resources for private purposes.

The goal of the economic system is to allocate resources among competing demands to produce the optimal level and composition of output. In order to meet this goal, the level and composition of output must be determined, a method of distribution must be developed and provisions must be made to meet projected growth in demand for goods and services (34).

Resource utilization is concerned with effective and efficient use of scarce resources. Effectiveness is concerned with achievement of goals, regardless of cost, and represents the quality of output achieved. Outcome standards are one method of determining effectiveness. Efficiency is concerned with achieving the lowest possible production cost per unit of output. For the health care industry, efficiency is determined as a cost per patient day, cost per discharge, or some other cost per unit of service. Efficiency studies focus on costs rather than on quality.

Managers are increasing their use of efficiency measures. In most cases, efficiency is measured by comparison with some preset standard. Unfortunately, not all standards can be applied universally. This may be related to lack of comparability of output or cost measures or lack of relevancy of certain cost concepts (32). For example, the cost per patient day in a small critical care unit may be very different from the cost per patient day in one critical care unit from a large teaching institution with several specialized critical care units. In another case, where certificate of need (CON) health planning regulation is used to determine which facility can expand services, cost may be a factor; however, the ultimate decision will probably be based on cost, quality of services, need, market analysis, and public relations efforts.

A nursing productivity model may provide a method of evaluating efficiency. Nursing productivity is defined as the efficient use of resources to accomplish certain defined and desired patient outcomes (34). However, a major concern with the use of a nursing productivity model is that they are often insensitive to the difference in time required to perform a task and time needed to measure knowledge of the client and provide appropriate education.

Effectiveness is concerned with the relationship between output and achievement of goals. A typical health care facility's goals include delivery of quality care along with financial solvency (32). Measuring effectiveness is more difficult than measuring efficiency because it is often difficult to quantify the relationship between output and goals. Outputs usually relate to more than one institutional goal. In the case scenario, maintaining solvency and reasonable costs are both institutional objectives. Developing a cardiothoracic surgery program may affect solvency negatively, yet, the increase in volume of critical care patient days may reduce the overall cost per patient day.

In order to balance the needs for both cost control and quality of services, the critical care nurse manager must evaluate the relationship of quality of care and cost to outcomes for patients. As a prerequisite to this endeavor, it is necessary to clearly establish desirable patient outcomes along with structure and process standards. Work by the American Association of Critical-Care Nurses has provided outcome standards for critical care nursing practice (35). These standards were established through the use of a consensus conference. While research validation remains to be accomplished, these standards provide a framework for evaluation of efficient and effective resource utilization by the critical care nurse manager.

Competition

In a market economy, competition is expected to have desirable effects on the price of goods and services. This occurs because firms seek to minimize production costs in order to effectively compete with other firms in pricing goods and services. Price becomes a function of the competition's price rather than a function of cost. While competition may occur on other levels, price competition is most important (36). If a health care organization cannot meet the competition's prices or achieve a break-even point, should the organization offer that service?

Two of the most sought after features of competitive markets, competition to reduce price and budget constraints that control spending, are noticeably absent or significantly diminished in health care markets (37). The uncertainty and risk of certain health care problems prompt patients and physicians to demand extra precautions in diagnosis and treatment. Furthermore, the availability of insurance makes physicians, providers, and consumers much less sensitive to price. Therefore, increases in price of health care services rarely alter demand, and competition rarely forces providers to reduce prices.

Competition in the health care delivery system began in the mid 1960s as the result of introduction of Medicare and Medicaid. These social programs removed the incentives for the elderly and poor to be concerned with the cost of health care services. Additionally, rapid growth of health care insurance coverage removed concerns about hospital costs for those with private insurance. Availability of adequate levels of external sources of reimbursement allowed competition to develop among hospitals without the usual constraints of price and budget (36).

Research results suggest that both proprietary and not-for-profit hospitals in competitive markets had higher costs under cost-based reimbursement than in markets dominated by only one or two hospitals (38). The higher costs were attributable to competition for physicians. Hospitals competed for physicians by providing additional facilities, the newest technology, and increased staffing. Health care insurers, such as Blue Cross and Blue Shield, either lacked sufficient market power to require hospitals and physicians to limit their costs, or did not use the market power they possessed.

In critical care several factors have influenced competition. First, physicians often choose hospital affiliation based upon the scope of services available at a particular facility. In order to capture an adequate share of the market, hospitals increase services, provide additional staff, and acquire the latest technology. Second, the complexity of health care delivery in our litigious society has created concern about the legal duty to have all available resources. Case law precedent suggests that a hospital will be held to a duty to have all available resources for the care of its patients unless it informs them, in advance, of any limitations (20, 39–40). This duty to have all available resources may be one of the considerations in the development of critical care units in small rural hospitals. And third, changes in reimbursement have forced hospitals to seek increasing shares of the most profitable patients. While ICU patients are not necessarily profitable in large teaching institutions or when there is a large percentage of uncompensated care, less resource intense ICU patients can be highly profitable for an institution.

Competition also may affect the quality of services provided by a health care facility. There is a frequency of care delivered that must be maintained to ensure competence. When hospitals compete for patients, frequency of service delivery may be inadequate. Critics of competition often cite the example of open heart surgery, where in 1989, 23% of hospitals with facilities for open heart surgery performed less than one per month, and 71% performed less than one per week (41).

In today's health care environment, competition has taken on new dimensions. No longer are hospitals merely competing for physicians; they are now competing for all of the resources necessary to deliver health care, and for patients to consume the services provided. Hospitals that fail to offer a full range of specialty services have difficulty both in competition for patients and affiliations with medical education programs. Salary issues and an inadequate supply of professional nurses, particularly in critical care, have created significant competition for manpower (42). External pressures to reduce the cost of health care, the increase of prepared health plans, and utilization review have contributed to competition for patients. The incentive to providers to offer lower priced services comes from increased volume of patients. Since cost per case can be lowered by increasing volume, the increased volume may improve or maintain profit margin.

In the case scenario, Hospital Y has provided ICU-CCU services in a combined unit. Specialized ICU patient needs have been referred to a major university teaching center. Operating a cardiovascular ICU may change the patient mix by increasing the numbers of longer stay and more critically ill patients. Such a decision may also increase the numbers of full-paying patients using the hospital facilities. A particular consideration in reaching this decision should be the frequency with which the CABG procedure will be performed at Hospital Y. Often in competitive markets, volume at each competing facility is reduced. Since there is a minimum volume necessary to maintain skill and training, volume projections may play a large role in the decision to expand services.

The teaching hospital may feel the effects of competition by "skimming" of less resource intense patients to Hospital Y. The net effect will be costlier treatment at the teaching hospital due to higher acuity within the subgroup of CABG patients and a potential increase in the uncompensated care delivered.

Regionalization and Regulation

The National Health Planning and Resources Development Act (NHPRDA) of 1974 was enacted in order to slow the rapidly escalating costs of health care through the prevention of unnecessary duplication of health care resources (43). In keeping with that legislation, certificate of need (CON) legislation was adopted in all states except Louisiana by 1979, and was included as part of the 1979 Amendments to NHPRDA (44). The purpose of CON was to control the proliferation of health care facilities.

Despite the decline in federal health planning interest, many states continue to use CON to control development of new health care facilities and the development of resource intense services. While there is wide variation in threshold levels by state, some combination of capital expenditure, addition of new health services and beds, and acquisition of new equipment is subjected to review. Programs, such as trauma, cardiothoracic surgery, neonatal intensive care, and transplantation come under CON regulation in many states (18).

Recognition of high cost of delivery of specialized services and limited demand for those services has led to development of regionalized models of care. The concept behind regionalization of services is to make high cost services readily available while limiting the number of facilities providing the services. The purpose is to assure cost effective quality outcomes based on adequate volume of service delivery. For example, it has been estimated that the start-up costs for a tertiary neonatal ICU exceed $1 million dollars for renovation or construction of space and equipment. Personnel may cost $45,000 dollars or more per bed per year. If the unit generates only a 20–30% occupancy rate, the operating loss will have to be passed on to other hospitalized patients. Low volume may also lead to lack of experience in certain types of care and increased patient risk.

Regionalization provides a method to assure appropriate allocation of scarce resources. However, regionalized approaches to health care delivery are often diametrically opposed to the competitive market, where supply and demand drive development of programs.

One of the issues of current concern in regionalized systems of care is the effect of capitated payment programs and contractual arrangements with inpatient facilities on traditional regional geographical boundaries. Contract arrangements between HMOs and hospitals do not respect traditional referral patterns, but rather, look to secure services at the lowest possible cost. Since the goal of rate control methods has been to limit cost, HMOs, PPOs, and insurers seek to contract with low cost providers. There is fear that institutions offering regionalized and more expensive services will lose their "normal" low cost patients to facilities that can provide care more inexpensively. This cost shifting to less resource intense patients has been a concern of insurers. The net result of eliminating cost shifting would be greater increases in the cost of those already costly services.

In the example, if Hospital Y skims the less resource intense CABG patients, the university medical center will need to demand even higher prices for the cost of its care. Allowing the medical center to maintain a reasonable patient mix can promote more reasonable costs for all patients.

SUMMARY

This chapter has presented information on economic influences in health care delivery. Nurse managers must be familiar with both unit based financial considerations and those factors that effect the overall position of the institution within the health care system. The key concepts explored include:

1. Supply and demand for health care services;
2. Impact of oversupply of services;
3. Market analysis;
4. Organizational financial positioning;
5. Debt management;
6. Efficiency and effectiveness in resource utilization;
7. Competition;
8. Regionalization.

Analysis of a case scenario is integrated throughout the chapter to facilitate the application of content to practice situations.

REFERENCES

1. Munoz E, Birnbaum E, Chalfin D, Mulloy K, Goldstein J, Wise L. The identifier concept: clinical parameters to stratify hospital patient costs for patients with hypertension. Heart & Lung 1988;17:550–554.
2. Rating America's best hospitals. U.S. News and World Report April 30, 1990;108:52.
3. Porter-O'Grady T. Take note. Aspen's Advisor for Nurse Executives 1990;5(5):1.
4. Higgins T. The woeful state of U.S. children's health. Healthweek June 25, 1990;4(12):17.
5. Sussman D, Wann, M. Controlling Medicaid costs a lingering concern in states. Healthweek 1990;4(9):1.
6. Hicks L, Boles K. Why health economics? In: Contemporary leadership behavior. 3rd ed. Glenview, IL: Scott Foresman 1990:425–432.
7. Feldstein P. Health care economics. 3rd ed. Albany: Delmar Publishers, Inc., 1988:80–82.
8. Raffel M, Raffel N. The U.S. health system: origins and functions. 3rd ed. Albany, NY: Delmar Publishers, Inc. 1990:221–322.
9. Grace H. Can health care costs be contained. Nursing & Health Care 1990;11(3):125–130.
10. Schulz R, Johnson A. Management of hospitals and health services. 3rd ed. St. Louis: C.V. Mosby Company, 1990:33–54.
11. Newhouse JP, et al. Some interim results from a con-

trolled trial of cost sharing in health insurance. New England Journal of Medicine 1981;305(25):1501.
12. Ernst & Young. OBRA 89: New reductions, regulations, and challenges. Ernst & Young, 1990:22–34.
13. AACN. Summary analysis of critical care nurse supply and requirements. Newport Beach, CA: AACN, 1988:1–8.
14. Aiken L, Mullinex C. The nurse shortage. The New England Journal of Medicine 1987;317(10):641–645.
15. Hartley S, Huey F. What keeps nurses in nursing? American Journal of Nursing 1988;88(2):181–188.
16. Penny M. Recruitment and retention of nurses in critical care. Nursing Management 1988;19(2):72R,72T,72V.
17. Jolma D. Relationship between nursing work load and turnover. Nursing Economics 1990;8(2):110–114.
18. Simpson R, Waite R. NCNIP's system of the future: a call for accountability, revenue control, and national data sets. N Admin Q 1989;14(1):72–77.
19. Roberts M, Minnick A, Ginzberg E, Curran C. What to do about the nursing shortage. New York: Commonwealth Fund, 1989.
20. Samson L. Predicting the marginal cost of direct nursing care for newborns. Ann Arbor: UMI, 1990:1–196.
21. Jones K. Feasibility analysis of preferred provider organizations. J Nsg Admin 1990;20(1):28–33.
22. Drew J. Health maintenance organizations: history, evolution and survival. Nursing & Health Care 1990;11(3):145–149.
23. Tibbitts S, Manzano A. PPOs: preferred provider organizations—an executive guide. New York: Pluribus Press, 1984.
24. Mullen P. Humana to buy leading Kansas City HMO. Healthweek 1990;4(12):5.
25. Kotler P, Carke R. Marketing for health care organizations. Englewood Cliffs, NJ: Prentice Hall, 1987.
26. American Hospital Association. AHA study reports changes, trends in 1980's. Reflections 1990;16(2):3.
27. Pauly M, Wilson P. Hospital output forecasts and the cost of empty hospital beds. Economic and Health Systems Research 1985;21(2):86–102.
28. Ehrat K. Neomodern health care: survival of the fittest. J Nsg Admin 1990;20(5):9–10.
29. Baptist A, Lameka R. Strategies for boosting outpatient care profitability. Healthcare Financial Management 1990;44(2):21–28.
30. Ives J, Kerfoot K. Pitfalls and promises of diversification. Nursing Economics 1989;7(4):200–203.
31. Garner J, Smith H, Piland N. Strategic nursing management. Rockville, MD: Aspen Publishers, Inc., 1990:95–118.
32. Cleverley W. Essentials of health care finance. 2nd ed. Rockville, MD: Aspen Publications, Inc., 1986:155–191, 371–408.
33. Mansfield E. Microeconomics: theory and application. 5th ed. New York: W. W. Norton & Co., 1985:5–17.
34. Hinshaw AS. Programs of nursing research for nursing administration. In: Henry B, Arndt C, Di Vincenti M, Mariner-Tomey A. Dimensions of nursing administration. Boston: Blackwell Scientific Publications 1989:251–266.
35. American Association of Critical-Care Nurses. Outcome standards for nursing care of the critically ill. Newport Beach, CA: AACN, 1990.
36. Feldstein P, pp. 245–248.
37. Altman S, Rodwin M. Halfway competitive markets and ineffective regulation: the American health care system. Journal of Health Politics, Policy and Law 1988;13(2):323–333.
38. Watt J. The comparative economic performance of investor owned chains and not-for-profit hospitals. New England Journal of Medicine 1986;314(2).
39. Garcia v. Memorial Hospital, 557 S.W. 2d 859 (Tex. 1977).
40. Perkes L. Medical malpractice-ostensible agency and corporate negligence. St. Mary's Law Journal, 1986;17:551.
41. Rand Corporation. 1989
42. Robinson J. Hospital competition and hospital nursing. Nursing Economics 1988;6(3):116–119.
43. Schneider W, Wing D. The National Health Planning and Resources Development Act of 1974. Clearinghouse Review, 1976;9:684.
44. Schonbrun L. Making certificate of need work. N Car L Rev, 1979;57:1259–1315.

Chapter 18

Hospital Organization

SUZETTE CARDIN

The critical care nurse manager in today's health care environment has to manage resources efficiently and effectively. To achieve this goal it is imperative that critical care nurse managers possess an overall organizational perspective. Awareness of the mission and goals of the organization that are a part of the strategic plan need to be incorporated into the nurse manager's financial management plan for the unit.

In most health care organizations, nurses are the largest group of providers. Nurse managers are at department head rank in most settings. Successful implementation of the role requires that the nurse manager incorporate the values of the organization and become a part of the organizational culture. The term organizational culture refers to a shared system of beliefs, values, and norms about the way the organization functions or the way things are done (1). Today's nurse manager is faced with the challenge of exploring the cultural characteristics of the organization and developing strategies and actions that will best match the current culture with the mission and environmental demands.

This chapter will examine aspects of the hospital's organization, structure, and the influence of the organization on the role of the critical care nurse manager. Analysis will include: the mission statement of the organization, structure and governance, rural and urban hospital settings, future predictions, and the role of the critical care nurse manager in the financial operation of the unit within a given organizational structure.

MISSION STATEMENT

Hospitals in the U.S. exist for the purpose of providing health care and most have a mission statement. The mission statement reflects the values, purposes, benefits, and priorities the hospital plans to contribute to a community. It shares beliefs and values and often mentions the scope of services offered. Developing a mission statement is complex, political, and requires planning and coordination with the governing body, medical staff, and administrative team. A clear mission statement facilitates planning, marketing, development of services, and public relations of the hospital. Some mission statements also identify the beliefs about the employees.

Historically, the mission statement incorporated three areas: (*a*) patient care, (*b*) teaching, and (*c*) research. The focus has changed, however, in light of the current prospective reimbursement system and the way in which hospitals have organized into for-profit institutions or multihospital systems. Table 18.1 shows examples of the mission of hospitals in a condensed form.

Today the mission statement identifies three aspects:

1. Community approach;
2. Services provided;
3. Financing (2).

Community approach refers to what group(s) are to be served by the organization and the depth of the involvement. The governing body usually establishes the domain under a charter which may limit the organization to providing only health care and related activities. The governing body must operate within the limits of state regulations. The term "services provided" refers to the scope and amount of care provided by the hospital. Services for a hospital include: acute and/or chronic inpatient care for adults and children; adult and/or pediatric outpatient care; alcohol and chemical dependency; behavioral medicine; education; home care; pre-hospital services; skilled nursing facilities; prevention programs; outreach programs; and residential care. Financing includes the willingness

Table 18.1. Common Distinctions between For-profit and Not-for-profit Organizations[a]

For-profit	Not-for-profit
Corporations owned by investors	Corporations without owners or owned by "members"
Can distribute some proportion of profits (net revenues less expenses) to owners	Cannot distribute surplus (net revenues less expenses) to those who control the organization
Pay property, sales, income taxes	Generally exempt from taxes
Sources of capital include a. Equity capital from investors b. Debt c. Retained earnings (including depreciation and deferred taxes) d. Return-on-equity payments from third-party payors (e.g., Medicare)	Sources of capital include a. Charitable contributions b. Debt c. Retained earnings (including depreciation) d. Government grants
Management ultimately accountable to stockholders	Management accountable to voluntary, often self-perpetuating boards
Purpose: Has legal obligation to enhance the wealth of shareholders within the boundaries of law; does so by providing services	*Purpose*: Has legal obligation to fulfill a stated mission (provide services, teaching, research, etc.); must maintain economic viability to do so
Revenues derived from sale of services	Revenues derived from sale of services and from charitable contributions
Mission: Usually stated in terms of growth, efficiency, and quality	*Mission*: Often stated in terms of charity, quality, and community service, but also may pursue growth
Mission and structure can result in more streamlined decision making and implementation of major decisions	Mission and diverse constituencies often complicate decision making and implementation

[a]Used with permission from McNerney WJ, et al. For profit enterprise in health care. Washington, DC: National Academy Press, 1986.

to provide charity care, the type of pricing the organization follows (e.g., competitive, lowest, market driven, or overpricing); and may specify the type of debt financing that will be used.

The need for all hospitals to generate profit on an ongoing basis is now an integral part of the mission statement in many hospitals across the country. The UCLA Medical Center mission statement is an example of a traditional mission statement from a large university medical center (Fig. 18.1).

The critical care nurse manager needs to carefully examine the corporate, organizational mission statement and value system. The statement provides clues to the culture of the organization. In looking at the mission statement, the nurse manager can identify the organization's objectives and priorities and check if there is congruence with one's own value system. This is crucial in the day-to-day existence of a nurse manager. If one believes that patient care is the highest priority, yet the organization is committed to education and research as the top priorities, how does the nurse manager function when there may be a conflict with the organization's mission? This is apparent in academic centers where medical education takes place at all levels. It is common for a critical care nurse manager to spend time and energy handling the issues and concerns that relate to the clinical nurse's concern for quality patient care when the

---

The mission of the UCLA Medical Center is to develop and maintain an environment in which the educational and scientific programs of the schools of the UCLA Center for the Health Sciences are integrated with exemplary patient care.

The conduct of the daily operations and the implementation of the long-term plans of the medical center reflect the mission. Continued success in achieving the mission's objectives will depend on the active partnership of the medical center's administration, staff, and medical staff and their commitment to excellence.

Figure 18.1. Mission of the UCLA Medical Center. (Used with permission from the UCLA Medical Center, Los Angeles, California.)

need of the organization is for education and research. In settings where there is conflict it is inherent in the role of the nurse manager to act as the patient's advocate and assist staff in balancing the institution's priorities with the patient's needs.

TYPES OF HOSPITALS

Hospitals in the U.S. are divided into two major groups, not-for-profit and for-profit. They are further subdivided by two major types of ownership, public and private. Not-for-profit hospitals include both public and private institutions. Public hospitals are supported by tax dollars appropriated by federal, state, or local governments. Private not-for-profit hospitals are usually owned by corporations or groups. These hospitals are established for the common good rather than for individual gain and are granted broad federal, state, and local tax exemptions.

For-profit hospitals are owned by private corporations or groups. They can declare dividends and distribute profits to individuals (2). Table 18.1 lists the common distinctions between for-profit and not-for-profit organizations.

An understanding of the breakdown of hospital organizations is essential for every nurse manager. The particular setting that the critical care nurse manager will function in is of significance to the successful implementation of the role. Table 18.2 outlines the five most common types of hospital organizations found in the U.S. Each has a different implication for the nurse manager, based on the mission of the organization and the financial structure.

The Community Hospital

The purpose of the community hospital is to provide personal health care in a manner that uses available resources most effectively for the community's benefit (2). Table 18.3 outlines the historical motivation for community hospitals.

The community hospital was the logical setting for the American Association of Critical-Care Nurses (AACN) demonstration project, since the typical intensive care unit (ICU) setting in the U.S. is similar to this setting. The findings which support high quality care, high nurse satisfaction, and exceptionally low nurse turnover—all at a minimal cost—have tremendous implications for the critical care nurse manager of the 1990s (3).

Private Corporations (Publicly Traded)

The community hospital located in a rural or urban setting may be an investor-owned corporation. It has only been in the last 20 years that investor-owned, for-profit organizations have appeared in the health care arena (4). For the critical care nurse manager the implications can vary. The positive benefits of the model are: (a) it provides new impetus of innovation; (b) it is more responsive to the needs and desires of patients and physicians; (c) approaches to management are financially sounder and more business oriented; and (d) it provides an important source of new capital for health services (4). There are, however, arguments against the model that have value as well. The three arguments are: (a) it is incongruent to the traditional mission and values of health care institutions; (b) it is a threat to the autonomy and

Table 18.2. Examples of the Mission of a Hospital

Type of Hospital	Mission	Type of Care Provided
Community	Health care	Community based: general medical-surgical, obstetrics, pediatrics
Investor-owned corporation	Profit Health care	General care, community health, ambulatory care, surgery
University medical center	Education Research Health care	Tertiary and research based care
Urban public	Health care for indigent	All types of health services
Government		

Military
  Public Health
  Veterans
	Combat readiness
	Research
	Health care
	Education
		Variety of health services, specific to population and facility

Table 18.3. Historical Motivation for Community Hospitals[a]

Motivation	Rationale
1. To be a good samaritan, and government support of the poor	1. Desire to aid the sick and needy because the aid itself has value or intrinsic merit
2. Personal health	2. Desire to improve one's health; ability to deal effectively with disease, disability, or death
3. Public health	3. Desire for health to be a social benefit, to reduce contagion and to assume a healthy workforce
4. Environmental health care	4. Desire to control cost of health care so health care is available to all
5. Economic gain for the community	5. Desire to make the community as a whole more economically successful

[a]Adapted from Griffith JR. The well managed community hospital. Ann Arbor, MI: Health Administration Press, 1987:39–40.

ideals of the medical profession; and (c) it does not provide medical care to people who cannot pay (4).

The Committee on Implications of For-Profit Enterprise in Health Care in 1986 investigated the quality of care issue as it relates to for-profit organizations. Limited data were available, and much were based on either successful accreditation of the hospital, qualifications of the medical staff, nursing personnel per census, and two surveys done by the American Medical Association (AMA) and American Hospital Association (AHA). The evidence that was available in 1986 did not support the fear that for-profit health care is incompatible with quality of care, not the belief that investor ownership might provide some assurance of quality (4).

University Medical Centers

The majority of university medical centers are located in large urban areas or on the campus of the university. The priorities in university medical centers are research, physician training, and patient care (5). Critical care units in these institutions are usually very specialized, have a different patient mix, and require different levels of expertise and care. At times, based on the priorities of the institution, the critical care nurse manager can be confronted with many different issues. Issues to be considered in light of financial constraints are listed in Table 18.4.

In our society the mission of the teaching hospital is becoming increasingly complex. Present day characteristics of teaching hospitals include:

1. Marked increase in the number of health profession students;
2. Doubling in the number of house officers;
3. Quadrupling of full-time medical faculty;
4. Marked increase in biomedical research and research training opportunities;
5. Mission changes from an emphasis on specialty training to a focus on primary care;
6. Centers for continuing medical education;
7. Expensive to maintain and the costs continue to escalate secondary to the training involved;
8. Research is essential; however, it is not a money making program;
9. Expected to provide state-of-the-art technology;
10. Need to provide services for the community (6).

Many teaching hospitals are now facing increasingly threatening and unstable environments. Challenges such as increased pressure to accept indigent patients and decreased financial support for medical education are among the major threats to university-owned or academic health centers (7). Table 18.5 provides a summary of university medical centers and some responses that have been formulated to help these centers survive the current competitive environment. Chapter 17 also provides insight into the current financial situation and

Table 18.4. Financial Constraint Issues in a University Medical Center

1. Does every patient have equal access to care regardless of the patient's ability to pay?
2. Who gets the transplant organ?
3. Do expensive tests continue to be ordered in spite of a limited prognosis?
4. Which patients receive first priority for admission when the critical care unit beds are full?
5. Does the do-not-resuscitate patient require unlimited resources?

Table 18.5. Summary of University Medical Centers in Response to Changes in Health Care Environment[a]

Strategy	Example	Potential Benefits	Extent of Use by UHs	Impact on Patient Care, Teaching, and Research
Diversification	UH hotels for patients, families	Added source of revenue; spread financial risk; cross-subsidize financial "losers"	Low-moderate	More emphasis on outpatient care with uncertain implications for teaching role; research from other industries shows mixed results for financial benefits
Vertical integration	UH-sponsored HMO, PPO	Attract/maintain referrals for inpatient admission; increase control over financing for care	Low-moderate	More emphasis on outpatient care; early research on community hospitals is encouraging
Horizontal integration	University hospital consortium	Economies of scale; manage competition with other providers	Moderate	Depends on specific initiatives developed by alliance members; now very popular in business and industry
Joint venture	UH-medical school joint ownership of diagnostic center and equipment	Vehicle to raise capital and minimize financial risk to partners; can be for-profit firm	Low-moderate	Research shows there are many ways that joint ventures can fail to meet partners' expectations; no research yet on joint ventures by UHs
Marketing	Television commercials; newspaper ads	Attract/maintain referrals and patients for inpatient and outpatient care; complement use of other strategies	High	Difficult to assess, but should only affect patient care and mix of patients
Political action	Lobbying for/against legislation in Washington	Prevent/encourage legislation that affects all major areas of UH performance	Moderate-high	Seems to have had high impact considering potential legislation that could influence all aspects of UH performance
Improve internal efficiency	Systems to monitor and reduce use of resources (e.g., personnel, equipment, drugs)	Cut costs to meet demands from purchasers and from competitors	High	Relatively high potential for adverse effects on number of indigents served; on quality/quantity of contribution to teaching and research

[a]Used with permission from Zuckerman HS. The strategies and autonomy of university teaching hospitals in competitive environments. Health and Services Administration 1990;35:110:111.

strategies that have been developed to cope with the current changes in the financial reimbursement structure.

Public Hospitals

Urban public hospitals provide most of the care for uninsured patients. Although they serve Americans at all income levels, caring for the uninsured and the indigent is the fundamental mission of the urban public hospital (8). These hospitals, interestingly enough, are only a small minority of nonfederal public hospitals in the U.S. In 1985, 60 urban public hospitals remained open. These hospitals were all large, with an average of about 500 beds, and were also major teaching institutions (8).

In public hospitals nurses are able to achieve a high degree of autonomy since collaboration is crucial for existence. Examples of collaboration are seen in the admission and discharge of patients, in the development and implementation of clinical protocols, and in the orientation of physicians to the unit. Quite frequently it is the nurse manager who is perceived as the "authority" in the unit.

Federal Hospitals

The federal health care system encompasses extensive and diverse services provided in both military and civilian facilities. Organizationally there are three distinct delivery systems and each falls under separate cabinet level departments in the federal government. Military health care is administered by the Department of Defense (DOD), public health programs are under the Department of Health and Human Services (DHHS), and veteran health care is provided by the Veterans Services Health and Research Administration (VSHRA) under the Department of Veterans Affairs. Combined these systems employ over 75,000 registered nurses (RNs) in over 400 hospitals and numerous outpatient departments, clinics, health stations, nursing homes, and home care agencies (9).

The centralized bureaucratic structure common to the federal health care system is often cited as the differentiating factor between public and private delivery models. However, many private hospitals are also structured along bureaucratic lines. The distinguishing difference from a financial perspective is that federal agencies are subject to policies and budget ceilings established annually by Congress. Funds appropriated to each department by Congress are then allocated to programs within the department. What dollar portion is allocated to individual hospitals, clinics, or services is of increasing concern to nurse managers. The federal deficit and pressures to control health care costs are national problems that affect both public and private health care providers.

In the federal sector each of the three systems is unique in terms of mission and population served. The military mission is to support forces in conflict (9). This entails a system that is ready to provide medical services in the event of combat. A system of active and reserve personnel meets this need. In peacetime the military operates over 500 facilities around the world including 168 hospitals that provide services to a beneficiary population (active military and retirees, including dependents, and dependents of deceased military personnel) of 9.3 million (9).

The DHHS mission is to "protect and advance the nation's physical and mental health; support and conduct medical, biomedical and health services research; support the development of health services and resources; prevent and control disease and substance abuse; and assure the safety of drugs, foods, cosmetics, medical devices, and radiation producing devices" (9). The mission is accomplished through agencies with responsibility for specific programs. Nurses in the Public Health Service (PHS) are classified as civil service or commissioned corps. The largest service is Indian Health Service (IHS). This program serves American Indians and Alaskan natives with 45 hospitals, six tribal hospitals, and numerous clinics and centers. Another major focus of DHHS is research. The National Institutes of Health (NIH), a 540-bed reseach hospital, has been designed through mission and resources to meet the public health needs of Americans. Other components of the PHS include acquired immune deficiency syndrome (AIDS) and organ transplantation programs, Centers for Disease Control (CDC), primary health care to underserved and migrant populations, services to patients with Hansen's disease, and services to federal prisoners, immigrants, and many others.

The mission of the Veterans Services Health and Research Administration is to provide care to veterans, administer education and training programs, conduct research, and support the DOD in the event of war or a national emergency. The VSHRA health care delivery system is extensive and varied, employing about 36,000 RNs in 172 medical centers, over 200 clinics, more than 100 nursing homes, and 17 domiciliaries (9). Nursing is career oriented in the federal system and offers clinical, education, administrative, and research tracts. Federal institutions offer unique opportunities to nurses through training and education, and research programs. Many medical centers are affiliated with universities and several employ nurse researchers with doctorates to promote the conduct and utilization of nursing research in the clinical setting. Geographic mobility is an advantage of VSHRA as nurses can transfer from one facility to another without loss of leave, retirement, and other benefits. Critical care units in tertiary care medical centers are similar to university medical centers and many of the characteristics listed previously for teaching hospitals apply to these units as well. Smaller veterans hospitals provide critical care services similar to community and rural hospitals and often refer patients to tertiary care facilities in the system. Nurses enjoy professional autonomy and interaction with physicians who are also employees of the hospital; this interaction promotes collaboration and collegiality.

Nurse managers in VSHRA are challenged with the same issues confronting health care in the private sector: cost constraints, nurse pay and compensation, the nursing shortage, an aging population, and higher acuity patients. Trends are toward more financial accountability for nurse managers, piloting creative programs for recruitment and retention, and exploring alternative delivery systems. Networking within the federal system offers opportunities to share innovations, successes, and failures. Coupled with the research resources available to VSHRA nurses, the system bears watching for creative solutions in the future.

Multihospital Systems

The structure of health care organizations is an ever-changing one. Multihospital systems are expanding rapidly. In 1986 approximately 40% of hospitals belonged to a multiinstitutional system, and by 1990 this figure is projected to be 60% (1). System consolidation has taken place along six levels. Table 18.6 outlines the various levels that are currently being implemented or are in place throughout the country.

In this structure the critical care nurse manager may find that profit is a high priority for the particular institution or it could be a not-for-profit institution and the mission is indeed a different one.

ORGANIZATIONAL STRUCTURE

Hospital organizations traditionally have been bureaucratic and hierarchical. This refers to the involvement of groups of individuals working on goals and objectives in a top-down approach often with many levels. Hospitals, like religious, social, community, and artistic activities, carry out the mission through a bureaucracy of individuals. Today, hospitals are changing from the hierarchical top-down approach to new structures. These structures include corporate, joint ventures, and internal design.

Corporate structures for hospitals have changed to meet challenges of competition, market demands, profit needs, and integration activities. The single hospital began to utilize a development foundation or a parent holding company for various for-profit and not-for-profit services and products. Some hospitals formulated for-profit real estate partnerships and other operating companies. In these ways hospitals can seek mechanisms to fund capital as opposed to depending on long-term debt. The hospital maintains control of all operations. The hospital may also align the medical staff with joint ventures and medical office buildings, and generate equity in order to fund needed projects.

Table 18.6. Multihospital Consolidation[a]

System	Focus	Examples
Large national hospital companies	Vertical and horizontal integration and diversification outside the hospital	American Medical International, Hospital Corporation of American, Humana
Voluntary affiliated systems	Provides members with access to capital, management expertise, joint venture opportunities	American Health Care System, Volunteer Hospitals of America
Regional hospital systems	Develop specialized markets to best meet market needs in their region of the country	Health West in Southern California, Health System in Phoenix, Baptist systems in Texas and Florida
Metropolitan based	Local	Henry Ford in Detroit, New York Health and Hospital Corporation
Special interest systems	Organized according to religious lines or teaching interests	Sisters of Mercy, Daughters of Charity, Adventist Health Care System
Independent free standing voluntary hospitals	High income communities with good health insurance coverage	Traditional community hospitals

[a]Adapted from Kaluzny AD, Shortell SM. Creating and managing the future. In: Williams SJ, ed. Health care management: A text in organization theory and behavior. 2nd ed. New York: John Wiley and Son, 1988:499–500.

Engaging in joint ventures with medical staffs is a recent change for hospitals. As competition, the high cost of technology, and cost constraints affect both hospitals and physicians, affiliations that meet mutual goals benefit both parties. Joint ventures involve each party contributing funds for an activity, service, or product in hopes of a financial return in the future. Such activities might be a joint venture for a magnetic resonance imaging (MRI) service or for an office building. Usually a joint venture is not managed by the hospital but is a separate corporation with members from each party serving on the board. Both parties benefit from marketing, planning, and management expertise. The legal arrangements are established to avoid any antitrust issues. Antitrust comes under the Sherman Antitrust Act which prohibits anticompetitive and monopolistic activities for businesses and health care. The act bans price-fixing, the creation of a monopoly which may lessen competition, agreements which limit expansion into new areas, and many restrictions that prevent competition (10).

Changes in the corporate structure and ownership of hospitals have raised legal issues related to tax status, business practices and accreditation, licensure, and certification (10, 11). Not-for-profit hospitals enjoy tax exempt status under Section 501(C)(3) under the U.S. Code. The two requirements to maintain tax exempt status are (*a*) net earnings cannot benefit any private party and (*b*) the hospital must operate for the public good. When a not-for-profit hospital enters into diversified business arrangements, questions regarding tax status are raised. These issues may become complex depending on the types and purposes of diversification. For example some business activities such as the hospital's involvement with a senior center may be tax exempt, while other businesses such as a physician office building or an ambulatory surgical center may fall under different tax codes.

Business practices may also be affected when organizations restructure. This is particularly true of joint ventures involving hospitals and physicians. Medicare and Medicaid fraud and abuse legislation is concerned with any activity that results in (or has potential for) increased costs. The primary issue is referral to providers for services when the referring party has an ownership interest in the agency providing the services. Discount arrangements for services also come under close scrutiny to ensure that practices are legal.

Antitrust legislation is the other area of concern in new business ventures. The purpose of antitrust legislation is to protect the free market system by ensuring competition. Any business practice that limits competition is subject to litigation under antitrust laws. Violations are generally related to price fixing, division of markets, group boycotts that are blatantly illegal, and practices that limit market competition (12). If hospital mergers create a monopoly in a certain geographic location the merger may be illegal. Collaborating on price by hospitals under separate ownership may be construed as price fixing, an illegal practice. Other examples that may violate antitrust laws are reducing duplicative services, agreements not to do business with certain suppliers, and consortiums of providers. While many of these business arrangements are aimed at decreasing costs while maintaining services, hospitals must consider new arrangements carefully to avoid legal ramifications.

Laws governing hospital certification, licensure, and accreditation fall under state statutes. New business ventures should be assessed carefully to identify any problems in complying with state regulations.

The last legal issue to be discussed here is the corporate practice of medicine. State medical practice acts vary but in some cases may conflict with hospital practices that could be interpreted as attempts to control physician practice. Use of alternative providers such as nurse practitioners is one example. Joint ventures, especially if physicians are employees of the hospital, may also be illegal. Nurse managers should be aware of the complex issues involved in restructuring organizations particularly when they participate in upper management planning.

Internal design involves the type of networks that link the individuals and assign accountability for part of the work load. The design shows reporting relations, areas of responsibility, and numbers of levels of management. In this way chain of command and span of control are identified. Internal designs are often pictured in an organizational chart. There are vertical, horizontal, matrix, and project types of internal design.

The vertical design is often found in large, complex medical institutions. The design may be pyramid in shape or tall with multiple layers and multiple cells in each layer. The layer and cells are normally organized by service or product. Like services are linked together and report to a higher layer in the established chain of command.

The horizontal design is often called the "flat" structure as it has very few layers and cells so that the top level manager is close to the employees. Often this structure eliminates the middle manager and empowers the employees to organize, plan, and implement the work. This decentralized structure enables decision making at the lowest level of the organization that has responsibility for program implementation.

The matrix design combines both vertical and horizontal layers in an integrated fashion. The grid that results shows accountability on the horizontal and vertical planes. Individuals have more than one supervisor. For example, the ABC Hospital uses a matrix design for its product lines. There are 12 product lines: cardiology, neuroscience, rehabilitation, oncology, pediatrics, renal and diabetic, geriatrics, women's health, psychiatry, surgery, ambulatory care, and pulmonary. Each product line has a product-line manager. Within the product line are many department managers who report to the product-line manager for the business and marketing aspects, and also to the manager of their functional area for aspects related to daily operations. Looking at the cardiology product line further defines this matrix concept. Within the product line are: nurse managers of the coronary care unit, cardiovascular surgery unit, and intermediate (telemetry) unit; manager of the cardiac cath lab; directors or managers from pharmacy, laboratory, housekeeping, cardiac rehab, nutrition, and respiratory therapy. The product-line manager discusses plans for marketing, physician needs, finances, and patient services, and sets goals to be achieved. Each manager reports to his or her respective department head for the clinical area of responsibility and day-to-day operations. This system requires excellent communication skills, trust, flexibility, and adult behavior.

The project structure of organizations organizes groups of individuals who have the needed expertise to work on a project or activity from inception to completion. Usually there is one project director who coordinates the project team. The organization may have many project teams. The project director may report directly to the chief executive officer (CEO).

The hospital organizes internally to meet mission, goals, and objectives. Responsibilities and accountabilities are identified to maximize expected outcomes of quality, cost control, and productivity.

Governance

Managing a hospital in a competitive, cost constrained, regulated environment requires good business direction. Hospitals must plan strategically, evaluate market share, remain profitable and productive, provide clinical expertise with quality outcomes, serve the community, offer new technology and services, and employ and retain many types of individuals. There are three key parts of governing or managing a hospital: (*a*) the governing board; (*b*) the medical staff, and (*c*) the administrative team. Each of these three groups affects each other and the hospital.

The governing body or board has been a traditional part of the hospital's structure. This group is at the top of the organizational chart having ultimate authority for strategic planning, establishing mission, overseeing all operations of the hospital and being responsible to the owners. This group is called the board of trustees, the board of directors, or the governing body. A chairperson is selected to oversee the activities of the board and lead the members to appropriate decision making. Boards vary in size and composition. Members may be influential community leaders, donors, representatives from religious, social, or philanthropic organizations, and physicians. To date few nurses have been appointed to the governing body. Board members are not hospital employees and usually receive no compensation for being a member.

The board ensures that profit goals are met, the needs of the community are served, quality is being improved, and operations are smooth and productive. The board may have various committees such as finance, audit, compensation for administration, quality, planning, and nominating. The board appoints the president or CEO, approves the annual and long-range budgets, appoints medical staff members, analyzes market demands, develops the strategic plan, considers issues affecting the hospital, and approves contracts and resolutions.

The medical staff members are appointed to the hospital by the governing body to provide quality clinical services. Often the chief of the medical staff may be a member of the governing body serving as the link between the two groups. The medical staff operates within approved bylaws, rules, and regulations which identify credentialing; active, courtesy, and inactive status; peer review process; and committee activities. The governing body approves medical staff bylaws, hospital appointments, and medical contracts for in-house physician service such as medical directors of various units, and coverage for the emergency, radiology, and pathology departments. The medical staff oversees training, education, quality care, and privileges of its members.

The administrative team is headed by the CEO who hires the other members such as the chief operating officer (COO), chief financial officer (CFO), chief nursing officer (CNO), chief information officer (CIO), and others. The administration implements the decisions from the governing body, monitors all hospital financial and operational activities, directs planning and marketing activities, plans, implements, and evaluates the annual budget, maintains information data bases, negotiates contracts with managed care groups and physicians, recruits and retains employees, represents the hospital at medical and community affairs, designs systems, responds to crisis, and ensures the highest quality care in the most efficient and effective way.

Communication among these three groups is critical for success. Orientation, education, and retreat activities help build relationships, outline expectations, and identify responsibilities. Nursing representation at board meetings, on medical staff committees and sections, and in the administrative circle provides a voice for patient care and the nursing clinical staff. The team concept in meeting quality, financial, and planning goals is advanced when nursing is a part of the governance structure.

CRITICAL CARE SETTINGS

The typical critical care unit in the U.S. is a mixed medical, surgical intensive care unit (ICU) or a coronary care unit (CCU) in a community of fewer than 300 beds (3). The critical care nurse manager needs to consider certain factors when doing the financial planning for the unit (refer to Chapters 6, 8, and 12). Factors to consider are whether the hospital is rural or urban, teaching or nonteaching, and whether the unit is a general or specialized care unit (5). Figure 18.2 shows the various types of units in various hospital settings. These are critical factors to consider when the critical care nurse manager is either planning the budget or analyzing the current financial status of the unit.

Rural and Urban Settings

The practice of critical care nursing in rural settings is very different from the practice seen in urban settings. The American Hospital Association identified 2580 hospitals as rural or small urban and the majority had fewer than 50 beds (13). Often these hospitals are less specialized and have less technology than the larger urban hospitals.

The rural hospital is frequently the largest or second largest employer in the community and its presence is often critical in attracting physicians and nurses as well as other business and industry to the community (14). In rural settings the ICU usually has two to four beds and is frequently an extension of the general care unit which offers all types of nursing care, the exception being obstetrics. Many nurses who work in rural settings, particularly in farming communities, work part-time to supplement the income of the family. Of the nurses working in the CCU and ICU at the American Association of Critical-Care Nurses (AACN) demonstration project hospital, 68% worked part-time (3). Nurses in rural hospitals function in a wide range of roles from being an adult generalist to a pediatric nurse to an emergency nurse and therefore must possess a variety of skills which becomes a challenge for the critical care manager. Low census, infrequent types of patient care problems, and the need to maintain a certain level of competency are challenges that a nurse manager in a rural setting has to consider. Maintenance of these skills can be costly and need to be factored into the financial planning for the unit or hospital.

Rural hospitals are facing increasingly unstable financial conditions and the trend is toward closing of rural hospitals (15). The results reported in one study were that nurses in rural settings worry about the viability of their institutions and their jobs. Low salaries, a general "wearing out," concern over costs to the institution, and the impact on their jobs are frequent concerns (16).

Various methods have been suggested to assist rural hospitals in surviving their current financial

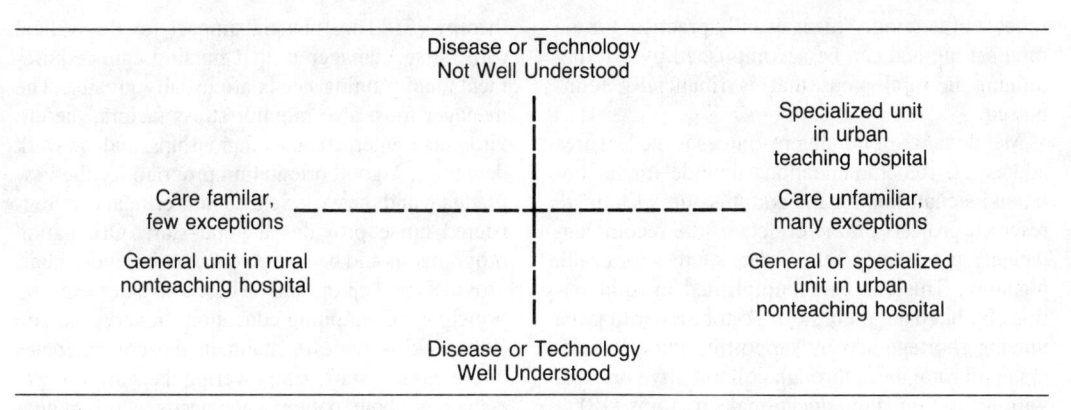

```
                        Disease or Technology
                          Not Well Understood
                                  |
                                  |               Specialized unit
                                  |                  in urban
                                  |               teaching hospital
     Care familar,                |               Care unfamiliar,
     few exceptions  _____|_____  many exceptions
                                  |
     General unit in rural        |               General or specialized
     nonteaching hospital         |                  unit in urban
                                  |               nonteaching hospital
                                  |
                        Disease or Technology
                          Well Understood
```

Figure 18.2. Comparison of various types of critical care units with complexity of patient problems and care provided. (Used with permission from Clochesy J. Planning for various settings in critical care. In: Cardin S, Ward C. Personnel management in critical care nursing. Baltimore: Williams & Wilkins, 1989.)

constraints. The Secretary's Commission on Nursing final report (9) identifies 16 specific recommendations grouped into six areas for relieving the overall shortage of nurses. The areas addressed are:

- Utilization of nursing resources;
- Nurse compensation;
- Health care financing;
- Nurse decision making;
- Development of nursing resources;
- Maintenance of nursing resources.

Many of the recommendations made by the commission will be difficult to implement in rural settings. Two of the recommendations for utilization of nursing resources address the use of adequate support personnel to allow nurses to concentrate on direct patient care, and the adoption of staffing patterns that recognize various levels of education, competence, and experience. In rural areas nurses have frequently taken over many of the ancillary tasks in order to provide for full employment, and they practice as multidisciplined generalists and need to keep this identity. A third recommendation is to automate systems, and using computers was suggested for the relief of time consuming report-writing in hospitals of more than 50 beds. However, in smaller hospitals it was felt that the precarious financial status prohibited automation.

The nurse compensation recommendation includes increasing pay, improving career retention with a one-time adjustment to increase relative wages, and developing strategies to allow compensation options and decrease the effect of pay compression. Rural hospitals are generally unable to offer the one-time rate increase to put the salary into proper adjustment, and salary compression is especially acute in these settings. However, some hospitals have been able to increase fringe benefits by offering part-time nurses full-time benefits.

The recommendation regarding health care financing suggests, among other things, that hospitals reallocate funds to raise salaries. This is difficult in rural hospitals. As noted in the December 5, 1987, *Hospitals* cover story: "Many rural hospitals are only a patient away from financial collapse or financial security. Their operating margins are so thin that one expensive or unreimbursed patient can push the hospital into the red" (17).

The three recommendations for nurse decision making include active participation in policymaking, a voice in governance of the organization, and employer recognition of nursing's clinical authority. These recommendations are appropriate to rural areas. Nurses working in rural areas have a great deal of autonomy in clinical decision making. Frequently nurses are highly respected in their communities, being second only to physicians in status.

Recommendations for development of nursing resources are related to improved financial assistance, reducing barriers to entry into nursing programs, development of relevant curricula, and promotion of a positive image of nursing. Rural hospitals need to offer more career mobility and develop collaborative models between hospitals and schools of nursing. This is usually practical for the rural setting and can be accomplished by offering training in rural areas that is financially reimbursed.

Maintenance of nursing resources is the last area addressed. Recommendations include implementation mechanisms for the commission's findings, research projects on the effects of the recommendations, and development of data sources for health planning. This can be accomplished in rural settings by having "their stories" told regarding the nursing shortage and by supporting nursing leadership in rural areas through collaborative projects with nearby nursing educational programs (18).

Strategies for rural hospitals to recruit and maintain competent staff stimulate creativity in the nursing organization. Many rural hospitals have successfully utilized licensed practical nurses (LPNs) and nurse aides under the supervision of an RN. Some rural hospitals network with a larger specialized hospital and may use radiotelemetry with phone access for interventions. Outreach education programs assist in competency maintenance. Some staffing and scheduling techniques that help rural hospitals cope with vacancies and retain staff are:

1. Job sharing. Two people fill a full-time position alternating hours worked in a pay period.
2. Work activity shifts. The shift starts and ends according to the work activity and may include an overlap time to cover peak work loads.
3. Use of 4-, 6-, 8-, 10-, and 12-hour shifts.
4. On-call and call back. Paying for a nurse to be on-call for the unit and receiving base wage rate plus overtime if appropriate when called back.
5. Use of cooperative care by involving the family members in meeting patient care needs.
6. Four night work week paid at full-time.
7. Crosstraining to all areas of the hospital and offering extra pay if crosstrained competently.
8. Self-scheduling. Each nurse fills out their own work schedule and negotiates with peers for coverage and changes.

As compared to the rural setting many urban hospitals have either one large ICU or a CCU as was noted in the demonstration project by AACN (3). Some hospitals have highly specialized units meeting select patient care needs. Patients in urban settings usually differ in the degree of specialized observation, therapeutic technology, and drug therapy (5). The financial impact for the critical care nurse manager is that nursing care requirements and training needs are usually greater. The manager must also monitor stress factors, the environment, interpersonal relationships, and the work demands. A good orientation program for the new graduate and the experienced non-critical care registered nurse provides a good start. Orientation programs should be competency based, individual, provide a preceptor, and be based on adult learning principles. Continuing education, in-services, and annual skills reviews maintain the competencies of the clinical staff. Empowering the staff to make decisions about patient care needs, work schedules, and unit activities assists in retention. The pursuit of certification in critical care promotes excellence in practice and self-esteem. The CCRN is a valued credential, and some hospitals require it and offer a differential.

Often critical care managers are concerned with the number of direct hours of care per patient day. Table 18.7 provides the number of direct care hours per patient day (HPPD) commonly provided in 1988 in urban hospitals. In 1987, it was determined that the range of nursing HPPD would escalate (see Table 18.8).

These findings were based on urban critical care

Table 18.7. Range of Critical Care Nursing Hours Predicted by Expert Panel[a]

Year	RN Hours per Patient Day
1988	14.5–22.0
1990	18.0–24.0
1995	20.0–26.0
2000	22.0–26.0

[a]Used with permission from Clochesy J. Planning for various settings in critical care. In: Cardin S, Ward C. Personnel management in critical care nursing. Baltimore: Williams & Wilkins, 1989.

Table 18.8. Average Number of Direct Nursing Care Hours Provided per Patient Day by Type of Unit[a]

Unit	HPPD
CCU	12–14
MICU	14–16
SICU	16–18
CTICU	18–24

[a]Used with permission from Clochesy J. Planning for various settings in critical care. In: Cardin S, Ward C. Personnel management in critical care nursing. Baltimore: Williams & Wilkins, 1989.

units and can be approximated to the rural setting. Nursing HPPD vary depending on patient population, length of stay, physical structure of the unit, skill mix, medical practices, administrative desires, community norms, and financial imperatives. The critical care manager must differentiate the worked hours from the total paid hours. Rural and urban hospitals adjust nursing HPPD for patients who require advanced technology and increased nursing care hours. These patients may be transferred to a tertiary care center. Some rural hospitals are participating in organized referral networks with urban or tertiary care centers for technology intensive services such as high-risk obstetrics or neonatal intensive care (14).

PREDICTIONS FOR THE FUTURE

As the critical care nurse manager looks to the future of health care, one needs to be creative, innovative, and be a risk-taker. Hospital organizations are being challenged by what was once a very safe, financially sound system that is now a system with a great deal of challenge and change. Table 18.9 outlines the major trends facing hospital organizations and the environment over time.

Critical care nurse managers need to have a vision and be prepared for the changes in the health care system. Figure 18.3 illustrates the changes that will be seen in the coming years and how one needs to prepare to meet these changes and challenges as they evolve over time.

SUMMARY

Critical care nurse managers are faced with many challenging dilemmas in their everyday practice whether they work in a large teaching hospital, community hospital, or small rural hospital. Critical to the implementation of their role is a sound understanding of the organization. To be successful, critical care nurse managers should look for the following characteristics in a well-managed hospital:

1. Formal mission statement which provides guidelines on major interests or directions;
2. Long-range plans for services, personnel, and capital requirements;
3. Annual environment assessments;
4. Annual review of capital expenditures and new program requests;
5. An annual review of each cost center;
6. Expectations should be clear at each management level;
7. Clear communication lines within the organization; it should flow in all directions;
8. Recognition of the interdependence of nursing, medicine, and clinical support services;

Table 18.9. Environmental Trends for the Critical Care Nurse Manager to Consider[a]

	Past (1950–1970s)	Present (1980s)	Future (1990 & beyond)
Cost containment	Not an issue—retrospective reimbursement	Emergent concern and shift to prospective reimbursement	Continual cost concerns and development of a fully capitated system
Social norms demographic composition	Provider dominated Aging of population not an issue	Changing consumer expectations Aging an emergent issue	Provider/consumer/employer patnerships Aging a major focus of activity
Technical development and assessment	Rapid development and implementation	Emerging efforts at assessment	Use of randomized trials and meta analysis
Health promotion/disease prevention	Not an issue	Emerging efforts	Major delivery efforts
Social experimentation	Emerging efforts	Pressure on accountability	Collaborative efforts between researchers and managers
Organizational arrangements	Cottage industry, large number of individual providers	Systems and consolidation	Mega systems both vertically and horizontally integrated

[a]Used with permission from Kaluzny AD, Shortell SA. Creating and managing the future. In: Williams SJ. ed. Health care management: A text in organization theory and behavior. New York: John Wiley & Sons, 1988:501.

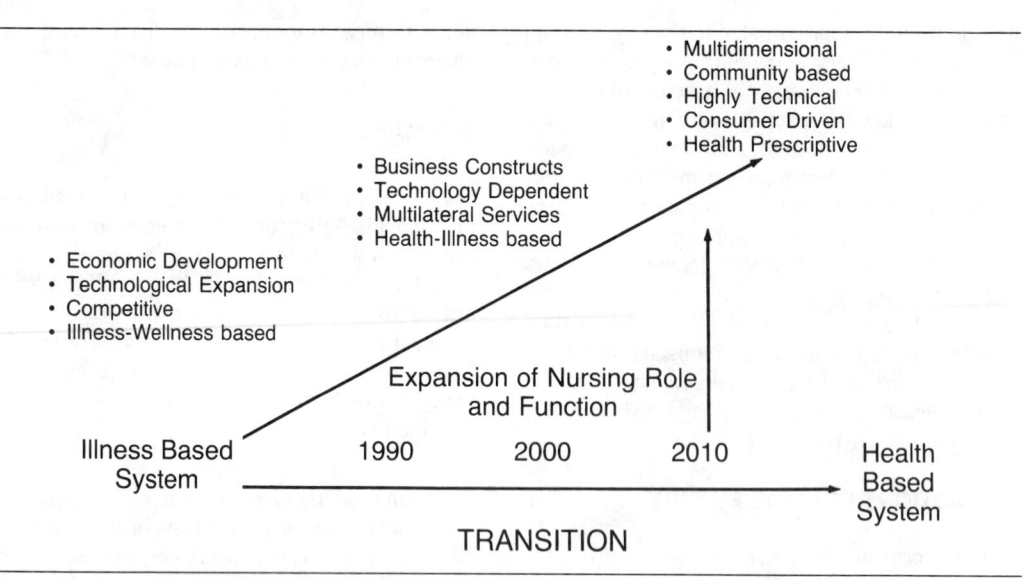

Figure 18.3. Health system in transition. (Used with permission from Porter-O'Grady T. Creative nursing administration. Rockville, MD: Aspen System Corporation, 1986.)

9. Expectations should be outcome oriented and allow for flexibility (19).

The critical care nurse manager in a well run, financially sound hospital organization will find that the organizational culture is easy to assimilate and translate into practice. Resources will be efficiently and effectively utilized and the goal of a financially stable critical care unit will be achieved.

REFERENCES

1. Kaluzny AD, Shortell SA. Creating and managing the future. In: Williams SJ, ed. Health care management: a text in organization theory and behavior. 2nd ed. New York: John Wiley and Sons, 1988:492–522.
2. Griffith JR. The well-managed community hospital. Ann Arbor, MI: Health Administration Press, 1987.
3. Mitchell P, Armstrong S, Forshee T, et al. American Association of Critical-Care Nurses Demonstration Project: Phase I Report. Newport Beach, CA: American Association of Critical-Care Nurses, 1988.
4. McNerney WJ, et al. For-profit enterprise in health care. Washington, DC: National Academy Press, 1986.
5. Clochesy J. Planning for various critical care units. In: Cardin S, Ward C, eds. Personnel management in critical care nursing. Baltimore: Williams & Wilkins, 1989:71–76.
6. Purcell E, ed. The role of the university teaching hospital: an international perspective. Port Washington, NY: Independent Publishers Group, 1982.
7. Zuckerman HS. The strategies and autonomy of university hospitals in competitive environments. Hospital and Health Services Administration 1990;35:103–120.
8. Altman SH, Henderson MG. Competition and compassion: Conflicting roles for public hospitals. Ann Arbor, MI: Health Administration Press, 1989.
9. Secretary's Commission on Nursing. Final Report Vol. 1. Washington, DC: Department of Health and Human Services, December, 1988.
10. Epstein JD. Legal structure of hospitals. In: Wolper LF, Pena JJ, eds. Health care administration. Rockville, MD: Aspen Publishers Inc., 1987:40–49.
11. Rosenfield RH, Mancino DJ, Miller JN. Health care joint ventures. In: Wolper LF, Pena JJ, eds. Health care administration. Rockville, MD: Aspen Publishers, Inc., 1987:204–211.
12. Fottler MD, Vaughan DG. Multi-hospital systems. In: Wolper LF, Pena JJ, eds. Health care administration. Rockville, MD: Aspen Publishers, Inc., 1987:252–253.
13. Secretary's Commission on Nursing, Vol. 11, Dec. 1988. Support Studies and Background Information: IV-1-15.
14. American Hospital Association. Environmental assessment for rural hospitals, 1988. Chicago: American Hospital Association, 1989.
15. American Hospital Association: Rural hospital closure: managment and community applications. Chicago: American Hospital Association, 1989.
16. Fuszard B, Slocum LI, Wiggers DE. Rural nurses, part I, surviving cost containment. Journal of Nursing Administration, 1990;20:7–11.
17. Robinson M. Rural providers ask: what's a hospital? Hospitals, December 5, 1987;61:51.

18. Fuszard B, Slocum LI, Wiggins DE. Rural nurses, part II, surviving the nursing shortage. Journal of Nursing Administration, 1990;20:41–46.

19. Griffith JR. Foundations of hospital organization. In: Kovner AR, Neuhasuer D. Health services management readings and commentary. 4th ed. Ann Arbor, MI: Health Administration Press, 1990

Chapter 19

Issues and Trends

DOLORES S. GOMEZ

A multiplicity of financial issues and trends have shaped what we call the health care industry as we know it. The final product, patient care, is provided in numerous "packages" aimed at meeting governmental, business, societal, and financial demands. These demands have placed extreme stress upon the health care industry. Hospitals in particular have felt the effects. Sound financial management in these turbulent times is mandatory for institutional survival.

To adequately meet the financial challenge facing today's hospitals, knowledge of the current issues and identification of present and future trends is needed. This chapter will describe these issues so as to bring clarity and understanding to the first-line nurse manager.

GOVERNMENT REGULATION

The financial impact of government intervention and regulation has literally changed the focus of the hospital industry from a retrospective payment system to a prospective payment system (PPS). After a decade of annual double-digit increases in total hospital costs, the federal government instituted a prospective payment mechanism aimed at decreasing Medicare costs. In 1982, the federal government passed the Tax Equity and Fiscal Responsibility Act (TEFRA), establishing limits on Medicare inpatient reimbursement per case. In 1983, Congress adopted the prospective payment approach of diagnosis related group (DRG) method of patient classification, whereby cases are sorted into similar discharge diagnoses with an equivalent length of stay and presumed equivalent cost. Public Law 98-21 was therefore enacted, which initiated a fixed payment schedule based on DRGs for Medicare (1).

The DRG classification consists of 23 major diagnostic categories and 490 diagnoses. The prospective payment system assumes that all hospitals will receive an equal proportion of patients with illnesses of similar severity within each DRG and that a similar level of care will be delivered. In essence, an averaging occurs to balance the financial losses of seriously ill patients with profits made on the less ill patients within each DRG. The message to hospitals was therefore quite clear. Those hospitals whose costs are less than the allocated payment will profit from their efficiency, while hospitals that are unable or unwilling to provide treatment below the allocated Medicare payment will incur financial losses (2).

The effects of the DRG prospective payment system were and still are far reaching. Hospitals that could not cut costs efficiently were thrown into financial chaos and many were forced to close. Between 1980 and 1983, 73 urban hospitals and 47 rural facilities closed their doors. Since the start of prospective payment, closures have risen to 128 urban and 116 rural hospitals. Hardest hit were small community hospitals functioning on minimal operating margins. Rural hospitals warrant particular attention, as they account for a greater share of closings now than they did in the past. From 1980 through 1985, 40% of total closures occurred in rural hospitals. In 1986, rural closures jumped to 52%, declining only slightly to 51% in 1987 (3).

The largest impact on the health care industry was a redefinition of how business is conducted. Hospitals are now forced to determine and control cost. Patient length of stay has decreased as patients are admitted later and discharged sooner. Gone are the days when a presurgical patient was admitted 2 days before surgery for tests and procedures. Outpatient and home care services have grown tremendously, as advances in medical technology coupled with case management and utilization controls have affected length of stay. As a result, inpatient acuity has increased and in-hospital resource utilization is compressed.

Reimbursement for capital expenditures is decreasing. Except for sole community hospitals, PPS capital payments were reduced 15% in fiscal year 1990 (4). Although some legislators feel that the cuts are not adequate, the combination of reductions in reimbursement for patient care and capital reimbursement has squeezed many hospitals and limited their access to capital. Creditworthiness has also been affected, as there is a direct link between profit margins and financial viability. As profit margins are narrowed and financial performance worsens, credit ratings decline (5).

Further legislation on Medicare capital reductions may be forthcoming. Proposals to Congress include "linking capital payment amounts to the degree of capacity utilization of particular facilities" (6, 7). In short, these proposals link capital payment to occupancy rates. Whether Medicare capital reductions continue to be across-the-board, incorporated into the prospective payment system, or linked to occupancy rates, it is clear that the future trend is a decrease in capital reimbursement to hospitals.

Medicaid

The Medicaid system is designed to finance health care for low income individuals. Medicaid programs, jointly funded by the state and federal governments, are administered by individual states. Although the federal government mandates certain basic services, states have wide latitude in determining eligibility and benefit criteria and can therefore limit access to services through eligibility criteria. Eleven states limit the number of covered hospital days. Provider reimbursement levels under Medicaid are low (8). These limits are so low that in California, for example, where individual hospitals contract with the state to provide care to "MediCal" patients, many hospitals choose not to contract with the state. The pre diem rate of reimbursement for Medicaid patients can be less than 50% of hospital charges (9).

Inner city hospitals that serve impoverished urban areas and rural hospitals have a larger proportionate number of Medicaid patients. Marginal reimbursement has placed these facilities in a precarious financial situation. Hospitals which have large percentages of both Medicare and Medicaid recipients are hardest hit. These "disproportionate share" hospitals are provided an increase in reimbursement to adjust for financial hardship caused by case mix and location. The fiscal year 1990 budget reconciliation bill again addressed the disproportionate share hospital issue. For discharges on or after April, 1990, urban hospitals with more than 100 beds that have more than 20.2% low-income and elderly patients will receive a 0.65 percentage point increase in Medicare payments for each percentage point that exceeds the 20.2% threshold. For rural hospitals with more than 100 beds and sole community hospitals, the disproportionate patient threshold is reduced to 30% from 45%. Hospitals that serve an entire community within a 35-mile radius are defined as "sole community hospitals." In addition, sole community hospital payment adjustment is increased to 10% (4).

Medicaid expansion and reform have been proposed by the Health Policy Agenda for the American People (8), a coalition of 172 public and private sector organizations. Proposed reforms include establishment of improved, uniform eligibility requirements across states, improvement in the scope and depth of coverage in state Medicaid programs, and increased provider payment rates. The cost of the reform would be approximately $9 billion dollars. Arguments for the reform state that a large portion of the costs would be offset by savings in current spending elsewhere in the system (i.e., reduce utilization of federal programs and programs for medically indigent). The proposed reform is costly, however, and actual expansion of the Medicaid program is questionable.

Governmental regulation will continue to influence the hospital industry since the government is a major third-party payor. In 1988, the government paid 42.1% of the total of $539.9 billion spent on health care. Of that, state and local government paid 12.9% and the federal government paid 29.2% (10). As the age of the population steadily increases, further changes will be forthcoming. The Medicare Catastrophic Coverage Act of 1988 is an example. The purposes of this legislation was to provide increased coverage for the elderly with prolonged inpatient hospital stays (11). It marked the largest expansion of Medicare benefits since 1965 when the program was created. Catastrophic benefits would have provided an unlimited number of days for inpatient care through payment of a single annual surtax. Repeal of the Medicare Catastrophic Coverage Act in 1989 was due to an outcry by the elderly in response to the amount of the surtax that was the program's key financing mechanism (12). Many seniors felt that catastrophic coverage duplicated private insurance that they already had for acute hospitalization. Coverage for long-term care needs was of greater concern and although the catastrophic plan improved benefits, it fell short of needed reform. As a result, issues surrounding the catastrophic plan convinced the American Association of Retired Persons (AARP) that a broader focus of health care coverage for the elderly is needed.

Managed Care

Changes in third-party reimbursement by the government have also had profound effects on the health insurance industry. There has been a proliferation of managed care programs in the form of health maintenance organizations (HMOs) and preferred provider organizations (PPOs). In addition, many indemnity insurers have developed managed fee-for-service plans. Government and managed care payors now provide 65% of all hospital revenues (13).

An HMO is an organized plan that guarantees the delivery of comprehensive health services to a voluntarily enrolled population at a prepaid fixed premium. HMOs that do not own hospitals must contract with hospitals to provide services to their enrollees. HMOs exert a large degree of control over costs by channeling subscribers into a closed provider panel. A closed provider panel is a specified list of physicians and/or hospital facilities that an enrollee must utilize to receive health care.

PPOs, sometimes referred to as preferred provider arrangements (PPAs), are contractual arrangements between a panel of health care providers (physicians and hospitals) and a purchaser of health care services (insurers and self-insured employers). PPOs give subscribers financial incentives (decreased charges) to encourage the use of specific providers. The specific providers in turn offer discounts from charges or accept a fixed payment rate such as per diem or per discharge. In addition, many PPOs require providers to agree to utilization review procedures such as preadmission certification.

HMOs and PPOs have grown due to the expectation that they control costs. Both HMOs and PPOs will continue to grow and increase enrollment. More than 50 million Americans have health coverage through HMO or PPO organizations. Industry reports estimate that this represents about 30% of the insured population. Some experts predict that nearly 90% of all Americans will be enrolled in a managed care plan before the year 2000 (13).

Profitability has declined dramatically for hospitals in the current health care market. As profits are no longer guaranteed, many hospitals in competitive areas have formed business ventures with medical groups and local physicians to develop local provider networks. These arrangements are generally termed independent practice association (IPAs). IPAs enable hospitals to negotiate fees with managed care plans or other purchasers. IPAs represent a bonding between physicians and hospitals. They are the newest and most popular form of HMO today and are expected to flourish in the 1990s.

The net effect of governmental restrictions and managed care is an emphasis on cost containment measures by hospital facilities. One way of managing utilization of resources and length of stay is through development of case management. Many models of case management exist (14, 15). Common elements of case management include: assessment, risk coordination and appraisal, treatment and care planning, service referral and treatment, monitoring, tracking and assessment of progress, evaluation, and provision of continuity and long-term accountability.

Case management models may be an extension of the primary nursing concept, a separate function within the hospital structure, or a contracted service. Other variations include HMO, state-based, industry, or insurance-based models. The primary goals of these later three types of case management programs are to control expenditures, control utilization, and cut costs.

The role of the case manager is viewed as that of "gatekeeper." The case manager's primary function is to ensure that quality care is provided in the most cost effective manner. The majority of case managers are registered nurses (RNs) with years of clinical experience. Depending on the case management model utilized and the setting, the case manager may have a varied clinical background. Some case manager RNs are experienced in discharge planning or utilization review and quality assurance programs. Inpatient case management may utilize the advanced clinician in an extended role, for example, the clinical nurse specialist or nurse practitioner. The American Nurses Association (ANA) describes nursing case management as "a health care delivery process whose goals are to provide quality health care, decrease fragmentation, enhance the client's quality of life, and contain costs" (16).

As hospitals rely more on managed care provider plans as a chief source of revenue, they will turn to case management models to assist in containing costs. Private case management firms are expanding and some hospitals may utilize these contracted services. In-house case management programs have been developed and have evolved from the utilization review and discharge planning functions or have developed alongside nursing delivery system models. Integrated case management and nursing delivery systems utilize case management plans or "critical paths" by which care is standardized so that specific clinical and financial outcomes are achieved within an allocated time frame (16, 17). The identified registered nurse, as case manager, is responsible and accountable to work with the multidisciplinary team to achieve the desired outcomes. Case management is quite clearly here to stay and will continue to provide significant opportunities for nursing through both increased professionalism and financial influence impacting the bottom line.

ACCESS TO CARE

Issues regarding access to care have become more pronounced in today's health care industry. There are approximately 37 million Americans who lack health insurance coverage (8, 18). Of this 37 million, about one-third of the uninsured are poor, another one-third are low income, and the rest are non-poor. Recent changes in the private insurance market, reductions in employer sponsored health policies, and limited availability of dependent coverage have contributed to the large and growing number of uninsured.

Medicaid, although designed to provide health care to the poor, currently covers less than one-half of the poverty population. Provider reimbursement levels under Medicaid are variable by state and often limit access to care. In California, for example, only contracted hospitals admit Medicaid patients, therefore limiting options in hospital services provided. In addition, fewer than 15 state Medicaid programs reimburse physicians on a usual, customary, and reasonable basis (10). The remaining states use fee schedules set at significant discounts. These large and growing gaps between Medicaid reimbursement and physician fees are a major factor limiting access to care as fewer physicians will accept Medicaid patients.

What about the uninsured? Clearly two-thirds of the 37 million uninsured are poor or have low income. Access to care is unavoidably tied to ability to pay. County and public facilities set up to treat the medically indigent are overcrowded, are poorly staffed, and at times are large distances from the recipient's home.

Traditionally, American medicine has avoided defining health care for the medically indigent as a basic right, and instead has attempted to recover the costs for such care from persons or entities other than the medically indigent individual. "Cost-shifting," the practice of increasing charges for services to third-party payors to recoup the cost of providing care to the indigent, was routinely utilized as a method to absorb or write-off charity care provided. However, with prospective payment, capitation, and managed care plans limiting reimbursement to hospitals, facilities can no longer shift the cost of care provided for the medically indigent. Thus, in a time when cost containment and profit are the buzz words of the hospital industry, the medically indigent are seen as a significant liability.

As such, a phenomenon known as patient "dumping" has occurred, in which medically indigent patients who are seen for emergency medical care are transferred or "dumped" onto the doorstep of public or county facilities. Patient "dumping" has had a major financial impact on public hospitals (20). Fewer community hospitals are admitting medically indigent patients, thus causing an increased burden on public facilities. Although the federal "anti-dumping" law called the "Examination and Treatment for Emergency Medical Conditions and Women in Active Labor" took effect in August, 1986, to prevent transfer of unstable emergency patients for economic reasons, variations of "dumping" still occur. Definitions of "emergency" and "stable condition" are utilized in broad terms as defined in the statute.

Current enforcement provisions subject hospitals and physicians who knowingly violate the law to civil penalties up to $50,000 for each violation (21). In addition, hospitals are subject to suspension or termination of their Medicare provider agreements. As of March 1990, a total of 104 hospitals have been found to be out of compliance with the "patient-dumping" regulations which took effect in 1986. Of those 104, 2 were terminated from federal programs, and 3 were suspended but allowed to participate after correcting problems (22). Even so, as long as the patient is "stabilized," a hospital is under no duty to treat the patient and therefore can transfer or send the patient elsewhere for care.

Access to care by the rural population is becoming a critical issue. Numerous closures of small, rural hospital facilities in the past several years have limited access to medical care. In some areas of Texas, individuals must travel hundreds of miles for hospital care. The rural poor or indigent are more limited in accessing charitable medical or hospital care.

The issue regarding access to hospital care is not limited to the poor, indigent, or rural populace. Managed care in the form of HMOs and PPOs limit subscriber's use of hospital care. HMOs control costs through the use of primary physician "gatekeepers" who keep tight control over hospital admissions through financial incentives for decreased utilization of hospital services. PPOs often require preadmission screening and certification, or a second opinion on hospital procedures. In addition, larger deductibles or co-payments can serve to deter utilization of hospital facilities for care.

As the cost of care rapidly increases and technological advances compound hospital costs, access to that technology becomes limited. An example of this is transplantation. Many third-party payors provide limited or no coverage for transplantation. In addition, transplantation is offered at few medical centers, because it is associated with high resource utilization and therefore is costly for the institution. Intensive care services are another example of costly technology for hospitals. Many hospitals limit the number of intensive care unit (ICU) beds available, relying on strict admission and discharge criteria to control access and use of the critical care unit.

Indigent/Uninsured

Health care for the indigent and uninsured is clearly an imposing challenge facing the nation. With over 37 million Americans without health insurance, it is expected that some form of national health insurance will be on the congressional agenda. Advocates of such a plan frequently point to the success of the Canadian health care system and propose the tailoring of such a system for the U.S. Arguments in favor of a national health program include: (a) reducing the cost by slashing bureaucratic waste, (b) improving health planning, (c) restructuring the way care is financed and eliminating financial barriers to access, and (d) preserving the physician-patient relationship (23). Arguments against national health insurance center around (a) potential deterioration of quality care, (b) the tremendous cost associated with such a program, (c) elimination of the free-market system of health care, and (d) public acceptance.

Other proposals aimed at providing care to the indigent and uninsured include expansion of the current Medicaid program. Proposals have been put forward by multiple groups including the Health Insurance Association of America, the Pepper Commission, and the Health Policy Agenda for the American People. The fiscal impacts of Medicaid expansion, in the face of budget cuts on the federal level, effectively leaves the issue of the indigent and uninsured unresolved.

Unresolved issues of marginal medical care, barriers to access, and crowded public hospitals continue as the plight of the indigent and uninsured. Charity care has become difficult for both hospitals and physicians as profit margins are squeezed by the prospective payment system, managed-care plans, and contractual arrangements. Health policy changes will be required in order to deal specifically with the issue of care for the poor.

HEALTH CARE POLICY

For several decades, Americans have considered health care as a right. Americans like the idea of high technology and space-age medicine. They believe, for the most part, that human life is sacred and should be saved at all costs. At the same time, Americans are outraged by the cost of health care today. Costs for Medicare and Medicaid are skyrocketing. Individual premiums for health insurance and out-of-pocket costs are increasing.

Some fundamental questions must be addressed by the nation to determine what shape the U.S. health care policy will ultimately assume. A few of these questions include:

1. Should universal access to all levels of health care be provided? If so, who should pay for it and how?
2. What should government's role be in determining health care access and coverage for technology?

3. Is the American public willing to spend more money on health care in the future? Or, will budget cuts be the focus of the agenda?
4. What should society's role be in providing health care to the aged and poor?

At the present time, national health care policy appears to be placing fingers in a dike ready to give way. Recent policy and program changes include: increased budget cuts across-the-board for both the Medicare and Medicaid programs, improved benefits for AIDS patients, reductions of capital payments by Medicare, increases in payments to disproportionate share hospitals, "anti-dumping" legislation, and reimbursement reduction for certain types of procedures (i.e., coronary bypass graft). In addition, reimbursement to facilities that perform less than a mandated number of specific procedures per year (i.e., open heart surgeries) may be in jeopardy.

Future health care policy will be determined by the ongoing issues facing the health care industry and nation today. These issues include:

1. Changing demographics. In 1980, 26 million people or about 11% of the population were 65 years or older. By the year 2010, nearly 14% or 39 million people will be 65 or older, and by the year 2050 almost 22% or 67 million people will be 65 or older (24).
2. Economic trends. Economic trends note increasing numbers of uninsured and less money available for the poor and indigent.
3. Technologic advances. For 3 decades, the U.S. has pumped billions of dollars into medical research and technology. Although many new technologies reduce inpatient costs by allowing care to be provided on an outpatient basis, new technology is responsible for more than one-half of the annual increase in cost of a patient day (25).
4. Societal issues. Payment for AIDS and other terminal illnesses has accounted for increased costs of medical care. The Center for Disease Control expects that by 1991 AIDS will be the leading cause of death for people aged 25-44 (21).
5. Hospital industry problems. Narrowed margins, decreased occupancy rates, hospital closures, and decreased access to capital will continue to affect the hospital industry.
6. Ethical dilemmas. Rationing of care; utilization of resources for the poor, elderly, or terminalpatient, technological advances that prolong or alter life; and biomedical research that may produce moral, ethical, and religious controversy continue to be issues facing the health care industry and society.

Physician payment reform is a policy initiative that is likely to be given serious consideration in the near future. In 1986, Congress created the Physician Payment Review Commission (PPRC) to advise it on reforms in Medicare policies for paying physicians. The PPRC has recommended a fee schedule for physician payment through usage of a resource-based relative-value scale (RBRVS). Fees would be set with the relative value of the different services determined by the cost of the resources used to produce the service (26).

Hospitals will be affected to some degree by adoption of a relative-value schedule for physicians. The effects on hospitals will depend on the volume response to changes in relative values. These may be hard to predict. For example, if surgery and radiology services increase in response to declines in price, then there could be an increase in service provided in hospital settings.

THE NURSING PERSPECTIVE

How do these issues and trends affect critical care nurse managers? The nurse manager is well qualified to take on the responsibility for managing patient care and the critical care unit in a cost effective manner. Nursing is the only service that has constant contact with the patient, assessing ongoing needs, and ensuring efficient delivery of services required. Additionally, nursing has the most direct interaction with the medical staff, providing the opportunity for joint problem solving, determining utilization of resources, and identifying and resolving potential complications.

The national movement to case-based and capitated payments to hospitals by third-party payors has placed focus upon the need to know costs associated with providing care to individual patients. Traditionally, the predominant technique for allotting and monitoring the utilization of nursing care resources in hospitals has been and continues to be the static "nursing hours per patient day." This concept of nursing care hours per patient day is one of fixed hours and fixed nursing costs per occupied bed, and is based on an assumption that all patients are equal in terms of nursing care requirements. Variations that exist when the unit of measurement is the individual patient rather than the occupied bed are not reflected in this gross monitoring technique of nursing resource utilization.

To manage resources effectively, the true costs of providing a particular service or product must be available. In the current prospective payment and contract-oriented health care reimbursement system, hospital managers must know true costs to manage effectively and negotiate profitable contracts with third-party payors. A valid patient classification system that links acuity of the patient's illness to the cost of nursing services is required and essential for cost accounting purposes. The critical care nurse manager can utilize classification and acuity data to monitor trends of resource utilization, allocate needed resources, and determine future budgetary requirements based on historical data.

Knowledge regarding nursing costs associated with particular DRGs can also be ascertained by a valid patient classification system (27). Sophisticated hospital information systems can utilize nursing cost data to determine the cost (and price) of nursing care by DRG. The critical care nurse manager can use this data to track high utilization DRGs in the critical care unit and therefore justify resource allocation and budgetary requirements. DRG outliers also require monitoring, as resource consumption in critical care is high compared to alternative care settings.

Models for third-party reimbursement of nursing care have been developed based on patient classification systems (28, 29). Through determination of the cost of nursing services and extracting the nursing charge from the traditional room rate, nursing units are converted to revenue producers with the ability to negotiate for managed care contracts, justify budgets and staffing, equate nursing with other revenue producing centers, and alter perceptions regarding cost of nursing services. Establishing nursing as a revenue center provides the economic accountability required to complement the professional care accountability that nurses currently have (30).

Arguments against establishing nursing as a revenue center point to the conflict between third-party reimbursement models and the movement toward the prospective payment system. Pressure on acute care institutions is severe, as they are often forced to assume the financial risk of providing care to an increasingly acute and needy patient population. Technological and pharmacological advancements, often very costly, compound the financial strain. At the bedside, institutional financial pressure often translates into demands for increased nursing productivity. Support services are often trimmed, which frequently results in nurses having to assume an increased number of nonnursing tasks. The AACN nursing economics task force suggests the following strategies to meet these challenges:

1. To explore the feasibility of developing models for contracted nursing service which include nurse ownership, profit sharing, and prospective rate negotiation.
2. Support legislation that recognizes the need to assure appropriate care for the disenfranchised.
3. Support research that provides data as to the impact of the prospective reimbursement system on the quality of service provided (31).

Management of the major nursing cost, nursing labor, is a challenging function of the critical care nurse manager role. Labor is the largest single expense in the hospital's operating budget. Nursing is the largest single labor group within the hospital and is therefore highly visible. In the intensive care unit nursing labor costs are proportionally higher relative to non-intensive care unit nursing labor costs due to the increased nurse:patient ratio provided. The critical care nurse manager can effectively manage labor costs through appropriate staffing and scheduling, and utilization of strategies to decrease nurse turnover.

Effective staffing and scheduling management entails both coverage of patient care requirements at an acceptable cost and attending to staff needs to promote nursing satisfaction. Critical care units must provide qualified staff for quality care delivery. However, undesirable schedule and work hours are cited as an important factor in the majority of resignations by nurses. Strategies that the critical care nurse manager can utilize as outlined by the AACN nursing economics task force are:

1. Identify and promote scheduling systems and technology that reflect innovation, flexibility and responsiveness to staff needs;
2. Encourage nurse manager and personnel collaboration regarding innovative scheduling and potential conflicts with labor laws;

3. Identify scheduling or support systems to empower nurses to develop self-schedules;
4. Encourage utilization and promote self-scheduling systems (31).

The cost of nursing turnover is a major source of avoidable expense in health care. The average cost to replace a nurse is estimated at $20,000 (32). The national recruitment expense in nursing advertising alone is approximately $3 billion per year. Additional money spent recruiting and orienting foreign nurses compounds the problem and cost, not to mention the ethical and cultural problems associated with this practice. Numerous reasons for the high turnover in nursing have been cited. Among these are burnout, inadequate salary compensation, working hours and conditions, staffing, lack of administrative support, poor nurse-physician relationships, absence of respect or recognition, fatigue and bureaucratic or political hassles (33). The critical care nurse manager is in a pivotal position to affect retention within the intensive care unit. Leadership style and management effectiveness of the nurse manager is a major aspect of retention of critical care staff (34). Strategies the nurse manager can utilize in the retention of intensive care unit staff include: use of a participative, collegial, leadership style; setting high achievable expectations regarding patient care, peer relationships, and communication; providing support for nurse control over practice; creating a climate of caring and recognition; use of creative staffing and scheduling regimes; and emphasis on the education and individual needs of the intensive care unit staff.

Results of the Magnet Hospital Study, conducted by the American Nurses Association, which focused on hospitals that attracted and retained professional nurses, identified key elements essential in hospital organizations for retention of nurses. These elements are: a participatory management style; strong, supportive quality leadership; decentralized organizational structure with nursing involvement in hospital committees; ample, qualified nursing staff; competitive salaries and benefits; flexible work schedules; presence of career ladders; high-quality care standards; professional practice models that incorporate autonomy and peer support; high value placed on education and teaching; professional image that is valued and respected; emphasis on professional growth and development; and continuous efforts toward improvement of the professional environment (35). It is important that these elements are present throughout the hospital organization. However, the nurse manager who can successfully operationalize these elements within the critical care unit setting will clearly have the greatest impact on retention of staff.

The AACN demonstration project was developed to attempt to expand knowledge regarding cost-effectiveness in critical care nursing. The general purpose of the project was to "demonstrate fiscal costs and patient-care effectiveness of critical care nursing by testing and demonstrating multiple nursing care protocols within selected management structures on a nationally-visible intensive care unit."

Cited as important for effective clinical outcomes were: (a) decentralized participative management, (b) an all-RN staff, (c) specialized knowledge of critical care nursing, (d) use of standards of care to guide practice, and (e) collaboration between nurses and physicians.

Outcomes of the AACN demonstration project are important in ascertaining strategies to decrease costs of intensive care nursing in the current prospective payment health care environment. Specific outcomes were:

1. Patient morbidity was 50% below predictions.
2. Turnover of nursing staff was 8% as compared to a national average of 25%.
3. Critical care nursing charges were only 11% of the total hospital bill, although the patients' median length of stay in critical care was one-third of the total hospital stay.
4. High morale and nursing satisfaction.
5. High physician satisfaction with effectiveness of nursing.
6. High patient satisfaction (36).

Critical care nurse managers can also affect overall cost by working collaboratively with physicians and hospitals administrators in determining appropriate utilization of intensive care unit resources. Historically, proliferation of ICU beds occurred due to advances in technology, the need for specialized nursing skills, revenue generation, and the perceived notion that increased observation and intervention affected patient outcome. As more intensive care beds became available, utilization of those beds increased. Non-critical patients often were placed in intensive care for reasons of "safety" or physician convenience. Reduction of inappropriate admissions to the ICU can be accomplished through the development and monitoring of admission and discharge criteria. The AACN guidelines for admission/discharge criteria in critical care define data sources and key elements needed to develop appropriate and objectives criteria for the admission and discharge of patients in the intensive care unit (37). Criteria must be written, implemented, and evaluated for each ICU setting by a multidisciplinary team which includes representation from medicine, nursing, and hospital administration.

Reimbursement under the prospective payment system has placed focus on resource consumption and utilization of ICUs. The current DRG reimbursement method provides significant financial incentives to limit both access and resource utilization within the intensive care unit. Studies have shown that DRG reimbursement does not meet the costs of intensive care services especially as patients older than 65 years of age demonstrate a longer length of stay, a greater severity of illness, a higher percentage of outliers, and a greater percent mortality as compared with patients younger than 65 years of age (38, 39). Patient outcome and utilization of ICU resources must be evaluated on an ongoing basis.

Improvement in utilization of the ICU requires the limiting of admissions, emphasis on reduced length of stay in the ICU, and reductions of inappropriate interventions (i.e., "No Code" designated patients). Case management in the intensive care unit can be an effective means to monitor utilization of the intensive care unit. Case manager collaboration with the critical care nurse manager, medical director, and primary nurse caring for the patient is essential.

Product-line management is a concept that is receiving much interest and attention in the health care industry. The movement from traditional to more innovative approaches, such as product-line management, is a result of the dramatic changes in hospital reimbursement. Benefits of product-line management include (*a*) quick identification of changes in the environment, patient demographics, case mix, etc.; (*b*) better understanding of the impact of change on the environment as well as more accurate simulations of new strategies; and (*c*) better allocation and control over resources and costs through quicker responses to changes, better implementation processes, and target marketing (40).

The critical care nurse manager may work in a hospital facility which has instituted some form of product-line management. Whether the hospital has adopted a parallel, product, or matrix structure to operationalize the product-line strategy, the critical care nurse manager is in an optimal position to influence the quality and cost of specific products which utilize critical care services. A challenge facing some nurse managers in critical care is the elimination of the functional and traditional lines of authority and replacement with product-line managers. In these hospital organizations, the critical care unit may report to a nonnursing product-line manager. An example of such an arrangement is where the cardiovascular intensive care unit reports directly to the cardiac product-line manager.

Fiscal management is an integral function within the role of the critical care nurse manager. The AACN position statement which defines the role expectations for the critical care manager identifies key administrative accountabilities for fiscal management of the intensive care unit. These include:

- Establishment of a valid statistical data base for budgetary decision making;
- Facilitation of the development of realistic annual budget which may include revenue, personnel, supplies, and capital equipment;
- Establishment of accurate nursing productivity measures;
- Regular review of budgetary variances to assure appropriate use of resources;
- Promotion of cost effective unit operations;
- Anticipation of the impact of institutional financial status on unit operations (41).

In these times of prospective payment, capitation, selective contracting, and managed care it is imperative that the critical care nurse manager be financially accountable for the performance of the intensive care unit. Accountability and responsibility are vital, as intensive care units are an expensive service in terms of labor costs, technology, and resource consumption.

FUTURE ISSUES AND TRENDS

Ongoing discussion of some sort of national health care insurance is likely to continue. Governmental spending for health care will continue to rise, and across-the-board cuts, a focus on health care for the poor and aged, and increased regulation are likely. Hospitals will continue to develop strategies for survival which are likely to include continued cost-cutting, reassessment of services offered, further development of outpatient services, reassessment of inpatient services offered, increased contracting with third-party payors, and organizational restructuring.

Focus upon patient outcomes will be a major indicator of quality of care. A great deal of research and development will be required to measure quality. Outcomes must be defined and measured, adjustments for differences in patient risk mix is essential, and quality assessment of technology usefulness is needed. Information systems will be further developed to assist in the management of quality care within the hospital industry.

Trends toward hospitals that specialize in certain types of services will continue. Full-service community hospitals are becoming an institution of the past. Tertiary-care hospitals or medical centers will become the hubs of technology and intensive care services. As such, there will be an ongoing demand for intensive care nursing.

REFERENCES

1. Scheeres D, Schoten D. DRGs and outliers in surgical critical care. The American Surgeon 1989;55(8):511–515.
2. Thomas F, Fox J, Clemmer T, Orme J, Vincent M, Menlove R. The financial impact of medicare diagnosis related groups: effect upon hospitals receiving cardiac patients referred for tertiary care. Chest 1987;91(3):418–423.
3. McCarthy C. DRGs—five years later. New England Journal of Medicine 1988;318(25):1683–1686.
4. Health policy week special report. Bethesda, MD: United communications group, December 4, 1989.
5. Traska M. Will operating margins limit access to capital? Hospitals 1988;62(2):38–44.
6. Staff. Reimbursement declines limit access to capital. Hospitals 1989;63(10):22–24.
7. Hemesath M, Pope G. Linking medicare capital payments to hosptal occupancy rates. Health Affairs 1989;8(3):104–116.
8. Thorpe K, Siegal J, Daily T. Including the poor: the fiscal impacts of medicated expansion. JAMA 1989;261(7):1003–1007.
9. U.S. Department of Health and Human Services. Health care financing program statistics: analysis of state medicaid program characteristics. HCFA, 1987.
10. Friedman E. Medicare and medicaid at 25. Hospitals 1990;64(15):38–54.
11. Federal Register. Medicare program: inpatient hospital deductible for 1990. HCFA;54(188).
12. Wagner L. Catastrophic collapse: is it a millstone or a milestone for health policy evolution? Modern Healthcare 1989;19(42):20–23.
13. Kenkel P. Meeting the challenge of managed care in hospitals. Modern Healthcare 1989;19(46):52–49.
14. Knollmueller R. Case management: what's in a name? Nursing Management 1989;20(10):38–42.
15. McKenzie C, Torkelson N, Holt M. Care and cost: nursing case management improves both. Nursing Management 1989;20(10):30–34.
16. ANA nursing case management publication. No. NS-32. Kansas City: American Nurses Association, 1988.
17. Del-Togno-Armanasco V, Olivas G. Harter S. Developing an integrated nursing case management model. Nursing Management 1989;20(10):26–29.
18. Schramm C. Healthcare industry problems call for cooperative solutions. Health Care Financial Management 1990;44(1):54–61.
19. Medicare and medicaid data book. Publication 03247. HCFA, 1986.
20. Ansell D, Schiff R. Patient dumping: status, implications, and policy recommendations. JAMA 1987;257(11):1500–1502.
21. Enfield L, Sklar D. Patient dumping in the hospital emergency department: renewed interest in an old problem. American Journal of Law Medicine 1988;13(4):561–595.
22. Hudson T. New patient transfer amendments pose problems for hospitals. Hospitals 1990;64(8):46–50.
23. Woolhandler S, Himmelstein D. A national health program: northern light at the end of the tunnel. JAMA 1989;262(15):2136–2137.
24. Burda D. The nation looks for new ways to finance care for the aged. Hospitals 1987;61(18):48–54.
25. Hicks L, Bopp K, Speck R. Forecasting demand for hospital services in an unstable environment. Nursing Economics 1987;5(6):304–316.
26. Griffith H. Capitol commentary, Physician payment reform: implications for nurses. Nursing Economics 1989;7(4):231–233.
27. Skydell B, Arndt M. The price of nursing care. Nursing Clinics of North America 1988;23(3):493–501.
28. Higgerson N, Van Slyck A. Variable billing for services: new fiscal direction for nursing. JONA 1982;12(6):20–27.
29. Stepura B, Miller K. Converting nursing care cost to revenue. JONA 1989;19(5):18–22.
30. Sovie M. Variable cost of nursing care in hospitals. Annual Review of Nursing Research, 1988;131–150.
31. American Association of Critical-Care Nurses. Nursing economics task force. Newport Beach, CA: AACN, 1988.
32. American Hospital Association. Protecting an endangered species. Program notes. November, 1987.
33. Alspach J. The shortage of critical care nurses: leadership survey results. Critical Care Nurse 1988;8(3):14–21.
34. Chamberlain S, Ruzanski J, Koczan S, Pingry A, Sirois C. Retaining qualified staff. In: Cardin S, Ward C, eds. Personnel management in critical care nursing. Williams & Wilkins, Baltimore: 1989:92–106.
35. McClure M, Poulin M, Sovie M, et al. Magnet hospitals: attraction and retention of professional nurses. Kansas City: American Nurses Association, 1982:83–98.
36. American Association of Critical-Care Nurses. Demonstration project. Newport Beach, CA: AACN, 1988.

37. American Association of Critical-Care Nurses position statement: Guidelines for admission/discharge criteria in critical care. Newport Beach, CA: AACN, 1987.
38. Munoz E, Josephson J, Tenenbaum N, Goldstein J, Shears A, Wise L. Diagnosis-related groups, costs, and outcomes for patients in the intensive care unit. Heart & Lung 1989;18(6):627–633.
39. Ahmad M, Fergus L, Stothard P, Harrington D, Sivak E, Farmer R. Impact of diagnosis-related groups' perspective payment on utilization of medical intensive care. Chest 1988;93(1):176–179.
40. Charns M, Smith L. Product line management and continuum of care. Health Matrix 1989;7(1):40–49.
41. American Association of Critical-Care Nurses position statement: Role expectations for the critical care manager. Newport Beach, CA: AACN, 1986.

Chapter 20

Future Directions

JOANNE M. DISCH

Over the past 10 years, health care has been characterized in a variety of ways: as turbulent white water, as an athletic contest, as big business, as chaos. The challenge has been to balance seemingly incongruent goals, e.g., to pursue dreams with discipline, to do more with less, to put out fires while planting trees. Rosabeth Kanter (1) captures the spirit of these dichotomous demands well:

> "Think strategically and invest in the future—but keep the numbers up today
>
> Be entrepreneurial and take risks—but don't cost the business anything by failing
>
> Continue to do everything you're currently doing even better—and spend more time communicating with employees, serving on teams, and launching new projects
>
> Know every detail of your business—but delegate more responsibility to others
>
> Become passionately dedicated to "visions" and fanatically committed to carrying them out—but be flexible, responsive, and able to change direction quickly
>
> Speak up, be a leader, set the direction—but be participative, listen well, cooperate
>
> Throw yourself wholeheartedly into the entrepreneurial game and the long hours it takes—and stay fit
>
> Succeed, succeed, succeed—and raise terrific children."

To function effectively today and throughout the 1990s requires flexibility, tolerance for ambiguity, creativity, people skills, and knowledge. For nurse managers, requisite knowledge includes an understanding of nursing practice, clinical issues, management principles, strategic planning, and personnel development. Additionally, the skillful nurse manager must appreciate the environment in which health care currently takes place.

This chapter looks to the future. Three major forces with 11 areas which promise to shape the health care environment significantly over the next 10 years are highlighted. Although their selection was largely arbitrary, they represent aspects of health care which (*a*) are heavily covered in health care literature, (*b*) consume a large share of resources, and (*c*) pose a particular challenge to financial management for nursing managers. This chapter also includes 10 mandates for action for successful managers of the 1990s.

The AACN *Scope of Critical Care Nursing Practice* provides a framework for organizing the forces. Based on Donabedian's model of quality assurance which includes structure, process, and outcome components, this book identifies critical care nursing as encompassing the critical care patient (and family), the critical care nurse, and the critical care environment (2). Thus, the major forces influencing financial management in the future are organized into sections on the patient, care givers, and the environment.

MAJOR FORCES

Patient

Severity of Illness

Patients receiving care within hospitals are sicker than their counterparts of the past. With decreased length of stay, increased utilization of outpatient services, and same-day admission process for many surgical patients, the acuity of inpatients has risen dramatically.

The prevalence of certain types of diseases is changing. We have seen a reduction in the incidence of communicable diseases such as tuberculosis and smallpox. However, as immunization programs have been neglected, an increase is occurring in diseases such as measles and whooping cough. The occurrence of "modern" disease, or those related to lifestyle patterns, e.g., AIDS, lung cancer, and cirrhosis, is increasing. A reverse trend in the U.S. over the past 20 years is the sharp decline in mortality from cardiovascular disease and the mortality from cancer. This trend is particularly true among younger people, but the decline of these diseases is also now reaching those over 54 years of age (3). The number of individuals with AIDS (or AIDS-associated conditions) continues to grow. As of early 1990, more than 132,000 cases had been reported to the U.S. Centers for Disease Control. During the first 4 months of 1990 alone, almost 15,000 cases were reported (4). As the century draws to a close, the anticipated life span has shifted well past 65, largely due to the changes in incidence of certain chronic diseases (5).

Measuring the severity of illness has been a focus of attention for a number of years with tools such as the therapeutic intervention scoring system (TISS), the acute physiology and chronic health evaluation (APACHE), the diagnosis related groupings (DRGs), and MedisGroups being developed (6). The need for valid and reliable tools that reflect differences in the severity of the patient's illness and that are linked to the use of costly resources has never been greater.

Age

"The aging of our society is the dominant demographic phenomenon of our time" (7). In 1900, 3 million persons were over 65 (4% of the population), today there are 30 million (12%) in this age group (7). Moreover, in the past 20 years, the number of "old-old" has increased exponentially: a 65% increase in the 75–84 year range, and a 174% increase for those 85 and older (8). Today, reaching the age of 85 can be a realistic goal for most people (3). It certainly has for each of the 30,000 people who annually celebrate their 100th birthday; by 2000, this number will reach 100,000 annually (9).

The elderly do disproportionately consume hospital resources. They are hospitalized twice as often and stay twice as long (10). Forty-five percent of critical care beds are occupied by persons over 65; and 50% of all inpatient, acute care admissions are for persons over 75. Furthermore, 77% of Medicare costs are incurred by elderly patients in the last 6 months of their lives (11).

Access to Health Care

In 1988, it was estimated that 35 million Americans have no insurance or other financial coverage for health care (12). A 1989 survey by the U.S. Census Bureau reported that, in a 28-month period, 28% of Americans were without health insurance coverage for some period of time (13).

Access to medical care for the poor, minorities, and uninsured has decreased as well (by up to 42% for some groups) as reported by a survey of 10,000 Americans. Available medical care is significantly underused. In this survey, one in six Americans with diagnosed serious, chronic illness; one in seven pregnant women early in their pregnancies; and one in five hypertensive patients had not seen a physician during the year. Additionally, 41% of patients with up to five serious symptoms did not contact a physician about these symptoms (14).

Interestingly, some data show that the elderly have better access to health care than most other groups, even those who are non-poor, insured, and working (15). Medicare provides general assistance to them and, with their perceived vulnerability, there may be greater likelihood of obtaining supplementary coverage. The group most at risk to experience access barriers to health care seems to be those individuals who are younger, low-income, uninsured, and non-white (15).

Consumer Participation

Patients and their families are deliberately and extensively being included as partners, decision makers, and stakeholders in health care today. While private insurance is covering a greater percentage of health care costs, Americans on average paid 26% of their health care bills out of pocket; almost one in five paid more than 40% of these costs directly (16). Americans paid $113.2 billion out of pocket for health care in 1988, up 10.5% from the previous year (17).

Moreover, employees covered under employer sponsored health insurance are experiencing increased costs through sharing of premiums, deductibles, and co-payments. For example, between 1980 and 1988, the following changes occurred: (*a*) the percentage of full-time employees in medium and large firms whose companies totally paid health care premiums fell from 72 to 51% (18, 19); (*b*) the percentage of workers in these firms with deductibles greater than $100 increased from 8 to 40% (17–19);

and (c) the percentage of workers in Health Maintenance Organizations (HMOs) increased from 3 to 19% (18, 19). In September 1990, faculty at Temple University in Philadelphia went on strike for several weeks, primarily over disagreements as to co-payment of health benefits (20).

Patients and their families are also speaking out more, declaring preferences, and expressing their views. Dissatisfaction with the way in which health care has been organized, delivered, and financed in the past has been reported (21). Due to the competitive market orientation in health care, patients are being viewed as key consumers and their input is being sought. Questionnaires, surveys, polls, and interviews are being used to solicit feedback and suggestions for ways in which care can be improved.

Care Givers

Demand for and Supply of Nurses

Today, there are 2,333,000 registered nurses (RNs); 96.7% of them women, 80% of them employed (54% full-time), and approximately 68% of them working in hospitals (22). Estimates for the demand for nurses over the next 10 years vary widely. They range from those of the Department of Health and Human Services (DHHS), which concluded that the supply of nurses was in balance with requirements (23), to the Secretary's Commission on Nursing (of the DHHS), which concluded that the reported shortage of nurses is "real, widespread, and of significant magnitude" (24).

Several factors increase the demand for nurses, among them the increased acuity and aging of the patient population, and increased dependency on sophisticated technology, the wage structure for nurses in relation to other care givers, the availability of alternative care providers, and the use of nurses in new roles and capabilities (e.g., operating room first assistants, quality improvement, preadmission screening, risk management, case management, insurance claims review).

The supply of nursing students, which previously was decreasing, seems to have levelled off and, in fact, has turned upward over the past year. Enrollment in nursing schools was up 8.9% in 1989 (22) and, hopefully, will continue in that direction. Factors which will positively affect this trend include increased nursing salaries, tuition support, improvement in the working environment, and a continuation in the shift by Americans toward careers in the service industries.

New Work Force

Over the past few years, it has become apparent that a different breed of individual is driving the work force. *Time* magazine wrote of the "twentysomething" generation and characterized them as well educated, skeptical, passive, indifferent to status, shrinking in numbers, but influential in work force impact (25).

In a similar vein, *Fortune* described "yiffies . . . for young, individualistic, freedom-minded, and few" (26). These new workers state that traditional lures, such as money, title, security, and promotions do not motivate. Rather, factors such as quality of life, personal relationships, job satisfaction, and personal fulfillment do.

Several implications arise from this philosophy of life and work. First, the work environment must support flexibility, creativity, and personal fulfillment. Second, with the decreasing pool of workers, health care managers must be sure to use them in their best capacity. Third, alternative manpower options must be developed to augment the productivity of the available professional workers.

Environment

Cost of Health Care

Health care costs continue their upward spiral. In 1988, health spending totaled nearly $540 billion, or more that $2100 for each of the 254 million people in the U.S. (17). Hospital and physician care accounted for more than 50% of the expenditures. Private sources accounted for over 60% of the financing: private health insurance (32%), out-of-pocket (26%), and other private sources (5%).

The percent of the gross national product (GNP) devoted to health care has gradually increased to 11.1% in 1989, from 10.4% in the previous year. Interestingly, in various surveys (16, 27), Americans have expressed the belief that this amount is not excessive and actually may be insufficient for what is needed. Americans are dissatisfied with the level of care available and outcomes realized.

Outcomes Measurement

Called the "third revolution in medical care" (28), the outcomes movement has gained momentum as a major force among quality and effectiveness initiatives. For example, the Joint Commission on Accreditation of Healthcare Organizations has aggressively moved toward assessing quality through evaluation of severity-adjusted outcomes. The Health Care Financing Administration and the Agency for Health Care Policy and Research have launched a national program directed toward (a) the evaluation of the effectiveness of medical interventions; and (b) the development of practice guidelines for major patient conditions. Financial support has also reflected this increased emphasis. Two years ago, funding for such activities was $1.9 million; more than $30 million is allotted in the 1990 budget (29).

Benefits from this approach are predicted to include improved guidelines for practice, better information for decision making for patients and physicians, and financial savings through elimination of unnecessary treatments. Whether these benefits result remains to be seen. Changes that have already occurred, however, include a greater development and use of a large computerized data base, and a clear recognition and acceptance of a broader range of outcomes. In addition to monitoring traditional outcomes such as morbidity and mortality, practitioners and policymakers are now tracking functional status, emotional health, consumer satisfaction, cognitive functioning, and quality of life.

Clearly, nursing is well placed for redirection of practice to focus on outcomes. First, much work has already been done on the development of standards. AACN recently published the second edition of the *Standards for Nursing Care of the Critically Ill* (30). The American Nurses Association (ANA) and speciality nursing organizations have also developed standards for the care of various patient populations. Second, AACN recently published *Outcome Standards for Nursing Care of the Critically Ill* (31). Not only is this document congruent with the national movement toward outcomes measurement, it is futuristic in that it includes research bases, where available, for the outcomes studied. Third, nursing's influence on some of the outcomes has been demonstrated and acknowledged. As policymakers move toward evaluating the cost effectiveness or cost-benefit analysis of certain procedures and care givers, nursing's contributions should become increasingly visible, positive, and necessary.

Technology

The role of technology in health care has continued to expand. Previously, patients were admitted without major, intrusive procedures or treatments; today these are the norm rather than the exception. New methodologies for diagnosis and treatment emerge daily. The proliferation of types of equipment, and multiple variations of each type, is staggering. The development of new drugs and other pharmaceuticals also represent new forms of technology.

Another source of technological advance is the new use of an old technology. Consider the hyperbaric oxygen chamber. Used in the past to treat the "bends" in deep-sea divers, it is increasingly being used to heal wounds and treat conditions associated with restricted blood flow. Currently, there are about 300 chambers in the U.S.; it is predicted that within 5 years, this will increase by 500–600 additional units. Costs for chambers range from $70,000 to $2 million for multichamber units (32).

New technologies also are spurred on by necessity. With patients being discharged sooner, equipment is needed in the home. For example, with the emergence of certain forms of long-term, chronic illness, such as ventilator dependence, some patients who previously would have stayed in the hospital are now being discharged to home. They continue to be dependent on the equipment while they complete recovery or maintain a new lifestyle.

Technology has numerous benefits, but also disadvantages. While many lives have been saved and diseases corrected, costs have been increased by some technological advances. In some instances, it has become the object of competition among care providers as evidenced by the head of one radiology department's comment, "Whoever has the most toys wins" (33).

Care has become increasingly dependent on technology; often the humanistic perspective has been compromised if not lost. We are finding that there is a double-edged sword with some of the successes. For example, in our country there are 10,000 individuals currently languishing in what is a new condition, persistent vegetative state (PVS) (34). We have discovered that the ability to achieve certain outcomes, particularly the prolongation of life through the use of technology, is often accompanied by ethical concerns.

Rationing of Health Care

For much of America's history, the tradition has been that health care is a right; health is a societal priority; and, if someone needs assistance attaining a certain level, society should help. All persons were equal, no one was better than another, and all should receive similar levels of care.

Recently, however, a change in thinking has occurred. Rather than guaranteeing a certain level of care, the focus has shifted to assuring that access to care is available (35). As mentioned earlier, our country still falls short of reaching this goal.

The role of rationing in health care has also received increased scrutiny. Some argue against rationing, citing ethical reasons; others say that resources are limited and rationing is essential. In reality, rationing of health care resources has occurred. Methods of rationing include: by age, by ability to pay, by disease condition, and by waiting time. For example, Callahan (36), has stirred debate by advocating care decisions according to age; many others disagree. Perhaps unique to the U.S. is rationing according to whom you know and how you plead your case to those who control resources, e.g., the campaign by Jamie Fiske's father to secure a liver transplant for her based on his access to the American Academy of Pediatrics.

More recently, the use of a raffle was effective as a rationing tool. This was used by the state of Pennsylvania for determining who would receive a scarce drug for schizophrenia (37). The point to remember in issues related to rationing is not whether it will occur, but under what conditions it will occur and with whom as decision maker.

Ethics in Health Care

As the prevalence of economic constraints has shaped decision making, several ethical issues have emerged, e.g., do-not-resuscitate orders, life-support termination situations, patient autonomy in decision making, and physician authority. Conflicting values and obligations have obscured the individual nurse's role and complicated the long-standing dictum, "Do no harm."

For many nurses, the focus on the business objective of profit conflicts with the objective of altruistic service. The studies of ethics and economics share several traits: (a) both serve as decision-making models in helping individuals approach current and complex health care issues; (b) both rely on extensive data bases: economics on objective facts (e.g., if this happens, then that will occur), ethics on specific values (e.g., if this value is held, then this action is appropriate); and (c) both are particularly relevant in times of scarcity.

As a result of the increasing focus on ethical issues and the acknowledgment that hospitals have a responsibility to provide an ethical climate for decision making, several institutional supports have emerged. The existence of ethics committees, ombudsmen, patient bills of rights, grievance panels, and discussion groups have greatly assisted the nurse and other health care professionals in their deliberation of appropriate courses of action. A recent survey, which gathered information from more than 700 hospitals, revealed that 67.8% had ethics committees and almost 20% had bioethicists on staff (38).

Mandates for Action

A review of major forces suggests several trends for nursing managers. First, prevention of disease and health promotion will be increasingly emphasized. In many areas, extensive use of technology with its excessive costs is not justified by outcome, especially in the terminal stages of life. Working with individual patients, their families, and the community promises to yield better outcomes of health with less costs. Data are already available that demonstrate, for example, $1 spent on prenatal care saves $3 in treatment and long-term care costs (39). Whether society, policymakers, and consumers of care sufficiently redirect their efforts toward prevention and health promotion remains to be seen.

Second, methods of rationing care that are explicit, thoughtful, and systematic need to be developed. Two areas often suggested as reasonable for rationing are high technology care for the aged and for the terminally ill. Whether intentional or not, limited access for certain populations also poses a form of rationing. Many mechanisms for rationing are evolving. One acceptable alternative to extensive rationing would arise from improvements in the efficiency and effectiveness of the health care delivery system itself. The health policy debate of the 1990s will focus on ways to limit rationing and improve access to health care.

Third, accountability-based models of care delivery and evaluation will be required. With the increased emphasis on outcomes of care, the contribution of individual practitioners to those outcomes will be increasingly monitored. Currently, differences among physicians in terms of their patients' morbidity, mortality, length of stay, and use of other hospital resources are tracked and, in many institutions, feedback on physician performance on these measures is given.

Comparable scrutiny over the outcomes of nursing performance will follow. The ability of nursing managers to correlate patient outcomes with the care provided by individual nursing personnel will become critically important. Accountability-based practice models, such as primary nursing and case management, will be essential for structuring care and clearly delineating responsibility and accountability. Aiken identified the need to decentralize decisions at the unit level, standardize procedures, and promote the use of secretaries on the units (40).

A fourth mandate is to monitor trends in health care costs and changes in health care financing closely. Predictably, health care costs will continue to rise; the slope of that increase, as well as the origin of cost increases and the nature of proposed solutions must be watched closely. Initiatives, such as national health insurance, managed care, consumer co-payments, and rationing of limited resources will continue to be offered as either solutions or partial remedies for the problem of escalating health care costs. Which initiatives are selected will impact significantly on patient care and nursing practice.

Developing skill in the use of computers is a fifth mandate. The voluminous amounts of clinical and management data generated within institutions, particularly within critical care units, require control, handling interpretation, and communication. The ability to access available data and generate needed reports quickly and accurately are two skills of increasing importance.

Mandate six focuses on improving nurse-physician relationships. The value of nursing in patient care currently is being acknowledged by physicians who utilize, appreciate, and support special knowledge, expertise, and nurse autonomy. This has not always been the case in nursing, where physicians treated nurses as subservient doers existing only to carry out physician orders. Today, new models are evolving. Collaborative practice models in geriatrics, oncology, cardiology, pediatrics, and psychiatry are being used by nurses and physicians who advocate this team practice approach. Participants in collaborative demonstration projects of RNs and MDs report more trust and confidence in each other's ability, improved satisfaction with work, and positive comments from patients (41).

The massive outcry by registered nurses across the U.S. in opposition to the American Medical Association's 1989–1990 campaign to create a new care giver called, "registered care technologist," shows that we still have a long way to go in improving relationships among nurses and physicians. The AMA did announce in mid-1990 the abandonment of this program due to a lack of places willing to pilot the project. The whole issue caused many physicians to seek input from staff nurses, focus on the nursing shortage, and look at interpersonal relationships. Hopefully, a new partnership will emerge of working together as colleagues for what is in the best interest of our patients. Positive communication styles, appropriate interpersonal relationships, and respect and trust will lead to new roles in an interdependent relationship.

Innovation and creativity in nursing are the seventh mandate. With the continued focus on reducing costs without compromising quality, nursing managers feel the pressure of developing new and better methods of care delivery. The concept of "all or none" may not work on every nursing unit with staff who seek greater flexibility, autonomy in practice, and professionalism. Nursing managers must assess current methods as they relate to quality outcomes and ask, "what can we do better to improve patient outcomes?" In asking thought-provoking questions, the manager stimulates contributions by the staff for the good of the patients. Creating a climate that promotes decisions initiated by staff facilitates a positive environment. Each clinical nurse brings ideas and solutions that, when nurtured and encouraged, promote the best outcomes. Morale and productivity can soar when the manager listens and supports more self-management through innovative and creative practice. Most nurses in critical care are creative problem solvers and thrive on being part of the solution.

Mandate eight requires exemplary leadership by nursing managers. Leadership involves making quantum leaps personally and professionally by developing breakthrough thinking (42). Skillfully communicating the hospital's mission, creating synergy, willingly taking risks, seeking failure, tolerating ambiguity, laughing, and flaming the passions of the joys of nursing will serve the nurse manager of the 21st century. Most nurse managers already work hard enough managing the moment-to-moment crisis, each one seemingly worse than the last. Continuing to function in this manner leads to more of the same: frustration: workacholic syndrome, codependence, and physical exhaustion. While the target is visible, nurse managers must be ready to take aim and fire, knowing that taking action leads to further adjustment and refinement. Failure to fire is failed leadership.

The ninth mandate instills quality improvement in the minds and actions of every care giver with each patient encounter. Quality is the product of nursing care and the outcome sought by patients, physicians, and nurses. We as nurse managers in critical care must instill a "no excuse" approach by focusing on quality improvement at every opportunity. This means reacting immediately to a quality issue, seeking facts, listening, being open and challenged by change, and preventing the problem from occurring again. This may mean looking at the systems and fixing the process. Every nurse who is part of the problem is part of the solution. Encouraging a team approach to evaluate the system issues promotes a quality improvement philosophy and empowers employees to action. The manager's goal is to eliminate hassles for the staff and barriers to quality outcomes. Quality stories, both good and bad, need to be shared at every clinical staff meeting, with the focus on what was done right and what can be changed and done better.

The tenth and last mandate supports the need for nursing research in all aspects of financial management of nursing care. Ingersoll and others reported in a 1990 article that gaps in nursing research exist in comprehensive cost-benefit and cost-effectiveness analyses, information about the effects of technology on patient care, evaluations of innovative care delivery methods, evaluations of information systems, and studies of ethical issues related to scarce resources (43). Not only must research be conducted in these areas, it must be utilized, shared, replicated, and supported. With tighter constraints on the health care dollar, nursing research may link the best methods for nursing care delivery with the best use of resources. Much work needs to be done in researching nursing management systems.

CONCLUSION

Nursing lives in an arena of enormous complexity, surrounded by a rapidly-changing environment. External and internal pressures push and pull nursing in different ways. Balancing the three major forces in the 11 areas of concern requires the skills of bright, creative, and resourceful managers. Ten mandates for action provide direction for the future.

REFERENCES

1. Kanter RM. When giants learn to dance. New York: Simon and Schuster, 1989:20–21.
2. American Association of Critical-Care Nurses position statement: Scope of critical care nursing practice. Newport Beach, CA: AACN, 1989.
3. Breslow L. A health promotion primer for the 1990s. Health Affairs 1990;9(2):6–21.
4. Zuercher A. A look at the latest U.S. AIDS projections. Health Affairs 1990;9(2):163–170.
5. National Center for Health Statistics. Health, U.S., 1987. DHHS Pub. no. (PHS)88-1232. Washington, DC: U.S. Government Printing Office, March, 1988.
6. Sixth report to the president and congress on the status of health personnel in the U.S. Washington, DC: Bureau of Health Professions, Health Resources Administration.
7. Omenn GS. Prevention and the elderly: appropriate policies. Health Affairs 1990;9(2):80–93.
8. U.S. Senate Special Committee on Aging. Aging America: trends and projections. Washington, DC: AARP, 1988.
9. Mezey M. Aging fact sheet (USA). Personal files, 1990.
10. Fein R. Medical care: medical costs. Cambridge, MA: Harvard University Press, 1986;82.
11. Fulmer TT, Walker MK. Lessons from the elder boom in ICUs. Journal of Geriatric Nursing 1990;7(3):23–27.
12. Wilensky GR. Filling the gaps in health insurance: impact on competition. Health Affairs 1988;7(3):133–149.
13. Nelson C, Short K. Health insurance coverage, 1986–1988. Current Population Reports, Series P-70, No. 17. Washington, DC: U.S. Census Bureau, March, 1990.
14. Freeman HE, Blendon RJ, Aiken LH, Sudman S, Mullinix CF, Corey CR. Americans report on their access to health care. Health Affairs 1987;6:6–18.
15. Hayward RA, Shapiro MR, Freemand HD, Corey CR. Inequities in health services among insured Americans. New England Journal of Medicine 1988;318(23):1507–1512.
16. Health care in the U.S. Poll No. 212 (Storrs, Conn.:

Roper Center for Public Opinion Research). Los Angeles: Los Angeles Times, March, 1990.
17. Levit KR, Freeland MS, Waldo DR. National health care spending trends: 1988. Health Affairs 1990;9(2):171–184.
18. U.S. Bureau of Labor Statistics. Employee benefits in medium and large firms. Washington, DC: GPO, August 1989.
19. U.S. Bureau of Labor Statistics. Employee benefits in medium and large firms. Washington, DC: GPO, September, 1981.
20. Collins H, Ellis L. Health benefits' cost causing strife on campuses. Philadelphia Inquirer September 10, 1990; B1.
21. Blendon RJ, Leitman R, Morrison I, Donelan K. Satisfaction with health systems in ten nations. Health Affairs 1990;9(2):185–192.
22. American Nurses Association. ANA media background sheet, 1990.
23. Thomas JW, Ashcraft MLF. Measuring severity of illness: A comparison of interrater reliability among severity methodologies. Inquiry 1989;26(4):483–492.
24. Secretary's Commission on Nursing: Final Report. 1988 Washington, DC: U.S. Department of Health and Human Services.
25. Gross DM, Scott S. Proceeding with caution: the twentysomething generation. Time 1990;136(3):56–62.
26. Deutschman A. What 25-year-olds want. Fortune 1990; 122(5):42–50.
27. Blendon RJ. The public's view of the future of health care. Journal of the American Medical Association 1988;259(2):3589.
28. Relman AS. Is rationing inevitable? New England Journal of Medicine 1990;322(5):1809–1810.
29. Epstein AM. The outcomes movement: will it get us where we want to go? New England Journal of Medicine 1990;323(4):266–269.
30. Sanford S, Disch J, eds. Standards for nursing care of the critically ill, 2nd ed. Newport Beach, CA: American Association of Critical-Care Nurses, 1989.
31. Kuhn RC, Ackerman SC, Barnsteiner JH, Turzan L, Tyler ML, Wotring KE, eds. Outcome standards for nursing care of the critically ill. Newport Beach, CA: American Association of Critical-Care Nurses, 1990.
32. Appleby CR. New uses for hyperbaric therapy make a splash. Healthweek 1990;4(16):10.
33. Pearlman E. When tech strategy is reduced to toy collecting. Healthweek 1990;4(16):16.
34. Angell M. Prisoners of technology. New England Journal of Medicine 1990;322(25):1806–1808.
35. Equity in health care debated. Hospitals August 1, 1983; 1983:17.
36. Callahan D. Setting limits: medical goals in an aging society. New York: Simon and Schuster; 1987.
37. Pa. plans 'lottery' to distribute costly new drug for schizophrenia. Phil Inquirer July 28, 1990; A1.
38. Lanken P. Personal communication, September 12, 1990.
39. Mason JO. A prevention policy framework for the nation. Health Affairs 1990;9(2):22–29.
40. Aiken LH. Charting the future of hospital nursing. Image: Journal of Nursing Scholarship, Spring 1990;22(2):72–78.
41. Stein LI, Watts DT, Howell T. Sounding board. The doctor-nurse game revisited. New England Journal of Medicine, 1990;8:'546–549.
42. Pritchett P. you2. Dallas: Quicksilver Press, 1990;1–14.
43. Ingersoll GL, Hoffort N, Schultz AW. Health services research in nursing: current status and future directions. Nursing Economics, 1990;4:229–238.

Glossary

Accounting. The act of classifying, recording, reporting, and summarizing quantitative information much of which is financial and interpreting results.

Accounting Concepts/Principles. Rules and guidelines used in performing accounting activities which are generally accepted.

Accounts Payable. Short-term debt owed to a creditor for products and services provided.

Accounts Receivable. Amounts owed to the organization by its customers for services rendered to them.

Accrual Accounting. A system of accounting in which revenue is recorded in the accounting period in which it is earned and expenses are recorded in the accounting period in which they are used. This procedure does not consider cash receipts or disbursements.

Allowance. An adjustment to revenues that reflects the difference from the actual amount charged to the amount billed such as bad debt, charity, and discounts. Also may be called an adjustment.

Application. A set of computer programs that perform a certain task such as payroll, order entry, and results reporting.

Archive. A copy that is saved for future reference or for recovery purposes in case the original data are damaged or destroyed.

Artificial Intelligence. The branch of computer science that involves using computers to simulate human thinking.

Asset. An economic resource owned by an organization or individual that can be exchanged for value.

Audit. An independent study and report of financial activities.

Automation. Refers to the use of machines to do work once done by people.

Bad Debt. An amount not paid by the customer, despite various efforts to collect, written off as an allowance.

Balance Sheet. A financial report listing assets, liabilities, and fund balances of an organization as of a specific date, usually the end of the month or fiscal year.

Base Wage Rate. The hourly rate of pay before all other wage enhancements.

Benefit. When a person is better off or an outcome has improved.

Benefit-Cost Ratio. Monetary benefits divided by monetary costs.

Board of Trustees (Directors). A group of individuals elected or appointed to oversee the financial and long-term objectives of an organization.

Bond. A legal contract where the issuer agrees to make specified interest payments and to repay borrowed principal at an agreed date of maturity.

Bond Ratings. Independent assessments by financial organizations of the potential risk associated with the bond offering and potential yield for investors.

Break-Even Level. The volume at which revenue and expenses are exactly equal resulting in no gain or loss.

Budget. A financial forecast of plans for revenue and expenses.

Budgeting. A systematic process that incorporates past and present information into decisions about financial requirements for the future.

Business Plans. A detailed formal document that presents the business being proposed or changed and what expected performance measurements and outcomes will be over a specified time frame.

Capital Asset. A long-term asset with a life of greater than one year, such as facility and major equipment.

Capital Budgeting. A process of planning and decision making on assets whose returns are expected to be longer than one year.

Capital Equipment. Major movable items of a certain value with a usable life of greater than one year.

Case Management. A patient care delivery system in which collaborative and coordinated management of care measures both clinical and financial outcomes.

Cash Flow. The amount of cash received (revenue) and cash paid out (expenses), also called the inflows and outflows of cash.

Centralized Budgeting. Budget planning and control done by top administration.

Certified Public Accountant (CPA). An individual who has studied auditing, accounting theory, business law, and accounting practices and successfully passes the national accounting examination.

Charge. Amount of money which has been set as the price or rate for a product or service.

Charity. Uncollected revenue from those who cannot pay.

Comparative Analysis. The act of making comparisons and then determining an action plan to be communicated to the parties involved.

Comparisons. Process of noting the similarities and differences from what was planned.

Competition. Provides for welfare maximization by preventing undue concentration of power and resources as well as the exploitation of the consumer.

Competitive Market. A free exchange system driven by the demand for, and supply, price, and quantity of goods and services.

Computer. A machine capable of executing and storing instructions on data.

Contractual Allowance. Formal contracts with third-party payors and providers to discount or adjust rates for services and products.

Contribution Margin. The amount that is the excess of revenues over variable expenses that contributes to the fixed costs.

Controlling. A management function of checking, directing, restraining, and regulating resources in comparison to objectives of plans and mission.

Copy. Transferring information to another location while leaving the original unchanged.

Cost. A monetary value assigned to an asset, service, or product which is incurred when used.

Cost Accounting. A financial system of identifying all the costs associated with a good or service.

Cost Allocation. The method of gathering costs in an organized fashion and assigning them to an account.

Cost-Benefit Analysis. The study of the relationship between costs and benefits, expressed in monetary terms.

Cost Center. A department that incurs costs.

Cost Feasibility. Expected costs compared to available resources.

Critical Path. A plan defining key events and expected outcomes at crucial times.

Current Assets. Cash and other assets that may reasonably be expected to be realized in cash, sold, or consumed during the normal operating cycle of an organization within one year.

Current Liabilities. Obligations that are expected to be satisfied either by the use of current assets or by the creation of other current liabilities which are due within one year.

Current Ratio. A common measure of liquidity determined by dividing current assets by current liabilities.

Cutback Management. A systematic process of downsizing programs and personnel in response to organizational change.

Data. Factual information

Data Base Management. The task of storing and organizing data in a bank for the purpose of retrieving information necessary or decision making.

Days:Cash-on-hand Ratio. Examines how many day's bills the cash on-hand would pay determined by the amount of cash divided by (expenses minus depreciation) divided by 365 days in a year.

Days:In Patient Accounts Receivable Ratio. Examines how many day's worth of revenues are represented in accounts receivable calculated by net accounts receivable divided by the net patient revenue divided by 365.

Debt:Equity Ratio. Illustrates the balance that the management of an organization has struck between the forces of risk (debt) versus cost (equity) calculated by long-term debt divided by fund balance.

Decentralized Budgeting. Budget responsibility and accountability at the lowest level of the organization that has knowledge and skill for responsible decision making.

Deductible Ratio. Measures the relationship of the gross operating revenues that will not be realized in cash because of deductions calculated by deductions from revenue divided by gross operating revenue.

Demand. Indicates the level of interest in or need for a particular type of health care service.

Depreciation. The accounting process for the gradual conversion of plant and equipment capitalized cost into expense due to wear and deterioration.

Diagnosis Related Groups (DRG). A patient classification system used by the Health Care Financing Administration for Medicare patients that sorts them into groups according to medical conditions.

Differential Accounting. Estimates how costs, revenues, and assets would be different if one course were adopted as compared to an alternative course of action.

Direct Cost. Costs that are directly traced to goods or services.

Direct Expense. Expenses that are traceable to an actual service or good.

Discount. A reduction from the full amount of a price or debt.

Disk. A magnetic computer memory device.

Diversification. Entry of a hospital into an expanded mix of health- or non-health-care-related businesses for vertical and horizontal integration.

Economic Forecasting. A technique using statistically estimated models to analyze conditions in the real world.

Economic Ordering Quantity (EOQ). The optimum quantity to be ordered each time an order is placed.

Effectiveness. Determination of goal attainment through production of outputs.

Efficiency. Achieving the lowest possible cost of production for the benefits delivered.

GLOSSARY

Electronic Mail. A process of sending and receiving information via a computer terminal.

Entity. A specific area of accountability or a going concern.

Equity. The excess of assets over liabilities.

Evaluation. A systematic process of analyzing inputs and outputs for the purpose of making decisions.

Ex Ante Cost-Benefit Analysis. Anticipated costs and benefits.

Expense. Those products or services consumed in operations of the business.

Ex Post Cost-Benefit Analysis. Actual costs and benefits realized.

External Audit. A formal examination or verification of financial records completed by an outside firm of public accountants or auditors.

Financial Accounting. The process of identifying, measuring, and communicating economic information to permit informed judgments and decisions by users of the information through three financial statements: the balance sheet, the income statement, and the statement of cash flows.

Financial Accounting Standards Board (FASB). A nongovernmental organization created in 1973 to develop new or modified generally accepted accounting principles.

Financial Management. The process of managing an organization's revenues, assets, and use in order to meet certain goals.

Fiscal Year. A 12-month period designated for the measurement of the financial operations of an entity or organization.

Fixed Assets. Assets that are tangible and relatively long lived known as plant, property, or equipment.

Fixed Asset Turnover Ratio. Illustrates how much the organization is able to use existing fixed assets to generate revenues calculated by total operating revenue divided by total fixed assets.

Fixed Costs. Costs that do not vary with volume.

Flexible budget. A process allowing for budget adjustments due to changes in volume, revenues, and expenses.

Floppy Disk. A computer storage medium made of magnetic coating covered with a protective plastic jacket.

Footnotes. Notes which accompany and are deemed an integral part of the financial statements which explain unusual occurrences.

Formative Evaluation. Focuses on program elements during the developmental and implementation stages of a program.

Full-time Equivalent. The equivalent of one employee working 2080 hours a year.

Fund Balance. The amount that remains after all the liabilities have been deducted from the assets; noted on the balance sheet.

General Ledger. A book containing all the accounting transactions.

Generally Accepted Accounting Principles (GAAP). Ground rules that govern financial accounting.

Goals. Broadly stated terminal outcomes.

Governing Body. Individuals or a group that has the ultimate authority for mission, plans, and decisions.

Graphics. Computer output devices such as screens and plotters used to produce pictures.

Gross National Product (GNP). The sum of all final goods and services produced in a given time period.

Hardware. All the physical elements in the computer such as integrated circuits and wires as well as the terminals and processors.

Income Statement. The accounting report that summarizes revenues and expenses of an accounting period.

Incremental Budgeting. A budget technique using the last year's base and adding or subtracting an amount calculated by predetermined criteria or projected change in services.

Indirect Cost. A cost that cannot be directly traced to a service, good, or person.

Indirect Expense. An expense which cannot be directly traced to a service, good, or person.

Inflation. A market-driven factor of a varied percentage applied to goods and services at certain time periods.

Information System. A manual or computerized method of providing data and reports to management for the purposes of planning and decision making.

Input. Any contribution to a system.

Intangible. Difficult to assign a monetary value due to being unclear or difficult to perceive.

Interface. Computer hardware and software whose purpose is to convert data from one form to another enabling different systems to communicate with one another.

Internal Audit. A formal examination or verification of financial records or activities completed by the organization's own staff of auditors.

Internal Rate of Return. A method of calculating the return on an investment that incorporates the time value of money.

Inventory. A detailed list of supplies, including quantity and value of items listed.

Inventory Turnover Ratio. The ratio most commonly used in analyzing the size of inventory calculated by total operating revenue divided by inventory.

Joint Venture. A financial undertaking by two or more parties for the purpose of making a profit.

Keyboard. A typewriter-like arrangement for typing various functions and numbers to enter information into a computer terminal.

Lease. An alternative to purchase for acquiring capital equipment.

Leverage. The amount to which the organization has equity to meet debt.

Liability. An obligation to outside parties arising from events that have already happened.

Line Item Budget. A detailed budget technique of listing each expense item on a separate line.

Liquidity. Refers to the organization's ability to meet its current obligations.

Liquidity Ratio. A measure of performance that focuses on how well short-term obligations can be met by looking at current liabilities and current assets.

Long-term Debt. Refers to debt or amount owed that will be repaid over a period of greater than one year.

Mainframe. A large computer occupying an environmentally-designed room that typically supports more than 100 users at a time.

Managed Care. A patient care delivery system organized internally or externally to maximize cost and outcome.

Management by Objectives (MBO). A budget and management technique that integrates goals and objectives throughout each level of the organization through planning, implementing, and evaluation for a given time period.

Managerial Accounting. A process of identifying, measuring, analyzing, preparing, interpreting, and communicating information about accounting that assists in meeting organizational objectives.

Marginal Cost. The cost of producing or consuming an additional unit.

Market Share. The proportion of business experienced compared to total business available in a certain area.

Master Budget. The total budget that consolidates the overall plans of the organization.

Matching. A concept of establishing the relationship of the revenues with the expenses.

Medicaid. A state administered program that provides medical care according to preestablished criteria.

Medicare. A federally-administered program for the elderly over aged 65 and the disabled.

Microcomputer. A computer in which the processing unit consists of a single integrated circuit known as the microprocessor, usually used by one person.

Minicomputer. A computer of intermediate size between a microcomputer and a mainframe computer that supports 10 to 100 users at a time.

Monitor. A visual display unit.

Net Income. The excess of all the revenues over all the expenses for a given period.

Net Present Value. A method of evaluating projects through the use of calculating the cost of capital for a project by discounting the expected future cash flows to the present.

Net Worth. The amount of surplus in an organization, also called owner's equity.

Nonoperating Revenue. The amount of revenue that comes from nonpatient sources.

Nonproductive Hours. Hours paid for time away from the usual work assignment such as sick time, vacation, or training time.

Nonquantification. No value is assigned to an intangible good or service because it is to difficult to do so.

Not for Profit. A term referring to the tax exempt status of an organization.

Objectives. Realistic, measurable, timely, and purposeful action.

Occupancy. A measurement of the percent of actual to total bed capacity.

Operating Budget. The plan that identifies expected revenues and expenses for a future time period, usually one year.

Operating Expenses. An expense generated by the day-to-day operations in conducting the business of the organization.

Operating Margin Ratio. The measure of overall profitability of an organization calculated by net operating income divided by total operating revenue.

Opportunity Cost. The maximum alternative gain that could have been realized if the service or product had been invested somewhere else.

Outcome. What results from something or the consequences of various actions and events.

Output. The quantity or the amount produced.

Overhead. The general costs of running a business that are indirect costs.

Patient Classification Systems. A method of differentiating among patients based on patient need in order to determine required care hours.

Payback. A method of determining the amount of time needed to recover, in the form of cash coming in, the initial dollars invested.

Payor. A person or group who owes a debt.

Payor Mix. A distribution of the number of individuals and organized subscribers paying for health care.

Planning, Programming Budgets (PPB). A budget technique that specifies objectives with a variety of alternatives for achievement including analysis of determining costs and benefit.

Price. The monetary value assigned to a good or service to be sold.

Processing. The performance of logical operations and calculations on information in real time.

Processing Unit. The part of the computer that includes the circuits that control the interpretation of execution of instructions.

Product-Line Management (PLM). A budget and business technique that relies on planning, managing, and marketing strategies to promote specific products or product-lines to consumers.

Productive Hours. Hours worked in performance of regular duties.

Productivity. The comparison of inputs to outputs and a measure of efficiency.

Profit. The excess of revenues over expenses.

Program. A set of interrelated activities carried out to accomplish a specific set of goals.

Rate Setting. The process of establishing a price to cover all costs.

Ratio. The relationship of one amount to another.

Ratio of Cost to Charge. A method of rate setting involving the determination of the relationship of all the costs in providing the service or good to the charge needed to generate a satisfactory margin.

Realization. The concept that recognizes revenues.

Relative Value Unit. An indexed number calculated on various procedures based upon the relative amount of supplies, labor, and equipment needed to perform the procedure.

Regionalization. An arrangement of services by geographic area.

Reimbursement. The amount paid for services previously rendered.

Reliability. Consistency and stability of a measure.

Responsibility Accounting. A system of accounting that accumulates, recognizes, and communicates historical and projected fiscal data throughout the organization and reflects the revenues and expenses for various centers which are responsible for the operations.

Return on Investment. A test of profitability calculated by the income or profit divided by the investment which was required to obtain the income or profit.

Revenue Center. The area of responsibility for revenues.

Revenues. The inflow of assets in exchange for services or products.

Risk. The probability of exposure to loss.

Semivariable Costs. Costs that vary with volume but not directly; a portion of these costs may be fixed.

Severity of Illness. A measure of a patient's condition as determined by clinical outcomes for the purpose of predicting outcome.

Shadow Prices. Any reasonable ascription of value assigned to a good not openly traded in the market.

Software. The set of programs that tell the computer what to do.

Solvency. Refers to the organization's ability to meet the interest costs and repayment schedules associated with its long-term obligations.

Standard. A concrete measure of something.

Statement of Cash Flows. A formal explanation of the sources and uses of resources and the changes resulting.

Strategic Planning. A process of determining long range goals and future directions.

Summative Evaluation. Focuses on the achievement of stated goals and objectives.

Support Department. Those areas of the health care facility that do not generate revenues from the patients.

Supply. The quantity of resources available.

Surcharge. The base amount plus an additional amount or percent.

Tangible. Resources that can be assigned a monetary value.

Third-Party Payor. An agency or group that contracts with hospitals and patients to pay for the care provided usually at a negotiated rate.

Times Earned Interest Ratio. The relationship between an organization's income and its interest requirements, calculated by net income plus interest, divided by interest.

Total Asset Turnover Ratio. Illustrates how much the organization is able to use existing total assets to generate revenue, calculated by total operating revenue divided by total assets.

Total Operating Revenue. A summary of the total patient care revenues and other operating revenues less any allowance (deductions).

Transactions. A recording of any event that affects the financial position of an organization.

Turnover. The percentage of employed nurses who leave their jobs during a time period.

Validity. The tool measures what it is supposed to measure.

Variable Cost. Those costs that vary with volume.

Variance. A difference of actual results from what was budgeted or expected to occur.

Vendor. A supplier of medical goods and services.

Working Capital. The amount of current assets in an organization over the amount of current liabilities and often refers to investments.

Work Load Index (WLI). A factored amount derived from required patient care hours applied to current work; the WLI is utilized to determine staffing levels.

Zero Base Budgets (ZBB). A budget technique that starts at ground zero without considering past accomplishments but focuses evaluation and justification on all programs and activities annually as though they were being started for the first time.

Index

Page numbers in *italics* denote figures; those followed by "t" denote tables.

Absenteeism, 203
Access to care, 15, 267–268, 276
 cost shifting, 247, 267
 for elderly persons, 276
 for high-technology procedures/resources, 268
 for medically indigent persons, 267
 patient "dumping," 267–268
 for rural population, 268
Accounting, 18–31
 accounting entity or going-concern concept, 19
 accounts payable, 21
 accounts receivable, 20–21
 accrual, 21–22, 22t
  advantages of, 22
  applied to hours worked and vacation time, 22
  vs. cash basis system, 22
  definition of, 283
  example of, 22
 allocation, 27, 28t
 bad debt, 24, 29, 33, 45, 244
 charges, 25
 concepts/principles of, 283
 continuing concern concept, 25
 cost, 208
  definition of, 284
 cost center vs. revenue center, 25
 cost valuation principle, 23
 costs, 26–27, 28t
 definition of, 18, 283
 depreciation, 27–29, 28t, 47, 112–113
 differential, 208–210
  definition of, 208, 284
  example of, 209–210
  steps in, 208–209
 duality principle, 23, 24t
 expenses, 25–26
 financial, 18–19, 285
 flow of revenue
  payment for supplies and equipment, 31
  purchase of capital equipment, 31
 functions of, 18
 generally accepted principles for, 285
 managerial, 18–19, 286
 matching and cost recovery principles, 23–24
 money measurement principle, 23
 objectivity principle, 24
 principle of materiality, 24
 process of, 18
 purpose of, 18
 rate setting, 29–30
 realization (recognition) principle, 21, 21t

 responsibility, 208, 287
 revenue, 25
 stable-dollar (stable-monetary-unit) concept, 23
 transactions, 19–20
Accounts payable, 21
 definition of, 21, 283
 discounts for rapid payment, 21
Accounts receivable, 20–21
 collection of, 20
 days: inpatient accounts receivables ratio, 284
 definition of, 20, 283
 factors affecting conversion to cash, 20
 precertification and, 21
 relation to cash flow, 20
Activity ratios, 51–52
Acute physiology and chronic health evaluation (APACHE), 276
Aging of population, 276
AIDS, 276
Allowance
 contractual, 33–34, 45, 284
 definition of, 283
Alternative care givers, 216–217
Alternative choice process, 208–210
 definition of, 208
 example of, 209–210
 steps in, 208–209
Antitrust legislation, 256
Application, 167, definition of, 283
Archive, definition of, 283
Artificial intelligence, 171
 definition of, 283
Assets
 accounts receivable, 20–21
 on balance sheet, 43–44
 capital, 113
  definition of, 283
 current, 20, 43–44
  definition of, 284
 definition of, 43, 283
 fixed, 44, 285
 fixed asset turnover ratio, 285
 liquidity of, 43
Audits, 47–49
 definition of, 48, 283
 external, 48, 285
 internal, 47, 285
 rules for, 48–49
Automation, 170
 definition of, 283

289

INDEX

Back injuries, 203–204
Bad debt, 24, 29, 33, 45, 244
  definition of, 24, 29, 283
  determinants of, 29
  difference from charity care, 29
  matching to revenue, 24
  prevention of, 29
Balance sheet, 43–44, 44t
  assets on, 43–44
  definition of, 283
  format of, 43
  fund balance on, 44
  liabilities on, 44
  time period of, 43
Bank loans, 115, 244
Bar code system, 157–159
Base wage rate, 124, 125t
  definition of, 283
Bedside computer systems, 170
Benefit-cost ratio, 226, 228, 228t, definition of, 283
Benefits
  definition of, 283
  employee (fringe), 87, 126, 190, 194–95
Bereavement leave, 191
Billing, 20
Board of Trustees (Directors), 257
  definition of, 283
Bond ratings, 51, 115, definition of, 283
Bonds, 115
  definition of, 283
  tax-exempt, 243–244
Bonus pay, 125
Break-even level, 29, definition of, 283
Budgeting
  centralized, 57–58, 283
  decentralized, 57–58, 284
  definition of, 57, 99, 283
  incremental, 285
  methods of, 66–80. *See also* specific strategies
    business plans, 77, 78t–79t
    cutback management, 66–69
    downsizing, 69–74
    product-line management, 74–77
Budgeting process, 32–33, 81–97
  administrative phase of, 39
  application of nursing process to, 32
  basis of budget development, 83
  budget cycle, 38–39
  calendar for, 40t, 83–84, 84t
  capital budget, 37–38, 38t, 89–90, 98–117. *See also* Capital budgeting
  communication of goals and objectives for, 39
  computerized assistance in management of, 90
  data collection, 32
    consistency/accuracy of reports used, 84
    sources for, 84–85
    types of data, 85
  determining fiscal year for, 38–39
  evaluation, 33
  expense budget, 87–89
  implementation, 33, 39
  integrated budget programming, 82
  organizational assumptions affecting, 84–85

  organizational prerequisites for, 82–83
  planning budget, 33
  presentation and approval, 39, 172–176
    articulation of unit's needs, 173–174
    chief nursing officer's role, 172–173
    congruence with institutional goals, 173
    final presentation checklist, 172, 172t
    finalizing budget package, 172
    hierarchy of approval process, 172, 173t
    responsibility for, 172–173, 173t
    strategies for approval, 174t, 174–176
  quantification of budget, 39
  roles of financial department, 39–41
  strategic planning and, 32, 33, 39, 41–42, 81–82
  use of forecasted data, 83, 85–87, 86t
  use of historical data, 83, 85, 86t
Budgets, 32–42
  advantages of using, 32
  continuous ("rolling"), 57
  definition of, 32, 56, 283
  development of, 58–60, 59t
    control stage, 59
    management stage, 59
    planning stage, 59–60
  expenses, 34t, 35, 36t
  flexible, 58, 179–180, 180t, 207, 285
  formats for, 60–66. *See also* specific formats
    comparison of, 60t, 77t
    line-item budgeting, 60–61, 286
    management by objectives, 62–64
    planning, programming and budgeting system, 61–62
    zero-base budgeting, 64–66, 66t
  master, 286
  monitoring and reviewing of, 41
  nurse manager's responsibility for, 56–57
  as operational plans, 81
  organization of hospital budget, 56
  profit, 35–37
  quantitative vs. qualitative components of, 32
  relation to strategic planning, 32, 33, 41–42, 81–82
  revenues, 33–35, 34t
  time encompassed by, 57
  types of, 37–38
    capital, 37–38, 38t, 98–117. *See also* Capital budgeting
    operating, 37, 144–162. *See also* Operating budgets
    personnel, 37, 118–130. *See also* Personnel budgets
    revenue, 37
Business plans, 230
  definition of, 77, 283
  description of, 77
  example of, 41–42
  master outline for, 78t–79t
  role of fiscal department in, 41

Call back pay, 126
Capital budgeting, 37–38, 38t, 89–90, 98–117
  application of nursing process to, 109
  approval process for, 99–100

capital equipment report for surgical ICU, 100, 101t
capital equipment requests, 96–97, 100, 102t
components of, 89, 98
definition of, 99, 283
depreciation, 27–29, 47, 112–113
discounted cash flow analysis for, 89
effect of prospective payment system on, 98
example of, 103–106
financial analysis techniques for, 110–112
  internal rate of return, 89, 111
  net present value, 89, 111
  payback method, 111–112
  return on assets, 112
  return on investment, 110–111
financial aspects of, 109–110
importance of hospital's organization for, 98–99
nurse manager's responsibility for, 98–100
purchase vs. lease decisions, 113–114
reasons for capital expenditures, 89
recording capital assets, 113
steps in, 89
  developing list of equipment with justifications and priorities, 100–103
  establishing unit goals and objectives, 100, 103
  evaluating present equipment for upgrading, 102, 106
  evaluating proposed equipment, 104t–105t, 106, 107t–109t
  installing and evaluating equipment, 103, 106
  selecting vendors, 102–103, 104t–105t, 106
strategic planning and, 99
terminology for, 99
timetable for, 89
Capital financing, 114–115, 243–244
costs of, 244
effect of prospective payment system on, 114
factors affecting decisions about, 244
long-term debt, 115, 244, 286
methods of, 115, 243–244
  bank loans, 115
  bonds, 115, 243–244
  equity financing, 115
  restricted funds, 244
sources of, 115
Capital investments, 240
Capital structure ratios, 51
Care hours per patient day, 269–270
direct, 120t, 120–121
indirect, 121
in urban hospitals, 260t, 260–261
variance reporting on, 189
Case management, 218, 266–267
critical paths in, 218
definition of, 283
effect on length of stay, 218
financial impact of, 218
hospital-based, 218
Cash flows
definition of, 283
statement of, 46–47, 48t
Catastrophic coverage, 265–266
Census

calculation of, 119, 120t
low, 207
Certificate of need legislation, 246–247
Certification pay, 124
Certified public accountant, 48, definition of, 283
Change in financial position, 46. *See also* Statement of cash flows
Charges, 25
definition of, 25, 283
determinants of, 25
for outpatient services, 241
ratio of costs to, 287
Charity care, 29, 33, 45, 267–268
definition of, 284
Chief executive officer, 172–173, 258
Chief financial officer, 39–41, 258
duties of, 39
role in business planning, 41
role in development of annual budget, 39–41
Chief information officer, 258
Chief nursing officer, 172–173, 258
Clinical nurse specialist, 203
Collaborative practice model, 217
Community hospital, 251, 252t
Comparative analysis, 110, 207, definition of, 284
Comparisons, 207
definition of, 207
Competition, 245–246
in critical care delivery, 246
definition of, 284
effect on price, 245–246
effect on quality of service, 246
in free market economy, 245
in health care delivery system, 245
for personnel, 246
rate setting based on, 30
Competitive markets, 245
definition of, 284
Computerized severity index, 6
Computers
access to, 165
artificial intelligence systems, 171
bedside systems, 170
definition of, 284
developing skills, 280
disks for, 284, 285
electronic mail, 169
expert systems, 170–171
hardware for, 164–166
  definition of, 285
  mainframes, 165–166
  micros, 166
  minis, 166
vs. nonautomated systems, 170
personal, 166
software for, 167–169
  data base management, 90, 168–169
  spreadsheets, 90, 167–168, *168–169*
  word processing, 168
use in managing budgets, 90
Consumers, 11–12
definition of, 11
elderly, 11–12

Consumers—*continued*
  expectations for health care, 11
  uninsured, 11, 267–268, 276
Continuing concern concept, 25
Continuing education costs, 155
Contractual allowances, 33–34, 45
  definition of, 284
Contribution margin, definition of, 284
Controlling, 198–210
  comparisons for, 207
  components of, 198
  decision making and, 207–210
    cost accounting, 208
    definition of, 207
    differential accounting, 208–210
    responsibility accounting, 208
  definition of, 198, 284
  expectations for, 201
  materials and inventory control, 204–205. *See also* Supplies
  nurse manager's roles in, 198
  participation in budgeting, 198–199
    collaboration with physicians, 199
    education, 199
    staff nurses' roles, 199
    worker satisfaction, 199
  personnel control, 201–204. *See also* Personnel control
  process of, *198*
  result of, 198
  of services, 205–207
    hospital on divert status, 205–207
    in-house maintenance, 205
    low census, 207
    nurse:patient ratios, 205
    nursing practice, 205
    procedures performed in unit vs. surgical suite, 205
  standards for, 199–201
    operating and capital budgets, 199
    quality control, 200–201
    reports, 200
    variance reporting, 200, 203t
    work improvement methods, 200
Copy, definition of, 284
Corporate structure, 241, 255–257. *See also* Hospitals, organizational structure of
Cost-benefit analysis, 226–228
  assigning value to benefits, 226–228
  calculations for, 228, 229t
  definition of, 284
  definitions of cost and benefit for, 228
  ex ante, 226
  ex post, 226, 285
  identifying costs and benefits for, 228, 229t
  methodology for, 228t
Cost-benefit ratio, 217
Cost centers, 25, 145
  definition of, 284
Cost distribution report, 145, *146*
Cost effectiveness analysis, 228–229
Cost feasibility
  analysis of, 229–230
  definition of, 284

Cost shifting, 247, 267
Cost valuation principle, 23
Costs, 5–6, 26–27
  allocation of, 27, 28t
    definition of, 284
  avoidable, 27
  categorization of, 26
  controllable vs. noncontrollable, 26
  definition of, 284
  direct, 26, 35, 45, 147, 284
  vs. expenses, 26
  fixed, 26, 88, 147, 285
  of health care in America, 12
  hospital cost per patient, 5
  incremental, 27
  indirect, 26, 35, 45, 147, 285
  for indirect departments, 26–27
  marginal, 286
  for medical ICU, 147–157
    dietary, 149–151, 152t
    drugs, 148–149, 149t–151t
    education and training, 154–156
    general supplies, 148–149, 149t–151t
    laboratory, 149
    library, 157
    minor equipment, 151–152, 153t
    nursing turnover, 5, 140, 156–157, 193–194, 271
    recruitment advertising, 153–154
    repair and maintenance, 152–153
    utilities, 153
  nursing, 5, 213–215. *See also* Nursing costs
  operating, 147–157
  opportunity, 27, 286
  of procedures related to outcome, 5–6
  vs. reimbursement for care, 215t, 215–216
  semivariable, 147, 287
  standard, 209
  variable, 26, 88, 147, 287
Critical care units, 258–261
  average length of stay in, 212
  costs of, 212
  fiscal management of, 272
  increase in, 212
  reimbursement for services of, 212
  in rural vs. urban hospitals, 258–261. *See also* Rural hospitals; Urban hospitals
  types of, 258, *259*
  utilization of, 6
    appropriate use of beds, 217–218
    diversion of low-risk patients to intermediate care units, 6
    effect of feedback to physicians, 6
    organization by severity of illness, 6
Critical paths, 218
  definition of, 218, 284
  deviations from, 218
Current ratio, 49, definition of, 284
Customer relations, 34–35
Cutback management, 66–69
  definition of, 67, 284
  downsizing, 69–74, 207
    effect on survivors of, 74
    implementation of, 69–74

objectives of, 69
restructuring for, 69
by seniority, 69
strategies for coping with, 69
factors affecting decisions about, 67
financial reasons for, 67
hospital closures/conversions and, 67
problems in declining organization, 68
staff reduction plan, 70t–73t
strategies for, 68–69
to adjust to decline, 68
layoffs and alternatives, 68–69
rationing, 68
to resist decline, 68
stretching, 68
stress related to, 68

Data
for budget planning, 32, 84–87
consistency/accuracy of, 84
forecasted data, 83, 85–87, 86t
historical data, 83, 85, 86t
sources for, 84–85
types of, 85
definition of, 284
for program evaluation, 225–230
analysis of, 226–230, 228t–229t
collection of, 225–226, 227t
sources of, 225
for program evaluation of
validity and reliability of, 225
Data base management
definition of, 284
software for, 90, 168–169
for variance reporting, 178–179
Days: cash-on-hand ratio, 50, definition of, 284
Days: inpatient accounts receivables ratio, 49, definition of, 284
Debt. *See also* Bad debt
accounts payable, 21
for capital financing, 114–115, 243–244
definitions related to
debt capacity, 244
debt service reserves, 244
debt: equity ratio, 284
financing methods, 115, 243–244
long-term, 115, 244, 286
sources of capital, 115
Decision making
alternative choice process, 208–210
definition of, 208
example of, 209–210
steps in, 208–209
contribution of program evaluation to, 221
decentralized, 218
definition of, 207
Deductible ratio, 52, 53, definition of, 284
Demand, 15. *See also* Economics
definition of, 234, 284
for health care, 235–239
case scenario of, 238–239
factors affecting, 235t, 235–236
implications for nurse manager, 238

methods for controlling, 15, 236–237
for nurses, 277
Depreciation, 27–29, 47, 112–113
definition of, 27, 284
determining remaining value of assets after, 28–29
double declining balance technique of, 112–113
estimating life of capital assets for, 113
formulas for calculation of, 28, 112
historical vs. replacement costs and, 113
inclusion in reimbursement schedules, 113
straight-line, 27, 112
sum-of-the-years-digits technique of, 112–113
Depreciation reserves, 244
Diagnosis related groups (DRGs), 4, 276
cost vs. reimbursement under, 215t, 215–216
definition of, 284
determining staffing needs by, 121
development of, 211
financial impact on hospitals, 212–213, 264
nonconsideration of severity of illness, 212
nursing costs determined by, 196–197, 197t, 213–215, 270
product-line management and, 75
used to plan operating budget, 145
Dietary costs, 149–151, 152t
Differential pay rates, 125
Discharge of patients, 7
Discounted cash flow analysis, 89
Discounts, 45
definition of, 284
legality of, 256
for prepaid health plan contracts, 240
Disk, definition of, 284
Diversification, 241–243, *242–243*, 253t
corporate models, 241, *242*
definition of, 241, 284
factors affecting decisions about, 243
horizontal integration, 241–243, *243*
joint ventures, 253t, 256, 285
vertical integration, 241, *243*
Divert status, 205–207
advantages of, 205
avoidance of, 205–207
disadvantages of, 205
Dollar variances, 191–193, 192t
Double declining balance technique, 112–113
Downsizing. *See* Cutback management
Drugs
forecasting costs of, 148–149, 149t–151t
monitoring inventory of, 204
Duality principle, 23, 24t

Economic ordering quantity, 204
definition of, 284
Economics, 13–14, 234–247
access to care, 15, 267–268
challenges for nurses, 15–16, 238
competition, 245–246
controlling expenditures, 15
definition of, 13, 234
demand for health care, 235–239
case scenario of, 238–239
factors affecting, 235t, 235–236

Economics—*continued*
    implications for nurse manager, 238
    methods of controlling, 15, 236–237
    financial repositioning, 239–244
        debt management, 243–244
        diversification, 241–243, *242–243*
        investment, 239–240
        marketing, 240–241
        prepaid health plans, 240
        reallocation of unused beds, 241
    free market system, 13
    function of economic system, 13
    Gross National Product, 14
    of health care sector, 14–16, 234–247
    market analysis, 239
    market equilibrium, 13–14
    optimization, 13–14
    professional practice acts, 15
    questions related to, 14
    regionalization and regulation, 246–247
    resource utilization, 244–245
    substitution and complements concept, 14–15
    supply of health care, 15, 237–239
        case scenario of, 238–239
        factors affecting, 237t, 237–238
        implications for nurse manager, 238
Education costs, 154–156, 191
Effectiveness, 244–245
    definition of, 284
    measurement of, 245
    program evaluation of, 224
Efficiency
    cost-benefit analysis of, 228
    definition of, 284
    measurement of, 245
    program evaluation of, 224
Elderly patients, 276
    access to care, 276
    funding health care for, 12
    use of health care system by, 11–12, 276
Electronic mail, 169
    definition of, 285
Employee benefits, 87, 126, 190
    variance reporting for, 194–195
Entity
    accounting entity, 19
    definition of, 285
Environment, 12
    assessment of, 205, 206t
    trends in, 261, 261t
Equipment. *See also* Capital budgeting; Capital financing
    capital, 283
    financing of, 114–115
    inventory report for, 200, 200t
    leasing of, 113–114
    minor, budgeting for, 151–152, 153t
    purchase report for, 200, 201t
    requests for, 96–97, 100, 102t
    surgical ICU report of, 100, 101t
Equity
    definition of, 285
    financing, 115

Ethical issues, 279
    in organ donation/transplantation, 13
    related to technology, 13
Evaluation
    definition of, 285
    formative, 221–222, 285
    impact, 222
    outcome, 222
    process, 222
    of programs, 221–231. *See also* Program evaluation
    summative, 222, 287
Expense analysis schedule, 92–93
Expense budget, 87–89
    components of, 87
    non-wage-and-salary portion of, 88–89
    wage and salary portion of, 87
Expenses
    vs. costs, 26
    definition of, 25, 45
    depreciation, 27–29, 28t, 47, 112–113
    direct, 26, 35, 45, 284
    on financial statement, 34t, 35
    fixed vs. variable, 26, 88, 147
    indirect, 26, 35, 45, 285
    line items for, 35
    operating, 25–26
        categories of, 45–46
    per patient day, 179–180, 180t, 191
    salaries, 35, 87
    supplies, 35, 88–89
Expert systems, 170–171

Falls, 203–204
Federal hospitals, 254–255
    centralized bureaucratic structure of, 254
    military, 254
    public health, 254
    veterans, 254–255
Financial Accounting Standards Board, 48–49, definition of, 285
Financial analysis techniques, 110–112
    internal rate of return, 89, 111, 285
    net present value, 89, 111
    payback method, 111–112
    return on assets, 112
    return on investment, 110–111
Financial management, 2–16
    costs, 5–6
    definition of, 285
    goals of, 31
    historical perspectives on, 2–3
    hospital perspectives on, 3–4
    integrative model for, ii
    myths about, 2
    nursing and, 4–5, 8–11
        accepting challenges and taking risks, 8–9
        application of nursing process, 9
        contingency theory, 9
        financial understanding of nurse managers, 9–11
        innovation and creativity, 9
        "Role Expectations for the Critical Care Manager," 8, 9, *10*, 144, 219

quality, 6–8
review of literature on, 5
utilization, 6
Financial repositioning, 239–244
debt management, 243–244
diversification, 241–243, *242–243*
investment, 239–240
marketing, 240–241
prepaid health plans, 240
reallocation of unused beds, 241
Financial statements, 19, 43–53
auditing of, 47–49
footnotes to, 46, 285
importance of understanding, 43
purpose of, 43
ratio analysis of, 49–53
activity ratios, 51–52
leverage or capital structure ratios, 51
liquidity ratios, 49–51
objectives of, 49
profitability ratios, 52–53
types of, 43–47
balance sheet, 43–44, 44t
income statement, 44–46, 46t
statement of cash flows, 46–47, 48t
Fiscal department, 39–41
development of annual budget by, 39–41
monitoring and reviewing budget by, 41
organization of, 39
role in business planning, 41
Fiscal year, 38–39, 46
definition of, 285
Flexible budgeting, 58, 179–180, 180t
Floppy disk, 163, definition of, 285
Footnotes, 46
definition of, 285
Forecasting, 83, 85–87, *86*
definition of, 83
economic, 284
least squares method of, 86–87, 87t, *88*
moving average method of, 86, 86t
for operating budget, 145–147
purpose of, 85
regression analysis for, 87
steps in, 86
types of methods for, 85–86
Full-time equivalents, 118–129. *See also* Personnel budgets
calculation of, 181–182
definition of, 285
determinants of, 118–122
factors which need not affect, 123–124
nonproductive hours as, 190t, 190–191
position control system for, 182–185. *See also* Position control
Full-time staff, 123
Fund balance, 44
definition of, 285
Future issues, 272–273, 275–281
care givers, 277
new work force, 277
supply and demand for nurses, 277
cost of health care, 277

environmental trends, 261, 261t
ethics in health care, 279
focus on patient outcomes, 273
health care policy, 269
mandates for action, 279–281
accountability-based models of care, 279–280
development of computer skills, 280
improvement of nurse-physician relationships, 280
innovation/creativity in nursing, 280
leadership by nurse managers, 280–281
methods of rationing care, 279
monitoring trends in health care costs, 280
nursing research, 281
prevention of disease/health promotion, 279
quality improvement, 281
national health care insurance, 268, 272
outcomes measurement, 273, 277–278
patients, 275–277
access to health care, 276
age, 276
participation in health care, 276–277
severity of illness, 275–276
rationing of health care, 279
reimbursement management, 218–219
specialized hospitals, 273
technology, 278

General ledger, 19–20
definition of, 285
Goals
for budgeting, 39
for capital budgeting, 100, 103
congruence of budget with, 173
definition of, 285
of financial management, 31
of programs, 221
for strategic management, 81
Going-concern concept, 19
Governing body, 257
definition of, 285
Government regulations, 264–267. *See also* Prospective payment system
effect of prospective payment system, 211–219, 264
Medicaid, 265–266
Graphics, 168, definition of, 285
Gross National Product, 14
definition of, 14, 285
health care consumption of, 14, 212, 277

Handwashing, 204
Hardware, 164–166
definition of, 285
mainframes, 165–166
micros, 166
minis, 166
Health care
accountability-based models of, 279–280
cost of, 12, 212, 234, 277
economic trends affecting, 234–247. *See also* Economics
effect of prospective payment system on, 212
ethics of, 279

Health care—*continued*
　factors influencing, *11*, 11–14
　　consumers, 11–12
　　economics, 13–14
　　Gross National Product, 14, 234
　　providers, 13
　　public policy, 12
　　social forces, 12
　　technology, 12–13
　financial challenges in, 13
　for indigent/uninsured persons, 11, 267–268, 276
　myths about, 2
　national system for, 268
　public policy on, 268–269
　rationing of, 2, 211, 279
Health maintenance organizations, 211, 240, 266
"Heavy" patients, 140
Hiring variances, 181–182
Holiday pay, 187, 190–191
Horizontal integration, 241–243, *243*, 253t
Hospital information systems, 163. *See also* Management information systems
Hospitals, 249–262
　appropriate use of critical care beds in, 217–218
　changes in pattern of health care in, 212
　closures/conversions of, 67
　community, 251, 252t
　contracts with prepaid health plans, 240
　"disproportionate share," 265
　diversification of, 241–243, *242–243*, 253t
　on divert status, 205–207
　environmental trends affecting, 261, 261t
　federal, 254–255
　financial impact of diagnosis related groups on, 212–213, 264
　for-profit vs. not-for-profit, 98–99, 245–246, 250t, 251
　of future, 13
　governance of, 257–258
　　administrative team, 258
　　governing body, 257
　　medical staff, 257–258
　horizontally integrated, 241–243, *243*, 253t
　internal design of, 256–257
　　horizontal, 257
　　matrix, 257
　　project, 257
　　vertical, 256–257
　low census in, 207
　marketing of, 240–241, 253t
　Medicare payments to, 213
　mergers of, 67
　mission statement of, 249–251, *250*, 250t–251t
　multihospital systems, 255, 255t
　organizational structure of, 241, 255–257
　　antitrust legislation, 256
　　corporate model with foundation, 241, *242*
　　joint ventures, 256
　　nurse retention and, 271
　　parent holding company, 241, *242*
　　tax-exempt status, 256
　　traditional corporate model, 241, *242*
　private corporations, 251–252
　public, 253–254
　reallocation of unused beds in, 241
　restructuring of, 67
　rural vs. urban, 258–261. *See also* Rural hospitals; Urban hospitals
　specialized, 273
　university medical centers, 252t–253t, 252–253
　vertically integrated, 241, *243*, 253t

Incentive weekend plans, 123
Income statement, 44–46, 46t
　adjustments on, 45
　definition of, 285
　expenses on, 45–46
　net income on, 35–37, 46
　purpose of, 44
　revenues on, 45
　synonyms for, 44
Independent practice associations, 240, 266
Indigent persons, 267–268, 276
Infection control, 203–204
Inflation, 23, 145–146, definition of, 285
Information, 163–171
　computerized management of, 163–164
　essential vs. nonessential, 166, *167*
　exchange of, 163
　flow of, 163, *164*
　gathering of, 163
　generation of, 163
　importance for decision-making, 164
　management of, 163–171. *See also* Management information systems
　nurse managers roles in management of, 163–164
　recording of, 163
　retrieval of, 163
Input, 136–137, definition of, 285
Intangible
　benefits of program, 226
　definition of, 285
Interest rates
　effect on debt financing, 244
　on investments, 239–240
Interface, definition of, 285
Internal rate of return, 89, 111
　definition of, 285
Inventory. *See also* Supplies
　control of, 204–205
　　bar code system for, 157–159
　　pilferage and, 205
　definition of, 285
　of drugs, 204
　turnover ratio, 285
Investment, 239–240

Job sharing, 68
Joint ventures, 253t, 256
　definition of, 285
Jury duty pay, 191

Keyboard, 164
　definition of, 285

Laboratory costs, 149
Layoffs, 68–74. *See also* Cutback management
Leasing, 113–114, 204
  advantages of, 114
  definition of, 286
  sources for, 114
  types of leases, 114
Least squares method, 86–87, 87t, *88*
Length of stay, 264
  effect of case management on, 218
  effect of prospective payment system on, 7, 212
  for ICU vs. general hospital patients, 212
Leverage
  definition of, 286
  ratios, 51
Liabilities, 44
  on balance sheet, 44
  current, 44
    definition of, 284
  definition of, 44, 286
  long-term, 44
Library costs, 157
Line-item budgeting, 60–61
  advantages and disadvantages of, 61
  definition of, 60, 286
  focus of, 60
  incremental budgeting and, 60
Liquidity, 43
  definition of, 286
Liquidity ratios, 49–51
  definition of, 286

Magnet Hospital Study, 271
Mainframes, 165–166
  definition of, 286
Maintenance costs, 152–153
Managed care, 211, 266–267
  case management, 266–267
  definition of, 286
  effect on access to hospital care, 268
  health maintenance organizations, 211, 240, 266
  increases in, 266
  independent practice associations, 240, 266
  preferred provider organizations, 211, 240, 266
  role of case manager, 266
Management by objectives (MBO), 62–64
  advantages and disadvantages of, 64
  areas addressed by objectives, 63
  criteria for objectives, 63
  decentralized structure for, 62–63
  definition of, 286
  development of, 62
  evaluation phase of, 62
  implementation phase of, 62
  philosophy of, 62
  planning phase of, 62
Management information systems, 163–171
  automation vs. nonautomation, 170
  definition of, 285
  essential vs. nonessential information, 166, *167*
  expert systems, 170–171
  hardware for, 164–166
    definition of, 165
  importance for decision-making, 164
  software for, 167–169
    data base management, 168–169
    definition of, 167
    spreadsheets, 167–168, *168–169*
    word processing, 168
  uses and misuses of, 169–170
Market analysis, 239
  financial assessment, 239
  market assessment, 239
  nurse manager's role in, 239
  provider assessment, 239
Market share, 239
  definition of, 286
Marketing, 240–241
  definition of, 240
  hospital, 240–241
Matching, 23–24
  definition of, 286
Materiality principle, 24
Medicaid, 212, 265–266
  definition of, 286
  eligibility for, 265
  expenditures for, 234
  proposed expansion of, 268
  proposed reforms for, 265
  provider reimbursement levels under, 265, 267
Medical practice acts, 256
Medical staff, 257–258
Medicare, 211–212
  Catastrophic Coverage Act of 1988, 265–266
  definition of, 286
  expenditures for, 212, 234
  payments to hospitals, 213
  prospective payment system and, 211
MedisGroups, 276
Mergers of hospitals, 67
Merit raises, 124–125, 202
Microcomputers, 166
  definition of, 286
Military health care, 254
Mini-computers, 166
  definition of, 286
Mission statement, 249–251, *250*, 250t–251t
Money market accounts, 239–240
Money measurement principle, 23
Monitor, 164
  definition of, 286
Moving average method, 86, 86t
Multihospital systems, 255, 255t

National health care insurance, 268, 272
Needle stick injuries, 203–204
Net income, 35–37, 46. *See also* Profit
  definition of, 286
Net present value, 89, 111
  definition of, 286
Net worth, definition of, 286
"No code" patients, 218

Nonproductive hours, 190t, 190–191
  definition of, 286
Nonquantification, 228, definition of, 286
Not for profit
  definition of, 286
  hospitals, 98–99, 245–246, 250t, 251
Nurse managers, 4–5
  budget responsibilities of, 56–57
  capital budgeting by, 98–100
  financial management responsibilities of, 8, 9
  financial understanding of, 9–11
  impact on profit, 37
  impact on revenues, 34
  implications of supply and demand for, 238
  information management by, 163–164
  leadership by, 280–281
  market analysis by, 239
  role expectations for, 8, 9, *10*
  role in controlling, 198
  role in product-line management, 272
  trends affecting, 269–272
Nurse:patient ratios, 120, 120t, 205
Nurses
  alternative care givers and, 216–217
  cost accounting applied to, 209
  development of education for, 4
  historical perspectives on, 4–5
  as managers, 4–5
  relationships with physicians, 280
  supply and demand of critical care nurses, 67
Nursing costs, 5, 213–215, 269–270
  determined by patient classification system, 213–215, 270
  labor. *See* Personnel budgets; Salary budget
  measured under prospective payment system, 213, 214t, 270
  strategies to decrease, 271–272
  third-party reimbursement for, 270
Nursing information systems, 163. *See also* Management information systems
Nursing research, 7t, 7–8, 281

Objectives
  of budgeting, 39
  for capital budgeting, 100, 103
  definition of, 286
  of downsizing, 69
  management by, 62–64. *See also* Management by objectives
  of programs, 222
  of ratio analysis of financial statements, 49
Objectivity principle, 24
Occupancy
  capital reimbursement and, 265
  decreases in, 212
  definition of, 286
  full-time equivalent positions based on, 119–120
On-call pay, 126, 202
Operating budgets, 37, 144–162
  application of nursing process to, 144
  assessment and planning for, 145–147
    cost distribution report, 145, *146*
    forecasting methods, 145–147
    patient diagnostic categories, 145
    determining complexity of, 145
  evaluation of, 159
  example of, 159–161, *161*
  implementation of, 157–159, 158t
    bar code system, 157–159
    computerized information system, 157–158
Operating costs, 25–26, 147–157
  categories of, 45–46
  dietary, 149–151, 152t
  drugs, 148–149, 149t–151t
  education and training, 154–156
  general supplies, 148–149, 149t–151t
  laboratory, 149
  library, 157
  minor equipment, 151–152, 153t
  nursing turnover, 5, 140, 156–157, 193–194, 271
  recruitment advertising, 153–154
  repair and maintenance, 152–153
  salaries, 118–130. *See also* Personnel budgets
  types of, 147
    direct vs. indirect, 26, 35, 45, 147
    fixed vs. variable, 26, 88, 147
    semivariable, 147
  utilities, 153
Operational plans, 82
Orientation hours, 190, 191
"Outcome Standards for Nursing Care of the Critically Ill," 7
Outcomes
  definition of, 286
  factors positively impacting, 271
  of programs, 226–228
    assigning monetary value to, 226–228
    direct vs. indirect, 226
    evaluation of, 222
    tangible vs. intangible, 226
  quality of care measured by, 273, 277–278
Output, 136–137, definition of, 286
Overhead
  definition of, 286
  positions, 122
Overtime, 125, 187
  alternatives to, 201

Paid time off, 190–191
Parent holding company, 241, *242*
Part-time staff, 123
Patient care units, 209
Patient classification systems, 120, 133–136, 134t–137t
  characteristics of, 134
  constant factors in, 135
  content validity of, 135
  definition of, 286
  developing standards for, 135
  development/updating of, 134, 135
    time studies, 135
    work sampling observation, 135
  factor type system, 134, 134t
  identifying indicators for, 135
  inter-rater reliability of, 134–135
  nursing costs determined by, 213–215, 270
  prototype system, 134, 134t

requirements for, 134
staffing calculations based on, 135–136, 136t, 159–160
staffing schedule based on, 136, 137t
used to plan operating budget, 145
Patient days, 180–181
expenses per, 179–180, 180t, 191
Patient "dumping," 267–268
Patient volume, 119, 120t
Payback
definition of, 286
method, 111–112
Payors
definition of, 286
government, 265
historical vs. current, 211
payor mix, definition of, 286
third-party, 287
Persistent vegetative state, 278
Personnel budgets, 37, 94, 118–130. *See also* Staffing
approval of, 129
components of, 118
determinants of full-time equivalent positions, 118–122, 181–182
bed capacity vs. occupancy, 119–120
calculation methods, 119
direct care hours per patient day, 120t, 120–121
indirect care hours per patient day, 121
management and other unit-based positions, 122
patient volume, 119, 120t
replacement time positions, 121–122
determinants of salary budget, 35, 87, 124–126
base wage rate, 124, 125t
differentials and bonuses, 125
employee benefits, 87, 125
merit or step increase raises, 124–125, 202
on-call and call back pay, 125, 202
overtime, 125, 187
specialty or certification pay, 124
supplemental staffing, 125, 188
development for CCU, 126–129
example of, 130t
factors which need not affect full-time equivalent positions, 123–124
incentive weekend plans, 123
minimum staffing, 123
part-time vs. full-time staff, 123
scheduling patterns, 123
student employees, 123–124
impact of how unit works on, 118
Personnel control, 201–204
absenteeism, 203
alternatives to overtime, 201
benefit time, 202
clinical nurse specialist, 203
clinical staff mix, 201
internal ICU pool of nurses, 202
merit raises, 202
on-call system, 202
scheduling patterns, 201
special projects, 202
staff education, 202

turnover, 203
workers compensation issues, 203–204
Philanthropy, 243
Physician Payment Review Commission, 269
Planning, programming, and budgeting system, 61–62
advantages and disadvantages of, 61–62
characteristics of, 61
definition of, 61, 286
implementation of, 61
Position control, 182–185, 201
advantages of, 182
steps in development of, 182–185
budgeting of FTEs, 182–183
never hiring above allowed level, 183–185
placing FTEs in staffing pattern, 183, 184t
reducing number of FTEs, 185
Precertification, 21
Preferred provider organizations, 211, 240, 266
Prepaid health plans, 240
Price. *See also* Rate setting
in competitive market, 245
definition of, 286
shadow, 287
of supplies, 204
Private hospital corporations, 251–252
Processing, 163, definition of, 286
Processing unit, 164
definition of, 286
Product-line management, 74–77, 257, 272
accounting orientation for, 75–76
advantages and disadvantages of, 76–77
benefits of, 272
definition of, 74, 287
diagnosis related groups and, 75
history in hospitals, 74
identifying hospital products for, 74–75
implementation of, 76
matrix organizational structure and, 74–75
nurse manager's role in, 272
strategic business units for, 75
Productivity, 136–138, 137t–139t
analyzing reports of, 185, 186t
calculation of, 137–138, 138t
definition of, 136, 137t, 287
definition of productive hours, 287
effect of balancing inputs and outputs on, 138
efficiency and effectiveness and, 137
employee morale and, 138
industrial, 136–137
nonproductive hours, 190t, 190–191
nursing, 245
patient care pathway and, 138, 139t
time for nurse to achieve 90–100%, 193
total budget, 191
ways of managing, 138
Profit, 35–37, 46
calculation of, 46
definition of, 35, 46, 287
ways nurse manager can impact, 37
Profitability ratios, 52–53
Program evaluation, 221–231
data analysis for, 226–230, 228t–229t
assigning value to program benefits, 226–228

300 INDEX

Program evaluation—*continued*
   cost-benefit analysis, 226–228, 228t–229t
      definition of, 226
      ex ante cost-benefit analysis, 226
      ex post cost-benefit analysis, 226
      recognizing program assumptions and alternatives, 228
      statistical methods for, 226
   data collection for, 225–226, 227t
   defining program for, 222–223
   definition of, 221
   designing project for, 224–225
   formative vs. summative, 221–222
   items considered in, 221
   program aspects analyzed by, 224–225
      context characteristics, 224
      participant characteristics, 224
      program characteristics, 224
      program costs, 224–225
      program outcome, 224
   purposes of, 221, 221t
      defining, 223
   recipients of results of, 223
   reporting findings of, 230t, 230–231
   sources of data for, 225
   stating questions for, 223–224
   steps in, 222, 222t
   validity and reliability of data for, 225
Programs, 221–223
   defining purpose of, 222–223
   definition of, 221, 287
   goals of, 221
   identifying target audience for, 222–223
   organization of, 223
   types of, 221
Prospective payment system, 3–4, 211–219. *See also* Diagnosis related groups; Reimbursement
   effect on average length of stay, 7, 212
   effect on capital budgeting, 98
   effect on capital financing, 114
   effect on health care, 212
   effect on profitability of critical care units, 67
   effect on quality of care, 6–7
   measuring nursing costs under, 213, 214t
   reimbursement for critical care under, 272
   sickness at admission and, 7
Public health programs, 254
Public hospitals, 253–254
Public policy, 12

Quality control, 200–201
Quality of care, 6–8
   AACN studies on, 7–8
   effects of prospective payment on, 6–7
   equality in, 15
   improvement of, 281
   patient outcomes as indicator of, 7, 273, 277–278
   role of critical care manager in, 8

Rate setting, 29–30
   based on competitor's rates, 30
   definition of, 29, 287
   determining rate adjustments, 30
   hourly rates, 30
   ratio of cost-to-charge method, 30
   relative value method, 30
   surcharges, 30
   steps in, 29–30
      allocation of expenses, 30
      determination of financial requirements, 29
      ensuring needed cash flow, 30
Ratio, 49, definition of, 287
Ratio analysis, 49–53
   activity ratios, 51–52
   leverage or capital structure ratios, 51
   liquidity ratios, 49–51
   objectives of, 49
   profitability ratios, 52–53
Ratio of cost to charge, 30, definition of, 287
Realization (recognition) principle, 21, 21t
   definition of, 287
Recruitment bonuses, 195
Recruitment costs, 153–154, 271
Regionalization, 247
   cost shifting and, 247
   definition of, 287
   purpose of, 247
Registered care technician, 217
Regression analysis, 87
Reimbursement, 211–219. *See also* Diagnosis related groups; Prospective payment system
   for capital expenditures, 265
   vs. cost of care, 215t, 215–216
   definition of, 287
   future management of, 218–219
   historical methods of, 211
   measuring nursing costs, 5, 213–215
      by patient classification systems, 213–215
      under prospective payment, 213, 214t
   under Medicaid, 265
   under prospective payment system, 211–213
   strategies affecting, 215–218
      appropriate use of critical care beds, 217–218
      cost vs. reimbursement, 215t, 215–216
      nursing case management, 216
      use of alternative care givers, 216–217
Relative intensity measures, 214
Relative value units, 209
   definition of, 287
Reliability
   definition of, 287
   of patient classification systems, 134–135
   of program evaluation data, 225
Repair costs, 152–153
Replacement time positions, 121–122
Resource based relative value scale, 13
Resources, 244–245
   allocation of, 244
   definition of, 244
   utilization of, 244–245
Restricted funds, 244
Retrospective reimbursement system, 3
Return on assets, 112
Return on investment, 110–111
   definition of, 287

Revenue, 25
 adjustments for bad debt, charity, and contractual allowances, 33-34, 45
 customer relations and, 34-35
 definition of, 25, 45, 287
 flow of, 30-31
 gross, 33
 on income statement, 33-35, 34t
 net, 34
 nonoperating, 33, 45, 286
 from patient services, 45
 sources of, 25, 33, 45
 total operating, 287
 variance reporting for, 196t-197t, 196-197
 ways nurse manager can impact, 34
Revenue centers, 25
 definition of, 287
Risk, 79t, 241, 244, definition of, 287
"Role Expectations for the Critical Care Manager," 8, 9, *10*, 144, 219
Rural hospitals, 258-260
 competency maintenance in, 260
 financial constraints on, 258-259
 ICU in, 258
 nurses' roles in, 258
 recruitment by, 260
 relieving nursing shortage in, 259-260
 staffing and scheduling techniques in, 260

Safety education, 204
Salary budget, 35, 87, 124-126
 base wage rate, 124, 125t
 differentials and bonuses, 125
 employee benefits, 126
 merit or step increases raises, 124-125, 202
 on-call and call back pay, 126, 202
 overtime, 125, 187, 201
 specialty or certification pay, 124
 supplemental staffing, 126, 188
Scheduling patterns, 123, 202, 270-271
Service contracts, 205
Severity of illness, 275-276
 definition of, 287
 diagnosis related groups and, 212
Shadow prices, 226, definition of, 287
Shared agreements, 156
 between employer and employee, 156
 between facilities, 156
Sick leave, 190-191
Software, 167-169
 data base management, 90, 168-169
 definition of, 287
 spreadsheets, 90, 167-168, *168-169*
 word processing, 168
Solvency, 49, 239, definition of, 287
Specialty pay, 124
Spreadsheets, 90, 167-168, *168-169*
Stable-dollar (stable-monetary-unit) concept, 23
Staff reduction plan, 70t-73t, 185
Staffing, 131-143. *See also* Personnel budgets
 alternative care givers, 216-217
 based on DRGs, 121
 based on patient classification systems, 120, 133-136, 134t-137t, 159-161
 costs of, 153-156
  recruitment advertising, 153-154
  training and education, 154-156
 determinants of, 132
 economic issues affecting, 270-271
 effect of standards of care and standards of practice on, 131-132
 hiring variances, 181-182
 hospital philosophy about, 132-133
 increases in, 213
 master plan for, 133
 methodology for, 142
 minimum, 123
 options and strategies for, 141-142
  matching hours to work load, 142
  self-staffing, 141
  supplemental staffing, 141
 part-time vs. full-time, 123
 position control system for, 182-185. *See also* Position control
 productivity and, 136-138, 137t-139t
 questions pertaining to, 131
 supplemental, 126, 141
 turnover, 140-141, 156-157, 271
  report on, 193-194, 194t
 unit plan for, 133
 unit policies and, 133
 variances in, 185-188
  analyzing productivity reports, 185, 186t
  holiday hours, 187
  inpatients and outpatients, 185
  overtime hours, 125, 187
  purchased hours (supplemental staffing), 125, 188
  regular hours, 187
  total volume, 187
 work load and, 133, 138-140, 139t-140t
Standards
 of care, 131-132
 definition of, 131, 132, 287
 outcome, 132, 244
 of practice, 131-132
 process, 131-132
 structure, 131-132
Statement of cash flows, 46-47, 48t
 definition of, 287
 purpose of, 46-47
 time period for, 47
Step increase raises, 124-125
Stocks, 240
Strategic management, 81
 definition of, 81
 goal of, 81
Strategic planning, 81-82
 capital budgeting and, 99
 definition of, 81, 99, 287
 market analysis for, 99
 process of, 82
 relation of budget to, 32, 33, 39, 41-42, 81-82
 responsibility for, 81
Strategy principles, 174t, 174-176

Strategy principles—*continued*
  analyzing conflict, 174–175
  cultivating allegiances, 175
  developing error-free strategy, 175
  estimating costs, 175
  executing decisive thrust, 176
  knowing situation, 175–176
  maneuvering for advantage, 175
  mobilizing with unity, 175
  moving spontaneously according to situation, 175
  positioning oneself for triumph and one's opponent for defeat, 175
  using camouflage, 175
  using information to one's advantage, 176
Student employees, 123–124
Sum-of-the-years-digits technique, 112–113
Supplemental staff, 125, 188
Supplies
  bedside assessment of, 205
  budgeting for, 35, 88–89
  charging patient for, 205
  control of, 204–205
  economic ordering quantity for, 204
  education about, 204
  evaluating inventory of, 204–205
  forecasting costs of, 148–149, 149t–151t
  free trial periods for, 204
  maintaining within proper area, 204
  negotiating best price for, 204
  pilferage of, 205
  standardization of, 204
  variance reporting for, 195–196
Supply, 15. *See also* Economics
  definition of, 234, 287
  of health care, 237–239
    case scenario of, 238–239
    factors affecting, 237t, 237–238
    implications for nurse manager, 238
  of nurses, 277
Support department, definition of, 287
Surcharges, 30
  definition of, 287

Tangible
  benefits of program, 226
  definition of, 287
Technology, 278
  affecting critical care, 12
  ethical dilemmas related to, 13
  impact on health care system, 12–13
  to prevent/control chronic health problems, 12
Teleconferences, 155–156
Temporary agency nurses, 188
"The Hospital Industry Financial Report," 49
Therapeutic intervention scoring system (TISS), 276
Times earned interest ratio, 51, definition of, 287
Total asset turnover ratio, 51, definition of, 287
Total margins, 212–213
Training costs, 154–156, 191
Transactions, 19–20
  credit vs. cash, 20
  definition of, 19, 287
  ledger of, 19–20
  records of, 19
Transplantation surgery, 268
  ethical issues in, 13
Treasury (T) bills, 240
Trends, 264–273
  access to care, 267–268
  effects on nurse managers, 269–272
  future, 272–273
  government regulations, 264–267
  health care policy, 268–269
Tuition reimbursement, 155
Turnover, 140–141, 203
  avoidable vs. unavoidable, 140
  computation of, 140
  costs of, 140, 156–157, 193–194, 271
  definition of, 140, 287
  identifying trends in, 140–141
  questions related to, 141
  report on, 193–194, 194t

Uncollectable acccounts, 2
Uninsured persons, 11, 267–268, 276
University medical centers, 252t–253t, 252–253
  characteristics of, 252
  financial constraint issues in, 252t
  mission of, 251t
  priorities of, 252
  responses to changes in health care environment by, 253t
Urban hospitals, 260–261
  direct care hours per patient day in, 260t, 260–261
  ICU in, 260
  nursing training needs in, 260
Utility costs, 153

Vacation pay, 22, 190–191, 195
Validity
  definition of, 287
  of patient classification systems, 135
  of program evaluation data, 225
Variance reporting, 178–197, 203t, 207, 208t
  allowable amount of variance, 200
  budget and patient outcome, 178
  data bases for, 178–179
  definition of variance, 287
  dollar variances, 191–193, 192t
  employee benefits, 194–195
  for expenses per patient day, 179–180, 180t
  flexible budgeting and, 58, 179–180, 180t
  hiring variances, 181–182
  nonproductive hours, 190t, 190–191
  orientation and other hours, 191
  patient days and, 180–181
  relationships: source of worked hours, 188–190
    acuity system and percentage of productivity, 188–189
    care hours per patient day, 189
    fixed hours, 189–190
  revenue variances, 196t–197t, 196–197
  staffing variances, 185–188
  supply expense variances, 195–196
  turnover, 193–194, 194t
Vendors, 102–106

definition of, 287
  selection of, 102–103, 104t–105t, 106
Vertical integration, 241, *243*, 253t
Veterans Services Health and Research Administration, 254–255

Word processing, 168
Work force, 12, 277
Work load, 138–140
  analysis schedule for, 95
  calculated by patient classification system, 138, 139t
  determinants of, 138
  matching hours to, 141–142
Work load index, 138–140, 140t
  definition of, 287
Work sharing, 68

Workers compensation issues, 203–204
Working capital, 47
  definition of, 47, 287
  sources of, 47

Zero-base budgeting, 64–66, 66t
  advantages and disadvantages of, 65–66
  characteristics of, 64
  criticisms of, 65
  decision packages for, 64–65
  definition of, 64, 287
  funding levels in, 65
  history of, 64
  instructions for, 66t
  purpose of, 64
  ranking process for, 65